Sheila Kay Cornwell

Janet Cornwell

Kay Robison

Kay Robison

2.75

303

NAME
SCHOOL

KAY

Beat

3610
291

39
37/66

66

66
3/9

Maralyn

Charles K.

Dorette F.

Brendas

Claude C.

Valoise J.

Charles M.

Lou ?

Shirley J.

Leon C.

John H.

Roy W.

Vickie W.

Larry C.

Lois H.

Janet ?

Martha P.

Potly R.

Ronnie C.

Virginia W.

Don M.

Marsha T.

Dave B.

Sarah H.

Donald C.

Betty J.

Becky C.

Peggy B.

Brenda J.

Ronald

Steve B.

Athyl B.

Johnnie W.

Vicki W.

Donavon W.

Marcia J.

Marvin's

Gladys A.

Chester

Mary Beth C.

Eva R.

Teresa T.

Melvin T.

Vickie

Ronnie A.

Elizabeth R.

Jimmie J.

Sherry J.

Kay J.

Ernie B.

chants and sailors were often insulted and sometimes beaten. Clearly it was the government's duty to arrange protection for American citizens in China.

In 1843 the United States sent a New Englander named Caleb Cushing to China. Cushing was a brilliant man who had learned a great deal about the Chinese and their traditions. In 1844 he won a treaty that granted the United States many trading rights and promised fair treatment for Americans in China.

After Cushing's visit trade with China boomed. Clipper ships won a big share of China's trade. The Chinese came to regard the United States as a friendly nation — perhaps their only friend, for other countries were seizing pieces of Chinese territory.

The Open Door Policy helped China.

The first threat to friendly relations with China came in 1900. A rebellion broke out in the Chinese capital, Peking (PE KING). The rebels were a fierce band called the "Boxers." Their slogan was "China for the Chinese." Their aim was to kill all foreign devils" or drive them out of China.

The Chinese government made little attempt to put down the rebellion. The Boxers murdered every white person they could find. In terror, foreigners in Peking fled to the legations (le GAY shuns) or offices of their ambassadors for safety. According to international law a legation must never be attacked, for it is in a sense foreign territory. But the Boxers cared nothing for international law. They attacked and besieged the legations for two months.

Inside the legation walls, missionaries, merchants, and government representatives waited in terror. They had little hope of rescue. But at last an international army, made up of troops from six nations, arrived just in time to save them.

China was punished for the Boxer Rebellion. For a time it looked as if her territory would be divided among the nations who had sent troops to Peking. But John Hay, American Secretary of State, helped block this scheme. Instead China had to pay a huge fine or *indemnity* (in DEM nih tee) to nations whose citizens had been injured. The United States received 24 million dollars of the indemnity, but later returned 18 million to China, because that much money was left after paying claims of Americans who had been injured. China used the money to send Chinese students to American schools and colleges.

China had many reasons to feel friendly to the United States, and especially to John Hay. Shortly before the Boxer Rebellion he proposed a new plan for European nations to follow in China. He called it the *Open Door Policy*. It provided that China should not lose any more of her territory and that all nations should have equal rights to trade in China. Other nations

The new possessions served as "stepping stones" by which Americans moved closer to Asia. Some American business firms established branches in Hawaii and the Philippines; then they looked longingly toward the vast markets of Asia. "If every Chinese bought just one dollar's worth of American goods a year that would add up to a business of over 400 million dollars," merchants pointed out.

This was not a new idea. American interest in China and Japan began long before the United States gained possessions in the Pacific. American merchants early saw the possibilities for trade with the region known as the *Far East*. The Far East may be defined as the countries of eastern Asia — China and Japan and their neighbors. (Europeans named this part of the world the Far East because it was far from Europe.)

The Far East has millions of hard working, skilful people. They produce many goods — spices, minerals and silks — that Americans want. And Americans would like to sell them machines, textiles, and farm products. For more than a hundred years Americans have dreamed of winning enough customers in the Far East for all the foods and manufactured goods they could not sell in the United States or Europe.

United States was friendly with China. The War for Independence was scarcely over when an American

The Far East has many lovely palaces and temples. Above is the Throne Room of the ancient royal palace near Seoul, Korea.

trading ship sailed across the Pacific, and into the South China port of Canton in 1784. With an eye to pleasing customers the ship was named *The Empress of China*. Canton merchants liked the quality of her cargo, especially the cotton cloth; the captain quickly traded his goods for silk, tea, and china dishes. The profits he made from one voyage more than paid the cost of building the ship.

Other merchants rushed to follow his example. From Philadelphia, Boston, and Providence ships set sail for the Far East. Trade with China grew steadily, bringing rich profits. But the United States government had no official relation with China.

In those days, when China was a great empire, the Chinese felt that other nations were inferior. This led to misunderstandings and then to serious trouble. American me

Glenn W. Moon
and
John H. MacGow

HE   OLT

PANY

GLENN W. MOON
has taught Social Studies at Burdick
Junior High School, Stamford, Connec-
ticut and is now principal of Walter R.
Dolan Junior High School in Stamford,
Connecticut.

JOHN H. MacGOWAN
is a teacher of Social Studies at Manhasset Junior High School, Manhasset,
Long Island, New York.

CONTENTS

AMERICAN PAINTINGS TELL THE STORY OF OUR LAND AND PEOPLE

On the following pages you will find a group of eight paintings that show some of the great periods and developments of American history.

First came the Indians, so the first painting, *Crow Indian Village* by George Catlin, gives you a glimpse of how the first Americans lived before the coming of the Europeans. The village, which has long since vanished, was in the region that is now the state of Montana.

The discovery of America is the subject of the second painting, *Landing of Columbus* by Albert Bierstadt. Notice how the Indians watch in fear and wonder as white people claim the land.

The third picture, which is a detail from a larger painting called *Penn's Treaty With the Indians* by Benjamin West, illustrates one of the key problems of the colonial period, how to establish peaceful relations with the Indians.

The colonial period ended in 1776 when the Declaration of Independence was signed. The fourth painting, *Declaration of Independence* by John Trumbull, shows the beginning of the American republic.

One of the great themes of American history is the westward movement. Even while the Declaration was being signed, pioneers were

crossing the mountains to the West. The fifth painting, *Daniel Boone Escorting a Band of Pioneers Through the Cumberland Gap* by George Bingham, shows an early event in the westward movement.

The sons of the pioneers grew up in the wilderness and many of them had a hard struggle to get an education. In the sixth painting, *Boyhood of Lincoln* by Eastman Johnson, Abraham Lincoln is seen studying by the firelight in his log cabin home, as many of the great men of the nineteenth century had to do.

The seventh painting, *Lackawanna Valley* by George Innes, shows a scene near Scranton, Pennsylvania, in the nineteenth century. It illustrates the growing strength and prosperity that came with the growth of railroads and new industries.

The eighth and last painting, *American Landscape* by Charles Sheeler, shows one of the modern factories which help make the United States the strength of the free world.

Thus these paintings tell part of the story of our land and its people from wilderness to world power.

The first Americans came from Asia.
Thousands of years ago a small group of hunters wandered into the northeast corner of Asia. Tired and shivering, they huddled around the campfire. The land was cold and dreary, and they had only a few skins to cover their bodies. The small children cried softly. It was a long time since they had tasted meat. Their fathers had little luck hunting, for they carried only rough clubs and stone-tipped spears.

Then one dark day, an older boy noticed something. He grunted and pointed. Quickly, the others gathered around him. They knew him well; he had sharp eyes and he did not get excited easily. The others looked to where he was pointing.

Sure enough, there were tracks on the ground — big tracks, perhaps those of a deer or a bison. Swiftly, silently, the hunters followed the trail. The tracks led across a narrow strip of land they had not seen before. After many miles the land widened into a vast wilderness.

Toward night the hunters found their deer and killed it. The tribe had a feast. For once their stomachs

were full. The hunters found other tracks and followed them. Slowly the tribe pushed southward. Year by year they moved away from their old hunting grounds in Asia.

Other tribes and hunters seem to have followed them. Probably, a path or trail gradually appeared. It led across the narrow strip of land. This strip was really a land bridge from Asia to America. And those long-ago hunters are believed to have been the first *immigrants* or newcomers to America.

This all happened in the far away time known as the *Stone Age*, between ten and twenty thousand years ago. The people of the Stone Age could not read or write, so they left no records. No one knows exactly when or how they came. But some evidence has been found in widely scattered places: a stone weapon, animal bones around what was probably an ancient camping place, the skeleton of a child who met its death sometime in the dim past before history began. From such meager evidence the story of the first Americans can be pieced together. But it is not complete or

Stone Age tribes lived chiefly by hunting. Ancestors of the Indians probably had reached this stage of development when they came to America from Siberia.

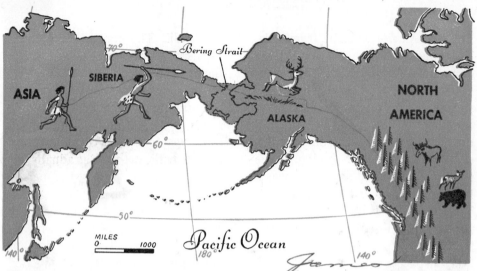

This map shows the route by which Stone Age ancestors of the American Indians are believed to have come from Asia to America thousands of years ago.

factual; and any account of early wanderings from Asia to America has to be based largely on theory and imagination.

It is thought that the tribes who came from northeastern Asia to America were the ancestors of the people now known as the American Indians. The part of Asia from which they seem to have come is now called Siberia (sy BEER ih ah). They are believed to have crossed into the part of America now known as Alaska. The map on this page shows the route by which they probably came to America.

After thousands of years a frightening thing happened. The land bridge between Asia and America sank under the icy waves of the water. The narrow channel where land used to be is now known as Bering (BARE eeng) Strait.

Immigration from Asia practically stopped. But the people who had already crossed into Alaska probably paid no attention. They seem to have kept moving south where the land was warmer and the hunting was better. Generations lived and died and left no record of their wanderings. At length, after many centuries, the immigrants found homes in almost every part of the American continents. They spread out and formed tribes.

Central and South American Indians built great civilizations. Most of the Indians continued to live by hunting and fishing. But some of them learned how to grow their food. Gradually they settled down in villages and became farmers. They discovered ways of weaving cloth and they found out how to make tools of metal.

When and how did this happen? No one knows exactly. Apparently it was a very slow process. Some-

4

times discoveries were made by accident. Sometimes one man improved a little on another man's discovery. Perhaps he found that corn grew better if he stuck a piece of fish in the ground near the plants. Or he found a way to put a sharper edge on his knife. Then he taught his son and grandson the new method. Progress was slow and difficult, but that is the way civilization develops.

The Indians who reached Central and South America found conditions there favorable to their needs. There were hills and valleys where they could hide from other tribes that were their enemies. The climate was warm and dry. And the soil was soft and loose in many places so it was easy for them to plant crops. Perhaps that is why the Indians of this region became more skilful and advanced than the tribes in North America. There may have been other reasons. No one really knows why great Indian civilizations developed in South rather than in North America. But that is what happened, for the ruins of their temples and cities are still standing.

In the region that is now Guate-

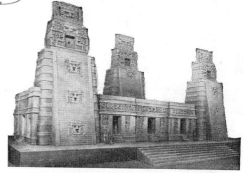

Maya Indians built lovely palaces in Yucatán as this reconstruction shows.

mala (GWAH tay MAH lah) and Mexico, a group of Indians called the *Mayas* (MAH yahs) made great progress. They built fine cities and beautiful temples. They developed an accurate calendar, and they learned to keep records. But wars and other troubles destroyed the Mayas. Deep in the jungles of Central America, scientists are still studying the ruins of their lost cities.

Another group of Indians called the *Aztecs* (AZ teks) also lived in Mexico. They took over or "borrowed" many discoveries of the Mayas, such as the calendar. The Aztec civilization was still flourishing when the Spaniards came.

Much farther south in Peru, there was another great Indian civilization, that of the *Incas* (ING kahs). They ruled over a vast area. They built many roads; some of their roads are still in use today. They wove beautiful cloth and made some of the finest articles of metal that the world has ever seen.

North American Indians believed in "the Great Spirit." In the part of

The ancient calendar stone of the Aztec Indians recorded time accurately.

America that is now the United States the Indians were less advanced. They spent a great deal of their time fighting off invading tribes. Climate and other geographic conditions were not very friendly to the growth of an Indian civilization. And perhaps the tribes that settled in North America were less ambitious or gifted than the Indians farther south. At any rate, it seems clear that the Indians of North America did not move forward so fast or so far as Indians of Central and South America.

All the Indians lived close to nature. They loved the beauty and the freedom of outdoor life. They believed that rocks, plants, the sun, and the wind all had spirits or souls like men. And over everything, they thought, ruled "the Great Spirit."

Villages and tribes sought to win the help of spirits by means of dances and other ceremonies. The farming tribes held dances to bring the rain and help the corn to grow. Their dances were not at all like modern social dances. They were more like religious ceremonies. Decked out in feathers and colorful costumes, the men marched, skipped, or jumped to the rhythm of drums or to words chanted by members of the tribe.

Religious leaders, called priests or "medicine men," were in charge of such ceremonies. They had great power in Indian affairs; chiefs and warriors sought their advice. Often they were the real rulers of the tribe.

However, the other Indians had some influence in making important decisions. The chiefs usually held council meetings where almost any matter might be discussed and everyone had a right to speak. The members of the tribe were usually related to one another; the family was the basis of the Indian's govern-

The map below shows where the five main groups of Indians lived.

ment. In a few tribes the women were badly treated; but as a rule they had great power.

The Indians loved their children dearly and treated them with great kindness. But children were expected to be helpful. They gathered wood for the fire and watched the tribe's cattle or horses. When a boy brought home the first animal he had killed with his own bow or spear, his proud father would probably hold a big feast.

When youngsters reached the age

people came back to the tribe there was feasting and rejoicing.

It is important to remember that not all Indians observed these ceremonies. Each group of tribes had different customs and they developed in different ways. As you can see on the map on page six there were five main groups of Indians in North America when the white men came. They were:

(1) The *Eastern Woodland Indians* who lived in the eastern part of the United States from Maine to Florida

The Indians of the Plains tribes lived by hunting the "buffalo" or American bison. Their horses were descendants of steeds brought to America by the early Spanish explorers.

of 13 or 14 they were considered men and women. They had to take part in long, difficult ceremonies to become members of the tribe. For example, a boy might go out into the desert or forest and remain there alone for many days. He fasted and prayed, hoping that a spirit would appear and give him guidance. A girl might stay apart from the tribe for several months under the care of an old woman. When the young

and as far west as the Mississippi River. Many of these eastern tribes made considerable progress. They learned to raise corn and beans. Some of them built wooden houses or "lodges" and lived in little villages. The names of many of the Woodland tribes are famous in American history: there were the Chippewas (CHIP eh wahs), Senecas (SEN eh kas), Mohicans (moh HEE kans), Delaware, Algonquins (al GONG kwins),

Marty

This Arizona Indian woman is grinding corn. She belongs to the Southwestern tribes.

and many others. In the South lived the Cherokees (CHAIR uh KEEZ) and the Seminoles (SEM ih nohls).

Perhaps the most famous of the Woodland Indians were the Iroquois (IHR oh kwoy) who lived along the Great Lakes. They included five tribes that joined together to help one another instead of fighting.

(2) The *Plains Tribes* were the Indians who lived farther west, beyond the Mississippi River. There were few trees in their country. Thousands of buffalo roamed over the rolling grasslands. The Plains Tribes were weak and poor until the white men came. Then they stole horses from the Spaniards or got them by trading. As soon as they had horses, the Plains Indians grew prosperous. They could gallop after the buffalo and kill them for meat. They made almost everything out of buffalo hide — clothing, tents, bags, and robes to sleep on.

The Plains Indians were always on the move, following the buffalo. They fought constantly to get the best hunting grounds. Even the names of the Plains Tribes sound like a battle cry. There were the Comanche (koh MAN chee), Cheyenne (shy EN), Sioux (SOO), Arapaho (a RAP a ho), Pawnee (paw NEE), and many more.

(3) The *Southwest Indians* inhabited the high, dry region that is now Arizona and New Mexico. In many ways they were the most progressive Indians north of Mexico. They raised corn, beans, and squash, and raised turkeys because they loved to wear their bright feathers. Out of stone and clay they built big dwellings where many families lived on different levels, somewhat like apartment houses. The Spanish ex-

The Seed Gathering Indians of the West had to work hard to keep alive. Notice how the Indians in the picture below are busy at many kinds of hand work.

Bell

plorers called such dwellings "pueblos," a Spanish word that means "villages." Some of the Southwest Tribes are called "Pueblo Indians." They include the Hopi (HOPE ee) and Zuñi (ZOO nyee) tribes.

(4) The *Seed Gatherers* were the Indians who roamed over what is now Nevada and eastern California. Few animals lived in this dry region so there was little hunting. The women gathered berries, roots, seeds, and nuts, and ground them into flour. They made beautiful closely-woven baskets to hold the seeds they gathered. The Shoshone (sho SHO nee) and Paiute (py YUT) tribes belonged to this group.

(5) The *Northwest Fishermen* lived on the rainy Pacific Coast in the land that is now Oregon and Washington. They fished and hunted and set traps. They also learned to carve wood and make fine canoes out of the trees that covered their land. The Northwest Indians included the Chinook (chi NOOK), the Nootka (NOOT kah), and the Yakima (YAK ih mah) tribes.

The Indians fought the white men. Thus, long before the white men came from Europe, the Indians came from Asia to all parts of America. They did not fill the land, however. There were probably only about a million Indians in the region between Canada and Mexico. That is less than the population of Detroit or Los Angeles today.

The number of Indians was small because they did not really know how to develop America's *natural resources* — that is, the soil minerals, water power, and other natural riches of the land. They might have gone on and developed great civilizations that could support a large population. But they moved forward too slowly. Their way of life was doomed when another group of immigrants appeared in America: white men from Europe whose knowledge and skill were far greater than that of the wisest Indians.

At first the Indians welcomed the white men. Later, when they realized they were going to lose their hunting grounds, they fought hard to drive them out. However, they never put up a united fight. The Indian wars went on for almost three hundred years, but they were mostly small-scale local affairs.

Some Indians remained friendly to the white men and helped them in many ways. But most of the tribes went on the warpath at one time or another. And they were savage, cruel fighters. They hoped to frighten the white men away.

Many settlers died when Indians attacked their villages. But in the end the Indians always lost. Finally, they had to settle down on *reservations*, or certain stretches of land the white leaders set aside for the Indians. Many Indians became sick and died of diseases the white men brought to America.

Today there are about 400,000 Indians left in the United States. A

Johnny

← **Burden basket made by California Indians**

great many of them still live on reservations, but in recent years a steady stream has left the reservations to get jobs in factories and on farms. In World War II and in the Korean War thousands of Indians fought with a bravery that their ancestors would approve

The Indians helped build modern America. Americans owe a great deal to the Indians. Some modern roads, such as "U.S. 40" include sections that were once Indian trails. Friendly Indians showed the early settlers the best way over mountains and across rivers. They showed them how to use canoes and snow-shoes. They taught them how to live in the woods and on the plains.

Perhaps the Indians' most important gift was food. Modern meals would lack richness and vitamins without corn, beans, squash, to-matoes, and potatoes. And life would be much duller without maple sugar, peanuts, chocolate, and chew-ing gum. All these were unknown to the white men before the discovery of America. The Indians also showed the settlers how to cook the new foods. They taught them how to prepare clambakes and corn roasts, and how to make popcorn, succotash, and hominy.

The Indians added new words and expressions to the English language, too. Everywhere you go in the United States you will find Indian names; cities, mountains, and rivers still bear the names the Indians gave

them. And Indian expressions are used in everyday speech. Americans talk of "going on the warpath" or "burying the hatchet." Indian games, such as lacrosse, are popular in some parts of the United States.

Europeans developed civilization in ancient times. Who were the white men who took over the land where Indian tribes had roamed for cen-turies? Why were they eager to leave Europe and take their chances in the American wilderness? To find the answers, it is necessary to look back to the early days of mankind.

About the time that the first hunters crossed from Asia to North America, other groups of early people were moving across Asia into Europe and North Africa. They progressed more rapidly than the inhabitants of the Americas. They developed great civilizations in Egypt and Asia Minor, and later in Greece and Rome. In the part of western Asia known as Palestine (PAL es tine), the great religious leader, Jesus

The fearsome mask pictured below was used by Northwest coastal Indians.

Jimmie

Christ, was born almost 2000 years ago. The Christian religion, based on Christ's teachings, later spread over Europe and America.

After centuries of rapid advance, there came a time of decay and decline. The great Roman Empire fell apart. There followed a period called the *Dark Ages* when it seemed as if civilization would die in Europe. But some books and ideas remained alive in Europe largely through the efforts of men and women who spent their lives in monasteries and convents copying ancient writings.

The Crusades stimulated trade and led to a revival of learning. The Dark Ages came at the beginning of a long period called the *Middle Ages*. The Middle Ages are so called because they came between ancient times and modern times. Toward the end of the Middle Ages, interest in science and education increased noticeably. Trade between Europe and Asia expanded. People in Europe learned about the riches of the East as a result of movements called the *Crusades* (kroo SAYDZ).

The Crusades were an attempt by the Christians of western Europe to win control of Palestine, the Holy Land where Christ was born. Thousands of people from western Europe traveled to Palestine to fight the Arabs and Turks who ruled the region and who were not Christians. The Crusaders failed to win permanent control of Palestine, but they caused a great increase in trade and a big change in business methods.

From Asia the Crusaders brought home spices, silks, lovely glass and chinaware, and beautiful jewels. Their families and friends wanted more of these luxuries, so trade increased. Travelers from Greece and Asia Minor began coming to Europe on business. Along with spices and silk, they brought books and new ideas, for these lands had managed to keep alive much of their ancient civilization.

The Crusades, the increase in trade, and new ideas from Greece and Asia led to a strange and wonderful period called the *Renaissance* (REN ah SAHNTS). The word renaissance means rebirth or revival. The entire period was marked by a revival of vigorous activity along artistic and intellectual lines.

The Renaissance began in Italy, for many reasons. Italy is near Greece and Asia, so it was the first part of western Europe that eastern scholars visited. Then too, the civilization of ancient Rome had never quite died in Italy. The Roman Catholic Church which has its headquarters in Rome also helped keep civilization alive in Italy.

Trade with Asia was slow and expensive. The Renaissance made Europeans, especially the Italians, wake up and pay attention to the world around them. They began to read books, and take an interest in painting and sculpture. They also looked for ways to increase business.

"God wills it!" shout the Crusaders, and Peter the Hermit blesses them. (Scene from a famous moving picture)

long, roundabout, dangerous way. They passed through the hands of many men and each one collected a profit. Robbers hid along the way and often stole a load of goods. And the rulers of the countries through which the goods passed demanded tax money. No wonder the products of the East were scarce and high priced!

The map on page 13 shows the three main trade routes to the East:

(1) The northern route started in Italy. It crossed the Mediterranean and led eastward over the Black Sea to the edge of Asia. Then it became a land route by which camels and traders traveled slowly across the vast plains of central Asia and finally reached China.

(2) The middle route was a combination sea and land route. It began in Italy and traveled across the Mediterranean Sea to the southwest corner of Asia. It followed the Tigris-Euphrates (TY grihs u FRAY teez) river valley to the Persian Gulf. Then it became a sea route that followed the coast of India and southeast Asia and finally reached the seaports of China.

(3) The southern route was mostly a water route. It ran from Italy to Egypt, then through the Red Sea and the Indian Ocean, around the edge of Asia to the Pacific Ocean and the coast of China.

The merchants of Venice and Genoa, the chief seaports of northern Italy, made big profits out of their eastern trade. But they were not entirely satisfied, and their customers were very much dissatisfied. Prices were very high because products from the East had to travel over a

Some people talked about a new route to the East. Notice that all three routes began in Italy. The

Italians had complete control, or a *monopoly* (moh NAHP oh lih), of the trade with Asia. People who lived farther west — the Spaniards, Portuguese, and English — had no part of the rich trade with the East. If they wanted silks or spices or eastern jewels they had to buy them from the Italians, and pay them a good profit. They began to think how nice it would be if they could find new routes to Asia — routes that would be under their own control.

Most people in Europe were still ignorant and bewildered. They thought that the world must be flat because it looked flat. If anybody traveled too far out into the unknown lands to the west, they thought he would fall off the earth. Perhaps he would be devoured by giant serpents. All sorts of horror stories were told about the region beyond the sunset.

However, there were educated, intelligent people in Europe who did not believe such stories. They thought the earth must be round. They had watched eclipses and had noticed that the earth's shadow on the moon was round. They had read the books of ancient Greeks which said that the earth was round.

They also thought the earth was small. If the earth was round and small, thoughtful Europeans reasoned, it should be possible to reach the East by sailing west. The idea was particularly attractive to the Spaniards and the Portuguese. If a way could be found to reach Asia by sailing west, they would be "in the front row." They occupied the southwest corner of Europe, so they could control the new westward route just as the Italians controlled the eastern routes.

The Vikings visited America in the year 1000. The scholars did not know it, but some daring seamen of

On the map below are shown the three main trade routes to the East in the days before America was discovered. Notice that all three routes started in northern Italy.

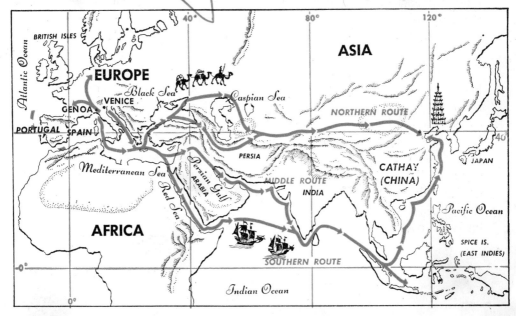

The Vikings go voyaging! This painting shows the discovery of Greenland.

Northern Europe had actually sailed westward years before. The *Vikings* (VY kings), as the skilful sailors of Norway and Sweden were called, dared to travel across the Atlantic Ocean. They built sturdy little ships. The typical Viking boat had a high prow decorated with the figure of an animal. Its square sails were striped in many colors. The whole ship was brightly painted and elaborately carved. By modern standards the ships were very small. It is amazing that the Vikings were able to cross the oceans in such boats.

In the ninth century the Vikings began to settle in Iceland. About a hundred years later, a leader they called Eric the Red sailed west from Iceland and discovered Greenland. He settled there; his son Leif (LEEF) grew up in Greenland. As soon as he was able, Leif Ericsson got a ship and began voyaging. Once on his way back to Greenland from Norway he was blown far to the southwest. He found a strange, rich land that he called Vinland, or Wineland, because grapes grew there in abundance. This happened about the year 1000 A.D.

Vinland was part of the eastern coast of North America; perhaps it was the region now called Newfoundland. Other Viking ships reached Vinland. Some of the warriors traveled inland. No one knows exactly where the Vikings landed or how much of America they explored. It is one of the puzzles of history, for they left no written records. They were good sailors, but they did not know how to read or write.

However, the story or *saga* (SAH ga) of Leif Ericsson's voyage was sung or recited over and over again, wherever the Vikings went. Probably it reached the ears of men in southern Europe who were dreaming of a westward route to Asia. It may have strengthened their determination to find such a route.

Marco Polo wrote about the East. The Viking stories do not seem to have impressed many people. They were probably regarded as fairy tales and soon forgotten. But the story of an Italian traveler named Marco Polo won the attention of scholars and common people alike.

Marco Polo was born in Venice in northern Italy about the middle of the thirteenth century. His father and uncle were merchants who often made trips to the East.

AMERICA AND EUROPE

When Marco was seventeen his father and uncle decided he was old enough to go with them on a trip to China, or "Cathay" as they called it. After many weary months and strange adventures they reached the palace of the Great Khan (KANN), or emperor, who ruled Cathay.

Marco Polo was a pleasant, intelligent young man. The Great Khan liked him so much he made him his adviser. He sent him to distant parts of the empire on business trips. The Polos stayed in the Far East for seventeen years. At last in 1295 they returned home with a great fortune in jewels. Marco Polo told fascinating stories of the palaces he had visited and the wonders he had seen.

The Polos did not long enjoy their wealth in peace. The next year a war broke out between Venice and the other great trading city, Genoa.

Marco Polo was captured and thrown into prison where he spent many months. There he dictated the story of his travels to a fellow prisoner. *The Book of Ser Marco Polo* still makes exciting reading. Polo described the wealth of the East in vivid words:

Rubies are found. . . . also sapphires and topazes and many other stones of price. . . . I can tell you the quantity of gold they have is endless. . . . a great palace is entirely roofed with fine gold. . . . all the . . . floors of its chambers are entirely of gold; the windows also are of gold.

Marco Polo traveled to the Far East. At the right is the Great Khan and the map below shows Polo's route.

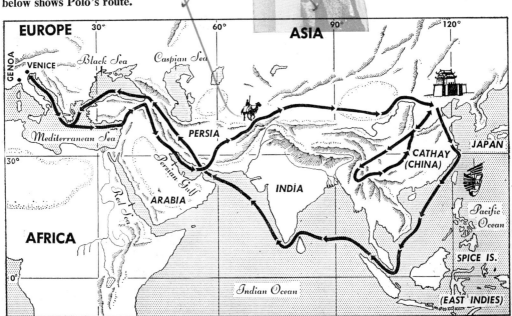

Some people laughed at Marco Polo's stories and called him a liar. He did exaggerate some things, but most of what he wrote was true. Sailors and mapmakers were especially interested in Polo's report of a great ocean beyond Cathay. They began to ask, "Is that ocean east of China the same ocean that is west of Europe?" Some scholars claimed that Marco Polo had seen the other side of the Atlantic and that a ship might reach China by sailing westward from Europe.

New inventions helped sailors. Because of the demand for eastern products and the stories of Marco Polo, interest in a western route to China increased steadily. But it is not likely that anyone would have dared to look for such a route if it had not been for certain new improvements and inventions.

The *compass* was one invention that gave sailors courage to try to

A boat compass is shown below. This invention encouraged exploration.

The astrolabe shown above helped sailors find their way by the stars.

cross the ocean. During the Middle Ages ships had to keep in sight of the shore, so they could steer by landmarks such as a hill or a church tower. When storms arose they were always in danger of being driven off their course and wrecked. Then some traveler from the East — it may have been Marco Polo — brought the compass to Europe in the 13th century. With the compass sailors could steer their ships accurately, even though they were out of sight of land. The compass always told them which way was north.

During the early years of the Renaissance, sailors learned to navi-

Andy

gate by studying the stars. They used an instrument called the *astrolabe* (AS tro layb) to find how far north or south they were.

Another discovery that gave sailors more courage was gunpowder. The Chinese had known about gunpowder for centuries; they used it for fireworks and celebrations. Gunpowder first appeared in Europe in the fourteenth century. Perhaps Arab traders introduced it, or perhaps a scholar from the East told Europeans how to make it.

Gunpowder soon changed methods of fighting in Europe. It was used to fire bullets and cannon balls. Ships began to carry cannons. This made it safer to approach a strange coast. Sailors with guns had

a big advantage over savage natives who had only bows or spears.

Another invention that encouraged people to explore was the printing press. During the Middle Ages, books were scarce and expensive because they had to be copied by hand. This was slow, tiresome work; only a few trained men knew how to do it. A book the size of the one you are reading would cost a thousand dollars or more. No wonder few people ever saw a book or learned to read! And you can see why it took a long time for people to learn about new discoveries and ideas.

About the year 1450, a German named Johann Gutenberg (GOO tehn berk) invented a printing press. This made it possible to print many

Gutenberg invented the printing press and so helped spread knowledge. In the picture below he and an apprentice demonstrate how his invention works.

copies of a book quickly and at a reasonable price.

Before the invention of the printing press, the discovery of a strange land or a new trade route was known only to the man who found it. He might tell his friends, but the story would get confused or lost.

The printing press changed things. Printed books made it possible for every discovery to be known all over Europe. The story of Marco Polo's travels was soon printed. It is believed that Columbus owned a copy of Polo's book and studied it.

Thus, there were many reasons why Europeans became interested in traveling to the East. First, the Crusades aroused interest in eastern lands and products. This led to an increase in trade and contact with eastern scholars that helped bring about a revival of learning. One result of the revival of learning was the improvement of methods of navigation and the spread of more accurate ideas about the shape of the earth. Remember, also, that people were growing discontented about the cost of silks and spices and the time it took to bring them from Asia.

The rulers of several European nations resented Italian control of the routes to the East. Competition and ill feeling among European nations were a new development that appeared toward the end of the Middle Ages. People in various parts of Europe became conscious of their own *nationality* — that is, they felt that together with their families, friends, and near neighbors they formed a nation. They usually spoke the same language and had similar customs.

As the nation grew bigger the people felt more and more that they "belonged together" and that they were capable of doing great deeds. And each ruler was eager to prove the nation's greatness. One way to prove it was to find new routes to the East, so that became a favorite project of several European rulers. Thus rivalry developed among the countries of Europe.

Prince Henry encouraged explorers. One of the new national states that had developed toward the end of the Middle Ages was Portugal. In the fifteenth century Portugal was one of the big powers.

Find Portugal on the map on page 13. Notice that it is on the western edge of Europe. It has a fairly long coast on the Atlantic Ocean. It is also near the Mediterranean Sea and Africa. Thus

West meets East. The page of an old manuscript below shows Europeans meeting Asiatics in the Middle Ages.

Portugal was a good place from which to start exploring.

Many Portuguese boys heard the call of the sea and became expert sailors. Portuguese captains commanded some of the most important voyages in history. Through their efforts, Portugal won rich colonies in Africa and Asia, some of which she still holds.

One man was largely responsible for Portugal's early success in trade and exploration. He was Prince Henry the Navigator, a younger son of the king of Portugal. He might have wasted his life in careless pleasure as many sons of royalty have done. But Prince Henry was truly a man of the Renaissance. He wanted to study and learn and increase knowledge.

As a young man, Prince Henry fought the Moors in North Africa. He became interested in the wild, unknown continent. For fifty years he encouraged sailors to explore the coast of Africa and the region beyond. He started a school where boys could learn navigation. He sent to Italy for men who could teach map making. Under his direction the astrolabe was improved, and sailors learned to use the compass.

Henry sent out many exploring expeditions. His men discovered several islands in the Atlantic that Europeans did not know existed: the Canary Islands, the Azores (a ZORZ), the Madeiras (mah DEER ahs), and the Cape Verde (VURD) Islands. These islands were called the "outermost lands" — that is, the farthest out from Europe. They proved important later on. When Columbus and other explorers started out on a long voyage across the Atlantic they stopped there to get food and water. Even today the islands are useful as landing fields for airplanes flying the Atlantic.

"Explore, trade, convert," Prince Henry urged the Portuguese, and they did as he asked. They kept looking for a new route to India and China. They believed that if they could only get around the continent of Africa they would reach the East.

In those days sailors were terribly afraid of Africa. Said one of them to Prince Henry: "Africa's hellish coasts are fringed with sea monsters, serpent rocks, and other fearsome creatures. There is the Devil's ocean that boils with fiery heat."

Díaz reached the Cape of Good Hope in 1486. Prince Henry laughed at such tales and encouraged sailors to keep sailing southward. At last, long after Prince Henry was dead, a brave captain named Bartholomew Díaz (DE ahs) reached the southernmost part of Africa. He found that the great continent narrows down to a point, or *cape*. In 1486, Díaz sailed around the cape and found a vast new ocean. The ocean Díaz found has ever since been called the

Indian Ocean for beyond it is India.

There, sad to say, Díaz had to turn back. His men were suffering from hunger and thirst. There was no map or chart to show the way across the new ocean. They had already sailed more than 3500 miles — the longest voyage any ship had ever made. And they still had to work their way back to Portugal.

Díaz had found what so many people were hoping for, a new route to India, but he could not follow it. He called the tip of Africa the "Cape of Good Hope," for he hoped some time to go on and reach India.

Vasco da Gama sailed around Africa to India in 1498. Díaz was never able to return and finish the trip to India. Another Portuguese explorer won

The map shows da Gama's route.

The map below shows da Gama's route.

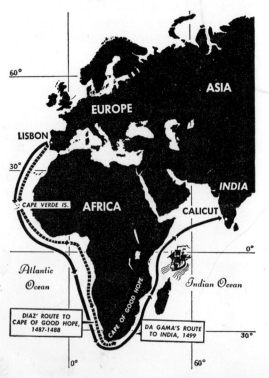

the glory of finding a new all-water route to the East. He was Vasco da Gama (GAH mah).

Twelve years after Díaz had to turn back, da Gama set sail. He had a chart Díaz had made to guide him around the coast of Africa. He sailed around the Cape of Good Hope and up the eastern side of Africa. He stopped often for food and water and to set up stations for trading with the natives. Then he boldly headed east across the Indian Ocean. In 1498 he dropped anchor in the harbor of Calicut, India.

It was a great day for Portugal. Da Gama loaded his ship with spices and jewels worth sixty times the cost of his voyage. He brought back a letter to the king from the Indian prince who ruled Calicut. It said:

A nobleman of your royal household has visited my kingdom, and his visit gave me pleasure. In my land is great abundance of cinnamon, cloves, ginger, pepper, and precious gems. What I would have from your land is gold, silver, coral, and scarlet cloth.

Trade with India soon made Portugal rich. Lisbon, the capital of Portugal, was for a time the busiest seaport in Europe. But the glory did not last. Spain also was looking for a new route and new lands to conquer. When Vasco da Gama returned he heard the news that, while he was gone, Spain had sent an expedition westward across the Atlantic. An Italian navigator led the Spanish expedition. You will read about him in the next chapter.

Chester *Jack*
Benny
"Well"

The Indians came to America from Asia thousands of years ago. The Indians of North America did not advance so far as the Indians of Central and South America. Most North American Indians lived mainly by hunting and fishing. Modern America owes much to the Indians. They showed early settlers how to raise corn, tobacco, potatoes, and other crops. They showed them how to follow old trails in the wilderness.

Great civilizations developed in Asia and Europe in ancient times. During the Middle Ages, a movement called the Crusades led to increased trade with Asia. In the fourteenth century a great revival of learning, or Renaissance, occurred. Europeans began to explore the world. New inventions, such as the compass, the astrolabe, the printing press, and gun powder, encouraged exploration.

There was a demand for a new route to the Far East. The old trade routes were long and dangerous. Spain and Portugal wanted to find routes they could control. Prince Henry of Portugal encouraged sailors to explore the African coast. In 1498 a Portuguese explorer, Vasco da Gama, sailed around Africa to India.

The Language of History

The following words appear in Chapter 1. Learn the meaning of each by looking it up in this book and in a good dictionary.

1. Crusades
2. Renaissance
3. monopoly
4. immigrant
5. Dark Ages
6. nationality
7. Viking
8. saga
9. Stone Age

What Happened Then

Be sure you know the important events connected with each of the following dates:

1. 1000 A.D.
2. 1450
3. 1498

Who's Who in History

Identify the following persons by referring to an encyclopedia and this textbook:

1. Leif Ericsson   3. Johann Gutenberg   5. Bartholomew Díaz
2. Marco Polo   4. Prince Henry   6. Vasco da Gama

Study Questions

1. **a.** From what part of the world is it thought that the ancestors of the American Indians originally came?
   b. By what route are they believed to have come?
   c. In what period of time is it thought they came to America?

2. What conditions in Central and South America were favorable to the development of Indian civilization?

3. **a.** Who were the Mayas?
   b. Where did they live?
   c. Mention three things the Mayas accomplished.

4. **a.** Who were the Aztecs?
   b. Where did they live?
   c. From whom did they borrow many discoveries?

5. **a.** Who were the Incas?
   b. Where did they live?
   c. Mention two achievements of the Incas.

6. Why did the Indians fight the white man?

7. List three contributions of the Indians to modern American life.

8. **a.** What were the Crusades?
   b. How did they encourage an increase in trade?

9. **a.** What was the Renaissance?
   b. Why did it begin in Italy?

10. **a.** Who were the Vikings?
    b. When did they visit America?

11. **a.** Who was Marco Polo?
    b. Why did his book stimulate interest in a new route to the East?

12. Name three inventions that encouraged voyages of exploration.

Chapter 2

COLUMBUS FOUND
A NEW WORLD

IF Columbus had sailed under his native flag instead of sailing for Spain the world's history might have been different. Why didn't he sail under the Italian flag? And why, for years, would no one offer gold to finance his expedition?

Spain reaped a fantastic reward for giving Columbus his little ships. After him came Spaniards whose names you may have read before: De Soto, Cortez, Coronado. And there were others, too, not so well-known, but as courageous. There was Pedro Cabral, for instance, who was blown off his course and landed in Brazil when he meant to go to India. There was Cabeza da Vaca whose story, a famous historian said, "is incredible and would have to be considered a legend except that it is true."

What drove these early explorers to cross and recross the Americas, defying terrible hardships? Was it greed? Love of adventure? Or was it eagerness to find the fabulous Seven Cities of which the Indians spoke?

As you read the chapter, keep these questions in mind. The answers will help you understand the whole Age of Discovery — that exciting time when two continents lay open to conquest, when a man of courage might find rivers and see mountains such as no European had known before.

Columbus believed the world was round. When Bartholomew Díaz sailed into the harbor of Lisbon, Portugal in 1486, an Italian sailor stood in the crowd that welcomed him. His name was Christopher Columbus. He came from Genoa, a center for trade with the East.

Christopher's father was a poor weaver, but he managed to send his son to school for a few years. Christopher studied Latin, geography, and navigation. He loved to look at old maps and charts. He did not care for his father's trade, so he became a sailor.

Columbus sailed all over the Mediterranean and even made a voyage to northern Europe. He visited England and may have reached Iceland. He probably heard stories of Leif Ericsson's discoveries.

Columbus was not ignorant or superstitious like most sailors of the time. He was a man of the Renaissance, eager for knowledge and new ideas. He knew that ancient Greek and Roman geographers had said the world was round. And his own observations convinced him that they were right. He also had read the story of Marco Polo's travels. Gradually Columbus became excited about the possibility of reaching the East by sailing westward.

Columbus sought aid in Portugal and Spain. Most people in Italy were not interested in new routes to Asia. They were satisfied to keep control of the old routes. Columbus got little encouragement in his homeland.

Columbus heard news of progress the Portuguese were making in navigation. Perhaps he dreamed of going to Lisbon, much as boys and girls in smaller towns now dream of going to New York. Then an accident helped him on his way. One day the Genoese ship on which he sailed was attacked. It sank near the coast of Portugal, and Columbus swam ashore. There he met and later married the daughter of one of Prince Henry's captains.

Columbus spent several years in Portugal. He tried to get the government interested in his idea of a westward route to Asia. But he had no luck. Perhaps the Portuguese were suspicious of him because he was a foreigner. They were so interested in finding a route around Africa they paid little attention to Columbus.

You will understand the problems of Columbus if you remember that three things were needed for a voyage of discovery: (1) ships, (2) men, and (3) money. He had none of these things himself. And how could a poor man hope to get them?

At the time it was very dangerous for a single ship to venture into a strange ocean. Often, when five or six ships were sent on a long voyage, only one or two came back. So Columbus felt he should have at least five ships. But men who owned ships were unwilling to hand them over to a poor Italian sailor.

When his wife died, Columbus left Portugal in discouragement. With

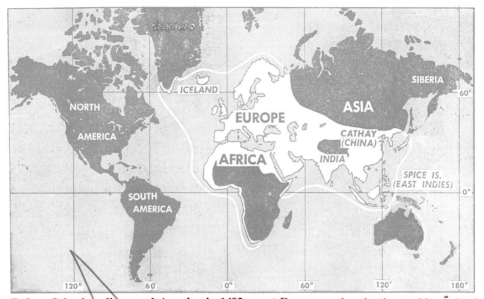

Before Columbus discovered America in 1492, most Europeans thought the world consisted only of the regions shown in white on this map. All the lands shown in solid color — North and South America, Australia, most of Africa and Asia — were unknown and undreamed of.

his little son, Diego (dee AY go), he made his way to Spain. Columbus tried to get Spanish officials interested in his plan. But he did not succeed. He even sent his brother to London to beg help from the English king; that effort also failed.

Years went by and Columbus grew older and poorer. Yet he never lost faith in his idea. At last he decided to go to France and try to interest the French court in his plan.

Queen Isabella of Spain decided to help Columbus. Columbus had to wait in port a few days for a ship to take him to France. He spent the time at a monastery near the town of Palos in Spain. Columbus was so wrapped up in his dream that he could talk of nothing else. The head of the monastery listened and be-

came convinced that Columbus really had a worth-while idea. So he used his influence to persuade Queen Isabella of Spain to see Columbus.

The Queen listened patiently to the Italian navigator. Columbus proudly demanded five or six ships, the title of admiral, and the governorship of any lands he might discover. He also demanded a ten per cent share of all gold and silver in the lands he expected to rule.

The Queen's advisers told her to refuse, but she could not make up her mind. For years she and her husband, King Ferdinand, had been fighting the Moors, who had invaded Spain from Africa. At last, the Moors were defeated. But the Spanish court had little money left to invest in what seemed a wild dream.

Columbus spent several years in

CHRISTOPHER COLUMBUS (1451–1506)

Teddy

"A strange boy, always watching the sea or looking at maps and sailors' charts." "Just a dreamer." Thus his neighbors in Genoa might have characterized young Christopher Columbus.

Columbus had a dream that he refused to give up in spite of poverty and disappointment. He believed he could find a new route to the Indies by sailing west. At last he persuaded Queen Isabella of Spain to give him a chance to prove his idea was right.

With three little ships and a handful of men he crossed the Atlantic Ocean. On October 12, 1492 he landed on an island he thought was part of China or Japan. He called the natives "Indians," thinking he had reached his goal, the Indies.

Columbus never realized he had made what was probably the greatest discovery of all time. Because of his faith in himself and in God's guidance he found a New World. Every year on October 12, millions of people in North and South America remember and honor the Italian navigator who discovered America in 1492.

Spain. Finally, he lost hope of getting help from Queen Isabella. Once more he started for France. Then Isabella made up her mind. She sent a messenger after Columbus. He returned; a few months later a contract was signed that gave Columbus most of what he asked.

Columbus sailed from Palos, Spain. The Queen appointed Columbus Admiral of the Ocean Sea, Viceroy, and governor of whatever territory he might discover. Instead of the five or six large ships he had asked for, he had to be content with three small ones: the *Santa Maria* (mah REE ah), the *Pinta* (PIN tah), and the *Niña* (NEEN ya).

The *Santa Maria* was the largest, so it became the flagship or the leader. It was only 90 feet long and it was in poor condition. The *Pinta* was only half as big as the *Santa Maria*, and the *Niña* was even smaller.

Columbus had a hard time finding crews to sail the ships. Few sailors wanted to sail west into the "sea of darkness." Columbus and his friends had to promise and coax. Men in prison were set free if they would join. Others were promised a share of gold that might be discovered.

Again and again the departure had to be delayed while the search for a crew went on. At last, men, ships, and supplies were ready. There were only eighty-eight men to sail the three ships — far less than the number needed.

Early on the morning of August 3,

1492, the little fleet left the port of Palos in southern Spain. It took nine days to reach the Canary Islands. There, both the *Niña* and the *Pinta* had to be repaired, so there were more delays. Then they sailed westward into the unknown. For seventy days, steady winds drove them across the Atlantic.

The sailors watched fearfully for serpents that were supposed to live in the ocean and swallow ships. Day after day passed with no sign of land. The sailors feared they would never get back to Spain. They begged Columbus to turn back, but his answer was "Adelante! Adelante!" ("Sail on! Sail on!") He told the crew he "had sailed to go to the Indies and would continue until he found them, with the Lord's help."

Columbus landed in the Bahama Islands. The men threatened to rebel. Perhaps they planned to throw Columbus overboard. Supplies were running low. The situation looked desperate. Then, on October 11, signs of land appeared. The next day, October 12, 1492, Columbus and his men landed on a tiny island in the Bahama Islands. He named it San Salvador; it was probably the island now known as Watlings Island. He spent many weeks sailing around nearby islands, looking for the mainland of Asia. He discovered the islands of Cuba and Hispaniola, or Haiti (HAY tih).

Everywhere he found friendly, brown-skinned natives. He called

Christopher Columbus, the Italian navigator, sailed for Spain and discovered America.

them Indians, for he thought he had found India. Columbus did not dream that North and South America lay between him and Asia.

On Christmas Eve, 1492, the *Santa Maria* was wrecked. Columbus hastened to sail home on the *Niña*. In Spain he received a hero's welcome. Everyone thought he had found a new route to Asia and the riches of the East.

In September, 1493, Columbus again set sail for "the Indies." This time he had 17 ships and 1200 men. He discovered Puerto Rico, and explored the Leeward Islands.

On a third voyage, in 1498, Columbus reached the mainland of South America. But nowhere did he find gold or the rich cities he expected. The Spanish government was disappointed; the Portuguese

were making big profits out of da Gama's discovery of a route to India by way of Africa.

Columbus found himself out of favor. His voyages had cost Spain a large sum and had brought little return, it seemed. In 1502 he began his fourth and last voyage across the Atlantic. This time he explored Central America from Honduras to Panama. Again he failed to find the riches of India.

The Italian navigator grew more and more puzzled. According to his map, the new lands were a part of India or China, but he could not find what he was looking for. There were no kings, no wise men, no gold, no palaces, no jewels or spices. Instead he saw endless woods and half-naked savages. They lived in huts. Some wore a few ornaments of gold, which they gladly traded for glass beads. To the end of his life Columbus did not know that in his search for India he had found a new world.

In 1506, two years after his last voyage, Columbus died in Spain. He was disappointed and bitter. He thought he had failed. But now he is honored as one of the greatest discoverers of all time.

Explorers wanted a northwest passage to Asia. "I opened the gates and others will enter at their pleasure," Columbus said shortly before his death. He spoke the truth. Within a few years Spanish, Portuguese, English, French, and Dutch ex-

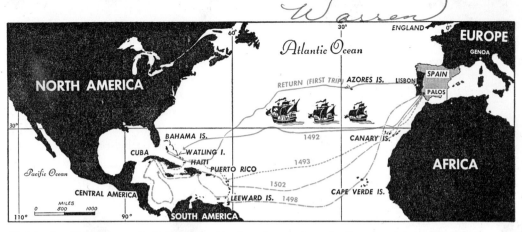

Christopher Columbus made four voyages to America as shown in the map above. He visited several West Indian islands and South America but not North America.

plorers were roaming up and down and across America.

Every time the explorers found a broad river or a big lake in North America, they hoped they had found a passage to India. The search for such a passage went on for centuries. The early explorers never found it, but because of their search North America was thoroughly explored.

The news of Columbus' voyages inspired many Spanish adventurers to sail westward. And Spain's rulers were eager to spread the Catholic religion to other lands. An Italian named Amerigo Vespucci (ves POOT chee) was a member of a Spanish expedition that visited South America in 1500. He seems to have been the first to say positively that this was a new region and not part of Asia. In his honor the geographers called the new lands America.

Ponce de León discovered Florida in 1513. The Spaniards gradually explored and started colonies on the islands now known as the West

Indies. They also made many visits to Central and South America. They were not much interested in the land to the north for it seemed to promise little gold. But in 1513 the governor of the island of Puerto Rico went exploring. He was Ponce de León (PAWN thay day lay OHN).

The Indians talked of the magic spring they called the Fountain of Youth. It was somewhere to the north on the mainland of North America. They said that anyone who drank from the spring would be cured of disease and would live forever. They also said that the Indians who lived near the spring wore many gold ornaments.

Ponce de León may or may not have believed in the magic spring. He certainly was interested in the gold ornaments. So he sailed

Ponce de León was attacked by Indians in Florida and later died of wounds.

north. On Easter Sunday, in 1513, he discovered a great peninsula. He called it Florida because the Spanish name for Easter is Pascua Florida. Florida means "full of flowers." Ponce de León never found the Fountain of Youth, but he was the first Spaniard to reach land that is now part of the United States.

Balboa discovered another ocean. In that same year, 1513, another Spaniard, Vasco de Balboa (bal BO ah) made a big discovery. Balboa had come to America seeking his fortune. He moved from place to place; he was often in trouble. Balboa got into debt and had to escape by hiding in a boat bound for Panama. At last, he reached Darien in Panama. Balboa was a kind man, and the Indians became fond of him. They told him that if he made a short journey westward he would find "great waters, very great waters."

Balboa listened eagerly. These waters might provide a way to get to the Indies. He did not hesitate.

With a few followers he crossed the narrow strip of land now known as the Isthmus of Panama (IHS mus of PAH na ma).

Indians led Balboa through the forest up a rocky path. When he reached the top of a mountain he suddenly saw spread before him the waters of a vast sea. No white man had ever seen those waters.

Balboa stood silent, amazed. Then, with a shout, he rushed down toward the shining waters. But he still had a long way to travel through rough, wild country. Finally, four days later, he reached the shore. In the name of Spain, Balboa claimed the new ocean and all the lands that touched it. Because he had traveled south he called it the South Sea. Later, the name was changed to the Pacific Ocean.

An Indian chief touched Balboa's arm and pointed southward. There, he told the explorer, was Peru, the land of gold. Balboa made plans to go to Peru, but in vain. His enemies accused him of being disloyal to the king. Balboa was put to death.

Magellan found a way around South America. Balboa's discovery of the new ocean proved that Columbus had not reached Asia but had found a new continent. Explorers kept trying to find a way to Asia. Nobody cared much about wild new lands. Trade was the big thing.

A Portuguese sailor named Ferdinand Magellan (mah JEL an) had a plan. He believed that if he kept

SPAIN'S EXPLORERS

sailing southwest he could find a way around the new lands. Then, he thought, he would reach Asia.

Portugal had no interest in Magellan's idea so he went to Spain. The Spanish king agreed to his plan and gave him five ships with full crews.

On September 20, 1519, Magellan set sail. For months he sailed south along the coast of South America, trying to find a channel or short cut to the West. At last, far to the south he found it. On the map you can find it easily, for it is still called the *Strait of Magellan*. (See map, p. 32.)

One of his sailors wrote: "It is a channel where waters are lashed by icy gales, and the rocky land is stark with eternal cold." Magellan and his men battled their way westward through the channel until they reached a great, quiet ocean.

Thankful for calm after storm, Magellan called his discovery the *Pacific Ocean* — a name that means mild or peaceful. He did not know it was the same ocean that Balboa had discovered at Panama, more than 3,000 miles to the north.

Magellan was soon to learn that Pacific was hardly the right name. The tale of his crossing reads like a terrible dream or nightmare. A gale sent two of his ships to the bottom with their crews. The remaining sailors waged a long battle with hunger, thirst, and weariness — and the dreadful disease called scurvy.

Magellan's ship sailed around the world. In spite of everything, Magel-

Balboa discovered the Pacific. Above he is shown claiming the ocean for Spain. The map below shows his route.

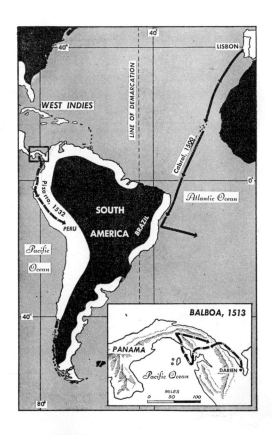

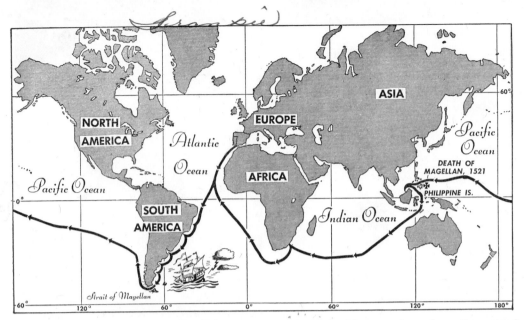

Magellan's expedition sailed around the world (1519–22). The map above shows the route of his ship, the *Victoria*. The explorer is shown in the picture below. He was killed by natives when he went ashore in the Philippines.

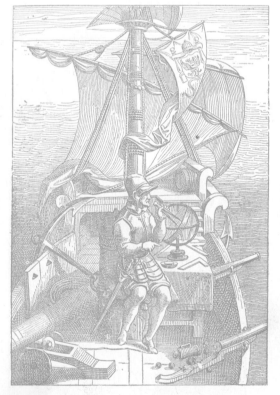

lan kept sailing west across the Pacific. Almost four months later he found a group of islands. He named them the Philippines (FILL ih peenz) in honor of Prince Philip, son of the Spanish king.

Locate the Philippines on the map on this page. Notice that they are close to the mainland of Asia. Magellan had proved it was possible to reach Asia by sailing west, just as Columbus and others had said. But Magellan never enjoyed his triumph. He was killed in a fight with natives on one of the Philippine Islands. His men hurriedly sailed away. They reached the Spice Islands, now called the East Indies.

By this time only two of Magellan's five ships were left. One turned back and tried to re-cross the Pacific. This ship was never seen again.

SPAIN'S EXPLORERS

The other ship sailed westward across the Indian Ocean, around Africa, and home to Spain.

Three years after the five ships had put out to sea with almost 300 men, the battered *Victoria* came back alone. On her decks were 18 men, so pale and worn that no one recognized them. They were the first men to sail around the world.

The voyage that Magellan planned, but did not himself finish, had many important results: (1) It proved that the world is round. (2) It proved that it is possible to reach the East by sailing west. (3) It proved that America is not part of Asia, but a vast new land. (4) It opened men's eyes to the real size of the earth.

Cortez conquered Mexico. After Magellan, most of the Spanish explorers concentrated on finding what wealth the American continents held. They realized that the long voyage across the Pacific to Asia was too dangerous for their little ships.

In March, 1519, a few months before Magellan started on his voyage, Hernando Cortez (kor TEZ) led an expedition from Cuba to Mexico. Cortez was a proud Spanish adventurer. With 600 men, he invaded the huge, wild land where thousands of Indians lived.

When he landed in Mexico, Cortez burned his boats so his men could not run away to Cuba. Then he fought his way inland to the capital of the Aztec Indians. On the way he captured an Indian girl who knew the languages of many tribes. Cortez had her baptized Marina. She helped him find his way and persuaded other Indians to give him food and other aid.

One of the legends or stories of the Aztecs was about a light-skinned god who had left Mexico long before. The fair god had promised he would

Hernando Cortez captured Mexico City in 1519. In the picture below the Spanish conqueror and his men are shown forcing their way into the capital of the Aztec Indians.

return some day. The Aztec Indians thought Cortez was the fair god. Their king, Montezuma (MAHN tee ZOO mah), received him with gifts.

But Cortez was cruel and greedy. He took the gold and jewels the Aztecs offered and demanded more. Then he made Montezuma a prisoner. Later, he destroyed the Aztec city and conquered all of Mexico. For over three hundred years after Cortez, Mexico remained a Spanish colony. That is the reason the people of Mexico speak Spanish.

Pizarro conquered Peru. Mexico was a rich prize but the Spaniards found even more wealth in Peru. You will recall that an Indian had told Balboa about the gold in Peru. Years afterward, one of Balboa's men became the conqueror of Peru. He was Francisco Pizarro (pih ZAHR oh). Like Cortez he was poor and he longed for gold.

Pizarro prepared carefully. He sailed down the west side of South America and spent some time on the coast of Peru. Later he returned with men and supplies. In 1532 he climbed the Andes mountains looking for the Indian ruler. The Inca emperor received him without fear.

The Indians of Peru were intelligent and skilful. They called themselves "the children of the sun." They did not think the handful of Spaniards could hurt them. Never did any people make a worse mistake!

The Spaniards had guns which the Indians had never seen. In a short

time Pizarro captured the chief cities of the Incas. He took the ruler as prisoner. The Incas filled a huge room with gold to ransom their ruler. Pizarro took the gold and then had the ruler choked to death.

Soon the Spaniards controlled all of Peru. The proud Inca Indians became slaves. One of Pizarro's officers, Pedro de Valdivia (val DEE vee ah), pushed south and conquered the region that is now Chile. Thus,

Francisco Pizarro conquered Peru and won the wealth of the Inca Indians.

Spain gained power over new regions and thousands of hard working Indians came under Spanish rule.

Cabeza de Vaca made a wonderful journey. The Spaniards failed to find much wealth in the land north of Mexico. They heard stories of fountains of youth and great cities full of gold, but they could not find such places. Many expeditions wandered across the southern part of what is now the United States.

In 1528 a small group of adventurers set out to explore Florida. They ran into trouble and hardships. First, their leader was killed. A man named Cabeza de Vaca (VAH kah), or "Cow's Head," took charge. He decided to reach Mexico by sailing across the Gulf of Mexico. But de Vaca lost his way and the

of Mexico eight years later, in 1536.

Cabeza de Vaca and his three followers were the first Europeans to cross Texas and the great Southwest. They found no gold, but they always hoped to find the Seven Cities of Cibola (SEE bo la), a wealthy far away region Indians talked about. "We ever held it certain," they reported, "that going toward the sunset we would find what we desired."

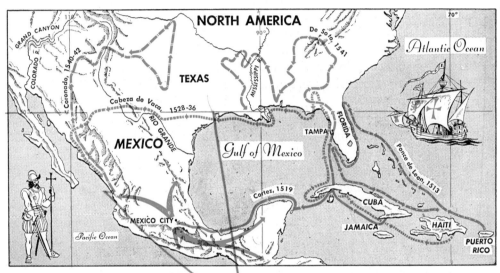

The map above shows the routes and discoveries of the early Spanish explorers in the Americas.

group landed in Texas. There they were captured by Indians.

Most of the men died the first winter. After years of captivity, Cabeza de Vaca and three of his men escaped. One was a Negro slave named Estéban, or Stephen. They wandered westward across the vast region that is now Texas, New Mexico, and Arizona. Then they turned south. After terrible hardships, they reached the west coast

De Soto discovered the Mississippi River in 1541. The Spanish expeditions to North America usually started out from the islands southeast of Florida. Find Cuba and Puerto Rico on the map on this page. Notice that these islands are convenient starting places for people planning to invade the mainland of the North American continent. Remember that Ponce de León came to Florida from Puerto Rico and

Cortez came to Mexico from Cuba.

Twenty years after Cortez, another Spaniard set out from Cuba. He was Hernando de Soto (dee SO toh), a brother-in-law of Balboa. He had fought with Pizarro in Peru.

De Soto reached Tampa, Florida, in 1539 with 720 men and more than 200 horses. His expedition was the best prepared and equipped that had so far set out to conquer the New World. De Soto was looking for the gold of the Seven Cities of Cibola. He hoped to find greater riches than Pizarro had won in Peru. He did not know that the Indians of North America were poor and backward.

In 1541 de Soto and his men reached and crossed the Mississippi River. They were probably the first white men to see the river that is still called the "Father of Waters."

De Soto's men tramped nearly halfway across North America, but they never found the gold or jewels they wanted. De Soto himself caught fever and died. He was buried in the great river he had discovered. His men wandered into northern Texas and then returned to the Mississippi. They followed the river to the Gulf of Mexico. A few of them lived to reach Mexico.

They had walked across a wilderness that is now Florida, Georgia, the Carolinas, Tennessee, Alabama, Mississippi, Louisiana, Arkansas, Oklahoma, and Texas! They did all this with only a few crude tools. Most of their food they found along the way. They had to fight Indians and fever and terrible loneliness. The expedition was considered a failure at the time, but it added much to the world's knowledge of the North Americas.

Coronado explored the Southwest. In spite of hardships and failure, the Spaniards still kept on searching. Some wanted to find gold. Others still hoped to discover a short cut to the Pacific and Asia.

In 1540 the Spanish governor of Mexico sent a young captain named Coronado (KOH roh NAH doh) to search for the rich cities of Cibola the Indians said were somewhere to the north. With about 300 horsemen and 1000 Indians, Coronado marched north into New Mexico.

Coronado found the famous cities of Cibola. They turned out to be the pueblos, or villages, of the southwestern Indian tribes. But there was no gold. Disappointed, Coronado pushed farther north. One of his lieutenants discovered the Grand Canyon of the Colorado River. Coronado marched across Oklahoma and into Kansas. "We shall go always a little farther; it may be beyond that last blue mountain barred with snow. . . ."

Coronado and his men saw many wonders: the Grand Canyon, the Great Plains, huge herds of buffalo. But there was never any gold. The expedition was a failure. Coronado and his men gave up in disgust. Friendly Indians guided them toward

De Soto discovered the Mississippi in 1541. Here he claims the region for Spain.

Mexico along an ancient path that later became the Santa Fe Trail.

The governor of Mexico dismissed Coronado in disgrace. Coronado had not found any treasure. But he had explored the Southwest and he had increased the world's knowledge.

Portugal claimed Brazil. Meanwhile, the Portuguese were making profits out of the African route to India. They were not much interested in the Spanish discoveries in the Americas. Sometimes, however, Portuguese ships were blown off their course. Notice, on the map on page 32, how close South America is to the west coast of Africa. You can understand how a Portuguese ship sailing south along the African coast might be blown across the Atlantic to the part of South America now called Brazil. That is what seems to have happened to Pedro Cabral (kah BRAHL) in 1500. He landed on the coast of South America and claimed Brazil for Portugal.

The Spaniards did not like Portugal's claim. They felt that all of the Americas should belong to Spain because Columbus had reached the New World first. But Spain had to let Portugal have Brazil because of an agreement that the two Catholic nations had accepted soon after Columbus discovered America.

This agreement was about the *Line of Demarcation.* It was a line that the Pope, as head of the Catholic Church, had suggested. He wanted to prevent disputes between the two nations so he drew a line on the map west of the Azores and Cape Verde Islands. It ran north and south through the Atlantic Ocean. All discoveries east of this line would belong to Portugal and all discoveries west of it would belong to Spain.

In 1494 Spain and Portugal agreed to move the line farther west, at a point west of the Cape Verde Islands. You can see the Line of Demarcation on the map on page 31. Part of Brazil lay on the Portuguese side of the line, so Brazil became a colony of Portugal. That is the reason the people of Brazil speak Portuguese today.

All the rest of South and Central America became the possession of Spain. Much of North America also came under Spanish control. California, Texas, and the Southwest were ruled as part of Mexico. Florida was a Spanish colony for more than three hundred years.

Thus, Spain won a great empire in the years after Columbus reached the New World. But other nations soon challenged the Spanish monopoly. France, Holland, and Great Britain all established claims and colonies in North America.

CHAPTER SUMMARY

Columbus was an Italian navigator. He sailed from Spain and discovered America in 1492. He was looking for a new route to India. He made three more voyages to the West Indies and South America.

Spain claimed North and South America. Soon after the discovery of America, Cortez conquered the Aztec Indians of Mexico and Pizarro conquered the Incas of Peru. De Soto discovered the Mississippi River. Coronado explored the southern part of North America. Balboa discovered the Pacific Ocean.

The early explorers wanted to find a way around America to Asia. They searched tirelessly for a northwest passage. Part of an expedition led by Ferdinand Magellan did reach Asia, and one of his ships sailed around the world.

Portugal claimed Brazil. A Portuguese explorer named Cabral reached Brazil in 1500. Spain and Portugal had agreed earlier to divide the New World between them. A Line of Demarcation was established between their possessions.

The Language of History

The following phrases appear in Chapter 2. Learn the meaning of each by using both this book and a good dictionary.

   1. Northwest passage   **2.** Line of Demarcation

What Happened When

Be sure you know the important events connected with each of the following dates:

   1. 1492   **2.** 1519–22   **3.** 1541

Who's Who in History

Identify the following persons by referring to an encyclopedia and this textbook:

1. Christopher Columbus
2. Ponce de León
3. Vasco de Balboa
4. Ferdinand Magellan
5. Hernando Cortez
6. Montezuma
7. Francisco Pizarro
8. Pedro de Valdivia
9. Cabeza de Vaca
10. Hernando de Soto

Study Questions

1. Write a short biography of Columbus telling (a) where he was born, (b) how he became interested in finding a new route to Asia, (c) his struggles to get someone to sponsor his expedition, (d) the names of his ships, (e) where and when he landed in America, and (f) why he died a disappointed man.

2. It has been said jokingly of Columbus that "when he started he didn't know where he was going; when he got there he didn't know where he was; and when he returned he didn't know where he had been." Explain the meaning of this statement. Do you think it is fair to speak of Columbus in this way? Why or why not?

3. Why was the New World called *America?*

4. Tell what each of the following discovered and give the dates of their discoveries:
   a. Ponce de León   b. Balboa   c. De Soto

5. What is wrong with the following statement: "Magellan was the first man to sail all the way around the world"?

6. How and when did Mexico become a Spanish colony?

7. Describe the conquest of Peru telling (a) who led the expedition, (b) why he was able to conquer the natives although they greatly outnumbered his group, and (c) how he treated the ruler of Peru.

8. What regions did Coronado explore?

9. How did Brazil happen to become a Portuguese colony?

10. Locate each of the following and tell its importance in the Age of Exploration:
    a. Florida
    b. Isthmus of Panama
    c. Strait of Magellan
    d. Philippine Islands

Chapter 3

THE FRENCH, DUTCH, AND ENGLISH EXPLORED NORTH AMERICA AND FOUNDED COLONIES

Slowly at first, then with mounting excitement, the New World became the center of attraction for men of courage in Europe. Spain and Portugal had divided the Americas between them and were gathering in the great wealth of the New World. But France, Holland, and Great Britain would not respect the Line of Demarcation. They began their own explorations.

In a burst of energy France sent out many great explorers, a number of them priests and missionaries, since France was a Catholic nation. Who were these brave men? Where did they go and what did they accomplish in America?

And what of the Dutch? World famous as bold businessmen, they could not be kept out of the New World. They seized the opportunity to colonize in America. But who did their exploring for them, and what region did they claim?

The British began late to colonize in America even though they had a strong claim to North America, thanks to the explorations of John Cabot and his son. And when they did colonize at last, their first attempts failed miserably. Why were they so slow to start? And what went wrong at first?

You will find the answers in this chapter as you watch nations gaining a foothold in the vast region that is America.

John Cabot claimed North America for England. Only five years after Columbus reached America, an English king, Henry VII, hired another Italian navigator to search for new lands. The man he chose to sail westward was John Cabot. Like Columbus, Cabot believed he could reach the East by sailing west.

In 1497 John Cabot sailed from Bristol, England. He reached the coast of North America about seven weeks later. He went ashore and claimed the territory for England. Later he spoke of it as the new found land. To this day, an island in the region is called Newfoundland. Cabot explored many miles of the coast; he sailed southwestward, perhaps as far as Maine.

The next year, 1498, Cabot sailed again to the North American coast. This time his son Sebastian seems to have sailed with him. Not much is known about the Cabots. The records show that the English king made John Cabot a gift; "Five pounds to him who found the new isle."

The money was good investment. Because Cabot was the first to reach the mainland of North America (Columbus only visited South and Central America), Great Britain claimed the whole North American continent. But for a long time the English were too busy at home to colonize the New World.

France sent explorers to America. Next, France decided to explore the New World. In 1523 King Francis I hired an Italian named Verrazano (VAIR raht SAH noh) to search for a route to the Indies through North America. Verrazano explored the coast from Nova Scotia to Florida. He was the first white man to sail into New York harbor. He found no short cut to China, but his voyage gave France a claim to North America.

Ten years after Verrazano's trip the French king sent another explorer to search for a northwest passage. He was Jacques Cartier (car TYAY), one of the most daring

The map below shows the route of John Cabot who reached the coast of North America in 1497 and claimed it for England.

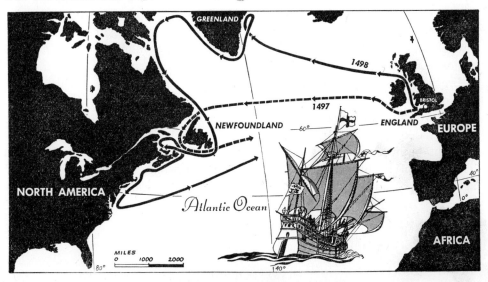

Cartier explored the St. Lawrence region and claimed it for France.

of the very early French explorers.

Cartier made several voyages to the coast of North America. In 1534 he discovered and named the Gulf of Saint Lawrence. In 1535 he sailed up the St. Lawrence River and anchored his ship under a great cliff called Quebec.

Cartier was sure the river would lead to China. He sailed on until he was stopped by the roar of great rapids. He called the rapids La Chine (luh SHEEN) which means China in French. The rapids are still called the Lachine Rapids in memory of what Cartier hoped to find.

Near the mouth of the St. Lawrence River, Cartier planted the French flag. He claimed the whole region for France.

French fishermen followed Cartier to North America. They fished along the Newfoundland coast. Some of them traded with the Indians and brought home furs as well as fish. The sight of beautiful furs encouraged hunters and traders to move up the St. Lawrence River to trade with the Indians. The fur trade brought wealth to the French and strengthened their claim to the region north of the St. Lawrence. They called the land by the name the Indians called it: Canada.

Champlain founded Quebec and New France. During the sixteenth century, France was too busy with religious disputes and civil wars to develop colonies. At last in 1589, a strong king, Henry IV, managed to restore order. One of his followers was a bold young fellow named Samuel de Champlain (sham PLAN). King Henry decided Champlain was the man to establish French settlements. It was a wise choice. Champlain well deserves the title of "Father of New France."

In 1608 Champlain founded Quebec, the first permanent French settlement in America. He also built a trading post at Montreal. Later, Champlain explored parts of New York and New England. There in 1609 he discovered a beautiful lake, now called Lake Champlain.

Champlain made friends with the Algonquin (al GONG kwin) and Huron (HYOO rahn) tribes of Indians. He helped them fight their enemies, the Iroquois Indians. This was a serious mistake. From that day on, the Iroquois always hated the French. They sided with the English and helped them defeat the French.

Meanwhile, other Frenchmen pushed westward. They discovered

42   EXPLORATION AND COLONIZATION

Samuel de Champlain, the Father of New France, made friends with the Algonquin Indians in Canada. Here he is shown demonstrating the white man's weapons.

the five inland waterways that are now called the Great Lakes. Two of the great French explorers were Louis Joliet (zho LYAY) and Père Marquette (pare mahr KET).

Joliet was a restless fur trader. Père (or Father) Marquette was a missionary who devoted his life to teaching Indians the Christian religion. At a little French trading post on Green Bay, Lake Michigan, the two men heard Indians speak of *mitchee seepee* (great flowing water). They thought it might be the passage to China that so many explorers had tried to find. But it was the Missis-

Joliet and Father Marquette are shown viewing the Mississippi in 1673.

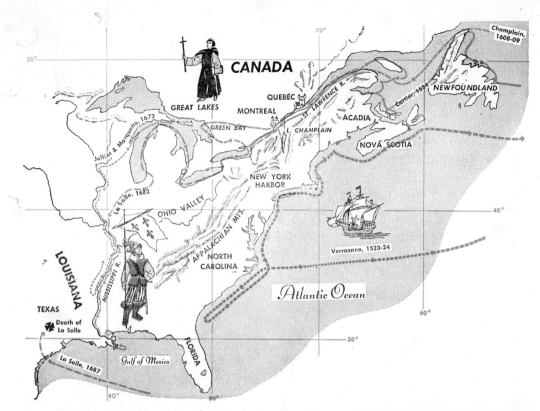

This map shows French explorations in America. France claimed Canada and the Mississippi Valley because of these explorations.

sippi River. They reached it with the help of Indian guides, in 1673.

In birch bark canoes the Frenchmen glided southward for many days. They could hardly believe that a river could be so big. From little villages Indians came to stare at the white men. Joliet was thinking, "What a place for the fur trade!" Père Marquette was thinking, "What a place to build a mission and teach these poor savages the Catholic faith!" They were hardly half-way down the river when their food began to run low and they had to turn back. By this time they had seen enough to realize the river did not lead to

the Pacific Ocean and Asia as they had hoped.

La Salle claimed Louisiana. Another Frenchman later reached the mouth of the Mississippi River. He was Robert Cavelier de la Salle (kah VEH lyeh deh la SAL), one of the greatest French explorers. He sailed up the Great Lakes and then crossed the land that is now Wisconsin to reach the upper Mississippi.

La Salle and his party went all the way down the Mississippi River to the Gulf of Mexico. On April 9, 1682, he went ashore and planted the French flag near the mouth of the

EXPLORATION AND COLONIZATION

EXPLORATION

SAILED FOR	EXPLORERS	DATE	WHAT THEY DID
SPAIN	Columbus	1492	Discovered America
	de Leon	1513	Discovered Florida
	Balboa	1513	Discovered Pacific Ocean
	Magellan	1519-22	Led first expedition around the world
	Cortes	1519	Conquered Mexico
	Pizarro	1531	Conquered Peru
	Coronado	1540-2	Explored the Southwest
	de Soto	1541	Discovered Mississippi River
	Menendez	1565	Founded St. Augustine, oldest city in the United States
PORTUGAL	Diaz	1486	First to round the Cape of Good Hope
	da Gama	1498	Rounded Africa to reach India
FRANCE	Verrazano	1524	Explored Atlantic Coast
	Cartier	1534	Discovered St. Lawrence River
	Champlain	1608	Founded Quebec
	La Salle	1682	Explored the Mississippi River to its mouth
ENGLAND	Cabot	1497	Explored the Labrador Coast
	Drake	1577-80	First Englishman to circumnavigate the globe
HOLLAND	Hudson	1609	Discovered the Hudson River

river. He claimed possession of the whole Mississippi Valley for France. And he called the region Louisiana in honor of Louis XIV of France.

La Salle had no idea how big was the valley of the Mississippi and its branches. It extended from the Appalachian (AP eh LAYTCH yun) Mountains in the East to the Rocky Mountains in the West. La Salle also did not know that De Soto had found the river long before and had claimed the territory for Spain.

France claimed the Mississippi Valley. The year after his trip down the Mississippi, La Salle returned to France. Then, with four ships he sailed from France again. This time he headed for the Gulf of Mexico. La Salle planned to sail up the Mississippi River.

But trouble hung over the expedition. Spaniards captured one ship; another was wrecked. Moreover, the Gulf Coast seemed the same everywhere. La Salle could not find the Mississippi.

By mistake, the explorers landed on the Texas shore. They tried to march overland to the Mississippi. It was a hard trip; the men grew tired and angry. They wanted to quit and return to France. When La Salle insisted they must go on, they murdered him.

Thus, La Salle died in 1687 — a failure, it seemed. But his explorations gave France a strong claim to the heart of America. Within a few years the French built a chain of forts along the Mississippi River. They also claimed the Ohio Valley as part of the Louisiana territory. You can imagine how all these claims led to trouble with England.

Hudson found a great river and harbor. Early in the 1600's another nation joined the race to find new lands and a new route to Asia. The people of Holland were greatly interested in trade with the East. Their little ships sailed to India and China and came back loaded with silks and spices. The Dutch East India Company was one of the busiest and most successful organizations in world trade. The Company sent Henry Hudson to find a passage to China.

The map below shows Henry Hudson's explorations in North America (1607–11).

EXPLORATION AND COLONIZATION

Henry Hudson is here shown on the shore of the river he discovered in 1609.

Henry Hudson was an Englishman who had already made two voyages of exploration. On April 6, 1609, he sailed from Amsterdam in the *Half Moon*, a sturdy little ship. He had a crew of twenty Dutch and English seamen. He reached Newfoundland in June and sailed south along the coast. Early in September he entered New York Harbor just as Verrazano had done almost a hundred years before.

Hudson explored the region more thoroughly than Verrazano. He found the mouth of the great river that empties into New York Bay. In his description of the region where New York City now stands, Hudson wrote an unconscious prophecy: "This is a very pleasant place to build a town on."

The *Half Moon* sailed up the river for 150 miles and reached the point where Albany now stands. Hudson kept hoping the broad, majestic river would lead west to China. At last he turned back, disappointed.

Hudson also discovered a huge bay in northeastern Canada on his fourth and last voyage. On the way home he ran into trouble; Hudson's men rebelled and took over the ship. They seized Hudson and his little son. They put them in a small boat with seven other men. Then they set them adrift to die.

Frobisher sought the Northwest Passage for England. England lagged behind Spain and France in settling the New World. The Spanish colonies boasted cities and universities before the English colonies even got started. St. Augustine, Florida, now the oldest city in the United States, was founded in 1565 — more than forty years before the first permanent English settlement. England was far away from the old trade routes to the East, all of which started in Italy. The English government was slow to realize that new trade routes across the Atlantic would increase British commerce.

True, an English king had sent John Cabot to North America in 1497. But for more than fifty years the English did nothing to follow up Cabot's exploration. They were too busy quarreling over religion and other issues to think about faraway lands. However, when red-haired Elizabeth became queen, the English began to take an interest in world affairs. In 1576 Sir Humphrey Gilbert wrote a book about the Northwest Passage. The book was widely read. It inspired several Englishmen to look for a way to China by going across or around America.

One sailor who was an old friend of Sir Humphrey started out as soon as he read the book. He was Martin Frobisher. On the map on page 46 you will find Frobisher Bay, which cuts into the northeastern part of Canada. Frobisher found the bay on his first voyage to America in 1576. He was sure it would lead him to China, but he had to turn back because of ice that blocked the bay. He made two more voyages to America, but he never found a northwest passage.

Drake was a daring sea captain. Another Englishman, Francis Drake, did much to advance Britain's position in the world. Drake was born in Devonshire on the southwest coast of England. He went to sea when he was ten; when he was twenty-two he was already captain of a ship. Drake was one of the great English "sea dogs" whose lawless attacks made life hard for the Spaniards. The fact that Spain and England were supposed to be at peace never bothered Drake.

On one voyage to Panama, Drake plundered several Spanish towns. He also happened to catch a glimpse of the Pacific Ocean. He murmured a prayer that he "might sail once in an English ship on that sea."

Drake's prayer was answered in a great voyage he began in 1577. He sailed around South America and through the stormy Strait of Magellan. Four of his five ships were wrecked or turned back. But Drake went on alone. He sailed up the Pacific Coast of South America, capturing ships and attacking Spanish towns in Chile and Peru.

Drake sailed around the world. Drake headed his ship north looking

Admiral Sir Francis Drake (below, left) was a loyal subject of Queen Elizabeth (below, right).

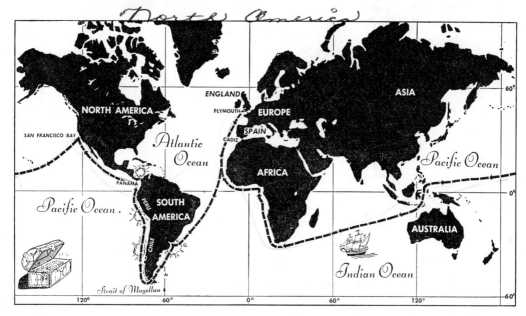

Francis Drake sailed around the world (1577–80). The map above shows the route of his ship, the *Golden Hind*. Drake was the first Englishman to circumnavigate the globe. He was knighted by Queen Elizabeth I of England as a reward.

for the western end of the North-west Passage. He wanted to find a short cut that would lead him to the Atlantic and home. He went north along the coast of what is now California, Oregon, and Washington. He entered a beautiful bay that was probably San Francisco Bay. He claimed the whole Pacific Coast for England and Queen Elizabeth.

By this time Drake's ship was loaded with treasure stolen from Spain. If he tried to sail back home along the South American coast and through the Strait of Magellan, the Spaniards would almost certainly capture him. And he could find no passage across North America. So he decided to turn west, across the Pacific, and sail home around the world.

His men were tired and supplies were low. It looked hopeless, but Drake's ship, the *Golden Hind*, made its way to India and around Africa. At times the ship was almost out of drinking water, but Drake sailed on.

At last, on September 26, 1580, the *Golden Hind* entered the port of Plymouth, England. The voyage had taken almost three years. Drake and the men under his command were the first Englishmen to sail around the world.

Drake brought back gold and jewels worth more than two million pounds (worth many times that amount in today's money). England was very proud of the daring captain. Queen Elizabeth herself came on board his ship and gave him the title of Sir Francis Drake.

Drake's voyage gave England a claim to the western coast of North America. But the Spaniards did not

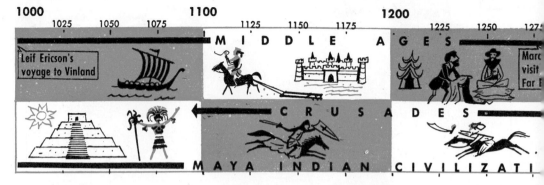

Above is a *time line*. This is a device to help you understand the order in which things happened. On a time line each century is allotted the same amount of space regardless of how many or how few things happened. This time line covers the time from 1000 to 1600.

recognize the claim; to them Drake was just a pirate. Drake cared little what the Spaniards thought. He kept on attacking Spanish colonies and ships. Once, he sailed into the harbor of Cadiz, Spain, burned many ships, and sailed out again. He called this "singeing the King of Spain's beard."

Eventually, the Spaniards sent a great fleet, or *armada* (ahr MA dah), against England in 1588. Drake and his friends sailed out to meet the clumsy Spanish ships. In quick time, their superior seamanship defeated the Armada. The Spanish ships tried to escape by going north and west around Scotland and Ireland. But a terrible storm came up and did much damage. Only one-half of the Spanish fleet managed to reach home. Spain's sea power was weakened. Perhaps more than anyone else, Drake helped make England mistress of the seas.

Humphrey Gilbert tried to found a colony. So far, England had started no settlements in America. Spain

and Portugal had many flourishing colonies. France was making money out of American fisheries and fur trade. England was far behind.

But something was happening in England. The spirit of the Renaissance at last reached the British Isles. Englishmen were awakening to the opportunities of world trade. Queen Elizabeth I was a strong, wise ruler. She inspired her people with a sense of patriotism. Englishmen felt ready, willing, and able to conquer the world for "good Queen Bess."

Sir Humphrey Gilbert was a man of the Elizabethan Age. In 1583 he went to Newfoundland and tried to organize a colony there. The attempt failed, perhaps because the land was so cold and lonely. Sir Humphrey started home, but he and his ship were lost in a storm near the Azores.

Sir Humphrey had a young half brother named Walter Raleigh (RAW lih). Sir Walter was a great favorite with Queen Elizabeth. There is a story that he once threw his velvet cloak over a puddle so the queen would not have to step in the mud.

EXPLORATION AND COLONIZATION

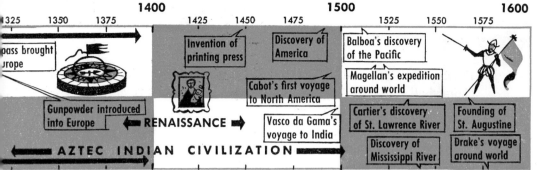

| 1400 | | | | | 1500 | | | | 1600 |

Notice that the earlier centuries are much less crowded than the later ones. Study this time line carefully, and try to remember which events happened first. Also try to understand how certain events may lead to other developments in later centuries.

Sir Walter decided to carry on his half brother's work and found a colony in America. This was a dangerous undertaking. Spain had threatened to destroy any American colonies that England founded; and the English Navy was not yet strong enough to defend faraway places.

Sir Walter Raleigh founded the Lost Colony. In spite of the danger, Queen Elizabeth gave Raleigh permission to start a colony. In 1585 Raleigh sent a colonizing expedition to the North Carolina coast. They landed on Roanoke (RO ah NOHK) Island. The first group of colonists soon became discouraged. They were happy when an English ship took them home the following year.

Raleigh was not the kind of man who gave up easily. In 1587 another group of colonists arrived on Roanoke Island. A month later a little girl was born to one of the families Raleigh had sent. Her name was Virginia Dare. She was the first child born of English-speaking parents in what is now United States.

The colony did not prosper. It was hard to find food. The Indians were unfriendly. The settlers quarreled among themselves. They longed to see a ship from England.

But the ship was delayed for three years. You will recall that this was the period when Spain sent her great Armada against England. No English ships could be spared to help a colony on the other side of the ocean.

When at last the relief ship came to Roanoke, not one of its people could be found alive or dead. What happened to Raleigh's colony is still a mystery. The only clue was the word "Croatoan" carved on a tree. There was another island named Croatoan where friendly Indians lived. Perhaps the colonists planned to go there, but no trace of them was found. Historians call the settlement the Lost Colony.

The failure of the Newfoundland colony, and the strange tale of the Lost Colony, discouraged other Englishmen. There were no new attempts to start an English colony in America for many years.

CHAPTER SUMMARY

France, Holland, and England sent explorers to America. England claimed all of North America because of John Cabot's voyage to New-foundland in 1497.

France claimed North America because of the explorations of Verrazano, Cartier, La Salle, and others. Samuel de Champlain was called the Father of New France. He founded Montreal and Quebec. French priests came to North America to teach Christianity to the Indians. La Salle traveled down the Mississippi and claimed Louisiana.

The Dutch sent Henry Hudson to America in 1609. He sailed up the Hudson River and claimed the region for Holland.

The English were slow to explore America. Martin Frobisher tried to find a northwest passage across America in 1576. Francis Drake explored the west coast of North America in 1579, and then completed his trip around the world in 1580.

Sir Humphrey Gilbert tried to found the first English colony in America in 1585. It was a failure. Sir Walter Raleigh tried to start a colony in North Carolina in 1585 and 1587. The settlers disappeared mysteriously and the settlement is called the Lost Colony.

The Language of History

The following words and phrases appear in Chapter 3. Learn the meaning of each by using both this book and a good dictionary.

1. settlement	3. armada	5. Elizabethan Age
2. missionary	4. time line	6. the Lost Colony

What Happened When

Be sure you know the important events connected with each of the following dates:

    1. 1497   **2.** 1534   **3.** 1565   **4.** 1585   **5.** 1588   **6.** 1609

Who's Who in History

Identify the following persons by referring to an encyclopedia and this textbook:

1. John Cabot
2. Jacques Cartier
3. Virginia Dare
4. Martin Frobisher
5. Henry Hudson
6. Francis Drake
7. Robert de La Salle
8. Walter Raleigh
9. Samuel de Champlain

Study Questions

1. On what did the British base their claim to North America?
2. Tell what each of the following men discovered or explored and the date of the discovery:
   a. Verrazano   b. Cartier   c. Father Marquette and Joliet
3. On what did the French base their claim to the Mississippi Valley?
4. Why is Champlain called "the Father of New France"?
5. Why were the Iroquois Indians unfriendly to the French?
6. Write a short sketch of the life of Francis Drake telling (a) why he attacked Spanish ships in peace time, (b) the date and reason for his voyage around the world, and (c) his part in the defeat of the Spanish Armada.
7. a. Who was Sir Walter Raleigh?
   b. Where and when did he try to start a colony?
8. Locate each of the following and tell its importance in the history of exploration:
   a. Louisiana
   b. Hudson River
   c. Newfoundland
   d. Roanoke Island
   e. Frobisher Bay
   f. Lake Champlain
   g. St. Lawrence River
   h. La Chine Rapids
   i. Quebec
9. a. What did Henry Hudson discover on his third voyage?
   b. For what country did he sail on this voyage?
   c. How did Hudson meet his death?
10. a. Why was Great Britain slow to start colonizing America?
    b. Why did the defeat of the Spanish Armada encourage British efforts to colonize America?
11. In a well-known advertisement Virginia Dare is pictured as an attractive young lady in modern dress. What is wrong with such a picture?

LET'S LOOK AT WHAT WE'VE LEARNED

Who were the first Americans and where did they come from?

It is believed that the first Americans were the ancestors of the people called American Indians. They seem to have come to America from Asia by way of the Bering Strait in the Stone Age, many thousands of years ago.

What events in Europe helped bring about the discovery of America?

1. The Renaissance caused many Europeans to become interested in exploring the world. 2. The invention of the printing press made it possible for news and ideas to spread rapidly. 3. The invention of the compass and the astrolabe helped sailors find their way. 4. During the Crusades, Europeans became acquainted with the products of Asia: silks, spices, and fine woods. A rich trade developed which was mostly under Italian control. The new national states, Spain, Portugal, France, and England, were envious of the Italians' trade monopoly. They wanted to find new routes to Asia.

When and by whom was America discovered?

Columbus, an Italian navigator, in the service of Spain, discovered America in 1492.

By whom were the American continents explored?

Most of the early explorers were sent out by Spain. Among them were: 1. Ponce de León, discoverer of Florida; 2. Balboa, who discovered the Pacific Ocean; 3. Cortez, conqueror of Mexico; 4. Pizarro, conqueror of Peru; 5. De Soto, who discovered the Mississippi River; and 6. Coronado, who explored the Southwest.

A Portuguese sailor, Cabral, discovered Brazil, which later became a Portuguese colony.

John Cabot, an Italian who sailed for England, was the first to visit North America.

The French sent several explorers to North America. Among them were: 1. Cartier, who discovered the St. Lawrence River; 2. Champlain, who founded Quebec; 3. La Salle, who explored the Mississippi Valley.

Henry Hudson explored and claimed the Hudson River Valley for Holland.

What part did the English play in the exploration of America?

The English did not become interested in America until long after the Spaniards were established in the New World. But they soon made up for lost time. Among the great English explorers were: 1. Martin Frobisher, who explored the northeastern coast of Canada in 1576; 2. Francis Drake, who sailed around the world (1577–1580) and claimed the Pacific coast of North America for England.

What was the Northwest Passage and how did it encourage exploration of North America?

For many years Europeans looked upon the American continents as merely an obstacle that blocked the way to Asia. They wanted to reach China and India and bring back the riches of Asia. For this reason, explorers tried to find a short cut to Asia across or around the Americas. They sailed up many rivers hoping to find their way to the Pacific coast and Asia. They did not find any northwest passage, but they did explore much of North America.

Connecting the Past with the Present . . .

Americans like to be on the go. The average American is never so happy as when he is going some place. This has long been characteristic of people who live in America. The ancestors of the Indians wandered from Asia to Alaska and then southward to every corner of the Americas. The Indians themselves were often on the move, looking for new hunting grounds. The explorers who came after Columbus wandered up and down the land, seeking riches or a new route to Asia.

The belief that something better, something strange and wonderful lies over the hill or beyond the horizon has long been part of America. Today, Americans think little of driving across the continent to find a new job and establish a new home. They are following a dream that was old when the first English settlers came to the New World.

Questions for Discussion and Review

1. List four inventions that encouraged exploration.
2. Name the five groups of Indians who lived in North America.
3. Name the two most advanced Indian nations and tell some of the things they were able to do. One nation was in Mexico and the other in Peru.
4. Many people believe that Leif Ericsson discovered North America almost 500 years before Columbus. Why do you think the trip by Columbus was more important?

5. Give two main reasons why the Spanish worked so hard at exploring the New World.

6. a. What was the Northwest Passage?
   b. Why were Europeans so eager to find it?
   c. Name three explorers who searched for it.

7. Explain why people in Brazil speak Portuguese today while almost all the rest of the people of South America speak Spanish.

8. a. Name five of the explorers who first traveled in what is now Canada and the northern United States.
   b. What country did each come from?
   c. What reasons did they have for making such dangerous expeditions?

9. a. What three nations claimed the Hudson River Valley?
   b. Which one first sent settlers there?

10. The defeat of what great navy made settlement on the Atlantic coast more inviting to other European people?

THE HISTORY LABORATORY

Human beings learn by doing. When you plan and carry through an activity or project you gain new skills and absorb facts that you remember. Here are suggestions for activities that you will find interesting and profitable.

Work With Maps . . .

1. On a map of the United States show the location of cities, mountains, rivers, parks, universities named after Columbus. Use a large atlas to look up places with names like Columbus and Columbia.

2. Make lists of places in the United States that have Spanish, French or Dutch names. Use an atlas.

WHAT AND WHEN

Discovery of America 1492   Cabot's voyage 1497   Magellan's expedition 1519-22

Committee Assignments . . .

Have the Bulletin Board Committee prepare a display to illustrate each of the chapters of this Unit.

Have a committee work out a program of readings, music, drawings, clothing, showing how the Indians lived before the arrival of the Europeans. The committee members might consult *Americans Before Columbus* by Baity and *The Book of Indians* by Holling.

Prepare a Scrapbook . . .

The Spanish Main was the scene of some of the most famous pirate stories ever written. Look up the meaning of the term in the dictionary. Then prepare a scrapbook called "The Spanish Main." Include the story of Spanish merchant ships and the pirates who attacked them, maps of the region, stories, clippings, and drawings of pistols, ships, treasure, flags, clothes, and forts.

Make Some Models . . .

Make clay, soap, metal, or wood models of some of the following:

1. the *Santa Maria*
2. a Viking ship
3. a pirate's pistol
4. a sea monster
5. the *Golden Hind*
6. an Indian village

(Consult the encyclopedia for pictures of these.)

Enlarge Your Vocabulary . . .

Make a dictionary of Spanish words and sayings which Americans use every day. Here are a few examples: hacienda, adios, sombrero.

For Dress Designers . . .

Sketch or make a dress for a doll in the style worn by Queen Isabella or Queen Elizabeth.

discovers St. Lawrence
1535

De Soto's discovery
of Mississippi River
1541

Drake's voyage
1577-80

Raleigh's "Lost Colony"
1587

CROATOAN

Wanted: Authors! . . .

You have probably read stories based on history, which have imaginary plots and characters. Pretend you write stories for a famous magazine and choose one of the following titles for your next tale:

a. "Eighteen Came Home." A story by one of Magellan's crew.

b. "The Terrors of the Deep." A sailor's report of monsters he claims to have seen near the edge of the world.

Keep a Notebook . . .

It is not easy to remember all the facts of history. A carefully kept notebook will help you recall the most important facts and remember the order in which things happen.

Select a notebook of the size and kind your teacher recommends. Then record in it the important dates, chief events, and leading people in each Unit. Be sure to include definitions of new words and phrases you learn.

You will find your notebook very useful when you have to prepare for tests and final examinations. And the "notebook habit" pays dividends all through life.

Let's Read About the Period Before 1492

BAITY, ELIZABETH, *Americans Before Columbus*, Viking, 1951.
*CLARK, ANN, *Secret of the Andes*, Viking, 1952. (a novel)
**ELLSBURG, EDWARD, *Spanish Ingots*, Dodd, 1936.
*GRAHAM, ALBERTA P., *Christopher Columbus, Discoverer*, Abingdon, 1950.
HOLLING, HOLLING C., *Book of Indians*, Platt, 1935.
KJELGAARD, JAMES, *Explorations of Père Marquette*, Random, 1951.
MITCHELL, HELEN and WILSON, W. N., *Ships that Made U.S. History*, McGraw, 1950.
SALOMON, JULIAN H., *Book of Indian Craft and Indian Lore*, Harpers.
SYME, RONALD, *Champlain of the St. Lawrence*, Morrow, 1952.
SYME, RONALD, *Cortes of Mexico*, Morrow, 1951.
WHITE, ANNE T., *Prehistoric America*, Random House, 1951.
*WHITE, ROBB, *Secret Sea*, Doubleday, 1947. (a novel)

* indicates easy reading
** indicates advanced reading

Unit 2

GREAT BRITAIN BECAME THE CHIEF POWER IN NORTH AMERICA (1607-1763)

WHAT HAPPENED to the British in the seventeenth century? After centuries of lagging behind other nations, they suddenly made the world pay attention to them.

After failure at first, the British founded several colonies that became solidly prosperous. But life in these colonies was different from anything the settlers had known back in England. Now they were living in a wilderness. How did they keep alive? Who was responsible for their success?

Britain grew stronger in America — the colonies grew larger — but Spain still claimed the whole region. And France had established forts and trading posts near the British settlements. What conflicts developed as the British colonies began to spread westward?

The answers to these questions are part of the story of the development of British colonies. This and the long struggle between Britain and France for control of North America make up the story you will read in Unit 2.

59

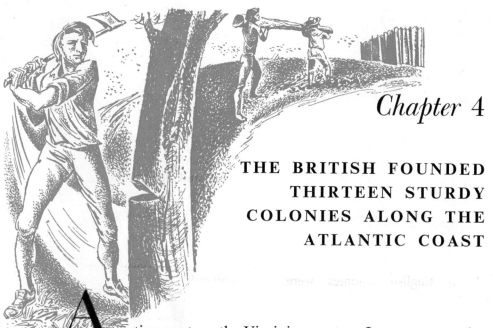

Chapter 4

THE BRITISH FOUNDED
THIRTEEN STURDY
COLONIES ALONG THE
ATLANTIC COAST

AT a tiny spot on the Virginia coast — Jamestown — the British founded their first successful colony, and the history of the American nation began. Thirteen years later another colony was started, this one at Plymouth, in Massachusetts. What troubles and suffering were endured to get the colonies permanently and safely established!

However, "nothing succeeds like success," and never was that saying truer than in colonial times. The British poured money into America. New colonies sprang up and grew larger until they outdistanced Jamestown and Plymouth. Who were the leaders responsible for Britain's success? Where did all the money come from?

British colonization was not just a business matter. Religion played a great part. At least four colonies were started as refuges for people who were suffering from religious persecution. Who were those people? Who were the men who took the lead in creating refuges for them?

From Jamestown in 1607 to Georgia in 1732, this chapter traces the establishment of the thirteen British colonies. Here is the story of America when it was just a string of little settlements on the edge of the Atlantic Ocean.

The defeat of the Armada cleared the way for British colonists. Five nations — Spain, Portugal, France, Holland, and Great Britain — had raised their flags in the Americas. It soon became clear, however, that flag raising would never win lasting possession of the new land. Only by sending settlers and homemakers could the land be held. The success of the Spanish colonies in South America proved this.

Cabot's discovery gave England a claim to North America, but no successful English colonies were founded until more than a hundred years later. You have already learned the reason for this. England was a small weak nation in Cabot's time. Spain was strong and the Spanish navy ruled the oceans. Not until Drake and other British seamen defeated the Spanish Armada could England begin to build colonies.

The destruction of the Armada in 1588 did not end Spain's empire. For many years Spain remained powerful in world affairs. But the defeat of the Armada did mark the beginning of a glorious age for Great Britain. Now the British could go forth to settle the New World.

As you learned in the last chapter, Sir Humphrey Gilbert and Sir Walter Raleigh had tried to found English colonies or plantations in America. A *colony* meant, originally, a group of men and women who left their home country to settle in a land far away. English colonies were often called plantations because people thought they were like young trees that are dug up by the roots and planted in a different soil and climate. Some transplanted trees live, others die, and so it was with the colonies.

Bad times in England encouraged settlement of America. It took great courage and determination to come to North America in the early seventeenth century. The land was an unknown wilderness where wild animals roamed. Terrible storms often lashed the coast. The Indians had already learned to distrust white men and attack new settlements. And the voyage to the New World was full of dangers. Many ships were lost trying to cross the Atlantic.

Why did people leave their homes in peaceful English towns to settle in an unknown wilderness? What drove them to gamble their lives and their children's lives? There were several causes. Some came for reasons that were *economic* (EE kho NAHM ik) — that is, connected with earning a living. Times were hard in England. This was partly because of a change in farming. The big landowners found sheep raising more profitable than the raising of grain. Many of them made sheep pastures out of their farms. They ordered the tenant farmers and laborers to leave. Thus, thousands of farm workers lost their homes and their jobs. Where were these people to go? How could they earn a living? They wandered into the cities looking in vain for work. Some became

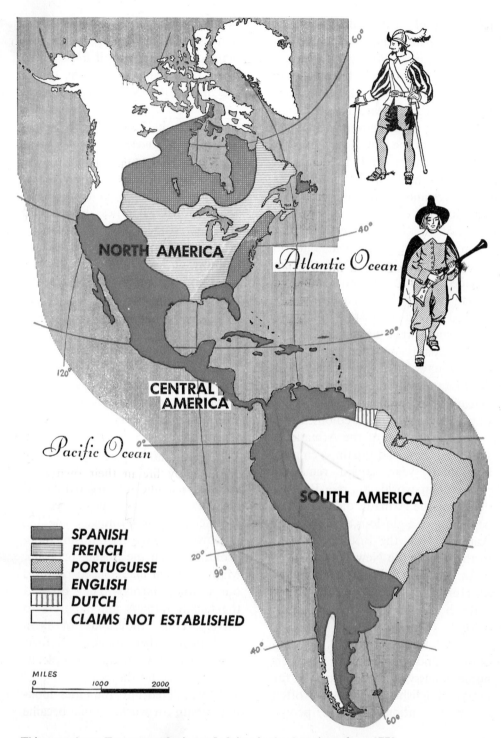

MILES
0   1000   2000

SPANISH
FRENCH
PORTUGUESE
ENGLISH
DUTCH
CLAIMS NOT ESTABLISHED

This map shows European colonies and claims in the Americas about 1750.

beggars and others stole. Many went to prison. To such homeless and disgraced men the colonies offered another chance.

Most settlers came to America with the hope of making a better living than was possible in Europe. Almost all the land in Europe was owned by noblemen. Ordinary men were lucky if they could rent some land from a noble. They had to give a large part of their crops to the owner. A man who owned even a little land was regarded as rich.

Imagine how English farmers felt when they heard they could get many acres of good land in America and pay for it in a few years out of the crops they raised! The news was wonderful, "too good to be true." Here at last was a chance to get ahead in the world. But only the bravest dared to seize the opportunity to gain land in the wilderness.

Some people hoped to get rich in a hurry. Other Englishmen hoped to find gold in America. Tales of Spanish treasure ships had excited the nation. People who could afford it crowded into a London theater to see a new play, *Eastward Ho!* One actor said to another, speaking of American Indians, "Why man, all their cooking pans are pure gold. The prisoners they take are chained with gold. As for diamonds and rubies, they go forth on holidays to gather them by the seashore to hang on their children's coats."

Talk like this brought adventurers to the American colonies. They did not want to work or build homes. They wanted to look for gold, fill their pockets, and hurry home. The treasure seekers did not make good colonists.

A few men came to America for the same reason that Marco Polo had gone to China. They wanted to trade with the natives. The ships that came back from America brought news that Indians would exchange beautiful furs — beaver, mink, or otter — for a knife or a handful of glass beads. To every colony came traders who hoped to gain wealth in a way that was somewhat slower but more certain than finding gold or diamonds.

A few men and boys came to America for the pure love of adventure. They wanted a change — something new and different. They were tired of the rules and regulations of the Old World. They longed to find a place where they could enjoy life in their own way. America has always attracted people who want freedom. Many of them became the pioneers and pathfinders who led the advance of civilization.

Many colonists sought religious freedom. Besides those who came to earn a better living or find treasure or adventure, some people came to America for religious reasons. In 17th century Europe, the law compelled most people to go to the church their ruler favored.

In every country there were brave

men and women who thought such laws were wrong. They wanted to worship God in their own way. But if they refused to attend the national or state church, the ruler might put them in prison, torture them, perhaps even kill them. In England, Pilgrims, Puritans, and Quakers were severely punished for their religion. In the German lands people of many faiths were abused.

Only in the New World across the sea was there hope of religious freedom. Four of the English colonies — Massachusetts, Rhode Island, Maryland, and Pennsylvania — were founded by people who wanted religious freedom.

Trading companies raised money for colonies. Thus, some people desired to come to America for economic reasons, some for religious reasons, and some because they loved adventure and freedom. But most of those who wanted to leave England were poor folk. Rich people seldom cared to leave their comfortable homes to settle in a wilderness!

But as Columbus and others had found out, it took a great deal of money to travel to America. Hundreds of workers were needed to make a successful colony. To hire or build ships and stock them with food for the trip cost many English pounds for each colonist. But that was out of the question. A working man of the time earned a few pennies for a day's work. He could not possibly save enough to pay for the trip.

The problem was solved by a few rich men who formed a business company, or a *trading company*. First they persuaded the King to give them a big stretch of land, or a *grant*. The King was anxious to have the land settled, so it was not hard to get a grant of land.

The next step was to raise money to start a colony. Sometimes the men who formed the company put up the money themselves. More often they raised the money by selling shares of stock in the company. (Business companies today still use this method to get money to build a new plant or start making a new product.) People who bought the shares received yearly payments or dividends out of any profits the company made.

The company hoped to make money by buying goods the colonists produced and selling them at a higher price. Then, too, after the colony was well started, the company would sell land to new settlers. The land had cost the company nothing. If some of it could be sold for a few cents an acre the company would still make money. It looked like a good investment. But there were so many unexpected dangers and losses that few of the companies ever earned profits. They did start successful colonies, however; America owes much to these companies.

The company would give certain people who wanted to go to America a share of stock, passage to America, and fifty acres of land. In return they had to work for the company until they had paid back the debt. Often they were able to repay in five or six years.

But not everybody could make such an arrangement. Usually the company chose men who had a good reputation and were experienced farmers. They expected them to bring their own farm tools and perhaps a horse or a cow and a pig. The very poor people who wanted to come to America had to sell themselves as "bond servants" or "indentured servants" for a number of years — usually seven. That meant that they agreed to work without pay for that period in return for their passage to America. After they had worked for their masters for the years agreed upon, they be-

came free men. Hundreds of them soon had farms of their own.

Jamestown was founded in 1607. One of the early trading companies was the Virginia Company of London, sometimes known as the London Company. Several businessmen who lived in London got together and formed the company. Their aim was to carry on the work of Sir Walter Raleigh and found a successful colony in America.

The leaders of the London Company were wise enough to learn from Raleigh's unhappy experience. They made careful preparations, for they did not intend to have the people in their colony starve to death. They bought three ships and a big supply of food, tools, and seed.

Next they sent 100 men across the ocean to prepare the way for those who were to come later. The pioneer band reached the region we now call Virginia in 1607. They settled near the coast on a river they named James in honor of the English king. (Queen Elizabeth had died four years

The map below shows early Virginia settlements. Note that they were near the coast. Jamestown was built on marshy ground so the capital later was moved north to Williamsburg.

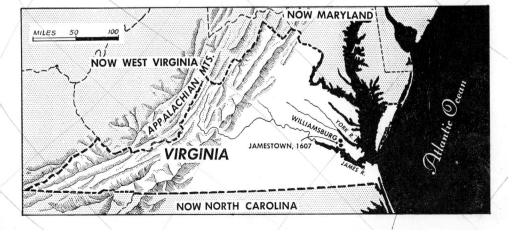

earlier, and the King of Scotland, James Stuart, had succeeded her.)

The new settlement was called Jamestown. It was the first English settlement to become well established in North America. The settlers might have chosen a better location if they had had more experience. The place was low and swampy and hard to defend against enemies. But there was plenty of fish in nearby Chesapeake Bay. On or near the shore were clams and oysters. The woods were full of turkey and deer. The sandy soil could be farmed.

However, the first colonists were a helpless lot. They were city folks who did not know how to keep alive in the wilderness. The company had accepted anyone who was willing to go. Many of the men spent all their time looking for gold. Nobody bothered to plant the seeds the company had sent. The summer drifted by; in the autumn there was no crop of grain or vegetables. The pile of food they had brought from England grew smaller and smaller.

Then came cold, damp, winter days — and famine. Many settlers became sick with fever. Often their only food was soup made from boiled bark. One of the colonists wrote sadly, "The many birds and beasts were wild and we unskilled and they suffered not much from us." So the colonists starved and died in the midst of plenty. Only forty were left alive in the spring.

John Smith saved Jamestown. In the midst of the trouble and suffering one man showed himself a leader with good common sense. He was

Below is pictured "The First Day at Jamestown." Note that few people seem inclined to work. They little dreamed what hardships were ahead.

Captain John Smith. At first the other colonists were suspicious of him. He loved to tell stories about great things he had done. No one knew much about him, except that he had fought in distant places.

When the leaders the company had selected proved unfit, Captain Smith took charge. He ordered everybody to work, saying, "He who will not work shall not eat." Smith made friends with some of the Indians. By skilful trading with them he got enough corn to keep the settlers alive.

John Smith was too active to stay in the wretched little settlement very long. The strange rivers and the dark forest attracted him. Like so many other adventurers he dreamed of finding a northwest passage to Asia. He explored the land around Jamestown hoping to find a path to the Pacific Ocean.

Smith did not remain away from the colony very long on his exploring trips. Often he brought back food from the Indians, and he always had an exciting story to tell. Once, he reported, a band of angry Indians suddenly surrounded him. They dragged him to their village and brought him before their chief, Powhatan (POW hah TAN). Powhatan called a council of his warriors and medicine men. The council decided that Smith must die. He was tied up and his head was laid on a huge stone. Two warriors raised their heavy clubs to crush it.

Suddenly, the chief's daughter,

Pocahontas saved John Smith's life, he said. This picture is taken from a recent movie about the early days in Virginia.

Pocahontas (POH kah HAHN tas), sprang from her seat by her father's side. She clasped the prisoner's head in her arms, and laid her own head on his. Chief Powhatan yielded to his daughter's wish. Smith was set free. The Indians even escorted him back to Jamestown.

The story of Pocahontas and Captain John Smith may or may not be true. There is no proof, except Smith's word, and he liked to tell "tall tales." But we do know that Smith made friends with Powhatan. Pocahontas later became a Christian. She married an Englishman named John Rolfe. He took her to England where she soon died.

Tobacco growing brought wealth. Early in 1608 two ships arrived from England with fresh supplies and more settlers, including a few women.

The tobacco plant brought success to the Virginia Colony. There was a big European market for "the Indian weed."

The new settlers were not much better than the first lot, but Smith made them all work.

The second winter was hard. Many settlers died of disease, but Smith's leadership pulled the colony through. In the spring of 1609 another and larger group of settlers arrived. Smith was injured when some gunpowder blew up. He returned to England.

Without his leadership the Jamestown colony's troubles grew worse. The winter of 1609–1610 was known as the "starving time." Disease, Indian attacks, and lack of food killed most of the colonists. But in the spring the ships came again with food and new settlers. Somehow the colony managed to keep alive and even grow stronger. Success was won at last, but at fearful cost of human life.

The leaders of the London Company learned to be more careful in choosing colonists. They sent over skilled workers and farmers — men who knew how to handle tools and who were not ashamed to work. They also sent some women to make homes for the men and boys.

The Jamestown settlers never found gold, but they discovered something else that brought them big profits: they began to grow tobacco. Europeans were eager to smoke this "Indian weed," so Virginia tobacco found a ready market. Slowly the land was cleared of trees, and big fields of tobacco brought wealth to the colony.

But there were never enough workers. In 1619 a Dutch ship brought twenty Negroes to labor in the fields. These were the first Negroes who came to the English colony. The planters welcomed them and treated them as indentured or bond servants. In time they were set free, but Negroes who came later remained slaves.

The first American legislature met in 1619. The new settlers started other towns nearby. People began to talk of the Virginia Colony. It was named in honor of Queen Elizabeth, who was called the Virgin Queen.

Jamestown slowly lost its importance. But it can never lose the glory of having been the first English colony that became well-established. It has another claim to fame. It was the first capital of Virginia; there the first American lawmaking body met in 1619.

At first the London Company had made the laws for the colony.

The settlers soon became unhappy about this arrangement. As Englishmen they were used to having a say in their government. The free air of the New World soon made them feel even more independent. Why should they take orders from a few men in England who happened to be head of the London Company?

About this time, new men gained control of the London Company. They were willing to listen to the colonists' wishes. They sent over a wise governor who let the planters choose men to speak for them, or represent them. The representatives were called *burgesses* (BUR jes es) because each was elected by the people of a *borough* or town.

The representatives came together and met as the *House of Burgesses* in Jamestown in August, 1619. That is a date to remember, for the House of Burgesses was the first lawmaking body in the colonies. For the first time, Americans sat down together and decided what rules they needed and what taxes they should pay.

Virginia's House of Burgesses was the first American Colonial legislature.

A. THE NEW ENGLAND COLONIES

The Pilgrims founded Plymouth in 1620. Thirteen years after the founding of Jamestown, another colony began far to the north. This was the Plymouth colony. The small group of men and women who founded it are called Pilgrims, a name that means wanderer. They came in a ship called the *Mayflower*.

In their home town, Scrooby, in the north of England, the Pilgrims were unpopular. They were poor and they were deeply religious. Their neighbors thought the Pilgrims were odd, because they met often to read the Bible and discuss its meaning. Sometimes government officials broke up such religious meetings, for in England everybody was supposed to attend the King's church.

The Pilgrims decided to go to Holland because they had heard that in Holland people could worship as they please. The Dutch welcomed them and did not interfere with their religious meetings. But life was hard in Holland. Food was high and wages were low. Even the children of the Pilgrims had to work twelve hours a day.

The Pilgrims often felt homesick. They did not like to speak Dutch; it made them unhappy to see their children forgetting English customs and the English language. Some of the Pilgrims began to think that they should have gone to America instead

The Pilgrims sailed from England on the *Mayflower.* This painting shows how the Pilgrims gathered and prayed for guidance as the voyage began.

of Holland. In a new land the children would have a better chance to get ahead — and they would also have the right to worship God in their own way. So back they came to England to make arrangements to go to America.

Somehow the Pilgrims managed to borrow money to buy land from the London Company and to pay their expenses on the *Mayflower.* They sailed from Plymouth, England late in the summer of 1620. A storm drove the *Mayflower* off her course

so the Pilgrims did not land on the territory of the London Company. In December, 1620, they landed far to the north in the part of Massachusetts now called Cape Cod.

They named their landing place Plymouth (PLIM uth), after the beautiful English town from which they had sailed. A big stone on which they are said to have stepped ashore from their boats is still preserved and is called Plymouth Rock.

The storm that had blown them astray proved to be a good thing.

The Pilgrims landed on the Massachusetts coast in December 1620. The painting below shows how the little group knelt and offered prayers of thankfulness after leaving the ship.

Since they were going to a part of the Atlantic Coast claimed by two companies but held by neither, there would be no governor to rule them. So, before they had even landed, the Pilgrims decided to form a government of their own. Their written agreement is now called the *Mayflower Compact* because they drew it up in the ship's cabin and all the men on board signed it. In it they agreed to "make just and equal laws

This is a model of the *Mayflower*, the famous little ship of the Pilgrims.

for the general good."

Next, they elected John Carver to be governor for one year. Carver, a member of the Pilgrim band, was the first governor elected in the American way, by free choice of his fellow men. Miles Standish was the military leader of the colony.

Hard work made the Plymouth Colony a success. Landing in the snow

and ice of winter, the Pilgrims faced the problem of shelter from the cold. The women and children stayed on shipboard for a few weeks, while the men erected a building to serve as a church on Sunday, and for community meetings and as a hospital at other times. William Brewster was the religious leader.

Next, the Pilgrims built a hut for each family. By then food was so scarce that for days at a time they lived on clams. Yes, and "thanked God," as Governor Carver wrote, "for abundance provided by the sea."

No enemies troubled the Pilgrims then or for years afterward, for a strange disease had killed most of the Indians around Plymouth. But the same or another disease fell upon the half-starved Pilgrims, causing at least one death in every family. John Carver died; William Bradford became governor in his place. When spring arrived, only half of the little Pilgrim group had lived through the winter. But not one wanted to go back when the *Mayflower* sailed away. Hopefully the Pilgrims planted corn from seed they found in a deserted Indian storehouse.

One day an Indian named Samoset (SAM oh set) appeared at Plymouth. The Pilgrims were badly frightened, but Samoset soon proved he was a friend. He brought his chief, the great Massasoit (MAS ah soit), to the colony. Later the settlers made a treaty of friendship with Massasoit that kept the peace for forty years.

The Pilgrims made a treaty of friendship with the Indian Chief, Massasoit.

Another Indian, Squanto (SKWAN toh), liked the Pilgrims so much that he made his home at Plymouth. He showed the colonists how to plant corn and where to hunt and catch fish. They were careful to dry some of the fish and to set aside a store of smoked meat. When winter came they would be protected against famine. They quickly developed a good fur trade with the friendly Indians. They sold the furs to English traders at a profit.

Because of their hard work and common sense, the Pilgrims avoided much of the troubles that made life hard for the Jamestown colonists. They harvested a good crop in the autumn of 1621. Grateful to God, Governor Bradford ordered a day of Thanksgiving. Massasoit and his

warriors came to the feast. It was the first Thanksgiving. Following the example of the Pilgrims, Americans still celebrate the Thanksgiving holiday each autumn.

The Puritans founded Massachusetts Bay Colony in 1628–30. The Pilgrims were not the only Englishmen who sought religious freedom in America. Another group called the *Puritans* founded a second colony in New England ten years after the Pilgrims came to Plymouth.

The Puritans were better-educated than the Pilgrims and they had more money. They did not want to make a complete break with the King's church as the Pilgrims had done. They just wanted to purify the church of certain practices they did not like. Hence, they were called Puritans.

The Puritans formed their own company and bought a large stretch of land from the King. King Charles also gave them a *charter* or plan of government. The charter provided that the colonists could run their affairs without interference from the English government. No one

The Pilgrims celebrated the first Thanksgiving time at Plymouth in the autumn of 1621. The picture below shows the feast they held, thanking God for the rich harvest.

COLONIZATION

NEW ENGLAND COLONIES				
Plymouth & Massachusetts	1620 1628	Plymouth Boston	William Bradford John Winthrop	Mayflower Compact Educational development
Rhode Island	1636	Providence	Roger Williams Anne Hutchinson	Religious freedom
Connecticut	1636	Hartford	Thomas Hooker	Fundamental Orders of Connecticut
New Hampshire	1623	Portsmouth	John Mason Benning Wentworth	Lumbering and shipbuilding
MIDDLE COLONIES				
New York	1614-24	New York Albany	Peter Stuyvesant John Peter Zenger	Fur trade; patroon system
New Jersey	1664	Princeton Trenton	George and Philip Carteret	Trade and prosperity
Pennsylvania	1682	Philadelphia	William Penn Benjamin Franklin	Religious freedom
Delaware	1638	Wilmington	Caesar Rodney	First log cabins built by Swedish settlers
SOUTHERN COLONIES				
Virginia	1607	Jamestown Williamsburg	John Smith Nathaniel Bacon	House of Burgesses Bacon's Rebellion
Maryland	1634	St. Mary's Baltimore	Cecil Calvert Charles Carroll	Religious toleration
The Carolinas	1663	Charleston	John Sevier	Production of rice, indigo, naval stores
Georgia	1733	Savannah	James Oglethorpe	Refuge for debtors; buffer colony

knows why King Charles was so generous to the Puritans, for he did not like them or their ideas. Perhaps the reason was the fact that the King was always short of money. The Puritans were willing to pay a high price for what they wanted.

After careful preparations, the Puritans sent eleven shiploads of colonists to New England. In 1630 they founded Boston and several other little towns along the Massa-chusetts coast. The settlements made up what was called the Massa-chusetts Bay Colony. John Win-throp was chosen governor. He was re-elected many times and soon be-came the colony's leading citizen.

Massachusetts Bay Colony grew rapidly when the government in England began to punish severely those who criticized the established church. Within ten years the colony had 20,000 settlers. Half a century

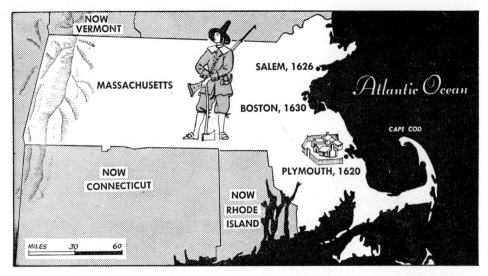

NOW VERMONT

MASSACHUSETTS

SALEM, 1626

BOSTON, 1630

Atlantic Ocean

CAPE COD

NOW CONNECTICUT

NOW RHODE ISLAND

PLYMOUTH, 1620

MILES 30 60

This map shows early settlements in Massachusetts. The Pilgrims settled Plymouth first. Later the Puritans founded several towns along the coast.

later the settlement at Plymouth was united with Massachusetts Bay Colony, because the Pilgrims had never been able to get a charter from the King.

Roger Williams sought freedom in Rhode Island. The Puritans were very religious people. Their ministers were the real leaders of the colony. They had come to America chiefly because they wanted to worship God as they pleased. But they were not willing to give the same freedom to people who differed from them. As one minister said, their idea was that persons of other religious beliefs "shall have free liberty to keep away from us." This situation led in a strange way to the founding of another colony in New England, the colony of Rhode Island. This is how it happened.

A fiery young minister named Roger Williams came to Boston in 1631. He did not like the way the colonists were conducting religious services, and he did not hesitate to say so in a loud voice. He also thought the Puritans were treating the Indians unfairly. He said that the land belonged to the Indians and that the King had no right to give it to the colonists.

This was dangerous talk. The Puritan leaders decided to get rid of Williams before he caused trouble with the King or the Indians. They ordered him to leave the colony and take the next ship back to England.

Roger Williams knew that if he went back to England he would probably be put to death by the King. So one bitter cold day in January, 1636, he fled from Massachusetts. He went to live with his Indian friends in the woods.

But Roger Williams had friends among the colonists. In the spring some of them joined him. He bought

FOUNDING THE THIRTEEN COLONIES

ROGER WILLIAMS (1603?–1683)

Banished! Tramping through the snow, scholarly young Roger Williams pondered his strange fate. A few years before, Massachusetts had welcomed him like a young prince. Yet now he was an outcast. Exhausted and cold, he stumbled along the icy path until he collapsed, shaking with fever. There, friendly Indians found him and cared for him.

Why did Roger Williams have to flee? "He's a dangerous man," the leaders in Boston warned. He dared to say the government must not interfere in religion. He claimed the King had no right to take the Indians' land. Roger Williams was dangerous because he believed in freedom!

In the spring friends came to the Indian camp to join him. Together they pushed on to what is now Rhode Island. There, in 1636, they founded a settlement. Williams named it Providence in memory, he said, "of God's merciful providence to me in my distress."

The colony became "a shelter for persons distressed of conscience." Rhode Island welcomed all religions. Like Roger Williams himself, it came to stand for freedom of thought.

land southeast of Massachusetts from the Indians. There he and his friends founded the town of Providence in June, 1636. It was the beginning of the colony of Rhode Island.

Roger Williams was not the only person who got into trouble for speaking his mind in Massachusetts. At about the same time, a lady named Anne Hutchinson dared to express her ideas about religion. She too was ordered to leave the colony. She and her family went to Rhode Island and founded a settlement not far from Providence.

After a time the settlements in Rhode Island were united to form one colony. Roger Williams had some good friends in England. They helped him get a charter for the colony. In spite of the unfriendliness of the people in Massachusetts, Rhode Island grew and became prosperous. Roger Williams really believed in religious freedom. He welcomed everyone. It is the glory of Rhode Island that it was the first colony to grant religious freedom.

Settlers from Massachusetts founded Connecticut and New Hampshire. Several other settlements were founded near the borders of Massachusetts Bay Colony. A minister named Thomas Hooker felt that the government of Massachusetts was not democratic enough. He led a group of his followers into Connecticut in 1636. There they founded a town they called Hartford. Other dissatisfied groups from Massachu-

setts made the dangerous journey through the wilderness. They founded New Haven and other towns near Hartford.

In 1639 the Connecticut settlements were united into one colony. They adopted a written plan of government called the *Fundamental Orders of Connecticut.* It was the first time in America that settlers wrote out a complete plan for governing a colony.

While Thomas Hooker and his followers were traveling south, other people from Massachusetts were traveling north to the region now called New Hampshire. They started several little towns: Dover, Portsmouth, Exeter, and Hampton. Later the towns were united to form the colony of New Hampshire. There were also settlements in the regions now called Maine and Vermont, but they did not set up separate governments until long after colonial days. For more than 150 years, there were only four New England colonies: Massachusetts, Rhode Island, Connecticut and New Hampshire.

B. THE MIDDLE COLONIES

The English took New York and New Jersey. Between the New England settlements and Virginia several colonies were founded. They were known as the Middle Colonies. This group included New York, New Jersey, Pennsylvania, and Delaware.

You will recall that the Dutch claimed New York because of the explorations of Henry Hudson.

The Dutch purchased the island of Manhattan from the Indians for $24 in 1626.

About 1626 the Dutch started a settlement on Manhattan Island, at the mouth of the Hudson River. They called it New Amsterdam. This was the beginning of New York City. The first leader of the settlement was a shrewd businessman named Peter Minuit (MIN U it). He persuaded the Indians to let them have the land in return for a gift of beads and small articles worth about $24. This was probably one of the greatest bargains in history, for Manhattan Island is now worth billions of dollars.

The Dutch company that bought Manhattan was mainly interested in the fur trade, but farming was also developed. Many rich Dutch families bought great estates along the Hudson. They brought over farmers to work the land for them. The farmers were only tenants and had few rights. The landowning families were called *patroons*. One patroon was named Roosevelt. You will hear much about the Roosevelt families in later American history.

The Dutch settlers did not have much to say about how they were governed. The governors sent over from Holland were very powerful. The most famous governor was Peter Stuyvesant (STI veh sant). Stuyvesant was a bad-tempered man with a wooden leg. He was nicknamed "Headstrong Pete." The settlers grew tired of his high-handed ways. They were not very sorry when English warships appeared in 1664 and took over the colony. England had always claimed the region on the basis of John Cabot's explorations.

The English changed the name of the colony to New York, in honor of the King's brother, the Duke of York. True to English custom, the settlers gained the right to elect representatives to make the laws.

Across the Hudson River from New York lies the region now called New Jersey. Dutch settlers early

Governor Stuyvesant of New Amsterdam.

crossed the river, hoping to get away from "Headstrong Pete." They farmed and traded with the Indians and grew rich. From that day to this, New Jersey has been a busy, prosperous section.

The English took over the New Jersey settlement along with New York. The Duke of York gave the region to his friends, Lord John Berkeley and Sir George Carteret.

The Swedes, Dutch and English ruled Delaware. The Dutch had tried to start a colony farther south in the region we call Delaware. The settlers mistreated an Indian warrior; in revenge his tribe came by night to burn the village. Not a man, woman, or child was left alive.

Next the Swedes decided to found a colony on Delaware Bay. They built a fort which they named Fort Christina in honor of their Queen. Later its name was changed to Wilmington. The Swedes worked hard. Their colony seemed to be a

great success. Then, without warning, Dutch Governor Stuyvesant appeared with warships and soldiers. Sternly he told the Swedes that they were on land belonging to the Dutch and must obey his orders. So New Sweden became Dutch and remained under Dutch rule until 1682. Then it was purchased by William Penn and became part of Pennsylvania for a time. But in 1702 Delaware became a separate English colony.

Penn founded a refuge for the oppressed. William Penn is one of the great men of the colonial period. He founded Pennsylvania, which means Penn's woods. It was one of the later colonies. It was started in 1681, sixty-one years after the Pilgrims came to Plymouth.

William Penn was a handsome young man who disgraced and saddened his parents for a strange reason: he was too religious, they thought. William's father was a British admiral and a friend of the King. In spite of this, William Penn chose to join the most unpopular and persecuted religious group, the Quakers, or Friends. He spent time in prison, but nothing could shake his faith.

When Admiral Penn died, it was found that the King owed him a large sum of money (about $80,000). William Penn felt sure that the King would never pay the money, so he asked for a grant of land in America. The King was glad to get rid of a debt so easily. It was not hard to

78   FOUNDING THE THIRTEEN COLONIES

give away land he had never seen and which did not really belong to him. In 1681 William Penn got a grant of 48,000 square miles — a territory almost as big as England.

Penn had a plan for his land. He decided to start a colony for poor people who wanted religious freedom and a chance to make a living by farming. To attract settlers, Penn used a method that is still popular today: he advertised. He printed short advertisements in six languages and sent them to many parts of Europe. The land-hungry people of Europe could scarcely believe it. Every man could have forty acres of good land for about $10, which he could pay out of his first crop. And he could worship as he pleased; no one would bother him.

Penn also hoped to make some money for his growing family out of the plan. Even if he sold the land for fifty cents an acre it would bring a big fortune. However, the expenses of starting the colony were great. Penn had to go deeply in debt. His creditors even had him put in prison when he could not pay all the bills.

Penn's plans made Pennsylvania a great success. One of the first and the wisest things Penn did was to make friends with the Indians. He sat down with them under a great tree and made a treaty of friendship. As long as Penn lived he carried out the treaty. The Indians also kept their word, so Pennsylvania in the early days was never attacked by Indians. But after Penn died, his family cheated the tribes and Indian wars raged over Pennsylvania.

On his first visit to America in 1682 William Penn made a careful plan for the chief city of his colony. He named it Philadelphia, a combination of Greek words that means "City of Brotherly Love." Philadelphia later became one of the great American cities. For a time, it served as the nation's capital. Today it is still called "the Quaker City" in honor of the people who founded it.

Another wise thing that Penn did

William Penn made a treaty of friendship with the Indians of Pennsylvania in 1682. Below he is shown negotiating with them. The treaty kept peace for years.

was to give the settlers a written plan of government which became famous as the Great Law. Penn was the sole master, or proprietor, of his colony. He could have ruled like a tyrant, but he was not that kind of a man. In the Great Law he ordered: (1) that all men would have freedom of religion; (2) that colonists would have the right to elect representatives to make the laws, subject to the approval of the appointed governor; (3) that every man who owned land or paid taxes should have the right to vote.

Thanks to the wisdom and generosity of William Penn, Pennsylvania was very successful from the beginning. Large numbers of Quakers came from all parts of the British Isles. The advertisements that Penn sent to other countries brought thousands of people who wanted freedom of religion. Shipload after shipload came from Germany, where wars and cruel laws had brought unhappiness. The Pennsylvania Germans, or Pennsylvania Dutch as they are incorrectly called, were hard-working, thrifty folk. They and their children helped make Pennsylvania a rich colony.

C. The Southern Colonies

Lord Baltimore founded Maryland. The Puritans and the Quakers were not the only people in England who suffered because of their religion. The Roman Catholics also were unpopular. A Catholic nobleman named George Calvert decided to start a colony where Roman Catholics could worship in peace.

The King gave Calvert 12,000 square miles of land on the shore of Chesapeake Bay, between Virginia and Pennsylvania. Calvert died before his preparations were complete; his son, Cecilius Calvert, Lord Baltimore, carried on the work. In 1634 about two hundred colonists, many of whom were Catholics, settled a town on the western shore of Chesapeake Bay. They named it St. Mary's. The colony was called Maryland in honor of the Mother of Christ.

Having learned a lesson from the suffering of the Jamestown settlers, Lord Baltimore was careful to choose colonists who were willing to work and who knew how. When the first autumn came, they had two crops: tobacco, which sold in England at a good price; and corn, which they shipped to Boston in exchange for dried codfish. They also filled their storehouses with fish and game they caught. There was no starving time in Maryland.

But the colony had its troubles. Settlers in nearby Virginia were not friendly. Later the Baltimores quarreled with the Penn family over the boundary between Maryland and Pennsylvania. The boundary dispute became so troublesome that Lord Baltimore finally sent over two skilful young surveyors named Mason and Dixon. The *Mason-Dixon line* which they drew to establish the boundary between Maryland and Pennsylvania later became famous as the dividing line between North and South.

The Carolinas became prosperous colonies. About the same time that Lord Baltimore was planning to settle Maryland, other people were thinking about settling the land south of Virginia. You will recall Sir Walter Raleigh's sad experience trying to found a colony on Roanoke Island.

In 1663 King Charles II gave a grant of land south of Virginia to eight nobles who were to be the *proprietors* (proh PRI eh ters), or owners. The proprietors sent over settlers who founded a town they called Charles Town in honor of the King. Later the name was shortened to Charleston. The colony was named Carolina, also in honor of the King, whose name in Latin was *Carolus.*

The proprietors governed the colony badly. There was constant trouble with the settlers who felt they had a right to run their own affairs. When the proprietors saw they could not make any money out of Carolina, they turned it over to the King. Later the colony was split into North and South Carolina, each with a royal governor and an elected assembly to make the laws.

The Carolina settlers found many ways to make money. They raised tobacco and rice. They also planted indigo, a plant used in making blue dye. They tapped the pine forests for tar and turpentine, which European shipyards needed to build ships. Within a few years Charleston was the busiest port in the South.

James Oglethorpe founded Georgia in 1733. Almost 125 years after the settlers at Jamestown built their first huts, the last of the thirteen original colonies was founded. It was Georgia, and the year was 1733.

Notice on the map on this page that Georgia was the farthest south of the colonies. It lay between the Carolinas and Florida. This was a

The original thirteen colonies.

dangerous spot in the early days, for Florida belonged to Spain. The new colony was open to attack from the Spaniards in the South and the Indians in the West.

The hero of Georgia, James Oglethorpe (O g'l thawrp), was different from most of the other men who had started colonies. He had no thought of getting any profit for himself. He wanted to help the poor and unfortunate.

Oglethorpe was the youngest son of a noble family. He entered Oxford University but soon left to fight the Turks. When he came back to England he was elected a member of Parliament, the English law-making body. One day he heard that an old friend had died of neglect in debtors' prison.

At that time, people were put in prison if they did not pay their bills. And there they had to stay until their debt was paid. Since they could not earn any money in prison, there was little chance they could pay. When Oglethorpe saw the misery of the people in debtors' prison he made up his mind to do something about it. He asked King George II to give him land in America where the debtors could have another chance.

Oglethorpe received a generous grant of land and a charter. He chose his colonists carefully. In 1733 he and a little band of thirty families founded the town that is now Savannah. The colony itself was called Georgia in honor of the King who ruled England at the time.

Georgia was a mild, sunny land. The soil was good. The settlers were soon shipping rice, indigo, lumber, tar, and turpentine, and many other products to England. Not many debtors came to Georgia, but Scotch and English workers were glad to come. Oglethorpe made it easy for them to get good land.

Oglethorpe made friends with the Indians, so there was little trouble with them in the early years. The colonists had to fight the Spaniards during the frequent wars between England and Spain. Georgia was called the Sentinel Colony, or the Buffer Colony, because it formed the border between the English settlements and Spanish Florida.

James Oglethorpe meant well and he accomplished much good. But he was a soldier and accustomed to giving orders. The settlers grew tired of having to accept his ideas. A quarrel developed. Oglethorpe went back to England. He turned the colony over to the King. In 1754 Georgia became a royal colony like Virginia. Today Oglethorpe University in Atlanta keeps alive the memory of the great-hearted soldier who founded the last of the original thirteen colonies.

James Oglethorpe, founder of Georgia.

CHAPTER SUMMARY

Jamestown was the first permanent British colony in America. It was founded in 1607. The first American legislature was established there in 1619. Plymouth, founded by the Pilgrims in 1620, was the second successful British colony. The Pilgrims drew up the "Mayflower Compact" which served as a basis of government for their colony. Plymouth was later merged with Massachusetts Bay Colony, which the Puritans established in 1630. The other New England colonies were Rhode Island, Connecticut, and New Hampshire.

The Middle Colonies were New York, New Jersey, Pennsylvania, and Delaware. New York was founded by the Dutch but was taken over by the British in 1664. Pennsylvania was founded by the great Quaker, William Penn.

The Southern Colonies were Virginia, Maryland, North and South Carolina, and Georgia. Lord Baltimore founded Maryland as a refuge for Roman Catholics. Georgia was the last colony to be established. It was founded by James Oglethorpe as a refuge for debtors. It served as a buffer colony, protecting the other colonies from the Spaniards in Florida.

The Language of History

The following words and phrases appear in Chapter 4. Be sure you understand the meaning of each. Consult the dictionary as well as your textbook.

1. colony	3. legislature	5. patroons
2. debtor	4. economic reasons	6. trading company

What Happened When

Make sure you know the important events connected with the following dates:

1. 1607   **2.** 1619   **3.** 1620   **4.** 1630   **5.** 1682   **6.** 1733

Who's Who in History

Be sure you know the part that the following played in the colonial period:

1. John Smith	**3.** Roger Williams	**5.** William Bradford
2. William Penn	**4.** Lord Baltimore	**6.** James Oglethorpe

Study Questions

1. What conditions in Europe in the 17th century encouraged people to come to America?

2. **a.** What mistakes did the London Company make in the founding of Jamestown?
   b. How was the colony saved and made successful?

3. Describe the founding of Plymouth including **(a)** the date, **(b)** the location, **(c)** the way the government was organized, **(d)** the leaders, and **(e)** reasons for the success of the colony.

4. **a.** State the chief differences between Pilgrims and Puritans.
   b. Name and locate the towns founded by the Puritans.
   c. Why was Roger Williams forced to leave Massachusetts?
   d. What colony did he found?

5. What were the Fundamental Orders of Connecticut?

6. **a.** Who founded New Amsterdam and for what purpose?
   b. How and when did Great Britain get control of New Amsterdam?
   c. What did the British call New Amsterdam and in whose honor was it named?

7. **a.** Why did William Penn receive a grant of American land?
   b. How did he attract settlers to his colony?
   c. Give three democratic features of the Great Law of Pennsylvania.

8. Write a paragraph about Maryland telling **(a)** its founder and **(b)** the reason for establishing the colony.

9. In a paragraph about the Carolina colonies tell **(a)** the founders, **(b)** chief city, and **(c)** reasons for prosperity.

10. In a paragraph on Georgia tell **(a)** its founder, **(b)** the purpose of its founding, and **(c)** why it was called the Sentinel Colony.

FOUNDING THE THIRTEEN COLONIES

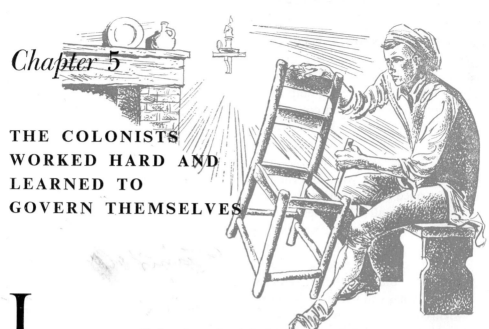

Chapter 5

THE COLONISTS WORKED HARD AND LEARNED TO GOVERN THEMSELVES

IMAGINE you are living in colonial times. At night you lie in bed in your log cabin wishing the wolves would stop howling so you can get some sleep. Tomorrow you must get up at daybreak to go to work in the fields. And you will have to carry your gun with you because two of your neighbors already have been attacked without warning by Indians.

What was it like to live in colonial times? Was life exciting or was it just a terrible struggle to keep alive? How did the settlers themselves feel about their way of life?

Colonists had big families. But what about the children — did they go to school? Did they have textbooks and homework? Did anybody go to college?

As a colonist, you would have been an American, but you would also have been a British subject. Can you imagine what it was like to be ruled by a king thousands of miles away?

Where would you have liked best to live: in the New England Colonies with their schools and churches, snowy winters and pleasant summers; or the Middle Colonies, busy and prosperous; or in the Southern Colonies, where you could be out of doors most of the year? As you read about the colonies watch how their geography influenced their ways of life.

The colonists faced many dangers. What was it like to live in colonial America? To answer this, imagine that you have come by ship to a new country. It is a wild country and it looks forbidding; it seems to be warning you: "Watch out!"

On one side is the ocean; the water separates you from the friends you once knew, but may never see again. On all other sides are woods. There are no houses, no roads, not even a path to follow. Hidden in the woods are wild animals, and Indians that may be dangerous. Now, what will you do? What problems must you solve if you are to make a home in the wilderness?

The settlers had four big problems. The first thing the settlers had to do when they landed in America was to find or make a place to live. They had to have shelter from storms, and cold, and wild animals.

Next they had to think about food. They usually brought a small supply with them; when it was gone they had to take what they could find or grow. Fortunately, they had no trouble finding drinking water, for there were many rivers and springs near the coast. And fuel for cooking, or for warmth in cold weather, was also easy to find; the land was covered with trees and bushes.

The settlers soon needed new clothing, too. The clothes they brought from Europe became ragged after a few weeks in the wilderness. Shelter, food, and clothing — these three were serious problems. But what worried people even more was how to get along with the Indians.

In the beginning, when Columbus came, the Indians were friendly. But the white men's mistakes and cruelty changed that. Almost every colonist went through at least one terrible Indian attack.

In Massachusetts, the early friendship with the Indians lasted until 1675. Then Chief Massasoit's son, known as King Philip, suddenly went on the warpath. He wanted to drive all white people from the land. "King Philip's War" lasted for two years. More than 600 white men were killed, as were 1200 women and children. The Indians also burned 52 towns and left more than a thousand farms without a house or barn standing. Finally Philip was shot and his tribe was defeated.

King Philip, son of Massasoit, led a war against New England colonists.

Log cabins solved the shelter problem.
Fortunately for the early settlers, there was plenty of building material. Every tree seemed to say, "Take me for your home."

The settlers in Delaware seem to have brought the log cabin idea from Sweden in 1638. They built their cabins quickly by laying logs one upon the other and notching the corners together. The children helped make the cabin weather-tight by stuffing the cracks, between the logs, with moss or clay. One or two small openings were cut in the logs and covered with oiled paper to let in sunlight. After dark, the only light came from the fireplace.

Near the roof was a low loft or attic reached by a ladder. Soon after supper children went up the ladder to sleep under the roof. Often the last sound they heard before they fell asleep was the howling of wolves.

All this, remember, was in early colonial days. After a few years some colonists had houses of oak and pine timber. These were built so well that some stand to this day.

And every town had a few mansions built of brick and filled with beautiful furniture brought by ship from Europe. But in the woods, on the edge of the settlement, the log cabin remained the typical dwelling. Abraham Lincoln and many other great men were born in log cabins.

Americans got plenty to eat. In the early days most colonists had to be hunters and fishermen. That was the

Chopping trees, hunting and fishing, the ever-present danger of Indian attack — all these were part of colonial life as the two pictures above show.

easiest way to get fresh food, but it was not very dependable. Most people who came to America hoped eventually to own land and become farmers. They brought seeds of grain and vegetables with them.

But first the land had to be cleared of trees. This was slow, hard work. The colonists killed thousands of trees by *girdling*, or cutting deep gashes in the bark. Then they burned some of the trees and scattered the

Most colonists lived on farms. Men and women worked hard, raising and harvesting crops and preparing food, as is shown in the two pictures above.

ashes to enrich the soil. Next they dug out the roots; then at last they had land on which to plant crops.

Friendly Indians showed them how to grow corn, beans, squash, and potatoes. The settlers also planted seeds of wheat and oats and many other foods they knew in the Old World. Cows, sheep, and pigs were shipped from England.

In a few years the settlers were eating well. Food was better and more plentiful than in Europe. Boys and girls born in the colonies grew taller and heavier than their parents.

Americans wore homemade clothes. A few rich colonists ordered new clothing from England. But most colonists had to make their own clothes. In all the colonies deer were very plentiful. Thousands of dried deer skins were sold or traded every season; soon, clothing of deer leather, or *buckskin*, became a common sight.

Linen and wool from colonial farms were made into men's clothing "for Sunday wear," and into women's dresses for all occasions. Almost every girl knew how to spin linen or woolen yarn on a spinning wheel. And almost every mother knew how to weave linen or woolen yarn into good cloth on a hand loom. They called the material *homespun* or *linsey woolsey*. It was not very pretty or fashionable, but it was comfortable and it wore well. Thus from their own farms and by their own skill, colonists produced their summer and winter clothing.

Beautiful furs of otter, beaver, mink, and other animals were plentiful in the colonies. But except in the far north — among Eskimos, for example — furs made very poor clothing. Indians wore them because they had nothing else; they were glad to trade furs for the white man's linen or wool.

Furs brought a high price in Europe, simply because it was the fashion for rich people to wear them. So colonial traders gave the Indians food or cloth in exchange for furs. Then they sold the furs in Europe, and with the money bought whatever they needed or could sell in America.

The colonies grew prosperous. The colonial period lasted a long time — from 1607 to 1775. As the years went by, life in the colonies became easier and more pleasant. Almost any man who worked hard got plenty to eat. The land was cheap and plentiful so he could soon have his own farm. He might even have a little extra money to buy luxuries made in England.

As the years went by, little corn patches became wide fields. They produced more food than the colonists could eat, so there was a surplus to send to England. From the great forests came timber and tar and turpentine — all needed in European shipyards. From the sea, New England colonists took fish. These they dried and sold in the West Indies at a big profit. Thus the fields and the forests and even the ocean brought wealth to the colonies.

Colonial clothing became gay and colorful. John Hancock, a rich Boston merchant, once appeared at noon in a red velvet cap, a long blue damask coat lined with velvet, an embroidered white satin waistcoat, black satin knee breeches, silk stockings, and red leather slippers.

The women also liked bright-colored silks and satins. And children of prosperous families dressed like their parents. George Washington, the Virginia planter who later became President, sent to London for clothing for his family. For his six-year-old stepson he once ordered "gloves and toys." For his stepdaughter, aged four, he ordered "12 pairs of gloves, 10 pairs of shoes, and 2 fans."

However, many colonists preferred a more simple way of life. Benjamin Franklin, a poor printer who became rich and famous, was one of these. When he moved into a new and larger house, his wife celebrated by buying a china dish and some silver spoons. Ben Franklin grumbled at such a waste of money. He said that his supper of mush and milk tasted good enough when he ate it out of a clay bowl with a wooden spoon.

Most colonists were farmers. Not all the colonists were rich. Then, as now, most people had to work hard and save their pennies. In colonial days, more than eighty per cent of the population — or about eight out of every ten persons — lived by

Massachusetts home, built in 1638.

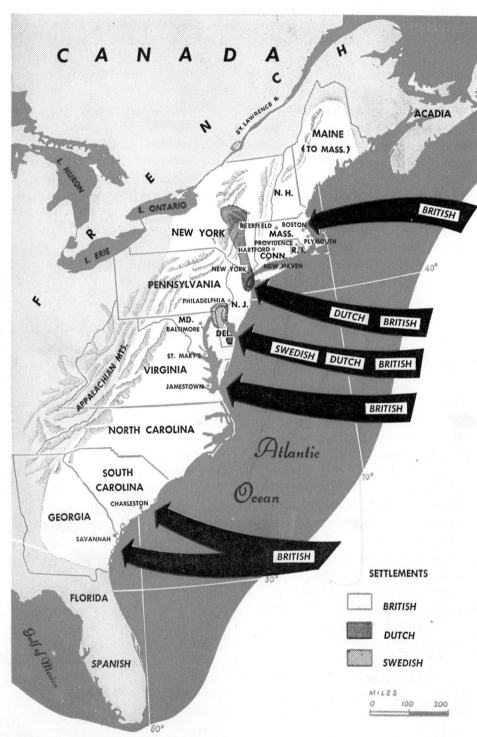

This map shows British, Dutch and Swedish settlements along the Atlantic seaboard.

farming. They raised crops of corn or tobacco and vegetables or fruit. They had a few sheep and pigs as well as cows and horses.

In New England and in the Middle Colonies, a farm was usually "worked" by one family. In the South there were some large plantations. There the work was done by slaves, and *indentured servants*. An indentured servant was one who had agreed to work for a certain period (usually from four to seven years) for his passage to America. But in the South, just as in the other colonies, most farmers had to work hard. There were only a few big planters, but they had great influence.

Each farming district had its village or town. There the farmers gathered to attend church on Sunday and, on other days, to buy and sell products and listen to the news. There was no radio or television to tell the news. At first the colonists had no newspapers, either, except those sent from England. Not until 1704, almost a hundred years after the founding of Jamestown, was a newspaper published in the colonies.

In each village there were a few workers who made a living by the skill of their hands. There was a blacksmith who shod the farmers' horses and repaired tools. Usually there were shoemakers and perhaps a hatmaker, and a cooper who made barrels and boxes in which goods were shipped overseas. There were also carpenters and boat builders, rope makers and candlemakers.

They worked in their homes or in little shops attached to their homes. Many great factories that now manufacture goods for all America started out as little shops.

Every village had a mill for grinding corn or wheat into meal or flour. Power to turn the mill wheels came from the rushing waters of a nearby stream. The mill was one of the first buildings the settlers erected. They had to have flour and meal to make bread and other favorite foods. The miller was an important person.

Cities grew and commerce developed. Some of the towns grew until they became cities. But there were no large cities in colonial times. Philadelphia, the largest town, had only about 28,000 people in 1769. There were not nearly so many people in all the colonies as there are in New York City or Chicago today.

But the little colonial cities like Boston, New York, and Charleston were centers of trade and wealth. They were the homes of the merchants, bankers, and lawyers. And in every town a few merchants soon gained power and respect.

The merchants grew rich by a three-step process. First, they saved some money and used it to buy supplies of tobacco or rice or wool or lumber. Second, they shipped the goods to Europe, or the West Indies, and sold them for more money than they had cost in America. Third, they brought back from foreign lands such products as tea, sugar, wine, and silk and sold them for more than they had paid.

Thus the merchants made a profit when they sold American goods in foreign lands. They made another profit when they brought European goods to America and sold them. But the profits did not come easily. The merchants had to work and worry and keep track of every barrel and box they bought and sold. They ran great risks, too. Sometimes their ships were lost in a storm or seized by pirates. So they earned their

In the first picture below you see a colonial kitchen. The second picture shows a typical fireplace. Both were favorite gathering places for people in colonial days.

y, hard work, and w to take risks. Almost anyone in the colonies had a chance to gain wealth and power if he worked hard and used his brains.

Americans worked very hard for several reasons. They wanted comforts and money of course. But they also felt that success was a sign God was pleased with them. Religion played a very important part in colonial life.

The colonists were deeply religious. Most people who came to America had strong religious convictions. They went to church regularly and listened to long sermons with interest. This was true in the southern colonies as well as in New England. Without strong religious faith the settlers probably could not have endured the hardships and suffering of the early days.

Church leaders had great influence in all the colonies. In New England, the ministers were the most powerful group. They were men of keen intelligence and deep faith. They never let the colonists forget their religious duties. "God sifted a whole nation that he might send choice grain over into this wilderness," a minister named William Stoughton told his audience in Boston in 1669.

The American colonies produced many outstanding religious leaders. One of the most famous was Jonathan Edwards of Connecticut. His father and grandfather were ministers, too. Jonathan graduated

The church shown above is in Sudbury, Mass. It was built in colonial days.

from Yale College at seventeen and became a minister two years later.

Edward's fiery sermons had a strong effect on his hearers. Hundreds of people were turned from wrongdoing. A "great awakening" of religious feeling swept the colonies partly because of Jonathan Edwards' work. Later he traveled among the Indians, teaching them Christianity. He wrote many books which students of religion still read.

The colonists had their own schools and textbooks. A clear sign of progress in the colonies was the increasing number of schools. The Puritans in New England were the first to provide free education. You will recall that the Puritans were very religious people. They wanted to make sure that their children learned to read the Bible. They also wanted to train boys to become ministers.

In 1647, only a few years after Massachusetts Bay Colony was founded, a law was passed there requiring towns to organize schools. The Dutch started schools in New York and New Jersey. The Quakers in Pennsylvania early organized schools for children whose parents were willing to pay a small fee.

In the southern colonies, however, there were few schools. This was mostly because the farms were far apart and it was hard for children to travel to school. Some planters hired teachers for their families, but the children of slaves or indentured servants had little chance at an education. And most of the English governors did not want schools. They believed it was easier to control people who could not read.

As a rule only the boys went to school. Girls were lucky if their mothers could teach them to read and write. Boys ʾ' not go to public school until ʾʾ ʾre eight or nine. Before th. if th. parents could afford it, they went to a "dame school." A woman whose husband had died often started a dame school in her home. She taught little children reading and writing and simple arithmetic.

At first, the only textbooks colonial children had were the Bible and a few other books brought from England. It was not long before a few

Here is a page of the *New England Primer*, a widely used colonial textbook.

teachers began to prepare their own textbooks. By far the most important and successful early American textbook was *The New England Primer*. For more than 100 years, most young Americans learned to read from its pages.

Colleges were established in the colonies. The teacher's word was law in early American schools. Most teachers were men. They did not hesitate to whip any boy who was stupid or troublesome. The boys dared not object. Of course, a great many quit school after a few terms. But those who stayed in school often became fine scholars.

When they could read Latin and Greek easily, these students were

"Now all together!" A house-raising bee meant teamwork, food, and fun for all.

ready for college. Some went to England to study. Others entered the two newly-established American colleges. These colleges educated boys to be ministers or lawyers.

Harvard was the first American college. The Puritans established Harvard in Cambridge, near Boston, in 1636. The South too had a fine college, William and Mary, at Williamsburg, Virginia.

By the end of the colonial period there were nine colleges in the colonies. Thus, even in the earliest days, Americans showed the strong interest in education that has become characteristic of the nation.

The settlers had some time for fun. Colonial people worked hard to earn a living. Perhaps that is why they got together to make a game of work at other times. When harvesting the autumn crop, for example, young and old people gathered for a "bee," so called because they were supposed to be as busy as a honey bee.

After the "bee" came the "treat," that is, supper or refreshments. Then a fiddler appeared on the scene, and all the "bees" danced in couples until somebody heard the rooster crow. That meant it was morning again, and time to go home.

The colonists had no radio or television, no movies or big league baseball games. Instead, they had to provide their own entertainment, and amuse one another. Among their evening amusements were telling of stories, working puzzles, guessing at riddles, playing blind-man's buff, cards, and dancing.

Some of the colonial leaders did not approve of dancing or card playing; they even got laws passed against such amusements. However, the *blue laws,* as they were called, had little effect.

Here is a letter a Puritan girl wrote to her mother. It tells of an evening party. It was a quiet little party, such as young Puritans often gave to a visiting friend:

We had a very genteel assembly at Mr. Soley's last evening, Miss Hannah being mistress of the ceremony. A large company assembled in a handsome room in the new end of the house. We had two fiddles, and I had the honor to open the diversion in a minuet (dance). Our treat was nuts, raisins, cakes, all in great plenty. For variety we played games, called Woo the Widow, Hunt the Whistle, and Thread the Needle.

Wrongdoers were punished severely. There was a darker, less pleasant side to colonial life. While some colonists were going to parties, others might be having trouble with the government officials. There were severe punishments for wrongdoing. Anyone who came into conflict with accepted ideas of right and wrong was likely to be punished in a way that held him up to public shame.

A man who drank too much, for example, might be *pilloried.* This meant that he would have to stand on a platform with his head and hands pushed through holes in a wooden framework called a *pillory.* The pillory was in the middle of the town. Those who passed by would laugh and point at him; sometimes they threw rotten eggs.

A man or woman who told lies or gossiped might be punished by the *ducking stool.* In this case the offender was tied to a chair at the end of a long pole and "ducked" into a pool of water. A man who wasted time or used bad language might be put in the *stocks.* This meant he would have to sit for hours with his hands and feet locked in a wooden board.

The pillory, the ducking stool, and the stocks were considered mild punishments. For serious offenses a prisoner might be whipped, or branded with a hot iron, or have his ears cut off. And a large number of crimes were punished by hanging. Today such punishments seem cruel and inhuman. But punishments in America were probably not so severe as in many other parts of the world in those days.

Virginia had trouble with Governor Berkeley. Strict as the laws were, the colonists do not seem to have complained much about them. Perhaps this was because they had helped to make the laws. You have already learned how the Jamestown settlers gained the right to help make the laws. In 1619, when they elected men to represent them in the House of Burgesses, democratic government began in America. There

COLONIAL PUNISHMENTS

The colonists frequently quarreled with their royal governors. Here Virginia leaders are shown arguing with Sir William Berkeley.

was nothing like it in the Spanish or Portuguese or French colonies.

The Virginia colonists took their right of self-government very seriously — more seriously than the leaders in England intended. In 1624 the London Company turned the colony over to King James I. The King sent over a royal governor to rule the colony in his name. After some years trouble developed between the governors and the House of Burgesses. Sometimes the governor thought he had the right to run the colony as he wished. The members of the House of Burgesses thought the governor should consult with them and take their advice.

The dispute over the power of the governor and the power of the colonial law-making body became a real quarrel after the King appointed Sir William Berkeley governor. Berkeley was hard to get along with. He did not like the idea of letting the people take part in the government.

Bacon's Rebellion was part of the fight for freedom. Berkeley liked money. He built up a large fortune trading with the Indians. He was so eager to protect his interest in the trade that he would do nothing to help the settlers when the Indians went on the warpath. He would not let the House of Burgesses send soldiers to protect the farmers who lived on the edge of Jamestown.

The Virginia settlers grew frightened and angry. A young planter named Nathaniel Bacon became their leader. In 1676 he defied the governor and led an attack on the Indians. Berkeley tried to make him an outlaw, but the people sided with young Bacon.

There was some hard fighting between Bacon's followers and Berkley's soldiers. Jamestown was burned. And the Governor had to give in. Then Bacon died suddenly of a fever. Berkeley captured his followers and had many of them put to death. The whole affair was called *Bacon's Rebellion*.

It looked as if the royal governor had won his battle against freedom-loving Americans. But the King heard the story. He realized that people might not go to America if they heard of such cruelty. So the King removed Berkeley. He sent a new governor who pardoned the rebels and gave Virginia more liberty.

A few years later the capital of Virginia was moved to the pleasant little town of Williamsburg. But the old struggle for power between the royal governor and the settlers went on. Often the settlers won.

In other colonies the same struggle took place. In the end the people of every colony won the right to elect representatives to make laws for the colony. They did not win complete self-government until after the Revolution.

The King could always *veto*, or forbid, any law passed by a colonial legislature. But he seldom did. The colonies were far away; the King and his advisers were busy with problems at home. So they usually let the Americans manage their own affairs. This policy gave the settlers good practice in running a government. It also made them more independent.

Town meetings gave Americans practice in governing themselves. The Pilgrims in Plymouth colony developed a very democratic form of government. This was the *town meeting* which Thomas Jefferson called "the best form of self-government ever invented by man." From Plymouth the town meeting idea spread all over New England and to parts of the Middle Colonies.

Many years later, when settlers moved westward into Kentucky and Ohio, one of the first things they did was to call a town meeting. There they made the rules of their settlement. You may have listened to "Town Meeting of the Air" on the radio. It follows to some extent the plan the Pilgrims developed.

This is the way the town meeting worked. At least once a year the people of the town met to talk over their problems and decide what to do. They also elected their leaders and agreed on the amount of taxes they would pay. If there was a sudden emergency, such as the danger of an Indian attack, they would quickly call a special town meeting.

At the town meeting every citizen had certain rights. He could speak his mind and say what he thought ought to be done. In other words, he had *freedom of speech*. This did not mean that he could tell lies or try to break up the meeting by causing unnecessary noise or delay. But as long as he spoke the truth or what he believed to be the truth, and acted like a sensible person, he was free to discuss and offer suggestions. He also had the right to vote for the town officers and representatives to the colonial legislature.

Out of the town meetings another right developed which is still very precious to Americans. This is *freedom of assembly* or the right of people to meet and discuss their problems. The royal governors and leaders in England did not like town

Below is a reconstruction of the Zenger or "freedom of the press" trial.

meetings. As you will see, this led directly to the Revolution — for the Americans would not give up freedom of assembly.

The Zenger trial increased freedom of the press. Another important right that Americans struggled for in colonial times was *freedom of the press.* This means the right of newspapers to publish an accurate account of things that have happened. It also means the right of newspapers to criticize the government.

Newspapers in England did not have much freedom in those days. They did not dare to criticize the government. In many parts of the world this is still the case. In Soviet Russia, for example, the people can read only what their leaders want them to read.

More than two hundred years ago, an American editor fought a battle that won a great increase of freedom for American newspapers. He was John Peter Zenger. Zenger was born in Germany and came to New York in search of freedom and opportunity. He and his wife, Anna, worked very hard writing and printing a little newspaper.

The royal governor of New York at the time was William Cosby. He was not a popular governor. He had done several unjust and dishonest things which he did not want to have known.

One day in 1733 he forbade a group of Quakers to vote in an election at a little town near New York City. When John Peter Zenger heard of this he denounced it in his newspaper as an act of tyranny. It was not the first time, he said, that the governor had used more authority than he had any right to use.

The Governor ordered Zenger arrested and thrown in jail. And there he stayed for eight long months. Governor Cosby planned to keep his prisoner out of sight until the town election was forgotten. But friends of Zenger insisted that, by all the laws of England, an accused man must have a trial in a court of justice. So Zenger was brought to trial in 1734. A jury of colonial men set him free with this verdict: "Men must be permitted to expose or to oppose unjust government by speaking or writing the truth."

Newspapermen are proud of this verdict. They call it "the morning star of American liberty." Zenger is the hero of freedom of the press, which became a part of the Constitution of the United States. He won for American newspapers the right to print criticisms of the government. The Zenger trial is a great landmark in the history of freedom.

Freedom of speech is part of town meeting.

CHAPTER SUMMARY

Most American colonists were farmers. They had to be self-sufficient. They cleared land and built log cabins. They raised their food and made their own clothes. They had to fight off many Indian attacks.

Hard work made the colonists prosperous. Philadelphia, Charleston, Boston, and New York became busy little cities. A profitable trade with European nations developed. The number of schools increased and colleges such as Harvard and William and Mary were founded. The colonists enjoyed parties and had many wholesome amusements. Punishment for wrong-doing was severe.

Americans learned the art of government in colonial days. In the town meetings everyone had a chance to express his opinion. The colonists often disputed the authority of the royal governors and usually they got their own way.

Freedom of the press became a cherished American right in colonial times. The Zenger trial won for colonial newspapers the right to criticize the government.

The Language of History

The following words and phrases appear in Chapter 5. Be sure you understand the meaning of each. Consult the dictionary as well as your textbook.

1. pilloried	**4.** town meeting	**7.** freedom of assembly
2. blue laws	**5.** dame school	**8.** freedom of speech
3. homespun	**6.** freedom of press	**9.** indentured servant

What Happened When

Make sure you know the important events connected with the following dates:

1. 1636	**2.** 1676	**3.** 1734

Who's Who in History

Be sure you know the part that the following played in the colonial period:

1. King Philip
2. William Cosby
3. William Berkeley
4. Nathaniel Bacon
5. Jonathan Edwards
6. John Peter Zenger

Study Questions

1. What four big problems faced the first settlers?
2. **a.** Who built the first log cabins?
   b. Why was the log cabin well-suited to the needs of the pioneers?
3. **a.** How did most colonists earn their living?
   b. Name four products that colonists sold to foreign lands.
4. **a.** Give two reasons why the Puritans insisted on having free public schools in every settlement.
   b. What were the "dame schools"?
5. **a.** Name two colleges established in colonial times.
   b. What was the chief purpose of colonial colleges?
6. **a.** In what ways did the colonists amuse themselves?
   b. What were the blue laws?
7. Write a paragraph about Bacon's Rebellion telling **(a)** the date, **(b)** the causes of the quarrel, and **(c)** the final result.
8. **a.** Explain what a town meeting is.
   b. Why is it considered one of the most completely democratic forms of government?
9. **a.** Who was John Peter Zenger?
   b. Why was he put in prison?
   c. If Zenger had lost his case, how would it have affected the development of American freedom?
10. Explain what each of the following was and tell its importance in colonial days:
    a. linsey woolsey
    b. buckskin
    c. the pillory
    d. *The New England Primer*

Chapter 6

THE BRITISH AND FRENCH FOUGHT FOR NORTH AMERICA

"JUST after we had passed a place called the Murdering Town, a party of French and Indians lay in wait for us. One of them fired at me not fifteen steps off, but fortunately missed. We walked all the remaining part of the night without any stop, that we might get the start so as to be out of reach of their pursuit, since we were assured they would follow our track as soon as it was light."

It was young George Washington who wrote those lines in December, 1763. The Governor of Virginia had sent him to warn off the French who were building forts along the Ohio River. The French replied with a warning that "the country belonged to them; that no Englishman had a right to trade upon those waters."

Washington carried this message back to the governor. It was on his way home that he was fired upon. And the bullet that fortunately missed him was one of the opening shots of the last French and Indian War.

Why did France and Britain fight a series of wars in the eighteenth century? Why did the Indians side with the French? What part did Washington play in the war?

This chapter tells the exciting story of the struggle between France and Britain for control of North America.

Louis XIV, the "Sun King" of France.

The British colonies were surrounded by enemies. Unfriendly neighbors watched the growth of the thirteen colonies with jealous eyes. The Spaniards held Florida and Mexico, as well as Central and South America. The French held the land north of the St. Lawrence River.

To the west, beyond the Appalachian Mountains, the rich valleys along the Ohio and the Mississippi rivers were Indian hunting grounds. Except for a few French forts and trading posts, the land on the other side of the mountains was still untroubled by the white man. France claimed the western valleys because La Salle and other Frenchmen had explored the region. But the British paid little attention to French claims. They had their own plans for trading and settling the West.

There was not much danger from the Spaniards to the south. After the defeat of the Spanish Armada in 1588, Spain left the British alone.

Except on the border of Georgia, British colonists seldom had to worry about Spain's ill will.

The French to the north were a serious danger. They encouraged Indians to attack British settlements. And French hunters and traders were seen more and more in the West. In those days France was strong and united. Louis XIV, who ruled France from 1643 to 1715, was a strong, ambitious leader. He liked to be called the "Sun King" for he thought he was the center of glory and civilization.

France and Great Britain were fierce enemies. The French and the English had been enemies for centuries. They had fought long bitter wars. Each regarded the other with contempt and distrust. France had a great army and was strong on land. England had a great navy and was a strong sea power. Each was ambitious to gain colonies and wealth.

Religion was another cause of hard feeling between the two nations. France was strongly Roman Catholic. Louis XIV would not let Protestants stay in France or settle in French colonies. The French were eager to spread the Roman Catholic faith in America. England had broken away from the Roman Catholic Church in the time of King Henry VIII (father of Queen Elizabeth). Most of the British settlers were Protestants. They feared the influence of the Roman Catholic priests in New France.

Thus, the stage was set for a terrible struggle. National pride and ambition, greed for colonies and wealth, memories of past wars, religious differences — all these helped plunge France and Great Britain into a series of four wars. For 73 years, from 1690 to 1763, France and Great Britain fought and made peace and fought again.

Battle and murder traveled along the "war road." The first three wars started in Europe, but the British colonies soon became involved. Sometimes the colonists first learned that war had broken out when some French officers led a raiding party of Indians against the British settlements. Much of the early fighting took place in northeastern New York along what the Iroquois Indians called the "war road." It led north from the Mohawk River — along the Hudson River, Lake George, and Lake Champlain — to the St. Lawrence River and New France.

The French wanted to control the war road and push south to the Atlantic Ocean. By doing this, they would split the English colonies in two, making it easier to win each half separately. It would also, they hoped, give them a harbor on the Atlantic Ocean that they could use all year. Their harbors on the St. Lawrence were often blocked by ice.

The French built several forts along the war road. The strongest was Fort Ticonderoga (TY kon duh ROH guh) at the southern end of Lake Champlain. On the map on page 104 locate the war road and Fort Ticonderoga. Note that this region lay between New France to the north and English colonies to the south and east. It was a vast wilderness of hills and lakes. Only the Indians really knew their way through it.

The French built Fort Ticonderoga (below). It was the strongest fortification on Lake Champlain. "Ti" was a keypoint in the wars between Britain and France. It still stands, but its guns have long been silent.

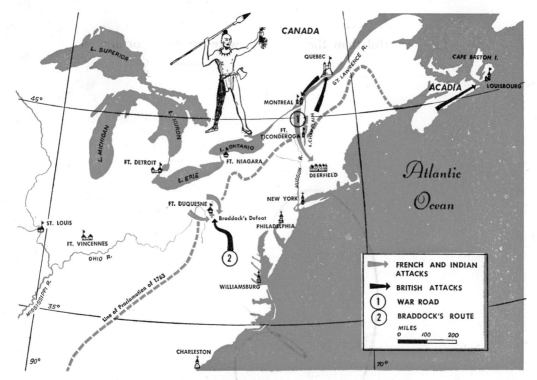

The French and Indian War was a struggle for control of North America. It began in the Ohio Valley and spread over the frontier. The map above shows the important battlefields. Note particularly the "war road" and the fortresses of Louisbourg and Quebec.

The people of New France had few rights. Life in the French colonies was quite different from life in the British colonies. Fishing and trading with the Indians were more important than farming. The government in France kept firm control over the colonies. There were no town meetings or colonial law-making bodies.

The population of New France was much smaller than the population of the British colonies, too. And it was spread over a much larger area. The French traders and fishermen seldom brought their wives to the wilderness. They planned to make some money and

then go back to France. Those who did settle down in Canada often married Indian women.

Most settlers in the French colonies had little chance to rise in the world. You have seen how a sturdy middle class of merchants and skilled workers developed in the British colonies. This did not happen in New France. The poor remained poor and oppressed, much as in France. Above them was a strong ruling class of government officials and rich landowners.

France kept many trained soldiers in America to defend the settlements. They were under command of the royal governor. This made

BRITISH AGAINST FRENCH

him much more powerful than the governors in the British colonies. French settlers did not argue with their governor, because he had the army on his side. Thus, democracy did not develop in New France.

The French were ready, willing, and able to fight. When war came, New France had several advantages over the British colonies. At a word from the governor, French soldiers and their Indian allies would rush to attack settlements in New York and New England. The British colonists had to defend themselves as best they could. As a rule, they got little help from England.

Many of the French governors, such as Count de Frontenac (deh FRAUN teh NAHK) were very capable men. They knew how to lead and how to fight. They made use of every advantage to strengthen New France. Along the border between French and English territory they built several strong forts — Fort Oswego, Fort Niagara, Fort Detroit, and many more.

As a rule, the French got along better with the Indians than the British did. Only the Iroquois Indians sided with the British. All the other tribes helped the French.

The French settlements were strongly united, while the British were divided into thirteen little colonies with little feeling of unity. French officials had much greater power over the people. When the governor of Canada issued an order, there were no delays or arguments.

It is no wonder that the war in America often went against the British. In the first three wars, more than a hundred villages in the British colonies were destroyed. Lonely farms on the edge of the settlements were raided again and again. Hundreds of men, women, and children were killed by Indians hired by the French.

French and Indians set the frontier aflame. A favorite target for Indian attacks was the struggling little vil-

Count Louis de Frontenac (below) was a strong, capable governor of New France.

The picture above shows the beginning of the attack on Deerfield in 1704.

lage of Deerfield in northwestern Massachusetts. It consisted of a church and a few houses. It was surrounded by a fence, or *stockade*, of wooden posts eight feet high. The settlers took turns guarding the stockade and watching for enemies. As the war went on, most of the men and boys had to leave Deerfield to fight with the colonial troops. Only a few were left to defend the town.

In February, 1704, a "war party" of about three hundred Frenchmen and Indians headed for Deerfield on snowshoes. They hid in the woods a few miles from the village. Day and night they watched for a chance to catch the settlers off guard.

A bitter storm from the northeast gave them their chance. It brought snow drifts and howling winds. At midnight the villagers were asleep, all but the sentinel. He left his post for a few minutes to warm his half-frozen hands at a fire.

Out of the dark woods came the enemy, like shadows in the storm. Easily they crept up a drift the wind had piled against the stockade. They leaped down into the village. The crash of muskets and Indian war whoops awakened the doomed settlers. The gloom was half-lighted by the flare of roofs set afire by torches of birch bark. Fifty people were killed and scalped. A hundred more, mostly women and children, were driven and dragged away to New France. Twenty died on the way. For every scalp, the governor paid a reward.

What happened at Deerfield happened on a smaller scale all along the frontier. At times Spain joined France and attacked the southern colonies. In 1704 Spanish ships attacked Charleston. Carolina settlers fought them for three days and drove them back to the West Indies. And in Georgia there were battles with Spanish and Indian invaders.

The British had trouble getting organized to fight. They were not united. The government in England failed to act quickly in the emergency. But the murder of Deerfield aroused a slow, deep anger in the men and women of America. They knew they could have no peace or safety as long as a French governor sat watching them across the St. Lawrence River. "New France must be destroyed!" became the battle cry.

Louisbourg was won and lost. On Cape Breton Island in Nova Scotia, the French built a ring of six forts around a good harbor. They called the place Louisbourg (LOO ee burg) in honor of their King. Several hundred soldiers and many cannons guarded the forts and the harbor.

BRITISH AGAINST FRENCH

France planned to use Louisbourg as a base for attacks on Boston, New York, and other seaports. Louisbourg was a constant threat to the British colonies. It was the strongest fortress that had ever been built in America. Both French and English naval officers thought it could never be captured.

New England men had a different idea, however. They had heard from scouts that Louisbourg was strong only on one side. All its cannon were mounted to shoot toward the front or harbor side. So the colonists decided on a daring attack.

In 1745 a little colonial army landed where no soldier in his right mind would expect an enemy to land. They chose a big marsh covered with high grass that was under water at high tide. A foolish place, it seemed — but the colonists knew what they were doing.

The marsh was just far enough away from the forts to be out of range of the guns. From a colonial supply ship came a few stoneboats, or flat platforms of planks, which farmers used for hauling rocks.

Placing each of their few small cannon on a stoneboat, 200 men dragged their artillery through mud and grass to the rear of the farthest fort. After battering it with cannon balls, they climbed over the wall on ladders. When the first fort surrendered they used its guns to batter the next fort. They captured that, too, and used its big guns in the same unexpected way.

The siege of Louisbourg went on for two months before England took any action. Then came three British warships from the West Indies to help the colonists. The warships kept out of the range of the fort's guns which might easily have sunk them. While tired American colonists pounded at the walls of Louisbourg, the British ships merely cruised offshore. They did capture

The picture below shows the fortress at Louisbourg in Nova Scotia. British colonists captured it in 1745, but it was returned to France three years later.

Young Washington carried a message to the French in the Ohio Valley in 1753.

to be kicked from one side to the other in a war game. But the American colonists had no use for a treaty that ignored their peace and safety. Some Americans began to think they would be better off if they were free from British rule.

The fourth war with France began at Fort Necessity. The last war that France and Britain fought for North America was different in three ways from all the others: (1) it began in North America; (2) it so roused England to the importance of her colonies that she sent a large number of soldiers and warships to help them; and (3) it marked the first appearance of a young man, George Washington, who later became the most honored of all Americans.

You will recall that both France and England wanted the Ohio Valley. But the French pushed into the area much faster than the British did. They built forts and trading posts at important points in the valley.

Governor Dinwiddie of Virginia sent 21-year-old George Washington to tell the French to get out of the Ohio Valley. The French received Washington politely, but went on with their plans. Washington reported that the French were getting ready to build another fort at the place where the Allegheny (AL uh GAY nee) and Monongahela (moh NAHN gah HEE lah) Rivers unite to form the Ohio River.

This is the point where the city of Pittsburgh now stands. It was

one French merchant ship that was bringing food to Louisbourg. But otherwise, they did nothing.

Yet, when the French commander raised a white flag, the British Commodore came ashore and claimed the right to receive the French surrender. Another right which he claimed, and got, was to take all the captured guns and war material home with him to England. Three years later Britain gave Louisbourg back to the French — much to the disgust of the colonists.

European nations seemed to regard any colony as a kind of football

the "gateway to the Ohio Valley." Settlers who wished to go west could travel by boat from this point, down the Ohio River, hundreds of miles to the middle of the country. If the French built a strong fort at the gateway, they could keep British settlers out of the Ohio Valley.

Governor Dinwiddie acted quickly. In 1754 he sent young Washington with 150 Virginia woodsmen to build a fort and keep the French out. Washington did his best, but he was young and lacked experience. Hurriedly he built a fort he called Fort Necessity. The French easily drove out Washington and his men. They built their own fort. In honor of the governor general they called it Fort Duquesne (duh KANE).

The French and Indian war had begun. Governor Dinwiddie realized it would take a large army to drive the French out of their new fort. He sent a message to England beg-

George Washington built Fort Necessity (below) but lost it to the French.

ging for help. The British government sent about 1400 trained soldiers, or "regulars." The commander was Major General Edward Braddock.

Braddock was a brave man and a soldier of long experience. But from the moment he arrived in America until he was shot, he did nothing but make mistakes.

Braddock knew nothing of the French and Indian way of fighting. He thought he had more than enough soldiers to defeat any force that the enemies could send against him. And he would take no advice from colonial officers who knew how to fight the French and Indians.

Braddock's first object was to capture Fort Duquesne. He boasted to Governor Dinwiddie and Benjamin Franklin, who was then Postmaster-General for the colonies:

To capture Fort Duquesne will hardly detain me more than two or three days. After that I shall proceed northward to the Great Lakes, if the season permits, and capture all the other French forts.

Braddock marched into a trap. Braddock's next mistake was to waste time. He arrived in Virginia in April, 1755. Fort Duquesne might have been won easily by quick action. But Braddock insisted on having many wagons to carry the mountain of baggage his officers and soldiers needed. He was furious when he heard the simple fact that there were no wagons or roads in Virginia.

More than a month passed before Benjamin Franklin was able to collect 150 wagons, with horses and teamsters, and send them from Pennsylvania. Then Braddock had to have a road made for the wagons. Almost two months slipped by while the road was built over the hills.

Braddock's army followed at a turtle's pace, only a mile or so in each day's march. With the army went a company of Virginia rangers, led by George Washington. Vainly they fretted at the needless delay. Braddock was in command, and they had to obey his orders.

At last, in July, 1755, the slow-moving army drew near Fort Duquesne. Colonial scouts reported that French soldiers and many Indians were hidden on three sides of an opening a short distance ahead. Again the colonists warned Braddock that Indians were dangerous when they fought on their own ground. He laughed at the warning and even called it cowardly.

The soldiers tramped forward shoulder to shoulder. They marched into the opening as if on parade. Suddenly there was a shrill war whoop. And from two sides came a deadly hail of bullets. Washington's rangers jumped behind trees, preparing to fight frontier fashion. But Braddock ordered them back into line. They obeyed; as a result most of them died.

For a few moments the regulars held steady, firing their muskets when their officers commanded. Not once did they see an enemy. Their bullets hit nothing but rocks and trees. Half of their comrades were killed, but still they obeyed orders until Braddock fell from his horse. Then panic hit them like a bomb. They fled in terror. They left their guns, their knapsacks — everything but their scalps — behind them.

Every officer but Washington was killed or wounded. Later he wrote his mother: "I luckily escaped unhurt, though I had four bullets

General Edward Braddock met defeat and death at Fort Duquesne, but the road he had built proved valuable in later times. It is now part of a great modern highway.

through my coat, and two horses shot under me."

Washington was able to rally some of the men and bring back a little order. The Indians were busy collecting scalps and loot; they did not pursue the retreating British. Washington's men carried the wounded Braddock into the forest.

Three days later Braddock died. His body was hastily buried in the middle of the road he had built. Before sunrise the soldiers marched over his grave. They did this to prevent the Indians from finding it and taking his scalp.

Long afterward, Braddock's road was traveled by settlers on their way to Ohio. Today it is part of "U.S. 40," the route that crosses the United States from coast to coast.

Braddock's defeat put the colonies in terrible danger. Braddock's defeat at Fort Duquesne was a bitter blow at Great Britain's power. Before the eyes of the colonists, the French, and the Indians, the British troops had failed miserably.

Now the French felt sure of victory. They thought that soon all the land from the Atlantic to the Mississippi would belong to them. They would wipe out the British settlements in a short time. In the future, they thought, French would be the language of North America. There would be no more town meetings, no more talk about the rights of the people.

The British colonists were fright-

ened and astonished. The flower of England's armies had gone down to defeat before a handful of French and Indian fighters. Now the colonists would have to depend entirely on themselves. What good was it to belong to the British Empire? What good did it do to pay taxes to England if English soldiers could not protect even themselves?

In anger and disgust, colonial Americans thought over the mess they found themselves in. They did not like it. They did not like the British authorities who were responsible. The idea of independence — of separating from Great Britain — began to seem attractive to some.

The worst effect of Braddock's defeat was its influence on western Indians. Only two tribes had sent their warriors to help the French. A dozen other tribes had waited to see how the battle between France and England would end. Now they decided to help the French. Like most people, the Indians wanted to be on the winning side. So their warriors joined in a war against the lonely settlements in the West — all the way from Maine to Georgia.

On the frontier, hardly a British trader or farmer escaped death. The Indians killed and burned without interference. They even invaded the settled areas near the coast.

The British sent another expedition against the French forts along Lake Ontario. It failed. An expedition against the French forts on Lake Champlain also failed. It

Rival Colonial Systems at War

FRANCE   ENGLAND

Centralized, autocratic government   Disunited colonial governments

Able, trained, military leadership   Military leadership untrained in American warfare

Friendship with a majority of the Indians   Friendship with only the Iroquois

Small scattered population – largely occupied in fur trading   Large stable population – with varied economic interests

looked as if the British colonies in North America were doomed.

The Acadians were driven from their native land. In the anxious days after Braddock's defeat, the English did a cruel thing to a group of French people called the *Acadians* (uh KAY dee ahns). The Acadians lived in Nova Scotia. In the second war with France, England won the homeland of the Acadians.

The Acadians were peaceful farmers. They asked only to be left alone to farm and practice their religion. But the English feared the Acadians were plotting to help the French win back Nova Scotia.

Without warning, in September, 1755, they marched thousands of the poor Acadians on board ships. They carried them away to southern colonies. Many children were separated from their parents and never found them again. Some Acadians reached Louisiana. Their descendants there are still called "Cajuns" (KAY juns). You can read the whole sad story in Longfellow's poem "Evangeline."

William Pitt saved England from defeat. The war dragged on for three bitter years. England sent warships and soldiers but they accomplished nothing. The French still held the forts on the Great Lakes and in the Ohio Valley. And they still held Louisbourg in Nova Scotia.

Then a new leader came to power in Great Britain. His name was William Pitt. He became head of Great Britain's government in 1758.

Pitt was not an army man but a political leader. But in two years he won victory after victory. From the minute he took charge, things seemed to go in Britain's favor. "I know," Pitt said, "that I can save this country and no one else can."

Pitt knew how to raise the spirits of the people in England and America. He picked good generals. He saw to it that they got the men and supplies they needed.

Pitt's leadership turned defeat into victory. A strong force of British and colonial soldiers again attacked Fort Duquesne. This time the French ran away without a fight. The fort's name was changed to Fort Pitt in honor of the British leader. Later the town that grew up there was called Pittsburgh.

And Pitt's orders sent British and colonial troops marching once more up the old war road along Lake George. The French saw them coming and blew up their forts at Ticonderoga and Crown Point. They fled across the river to Quebec.

William Pitt (below) led the British to final victory in the French and Indian War.

Quebec was the key to the defense of New France. Quebec was the strongest fort of all. It seemed that the British could never capture it. The French had worked for years to strengthen Quebec. They knew that if they lost Quebec they would lose all their American colonies.

The fort stood on a high, sheer cliff overlooking the St. Lawrence River. Soldiers in the fort could see up and down the river for miles. It seemed impossible that enemy soldiers could capture the fort.

William Pitt made careful preparations for the attack on Quebec. He sent a large part of the British fleet to America. He also sent an army of several thousand men. To command the attack he chose a 33-year-old officer named James Wolfe.

Wolfe did not look much like a military hero. He was a little fellow and not very strong. He liked to study and was especially fond of poetry. But he knew how to fight.

The son of a general, Wolfe joined the army at the age of fourteen. He became a general when he was 31. He played an important part in the recapture of Louisbourg in 1758. His skill and daring so impressed Pitt that he passed over many older men and put Wolfe in command.

The French commander at Quebec was Louis de Montcalm (deh mawn KAHLM). In many ways Montcalm and Wolfe were much alike. They were both young generals, full of fire and determination.

All summer long General Wolfe threw his men against the French defenses. Every attack failed. September came and the days grew cold. Navy leaders warned Wolfe that the ships must soon sail away or be frozen in the river all winter.

Wolfe won Quebec by a daring attack. General Wolfe was terribly discouraged. He became ill with fever and worry. It looked as if his attempt to capture Quebec had failed. But Wolfe decided on one more at-

French retreat from Quebec (below) marked the turning point of the war.

tack. He made his men climb a steep rocky path up the cliff. The French had stationed only a few guards there, for they thought nobody could climb the cliff there.

In the middle of the night British soldiers landed on the beach and began climbing. Somehow they pulled themselves over the rocks and up the cliff. They reached a level field some distance outside the fort. The space was called the *Plains of Abraham* because it belonged to a farmer named Abraham.

At sunrise, the astonished French found 4000 British soldiers lined up ready for battle outside the walls of Quebec. Montcalm had to come out and fight an open battle.

The fighting was bloody. In a short but decisive battle the French were completely defeated. Wolfe was wounded three times. He lived just long enough to learn that his men had won. "Now God be praised," he said. "I will die in peace."

Montcalm also fell wounded. His last words were, "Thank God, I shall not live to see the surrender."

The capture of Quebec in 1759 and the fall of Montreal the next year practically ended the war in America. France and Britain fought a few more battles in Europe and Asia. Everywhere the British won.

The Treaty of Paris (1763) ended French power in North America. The treaty of peace was signed at Paris in 1763. France surrendered Canada to Great Britain. She gave up all claims to the Mississippi and Ohio Valleys. And she turned New Orleans and Louisiana over to Spain.

France was able to keep only two small islands near Nova Scotia and two islands in the West Indies. She lost all her important American possessions. Great Britain became supreme in North America.

However, the influence of France in America did not end completely. The people of Quebec continued to speak French. Today, their descendants live in Quebec. They cherish the customs and the language of the settlers who came to New France three hundred years ago.

In Louisiana, "the land of Louis," French influence is strong. There the legal system is based on the law of France. Instead of counties Louisiana is divided into parishes, just as French provinces once were. New Orleans owes much of its beauty and charm to its French style of architecture. And the people of New Orleans still follow many French traditions. The city is famous for French cooking and its *Mardi Gras* (MAR dih GRAH) celebration.

Other American cities, such as St. Louis and Terre Haute, owe their names to French explorers and settlers. French rule disappeared from North America after 1763, but the French traditions and civilization have enriched American life.

Chief Pontiac aroused the Indians on the frontier. To American colonists, the Treaty of Paris meant safety

Pontiac tried to drive the British from Ohio, but finally had to surrender.

fought on the French side at Fort Duquesne. And he had little respect for British soldiers.

When the British moved into the French forts on the frontier, Pontiac decided that he and his warriors would drive them out. He traveled north and south, from tribe to tribe. He convinced the Indians that they were doomed if white people were allowed to move west. Pontiac was so clever and quiet that the colonists got no warning of his plans.

Then, at a secret signal from Pontiac, forty tribes took the warpath all over the frontier. They caught the colonists and the British soldiers off guard. They captured all but three of the frontier forts. In each battle they killed and scalped and burned. The uprising was much like King Philip's War against the New England colonists almost a hundred years before.

Pontiac's War lasted from May until November, 1763. The Indians were defeated at Fort Pitt and at Fort Detroit. Several tribes signed treaties and Pontiac finally submitted.

The British issued the Proclamation of 1763. Pontiac's uprising frightened the government in London more than it did the settlers in America. The French and Indian War had already shown the danger of Indian attacks. Pontiac's uprising made it clear that the frontier was not safe from Indian raids.

The British government wanted to make friends with the Indians. They

and the end of trouble with France. They started making plans for settling the land beyond the mountains. Ever since Braddock's defeat settlers had hesitated to move westward. Now the way was clear, they thought.

But the Indians still blocked the way. They did not want white men settling on their hunting grounds. They had lost the land along the coast long ago. They were determined to stop further settlement.

The French had scarcely left America when a frightful Indian uprising occurred. It was known as Pontiac's War or Pontiac's Conspiracy. Pontiac was a great chief among the Ottawa Indians. He had wanted to take over the fur trade out of which France had made big profits. They also wanted to protect the colonies from Indian attacks.

The leaders in England did not bother to talk about the problem with the colonists. They were not very pleased with the colonists at the time. They felt that the people in the colonies had not given as much support to the fight against France as they should have given. The colonists, of course, felt that they had done more than their share and that they had not had much real help from Britain. Relations between the colonists and the mother country were already getting chilly.

Without a word to the colonists, King George and his advisers took decisive action. The King issued the Proclamation of 1763. It announced that settlers would not be allowed to enter the western lands. These were to be reserved for Indians.

The Proclamation of 1763 aroused great anger in America. To the colonists it seemed that the British government was trying to steal the fruits of victory from them. For years they had dreamed of settling the West. They had suffered the terror of Indian attacks; they had fought the French again and again. Now the king and his advisers forbade them to enter the land for which they had fought.

The colonists disliked Great Britain's new policy. The colonists already had some grievances against Great Britain. They did not like the way the mother country had traded forts and colonies with France at various times during the long series of wars. They were very tired of being involved in Great Britain's wars.

The colonists now felt safer in opposing the government in London. They no longer had to fear the French. And they felt reasonably sure they could handle the Indians and the Spaniards. For more than a hundred years they had been fighting off Indian attacks. During the French and Indian War they had learned that British soldiers would not fight frontier fashion. They had little respect for British armies.

The colonists, you see, were growing up. They were feeling their own strength. They did not want British interference. The Proclamation of 1763 was a blow to their pride. They did not intend to be treated like children and ordered to stay out of territory they considered their own.

The leaders in London behaved like stern parents. They decided they were going to make their stubborn, headstrong colonists do as they were told! The colonists were going to pay a good share of the bills for the war Britain had fought for them. Laws about trade and taxes were going to be enforced strictly.

Thus, Great Britain's victory over France helped cause trouble with her colonies. Twelve years after the signing of the Treaty of Paris, the American colonists were in open rebellion.

CHAPTER SUMMARY

Britain and France fought four wars between 1690 and 1763. The thirteen American colonies were involved in all the wars. Both Great Britain and France wanted to control North America. Both claimed the Ohio and Mississippi River Valleys. Most of the Indian tribes sided with the French. In 1754 the French drove George Washington and his men out of Fort Necessity.

At first the war went against the British. General Braddock suffered a terrible defeat at Fort Duquesne in 1755. When William Pitt became Prime Minister the situation improved. He was the strong leader needed for victory. The French lost fort after fort. In 1760 General Wolfe captured the great stronghold of Quebec. France was soon completely defeated. In the Treaty of Paris of 1763 France lost all her American colonies except a few islands.

Britain issued the Proclamation of 1763. Chief Pontiac wanted to keep the English out of the Ohio Valley. The British wanted to be friends with the Indians. Thus the Proclamation ordered settlers to stay out of the Ohio Valley. This angered the American colonists. Bad feeling against the mother country increased rapidly.

The Language of History

Be sure you understand the meaning of the following words and phrases. Consult the dictionary as well as your textbook.

1. war road	**3.** stockade	**5.** Proclamation of 1763
2. policy	**4.** traditions	**6.** peace treaty

What Happened When

Make sure you know the important events connected with the following dates:

1. 1755	**2.** 1759	**3.** 1763

Who's Who in History

Be sure you know the part that the following played in the colonial period:

1. Louis XIV	**4.** Edward Braddock	**7.** Louis de Montcalm
2. James Wolfe	**5.** William Pitt	**8.** Count de Frontenac
3. Pontiac	**6.** Benjamin Franklin	**9.** George Washington

Study Questions

1. Give three reasons why France and Great Britain were unfriendly in the 18th century.

2. Point out two important differences between French and British colonies in North America. What advantages did the French have when war came?

3. Discuss Braddock's defeat telling (**a**) the date, (**b**) where it occurred, (**c**) Braddock's mistakes, and (**d**) results of the defeat.

4. Discuss the Acadians telling (**a**) where they lived, (**b**) why the British feared them, (**c**) what happened to them, and (**d**) the name of a poem that tells their story.

5. Explain how William Pitt's leadership helped Great Britain win.

6. State three provisions of the Treaty of Paris of 1763.

7. Point out two ways in which modern America still shows the influence of early French rule.

8. Write about Pontiac's Conspiracy telling (**a**) its purpose, (**b**) why it frightened British leaders, and (**c**) why the British were eager to make friends with the Indians in the Ohio Valley.

9. **a.** What did the Proclamation of 1763 say?
   b. Why did the Proclamation anger the colonists?

10. Explain why the French and Indian War led to bad feeling between the British government and the American colonists.

11. Locate each of the following and tell its connection with the events of the French and Indian War:

a. Deerfield	**c.** Quebec	**e.** Fort Ticonderoga
b. Louisbourg	**d.** Fort Duquesne	**f.** Braddock's Road

LET'S LOOK AT WHAT WE'VE LEARNED

Why were the British slow to start colonies in America?

A nation must be rich and powerful to found successful colonies. For a long time the British had to strengthen their government and build up their navy. They had to defeat Spain, the most powerful nation of the time. In the reign of Queen Elizabeth Britain became a great power. After that the British were able to begin colonizing.

For what purposes were the British colonies founded?

Most colonies were started to make money for those who financed the settlement. Some colonies were founded as refuges from religious persecution in Europe. Roger Williams started a colony in Rhode Island for those who wanted religious freedom. Maryland was intended to be a refuge for Roman Catholics. William Penn founded Pennsylvania as a refuge for the Quakers.

Many came to America to start life anew. James Oglethorpe founded Georgia to provide opportunity for unfortunate debtors.

Where and when did the British make their first permanent settlements?

The first permanent British colony was founded at Jamestown, Virginia, in 1607. In 1620 the Pilgrims landed at Plymouth on the New England coast. In 1630 the Puritans founded Massachusetts Bay.

What and where were the original thirteen colonies?

The thirteen colonies were located along the coast of the Atlantic Ocean from Canada to Florida. In the north were the New England colonies of Massachusetts Bay, Rhode Island, Connecticut, and New Hampshire.

Between New England and the Southern Colonies lay the Middle Colonies: New York, Pennsylvania, New Jersey, and Delaware.

Between the Middle Colonies and Florida lay the Southern Colonies of Virginia, Maryland, North and South Carolina, and Georgia.

How did the colonists earn a living?

Most colonists were farmers. In the South they raised tobacco, rice, and indigo; in the North they grew corn and wheat. A few colonists were skilled as blacksmiths, shoemakers, candlemakers, and printers.

In New England, fishing and shipbuilding were important industries. Some colonists hunted and traded with the Indians for furs.

How did colonial children get an education?

Many children, especially girls, got little education. They learned to read at home from the *New England Primer*.

In New England every town had to provide a public school. Most of the Middle Colonies also had public schools. In the South rich planters hired tutors for their children. Several colleges were started in colonial days. Harvard was the first, and William and Mary College in Virginia was the second in the colonies.

What rights did the British colonists have?

As British citizens they helped make laws and levy taxes. They had freedom of assembly and the right to a jury trial. Later they successfully asserted their right to freedom of the press.

Why did Britain and France fight often between 1690 and 1763?

The two nations differed in religion. They both wished to become world powers and control North America.

How did the end of the French and Indian War affect British colonists?

They no longer feared the French and did not need British protection. They were angry when the British kept them out of the new western lands. The colonists became dissatisfied with British rule.

Connecting the Past with the Present . . .

Freedom of thought, freedom of religion, a chance for everybody to get ahead if he works hard — these are the things you take for granted. "It's part of being an American," you say, and you are right. How did such rights and privileges get established in the first place?

Long ago in colonial days Americans like Roger Williams, Nathaniel Bacon, and John Peter Zenger fought and suffered for freedom's sake. They helped establish the idea that individuals should be allowed to develop their own ideas and abilities. Long before America became independent, the colonists were learning to stand straight and to speak their own minds. In quiet little towns along the Atlantic seaboard, men — and women too — carried on a ceaseless struggle against oppression. Roger Williams nearly died in the wilderness. John Peter Zenger spent weary months in jail. Anne Hutchinson was driven from Massachusetts. Thirteen of Nathaniel Bacon's followers were hung. They paid a heavy price for defying tyranny, and they made a great gift to you and to all Americans: the heritage of freedom.

Questions for Discussion and Review

1. Explain the three steps by which colonial merchants got rich trading American goods for foreign goods.

2. Make a list of reasons why people left Europe to face the hardships of life in the New World.

3. Describe the kind of building which met the need for good, cheap, and quickly built shelter for frontier families.

4. What were three differences between southern farms and northern farms during the colonial period?

5. Compare a colonial school with your school. If you could choose, which school would you go to? Why?

6. What three nations claimed great areas of North America before the Treaty of Paris of 1763?

7. What territory did the French lose by the Treaty of Paris?

8. Indians fought on both sides in the struggle for North America. Which tribes or groups of tribes fought for the English, and which for the French?

9. Compare the French colonists with the English colonists in regard to the following: occupations, religion, language, customs.

10. List four causes of the wars between the French and English.

THE HISTORY LABORATORY

Human beings learn by doing. When you plan and carry through an activity or project you gain new skills and absorb facts that you remember. Here are some suggestions for activities that you will find interesting and profitable.

Be a Pioneer . . .

There are still many frontiers in this world to which pioneers are moving. Parts of Asia, Africa, South America, North America, and

WHAT AND WHEN

Founding of Jamestown 1607   House of Burgesses 1619   Founding of Plymouth C 1620

perhaps Antarctica will look back to the twentieth century as their colonial days.

Organize a band of settlers within your class who will plan a move to one of these frontiers. Choose a place to go, find out what you would need when you arrived there, select a leader for the expedition, investigate how much money you would need, etc. A good source for this kind of project is *The National Geographic Magazine*.

Have a Party . . .

Why not make your next party a "bee" like one of those described in this unit? You could dress in colonial costumes, play colonial games, eat colonial style food and have colonial decorations. *Calico Bush* by Field and *Child Life in Colonial Times* by Earle are books which can supply some of the information you will need to help plan such a "bee."

Be a dramatist . . .

Write a play describing a day in a colonial school. You might present this as an assembly program. Your teacher may have some special stories about one-room schools to tell you. Another place you will be able to find out about our first schools is in *John Adams and the American Revolution* by Catherine Bowen (Little, Brown and Co., 1950). The first nine chapters relate several stories about John Adams' experiences as a student and as a teacher.

Town Meeting Today . . .

Hold a town meeting to discuss one of the following problems. (For suggestions about how to hold such a meeting see Wines and Card, *Come to Order!*)

a. Pretend that you are in a frontier village. It is proposed that all men and boys over 14 must take military training to protect the village against Indian attack.

settle Manhattan 1624   Bacon's Rebellion 1676   Trial of Zenger 1734   French-Indian Wars end 1763

b. Imagine that you live in a colonial town that has no school. Have the town meeting discuss whether or not a school should be built and children required to attend.

Build a Town . . .

Make a model of an early settlement. You might include a church, a village common, a mill, a shoemaker shop, a general store, a blacksmith shop, a boat shop, a candlemaker shop, a rope-maker shop, a hatmaker shop, a carpenter's shop, and a schoolhouse. The models can be made from clay, paper, wood, or metal.

Be a Reporter . . .

Write a newspaper account describing the trial of John Peter Zenger. Be sure to include the opinions of various people you might have talked to, such as Governor Cosby, Anna Zenger, a Quaker leader, and one of Zenger's neighbors. You will find Galt's *John Peter Zenger* helpful.

Let's Read about Colonial Days

*ANDERSON, A. M., *Squanto and the Pilgrims*, Watts, 1949.
*BLEEKER, SONIA, *Indians of the Longhouse*, Morrow, 1950.
BRILL, ETHEL C., *Madeline Takes Command*, McGraw, 1946.
**COOPER, JAMES F., *Last of the Mohicans*, Dodd, 1951.
COURNOS, JOHN, and NORTON, SYBIL, *Pilgrimage to Freedom: The Story of Roger Williams*, Holt, 1953.
EARLE, ALICE, *Child Life in Colonial Days*, Macmillan, 1899.
EATON, JEANNETTE, *That Lively Man, Ben Franklin*, Morrow, 1948.
EDMONDS, WALTER, *Matchlock Gun*, Dodd, 1941.
FIELD, RACHEL, *Calico Bush*, Macmillan, 1931.
**GALT, THOMAS F., *Peter Zenger, Fighter for Freedom*, Crowell, 1951.
HALL–QUEST, O., *How the Pilgrims Came to Plymouth*, Dutton, 1946.
HAVILAND, VIRGINIA, *William Penn*, Abingdon, 1952.
LENSKI, LOIS, *Indian Captive*, Lippincott, 1941.
McGINLEY, C. J., *Historic Models of Early America*, Harcourt, 1947.
MEADOWCROFT, E. L., *The First Year*, Crowell, 1941.
MEIGS, CORNELIA L., *Mounted Messenger*, Macmillan, 1943.
**ROSS, FRANCES, *Land and People of Canada*, Lippincott, 1947.
SHIPPEN, KATHERINE B., *Lightfoot*, Viking, 1950.
**YATES, ELIZABETH, *Amos Fortune: Free Man*, Aladdin, 1950.

* indicates easy reading
** indicates advanced reading

Unit 3

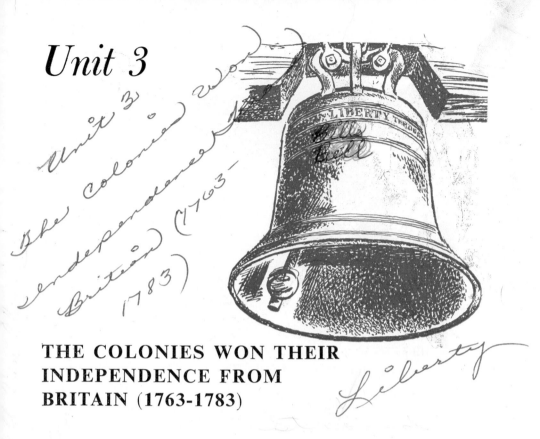

THE COLONIES WON THEIR INDEPENDENCE FROM BRITAIN (1763-1783)

IN 1763 GREAT BRITAIN was the mightiest power in the world. The French had been beaten decisively, and the British were supreme in North America. The American colonists loyally rejoiced in the triumph of their motherland.

Yet within twenty years Britain lost its thirteen original colonies in North America and suffered a complete and humiliating defeat as well. How did it happen? Why did Britain lose the loyalty of her colonists? What mistakes did she make that turned their affection into hatred?

A handful of colonists defeated an Empire! Where did they get money, weapons, and supplies? What part did France play? Time after time, ragged Americans were more cunning than Britain's finest generals. Who were the American leaders who achieved such miracles?

The answers are part of the story told in this Unit — the story of a quarrel that grew into the Revolution, out of which emerged a free and independent nation: the United States.

125

Chapter 7

DISPUTES
WITH BRITAIN LED
TO THE DECLARATION
OF INDEPENDENCE

THIRTEEN was an unlucky number for the British after the French and Indian Wars. By the Treaty of Peace of 1763 they had driven the French out of North America. Canada, the Ohio Valley, the rich fur trade — all these fell into Britain's lap. Then only thirteen years later the thirteen colonies declared their independence.

Who was to blame? The British leaders said the colonists were. The colonists blamed the king and his advisers. Clearly somebody must have made a mistake or a whole series of mistakes. Was there no chance to patch up the quarrel? What acts led to violence? Who were the American leaders who broke away from the mother country?

The Revolution began in New England. The first blood was shed in and around Boston. Why did it begin there rather than in the Middle Colonies or the South? And why did the other colonies come to the aid of Massachusetts? There was little love between colonies as a rule. Why then did Pennsylvania, Virginia, and the rest send men, money, and supplies to Boston as soon as they heard news of Lexington and Concord?

Answers to these questions are all part of the story told in this chapter — the story of the events that led to American independence.

126

The British and the colonists did not understand one another. John Adams once said that the American Revolution took place long before the actual fighting began. "The Revolution was in the minds and hearts of the people." He meant that Americans had grown sick and tired of British rule. The dictionary defines *revolution* as "a complete change in government." At the beginning of the quarrel, there were probably few Americans who wanted a complete change of government. However, they were growing dissatisfied.

The colonies changed a great deal in the hundred and fifty-six years after the founding of Jamestown. From the starving band of Virginia settlers, there developed a prosperous nation of farmers, merchants, skilled and unskilled workers. Land-hungry families looked longingly toward the West. They defied the Proclamation of 1763 and settled where they pleased.

You will recall that for many years after the colonies were started, the King and his advisers paid little attention to American affairs. They let the settlers run their own affairs and struggle along as best they could. This policy of neglect proved healthy for the colonists. They learned to depend on themselves.

After the French and Indian War, leaders in Great Britain changed their policy. They suddenly decided to be strict — to pay close attention to colonial affairs. People in America did not understand the change,
and they did not like it. The more Britain tried to interfere, the more the colonists resisted. At last the quarrel turned into a real war.

The cause of the American Revolution was an honest misunderstanding. Both sides were right on some points and wrong on others. Unfortunately, neither tried to see the other side's point of view.

Great Britain felt the colonists owed a great debt. Here is the way British leaders looked at the colonial problem:

(1) The colonies existed for the benefit of Great Britain. Many people in England had poured out a huge amount of money and supplies to establish the colonies. Men like William Penn had used up fortunes founding colonies. The trading companies had invested thousands of pounds in America; in return they had received only moderate profits and sometimes nothing. In return for all this, Britain felt that the colonies should trade only with the mother country. They should raise the crops that Britain needed. They should *not* try to manufacture goods to compete with British products.

(2) Great Britain had used her navy and her armies to defend the colonies. Many British soldiers and sailors had died in America.

(3) The colonies had not co-operated well in the fight against France. Some colonial legislatures had been slow to vote supplies for the war. Some Americans had

traded with the French West Indies.

(4) The wars with France had been very expensive. Great Britain was deeply in debt. British leaders felt that the colonists should help pay for the wars. After all, they reasoned, the wars had been fought partly to protect the colonies.

In the past, colonists had managed to get out of paying most taxes Great Britain had tried to impose. They even traded directly with the French and Spanish in spite of laws that forbade such trade. And Americans smuggled great quantities of goods — that is, they brought products from foreign nations into the colonies without paying taxes. The British decided this must stop.

(5) Most of the Indian tribes were unfriendly to Great Britain. British leaders were eager to win the friendship of the Indians for two reasons. They wanted to take over the rich fur trade that France had carried on. They also wanted to protect the colonies from Indian attack.

The colonists resented British control.
Some Americans agreed with the British point of view. They were loyal to the mother country in spite of everything. They were called Loyalists or Tories. (Tory was the name Englishmen gave to people who were friendly to the King; those who were not so friendly to the King and who were more willing to make changes in the government were called Whigs.) Many of the richest people in America were Tories. One

of them advised his fellow Americans:

Let us behave like good children who have received undeserved blows from a loved parent. Let us complain to our parents; but let our complaint speak the language of obedience and respect.

But Americans such as Samuel Adams, "father of the Revolution," had no use for this advice. They felt that Britain had not acted like a loving parent, but like a cruel stepmother. Here are some arguments of American rebel leaders:

(1) The colonists had brought to America a great heritage of liberty. Their ancestors had fought for the right to vote, the right to a trial by jury, and other rights of Englishmen.

Over the centuries, Englishmen had won certain important statements of liberty from the Kings: The Magna Carta, or Great Charter, the Petition of Right, and the Bill of Rights. These documents clearly stated that Englishmen could not be taxed without their consent, or put in prison without a trial.

The colonists felt the King had no power to tax them without their consent. Nor, simply because they lived in America, should he restrict their freedom. They believed they had all the rights of Englishmen. But the government in London seemed to look upon them as inferior people who existed just to serve the interests of Great Britain.

(2) The colonists felt that Britain had not cared for their interests during the wars with France. They had been left to defend themselves.

They had captured Louisbourg and then had watched Britain hand it back to France. And they remembered Braddock's stupid, unnecessary defeat and how it had endangered all the colonies.

(3) Like most people, the colonists did not like to pay taxes. They were willing to pay taxes to run their own local governments in America; but they did not feel they should pay taxes to England. After all, they could not send men to represent them in the British Parliament. Why then should Parliament pass laws and try to tax them? "No taxation without representation!" became the American motto.

(4) American colonists were ambitious and eager to get ahead. They wanted to start factories and make the goods they needed. They wanted to ship tobacco and fish and rice to European nations that were willing to pay a good price for these products. They felt that the more they produced and sold, the more prosperous they would become. Everyone would benefit, even the people in England.

But the British government interfered with American trade. Americans could not start factories because the British feared they would take business away from the mother country. When Parliament passed new laws to regulate colonial trade, Americans grew angry.

(5) Americans did not need British help any more. They felt strong and confident. They knew they could govern themselves because they had

Americans opposed the Stamp Act vigorously. The picture shows a protest parade.

been doing it for years. They had some idea of the rich land and resources in the region west of the thirteen colonies. They felt they could develop a great nation, "a land of promise." But they feared the British government would always hold them back and interfere.

After 1763 British interference increased. Soon after the colonies were founded, the British government began passing laws, or *Navigation Acts*, to regulate colonial trade. The laws, however, were seldom enforced. And the colonists were able to get around them. They managed to trade with foreign nations — and they seldom paid taxes on the trade.

But after 1763, things changed. The British government passed new laws and made a determined effort to enforce them. They sent soldiers to the colonies and ordered Americans to find shelter for them.

The colonists did not want the soldiers. They did not need them in time of peace. They felt it was not fair to make them provide places for the soldiers to live. Parliament paid no attention to American objections. The soldiers settled down in the colonies. Everywhere they caused trouble. Americans called them "Lobster-backs" because they wore red coats that resembled the color of boiled lobsters.

Why did Britain insist on sending soldiers to the colonies? Because she was determined to collect more taxes and stop smuggling. The soldiers would help enforce tax laws.

The man behind the new English policy was George Grenville. He was Chancellor of the Exchequer (ex CHECK er), a position something like that of the Secretary of the Treasury in the United States today. It was his job to find money to pay the government's bills.

The Stamp Act of 1765 made Americans angry. Grenville persuaded Parliament to pass a law called the Stamp Act of 1765. The purpose of the Stamp Act was to get money out of the colonists. It required Americans to buy stamps printed in England and use them in all sorts of business deals. The stamps were like those you now see on packages of cigarettes.

For example, a colonist who published a newspaper was supposed to put a penny stamp on every paper he sold. That was really a big tax, for newspapers were then very small and a penny was worth several times what it is today. A boy who graduated from college had to put a dollar stamp on his diploma. The trader who sold a horse was required to put a two-dollar stamp on the bill of sale. The farmer who sold a farm had to put a fifty-dollar stamp on the deed, or legal paper, which proved that he owned the land. The money that Americans had to pay for the stamps went to England, of course. The English government used it to help pay debts.

Englishmen thought the tax was a fine idea. The colonists did not agree. The Stamp Act hit them in a very sensitive spot — their pocketbooks. And they felt it violated one of the most precious rights of Englishmen: they were being taxed without their consent.

The Proclamation of 1763 had caused the colonists to grumble. Now, in 1765, the Stamp Act brought open defiance. A Virginian was one of the first to speak out. Patrick Henry, a young storekeeper who had studied law, stood up in the House of Burgesses and shouted: "Taxation without representation is tyranny. . . . If this be treason, make the most of it!"

Patrick Henry's words inspired the House of Burgesses to condemn the Stamp Act. The lawmakers did this by passing a series of statements, or *resolutions*, against the Act. Other colonies also opposed the stamp tax. Many people quietly refused to buy the stamps. In some places a mob forced the stamp seller to resign or chased him out of town.

Parliament had to repeal the Stamp Act. The colonies had always been slow to work together. Each was suspicious of the others. But — for awhile, at least — the stamp tax made them forget their differences. James Otis, a leading Boston lawyer, suggested that the colonists take united action against the stamp tax. As a result, a Stamp Act Congress met in New York in October, 1765. Nine colonies sent representatives. The Congress sent a respectful appeal to the King and Parliament. It said the law was unjust and would surely bring trouble.

Grenville and the other British leaders paid no attention to the appeal. Then the colonists tried something more effective: they refused to buy British goods. Hundreds of businessmen in New York, Philadelphia, Boston, and other cities signed promises that they would not buy goods from England. Today, such a united refusal to buy would be called a *boycott*.

British merchants became frightened. They faced ruin if they could not sell their goods in America. So they begged Parliament to repeal or cancel the Stamp Act. The merchants' appeal caused hot debate in Parliament. George Grenville wanted to use the British Army to

Repeal of the Stamp Act brought rejoicing. Here colonists read the news.

force the colonists to obey. But wise old William Pitt said the colonists were in the right. He advised Parliament to get rid of the law. Parliament gave in and repealed the Stamp Act in 1766.

Americans were happy and excited when they heard the news. Stores and shops closed; everybody had a holiday. But the rejoicing came too soon. The trouble was not over. Parliament had not given up its attempt to tax the colonists.

George Grenville soon lost his power and his job, but another man carried on his ideas. He was Charles Townshend. He became Chancellor of the Exchequer in 1766. The government badly needed money, so in 1767 Townshend got Parliament to pass new tax laws for America.

The Townshend Acts aroused opposition. The Townshend Acts, as they were called, provided that:

(1) The colonists would have to pay taxes on paint, glass, paper, tea, lead, and many other imports.

(2) The money raised by the new taxes would be used to pay royal governors and other British officials in America. No longer would officials have to depend on colonial legislatures for their pay. Thus, the

colonists would lose a powerful weapon they had used to influence royal governors.

(3) British officials could get search warrants or *writs of assistance*. These writs gave them power to search the home and storage place of any colonist they suspected of smuggling goods. This angered the colonists even more than the new taxes. It is an old English saying that "every man's house is his castle." Writs of assistance disregarded the ancient right or custom. Officials could easily get a writ and then come bursting into anyone's home or store.

(4) The Townshend Acts also forbade New York's Assembly, or legislature, to hold meetings. The Assembly had refused to give money for the support of the British soldiers sent to the colony. Now it was being punished. People in other colonies realized that if New Yorkers could lose the legislature so easily, it might soon be their turn.

Once more Americans united to fight "taxation without representa-tion." They refused to buy British goods. This time the fight lasted longer. For three years Great Britain tried to enforce the Townshend Acts. They sent more soldiers to the colonies. Two regiments led by General Gage arrived in Boston.

Merchants in almost all the colonies refused to bring in goods from Britain. Imports fell off almost fifty percent. The British spent almost a million dollars trying to collect the new taxes. They received in taxes only about $1500. The Townshend Acts failed just as the Stamp Act had.

In 1770 the British government gave in. Parliament repealed, or canceled, all the Townshend Act taxes except the one on tea. The tax on tea was kept to remind colonists Britain had the right to tax them.

Many Americans drew a long breath of relief when Parliament repealed the Townshend Acts. They thought that the quarrel was over. They expected relations with the mother country to become friendly once more. But a few men, like

The Boston Massacre, shown below, was the first bloodshed of the Revolution. On March 5, 1770 British soldiers fired at people who had been annoying them.

Samuel Adams of Massachusetts, warned that trouble would arise again. The dispute was too serious and deep-seated. This was shown by the Boston Massacre.

The Boston Massacre created bitter feeling. Just before the repeal of the Townshend duties, a serious clash occurred between British troops and a group of colonists. It happened in Boston where feeling between Red Coats and townspeople was growing.

One cold March day in 1770 some carefree boys had a snowball fight in Boston. On their way home they saw a soldier walking back and forth on guard duty. They promptly began to throw snowballs at him. To them it was just fun, but the soldier became frightened. He called for help. Soldiers rushed to aid him.

The noise brought men and boys running from all directions. Both sides hurled insults back and forth. Suddenly an excited young officer yelled a command. The soldiers thought he said "Fire!" They fired their muskets. When the smoke lifted, eleven of the crowd lay dead or wounded in the snow.

This was the *Boston Massacre* (MASS ah ker). It was the first time blood was shed in the quarrel between Great Britain and the colonists. Some people call the Boston Massacre of 1770 the opening fight of the War of Independence.

Boston was in an uproar after the Massacre. Angry citizens, led by Samuel Adams, told the governor to get the troops out of Boston. The governor did not want any more trouble, so he sent the soldiers to an island in Boston Harbor.

News of the Boston Massacre spread quickly. People in the other colonies asked themselves, "Will we be next?" The feeling against Great Britain became more bitter. Repeal of most of the Townshend duties — soon after the Boston Massacre — helped restore good relations. But the Massacre was not forgotten.

Samuel Adams wanted the colonists to keep in touch with one another so they could act quickly in case of trouble with the British. He started committees of correspondence in every Massachusetts town. Members of the committees wrote articles for the newspapers. They also wrote to leaders in other colonies. The plan worked well. Virginia borrowed Adams' idea and set up a committee. Soon there were committees of correspondence in most of the colonies. They helped unite the people and strengthened opposition.

The Tea Act caused trouble in Boston. You will recall that the British government kept the tax on tea when the other Townshend duties were repealed. This caused some trouble. Certain Americans stopped drinking tea because they did not want to pay the tax. In colonial days, when almost everyone drank a great deal of tea, this was a real sacrifice.

In 1773 Parliament passed a new law called the Tea Act. It permitted the British East India Tea Company to send tea to the colonies without paying any taxes. The colonists, however, would still have to pay a tax on the tea they bought.

The purpose of the Tea Act was to help the East India Tea Company sell a huge supply of tea it had on hand. The Company was given the right to open branch stores and sell directly to the colonists. But American businessmen did not like this idea. It meant that the East India Company would be able to sell tea far more cheaply than Americans could.

Samuel Adams declared it was all a trick to force the colonists to pay unjust taxes. All over the colonies there was opposition to the new plan. American leaders warned the East India Company not to send its tea to the colonies. But the Company paid no attention.

Ships loaded with tea arrived in several American seaports. In some cities the ships were refused permission to unload. They went back to England, and there was no trouble. But in Boston, Governor Hutchinson would not let the ships be sent back. His sons had been appointed agents of the East India Company to sell the tea. The people of Boston, however, would not let tea be unloaded. Neither side would give in.

On the evening of December 16, 1773, thousands of Boston citizens met to talk over the problem. Samuel Adams was in charge. Governor Hutchinson sent word that he would never permit the ships to be sent back. Adams decided it was time for action. He gave a secret signal. Suddenly the crowd heard Indian war whoops. A group of colonists, dressed as Indians and carrying hatchets, rushed to the wharf and climbed on the tea ships.

They used their hatchets to break open the tea chests. Silently they worked through the night, throwing

The "Tea Party," pictured below, was Boston's answer to Great Britain's attempt to make the colonists pay a tax on their tea. Men disguised as Indians dumped the tea into the harbor and so started the nation on the road to independence.

all the tea (342 chests) into the harbor. Ninety thousand dollars' worth of tea mixed with sea water! That was the Boston Tea Party.

England passed the Intolerable Acts.
King George and Parliament were in a rage over the destruction of tea in Boston. This was outright defiance! Boston must be taught a lesson. Early in 1774 Parliament passed a series of laws to punish Boston and Massachusetts. The laws were so harsh that Americans called them the Intolerable Acts, meaning they were too hard to be endured.

One law closed the port of Boston. No ships could enter or leave the harbor. This destroyed the town's trade and threatened the people with starvation. The port would remain closed until Boston paid the East India Company for the damage done at the Tea Party.

Another law put Massachusetts under military rule. The whole colony had to obey the orders of a British general. The people could not hold town meetings. They had nothing to say in the government. To enforce the new laws Britain sent 10,000 additional soldiers.

If Parliament could destroy Massachusetts' government and threaten Boston with starvation, no colony was safe. From New Hampshire to Georgia, the colonists met. They decided that something must be done to help Massachusetts. The committee of correspondence wrote letters and promised action. Virginia sent out a call for an assembly of representatives from all colonies.

The First Continental Congress met in Philadelphia. Fifty men from all the colonies but Georgia met in Philadelphia in September, 1774, to protest against the Intolerable Acts. The meeting later became known as the First Continental Congress. It was called "Continental" because it represented British colonies on the North American continent.

The Congress passed resolutions against the Intolerable Acts. It appealed to King George to right the wrongs that had been done. The Congress also agreed not to buy anything from Great Britain, or to ship any goods there, until American rights were recognized.

The answer of King George and Parliament to the appeal of the Continental Congress was to send more troops and warships. The colonists, in turn, gathered powder and guns. In Massachusetts' towns, men formed military companies and drilled regularly. They called themselves *Minutemen*, for they meant to be ready to fight at a minute's notice.

British General Gage put his men to work fortifying Boston. He received orders from London to strike fast and crush the rebellion at the first opportunity. Everywhere people wondered if war was coming. In March, 1775, Patrick Henry declared:

Gentlemen may cry, "Peace! Let us have peace!" but there is no peace. The war is actually begun. The next

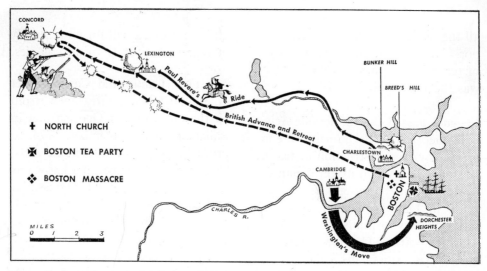

The map above shows the beginning of the Revolution in New England. The first battles took place in April 1775 at Lexington and Concord not far from Boston.

gale that sweeps from the north will bring the clash of resounding arms.

Why stand we here idle? What is it that gentlemen wish? What would they have? Is life so dear or peace so sweet as to be purchased at the price of chains and slavery? Forbid it, Almighty God!

I know not what course others may take; but as for me, give me liberty or give me death.

Americans "fired the shot heard round the world." When Gage heard that the colonists had collected powder and other military supplies at Concord, he thought he saw a chance "to teach the rebels a lesson." He sent about eight hundred soldiers to Concord. His troops were to cross the Charles River by boats, and march all night. On the way to

These silver spurs were made by Paul Revere whose famous midnight ride helped summon Americans to fight in April 1775.

Concord they would stop at Lexington to arrest two American leaders, John Hancock and Samuel Adams. Gage planned to try Hancock and Adams for treason.

The Americans had spies in Gage's army. They found out about his plan before he made the first move. Hardly were his soldiers in their boats before a light flashed in the tower of Boston's Old North Church. On the other side of the river four men were waiting on horseback. When they saw the light, they galloped off to alarm Minutemen in every town within forty miles. You have probably read about one of the riders in Longfellow's "Paul Revere's Ride."

The British soldiers reached Lexington at dawn, April 19, 1775. They were too late. Hancock and Adams had been warned. They left hours before the British arrived. On the village "green," or outdoor meeting place, fifty Minutemen stood

waiting, leaning on their guns. Their leader was Captain Parker.

A British officer ordered the Minutemen to lay down their arms and go home. Quietly, Captain Parker answered, "Steady, men. Don't fire unless you are fired on. But if they want war, let it begin here." The one-sided fight at Lexington, fifty against eight hundred, was quickly over. Nineteen of the Minutemen fell dead or wounded. When the others were driven to cover, the British hurried on to Concord. They had hardly begun to hunt for hidden military stores when the fire of gunshot sounded behind them. This was the "shot heard round the world." It came from Concord Bridge where the British had left a strong guard.

Minutemen of other towns had heard the call of night riders. They,

The leaflet above told America the names of those who fell at Concord.

too, came to join the fight. Fearful of being surrounded, British officers ordered their men to march back to Boston. A terrible march it was, through a double line of fire. The Minutemen knew every inch of the land on which they were fighting. British soldiers ran down an open road "like a flock of sheep chased by dogs." Hidden behind trees and walls on both sides, Minutemen fired

The American Revolution began at Lexington, Massachusetts on April 19, 1775. Below is an old picture of the battle, drawn several years after the event. Notice how the sharpshooting Minutemen are skillfully making use of the protection offered by rocks, trees, and hills.

Here Ethan Allen, leader of the Green Mountain Boys, orders the British Commander to surrender Fort Ticonderoga.

at them with deadly aim. The red coats of the British soldiers made fine targets. General Gage had to send two more regiments with field guns to rescue his men.

Day-and-night riders carried the news of Lexington and Concord to all the colonies. Everywhere people asked the same fearful question: Does it mean war?

The Green Mountain Boys captured Ticonderoga. The Americans badly needed guns and other military supplies. They knew the British kept artillery and ammunition at Fort Ticonderoga on Lake Champlain. In the wild Vermont country, a man named Ethan Allen decided on a bold attack. For sometime he had been drilling a group of men he called "the Green Mountain Boys." They were ready for action.

On May 9, Allen led 82 men across Lake Champlain. They arrived at Fort Ticonderoga very early in the morning on May 10. The sleepy British seemed to have heard nothing about the fighting at Lexington and Concord.

Allen pounded on the gate and ordered the British to surrender. When the British commander asked by what authority Allen demanded entrance, the Vermonter is said to have replied, "In the name of the great Jehovah and the Continental Congress!" The surprised British gave up the fort without a fight. Within a few hours the Americans were loading Ticonderoga's artillery on ox-sleds. Over the hills and icy paths they dragged the heavy guns to Boston.

Washington became Commander-in-chief. The day Ticonderoga fell, another great event took place: the Second Continental Congress met in Philadelphia's Independence Hall. The town was full of excitement. Everyone knew that King George had refused to see the messenger the First Continental Congress had sent to him. Parliament had refused even to read the petition from America. The new Congress had a war on its hands.

Many great men came to Philadelphia as delegates in 1775. Among them were Benjamin Franklin, John Hancock, John Adams, George Washington, and Thomas Jefferson. Philadelphia gave them all a warm welcome. There were parties and

QUARREL WITH BRITAIN

parades. But the delegates felt serious and troubled. It was a big undertaking to prepare for war against a mighty empire.

First it was necessary to raise an army. Congress asked each colony to send companies of riflemen to help the Minutemen fighting the British around Boston. The next question was, Who will be the Commander-in-chief of the new army?

Many people felt the commander should come from New England, where most of the fighting so far had taken place. But New Yorkers thought one of their leaders should have the honor. The delegates settled the dispute with a compromise. They chose a man from the South, George Washington.

A few days later, General Wash-ington started north to join the men who had fought at Lexington and Concord. The journey took more than two weeks. Before Washington reached Massachusetts, a bloody battle was fought in Boston.

The British won a costly victory at Bunker Hill. For weeks after the fight at Concord bridge, volunteers came from all directions to help fight the British. General Gage soon found that he and his men were "bottled up" in Boston. Food and supplies began to run short.

Again and again, General Gage sent a company of soldiers out of Boston to gather fresh meat or vegetables. The result was almost always the same: his soldiers were shot or captured or driven back to

In the picture below Washington is seen in the Continental Congress accepting appointment as Commander-in-Chief. John Hancock, President of the Congress, sits at the left.

At Bunker Hill Americans put up a stiff fight against trained British troops.

town by enemies they could not see. Minutemen fought in the Indian way, which was to keep under cover.

On the morning of June 17, 1775, Gage had startling news. Tory spies told him that a thousand rebel soldiers were digging trenches on Breed's Hill, which overlooked Boston from the north. A few cannon mounted on this hill might drive every warship out of the harbor. Then the British army of occupation would be left to starve or surrender.

Gage sent three thousand soldiers under General Howe to drive the rebels out of their trenches. It was to be pitched battle at last, both sides fighting in the open.

Twice the British charged, and twice they had to fall back with great loss. More regiments came to help them. A third time they charged. And this time they won. The rebels had to give way, obeying the sad order to retreat. They had used up their small stock of powder, and they were outnumbered three to one. Even so, they retired in good order to Cambridge, near Boston.

The fight on Breed's Hill, usually called the battle of Bunker Hill, was a small victory the British gained at fearful cost. For the Americans, who had twice driven back a charge of British regulars, Bunker Hill was a surprising triumph.

The thought of such a near-victory roused the colonists like the call of a bugle. It inspired them, united them. The battle had been fought by New England men; but now from the Middle and Southern colonies came company after company to join in the struggle. Two weeks after the battle, Washington reached Cambridge. There he took command of his troops.

So an army was formed. It was called the Continental Army, for it consisted of men from all the colonies. Americans were no longer fighting separately, but all together for a common cause.

Washington scared the British out of Boston. Washington soon proved his fitness to command. There was something in him, some rare quality of power combined with courtesy, that made the officers trust him. But it was harder to win the Minutemen. They had gathered for just one thing, to drive the British Army out of Boston. They wanted to get the job done and go home.

Washington knew that the impatient troops were facing not a battle to be won in an hour, but a long war that only trained soldiers could win. So he kept them drilling during the winter of 1775–76.

All winter the British troops stayed quietly in Boston. General Gage had to go home in disgrace because he had failed to crush the rebellion. General William Howe took his place. Howe was a cautious man who had learned to respect American fighters at Bunker Hill. So he waited for Washington to make the first move.

In the spring, Washington felt strong enough to act. His men were fairly well drilled. The artillery captured at Ticonderoga had arrived.

One dark night he sent troops to seize Dorchester Heights, a hill that overlooked Boston Harbor from the south. Hurriedly, the men dug trenches and mounted the big guns. Then the rest of the army moved in.

In March, 1776, General Howe found himself gazing up at a strongly entrenched army. Too late he realized that Washington's cannon could now destroy the British warships in the harbor, or drive them out to sea. Then his army would be trapped.

Howe made a quick decision. He marched his men on board the ships. The whole British force — army and war fleet — sailed away to Halifax in Nova Scotia.

The British left in such a hurry they left behind a huge store of tents, blankets, and other military goods. Continental troops, shivering in the snow and rain, were badly in need of tents and blankets. Imagine how they felt when they got them without firing a shot!

Americans fought against handicaps. The small American Army moved into Boston as soon as the British left. The fighting was practically over in New England. But in the other colonies the war was just beginning. As you will see, General Howe and his army soon came back and attacked New York. The war then moved to the Middle Colonies. It dragged on for five more weary years — until 1781.

Why did the war last so long? There were many reasons. The Americans were always short of guns, military supplies, and money. They had to fight not only the British troops but large numbers of Tories or Loyalists who sided with the King.

The soldiers in the American Army were all *volunteers*. That means they joined the army of their own free will. Usually they enlisted for a few months. When the time was up many of them went home, even though the army was in the middle of a campaign. So Washington's army was constantly changing in size. He never could count on more than a few thousand men. And Congress

British rifle captured in Revolution

found it hard to find money and food even for them.

Americans had important advantages. How were the Americans able to hold out in spite of such weaknesses? Fortunately, they had several advantages which in the end proved decisive. First and most important, they were fighting for their freedom. They had a burning faith in the rightness of their cause.

Second, they were fighting in their own country, often in their own neighborhood. They knew the roads, hills, and rivers, and how to move around quickly. The British soldiers, on the other hand, were fighting in a strange land for a cause they cared little about. Many of them had been forced into service. They received little pay. It was easy to understand why they did not fight with much spirit.

Third, a great many Americans knew how to handle a gun and shoot straight. They were used to defending themselves against Indian attacks. They knew how to hunt and take care of themselves in the woods. They were good fighting men.

Fourth, the Americans did not fight alone. Many fine soldiers came to help them. There was the young French nobleman, Lafayette. From Germany came Baron von Steuben (STOO ben), who helped drill the raw American troops. And from Poland came Pulaski (pyu LAS kih) and Kosciusko (KAHS ih us

Lafayette (top) and Kosciusko (above) were among the European friends of liberty who fought in the American Revolution.

koh) to support the cause of liberty.

The government of France sent money and supplies to strengthen the fight against England. The French had not forgotten their defeat by the British. They wanted revenge. They wanted England to lose her colonies.

Fifth, Americans had the advantage of good leadership. Washington lost many battles, but he always managed to keep his army together and attack once more. British officers called him "the old fox." He made use of every advantage. Best of all, he was patient and stubborn. He never gave up.

King George hired Hessians to fight. Disputes over taxes and the rights of colonists led to shooting and killing in Massachusetts. When the British troops left Boston, Americans felt puzzled and worried. What was going to happen next? Many people still hoped that some way would be found to settle the trouble. They honestly wanted to be friends with the King and stay in the Empire.

But King George and his friends failed completely to understand the Americans. They thought the only way to deal with the stubborn, rebellious colonists was to crush them by force. So England sent another fleet of warships and thousands of soldiers to New York. It was hard to find enough soldiers in Britain, so the King hired troops from a part of Germany called Hesse. He paid a German prince to send thousands of soldiers called Hessians (HESH ans) to fight in the colonies.

Sending the Hessians was a terrible insult to American pride. Imagine how people felt when they heard that their own king had hired foreign soldiers to attack them! Then and there, many colonists decided they were through with England and wanted to be independent. Then British officials began stirring up Indians to attack settlements in New York and Pennsylvania. Men, women, and children were scalped or burned as the tribes took the warpath. Americans lost all love for the king who used such methods.

Tom Paine called for independence. Everywhere in the colonies there was talk of independence. In the homes, on street corners, in town meetings, outside the churches after religious services, people argued about the idea.

A little paper-covered book, or pamphlet, helped Americans make up their minds. It was called *Common Sense*. A man named Thomas Paine published it in 1776.

Paine was a printer who got into trouble in England for criticizing the government. He knew how to use words as if they were stones or clubs to fight injustice. He came to America in 1774 and soon became involved in the quarrel with Britain.

Paine found work as a printer in Philadelphia. There he wrote and published *Common Sense*. It sold for a penny, and it is one of the most important books in history.

Tom Paine said it was silly for a big country like America to be ruled by a little island on the other side of the ocean. He pleaded for the colonies to break free of foreign control and become a home for all who loved freedom.

Americans bought thousands of copies of *Common Sense*. They read and quoted it to one another. Washington had it read to his men. Teachers read it to their classes. *Common Sense* became a "best seller."

Jefferson wrote the Declaration of Independence. After all the discussion, the question of independence was now brought up in the Second Continental Congress. Early in

June, 1776, Richard Henry Lee of Virginia offered a motion, or resolution: "Resolved, that these United Colonies are, and of right ought to be, free and independent states."

A committee was appointed to prepare a statement, or *declaration*, telling why the colonies felt they must separate from Great Britain. The committee included many wise, experienced men: Benjamin Franklin of Pennsylvania, John Adams of Massachusetts, Philip Livingston of New York, Roger Sherman of Connecticut. They decided to let Thomas Jefferson, a young lawyer from Virginia, write the declaration.

Adams and Franklin made a few changes in Jefferson's work. Then it was presented to Congress. The delegates spent several days debating and *amending*, or changing, what Jefferson had written. On July 4, 1776, Congress adopted the Declaration of Independence.

The Declaration of Independence is one of the great documents in the history of freedom. You will find a copy of it on page 620 of this book. It is not very long and it is not hard to understand. After a brief introduction comes a statement of the principles of government that the delegates believed in:

We hold these truths to be self-evident, that all men are created equal, that they are endowed by their Creator with certain unalienable Rights, that among these are Life, Liberty and the pursuit of Happiness.

The second part of the Declara-tion consists of a list of grievances against King George III. It describes the efforts of the colonies to get justice. The Declaration ends by proclaiming that the colonies are now free and independent.

Every member of Congress who signed the Declaration knew he was risking his life. If he fell into British hands, he would be put to death as a traitor. Benjamin Franklin said, with grim humor, "We must all hang together or assuredly we shall all hang separately."

The first to sign was John Hancock, the president of the Congress. You have met him before, as one of the patriots that General Gage tried to catch at Lexington. Hancock wrote his name large and black. "There," he said, with a final flourish of the quill pen, "King George can read that without his spectacles!" He was followed by other delegates, representing all the colonies.

Swift horsemen carried news of the Declaration to every town in the colonies. Patriots came out to celebrate by ringing churchbells and lighting bonfires. Tories, who sided with the King, stayed at home behind closed doors. Both sides knew that from now on there would be no more efforts to settle the quarrel peaceably. There would be no more appeals to the King and Parliament. The War for Independence had begun. Thus, in a time of danger and alarm, the nation was born.

CHAPTER SUMMARY

After 1763, Britain treated her colonies more severely. She tried to collect new taxes and stop smuggling. The colonists resented British interference. By united opposition they forced Parliament to repeal the Stamp Act of 1765 and the Townshend Acts of 1767.

The Tea Act led to violence. In Boston, a large quantity of tea was destroyed at the "Boston Tea Party." Parliament, to punish Boston, passed the Intolerable Acts. The other colonies sent delegates to the First Continental Congress and prepared to help Boston resist.

Lexington and Concord were the first battles of the Revolution. The Second Continental Congress appointed Washington Commander-in-chief. Early in 1776, the British were forced out of Boston. The fighting moved to New York and the other middle colonies.

The colonists gradually moved toward independence. The hiring of Hessian troops to fight in America, and the encouragement of Indian attacks, disgusted Americans with British rule. Tom Paine's pamphlet, *Common Sense*, convinced thousands that America should be independent. The Declaration of Independence was signed at Philadelphia on July 4, 1776.

The Language of History

Be sure you understand the meaning of the following words. Consult the dictionary as well as your textbook.

1. revolution	5. tyranny	9. writs of assistance
2. Parliament	6. boycott	10. unalienable rights
3. Minutemen	7. smuggle	11. pursuit of happiness
4. Hessians	8. Tory	12. representation

What Happened When

Be sure you know what important events happened on the following dates:

1. 1765	2. 1770	3. 1773	4. 1775	5. 1776

Who's Who in History

Tell what part each of the following played in the Revolution:
1. Samuel Adams   3. Ethan Allen   5. King George III
2. Paul Revere   4. Thomas Paine   6. Patrick Henry

Study Questions

1. Why did the British government decide to govern the American colonies more strictly after the French and Indian War?
2. Explain what the colonists meant by their motto, "no taxation without representation."
3. Discuss the Stamp Act telling (a) the purpose, (b) when it was passed, (c) why Americans disliked it, and (d) why it was repealed.
4. The dictionary defines massacre as "the killing of a number of human beings under circumstances of atrocity or cruelty." Do you think the Boston Massacre fits this definition? Why or why not?
5. Describe the Boston Tea Party telling (a) the date, (b) the causes, (c) what happened, and (d) how the British government responded.
6. a. Why did the British set out for Lexington and Concord?
   b. How did the colonists learn of the British plan?
   c. What was the result of the fighting at Lexington and Concord?
7. Why did the British leave Boston in 1776?
8. a. What advantages did the Americans have in the War for Independence?
   b. What handicaps did they have to overcome?
9. Tell the part each of the following played in the Revolution:
   a. Samuel Adams   c. Paul Revere   e. Thomas Paine
   b. James Otis   d. Patrick Henry
10. a. Why did the colonists decide to declare their independence?
    b. Who wrote most of the Declaration of Independence?
    c. On what date was the Declaration adopted?
    d. Put in your own words three things the Declaration said.

Chapter 8

AFTER A LONG, HARD WAR AMERICANS WON THEIR INDEPENDENCE

"IT was in the field when they came to the last act of the drama that the spirit and pride of the British soldier was put to the severest test: here their mortification could not be concealed. Some of the officers appeared to be exceedingly chagrined . . . and many of the soldiers manifested a sullen temper, throwing their [guns] on the pile with violence as if determined to render them useless." Thus an American soldier described the British surrender as he watched it at Yorktown.

How were the proud British brought to such a defeat?

At the beginning of the Revolution everything favored Britain. Poorly equipped, without training, with no sure source of money or supplies, Americans lost battle after battle — but they won campaigns. How did they do it?

Year by year the fighting moved from colony to colony, finally to end in the South. Which battle marked the turning point of the war? What period was "the darkest hour of the Revolution"?

American soldiers often went cold and hungry in the middle of a rich countryside. What foreign help did they receive and from whom?

The answers to these questions make up the story of how the War for Independence was won — the story told in Chapter 8.

The British captured New York.
Great Britain had failed to crush the rebellion in New England. Washington had forced the British out of Boston without even a fight. So British leaders decided to let New England alone for a while. They planned to attack rebels in the Middle Colonies, instead.

The British hoped to "divide and conquer." If they could smash the rebellion in the Middle Colonies, New England would then be cut off from help. All through the revolution, this was the British policy. The future looked black.

In July, 1776, four months after he left Boston, General Howe landed in New York City. He had a large army. When his brother, Admiral Richard Howe, arrived with several warships, General Howe had 30,000 men backed up by a strong fleet. He planned to conquer New York.

Washington learned of the British plans before they had made a move. He marched his small army from Boston to New York. But he did not have enough men or guns to hold the city. There were battles on Long Island, on Manhattan Island, and north of Manhattan at White Plains. Each time Washington had to retreat, for he was outnumbered.

If Howe had acted quickly, he might easily have surrounded the American Army. He could then have ended the war. But he felt sure he had Washington in a trap, so he did not hurry.

He was too slow, however, and Washington was able to get out of New York in the autumn of 1776. More than two thousand Americans were captured. Washington also had to leave behind badly needed supplies. He retreated westward, across New Jersey, to Pennsylvania. The future looked black.

Americans won surprising victories at Trenton and Princeton. The British believed they had crushed the rebellion. But Washington fooled them. He suddenly turned, in New Jersey, and made two attacks.

In those days, armies did not usually fight in the winter. When snow began to fall, they settled down in a town or a fort. They made this their "winter quarters."

Howe and his men settled comfortably in New York City. Only a few regiments remained in Trenton and Princeton to hold the New Jersey colony. Scouts reported to Washington that two of the hated Hessian regiments were stationed in Trenton on the Delaware River.

On Christmas night, 1776, the Hessian soldiers were drinking and making merry. Snow was falling; the river was full of ice. This was the night Washington chose to strike.

With a few companies of picked men, he crossed the river by boat. He attacked in the morning. The Hessians, in drunken sleep, were taken completely by surprise. They had to surrender.

The Americans captured nearly a thousand prisoners. In the gray

WAR OF INDEPENDENCE

dawn, Washington and his handful of men returned to their own quarters. They brought back six cannon, 1200 muskets, and a large amount of powder, food, and other supplies.

A few days later, in January, 1777, Washington struck again. This time he attacked British troops at Princeton, several miles from Trenton. He defeated two British regiments and captured the supplies they were guarding. Howe sent General Cornwallis with six regiments hoping to surround Washington's men on their way back to Pennsylvania. Cornwallis was sure of success. He boasted, "We have run the old fox down at last. In the morning we will bag him with his whole army."

In the morning, however, the Americans were gone. They did not march westward, to Philadelphia, as Cornwallis expected. Instead, they marched north to Morristown, New Jersey, where they settled down in new winter quarters. Once more "the old fox" had escaped.

Nathan Hale gave his life for America. The victories at Trenton and Princeton put new heart into the American cause. The Second Continental Congress, meeting in Philadelphia, decided the gallant little army should have its own flag. On June 14, 1777, Congress passed a resolution. It said that "the flag of the United States should be thirteen stripes alternate red and white, that the Union be thirteen stars white in a blue field." Today, Americans cele-

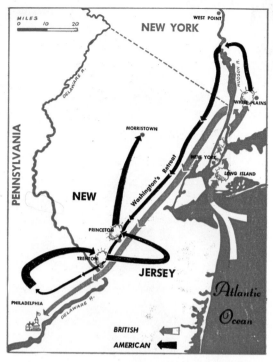

The victories at Trenton and Princeton revived faith in the American cause.

brate Flag Day on June 14 in memory of the action taken in 1777.

The sight of the new flag stirred the hearts of the people. They made up their minds to keep fighting in spite of discouragement. The story of a brave young man, Nathan Hale, also inspired the Americans.

Nathan Hale was a young school teacher from Connecticut. When he heard of the fighting at Lexington, he joined a Connecticut regiment. He soon became a captain, and was sent to New York.

One day, in 1776, General Washington called for a volunteer to go behind the British lines on Long Island and in New York City. He needed information, and he wanted

Nathan Hale died for freedom. Here he is shown about to mount the scaffold, saying, "I regret that I have but one life to lose for my country."

a spy. The job was very dangerous. If a soldier were caught in uniform behind enemy lines, he would be treated as a prisoner of war, but if he were caught spying in civilian clothes, he would be put to death.

Nathan Hale stepped forward and offered to do the job. Dressed as a teacher looking for work, he wandered from village to village near the British camps. He drew pictures of fortifications and found the facts that Washington wanted.

Hale was on his way back when he met a relative who was on the Tory side. The relative pointed him out as a spy to the nearest British officers. They searched Hale and found evidence of his guilt. He was taken to Howe's headquarters in New York City and condemned without a trial.

At sunrise, the next morning, the British led Hale to the gallows. As the rope was drawn around his neck, he was asked: "Have you anything to say?" Quietly, he answered, "I only regret that I have but one life to lose for my country."

General Burgoyne had a plan that failed. The war in America dragged on. King George and Parliament grew more and more impatient. They wanted to crush the rebellion quickly. In 1777, they decided on a "knockout" blow. They planned a three-way attack that would smash American resistance once and for all.

The man who thought up the plan was General John Burgoyne (bur

GOYN). He was a fine officer, but an unlucky one, as you will see. The main points of the plan were three: (1) Burgoyne would lead a large army down the old war road from Canada to the Hudson River; (2) General St. Leger (saint LEJ ur) would lead another army away from Canada across Lake Ontario to Oswego, New York, and march east through the Mohawk Valley to join Burgoyne at Albany; (3) General Howe, meanwhile, would lead his army from New York up the Hudson Valley. All three armies would meet near Albany.

Study the map on this page. You will notice that Burgoyne's plan aimed to wipe out all resistance in New York State. Also, it was supposed to cut off, or separate, New England from the other colonies.

Burgoyne carried out his part of the plan. He marched into New York State with about 8000 British and Hessian soldiers. He pushed slowly south toward Albany. And, when he reached the Hudson River, he wrote to King George: "My march is a triumphal progress."

Then the British began to run short of food. So Burgoyne sent several hundred of his Hessian soldiers eastward, into Vermont, to find supplies. But the Green Mountain Boys, led by Colonel John Stark, were waiting for them. At the battle of Bennington, they killed or captured the Hessians almost to the last man.

Meanwhile, General St. Leger was failing to carry out his part of the plan. While on his way to Albany, St. Leger met a small American force. The Americans defeated St. Leger's men, in the battle of Oriskany, and sent them running back to Canada.

It was General Howe, though, who really spoiled Burgoyne's plan. For some reason that is still not clear, Howe made no effort to join Burgoyne. Instead, he and his men boarded ships in New York harbor, and sailed away to invade Pennsylvania. There he beat Washington in

The map below shows the Saratoga campaign. Defeat at Saratoga in 1777 ended Britain's attempt to isolate New England. It was the war's turning point.

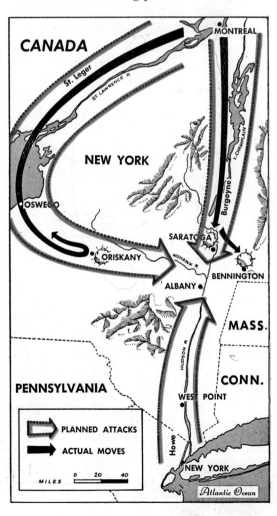

two battles, and captured Philadelphia. But he ruined Burgoyne's campaign by his failure to cooperate.

The battle of Saratoga was the turning point of the war. Burgoyne was now in a desperate spot. He had reached Saratoga (SAR ah TO gah), a few miles north of Albany. In front of him stood a strong American army. In back of him, companies of Minutemen blocked any retreat to Canada. Burgoyne was trapped. He fought a three-day battle at Saratoga, trying hard to force his way out. But it was no use. On October 17, 1777, Burgoyne surrendered. He and all his men became prisoners of war.

The battle of Saratoga was the turning point of the Revolution. Even foreign nations now felt that the Americans had a good chance to win. The French had secretly been sending help to the rebels. Now they increased their aid. Soon they made a treaty of alliance.

Washington's army spent a terrible winter at Valley Forge. American hopes rose high after the Saratoga victory. But the war was not over yet. There remained months, even years, of suffering and disappointment before independence was won.

Washington did not take part in the battle of Saratoga. He was near Philadelphia, at Valley Forge. He stayed there because he wanted to keep General Howe from conquering all of Pennsylvania.

Washington and his men went into winter quarters at Valley Forge after the British captured Philadelphia. And it was a grim winter for Washington's army. The weather was bitter; there was not enough food. Many of the soldiers became sick, for they suffered terribly from cold and hunger.

Twenty miles away, General Howe and the British danced and feasted in Philadelphia. But at Valley Forge, American soldiers bound their bare,

At Valley Forge, Pennsylvania, George Washington and his men spent a terrible winter in 1777–8. Below, Washington visits his ragged troops and sees bloody footprints in the snow. This was the most heartbreaking period of the Revolution.

bleeding feet in rags — and kept on drilling in the snow.

Two financiers helped win victory. You may wonder how the American Army managed to hold together in the face of so many hardships, disappointments, and defeats. Partly it was Washington's leadership. Partly it was a fierce determination to be free that the soldiers felt. But something else was necessary. The finest general and the bravest soldiers could not have kept on fighting for years without food and supplies.

The chief credit for financing the Revolution belongs to two men, Robert Morris and Haym Salomon. Morris was a wealthy business man that Congress put in charge of colonial finances. He often used his own money and went in debt to buy food and guns for Washington's men.

Haym Salomon was a Polish Jew who had worked for liberty in Europe and who had been forced to flee to America. He went into business, and soon became a rich man. When the Revolution came he worked for the cause of freedom.

Salomon knew many wealthy people in France and Holland; he persuaded them to lend money to help the American cause. Like Robert Morris, with whom he worked, Salomon used his own fortune to buy things the army needed. He equipped several regiments at his own expense.

Twice the British captured Salomon while he was traveling to and from military headquarters. He was thrown into prison and suffered such hardships that his health was ruined. He died a few years after the Revolution ended; most of the money he had advanced to the young republic was never repaid. The lives of Morris and Salomon show how men who never carry a gun on a battlefield may be heroes of liberty.

Americans lost an opportunity at the battle of Monmouth. Somehow, the Continental army managed to live through the terrible winter at Valley Forge. In the spring, things improved. There was good news from France; King Louis had recognized American independence. The French government had signed a treaty of alliance with the United States. France was at war with Great Britain. So Americans were no longer fighting alone. France was going to send an army, and a fleet of warships, to America.

In Philadelphia, the British heard the news, too. Sir Henry Clinton was in command. He had replaced General Howe, who was in disgrace for his failure to wipe out Washington's army. Sir Henry worried about the news from France. He was afraid the French might capture New York, which the British now held. So he decided to give up Philadelphia, and move back to New York.

When Clinton left Philadelphia, Washington followed him. After the long agony at Valley Forge, American soldiers wanted to see action. They were well trained after von

"The Heroine of Monmouth," they called Molly Pitcher, shown above. When her husband was killed she took his place at the gun and helped keep it firing throughout the battle.

Steuben had drilled them all winter.

The British hurried away from Pennsylvania, across New Jersey. They were almost on the run, trying to reach safety in New York. Washington stayed right at their heels. At Monmouth, New Jersey, he ordered an attack. But one of his officers, General Charles Lee, failed to obey orders. So most of the British escaped to New York, where they felt safe under the guns of their warships. Washington then led his troops around New York, to White Plains. He and his army watched the British constantly, hoping for a chance to destroy the enemy.

For the next three years, Washington and Clinton played a waiting game. Clinton sat in New York. Washington watched. But Washington was never able to attack.

There were no more big battles in the Middle Colonies. When at last the time for a decisive battle came, it was fought in the South.

Benedict Arnold tried to betray West Point. Sir Henry Clinton was a careful man. He would not take the risk of attacking Washington's army. But he tried to win control of the Hudson Valley by plotting with Benedict Arnold.

Benedict Arnold was one of Washington's officers. He had fought bravely in many battles. Earlier in the war, he had led an unsuccessful campaign to conquer Canada. Later, however, he was largely responsible for the victory at Saratoga. But Arnold felt that he had not been treated fairly. Younger men were being promoted over his head.

Then Arnold married the daughter of a Tory. They lived extravagantly, and Arnold soon found himself in debt. His work suffered; Washington was forced to scold him publicly for carelessness in keeping military records. Arnold was bitterly angry. He wanted revenge.

Washington really liked and admired Arnold. He felt that the man had been unlucky. So when Arnold asked to be placed in command of West Point, Washington agreed.

Study the map on page 151. You will see that West Point is located on the Hudson River. In the days of the Revolution, it was a very important fort. As long as Americans held West Point, they controlled the Hudson River. They needed this river to bring supplies from New England to Washington's army.

Benedict Arnold decided to betray the Americans. In 1780, he sent word to the British General in New York that he would show him how to capture West Point without a fight.

John André was hanged, but Arnold escaped. General Clinton jumped at the chance to win control of West Point. He promised to give Arnold a large sum of gold and to make him a British general.

Clinton sent a young English officer, Major John André (AHN dray), to arrange for the capture of West Point. André disguised himself by dressing as a Quaker merchant. Thus he became a spy. He met Arnold secretly at night. Arnold gave him a plan of the fort, and written instructions to attack at a certain point that would be left unguarded. André hid the plan and Arnold's instructions in his shoes.

On his way back to New York, the British spy met three Americans. One of them was wearing the coat of a captured Hessian soldier — perhaps it was the only coat he had. André said, "You gentlemen must be of the Royalist party."

They did not reply, but André kept talking. Perhaps he was lonesome or frightened. He tried to win the confidence of the men by telling them he was an English officer on important business.

That was enough for the Americans. They promptly marched him to the nearest military post. André begged them to let him go. He offered them gold, any amount of gold, if they would set him free.

At the military post, André was searched — his boots first of all. The plot was as plain as a fly in a cup of milk. André had many friends, both English and American. They did their best to save him, but their pleas were in vain. He was a spy and he had to pay the penalty. He was given a trial and then was put to death by hanging.

Arnold, meanwhile, had escaped to a British ship. He fought on the British side until the end of the war.

The picture below shows the capture of John André to whom Benedict Arnold had given the plans of West Point.

Long afterward he died in London, disgraced and friendless. His name has come to mean "traitor."

The British had Indian allies. On the frontier, far from New York and Philadelphia, other Americans were doing their part to help win independence. Washington and his officers paid little attention to the war in the West. It seemed of small importance at the time. But it won a vast region for the United States when the peace treaty was made.

You will recall that Americans were greatly interested in the Ohio Valley. They called it the "Northwest Territory," because it was northwest of the original settlements. As you can see on the map on this page, it included the land between the Ohio River and the Great Lakes.

The French built many forts in this area. But British soldiers had held the forts since the end of the French and Indian Wars. The forts were now commanded by Colonel Henry Hamilton, whose headquarters were at Fort Detroit.

Hamilton, and other British officers in the Northwest forts, encouraged the Indians to attack Americans. They planned terrible raids on pioneer settlements. Hamilton paid money for every American scalp the Indians brought him.

It was clear that Americans would not be able to settle in the Northwest while the British held the frontier forts. A Virginian, named George Rogers Clark, decided to do something about it. He knew the horror of Indian raids. He said the only way to stop such raids was to capture the forts where the Indians got muskets and supplies.

Clark went to see Patrick Henry, who had been elected governor after the royal governor was driven from Virginia. Patrick Henry agreed with Clark about the Northwest forts. He persuaded the Virginia legislature to provide money for an expedition. The money was used to buy food,

The map below shows the campign of George Rogers Clark. With a handful of men he traveled into the Northwest Territory and captured Kaskaskia and Vincennes. As a result the whole region became part of the United States.

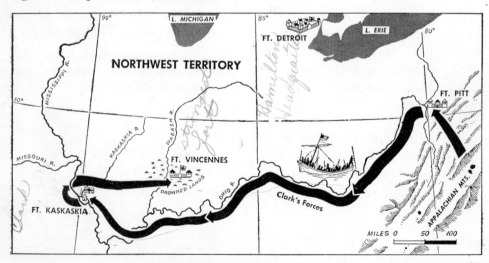

blankets, and guns for 150 men who were willing to go with Clark.

In the spring of 1778, Clark and his men walked from Virginia to Fort Pitt (now Pittsburgh). From there they sailed down the Ohio River for hundreds of miles. Near the mouth of the river they left their boats. Swiftly and quietly, they marched overland to Kaskaskia on the Mississippi. Taking the British completely by surprise, they captured the fort without a fight.

When British Colonel Hamilton heard that Kaskaskia was lost, he left Detroit in a hurry. He went to Vincennes on the Wabash River. That was one of the strongest forts; it had a garrison of about 500 men.

By February of 1779, Hamilton was feeling safe and comfortable at Vincennes. For miles around the fort, icy water covered the swamps and forests. The region was called the "drowned lands." And Hamilton felt sure that he could not be attacked — not, at least, until the land dried out in the spring.

Clark and his men, however, liked to do the unexpected. Half-starved, wet and cold, they made an heroic march through the "drowned lands."

At last, one evening they reached Vincennes. The British were sound asleep. Clark and his men easily captured the fort with all its supplies. For the first time in weeks, Clark's men could sleep warm and dry. They took Hamilton back to Virginia as a prisoner of war.

John Paul Jones won a great victory at sea. While Clark was seizing frontier forts, other daring commanders were attacking British ships. Many New Englanders had put guns on their fishing boats and merchant ships. Such vessels were called *privateers*. They operated with the approval of the American government. The privateers captured many British trading ships. The royal navy was kept busy, angrily trying to catch the privateers.

At the beginning of the Revolution, the colonies had no warships. In 1775, the Continental Congress started the American navy by voting to build thirteen fast cruisers.

The British easily destroyed most of the new cruisers while they were being built. But a few reached the open sea, where they did considerable damage. Under such gallant captains as Esek Hopkins and John Barry, they boldly sailed into the English Channel to fight.

The greatest of the American

The capture of the British warship, *Serapis*, by John Paul Jones, September 23, 1779, is shown in the drawing below.

naval heroes was John Paul Jones. Born in Scotland, he sailed to Virginia as a ship's cabin boy at the age of twelve. He studied every book of navigation he could find. He made many voyages and learned to know almost every bay and cape along the coasts of Europe and America. Jones was one of the first to offer to fight the British at sea.

On his first voyage, which lasted six weeks, Jones captured sixteen British merchant ships. In 1777 Congress made him captain of a new warship, the *Ranger*. He boldly raided the British coast and burned several ships. He even went ashore and captured a town. Jones destroyed the town's fortifications, and sailed away without losing a man.

John Paul Jones had his greatest adventure in 1779. The French king gave him a clumsy, old merchant ship. Jones repaired it, and turned it into a ship of war. He named it the *Bonhomme Richard* (boh NAWM ree SHAHR) in honor of Benjamin Franklin, who published "Poor Richard's Almanac."

Jones sailed around Ireland and Scotland and captured many ships. But on his way back to France, he met two large British warships. It looked bad for John Paul Jones, but he did not hesitate. He attacked the larger ship, the *Serapis* (see RA pis).

After some hard fighting, Jones ordered his men to stop firing. He then brought his ship close to the enemy. The British commander thought Jones was ready to surrender. He shouted through a trumpet, "Have you struck your colors?" Back came the startling answer, "I have not yet begun to fight."

The truth was that the American ship was in danger of sinking. When the ships touched sides, Jones quickly tied them together. His men dashed on the deck of the *Serapis*. There was desperate hand-to-hand fighting. Over half the Americans were killed or wounded. But they captured the *Serapis*. They also captured the smaller British warship.

Jones put his own crew on board the *Serapis*, and sailed back to France. Behind him, the old *Bon Homme Richard* went to the bottom of the sea.

The British tried to conquer the South. In 1779, the British government decided to try a new plan: they would conquer the southern colonies, one by one. The British had failed to crush the rebellion in New England. They had failed again at Saratoga. But in the South they hoped for better luck.

So in 1779, the fighting moved to the South. The British struck first at Savannah, Georgia. The battle was bloody. Brave, young Count Pulaski was killed, along with hundreds of Americans. But Savannah was captured. Soon the British held every important town in Georgia.

Charleston, South Carolina, was next. British warships sailed into the harbor early in 1780. A large British army landed. It was a long,

158

hopeless fight. The American commander, General Lincoln, had to surrender with all his men.

In August of 1780, another American army was surprised and badly beaten near Camden, South Carolina. It looked as if the British commander, General Cornwallis, would soon control the Carolinas.

Suddenly, in the dark, discouraging autumn of 1780, there was news of an American victory in North Carolina. At Kings Mountain, a few hundred American frontiersmen surrounded a force of 1200 Red Coats and Tories. The Americans lost only twenty-eight men, and they captured the entire enemy force.

When Washington heard news of British attacks in the South, he sent General Greene to the Carolinas. Nathanael Greene was, next to Washington, probably the best general in the American Army. He quickly gathered together the scattered troops who had escaped capture. In a few weeks, he had about four thousand men. They were ragged and hungry; some lacked guns.

Greene's plan was to fight and run. He wanted to draw Cornwallis and his men away from the sea coast, where they were getting supplies from British warships. So he attacked unexpectedly, and then retreated — with Cornwallis hurrying after him. At a favorable spot, Greene halted, fought again, then made another retreat.

When Cornwallis had chased Greene for about two hundred miles,

he suddenly realized what was happening. He was far from his base of supplies. Along the way he had left his heavy cannon and other supplies in order to move faster. His men were worn out by the wild chase in a strange country. Food was running low.

Now it was Cornwallis' turn to retreat. He went back to the coast to be near the British fleet. General Greene had lost every battle — but he had won the campaign! The British now held only Savannah, Charleston, and a few other sea ports. The rest of Georgia and the Carolinas were in American hands.

Cornwallis tried to conquer Virginia. The British War Office ordered Cornwallis to try to conquer Virginia next. It looked as if it would be easy to overrun Virginia. Nearly every Virginian old enough to fight had left to join Washington in the North or Greene in the South.

The only armed force in Virginia consisted of a few companies of Continental troops and a number of untrained woodsmen. To command them, Washington appointed Lafayette (lah fay ET), the gallant young French officer who had come at his own expense to fight for liberty.

Lafayette had fought with General Greene. He had learned how to fight and get away, so he followed this plan: he would make an unexpected attack and cut off supplies at one point. A few hours later, he would strike at another point miles

BATTLE OF KING'S MOUNTAIN

CAMPAIGNS OF THE AMERICAN REVOLUTION

YEAR	WAR IN NEW ENGLAND	WAR IN MIDDLE STATES	WAR IN SOUTH AND WEST
1775	April 19—Lexington and Concord June 17—Bunker Hill July 3—Washington takes command		
1776	March 17—British leave Boston (War moves to middle states)	Nov. 16—British capture New York Nov. 28—Washington defeated, retreats to Pa. Dec. 26—Washington crosses Delaware, captures Trenton	
1777		Jan. 3—Washington wins Battle of Princeton Aug. 6, 16—Americans win at Oriskany and Bennington Oct. 17—Battle of Saratoga (turning point of war)	
1778		Winter, 1777-8—Washington at Valley Forge June 18—British retreat from Philadelphia to New York June 28—Battle of Monmouth	George Rogers Clark conquers Northwest
1779		War Moves to South	
1780			Oct. 7—Battle of Kings Mountain
1781			Jan. 17—Battle of Cowpens March 15—Battle of Guilford Courthouse Oct. 19—Cornwallis surrenders at Yorktown, fighting ends

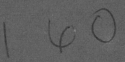

away, capturing a few men and guns.

Cornwallis disliked such warfare. He complained bitterly that it was not according to rules. Gentlemen, he said, did not fight that way! After a few attempts to trap Lafayette, he went into winter quarters at Yorktown, Virginia.

Notice the map on this page. Yorktown is on a peninsula that sticks out into Chespeake Bay; it is almost surrounded by water. To Cornwallis, this seemed a good, safe place. British warships in Chesapeake Bay would protect him; Washington was far away in the North, and Greene was far away in the Carolinas. Young Lafayette did not have enough men to fight a pitched battle. Cornwallis yawned. It looked like a long, safe winter ahead.

Washington seized an opportunity. Washington was still waiting for a chance to strike at Clinton's army in New York. His men were hungry. They had not been paid for months. Things were almost as bad as they had been at Valley Forge.

Suddenly the situation began to improve. Count de Rochambeau (RO shawm BO) and an army of 8000 men arrived from France. And word came that French warships in the West Indies were sailing toward Chesapeake Bay.

Next, Washington heard from Lafayette that Cornwallis had settled down on Yorktown peninsula. In a flash he saw his great chance. The French fleet would sail into Chesapeake Bay, and stop Cornwallis from getting away by sea. Washington's men and the newly arrived French troops would march quickly to Virginia, and block the western side of Yorktown peninsula. Cornwallis would be trapped.

Washington's plan worked. His army and the French troops marched away quickly and silently. They were in Virginia before Sir Henry Clinton knew they had left their camp in the North. The French fleet sailed into Chesapeake Bay at the right moment; the British warships, which should have been protecting Cornwallis, were in the West Indies at the time.

Cornwallis was a brave man. He

Below are shown the southern campaigns which ended with the surrender of Cornwallis.

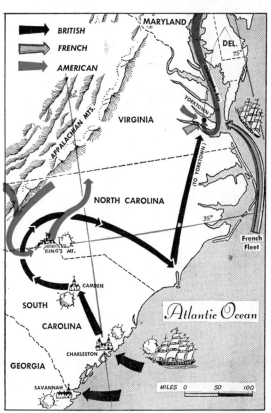

BENJAMIN FRANKLIN (1706–1790)

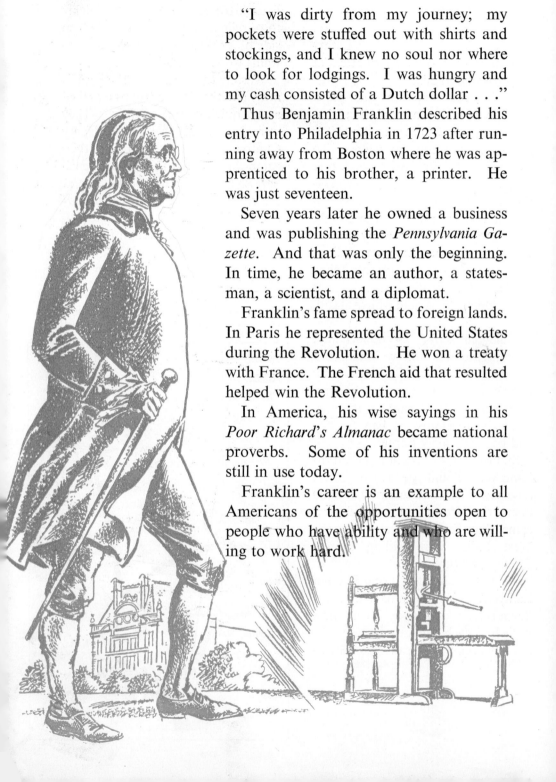

"I was dirty from my journey; my pockets were stuffed out with shirts and stockings, and I knew no soul nor where to look for lodgings. I was hungry and my cash consisted of a Dutch dollar . . ."

Thus Benjamin Franklin described his entry into Philadelphia in 1723 after running away from Boston where he was apprenticed to his brother, a printer. He was just seventeen.

Seven years later he owned a business and was publishing the *Pennsylvania Gazette*. And that was only the beginning. In time, he became an author, a statesman, a scientist, and a diplomat.

Franklin's fame spread to foreign lands. In Paris he represented the United States during the Revolution. He won a treaty with France. The French aid that resulted helped win the Revolution.

In America, his wise sayings in his *Poor Richard's Almanac* became national proverbs. Some of his inventions are still in use today.

Franklin's career is an example to all Americans of the opportunities open to people who have ability and who are willing to work hard.

tried to fight his way out of the trap, but it was hopeless. He had to surrender his army and a vast store of military supplies.

Eight thousand British soldiers marched out and laid down their guns between silent lines of French and American troops. Cornwallis gave up his sword. The band played a lively tune called "The World Turned Upside Down." The date was October 19, 1781.

The Treaty of Peace was signed in Paris in 1783. "Cornwallis is taken!" shouted the town criers all over America. In Philadelphia, citizens rushed from their beds and filled the streets. Bells rang and cannon boomed. Congress met at dawn to hear the report Washington had sent. Then the members went to church to "return thanks to Almighty God" for their victory.

News of the surrender was a stunning blow to the British. King George screamed wildly, "It is all over!" The people of London asked the King to "put an end to the unnatural and unfortunate war." Lord North, the Prime Minister, had to resign. Almost everyone in England wanted to end the war.

British commissioners were appointed to make peace. Congress sent Benjamin Franklin, John Jay, and John Adams to meet with the British commissioners in Paris. The treaty of peace was signed in 1783. Its most important provision announced, "His Britannic Majesty

This picture shows the British surrender at Yorktown in 1781, which marked the end of fighting in the Revolution.

acknowledges the United States to be free, sovereign, and independent."

Thus Britain gave up the thirteen colonies. She also surrendered the whole Northwest Territory. This was the vast region that George Rogers Clark had won.

The treaty was generous to America in many ways. The territory of the United States was to stretch from the Atlantic coast to the Mississippi, and from Canada to Florida. American fishermen could continue to fish off Newfoundland and in the Gulf of St. Lawrence.

So it happened that the United States took its place among the nations of the world. Americans agreed that the treaty was a good ending to a bad war. They looked ahead with sober confidence. They were going to build a great free nation such as the world had never seen.

CHAPTER SUMMARY

The War moved from New England. In 1776, the British captured New York. Washington and his army escaped. On the morning after Christmas, 1776, Washington defeated the Hessians at Trenton. Early in 1777, he won a victory at Princeton.

Americans won the Battle of Saratoga. General Burgoyne's surrender at Saratoga in 1777 was the turning point of the war. It helped bring about an alliance with France.

Washington's army spent a terrible winter at Valley Forge. In the spring, 1778, they pursued British troops from Philadelphia to New York. An indecisive battle was fought at Monmouth.

George Rogers Clark made an expedition to the Northwest. With a few frontiersmen, he defeated the British at Kaskaskia and Vincennes. They won the Northwest Territory for the United States.

The American Navy won several victories. John Paul Jones raided the British coast and captured two warships.

In 1779, the fighting moved to the South. General Nathanael Greene drove the British back to the sea coast. The War ended at the Battle of Yorktown. Washington and the French fleet cut off the British retreat. Cornwallis surrendered October 19, 1781. The British signed the Treaty of Paris in 1783, recognizing American independence.

The Language of History

The following words and phrases appear in Chapter 8. Be sure you know the meaning of each.

   1. Northwest Territory   **2.** privateers

What Happened When

Be sure you know what events happened on the following dates:

   1. 1777   **2.** 1781   **3.** 1783

Who's Who in History

Be sure you know the part that each of the following played in the Revolution:

1. Cornwallis   3. John Burgoyne   5. Marquis de Lafayette
2. Nathan Hale   4. Nathanael Greene

Study Questions

1. **a.** Why were many Americans very discouraged when Washington left New York in 1776?
   b. What were the results of the battles at Trenton and Princeton?

2. Why is the battle of Saratoga called "the turning point of the Revolution"?

3. Why was there so much suffering at Valley Forge?

4. What region did George Rogers Clark win from the enemy?

5. Discuss the war at sea, including **(a)** the part played by privateers, **(b)** the beginning of the American Navy, and **(c)** the victories of John Paul Jones.

6. Where are the following and what happened there during the Revolution?
   a. Bunker Hill   **c.** Bennington   **e.** King's Mountain
   b. Ticonderoga   **d.** Oriskany   **f.** Yorktown

7. Tell the part the following played in the Revolution:
   a. John Burgoyne   **c.** John Jay   **e.** John Paul Jones
   b. Robert Morris   **d.** John Adams   **f.** Haym Salomon

8. Who said each of the following and under what circumstances?
   a. "I only regret that I have but one life to lose for my country."
   b. "My march is a triumphal progress."
   c. "I have not yet begun to fight."

9. **a.** Where was the treaty of peace with Great Britain signed?
   b. What was the date?
   c. State three provisions of the peace treaty.

10. Show how Washington and the French trapped Cornwallis.

LET'S LOOK AT WHAT WE'VE LEARNED

What were the causes of the American Revolution?

The colonists and the British leaders did not understand one another. The colonists felt they had all the rights of Englishmen and should be let alone to run their affairs. British leaders felt that the colonies existed to benefit the mother country. They wanted to get money out of the colonies to help pay the costs of the French and Indian Wars.

When the British government tried to collect new taxes, such as the Stamp Tax, the colonists protested. Bad feeling increased, and the trouble came to a head when the British tried to force the colonists to pay a tax on tea. At the Boston Tea Party, a few Americans dumped several tons of tea into Boston Harbor. When the British government passed the Intolerable Acts to punish Massachusetts, the people in the other colonies sent aid. The British planned to crush the revolt by arresting some of the American leaders and seizing the powder stored at Concord. The battles of Lexington and Concord resulted.

Why and where did Americans declare their independence?

After several battles with British troops, many Americans came to feel there was no hope of a peaceful settlement. When King George hired German troops to fight the colonists, he killed the loyalty of many Americans. The publication of *Common Sense* by Thomas Paine helped convince Americans they should get out of the British Empire. On July 4, 1776, in Philadelphia, the Second Continental Congress adopted the Declaration of Independence.

What were the chief battles and campaigns of the Revolution?

The Revolution began in New England at Lexington and Concord. The British won a costly victory at Bunker Hill in June, 1775. The following spring, Washington forced the British out of Boston.

In 1776, the war moved to the Middle Colonies. The British captured New York. Washington won victories at Princeton and Trenton. The turning point of the war was the Battle of Saratoga, October 17, 1777.

Washington and his men spent the terrible winter of 1777–1778 at Valley Forge. On the frontier, George Rogers Clark and his men won victories at Kaskaskia (1778) and Vincennes (1779). American privateers destroyed or captured many British merchant ships. John Paul Jones defeated and captured two British warships (1779).

In 1779, the war moved to the South. The British captured several ports, but were not able to win permanent control of the Southern Colonies because of the clever tactics of General Greene. The British Army, under General Cornwallis, went into winter quarters at Yorktown. There, Washington's army cut off their retreat by land and the French fleet cut off their retreat by sea. Cornwallis surrendered, and the war was over.

How did the French help win American independence?

After the victory at Saratoga, France signed a treaty of alliance with the United States. A French army and a French fleet were sent to America. French help made the victory at Yorktown possible.

What were the provisions of the treaty of peace?

1. Great Britain recognized American independence. 2. The United States gained the Northwest Territory. 3. American fishermen could continue to fish off Newfoundland.

Connecting the Past with the Present . . .

Suppose the Revolution had failed? What differences would it make in your life today? For one thing, the Fourth of July would be just another day; for nobody would remember the Declaration of Independence. And instead of being America's greatest hero, George Washington would probably have been shot as a traitor and his birthday would be forgotten.

You would be singing "God Save the Queen" instead of "The Star Spangled Banner" and swearing your loyalty to the British ruler instead of pledging allegiance to the flag and the republic for which it stands. Perhaps you wouldn't be living in America at all. It is quite possible that your ancestors — or some of them — would not have decided to leave the Old World if the Revolution had failed. Canada, which remained under British rule, has attracted only a few immigrants compared to the number who came to the United States.

If the United States had remained in the British Empire it probably would have developed more slowly, as Canada has. Winning independence gave Americans increased self-confidence. They "went all-out" to make their country powerful and successful. Thus they built a new nation "conceived in liberty and dedicated to the proposition that all men are created equal."

Questions for Discussion and Review

1. Explain what is meant by this statement about causes of the Revolution: "Both sides were right on some points and wrong on others."

2. Give two reasons why Britain felt the colonists owed her a great debt. Tell how Samuel Adams would have answered such claims.

3. List four ways Britain interfered in colonial affairs after 1763.

4. Why did the colonists feel the *writs of assistance* were unjust?

5. List four transactions for which stamps were necessary under the Stamp Act.

6. What was the name of the assembly which met in protest against the Intolerable Acts? What action did it take?

7. Name three soldiers from other lands who helped win American independence.

8. Who were the Tories?

9. Why did the British call Washington "the old fox"?

10. What was the last important battle of the Revolution? Who was the American commander? What was the date? The result?

THE HISTORY LABORATORY

Human beings learn by doing. When you plan and carry through an activity or project you gain new skills and absorb facts that you remember. Here are suggestions for activities that you will find interesting.

Plan a Campaign . . .

Organize the class or part of it as George Washington's staff. Plan the strategy of one of his most successful campaigns. The staff work

WHAT
AND
WHEN

Passage of the Stamp Act 1765

Boston Tea Party 1773

Lexington and Concord 1775

should include communications, ordnance (guns and ammunition), supplies, food, map makers, engineers (road builders, bridge builders). The staff must receive its information about the enemy from spies and scouts and captured dispatches. Use your imagination. For information you need study the maps and the story of the Revolutionary War in this textbook and others; then look up "American Revolution" or "American War for Independence" in a good encyclopedia.

Learn the Story of the Flag . . .

Trace the beginnings of the American flag from early colonial times until the adoption of the Stars and Stripes during the Revolution. Information may be found in *American Citizens' Handbook* by J. E. Morgan (National Education Association, 1951) and in *Flags of All Nations* by Smith and Taylor (Crowell, 1950).

Make a Picture Record . . .

Make a picture calendar for the class with illustrations showing the important events of the period from 1763 to 1783. For exact dates of events refer to your textbook, the *Encyclopedia of American History* by Morris (Harper, 1953) or any standard encyclopedia.

Follow Paul Revere . . .

Have a group plan a class program for the reading of "Paul Revere's Ride" by H. W. Longfellow. Several readers can take part. Others may provide background music and art work to illustrate the story.

Calling All Authors . . .

Write a short story or essay on one of the following topics:
The Shot Heard Round the World. (Imagine you were at the battle of Concord.)
Cold and Hungry. (Tell the story of two soldiers at Valley Forge.)

| ...ation of Independence 1776 | Battle of Saratoga 1777 | Cornwallis' surrender 1781 | Peace with Britain 1783 |

The Tea Party. (Imagine you were an "Indian" who dumped the tea.)

Prepare a Scrapbook . . .

Make a scrapbook illustrating the Revolution. Illustrate such famous phrases as "the shot heard round the world," and "the Spirit of 1776."

Make Your Own Atlas . . .

Prepare an atlas of maps showing the battles and campaigns of the Revolution. Study the maps in this Unit and consult Adams' *Atlas of American History*, (Scribners, 1943.)

Illustrate History . . .

Make a model or a diorama of a scene at Valley Forge during the winter of 1778. Show ragged, barefoot soldiers drilling under the direction of General von Steuben.

Let's Read about the Revolution

ALLEN, M. P., *Battle Lanterns*, Longmans, 1949.
BAKELESS, JOHN, *Fighting Frontiersman*, Morrow, 1948.
*BROWN, VINSON, *John Paul Jones*, Watts, 1949.
**DESMOND, ALICE C., *Martha Washington — Our First Lady*, Dodd, 1942.
EDMONDS, WALTER D., *Wilderness Clearing*, Dodd, 1944.
ELLSBURG, EDWARD, *"I Have Just Begun to Fight!"* Dodd, 1942.
FORBES, ESTHER, *Johnny Tremain*, Houghton, 1943.
FORBES, E., and WARD, L., *America's Paul Revere*, Houghton, 1946.
*FOSTER, GENEVIEVE S., *George Washington*, Scribner, 1949.
FOSTER, GENEVIEVE S., *George Washington's World*, Scribner, 1941.
HAWTHORNE, HILDEGARDE, *Give Me Liberty*, Appleton, 1945.
HINTERNHOFF, JOHN, *Barry's Boys*, Holt, 1952.
*HOLBROOK, STEWART, *America's Ethan Allen*, Houghton, 1949.
NOLAN, JEANNETTE C., *Treason at the Point*, Messner, 1944.
NORTON, S., and COURNOS, J., *John Adams: Independence Forever*, Holt, 1954.
ORTEN, HELEN, *Hoof Beats of Freedom*, Lippincott, 1936.
ROSS, FRANK, JR., *Ben Franklin's Inventions*, Lothrop, 1952.
SKINNER, C. L., *Silent Scot, Frontier Scout*, Macmillan, 1925.
UPDEGRAF, F. M., *Coat for a Soldier*, Harcourt, 1941.

* indicates easy reading   ** indicates advanced reading

170

PHYSICAL MAP OF NORTH AMERICA

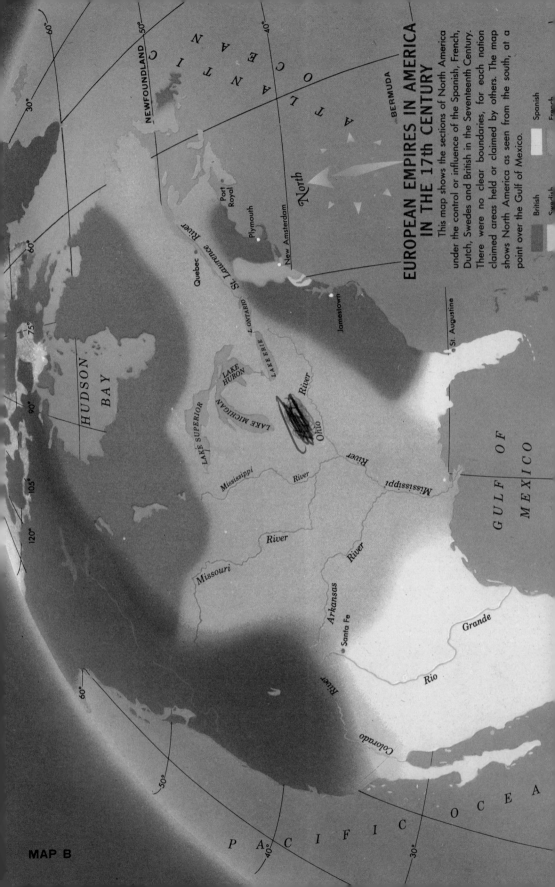

EUROPEAN EMPIRES IN AMERICA
IN THE 17TH CENTURY

This map shows the sections of North America
under the control or influence of the Spanish, French,
Dutch, Swedes and British in the Seventeenth Century.
There were no clear boundaries, for each nation
claimed areas held or claimed by others. The map
shows North America as seen from the south, at a
point over the Gulf of Mexico.

British   Spanish

Swedish   French

MAP B

DSON
BAY

HUDSON'S BAY COMPANY
(BRITISH)

NEW FRANCE

ACADIA

Isle Royale
(French)

Louisburg

LAKE SUPERIOR

Sault Ste. Marie

Fort Michilimackinac

LAKE MICHIGAN

LAKE HURON

Fort La Boye

Detroit

LAKE ERIE

St. Lawrence River

Quebec

Montreal

Fort Frontenac

LAKE ONTARIO

Fort Niagara

NEW HAMP- SHIRE

MASSACHUSETTS

Boston

CONN.

RHODE ISLAND

NEW YORK

Philadelphia

PENNSYLVANIA

NEW JERSEY

DELAWARE

MARYLAND

APPALACHIAN MOUNTAINS

BRITISH COLONIES

VIRGINIA

Ohio River

Fort de Chartres

Vincennes

FRENCH LOUISIANA

Missouri R.

River

Ohio

Arkansas Post

kansas River

Natchitoches

Mississippi River

New Orleans

Mobile

Pensacola

NORTH CAROLINA

SOUTH CAROLINA

Charleston

GEORGIA

St. Augustine

SPANISH FLORIDA

ATLANTIC OCEAN

GULF OF MEXICO

North

CUBA
(SPANISH)

50°

60°
40°

30°

75°

90°

The
THIRTEEN COLONIES
ABOUT 1750

This is the way Britain's thirteen colonies looked to
settlers voyaging westward from Europe in the mid-18th Century.
Note how the settled areas clung to the seacoast in a thin
line stretching from New England to Georgia.

British Settlements
Chief Spanish Areas
French Settlements
Unsettled
Forts

Copyright by C. S. HAMMOND & Co., N. Y.

MAP C

SARATOGA

CONCORD

NORTH CHURCH

DELAWARE CRO

FORT TICONDEROGA

VALLEY FOR

KINGS MOUNTAIN

GREENE'S CAMPAIGNS

YORKTOWN

INDEPENDENCE

DON'T TREAD ON ME

90° 75° 60°

60°

HUDSON BAY

HUDSON'S BAY COMPANY (BRITISH)

50°

LAKE SUPERIOR

Fort Michilimackinac

CANADA (BRITISH)

Quebec

NOVA SCOTIA (BRITISH)

LAKE MICHIGAN

LAKE HURON

Montreal

St. Lawrence River

Fort Edward Augustus

Fort Ticonderoga

Detroit

LAKE ERIE

LAKE ONTARIO

Fort Niagara

Saratoga ❷

Concord
Boston ❶

Fort St. Joseph

Fort Pitt

Ohio River

New York

Trenton

Monmouth

Valley Forge

40°

Cahokia

Vincennes

Philadelphia

Kaskaskia

Clark's Expedition in the West 1778-9

Yorktown ❸

SPANISH LOUISIANA

Mississippi River

THE THIRTEEN COLONIES

French fleet at Yorktown 1781

Cowpens

Guilford Court House

Kings Mountain

ATLANTIC

Moores Creek

OCEAN

Charleston

Savannah

Natchez

Baton Rouge

Mobile

New Orleans

North

FLORIDA (BRITISH)

GULF OF MEXICO

THE AMERICAN REVOLUTION

30°

This map shows the major campaigns of the War of Independence. Note that the fighting began in Massachusetts ❶, and moved to the middle states. The war reached its turning point at Saratoga ❷, moved to the South, and ended at Yorktown ❸

75°

Copyright by C. S. HAMMOND & Co., N. Y.

MAP D

Unit 4

AMERICAN STATES FORMED A STRONG UNION UNDER THE CONSTITUTION (1783-1789)

"I FEEL UNEASY and apprehensive, more so than during the war," John Jay wrote in 1786. He was not alone in his fears. Washington himself wrote, "I am mortified beyond expression when I view the clouds that have spread over the brightest morn that ever dawned upon any country. . . . To be more exposed in the eyes of the world, and more contemptible than we already are, is hardly possible."

What had happened to the nation that two of its most capable leaders should despair of the future? Why was the United States "contemptible in the eyes of the world"?

Men like Washington and Jay were not the kind to sit around and do nothing when their country seemed to be in danger. What did they do to remedy the situation and how successful were their efforts?

That is the story of Unit 4 — the story of how in a time of trouble and uncertainty, far-seeing men wrote the Constitution that still governs the American nation.

171

Chapter 9

A TIME OF TROUBLE AND UNCERTAINTY FOLLOWED THE REVOLUTION

AND they lived happily ever after."

That is what some Americans expected to do after the United States was free of King George and his haughty ministers and all the regiments of Red Coats. However, life after the Revolution proved just as complicated as ever — though in a different way. Now that there was no King or Parliament, how was the United States to be governed? Where was the money to come from to run the government?

Nobody knew the answers. Americans had to deal with each problem as it arose, making compromises and working their way out of humiliating situations.

Neighbors were a problem. How could the young, struggling republic make powerful nations like Britain and Spain respect its boundaries and its rights? Coming closer to home, how could the nation make its own people behave and cooperate with one another? The states were jealous of one another, arguing bitterly and continuously about boundaries, trade, and other matters.

How the young republic struggled with these and other problems makes up the subject matter of this chapter.

The American Revolution influenced other nations. The long war was over. The thirteen colonies were now free states. Americans had won a great victory. And they had won it by fighting together — a fact some of them forgot.

The American Revolution is a great event not only in the history of the United States but in the record of the human race. Individuals in many other nations were filled with hope when they heard of the revolt. If Americans could get rid of unjust rulers and set up their own government, surely other people had a chance to win liberty, too.

The French Revolution began only six years after Americans won their independence. There is no doubt that the success of the American Revolution helped inspire Frenchmen to fight for liberty. In South and Central America, news of the Declaration of Independence also had a striking effect. It encouraged a few brave men to dream of freedom. Several years later, Central and South America threw off foreign rule. The Spanish colonies gained courage to revolt partly because of the American Revolution.

However, some people in America were not happy about the Revolution. They were the Tories or Loyalists. Seventy thousand of them had to leave the United States in a hurry. They lost homes and possessions.

Thousands of Tories fled to Canada. For various reasons, Canada was still loyal to Great Britain. During the Revolution the Continental Congress had tried hard to get Canada to join in the fight against Britain. But the French Canadians were not interested. They felt sure they were being treated fairly by the British government. They were allowed to go on speaking French; no one interfered with their religion. Why should they fight to help these faraway neighbors who were different in language and religion?

So Canada stayed inside the British Empire. The Tories who fled from the United States helped strengthen Canada's loyalty to Great Britain. They taught their children to love Britain and hate the United States.

Thus the United States started

Tories had to flee to Canada. In the picture below a family of Loyalists is being driven from their home.

out with an unfriendly neighbor on the northern border. The new nation had other troubles as well. The first few years after the Revolution were full of worry and danger.

The states were jealous and unfriendly. After the war each of the thirteen colonies became an independent state. Each state claimed the right to coin its own money and to deal with foreign nations. For example, Massachusetts businessmen would not accept Pennsylvania money; New York taxed goods brought in from Connecticut. This led to quarrels and confusion.

Many leaders realized that the states needed to work together under a strong national government. But most people didn't like the idea. They had fought a long, hard war to break away from British control. They had no desire to set up another government that would interfere with their affairs.

Men like Samuel Adams and Patrick Henry feared that a strong national government would mean the end of liberty. They had fought for freedom and they meant to keep it. So for several years they tried to get along without a strong union.

Such devotion to one geographical region and its people is known as *sectionalism*. Devotion to the whole country and its people is called *nationalism*. So far nationalism had not developed very widely in the United States.

As a result, Americans were not a united people in 1783 or for a long time afterward. Today if you ask a citizen of the United States, "What is your country?" he will answer proudly, "The United States is my country." But in the early days the United States was merely a name. People were loyal instead to the state where they lived.

It was hard for Americans to understand one another, for the ways of living were different in various parts of the country. In the northern states there were many small farms and shops. Most families owned their own homes. They farmed a few acres or worked in a shop attached to their own home. Everywhere there were small communities; most people lived near a village.

In the South, however, the population was spread out over a wide area. There were a few large plantations where slaves raised tobacco and rice; the plantation owners had great influence. But there were many poor farmers in the South who struggled along, trying merely to make a living.

The West was different, too. In Ohio, Kentucky, and Tennessee, life was more difficult than in the eastern settlements. There was always the danger of an Indian attack. People had to make almost everything they used, for there were few stores and no factories. By today's standards almost everybody was poor. Everyone had to work hard to keep alive.

Thus, each section had its own problems and its own way of life.

Europeans expected the United States to collapse. Foreigners expected the new nation to fail. An English visitor who traveled widely wrote:

The clashing interests of Americans, with their differences of government and manners, indicate that they will have no center of union, and no common interest. They never can be united under any form of government whatever. To the end of time they will be divided into little states.

You have probably read and studied enough about America to know how wrong that Englishman was. But in the last part of the eighteenth century, most Europeans and many Americans agreed with him. It seemed hopeless to try to make a nation out of little states.

The population was small and scattered. There were only about four million people in the United States in 1790 — about the population of Chicago today. There were few roads and they were all in bad condition. Travel was slow and very difficult. For example, it took Washington two weeks to travel from Philadelphia to Boston at the beginning of the Revolution.

European leaders waited happily for the United States to fall apart. They hoped they would be able to grab some American territory.

The map below shows the United States in 1783 when the war with Great Britain was over. Notice that the new country extended to the Mississippi River.

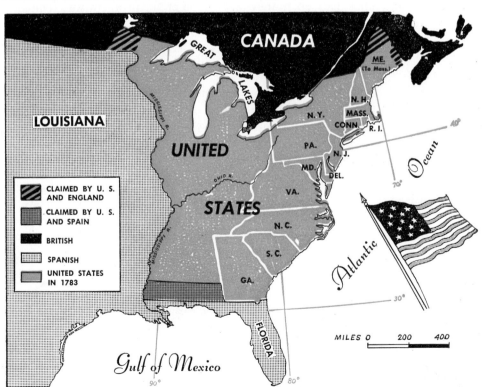

CANADA

LOUISIANA

UNITED STATES

GREAT LAKES

MISSISSIPPI R.

OHIO R.

ME. (To Mass.)

N. H.
N. Y.   MASS.
CONN.   R. I.
PA.
N. J.
MD.
DEL.
VA.
N. C.
S. C.
GA.
FLORIDA

Atlantic Ocean

40°
70°
30°
90°   80°

Gulf of Mexico

CLAIMED BY U. S. AND ENGLAND
CLAIMED BY U. S. AND SPAIN
BRITISH
SPANISH
UNITED STATES IN 1783

MILES 0   200   400

Spanish officials in Florida and Louisiana tried to persuade settlers in the Southwest that they would be better off to join Spain. The British did not get out of the Northwest forts as they promised.

European leaders believed that the United States could not succeed because the new nation was a *republic;* that is, it had no king. The idea of trying to govern a nation without a king seemed dangerous and unwise.

The United States had many financial problems. For several years, after the Revolution, the American states seemed to be in the danger of losing their independence. In addition to disputes with foreign powers, the new nation had serious problems at home. Business was bad. Many people, especially the small farmers, were in debt. They had no money to pay their debts or taxes. Merchants found it hard to sell American goods in foreign countries. They lost many of their old customers in Great Britain. And British officials did their best to discourage trade with the United States. Because Americans were no longer part of the British Empire, many British ports — especially those in the West Indies — were closed to Americans.

To make matters worse, the nation and the states were deeply in debt. During the war the Continental Congress had borrowed money in France and Holland. The money had been used to buy guns and powder and had helped to win the war. But the borrowed money had never been repaid. And Congress had no way to get money to pay the debts.

After the war each state also had a large debt to pay. Some states made arrangements to pay their debts, but others did not. So the *credit* of both the nation and the states was in danger. This meant that in the future people who had money to lend might not be willing to trust the United States.

The credit problem was related to the problem of currency. During the Revolution, Congress had printed millions of dollars of paper money. Each paper dollar was just a promise that the government would pay gold or silver later on. Many people had no faith in the government's promise to pay. As the years went by, it began to look as if they were right.

Below is shown paper money of the Continental Congress. The bill on the left was marked $2; the one on the right, $40; but they would actually buy only a few cents worth of goods.

More and more people lost faith in the paper money which they called "Continental currency." No one wanted paper money. Its value, or purchasing power, grew less and less. For example, you had to pay one thousand dollars in paper money for a suit of clothes that you could buy for ten dollars in silver or gold.

Many states also printed paper money that had little value. Other states tried to keep on using English money. And no state would accept the money of another state at full value. For example, a silver coin worth twelve cents in New Jersey might be worth only nine cents when you crossed the Delaware River to Pennsylvania, or only six cents when you crossed the Hudson River to New York. Imagine how hard it must have been to buy and sell under such conditions!

The remedy was plain to Washington and certain other leaders. They felt that the nation had to have a government strong enough (1) to tax the people of all the colonies and (2) to issue sound money that would be accepted in all parts of the United States. However, it took years of discussion and hard times to convince the nation that Washington was right.

There had been many attempts at union. Earlier in American history, far-sighted men had tried to form a real union. Each time, suspicion among the settlers defeated the attempt. In 1643, only a few years after the Pilgrims landed at Plym-

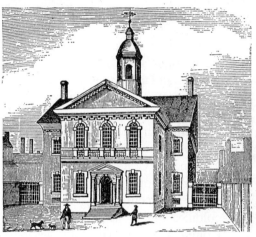

The top picture shows a poster urging the colonies to unite. The second shows Carpenter's Hall, Philadelphia, where the Continental Congress met.

outh, four New England colonies formed the United Colonies of New England. The purpose of the union was to settle quarrels over boundaries and to provide for defense against the Indians. But the union fell apart after a few years, because none of the colonies would give up real power.

The next attempt at union came a century later (1754), at the beginning of the last French and Indian War. A call went out to all the colonies, asking them to send delegates to a convention at Albany, New York. Only nine colonies sent delegates.

At the Albany convention a plan of union was drawn up by Benjamin Franklin. According to his plan, each colony would send representatives to a council. The council would have power to deal with the Indians and to provide for defense.

But the Albany Plan of Union never had a chance. The British government would not approve it because it gave the colonies too much power to manage their own government. And every colony rejected the plan because they did not want to give up any power to a central government such as the proposed council.

The third attempt at union was the Continental Congress. As you know, it came about when King George and Parliament tried to bring the colonies under strict control. The Congress consisted of delegates elected from every colony. Its prime purpose was to hold the colonies together until independence was won.

It was, at best, a very weak kind of government. It lacked two powers that a strong government must have: one, to make and enforce a law; the other, to raise money by taxation. The Congress could only advise each colony what to do. It could merely ask the colonies for money.

As time and the war went on, the Congress took to itself more and more power. It raised an army, enlisted soldiers and sailors, borrowed money in the name of all the colonies, and even made a treaty with France.

Thus the Congress acted like a strong government, but without any legal right to do so.

The Continental Congress was much like an alert man or boy who steps out into a street crowded with automobiles when the traffic lights are not working — and directs traffic. He has no uniform, no badge of authority; but drivers obey his signals because he is helping them avoid trouble. So the thirteen free colonies silently agreed to be governed, for a while, because the Congress was doing its best in time of danger.

The states adopted the Articles of Confederation (1781). Congress did a good job in spite of difficulties that might well have crushed an older and stronger government. But many Americans worried about the situation. They did not think it was right that Congress had to act without any clear statement of powers. So a plan of union was drawn up.

This plan, called the *Articles of Confederation*, was drawn up soon after Congress adopted the Declaration of Independence. *Confederation* means an association or form of union. And the word *Articles* referred to the various parts of the agreement, or statements, by which the states were going to be united.

For months, the men in Congress talked over the plan outlined in the Articles of Confederation. They made many changes. Then they sent the plan to the state legislatures for their approval. Some states approved the Articles quickly; others debated the question for years. At last, by March 1781, all the states had approved or *ratified* the Articles.

The Articles of Confederation did not set up a strong government — far from it! The states were still powerful. Each state had one vote in Congress. Nine votes were needed to pass any law. That meant that nine states had to agree before Congress could do anything. If five states voted against a proposed law, they could keep the other eight from passing it.

One part of the Articles of Confederation said Congress could borrow money to pay soldiers or build ships. But it still could not *tax!* That is, Congress could not require anybody to pay any money to help run the government; it could only ask the state governments for money. As it turned out, some states contributed and some states did not. Thus, Congress was always in need of money. Often, there were no funds to pay the soldiers.

You may wonder why someone didn't try to change the Articles of Confederation to give Congress more power. The trouble was that the Articles could not be changed unless every state agreed, and there was always at least one state that voted against any amendment.

The national government was weak under the Articles of Confederation. During and after the Revolution, Congress struggled along trying to fight a war, make peace, and hold the states together. From 1781 to 1787, the Articles of Confederation provided the only national government the United States had.

Soon after the War for Independence was won, a startling event occured. It showed the weakness of the Articles in a way that everyone could understand.

When the war ended, hundreds of

The map below shows the Northwest Territory, governed by the Ordinance of 1787.

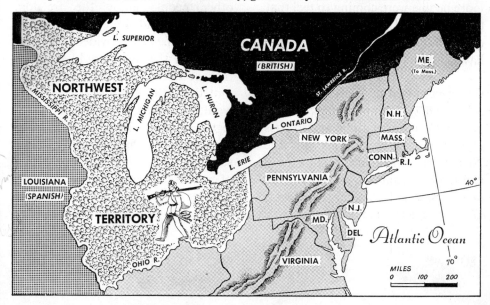

soldiers had been fighting for years without getting paid. They refused to disband and go home as General Washington ordered. One company marched to Philadelphia, entered the hall where Congress was meeting, and demanded pay.

There were brave men in that Congress; but there was no money in the treasury. Hoping to satisfy the soldiers, they sent a committee to try to borrow a little money. The committee went first to the Pennsylvania legislature, then to Philadelphia's city council. Both refused to give or lend. Quietly then, the Congress adjourned and walked out of the hall by the back door. The soldiers slowly drifted away. But Congress did not dare to meet again in Philadelphia. The meeting place was changed to Princeton. A handful of soldiers had forced the Congress of the United States to flee.

Even before this alarming example of Congress's weakness, Washington had called the Articles of Confederation "a rope of sand." More and more people were coming to feel that the Articles of Confederation were out of date and that the country must have a new and stronger government.

Congress passed the Northwest Ordinance (1787). In spite of its limited power, Congress did manage to pass one important law. This was the Northwest Ordinance, sometimes called the Ordinance of 1787. An *ordinance* is a law. The Northwest Ordinance, as you may have guessed,

was a law that referred to the Northwest Territory.

Several states claimed to own all or part of the Northwest Territory which George Rogers Clark and his men had won. The conflicting claims made it impossible for anybody to govern the region. The states finally agreed to give up their claims and let Congress govern the territory.

At last Congress had power to do something, even if it was only to make rules for the frontier! The members of Congress drew up a wise and careful plan for governing the Northwest Territory. Thomas Jefferson, who had written most of the Declaration of Independence, drew up the plan for the Northwest. Congress did not accept all of Jefferson's plan, but many of the basic ideas were his. Jefferson had great faith in education and in the common man. So it is not surprising that the Northwest Ordinance is one of the best laws ever written.

The Northwest Ordinance proved that Congress believed in letting other people enjoy the freedom Americans had fought for in the Revolution. It provided that the people in the West could organize their section into a state and be admitted to the Union. New states would have the same rights and privileges as the original states. The Ordinance also contained a clear statement of the rights and privileges of citizens in the Northwest Territory.

Some of the provisions of the Northwest Ordinance are still used

in the government of certain American territories. Most of the states that have entered the union since the Revolution have been governed according to the plan of this law. Thanks to the wisdom of Jefferson and other members of Congress, it has been possible for the United States to grow in an orderly manner.

Five states were formed from the Northwest Territory. They were Ohio, Indiana, Illinois, Michigan, and Wisconsin.

Washington led a movement to strengthen the government. The Ordinance of 1787 was the one great achievement of Congress under the Articles of Confederation. Almost everything else Congress tried to do

was a failure. There was open defiance of the government.

In Massachusetts, a hero of the Revolution, named Daniel Shays, led an uprising in 1786 that lasted for several months. With more than a thousand men, he tried to seize the military storehouse at Springfield. The national government could do nothing to stop such uprisings. Shays' Rebellion was finally crushed by Massachusetts troops.

Shays' Rebellion really frightened thoughtful citizens. It seemed as if discontented farmers in Massachusetts and elsewhere were trying to start another revolution. All over America, leading men agreed that "something must be done."

George Washington had long been

Below is a scene in Shays' Rebellion (1786). The farmers have seized a courthouse. They aimed to stop local officials from selling their farms for debts. The uprising convinced many people of the need for a stronger national government that could stop defiances of law.

GEORGE WASHINGTON (1732–1799)

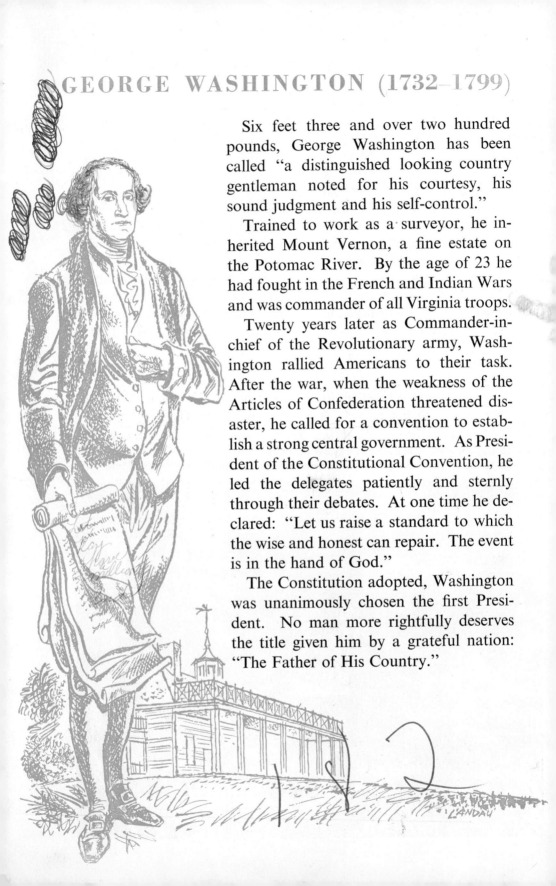

Six feet three and over two hundred pounds, George Washington has been called "a distinguished looking country gentleman noted for his courtesy, his sound judgment and his self-control."

Trained to work as a surveyor, he inherited Mount Vernon, a fine estate on the Potomac River. By the age of 23 he had fought in the French and Indian Wars and was commander of all Virginia troops.

Twenty years later as Commander-in-chief of the Revolutionary army, Washington rallied Americans to their task. After the war, when the weakness of the Articles of Confederation threatened disaster, he called for a convention to establish a strong central government. As President of the Constitutional Convention, he led the delegates patiently and sternly through their debates. At one time he declared: "Let us raise a standard to which the wise and honest can repair. The event is in the hand of God."

The Constitution adopted, Washington was unanimously chosen the first President. No man more rightfully deserves the title given him by a grateful nation: "The Father of His Country."

worried about the situation. The year before Shays' Rebellion he arranged a meeting at Mount Vernon, his plantation on the Potomac (poh TOH mack) River. Representatives came from Virginia and Maryland. The first purpose of the meeting was to try to settle a dispute about the use of the Potomac River.

The men who attended the meeting were soon able to settle the dispute over navigation on the Potomac. Then they began to discuss the weakness of the Articles of Confederation and other problems that were trou-

Mount Vernon (above) heard many anxious discussions of government problems.

bling the nation. But they knew their little meeting at Mount Vernon could not settle such big problems. They sent out a message asking all the states to send representatives to a meeting at Annapolis (uh NAP oh lis), Maryland, the next year.

Only five states bothered to send delegates to the Annapolis meeting. Imagine how discouraged the members felt! "What's the use of trying to do anything?" they must have asked themselves. But one young man was not discouraged. He was Alexander Hamilton, the restless little delegate from New York.

Hamilton stood up at Annapolis and made a suggestion. Call another meeting, he urged; this time let Congress send out the invitations. The states would be more likely to send representatives to a meeting that Congress called.

Hamilton's idea worked. After some delay, Congress agreed to call a meeting or *convention*. The purpose of the meeting was to change or amend the Articles of Confederation. The states were asked to send delegates to a convention in Philadelphia in May, 1787.

Alexander Hamilton (below) was a leader in efforts to strengthen the central government.

CHAPTER SUMMARY

The American Revolution changed world history. The French Revolution, six years later, and the revolt of the Spanish colonies in South and Central America were to some extent inspired by the example of the United States.

The Articles of Confederation were adopted in 1781. This document gave Congress power to borrow money, but not the power to tax. The states were still powerful; nine of them had to agree before Congress could act. The national government remained weak.

Congress passed the Northwest Ordinance in 1787. It allowed people in the West to form states and be admitted into the Union. The new states, and their people, were assured the same rights as the original states.

Shays' Rebellion in 1787 worried thoughtful citizens. Washington and other leaders wanted a stronger government. They wanted Congress to have power to tax and power to issue sound money. In Annapolis, Maryland a meeting was held to discuss the weakness of Congress. It accomplished little, but it led to the meeting in Philadelphia of the Constitutional Convention.

The Language of History

Be sure you know the meaning of each of the following terms as it is used in this chapter.

1. sectionalism
2. nationalism
3. republic
4. ratified
5. convention
6. tax
7. Articles of Confederation
8. Northwest Ordinance
9. Continental Congress

What Happened When

The following dates are important in American history. Make sure you know the important events that occurred on each date.

1. 1643
2. 1754
3. 1781
4. 1787

Who's Who in History

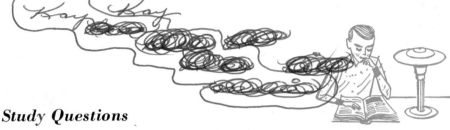

What part did the following play after the Revolution?
1. Samuel Adams   3. Daniel Shays   5. George Washington
2. Patrick Henry   4. Alexander Hamilton 6. Thomas Jefferson

Study Questions

1. What influence did the American Revolution have on oppressed people in other parts of the world?

2. Why were Canadians unfriendly to the United States for a long time after the Revolution?

3. Why were Samuel Adams and Patrick Henry against a strong national government?

4. List three problems that troubled the United States in the years immediately following the end of the Revolution.

5. Discuss the Albany Plan of Union telling (a) when it was proposed, (b) who wrote it, (c) what it provided for, and (d) why it was never approved.

6. Discuss the Articles of Confederation telling (a) when they were adopted, (b) three weaknesses of the Articles, and (c) why it was almost impossible to change them.

7. Write a paragraph about the Northwest Ordinance telling (a) two provisions, (b) when and by whom it was passed, (c) five states that entered the Union under its provisions.

8. Explain the importance of Shays' Rebellion giving (a) aim, (b) when and where it occurred, and (c) what it indicated about the national government.

9. a. Name two leaders in the movement to strengthen the national government.
   b. What happened at the meetings at Mount Vernon and Annapolis?

10. a. Where and when did the Constitutional Convention meet?
    b. What was its purpose?

Chapter 10

CAPABLE, FAR-SEEING MEN
WROTE THE CONSTITUTION
IN 1787

"To what do you attribute your long life?" a reporter asks Uncle Sam in a recent newspaper cartoon. "Blessed if I know," replies Uncle Sam, "unless it's my Constitution!"

The Constitution has certainly contributed much to the soundness of America. Yet in 1789 the men who wrote it were doubtful about its value. Some even refused to sign it.

Who were the men who labored through hot summer months to devise a government for the republic? Why did some of their Revolutionary War comrades refuse to attend the Constitutional Convention?

The proceedings of the Convention were to be secret. How then did so much of what happened become known? Who recorded it?

Basic disputes almost wrecked the Convention. How were they settled? What part did Washington and Franklin play in persuading the delegates to accept various compromises?

When the Convention's work was done, the battle had only begun. It was necessary to get the approval of the states. Who led the fight for ratification? What promise did the friends of the Constitution have to make to win votes?

These are the key questions to keep in mind as you read in this chapter the great story of the making of the Constitution.

The Constitutional Convention met in Philadelphia. One rainy day in 1787 representatives from twelve states met together in Philadelphia. Every state except Rhode Island had accepted the invitation to send delegates to a convention in Philadelphia.

The original purpose of the Philadelphia convention was to change, or *amend*, the Articles of Confederation. But the delegates soon decided it was better to start all over and write a completely new plan of government. The Articles of Confederation were too weak and unsatisfactory to try to repair them.

So the men at Philadelphia went ahead and wrote a new plan of government. The plan they wrote is called the Constitution of the United States. (A *constitution* is a fundamental law or statement according to which a country or region is governed.) The meetings at Philadelphia, in 1787, have ever since been called the *Constitutional Convention.*

The delegates met in the very same hall where the Declaration of Independence had been signed. It was a beautiful old room, with tall windows on two sides. All through the hot summer the windows remained shut, so that no one could stand outside and listen. And sand was spread thickly over the rough cobble stones of the streets to deaden the noise of wagons passing by. The delegates could stand the heat, but they had to have a quiet place to work.

One of the first and wisest things the delegates did was to elect George Washington chairman, or President, of the convention. It was his job to keep the discussion going in an orderly manner. Everyone had great respect for George Washington, so he

Independence Hall (below) where the Declaration of Independence was signed was also the meeting place of the men who wrote the Constitution.

had no trouble keeping any order.

Most of the delegates were young men, but one was very old: Benjamin Franklin, the Philadelphia printer who was world famous for his knowledge and common sense. Franklin was eighty-one years old and quite sick. He knew he did not have long to live. He had to save his strength, so he took no active part in the arguments that developed. Sometimes he seemed to fall asleep.

But Franklin always knew what was going on. He knew when to open his eyes and say something wise or funny. If the argument became bitter — if cruel things were said — Franklin would put in a few words and somehow bring about agreement. He was called the "peace maker" of the convention.

Many famous leaders of the Revolutionary War period were absent from the convention. Thomas Jefferson was in Paris, representing the United States to the French government. John Adams was in London serving as America's first minister, or representative, to the British government. Patrick Henry refused to attend the meetings in Philadelphia; he wanted no part of any effort to change the Articles of Confederation. And Samuel Adams and John Hancock were not elected delegates. Thus, for various reasons, many of the men who opposed a strong national government did not take part in the convention.

Fifty-five delegates came to Philadelphia, but many of them did not

James Madison of Virginia is often called the "Father of the Constitution."

attend the meetings regularly. At most of the meetings about thirty-five were present — just about the same number there are in a history class.

The delegates were well-educated and experienced in politics. Washington and Franklin were the best-known delegates, but there were many other outstanding men in the convention. From Virginia came James Madison, sometimes called the "Father of the Constitution." He kept a "journal" or record of the things that happened at each meeting. It is the chief source of information about the Constitutional Convention.

New York was represented by Alexander Hamilton, the brilliant young man who had served Washington as a secretary and "aide" during the Revolution. He later won fame as the first Secretary of the Treasury. Another famous young delegate was Gouverneur Morris of Pennsylvania,

THE CONSTITUTIONAL CONVENTION

Benjamin Franklin was the oldest and wisest delegate to the Constitutional Convention.

Gouverneur Morris took an active part in the discussions at Philadelphia.

who was equally gifted at talking and writing. He took part in all the big debates and then put into writing the points the delegates agreed on.

The other delegates were not so well-known, but they were all capable men. Over half of them were lawyers. There were some planters and merchants, too, and a few doctors and teachers. Most of the delegates had taken part in the Revolution and in the Continental Congress. They were leading citizens.

The delegates realized that their country was still in great danger, for the national government was weak. So they were determined to create a strong central government. The serious attitude of the delegates is shown by these words that one member, George Mason, wrote to his son:

The eyes of the United States are turned upon this assembly, and the peoples' expectations are raised to a very anxious degree. God grant that we may be able to satisfy them by establishing a wise and just government.

In this spirit the delegates worked day after day through the hot summer months. Some grew tired and went home. It was impossible, they said, to form a plan that all the states would accept. But the others kept on.

The delegates often disagreed. Under Washington's leadership, the delegates tried to make the best plan they could. But it was not an easy task. The delegates from the South disagreed with the delegates from the North. Delegates from the large states believed their states should have more power than the small states. And delegates from the small states feared that their states would be treated unfairly by the large states.

Any of these disputes might have caused the convention to fail, but the delegates always ironed things out. They were able to compromise (KAHM pro mize); that is, each side won certain points but had to give in on certain other points. This kind of settlement did not completely satisfy anybody, but it did give each side part of what it wanted. The ability to compromise was one big reason why the delegates were successful.

Thus, with all sides willing to compromise, the Constitution of the United States was finally written. It provided the framework for a new kind of government. There was much work and debate, however, before the document was completed.

A Federal form of government was created. Washington and some of the delegates wanted the new government to have a great deal of power. They wanted to take away most of the power of the states and give it to the national government. But other delegates were afraid to go so far. They were afraid the national government would become too powerful.

So it was decided to let the national government have power over certain things and to let the states keep control over others. The national government would have power: (1) to coin money; (2) make treaties; and (3) make rules for trading with foreign nations. But the states would have power to: (1) run public schools; (2) build highways; (3) pass marriage and divorce laws; and (4) regulate many other local and regional matters. No state could make a treaty with a foreign nation. Thus the power was divided.

A system where power is divided in this way is called a *federal* form of government. Today Americans live under a federal system. This means that every citizen is ruled by the government of his state and also by the national government.

Delegates from the convention agreed that laws for the whole country should be passed by a Congress elected from all the states. But they disagreed instantly when the question arose, How many representatives may each state send to the Congress? Some wanted each state to have one vote, as in the Continental Congress. Others thought the number of votes each state had should depend on the size of the state.

Delegates from the small states claimed that size had nothing to do with the matter. They said that a small state, like a small person, has exactly the same rights as a larger one. New Jersey delegates told the convention bluntly that their little state would never accept the Constitution unless it had as many representatives as any large state.

Delegates from Virginia and other large states thought that they should have a larger representation in the Congress. It is a basic principle of justice, they claimed, that when people are divided over a question of government, the *minority* or smaller

group must give way to the *majority* or larger group. Pennsylvania delegates insisted on this point. They told the convention that their state would not accept the Constitution unless it had more representation than a small state like New Jersey.

So it came about that the convention had to choose between two plans: the *New Jersey Plan* which the small states favored and the *Virginia Plan* which the large states wanted. The New Jersey Plan, as you might guess, gave equal representation in Congress to all states. The Virginia plan provided for representation according to population.

After a long and stormy debate the convention agreed on a compromise that seemed fair to both sides: each state would elect representatives to a national lawmaking body called the Congress. But Congress would consist of two branches or parts: a House of Representatives and a Senate. A law for the whole nation must be passed by both branches.

In the House of Representatives each state, however small, would have at least one representative. The larger states would send additional representatives according to the size of their population.

But in the Senate all states, large or small, would have the same number of representatives, called *Senators*. Each state would have two Senators, regardless of its size. Thus the dispute over representation was settled by a compromise: the large states got their way in the House of Representatives and the small states got their way in the Senate.

The system of checks and balances was adopted. The argument between the large and small states was the most serious dispute that arose in the Constitutional Convention. Once it was settled, the work went ahead more smoothly. The delegates agreed it was necessary to have someone in charge of enforcing the laws. So they created the position of the *President*. (The word president comes from the Latin and means "one who sits in front.")

Then some of the delegates began to worry. They pointed out that the President could easily grow too powerful — he might destroy the nation's liberty and rule like a king! To prevent this, the Constitutional Convention decided to set up a system of *checks and balances*. They divided the government into three branches: legislative, executive, and judicial. Each branch of the government checks on the other two; the purpose of this is to keep any one from becoming too powerful.

This is the way the system of checks and balances works. The national government is made up of (1) a *legislative* branch called Congress which makes the laws; (2) an *executive* branch, consisting of the President, his advisers, and assistants who enforce the laws; (3) a *judicial* branch consisting of the judges of the Supreme Court and lower courts who explain the laws.

CONSTITUTIONAL GOVERNMENT IN THE UNITED STATES

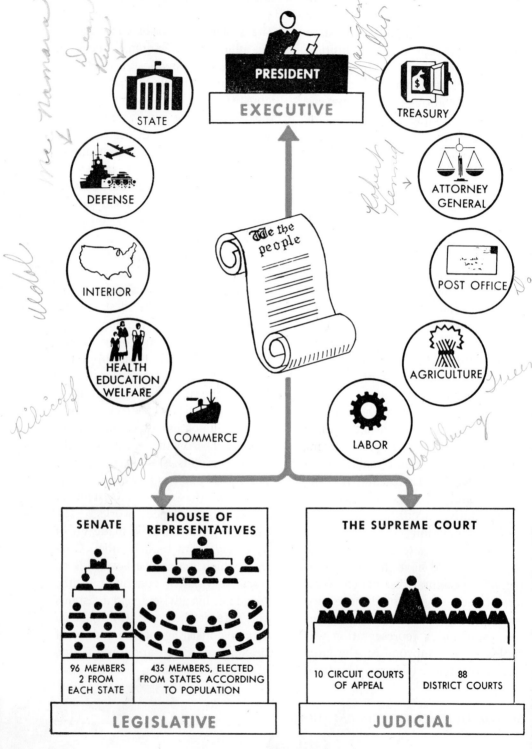

Each of the three branches has a way of checking the power of the others. For example, the President can *veto* or vote against a bill Congress has passed. But Congress can override or wipe out the President's veto if two-thirds of the members vote to pass the law again. And the Supreme Court can check both Congress and the President by declaring a law unconstitutional.

The Constitution is brief, clear, and to the point. Gradually the new plan of government was written. Each part was carefully thought out and talked over. The delegates to the Philadelphia convention — the "Fathers of the Constitution," as they are called today — drew upon their own experience in running state and colonial governments. Reaching back into English history, they included some ideas and methods their ancestors had developed long ago.

The American Constitution contains features that had worked well in state constitutions, colonial charters, and English political documents. It did not contain a great deal that was new; it was based, instead, on the wisdom of experience.

You will find a copy of the Constitution at the back of this book on page 625. As it is discussed, you should consult the document itself. To make it easier for you to find different parts of the Constitution, each paragraph is numbered consecutively from 1 to 123. Throughout this book whenever reference is made to a provision of the Constitution, the numbers appear in brackets to show which paragraph you should look up. Here is an example: The Constitution decided that Congress should have two houses [1].

Notice that the Constitution begins with a *preamble* or introduction. The preamble states the reasons why it was felt necessary to write a new plan of government. The Constitution, as it was written in Philadelphia, consisted of seven main parts or "Articles." Later, changes or *Amendments* were added.

Article I [1–53] of the Constitution tells how Congress is to be set up and what it can do. Article II [54–66] is about the Executive Department, that is, the President and Vice-President. Article III [67–72] deals with the judicial branch or the federal courts and judges. Article IV [73–79] discusses the relation of states and national government.

Article V [80] desrcibes the way the Constitution can be changed or amended when it seems necessary or desirable. Article VI [81–83] contains some general statements about the public debt, the laws, and the oath which officials of the United States must swear. Article VII [84] tells how the Constitution was to be ratified or approved by the states.

The Constitution was signed September 17, 1787. Seven Articles spread over a few pages! — that was all the delegates had to show for almost four months' work. It did not seem much at the time. The delegates were not very pleased with their work. "It's just a bundle of compromises!" said one man. Others remarked sadly, "Well, it was the best we could do under the circumstances."

On September 17, the delegates held their last meeting. The secretary read the Constitution in its final form. Then Benjamin Franklin started to make a speech. He tried to stand up, but his legs were too weak. He sank back in his chair. James Wilson read the speech.

Franklin admitted that he did not like some parts of the Constitution, but he added:

I am sure of this: that the combined wisdom of so many thoughtful men is certain to be sounder as a whole than anything any one of us could have written alone. So I hope each of you will join me . . . and show your approval of the whole effort by signing it, and supporting it before the people.

Thirty-nine delegates agreed with Franklin. They signed the document although they did not feel very proud or satisfied. Many signed chiefly because they had faith in the amending process described in Article V [80]. They felt the Constitution could be changed or amended to make it more satisfactory, so they signed.

As the delegates signed their names, Franklin told a story. Over and over, during the meetings, he said he had looked at the President's chair. A picture of the sun was painted on the chair. Franklin had not been able to make up his mind whether the sun was rising or setting. "Now, at length," he added hopefully, "I have the happiness to know it is a rising, and not a setting sun."

The real test, however, was still to come. Would the nation accept the Constitution? The states would have to call special conventions to consider the plan. When and if nine state conventions voted in favor of the Constitution, the new government could be started.

The states slowly approved the Constitution. It took a long hard fight to get the Constitution adopted. Many people did not like the new plan. In France, Thomas Jefferson wrote to James Madison, telling him that the Constitution should have a *bill of rights*. Jefferson meant that the document should contain a statement that guaranteed everyone freedom of speech, press, religion, and the right to a trial by jury.

There were other reasons why people opposed adopting the Constitution. Some feared it would set up a government so strong it might take away the rights of the states. They had just got rid of one strong government — the rule of Great Britain — and they did not want to create another one. Certain merchants were afraid that under the new plan Congress would interfere too much with foreign trade. Some southerners did not like the provision of the Constitution that would permit the new government to forbid the slave trade after 1808.

Small farmers were suspicious; they thought the new government would be controlled by big landowners or businessmen. So for many reasons opposition was strong.

During the fight to get the Constitution adopted, Alexander Hamilton was very busy. He wrote letters to the newspapers urging people to vote for the Constitution. He persuaded James Madison and John Jay to write letters also. Later, the letters were printed in pamphlets and then in a book called *The Federalist*. The articles were clear and forceful. They won many friends for the new plan.

Slowly the states voted to approve the Constitution. Delaware was first, then Pennsylvania. A little later, New Jersey, Georgia, Connecticut, Massachusetts, Maryland, and South Carolina ratified. Eight states — but nine were needed.

At last, in June, 1788, the New Hampshire convention voted to approve. Now the new government could be formed. But two large and powerful states still delayed; in Virginia and New York the fight was close, but eventually Virginia and New York ratified. North Carolina and Rhode Island were the last to come under "the new roof," as people were calling the Constitution. The Constitution really went into effect in 1789.

A Bill of Rights was added in 1791. Those who did not want the Constitution to be adopted were called *Anti-federalists*. This was because

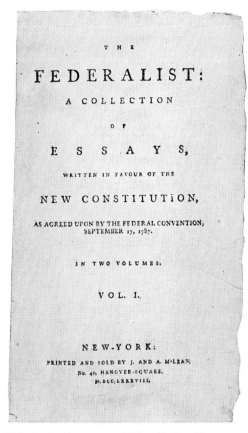

THE

FEDERALIST:

A COLLECTION

OF

E S S A Y S,

WRITTEN IN FAVOUR OF THE

NEW CONSTITUTION,

AS AGREED UPON BY THE FEDERAL CONVENTION, SEPTEMBER 17, 1787.

IN TWO VOLUMES.

VOL. I.

NEW-YORK:

PRINTED AND SOLD BY J. AND A. M'LEAN, No. 41, HANOVER-SQUARE. M,DCC,LXXXVIII.

This is the title page of *The Federalist*, a group of articles favoring the Constitution.

anti means "against," and they were against a strong federal government. Anti-federalists had opposed the Constitution because, they argued, it said a thousand words about government but not one word about personal liberty.

It is quite true that the Constitution said little or nothing about personal liberty. As one of the fathers of the Constitution explained, "It never occured to us that personal liberty could ever be endangered in this country." The states had safeguarded personal liberty in the state

BILL OF RIGHTS   195

Congress of the United States

Begun and held at the City of New York
on Wednesday the fourth of March one thousand seven hundred and eighty nine

Freedom of Religion

Freedom of Speech

Freedom from unreasonable searches

Right to assemble

Right to petition

Some Highlights
of the
of Rights

Right to jury trial and counsel

Right to summon witnesses

No illegal loss of liberty

No excessive bail or fines

Just compensation for property

constitutions that they adopted after the Declaration of Independence. The members of the Constitutional Convention did not think it was necessary to repeat a list of American rights in the Constitution.

But many people disagreed. They felt there should be no doubt about a matter of great importance. In the convention called by Massachusetts the members insisted that a list of ten personal liberties should be added to the Constitution. Other state conventions voted to adopt the Constitution *on condition* that these rights were made a part of it.

So it happened that ten amendments to the Constitution were quickly added, all at once. In 1791 they became part of the Constitution. Among the liberties which they protected were freedom of religion, of speech, of the press, and of peaceable assembly, that is, the right of citizens to meet and discuss any matter of importance. The chart on page 196 lists the ten rights guaranteed by the new amendments. On pages 636–638 at the back of this book you will find the full text of the first ten amendments. These first ten amendments were called the Bill of Rights. The American Bill of Rights was named after the British Bill of Rights, a famous law which Parliament passed in 1689 to protect the people against selfish and unjust kings.

The Constitution grew out of American experience. And so the American nation weathered the storms of the first years after the Revolution. The country had gone through a time of trouble and despair. Now the future looked brighter. The men of the Constitutional Convention had written a wise and workable plan for a strong government. Its roots were deep in the past. Because it was based on experience and good sense and respect for people's rights, the Constitution was a success.

Today, after more than one hundred and sixty-five years, the Constitution is still strong and growing. A great English statesman, William E. Gladstone, has rightly called it "the most remarkable work . . . produced by the human mind at a single stroke. . . ."

Americans owe a great debt to the men who worked so hard in Philadelphia in 1787. The Constitution they wrote is one of the factors that has helped the United States become the leader of the free world.

Freedom of Religion, guaranteed by the Bill of Rights, is dear to Americans as the picture below emphasizes.

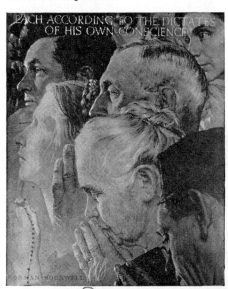

EACH ACCORDING TO THE DICTATES OF HIS OWN CONSCIENCE

NORMAN ROCKWELL

CHAPTER SUMMARY

The Constitutional Convention met in Philadelphia in 1787. The delegates were determined to create a stronger government. They disagreed about many things, but finally — after four months — the Constitution was written. The Constitution provided for a federal form of government. Each citizen must obey laws of both country and state.

A Congress of two Houses was established. The Senate is made up of two members from each state. The number of members each state sends to the House of Representatives depends upon its population.

A system of checks and balances was provided. The national government has three branches: legislative, executive, and judicial. Each of the three branches has a way of checking the powers of the others.

The Constitution was signed September 17, 1787. In June, 1788, the Constitution was ratified or approved by nine states and went into effect. A Bill of Rights was added in 1791. It consists of the first ten amendments and assures the people of individual liberties. It guarantees freedom of religion, of speech, of the press, and of assembly.

The Language of History

Be sure you understand the meaning of each of the following terms as it is used in this chapter. Consult a large dictionary as well as your textbook.

1. amend
2. veto
3. judicial
4. constitution
5. compromise
6. executive
7. federal form of government
8. system of checks and balances
9. legislative

What Happened When

Be sure you can connect an event with each of these dates.

1. 1787
2. 1789
3. 1791

Who's Who in History

Make sure you know the part each of the following played in the writing or ratification of the Constitution:

1. George Washington
2. Benjamin Franklin
3. Alexander Hamilton
4. Gouverneur Morris
5. John Jay
6. James Madison

Study Questions

1. Name three famous leaders of the Revolutionary Period who did not attend the Constitutional Convention. 188

2. Where would you probably find the most reliable information about what happened at certain meetings of the Convention?

3. a. List three leading delegates to the Convention.
   b. How many delegates attended the meetings regularly?

4. a. What was the occupation of a majority of the delegates?
   b. What previous political experience had most of them had?

5. a. On what point did the delegates from large states and delegates from small states disagree?
   b. How was the dispute settled?

6. a. What is a federal form of government?
   b. State two powers given the national government by the Constitution.
   c. State two powers reserved to the states.

7. a. What is the purpose of the system of checks and balances?
   b. Name the three branches of the federal government.
   c. Give an example of the way one branch of the government can check another branch.

8. What criticisms were made of the Constitution before ratification?

9. a. What was *The Federalist?*
   b. Who wrote it?

10. a. What are the first ten amendments called?
    b. When were they adopted?
    c. Mention three rights guaranteed by these amendments.

LET'S LOOK AT WHAT WE'VE LEARNED

What problems faced the United States after the Revolution?

1. Americans were loyal only to their own state. The population was small, roads were bad, and communication was difficult. 2. Money was scarce, and both the nation and the states owed big debts for the expenses of the Revolution. 3. Foreign nations were unfriendly.

How was the United States governed during and after the Revolution?

The chief governing body was Congress. There was no President. The basis of the government was the Articles of Confederation. Under them most of the power belonged to the states. The national government was weak.

What was the Northwest Ordinance and why is it important?

Congress passed the Northwest Ordinance in 1787, outlining the government of the frontier. The Ordinance directed that the people of the territories should be self-governing in part. When the population increased, new states would be formed out of the territory.

Why was the Constitutional Convention called?

Many American leaders such as Washington and Hamilton were greatly worried about the weakness of the Articles of Confederation. Their meetings at Mount Vernon and Annapolis led to the calling of the Constitutional Convention in 1787 to strengthen the national government.

Who were the leading members of the Constitutional Convention?

Most of the delegates had taken part in the Revolution and in state governments. The best known were: George Washington, who served as chairman; Benjamin Franklin; James Madison, "the Father of the Constitution."

What were the most important disputes in the Constitutional Convention and how were they settled?

The most serious was over the number of representatives for each state in Congress. The large states wanted representation according to population. The small states wanted equal representation, regardless of size. A compromise provided that Congress would consist of two houses. In the lower house, representation would be according to population. In the upper house, or Senate, each state would be represented by two Senators.

What kind of a government did the Constitution provide for?

A federal form of government was established. Under this plan, power was divided between the national government and the states.

What is the system of checks and balances and what is its purpose?

The purpose of the system is to keep any person or branch of the national government from becoming too powerful. The government is divided into three branches: legislative, executive, and judicial. Each branch checks on the other branches.

Why were many people against the adoption of the Constitution?

They were afraid the government it outlines would be too powerful. They objected especially to the fact that there was no Bill of Rights. Several states would not approve the Constitution until Hamilton and other leaders promised to see that a Bill of Rights was added.

Connecting the Past with the Present . . .

You can be President. You can be elected to the Senate or the House of Representatives. You can be appointed to the Supreme Court. Who arranged it so that any American can rise to the highest offices in the land? The Fathers of the Constitution planned it that way in 1787. In the document they made it very clear that the top positions in the government were open to those who possess ability and experience. There are no financial, religious, or social qualifications. So far as the Constitution is concerned, the race is open to all.

This may not seem anything to get excited about now. But in 1787 it was a tremendous step forward. In the Old World lands, a person had little chance to win a position of power unless he or she was born into the nobility. The men who wrote the Constitution might easily have arranged things according to Old World ideas. There was some talk of having a king as head of the government, but it was never taken seriously. The Fathers of the Constitution believed that everyone should have a chance to rise to a position of leadership. They felt that only if the offices of government were open to everyone could there be real democracy. Thanks to their efforts any American can have the opportunity to play an active part in running the government of his country.

Questions for Discussion and Review

1. List some of the countries whose people were encouraged by the American Revolution to revolt against their unjust rulers.
2. Why did many Americans fear a strong national government?
3. List some of the difficulties which troubled the thirteen states after the Revolution.
4. What is meant by: "It's not worth a Continental"?
5. Give an example of how little authority the Articles of Confederation gave to Congress in matters of taxation and finance.
6. The Northwest Ordinance was a very successful law. When was it passed? What did it regulate? How long have some of its provisions been used?
7. Why do you think that the delegates to the Constitutional Convention agreed not to tell what was done or said in the Convention?
8. **a.** Name five famous Americans of 1787 who did not attend the Constitutional Convention.
   b. Name five delegates to the Constitutional Convention.
9. Explain the compromise that was agreed on to give fair representation to all the states in the national Congress.
10. Which article of the Constitution tells how the plan was to be ratified?
11. **a.** Who were the Anti-Federalists?
    b. What amendments to the Constitution did they help to have adopted?

THE HISTORY LABORATORY

On the opposite page are suggestions for activities that you will find interesting and profitable.

WHAT AND WHEN

Albany Plan of Union 1754   Articles of Confederation 1781   Northwest Ordina 1787

ALBANY PLAN OF UNION

JOIN, or DIE.

4 Leaf Clover

Arrange a Display . . .

Make a wall display for your classroom illustrating the steps a bill must go through to become a law. For information consult an encyclopedia or the pamphlet *Congress in Action* by Smith and Riddick.

Write a Story . . .

There are many exciting jobs in the United States government. Write a story with one of these titles, or make up your own. Be sure to look up the background facts for your story:

"I Guard the President." Imagine you are a United States Secret Service agent and write an account of your experience.

"The Twenty-five Dollar Bill." Imagine you are an employee of the Treasury Department. Tell how you and other "T-Men" smash a counterfeiting ring.

"Code Breaker." Imagine you are a member of Army Intelligence. You have twenty-four hours to learn where the enemy will attack.

Woman's Place . . .

Make a scrapbook showing how women play a part in governing the nation. Illustrations for this project can be found in newspapers and magazines, especially women's magazines.

Take a Field Trip . . .

Make a list of all the public buildings in your community. Tell what activities of government are carried on in each. Learn which government officials are in charge of each activity. After you have all this information, plan a class trip to one or more of the buildings. A committee should be chosen to make arrangements with local officials for the trip.

ng of Constitutional Convention
1787

Ratification of Constitution
1788

Bill of Rights
1791

Take Some Pictures . . .

Make a picture album of government in your home community. Take snapshots of buildings, people, parks, and equipment. You might separate your album into two parts, one showing the services of the federal government and the other those of your state and local governments.

Follow the Tories . . .

Follow up the story of the men and women who chose to leave the United States after the Revolution and remain British subjects rather than become citizens of the new nation. You can get information on this subject by writing to the New Brunswick Bureau of Information, Frederickton, N.B., Canada, or to the Nova Scotia Bureau of Information, Halifax, N.S., Canada. You may also find the following books helpful: *Readings in Canadian History* by George W. Brown (Dent, 1940) and Kenneth Robert's novel *Oliver Wiswell* (Doubleday, 1940).

Let's Read about the Constitution and the Federal Government

BAILARD, V., and McKOWN, H. C., *So You Were Elected!* McGraw, 1946.
DESMOND, ALICE CURTIS, *Alexander Hamilton's Wife*, Dodd, 1952.
ELTING, M., and GOSSET, M., *We are the Government*, Doubleday, 1945.
**FARRAND, M., *Fathers of the Constitution*, Yale University Press, 1921.
FINDLAY, B. A., and FINDLAY, ESTHER, *Your Rugged Constitution*, Stanford University, 1950.
HARTMAN, GERTRUDE, *Making of a Democracy*, Day, 1941.
**JOHNSON, GERALD W., *This American People*, Harper, 1951.
McFEE, MRS. I. N. C., *How Our Government is Run*, Crowell, 1946.
MOSES, BELLE, *John Marshall*, Appleton, 1938.
SMITH, GEORGE and RIDDICK, FLOYD, *Congress in Action: How a Bill Becomes a Law*, National Capitol Publications, 1949.
*TURNER, MINA, *U. S. Means Us*, Houghton, 1947.
WELCH, EARL, *Cradle of Our Nation*, Holt, 1949.
*WITTY, PAUL A., and KOHLER, J., *You and the Constitution of the United States*, Children's Press, 1948.

* indicates easy reading
** indicates advanced reading

Unit 5

THE NATION GREW STRONG IN SPITE OF UNFRIENDLY NEIGHBORS (1789-1823)

THE UNITED STATES had a fine new Constitution in 1789, and most people felt cheerful about the future. However, the plan was still just a piece of paper. The government had still to be organized. Who was going to do it?

The country was in debt and without a sound currency. The government would need money; would the people accept new taxes?

On the frontier, the Indians were restless, stirred up — it was said — by British agents. Westward-moving settlers had to be protected. In the Mississippi Valley the situation was more explosive. Spain owned the river down which western farmers must ship their crops to market. Could the government help the westerners?

As you read this Unit keep in mind these questions: (1) How was the government organized and credit established? (2) How did Americans win the right to use the Mississippi? (3) How did the United States win respect from other nations?

Chapter 11

UNDER WASHINGTON'S LEADERSHIP THE NEW GOVERNMENT WAS FIRMLY ESTABLISHED

"We found the stairs covered with carpeting and the rails hung with crimson. The President was received by the Governor and the citizens in the most brilliant manner. Here he was met . . . by many of his old and faithful patriots who had borne the heat and burden of the day with him . . . and who now joined in the universal chorus of welcoming. . . . The streets were lined with inhabitants as thick as the people could stand."

Thus, in a letter to his wife, one of the spectators described the scene when Washington came to New York to take the oath as President.

It was a great day for Washington and the nation, but after all the shouting was over the hard work began. How did the President go about starting a new government? What help did he ask for and get? Who were his chief assistants? How did he find money to pay the bills?

Not everyone was ready to obey Washington and Congress. How did the President deal with defiance and rebellion? What did he do when the news came that the Indians along the Wabash had taken the warpath?

You will find the answers in this chapter as you read the story of how the government was organized under the Constitution.

Washington was the first President. Washington hurried home to Virginia after the Constitutional Convention. His heart's desire was to remain at Mount Vernon. But America needed him. The Constitution had created the position of President, or head of the government. There was no doubt about the man the nation wanted for President: George Washington. He was "first in war, first in peace, and first in the hearts of his countrymen."

The Constitution directed that the President be chosen by the *Electoral College*. This method involved several steps. First, each state legislature appointed a certain number of men called *electors*. Next, each group of electors met in their state capital and voted. Then the ballots were sent to Congress, where they were counted. Presidents are still selected officially by the Electoral College. However, since electors are now chosen by vote of the people, the method has become more democratic.

It was easy to count electoral votes in 1789. Every ballot had the name Washington written on it! So once more Washington had to ride away from Mount Vernon, looking back sadly at his beautiful home.

John Adams of Massachusetts was chosen Vice-President. He had just returned from England. It took time for the new leaders to reach New York, the first capital of the government under the Constitution. Because of spring floods the roads were worse than usual. Time after time carriages were stuck in the mud.

Along the way, people gathered to honor Washington. Children threw flowers in his path. At last, on

Washington leaves Mount Vernon (below). Answering his country's call, he says goodbye to his family and departs for New York and his inauguration as first president.

Here Washington is inaugurated as President amid rejoicing of the people.

April 30, 1789, Washington stood on the balcony of Federal Hall in New York City. He placed his hand on a Bible and took the oath of the President of the United States.

The crowd cheered wildly. Washington nodded and smiled in his dignified way. Then he went inside and made a speech to Congress. The new plan was getting started!

Washington chose a Cabinet. It was a tremendous job to organize the government. Washington and his advisers had only the brief outline in the Constitution to guide them. They had few old customs or rules.

Washington knew that he had to have help. The Constitution gives many duties to the executive, or law enforcing, branch of the government. No one man could handle them all. So, to assist the President, Congress created five departments. Each was to deal with one group of problems.

First and most important was the Department of State. Its job was to handle relations with foreign nations. Washington chose his neighbor, Thomas Jefferson, to be head of this department, or "Secretary of State." Jefferson was serving as American representative in France. He did not return to America for several months.

Next, Congress established the Treasury Department. The financial affairs of the United States were still in a weak condition. Someone had to find money to run the government. Washington knew the man to head the Treasury Department: Alexander Hamilton, who had been his aide during the Revolution. Hamilton understood the problems of money and banking. His knowledge helped put the nation on a sound financial basis.

To look after defense, Congress created the War Department. Washington appointed one of his generals, Henry Knox of Massachusetts, the first Secretary of War.

Later, Congress set up the Post Office Department to supervise the mail. Samuel Osgood was the first Postmaster General. Still later, Congress created the position of Attorney General. Edmund Randolph of Virginia became the first Attorney General. It was his job to advise the President on legal matters.

Washington often consulted with the heads of departments. They held regular meetings to talk over problems. Out of these meetings developed what is called the *Cabinet*. This is a council that advises the President; it is composed of department heads. There is nothing specific in the Constitution about the Cabinet. But it developed and became a traditional part of the government. From time to time Congress established new departments, so the Cabinet now is larger than it was in Washington's time.

Congress passed a tariff law. As soon as the government was organized, Washington and his Cabinet went to work on their biggest problem: money and how to get it. They had to find a way to pay debts, and meet many expenses.

Only a few hundred people worked for the government in those days, but they had to be paid. Money was needed to pay for ships and guns to defend the country. Under the Constitution, Congress for the first time had the power to tax — that is, to make people pay money to support the government.

Americans have never liked to pay taxes. But it is important to remember three things about taxes: (1) Every government must have money to operate or it will go to pieces. You have seen how troubles multiplied under the Articles of Confederation because Congress could not get money. (2) The only way a government can get money is

Washington is shown, below left, with his Cabinet. Next to him is Secretary Knox (War), then Hamilton (Treasury), Jefferson (State), and Attorney-General Randolph.

by taxing people in one way or another. (3) Taxing people means taking money out of your pocket, and everyone else's pocket.

Money the government gets by taxing is called *revenue*. Washington and Hamilton decided the best way to get revenue was to put a tax, or *tariff*, on goods brought to the United States from foreign countries. They persuaded Congress to put a tax on hundreds of *imports* or goods Americans bought from foreign countries. For example, every pound of tea that came into the United States was taxed six cents.

You will recall what an uproar Americans had raised when England tried to tax tea. But things were different now. It was their own government that was taxing them, so they did not complain very much. In a few months the tariff law brought in two million dollars. This was enough to pay most of the bills for a year.

Hamilton drew up a four-point program. Washington and Hamilton realized the government would soon need more money than the tariff would bring in. The United States still owed debts to foreign nations and to its own citizens. Some of the states also were in debt. There were other financial problems. Hamilton thought over the situation carefully. Then he drew up a four-point program for curing America's financial troubles.

The program included: (1) paying the national debt; (2) having the federal government take over and arrange to pay states' debts; (3) raising revenue by taxes on whisky and other liquors; and (4) establishing a Bank of the United States. Here is how Hamilton explained his program:

First, Hamilton declared, the United States must pay its debts. He suggested that each year the Treasury set aside some of the tax money it received. This would be used to pay the debts in an orderly, dependable way. When people saw the United States was steadily paying its debt they would have faith in the country's honesty. This would win respect at home and abroad — that is, it would establish the nation's *credit*. Hamilton easily persuaded Congress to adopt this part of his plan.

What about state debts? That was the next problem. Hamilton felt they should be paid. He believed the national government should take over state debts and arrange to pay them along with the national debt. Congress was not so ready to accept this idea. Virginia and a few other states had paid their debts. It did not seem fair to tax Virginians to pay the debts of northern states. The debate dragged on for many weary months.

During the argument, Jefferson came back from France. Hamilton explained the situation to him. Jefferson was not much interested in state debts, but he was interested in another question: where would the permanent capital of the United States be located? Jefferson and other southerners wanted the capital to be in the South. Hamilton and the northerners felt the capital should be some distance north of the Potomac River. In those days the settled area of the country did not yet extend much beyond the Allegheny Mountains so it was taken for granted that the capital should be located near the Atlantic coast.

Once again the ability to compromise saved the day. Jefferson agreed to help Hamilton win votes, to have the national government take over the state debts. In return, Hamilton promised to help Jefferson win votes to have the national capital located in the South.

Thus Hamilton won approval for the second part of his program. And Congress voted to build a permanent capital on ten square miles of land along the eastern shore of the Potomac River. The region belonged to Maryland, so it was considered southern territory. It was just a stretch of wilderness. Maryland agreed to give the land to the national government. Congress named the area the *District of Columbia.* The capital city was named Washington in honor of the President. The government did not move to Washington until 1800, for it took years to build the city.

Congress put a tax on liquor. Hamilton knew it would take a great deal of money to pay debts and build a new capital. So, as the third point in his program, he called for new taxes. He asked Congress to tax many goods made in the United States. The new tax was to be called an *excise* (EK size) tax.

The word "excise" comes from a Latin word meaning to "cut out" or "take out." It refers to the fact that long ago in Europe a farmer who brought a load of food to town had to give some of it to tax collectors. They took away, or excised, part of the load and sold it to get money to run the government.

The men in Congress thought the excise would be an easy way to collect money. So they passed a law taxing whisky and other liquors. Many of the people who had to pay the tax on whisky were poor farmers in western Pennsylvania. They raised grain and made it into whisky because whisky was easy to transport and to sell. You can see why they did not like the whisky tax! Later, when the government sent agents to collect the tax, there was trouble.

The Bank of the United States was organized in 1791. As Hamilton pushed ahead with his program, he made enemies. Jefferson and other southerners did not like the way Hamilton arranged to pay the national and state debts. Western farmers did not like the whisky tax. A split developed between those who liked Hamilton's program and those, like Jefferson, who opposed it.

Secretary of the Treasury, Alexander Hamilton, addresses his fellow directors of the first Bank of the United States. The Bank was a key point in Hamilton's great financial program to strengthen the credit and currency of the United States.

Hamilton paid little attention to his enemies. He felt he was right, and he was determined to have his way. But when he announced the fourth point in his program even he was surprised at the storm it caused!

The fourth point recommended establishment of a national bank. Hamilton asked Congress to set up a "Bank of the United States." People could buy shares in the Bank. Each share would cost $400. The government would buy 5000 shares, and would sell 20,000 shares to the public. When all the shares were sold, the Bank would have $10,000,000 in capital. It would be rich and strong.

Hamilton claimed the Bank would help everybody. It would be a safe place to keep money collected in taxes. It would issue paper money, or "bank notes," worth the same amount in every state; this would help provide the sound money business needed. The Bank would help make the government strong. Everyone would have increased confidence in the government.

Jefferson and his friends were against the Bank. They said it was a trick to get all the money in the country into the hands of a few bankers. There were bitter debates in Congress. But Hamilton won. Washington sided with Hamilton, and Congress voted to establish the Bank of the United States. Thus, Hamilton had won approval for the four parts of his program.

Political parties developed in Washington's first term. Jefferson was so angry he wanted to resign as Secretary of State. Washington persuaded

212   ESTABLISHING THE NEW GOVERNMENT

him to remain in the government a while longer, but the bad feeling between Jefferson and Hamilton grew worse. Out of the quarrel, two political parties developed.

A *political party* is a group of people who have the same ideas about the way the government should be run. The group is united, and has a leader. The party members want to control the government and put their ideas into effect.

People who believed in Hamilton's ideas formed the Federalist Party. They wanted a strong government. They favored the Bank of the United States. Many were businessmen, and they felt that Hamilton's policies were good for business.

People who liked Jefferson and his ideas formed the Democratic Republican Party. They feared a strong government, and they did not like the Bank of the United States. Many were poor farmers and working men. They felt that Hamilton's policies were going to hurt them.

The quarrel between Jefferson and Hamilton made Washington unhappy. He did not like to see the nation split into opposing groups. Political parties, he felt, would ruin America.

But, in this instance, Washington was wrong. Political parties have since proved to be a help in running the government. One party checks on the other, so that no group becomes too strong. And political parties give people a chance to express their opinions. They also give men and women a chance to get experience in politics.

As time went on the political parties changed their names or disappeared. New parties and new leaders arose, but the basic ideas remained much the same. The Republican Party of today resembles the Federalist Party in some ways. The Democratic Party of today favors some of Jefferson's ideas. So both political parties today trace their ancestry to the days when Washington was President.

A new kind of money was adopted. The struggle between Jefferson and Hamilton went on for a long while. For several years Hamilton was the winner. The Federalists controlled the government from 1789 to 1801.

Thomas Jefferson (below) vigorously opposed Hamilton's financial plans.

Hamilton's financial program proved successful, and America grew prosperous. The population increased rapidly. Two new states entered the Union: Vermont in 1791 and Kentucky in 1792. The young country was growing and spreading out. Within a few years, Tennessee and Ohio gained enough settlers to become states.

Everywhere people felt hopeful. They could see that their national government was firmly established. The Bank of the United States provided the country with sound paper money that had the same value all over the United States.

Businessmen still had *currency* troubles, that is, trouble with the kind of money used in exchange for goods. When Americans sold grain, fish, and lumber to customers in foreign lands, they were paid in gold or silver coins. In many parts of America merchants still figured prices in English "pounds and shillings." The pound was the unit of English money, somewhat like the modern American dollar but greater in value. The shilling was a smaller coin some-

The picture below shows President and Mrs. Washington looking at the first coins issued by the United States Mint. The new nation badly needed sound currency and at last achieved it in Washington's administration. The coins shown represent various types used in the early days.

Above are shown the buildings of the first United States Mint, established in Philadelphia in 1792. Note the muddy condition of the street near the Mint.

what like the modern American quarter. As business increased, more and more English, French, and Spanish coins came into the country. But foreign coins did not have the same value in all the states.

For example, an English sovereign (a gold coin worth 21 shillings) might buy goods of that same value in Charleston, but be worth only 18 shillings in Philadelphia. Whenever a storekeeper received French or Spanish coins, he had to ask himself, "Just how much is this coin worth?" Then he had to figure the value of the coins, and convince his customer he was right.

Another trouble was that many coins had been "clipped," that is, someone had cut or filed off part of the gold or silver for his own use. The result, as Washington said, was that the man who sold goods needed a pair of scales with which to weigh each gold or silver coin before accepting it. Worse still, many coins were *counterfeit* (KOWN ter fit),

which means that someone had made a coin of some cheap metal (lead, for example) by dipping it in a solution of gold or silver and then stamping it. Such coins were hard to identify.

The first step in solving the problem was to establish a new American currency with the dollar as the main unit of value. It was based on the *decimal* system. The word "decimal" means "by tens." Ten cents make one dime. Ten dimes make one dollar. This was simpler than the English or Spanish or French system because almost anybody could multiply or divide by ten. If you spend even a short time in a country that does not have the decimal system of currency, you will soon realize the convenience of the American currency system.

The next step was to set up a *mint* in Philadelphia. The word "mint" means a place where certain metals are melted and coined into money. The new coins proved stable, that is, the value remained the same everywhere. A dime, for example, would buy ten cents worth of goods in any state. The success of the first United States mint was great.

Washington was unanimously re-elected. It took all of Washington's first term to organize the government, and to put Hamilton's program into effect. In 1792 Washington was triumphantly re-elected; again he won every electoral vote.

Washington's second term was full of problems. Hamilton and Jefferson continued to quarrel. In 1793 Jefferson resigned as Secretary of State, partly because he could no longer work with Hamilton. War broke out in Europe; troubles with foreign nations increased.

Western farmers continued to grumble about the tax on whisky. When revenue agents came to collect the tax, they were driven off — with a warning not to come back. Washington sent the angry farmers this message: "Congress has passed the law, and it is my duty to enforce it. If you don't like the law, you are free to elect representatives who will change it."

The farmers paid no attention. In 1794 hundreds of them gathered and defied the government. They sent a messenger to tell Congress the whisky tax would never be paid, and could not be collected. This was the Whisky Rebellion. It was the first challenge to the government.

Washington did not hesitate. The national government now had power to enforce its laws. Washington sent 15,000 soldiers to put down the rebellion. When the troops reached western Pennsylvania, the rebellion faded away like smoke. Not a man was hurt, and there was no more trouble collecting the tax. The

The Whisky Rebellion (1794) challenged the authority of the new government. Below, frontier farmers are shown loading liquor on wagons to be carried to market.

Above is a scene from the Battle of Fallen Timbers (1794) where Anthony Wayne and his men defeated the Indians of the Ohio region. The victory subdued the Indians and made it safer for settlers to go to the Northwest Territory.

government had proved its ability to keep order. However, western farmers did not forgive or forget the affair. They blamed Hamilton and the Federalist Party for their troubles, and became Jefferson's followers.

"Mad Anthony" Wayne crushed an Indian uprising. In 1794, two Indian tribes in the Ohio Valley took the warpath. Settlers were pouring into the region; the Indians wanted to drive them back. The governor of Ohio, General St. Clair, led an army of 1800 men to protect the settlements, but he walked into a trap the Indians had set on a branch of the Wabash River. Half of St. Clair's army was killed. The rest were hunted like foxes through the woods. Encouraged by victory, Indians of many tribes set out to kill the whites or drive them out.

Here was a challenge Washington had to meet. He put General Anthony Wayne at the head of a powerful expedition. Wayne had fought in the Revolution and was known as "Mad Anthony."

At a place called Fallen Timbers in northwestern Ohio, Wayne defeated the Indians and sent them running in all directions. They lost all desire to fight against "Chief Who Never Sleeps," as they called Wayne. The next year they signed a treaty; they promised not to interfere with settlers in the Northwest Territory. Wayne's victory made the Ohio country a safer place for homemakers. Americans felt new faith in the government which had proved its power.

CHAPTER SUMMARY

Washington was the first President of the United States. John Adams was Vice President. Both men were chosen by the electoral college. Congress created a Cabinet to help the President.

The government needed money. More revenue was needed than the tariff supplied. Secretary of Treasury Hamilton drew up a four-point program to (1) pay the national debt, (2) have the federal government take over state debts, (3) raise revenue by taxes on whisky and liquors, (4) establish a Bank of the United States. A new currency was adopted based on the decimal system: ten pennies made one dime, ten dimes made one dollar, and so on.

Jefferson and Hamilton disagreed. Their quarrels led to the development of two political parties. The followers of Hamilton formed the Federalist Party; they favored a strong national government and a national bank. Jefferson's followers formed the Democratic Republican Party; they opposed the Federalists.

Washington was unanimously re-elected in 1792. He put down the Whisky Rebellion. At Washington's command, "Mad Anthony" Wayne crushed an Indian uprising in the Northwest Territory.

The Language of History

Be sure you know the meaning of the following words and phrases as they are used in this chapter.

1. electoral college	4. Cabinet	7. tariff
2. decimal system	5. currency	8. import
3. political party	6. revenue	9. excise

What Happened When

The following dates are important in American history. Make sure you know the events that occurred in these years.

1. 1789	2. 1791	3. 1792	4. 1794

HALL OF FAME

Who's Who in History

Make sure you know the part each of the following played in the early years of the American Republic.

1. George Washington   3. John Adams   5. Thomas Jefferson
2. Alexander Hamilton   4. Anthony Wayne   6. Edmund Randolph

Study Questions

1. Why did Washington take the oath of office as President in New York City rather than in Philadelphia or Washington, D. C.?

2. Name four members of Washington's Cabinet and tell the department each one headed.

3. State three purposes for which the government needed money in 1789.

4. **a.** What was the main purpose of Hamilton's financial program?
   b. List the four points of the program.

5. How did it happen that Washington, D. C. became the permanent capital of the United States?

6. **a.** Who owned the Bank of the United States?
   b. State two services the Bank performed for the country.

7. Why did Jefferson and his friends oppose the Bank of the United States?

8. **a.** What is the difference between an excise and a tariff?
   b. Why did the tax on whisky cause trouble?

9. **a.** How was the Whisky Rebellion settled?
   b. Washington's action in the Whisky Rebellion won increased respect for the federal government.   Why?

10. Explain how Wayne's victory at Fallen Timbers encouraged people to go west.

Chapter 12

THE REPUBLIC
WON THE RESPECT
OF FOREIGN POWERS

In 1800 "Long Tom" Jefferson rode into Washington to take over the Presidency from unlucky John Adams who had succeeded Washington. He faced many serious problems, particularly in dealing with foreign nations. What had happened in the eleven years since the adoption of the Constitution?

Under Washington's leadership many of the problems inside the country had been solved. But when were foreigners going to learn to respect the United States?

The Spaniards were especially troublesome, but the British were unfriendly, too. They kept interfering with trade, seizing American ships and sailors. What was the reason for their meddling? Worst of all, a quarrel with France was having unfortunate effects on American political affairs.

This chapter is chiefly about America's relations with foreign countries in the period from 1789 to 1805. As you read it, keep in mind these key questions:

1. How did the United States come to an agreement with Spain?

2. Why did France cease to be an ally?

3. How was war with Britain postponed?

4. How did disagreements over foreign policy help bring about the election of Jefferson?

American foreign relations began during the Revolution. While Washington and his advisers were setting up the government, serious problems were arising. Some, like the Indian rebellion, were quickly solved. But others, especially troubles with foreign nations, were not easy to handle.

Dealings with foreign nations belong to the branch of government activities known as *foreign relations*. Just as a man has to work with and compete against other men to get money for his family, a government must deal with other nations to protect and help its citizens.

Before the Revolution, colonists had little or nothing to do with foreign relations. Such important matters were handled by the British government. Not until the colonists declared their independence did American foreign relations begin. During the Revolution, Benjamin Franklin made a *treaty*, or solemn written agreement, with France. Then, at the end of the Revolution, the United States signed a treaty of peace with Great Britain. Both treaties soon began to cause trouble.

At the end of the Revolution, most leading nations formally recognized the independence of the United States. But they did not have much respect for the young nation. They did not hesitate to interfere in American affairs. There was trouble with Spain over the right of Americans to use the Mississippi River. There was also trouble with the British, for they refused to get out of the Northwest forts as they had promised in the peace treaty. Worst of all, a serious misunderstanding developed with America's friend, France.

Spain controlled the Mississippi River. You will recall that France helped the United States fight Britain in the Revolution. Spain also joined the fight against Britain. For this reason, France and Spain had a hand in the treaty of peace. By the treaty, Spain gained control of Florida once more. She was also allowed to keep control of New Orleans and the Louisiana Territory which France had turned over to her in 1763. In return, Spain promised to let Americans sail down the Mississippi River and use docks at New Orleans.

People in Ohio, Kentucky, and Tennessee produced large amounts of meat, grain, and lumber. They needed to use the Mississippi to transport their products to customers in eastern United States and in Europe. There were no good roads from the West to the Atlantic Coast, so the river was the only way they could send products to market.

Westerners usually sent their goods down the Mississippi on "flat boats" that they made themselves. But at New Orleans the goods had to be unloaded and put on board a well-built ship, strong enough to sail the ocean. Sometimes it took time to find a ship that was going where a farmer or lumberman wanted to send his products. So it was often necessary to store goods in New

Old New Orleans has many lovely ironwork balconies. The one above is characteristic of the oldest part of the city. The iron was usually brought from Spain.

Orleans for weeks. The privilege of landing and storing goods there was called the "right of deposit."

Imagine how westerners felt when Spain suddenly broke the treaty and closed the Mississippi River to American boats! Spanish officials forbade American ships to dock at New Orleans. They took away the "right of deposit." Westerners could no longer send their products down the Mississippi River. Yet they had no other way to get their products to market. Spain's action seemed to mean death for western trade.

The Pinckney Treaty improved relations with Spain. Angry frontiersmen threatened to settle the dispute with their guns. British agents took advantage of the situation: they circulated through the West, urging settlers to come back under Great Britain's protection. And Spanish officials hinted that if the westerners would join Spain, they could use the river freely.

Something had to be done quickly. If westerners could not use the Mississippi, they would either start a war or leave the Union. The country was in no condition to fight a war, but it could not afford to lose the West. Somehow westerners' rights had to be protected.

Washington sent Thomas Pinckney to Spain to try to arrange a settlement. The Spanish Court was unfriendly to Pinckney. Spanish nobles looked down their noses at the representative of a mere republic. But Pinckney knew how to get along with people. He made use of every argument, and at last he won an

EARLY FOREIGN RELATIONS

agreement, the Pinckney Treaty of 1795.

In the Pinckney Treaty, Spain once more agreed to let Americans use the Mississippi and unload goods at New Orleans. The treaty also settled a dispute over the boundary of Florida. It cleared up most of the difficulties with Spain for a time. But it was not the end of conflict. As long as Spain owned Florida and New Orleans there would be trouble in the Southwest.

The British interfered with American trade. In the North, along the Canadian border, there was more trouble. The British and the Canadians recognized American independence, but they were not ready to be friends. Great Britain had agreed to give up the Northwest Territory; still, year after year, she held on to the forts at Detroit, Mackinac, Niagara, and other points along the frontier.

The British showed their unfriendliness in other ways. They stopped many American ships from trading with British colonies in the West Indies. They also stopped Americans from trading with French colonies. This was a blow to American commerce. Americans accepted the fact that Britain had the right to keep other nations from trading with her colonies. But when the British tried to stop Americans from trading with French colonies in the West Indies, the United States really became angry.

Why did the British want to stop Americans from trading with France? The answer was that Britain and France were at war. So Britain did not want France to get supplies.

The War between Britain and France was partly a result of the French Revolution, which began in 1789, six years after the American Revolution ended. It was a revolt by the French people against their rulers. The French king and queen and many nobles were put to death. This shocked the rulers of other European nations. Soon war broke out between France and many of her neighbors.

The fighting between Great Britain and France lasted for many years. The United States tried hard to be *neutral*, that is, to stay out of the quarrel. But neither the French nor the British would permit this. The French thought the United States should help them in return for aid France had given during the Revolution. The British felt they were fighting for freedom and justice and that the United States should help them.

The British navy soon drove most French merchant ships from the sea. But France was able to get food and supplies from her colonies, for American ships were ready to carry goods from the West Indies to French ports. Naturally, the British wanted to stop the French from getting supplies that would help them keep on fighting. British warships began to capture American boats trading with the French and their colonies.

Interfering with the West Indian trade was bad enough, but the British did worse. They began seizing, or *impressing*, sailors on American ships. British warships were always short of men. It was hard to get anyone to serve in the British navy where sailors were often beaten, half-starved, and overworked. Many British sailors took the first chance to desert. Some took jobs on American ships, where they got better treatment.

John Jay (below) was a New York aristocrat who made an unpopular treaty with Britain.

Such desertions made British commanders furious. They began stopping every American merchant ship they met to search for deserters. They seized or "impressed" any British-born sailor they found. It did not matter if the men had become American citizens. "Once an Englishman, always an Englishman" was Britain's motto.

Sometimes, British commanders made a mistake and seized men born in America. The victims were forced to serve in the British navy. Sometimes they could not return to their homes for years.

John Jay made an unpopular treaty with Britain. Impressment, interference with American trade, failure to get out of the Northwest forts — all aroused anger in the United States. It would have been easy to drift into another war with Great Britain. But Washington knew that America was still weak. Another war so soon after the Revolution might ruin the United States.

Washington sent John Jay to London with orders to make an agreement that would prevent war, at least for a while. Jay was an intelligent, well-educated man. He had fought in the Revolution, and had helped write the Constitution.

Jay did his best to settle the disputes. He had a great deal of patience and he needed it, for the British were not much interested in arranging a settlement. They were busy fighting with France, and felt they had no time to listen to American complaints.

Under the circumstances it is remarkable that John Jay won any agreement. But he did. He got the British to sign a treaty. In this Jay Treaty of 1795 the British promised once more to give up the Northwest forts. The treaty also settled a few other disputes. But the British absolutely refused to stop searching ships and impressing sailors.

Imagine how Americans felt when they read the Jay Treaty! It seemed as if John Jay had given in to the British. Some newspapers called Jay a traitor. Even the President was blamed. The newspapers said so many harsh things about him that Washington declared: "I would rather be in my grave than submit to such treatment."

It is true the Jay Treaty left many things unsettled. But it did delay war with Britain for several years. It gave the country a "breathing spell," and got the British out of the Northwest Territory. Fort Niagara, Fort Detroit, and five other frontier posts became American property.

France expected Americans to help her fight Britain. While Pinckney and Jay were trying to settle disputes with Spain and Britain, a new quarrel was developing with France. When France went to war with Great Britain in 1793, Frenchmen expected the United States to help them. "We helped you," they reminded Americans. "Now it's your turn."

Sailors were forcibly impressed (top) and there were mock hangings of Jay because his treaty said nothing about such abuse.

Many Americans agreed. Jefferson and his followers, the Democratic Republicans, were friendly to France. But Hamilton and his followers, the Federalists, were more conservative. They did not like what was happening in France; they were disgusted by the French Revolution and the killing of the French rulers. The Federalists felt America should have as little to do as possible with such events.

Citizen Genêt of France got a chilly reception from President Washington.

Washington agreed with the Federalists. His policy was to keep the United States at peace no matter how strong the temptation to fight. So he issued a statement, called the *Neutrality Proclamation* (PROK luh MAY shun) of 1793. In this statement he declared the United States was at peace with Great Britain and France, and intended to remain at peace. He warned Americans not to take sides against any of the warring nations.

Just before Washington issued the Neutrality Proclamation, a French representative arrived in Charleston, South Carolina. His name was Edmond Charles Genêt (juh NAY). He was a brilliant man in many ways, but he lacked common sense.

The Democratic Republicans in Charleston and all along the way to Philadelphia gave Genêt a great welcome. Somehow he got the idea that all Americans were ready to fight for France. Without waiting to talk to Washington, Genêt urged American ship owners to go out and capture British merchant ships. He also started to organize men for attacks on Canada and Florida!

These actions might have involved the United States in the war between Britain and France. That was what Genêt wanted. He was furious when he read Washington's Neutrality Proclamation. He threatened to appeal to the people over the President's head. This was too much even for Washington's patience. He told the French government that Genêt was no longer welcome. He asked France to *recall* Genêt, that is, to order him home. The French government agreed to do so.

Genêt had failed completely to win friends for France. He decided, however, to stay in the United States. His party was out of power in France and, if he had returned, he would almost certainly have been put to death.

American neutrality caused a quarrel with France. Trouble with France increased steadily. The French did not like it when the United States made the Jay Treaty with Great Britain. They felt Americans were turning their backs on their old friends. French warships began seizing American merchant ships. It looked as if the United States might even go to war with France.

Relations with France were in bad shape when Washington's second term came to an end. He probably could have won the election again, but he was tired. He wanted to go back to his plantation.

Just before the end of his second term, Washington wrote some advice to the nation. In his *Farewell Address*, he urged Americans to work together and trust one another. He advised them "to steer clear of permanent alliances" with other nations. Neutrality, Washington felt, was the best policy. "Why quit our own to stand on foreign ground?"

In 1796, another President was chosen. He was John Adams of Massachusetts. Adams had been Vice-President under Washington, and he belonged to the Federalist Party. He continued Washington's policies and the United States refused to take sides in the war.

During Adams' term, trouble with France grew steadily. President Adams wanted to bring about friendlier relations. He sent three wise and experienced men to Paris: John Marshall, Charles Pinckney, and Elbridge Gerry. He told them to try to arrange a new treaty that would end the quarrel.

The XYZ Affair aroused American anger. When the three Americans reached France they were not permitted to meet any members of the French government. They had to wait a long time, as if they were strangers. At last they were told that three "agents" of the government would conduct the business. The agents informed them, first of all, that a treaty of any kind would cost "a great deal of money." The United States would have to offer a "gift" of $250,000 and then contribute 10 million dollars as a "loan" to France to help fight England.

The Americans were shocked, but they kept their heads. They asked the French agents to put their terms in writing. Then they came home and told President Adams.

The President laid the matter before Congress. He did not name the French agents, but referred to them as Mr. X, Mr. Y, and Mr. Z. For this reason the incident is known as the *XYZ Affair*.

When news of the XYZ Affair reached the people, the result was like an explosion. Americans were furious at the insult. "Millions for defense but not one cent for tribute" became the battle cry.

Congress voted to raise an army of 10,000 men. A Navy Department was organized; its first work was to fit out three warships. Their names, *Constitution, United States, Constellation*, are famous in naval history. Many swift merchant vessels were bought, armed, and sent out to

The *Constitution*, nicknamed "Old Ironsides," fought French warships in 1798.

fight against the French warships.

The nation was really at war with
France. But it was an "undeclared"
war. It is so called because the
Constitution [35] gives Congress the
power to declare war, and Congress
did not do so. For two years French
and American ships fought.

Adams won a settlement with France.
The President stayed calm in the
middle of the excitement. He was
determined to make peace. Like
Washington, he realized young
America could not stand the waste
and expense of a big war. So Adams
watched for a chance to get an agreement with France.

Meantime, the government of
France was changing rapidly. The
French Revolution came to an end.
A new leader, Napoleon, seized
power in 1799.

Napoleon was a soldier eager for
glory. He kept France at war with
Britain and other European nations
until he was finally defeated in 1815.
The period he was in power is known
as the *Napoleonic Era*, and the wars

he fought are the *Napoleonic Wars*.

Napoleon was too busy in Europe
to fight a war with the United States.
So he was almost as eager as President Adams to end the quarrel. He
agreed to receive an American representative with respect.

Once more President Adams sent
a group of men to France to get a
treaty. This time the attempt was a
success. In 1800 the United States
signed an agreement that ended the
"war" with France. It also ended
the old treaty of alliance and cleared
up the misunderstanding about
American neutrality in the war between France and Britain.

Thus Spain, Great Britain, and
France made treaties with the young
American nation. European countries were beginning to accept the
United States on something like
equal terms. It was a struggle, but
the American government slowly
won the respect of other nations.

**The Federalists lost, and Jefferson
won, in 1800.** Ending the undeclared
war with France did not make Adams
popular. He was a most unlucky
President. He did his best, but he
could not make friends or even get
along with his own party.

The struggle between the Federalist
Party and the Democratic Republicans grew more intense while Adams
was president. Jefferson and his
followers made savage attacks on
the Federalists. Many newspaper
editors were Democratic Republicans, so the newspapers were full of

criticisms of the Federalist Party.

The Federalists decided to stop such attacks. They got Congress to pass four laws that provided severe punishment for anyone who criticized the President or Congress. The laws were called the *Alien and Sedition* laws (ALE yen *and* suh DIH shun). They were bad laws, for they interfered with freedom of speech and freedom of the press.

In Virginia and Kentucky the state legislatures adopted a group of statements opposing the Alien and Sedition Laws. These statements were called the *Virginia and Kentucky Resolutions*. Thomas Jefferson wrote the Virginia Resolutions and James Madison wrote the Kentucky Resolutions. The Resolutions declared that under the Constitution Congress had no right to pass such laws. Therefore, the laws were unconstitutional and the states did not have to obey them.

The idea that states may decide whether or not a law is constitutional is called the *Doctrine of Nullification* (NUL ih fih KAY shun). It was stated for the first time in the Virginia and Kentucky Resolutions. You will hear more about nullification later, for it became involved in the dispute that led to the War Between the States (1861–1865).

The Federalists became very unpopular because of the Alien and Sedition laws. Americans would not stand for interference with their liberties. So the Federalist Party lost the election of 1800. John Adams went out of office after only one term as President. This defeat marked the beginning of the end for the Federalists. The party went out of existence fifteen years later.

The Democratic Republicans won the election of 1800 by a big majority. They were the party of the small farmers and workers. Jefferson, leader of the Democratic Republicans, became President.

Americans taught Tripoli a lesson. Jefferson was just as determined as the Federalists to make other nations treat Americans with respect. He soon had an opportunity to show the world that the United States would defend its right.

This time trouble arose far away in North Africa. At that time, there were four little nations on the coast

Napoleon (below) was too busy fighting Britain to fight America in 1800.

The United States fought a successful naval war with Tripoli. Hero of the war was Stephen Decatur who is shown boarding an enemy gunboat during an attack in 1804. With him is Midshipman Thomas MacDonough (left) who later became famous in the War of 1812.

of North Africa: Morocco (moh ROK oh), Tunis (TU nis), Algeria (AL JEER ih ah), and Tripoli (TRIP oh lih). They were called the Barbary (BAR buh ree) States, partly because they treated strangers in a barbarous, or cruel way.

The Barbary States claimed the Mediterranean as their private sea. Their warships seized any trading ship that dared to enter the Mediterranean without first paying them a bribe or tribute. This went on for years. Many ships were captured; their cargoes were stolen and their crews made prisoners. After each capture a message was sent to the prisoners'

home country, saying: "Either send a ransom in gold or your countrymen will be sold into slavery."

For many years the Barbary Pirates had been a terror to sailors. Britain, France, and Spain paid them a yearly tribute for the privilege of trading with Mediterranean countries. The Americans, of course, had to look out for themselves.

It happened while Jefferson was President that the ruler of Tripoli demanded a much larger tribute than usual from American trading ships. Jefferson was a man of peace, but this demand was too much for him. When he refused to ask the Congress

EARLY FOREIGN RELATIONS

to grant it, Tripoli declared war on the United States. In answer, Jefferson ordered four warships to the Mediterranean Sea.

The Tripolitan (trih POL ih tan) War, as it was called, lasted from 1801 to 1805. American sailors showed thrilling courage in the face of great odds. Stephen Decatur (de KAY ter) was one of the many heroes of this war.

One of the American ships, the *Philadelphia*, was captured during a storm and taken into the harbor at Tripoli. That night Decatur and a picked group of men took a small boat and slipped into the harbor. There they set fire to the *Philadelphia*. In spite of fierce fire from enemy guns, they escaped without losing a man. British Admiral Nelson called this venture "the most bold and daring act of the age." As a reward, Decatur was made a captain although he was only twenty-five years old.

The American ships set up a *blockade* to Tripoli — that is, they kept ships of all nations from entering or leaving the harbor. When food and other supplies began to be scarce, the ruler of Tripoli gave in. He agreed to make a treaty of peace favorable to the United States.

Tripoli had learned a lesson. But the other Barbary States still demanded tribute from the United States. Finally, several years later, America sent Captain Decatur with ten ships to stop Algeria from seizing American sailors. In one month's fighting, Decatur captured two warships and sailed into the harbor of Algiers. He forced the ruler to sign a treaty promising to stop interfering with American commerce. Decatur also won the release of all American prisoners. There was no more trouble with the Barbary States.

The picture below shows the burning of the American frigate *Philadelphia* in 1804. The ship had run aground and had been captured in Tripoli harbor. Young Stephen Decatur and his men secretly got aboard, set fire to the ship, and escaped.

CHAPTER SUMMARY

America had many problems after the Revolution. Spain refused to let Americans use the Mississippi River; Britain refused to get out of the Northwest forts; France expected help in her war against Britain. The Pinckney Treaty, in 1795, improved relations with Spain. Americans gained the right to use the Mississippi and the "right of deposit." The Jay Treaty, in 1795, got the British out of the Northwest forts.

The French disliked the Jay Treaty. They began to seize American ships. The XYZ Affair further aroused American anger. An "undeclared war" broke out between France and America.

Washington retired at the end of his second term. John Adams, a Federalist, was chosen President in 1796. But the Federalists became unpopular after passing the Alien and Sedition Laws interfering with freedom of speech and press. They lost the election of 1800 to Jefferson who continued the policy of neutrality in European affairs.

When Jefferson was President, America fought Tripoli. America refused to pay the tax that the Barbary States demanded for use of the Mediterranean Sea. The United States won a favorable treaty.

The Language of History

Be sure you understand the meaning of each of the following.

1. foreign relations	**4.** treaty	**7.** Napoleonic Era
2. right of deposit	**5.** neutral	**8.** nullification
3. Farewell Address	**6.** impressment	**9.** recall

What Happened When

What important events occurred on each of the following dates?

1. 1793   **2.** 1795   **3.** 1796   **4.** 1800

Who's Who in History

Make sure you know the part each of the following played in the foreign relations of the new republic.

1. Thomas Pinckney
2. Edmond Charles Genêt
3. John Jay
4. John Adams
5. Napoleon
6. Stephen Decatur

Study Questions

1. **a.** Why was the right to transport goods down the Mississippi River so important to the settlers on the frontier?
   b. By what treaty did Americans gain the right to use the Mississippi River and unload goods at New Orleans?

2. State three grievances the United States had against Great Britain in Washington's administration.

3. **a.** Why was the Jay Treaty unpopular?
   b. What did it accomplish?

4. Why did Washington issue his Neutrality Proclamation of 1793?

5. What mistakes did Genêt make?

6. What did Washington advise in his Farewell Address?

7. What was the XYZ Affair?

8. How did President Adams finally settle the quarrel with France?

9. **a.** Why were the Alien and Sedition Laws a threat to democracy?
   b. What idea or doctrine was set forth in the Virginia and Kentucky Resolutions?

10. What was the cause of the Tripolitan War?

11. What did the United States gain by fighting the Barbary States?

Chapter 13

"At about half past six o'clock in the evening, after the firing had ceased, I went on deck, and there beheld a scene which it would be difficult to describe: all the *Guerrière's* masts were shot away, and as she had no sails to steady her, she lay rolling like a log in the trough of the sea. Many of the men were employed in throwing the dead overboard. The decks were covered with blood. . . . Several of the guns got loose and were surging to and fro from one side to the other."

Thus an eye-witness described the British warship *Guerrière* after its losing battle with the American ship *Constitution* in the War of 1812.

The War of 1812 is sometimes called "the fight for a free sea." What events led to America's second war with Great Britain? How could the tiny American Navy administer such a defeat to the British who boasted they ruled the waves?

This chapter tells the story of the War of 1812. As you read it try to measure its true significance and its influence on later American history.

Jefferson wanted to buy New Orleans. Under Washington and Adams the United States made steady progress in foreign relations. But serious problems did not disappear overnight. Jefferson struggled with most of the same difficulties earlier Presidents faced.

There was the question of American rights on the Mississippi River. Spain owned the Louisiana Territory, which included the west bank of the river and New Orleans. Westerners feared the possibility that Spain might forbid them to use the river. Thanks partly to luck and partly to the ability of his representatives to act quickly and decisively, Jefferson was able to end this problem forever. Here is how it happened:

Early in his administration Jefferson heard startling news. Napoleon, the strong man of France, had persuaded Spain to sign a secret agreement giving Louisiana to France. Jefferson was alarmed. He did not want New Orleans in French control.

Americans would find it much harder to deal with Napoleon than with Spanish officials. The future looked dark. France would probably try to close the Mississippi to Americans forever.

To avoid such a possibility, Jefferson decided on a bold plan: the United States would try to buy New Orleans and the mouth of the Mississippi River. He sent James Monroe to Paris to help Robert Livingston, the American minister in France, to arrange the purchase.

The United States bought the Louisiana Territory. When the Americans made their offer, they had a pleasant surprise. Napoleon was willing to sell not only New Orleans but the whole Louisiana Territory! But he asked $15,000,000. It was all or nothing. They must buy an empire to get a city.

Why was Napoleon willing to sell such a valuable territory? He needed money to launch a new attack on England. A second reason was his fear that the British navy might soon seize Louisiana; he thought it best to sell the region while he could. A third reason was that Napoleon had become discouraged with colonies. In Haiti, the French colony in the West Indies, a bloody rebellion had cost the lives of thousands of French soldiers.

James Monroe (below) went to Paris to help arrange the purchase of New Orleans.

THOMAS JEFFERSON (1743–1826)

When the German scientist, Baron Humboldt, called at the White House he noticed a newspaper that was always full of poisonous abuse of President Jefferson.

"Why are these lies allowed?" demanded the Baron. "Why do you not have the editor fined and imprisoned?"

Jefferson said, smiling: "Put that paper in your pocket, Baron, and if you ever hear anyone question the reality of our liberty or the freedom of our press, show this paper and tell where you found it."

Thomas Jefferson really believed in freedom, even when it hurt him personally. Tall, awkward, carelessly dressed, and informal in manner, he impressed some people as lacking in dignity. Nevertheless, he was a true Virginia gentleman and one of the most scholarly of American presidents.

In Jefferson's administration Louisiana was purchased and explored, and the Tripolitan War was fought and won. However, Jefferson would probably prefer to be remembered for his insistence on simplicity and economy in the government.

The Americans hesitated. They had no authority to spend so much money (Jefferson had authorized them to spend no more than $10,000,000). They could not consult with Jefferson, for in those days there were no cables or telephones. But the situation demanded immediate action. They drew a deep breath and signed an agreement to buy Louisiana for $15,000,000. The year was 1803.

The Louisiana Purchase was the greatest real estate bargain in history: 828,000 square miles at about three cents an acre! The region was enormously rich in natural resources. It was so big no one knew just where the exact boundaries were. It was as large as the original area of the United States. As the map on this page shows, the Louisiana Purchase extended from the Mississippi River to the Rocky Mountains and from Canada to the Gulf of Mexico.

Thus in one giant step the United States doubled its territory. The American flag was raised over the Mississippi Valley and the city of New Orleans. The Louisiana Purchase made it practically certain that the United States would one day become one of the world's great powers.

Britain and France continued to interfere with American trade. The Louisiana Purchase was the big achievement of Jefferson's administration. In other fields progress was slow and problems were many. The war in Europe dragged on. The British and the French continued to seize American ships; the British kept on impressing American sailors.

The map below shows the Louisiana Territory which Jefferson purchased from France in 1803. It doubled the area of the United States and gave the nation control of the Mississippi.

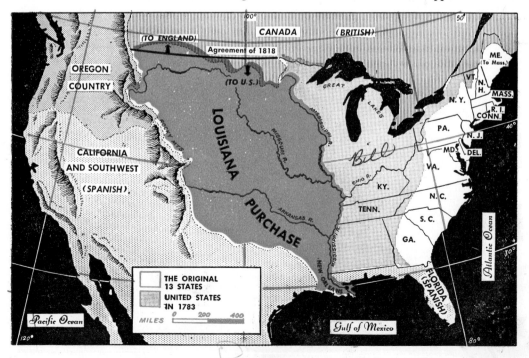

The British were willing to have American ships bring supplies to their ports, but they did not want Americans to trade with France. The French, on the other hand, were glad to get American products, but they wanted to stop American ships from going to Britain. So both British and the French seized American ships, and with every captured ship a valuable cargo was lost.

France and Britain dared to treat Americans in this way because the United States was still weak and lacked military strength. Like Washington, Jefferson knew that the country needed years of peace in order to grow strong.

Jefferson knew that France and Great Britain needed America's trade. So he decided upon a plan: if Americans suddenly stopped bringing any goods, Europe would soon feel the loss. By cutting off supplies, United States would make Britain and France realize how important American trade was to them. Then, Jefferson hoped, they would stop interfering with American trade.

To carry out his plan, Jefferson persuaded Congress to pass the *Embargo Act* of 1807. (An embargo is a government announcement that forbids ships to enter or leave its ports.) This law forbade American ships to leave for foreign ports. It practically stopped foreign commerce for more than a year.

The Embargo Act was a failure. The Embargo did much harm — to the United States. American sailors were thrown out of work. American ships lay idle in the harbors. Cargoes rotted on the docks. Farmers found they could sell only a small part of their grain or cotton. Hard times came back to American homes.

To Jefferson's disappointment, the Embargo had little effect on France or Britain. They were able to get food and supplies in other ways. If the Embargo had continued for years it might have caused shortages in

American shipping suffered because of the Embargo Act passed in 1807. Many sailors like the one in the picture below were thrown out of work, while ships stood idle.

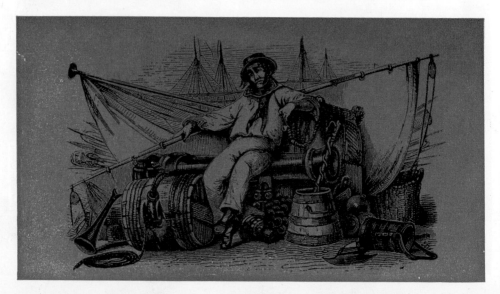

Britain and France; but United States could not wait. The American people demanded an end to the Embargo. It was *repealed*, or withdrawn, just before Jefferson left office.

In spite of the failure of the Embargo, Jefferson remained popular. He served a second term, then decided to retire. His successor was his friend, James Madison. Madison had helped write the Constitution and had served as Secretary of State under Jefferson.

The "War Hawks" wanted action.

When Madison became President in 1809 he tried to follow Jefferson's peace policy. But Americans were tired of insults. Bitterness against Britain increased steadily, for the British were interfering again with American trade.

The French interfered with American trade, too. But people did not feel so angry at France, for France had helped win American independence. And the French did not make a practice of impressing sailors.

So the nation slowly drifted toward war with Great Britain. Older Americans had bitter memories of British injustice during and after the Revolution. And the younger people were eager for a fight. They blamed British leaders in Canada for stirring up Indian trouble on the frontier and they thought the time had come for a showdown.

In Congress a group of energetic young men kept shouting for war. Most of them were from the frontier

Henry Clay of Kentucky was one of the "War Hawks" who demanded war with Great Britain from 1810 to 1812.

districts. They were nicknamed "War Hawks." Prominent among the War Hawks were Henry Clay of Kentucky and John C. Calhoun of South Carolina.

The War Hawks felt that Canada should belong to the United States. Why not seize Canada right away while Britain's armies and ships were fighting Napoleon? They also had their eyes on Florida, hoping to grab that region at the first opportunity. The War Hawks had no sympathy for the cautious policies of Washington and Jefferson.

In 1811, when the Indians went on the warpath in Indiana Territory, Americans exclaimed: "The British are in back of it!" And to some extent they were right. The governor of Canada and British fur traders were encouraging Indians to revolt.

The leader of this uprising was

Tecumseh (top) led an Indian uprising that was crushed by General William Henry Harrison at the Battle of Tippecanoe (above).

a great Indian named Tecumseh (tee KUM sa). He and his brother, who was called "The Prophet," were trying to unite the tribes against the white man's invasion.

The Governor of Indiana Territory, General William Henry Harrison, finally defeated Tecumseh and his followers at the Battle of Tippecanoe (TIP uh kuh NOO). But the Indians were not permanently conquered. People on the frontier felt there would never be peace with the Indians until the British were driven from Canada.

However, the chief cause of the second war with Britain was interference with American trade. Strangely enough, the British were preparing to end their policy of seizing neutral ships when Congress declared war in June, 1812. If radio communication had existed, there might have been no war, for people on both sides of the Atlantic would have been better informed.

The United States entered the War of 1812 with many handicaps. In spite of the loud talk of the War Hawks, the United States was not united in support of war. Eastern merchants were making money from trade with Europe, even though the British seized many ships. War with England would stop all American trade and end profits until the fighting was over. Partly for this reason, the war was unpopular in the East.

The United States was not really prepared for war. The army was small and badly organized. Most of the officers were men who had fought in the Revolution. Many were now old and uncertain. Other officers were young and inexperienced. Guns and various war supplies were scarce and poor in quality. The government lacked money to carry on a war.

How could the United States defend itself under such conditions? There were certain factors in the nation's favor. Great Britain was

240

fighting Napoleon and could not give full attention to war with the United States. Then, too, Americans were fighting on their own ground. They knew the country, which is a great advantage in war. And the American navy was in fine condition. It consisted of only sixteen sea-going boats, but officers and men were efficient and well-trained.

There were victories at sea and disasters on the frontier. Soon after war was declared, American sailors showed their skill in a head-on clash with a British warship. On August 19, 1812, an American warship, the *Constitution*, fought the British *Guerriere* (gare YARE). Within half an hour the British ship was sunk.

A few months later the *Constitution* destroyed a British warship off the coast of Brazil. After this battle the *Constitution* was nicknamed "Old Ironsides" because of her ability to resist the enemy's guns. The naval victories gave new courage to the American people who were deeply worried by the army's failures.

The war on land went badly from the start. Henry Clay and other leaders talked of "winning the war in six weeks" but it did not work out that way. They hoped to seize Canada before British troops could cross the Atlantic to defend it. So three small armies were hastily assembled. The plan was to invade Canada at three different points. One army would march down the old war road, along Lake Champlain, to Montreal. Another would cross into Canada by way of the Niagara River, a few miles from Niagara Falls. The third would attack Canada from Detroit.

All three attacks failed. The worst blow came when the army at Detroit surrendered without firing a shot. The whole Michigan Territory fell into British hands. Too late, the War Hawks learned that a successful invasion requires well-trained armies and careful, expensive preparations.

The picture below shows the victory of the *Constitution* ("Old Ironsides") in her battle with the British warship, *Guerrière*, August 19, 1812 near Nova Scotia.

When Tecumseh and his Indian followers saw how weak American military force was, they joined the British and went on the war path. They captured a fort where Chicago now stands and scalped every one of its defenders. General Harrison, who had defeated the Indians at Tippecanoe, now assembled a new army in the West. He set out to recapture Detroit. But he made little progress against the combined forces of the British and Indians. It looked as if the British might capture the Northwest and make it a British province.

Perry won a victory on Lake Erie in 1813. British hopes were shattered, however, by an unexpected defeat on Lake Erie. To attack the Northwest, the British had to bring supplies from Canada across Lake Erie. So control of the lake was essential. The British did not worry about that, for they had six warships to guard their supply line. The Americans had only a few gunboats.

But out of sight of the British, in a hidden harbor on Lake Erie, a young American naval officer, Oliver Hazard Perry, was building a fleet of ships. He kept his ship builders working like beavers. They cut down trees along the shore for timbers and planking. Sails, ropes, and guns for the ships were brought from Philadelphia, hundreds of miles away.

When the boats were ready Perry sailed boldly out on the lake. The

British rubbed their eyes in amazement. Perry had ten strongly-built ships that carried a total of fifty-five guns. He attacked the British at Put-in-Bay, near the western end of the lake. The Battle of Lake Erie lasted more than three hours.

The air was still heavy with powder smoke when Perry reported to General Harrison. "We have met the enemy and they are ours!" He had captured the whole squadron: two ships, two brigs, one schooner, and one sloop. In the history of the British navy it was the only squadron that ever surrendered.

British invasions were beaten back. Loss of the battle on Lake Erie spelled disaster for the invading British army. To escape capture or starvation, the commander ordered a retreat. On reaching Detroit, he blew up the fort, burned his supplies, and crossed to Canada. Close at his heels came General Harrison with his frontiersmen. The two forces met in the battle of Thames (TEMZ) River, north of Lake Erie. The British lost. Tecumseh was killed and his warriors were scattered. The threat to the Northwest was ended.

However, war continued farther east. In 1813, Americans invaded Upper Canada and burned many public buildings in its capital city, Toronto (or York, as it was then called). Fighting raged back and forth across the strip of land between Lake Erie and Lake Ontario. Buffalo was burned. Near Niagara Falls there were battles at Chippewa and Lundy's Lane. The American invaders were driven back. Neither side was able to hold territory.

British forces were growing stronger. Napoleon had been overthrown and the war in Europe was almost over. Great Britain now sent thousands of soldiers from Europe to defend Canada. In 1814 British commanders planned to invade northeastern New York and push south by way of Lake Champlain. Once again the old war road was to become a battlefield.

A young American naval officer, Thomas MacDonough (mack DAHN uh) spoiled British plans. MacDonough had served under Stephen Decatur in the Tripolitan War and knew how to surprise an enemy. In 1814, he was in command of a tiny fleet on Lake Champlain.

The British had to get control of Lake Champlain to protect and supply their army as it marched south. British warships attacked MacDonough's fleet near Plattsburg on September 11, 1814. They expected to sink the Americans in a few minutes, but the battle lasted for over two hours.

By superior skill and planning, MacDonough seized or destroyed four large British ships. It was a complete disaster for the British. Their army had to retreat to Canada. The British commander went home in disgrace. Once again the navy had saved American territory from invasion.

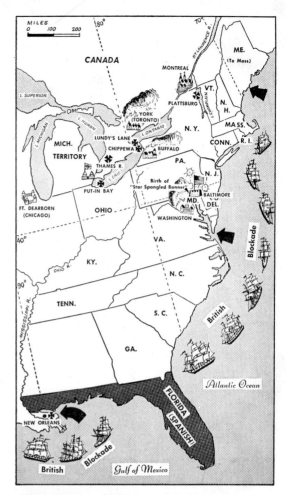

This map shows the most important battles and campaigns of the War of 1812.

The British burned Washington. Unfortunately, the navy could not be everywhere at once. A handful of ships could not protect thousands of miles of coastline. The British had hundreds of warships and they soon drove American warships off the oceans. Then the way was open for attacks on the American coast.

A British expedition attacked and captured the coast of Maine (then part of Massachusetts). Another

British army landed in Maryland in 1814 and marched on Washington. They burned the Capitol and the White House — in revenge, they said, for the burning of Toronto. Then they sailed away, while the people of Washington drifted back to look at the wreckage.

The same invaders planned to capture Baltimore, but the city put up a stubborn defense. Maryland troops drove off a landing party. For thirty hours the British fleet attacked Fort McHenry in Baltimore Harbor.

An American named Francis Scott Key was held prisoner on a British ship during the attack on Baltimore. All night he watched the shore. In the morning he was overjoyed to see the American flag still flying over the fort. The experience inspired him to write the words of *The Star Spangled Banner*. Set to an old tune, his verses have since become the national *anthem*, or patriotic song.

The British sailed away from Maryland, but a few months later they prepared another invasion. This time they tried to invade the Southwest. They planned to seize New Orleans and get control of the Mississippi River. They landed more than seven thousand trained soldiers near New Orleans. Over fifty British warships protected the landing.

Andrew Jackson won the Battle of New Orleans. The American commander in the New Orleans area was a frontiersman named Andrew Jackson. As a boy he fought in the Revolution and was taken prisoner.

The picture below shows a scene from the Battle of Plattsburg on Lake Champlain where Thomas MacDonough won a great naval victory for the United States in 1814.

The Battle Of New Orleans

Here is a scene from the Battle of New Orleans, January 8, 1815. Andrew Jackson (right) won a great victory against the British and as a result became a great national hero.

At that time, a British officer ordered him to black his boots. When the boy refused the officer struck him with a sword, cutting his arm to the bone. Andrew Jackson never lost the scar of that blow and he never stopped hating the British.

When war broke out in 1812 Jackson was living on the Tennessee frontier. He became the commander of a frontier regiment. "He's tough," said one of his men. "Tough as Hickory," agreed another man; from then on, Jackson was "Old Hickory."

Jackson and his men won several battles in the Southwest. President Madison was so pleased to find a man who could win that he put him in charge of the defense of New Orleans. In one month Jackson built trenches and set up guns.

When the British attacked on January 8, 1815, Jackson and his men were ready. Columns of the finest British troops — soldiers who had defeated Napoleon — marched into the deadly fire of the frontiersmen. It was a complete defeat for the British. They lost their three top officers. More than two thousand British soldiers were killed or wounded. Only thirteen Americans were killed.

The Battle of New Orleans was the greatest land victory of the war. It made Jackson a national hero. For Americans, the war seemed to end in a blaze of glory. Actually, the battle had no effect on the outcome. Two weeks before, on December 24, 1814, American and British representatives had signed a peace treaty at Ghent (GENT) in Belgium. Weeks after the Battle of New Orleans, sailing ships brought the news to America.

The second war for independence brought lasting peace with Britain. The Treaty of Ghent simply said fighting was to stop. Neither Britain nor the United States lost any territory. The treaty said nothing about neutral rights or impressments, the chief causes of the war. Reading between the lines, it is clear that both nations were tired of war. Many people on both sides now realized that the war never should have begun.

However, the War of 1812 had many good results. Americans felt an increased love for their country. They lost interest in European quarrels and concentrated on developing the United States. They became *nationalistic* or devoted to the whole nation instead of just their own section. Manufacturing grew rapidly during the war, when it was impossible to get goods from Europe. After the war, factories and industries continued to expand.

Strangely enough, the war improved relations between America and Britain. Each learned to respect the other's fighting ability. The British never again tried to treat the United States without respect.

Three years after the war, both governments agreed there should be no warships on the Great Lakes. Later the idea was extended to the land boundary between the United States and Canada. As a result, there are no troops or warships on the northern border of the United States today. This sensible arrangement has saved much expense.

Spain and Russia had designs on the Americas. The United States steadily grew stronger as the years went by. Americans demanded and after a while got respectful treatment from foreign nations.

Some years after the War of 1812 the United States proclaimed a new foreign policy. It was the *Monroe Doctrine*, which President James Monroe announced in 1823.

The Monroe Doctrine warned other nations not to interfere in North and South America. Why did President Monroe feel it necessary to issue such a warning? The answer lies in certain events in Europe during and after the Napoleonic Wars.

The American Revolution had inspired some people in Central and South America to fight for freedom. About 1806, a series of revolutions began that slowly won independence for most of Spain's American colonies. The Napoleonic Wars in Europe helped, because they kept Spain too busy to take strong action against her rebellious colonies.

But when the Napoleonic Wars were over, Spanish leaders wanted to regain control of Central and South America. They tried to get other European countries to help them. Spain belonged to an alliance that aimed to crush democracy.

France, Austria, Prussia, and Russia were members of this alliance. For a time it looked as if they might send an army to South America to overthrow the new governments. The United States was alarmed at the idea. If European powers could overthrow freedom in South America, they might soon attack United States.

At about the same time Russia

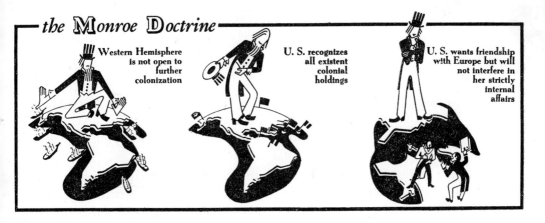

the Monroe Doctrine

Western Hemisphere is not open to further colonization

U. S. recognizes all existent colonial holdings

U. S. wants friendship with Europe but will not interfere in her strictly internal affairs

was trying to get control of the west coast of North America. The United States did not want Russia or any other European nation claiming new territory in the Americas.

President Monroe issued a warning. President Monroe talked the matter over with his Secretary of State, John Quincy Adams. Together they wrote a few short, clear paragraphs that have come to be known as the Monroe Doctrine.

In his message to Congress in 1823, President Monroe declared that: (1) the American continents would no longer be considered open to future colonization by any European powers; (2) the United States would consider any attempt by European powers to interfere in the affairs of independent American nations as "dangerous to our peace and safety"; (3) the United States would not interfere with existing European colonies in the Americas.

The Monroe Doctrine became a great foreign policy. What did the great powers of Europe think of such plain

talk from the head of a young nation? Strange as it seems, Great Britain agreed with Monroe. She did not want Spain to regain her colonies because British merchants had built up a profitable trade with Central and South America. If Spain won back her colonies she would forbid them to trade with Britain.

So the British gave full support to the principles of the Monroe Doctrine. Spain, Russia, and other European nations had no wish to fight United States and Great Britain. So Spain did not regain her colonies and Russia withdrew from the west coast.

The Monroe Doctrine became an important American foreign policy. In recent years Canada and the republics of Central and South America have joined United States in upholding its principles.

"OH, SAY CAN YOU SEE . . . ."

CHAPTER SUMMARY

Jefferson bought the Louisiana Territory in 1803 for $15,000,000. Congress passed the Embargo Act of 1807 stopping trade with Britain and France. It was a failure. Jefferson retired after two terms. Madison, the fourth President, tried to continue the policy of peace, but the "War Hawks," led by Clay and Calhoun, demanded action.

The United States went to war with Britain in 1812. The causes were: (1) British interference with American trade, (2) British encouragement of Indian attacks in the Northwest Territory, (3) American desire to gain territory in Canada and the Southwest.

The War of 1812 was disappointing. Early campaigns failed, but the Navy won victories at the Battles of Lake Erie and Plattsburg. Heroes of the war were Oliver Hazard Perry, General William Henry Harrison, Captain Thomas MacDonough, and Andrew Jackson. Francis Scott Key wrote the words to the *Star Spangled Banner* during the British attack on Baltimore. The peace treaty was signed at Ghent in 1814.

The Monroe Doctrine was proclaimed in 1823. The fifth President, James Monroe, warned other nations not to interfere in the Americas.

The Language of History

Be sure you understand the meaning of the following words and phrases as they are used in this chapter.

1. Louisiana Purchase   3. embargo   5. repeal
2. nationalistic   4. War Hawks   6. anthem

What Happened When

Connect each of the following dates with important events in American history.

1. 1803   2. 1807   3. 1812   4. 1814   5. 1815   6. 1823

Who's Who in History

HALL OF FAME

Make sure you know the part each of the following played in the events described in this chapter.

1. Robert Livingston
2. Thomas Jefferson
3. John Quincy Adams
4. Francis Scott Key
5. Henry Clay
6. James Monroe
7. Tecumseh
8. James Madison
9. Oliver Hazard Perry
10. John C. Calhoun
11. William Henry Harrison
12. Andrew Jackson

Study Questions

1. **a.** Give the boundaries of the Louisiana Territory.
   b. How much was paid for it?

2. **a.** What did the Embargo Act forbid?
   b. Why was the Act a failure?

3. State three causes of the War of 1812.

4. Locate each of the following places and tell what happened there during the War of 1812:
   a. Detroit
   b. Put-in-Bay
   c. Ghent
   d. Plattsburg
   e. Lundy's Lane
   f. New Orleans
   g. Fort McHenry
   h. Washington, D.C.
   i. Toronto or York

5. **a.** Why did American attempts to invade Canada fail?
   b. Name three naval victories of the War of 1812.

6. Why did the British burn Washington?

7. Describe the circumstances under which the *Star Spangled Banner* was written.

8. **a.** What did the Treaty of Ghent say?
   b. What two important disputes were not mentioned in the treaty?

9. State three results of the War of 1812.

10. **a.** What dangers caused President Monroe to announce the Monroe Doctrine?
    b. State three provisions of the Monroe Doctrine.
    c. When was the Monroe Doctrine announced?

LET'S LOOK AT WHAT WE'VE LEARNED

What were the chief achievements of Washington and his advisers?

They organized the federal government as outlined in the Constitution. They put the country on a sound financial basis. They put down the Whisky Rebellion and crushed an Indian uprising. They improved relations with Spain and Great Britain.

What were the main points of Hamilton's financial program?

1. He made arrangements to pay the national debt. 2. He persuaded Congress to let the national government take over the state debts. 3. He raised revenue by means of a tariff and an excise tax on liquor. 4. He persuaded Congress to establish the Bank of the United States.

Why and when were political parties organized in the United States?

Supporters of Hamilton's financial program helped put it into practice. They were chiefly businessmen, large landowners, and successful lawyers. They were called Federalists.

Thomas Jefferson and his friends disliked Hamilton's ideas. They opposed the Bank of the United States. After the establishment of the bank in 1793 they formed a political party called the Democratic-Republicans. They were chiefly small farmers and working people.

What foreign policy did Washington favor?

He wanted the United States to keep out of European quarrels. His Farewell Address advised America to avoid permanent foreign alliances.

Why did Jefferson win the election of 1800?

The Federalist Party was disliked by the common people. It had passed the Alien and Sedition Laws interfering with freedom of speech and press. Jefferson was popular for his democratic ideas, so he won.

What were the main achievements of Jefferson's administration?

He purchased the Louisiana Territory from France in 1803 for $15,000,000. Jefferson also stopped Tripoli from interfering with American commerce in the Mediterranean. But he could not stop Britain and France from interfering with American trade, although he avoided war.

Why did the United States go to war with Great Britain in 1812?

1. The British were seizing American ships and impressing sailors. 2. In the West, British agents were believed to be stirring up Indians. 3. Many people felt bitter about things that happened in the Revolution.

4. Many westerners wanted a chance to seize Canada and Florida.

What were the results of the War of 1812?

The United States did not lose any of its territory. Americans lost interest in Europe and concentrated on developing their own country. During the war, American manufacturing made great progress because people could not buy English goods. Relations with Britain and Canada improved after the war.

Why and when was the Monroe Doctrine announced and what did it say?

It was in a message President Monroe sent Congress in 1823 to combat the danger of Spain's attempt to regain her Latin American colonies. Russia also was threatening expansion in the West. President Monroe told other nations: (1) Do not try to establish new colonies in North, Central or South America; (2) the United States will not interfere with colonies already established; (3) if foreign nations try to overthrow independent Latin American republics, the United States will fight.

Connecting the Past with the Present . . .

You probably know the expression "sound as a dollar." Everybody knows what it means. The American dollar is a standard of value almost everywhere. In some of the most remote parts of the world you can win quick attention and respect by displaying an American bill.

It was not always so. In the time of the Revolution and for many years afterward American money was definitely not in demand. People preferred British or French or Spanish currency. No one knew for certain just how much an American bill was worth, if anything. The money issued by the Continental Congress had so little value that a barber papered his shop with it, and "not worth a continental" became a common saying people used when they wished to express contempt.

All that was changed in Washington's first administration, thanks largely to Alexander Hamilton. By means of his four point financial program he put the American nation on a sound financial basis where it has remained ever since.

Thus it is largely because of the concentrated efforts of Washington and his advisers that American money became a valuable medium of exchange and one of which all Americans can be justly proud.

Questions for Discussion and Review

1. Explain the part the electoral college plays in electing a President of the United States.

2. What is the President's Cabinet?

3. Give the provisions of (a) the Neutrality Proclamation of 1793 and (b) the Monroe Doctrine.

4. How did the battle cry "millions for defense but not one cent for tribute" spring from the XYZ Affair?

5. Why is the Louisiana Purchase called "the greatest real-estate bargain in history"?

6. What American rights were endangered by the Alien and Sedition Laws?

7. Why was the *USS Constitution* called "Old Ironsides"?

8. What naval battle ended the British invasion of the Northwest?

9. How was an invasion of the United States by way of the Lake Champlain-Hudson River route stopped?

10. What battle was fought after the war had been over for two weeks? Who was the American leader?

11. List four results of the War of 1812.

THE HISTORY LABORATORY

Here are suggestions for activities that you will find interesting and profitable in connection with your study of this Unit.

Be a Real Estate Expert . . .

Compare present property values with the price paid for Louisiana. Start with the value of local buildings. These you can find by con-

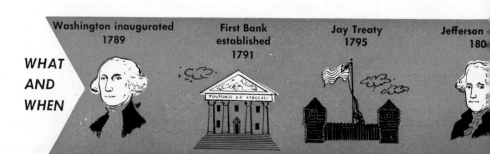

WHAT
AND
WHEN

Washington inaugurated
1789

First Bank
established
1791

Jay Treaty
1795

Jefferson
180

sulting real estate agents, bank officials, or local government officials. For other comparisons find the cost of airplanes, battleships, or manufacturing plants. Another project would be to investigate old real estate values in your locality, as far back as 1803, if possible.

Write a Letter . . .

Imagine you are a government official during Washington's administrations and that your brother is in the Northwest Territory. Write him a letter describing Washington's inauguration; then write another letter dated eight years later, discussing what Washington said in his Farewell Address.

Prepare an Exhibit . . .

Show how the British fleet blockaded France during the Napoleonic Wars and kept American ships from delivering their cargoes. Suggestion: Use flour, salt, and water to make a map of France; make miniature boats and place them on the exhibit to show the positions of British and American ships. Color the map and label the seaports.

Spread Propaganda . . .

Pretend you are one of the "War Hawks." Prepare handbills, cartoons, and posters to arouse the country against Great Britain.

For Those who Like to Write . . .

1. Write short biographies of the first six Presidents of the United States. If possible attach pictures of each. For information, consult an encyclopedia or James Morgan's *Our Presidents* (Macmillan 1949).

2. Prepare a radio-TV script telling the story of the pirate, Jean Lafitte, who helped Andrew Jackson defeat the British at New Orleans. For information consult *Black Falcon* by Sperry (Winston, 1949) or

olitan War
801-05
Embargo Act passed
1807
War of 1812
1812-15
Monroe Doctrine
1823

Pirate Lafitte and the Battle of New Orleans by Tallant (Random, 1951).

3. Write a play based on these facts: British forces burn Washington, D.C. and attack Baltimore. A stout defense routs the enemy and inspires Francis Scott Key to write "The Star Spangled Banner."

4. Imagine you are a newspaper reporter who interviewed Dolly Madison. Write a feature article on this First Lady of the land, how she felt and what she did when her home, the White House, was burned. Consult *Glamorous Dolly Madison* by Desmond (Dodd, 1946).

Prepare an Oral Report . . .

Give a talk describing life in the young American Navy during the War of 1812. For information see Ralph Paine's *Fight for a Free Sea* (Yale University Press, 1921). You might illustrate your talk with drawings or pictures of ships, weapons, and uniforms.

Build a Ship . . .

Make a model of "Old Ironsides" or another famous ship of this period. It can be made of wood, metal, or soap. For pictures of famous ships look in the encyclopedia and in Leeming's *Brave Ships of England and America* (Nelson, 1941).

Let's Read about the Early Days of the American Republic

*COBB, BERTHA B. and COBB, ERNEST, *Adam Lee*, Putnam, 1938.
CRAWFORD, PHYLLIS, *"Hello, the Boat!"* Holt, 1938.
DuSOE, ROBERT C., *Your Orders, Sir*, Longmans, 1953.
HINTERNHOFF, JOHN, *Barry's Boys*, Holt, 1952.
HUNGERFORD, E. B., *Fighting Frigate*, Wilcox, 1947.
LOWE, CORINNE B., *Knight of the Sea*, Harcourt, 1941.
MEADER, STEPHEN, *Down the Big River*, Harcourt, 1924.
*MEIGS, CORNELIA, *Wind in the Chimney*, Macmillan, 1934.
NOLAN, JEANNETTE C., *Andrew Jackson*, Messner, 1949.
**PAINE, RALPH D., *Fight for a Free Sea*, Yale University Press, 1921.
PARKS, E. W., *Little Long Rifle*, Bobbs Merrill, 1949.
SPERRY, ARMSTRONG, *Danger to Windward*, Winston, 1947.
SUTTON, MARGARET, *Jemima, Daughter of Daniel Boone*, Scribner, 1942.
WEIL, ANN, *My Dear Patsy*, Bobbs, 1941.
WILSON, HAZEL, *The Story of Mad Anthony Wayne*, Grossett, 1953.

* indicates easy reading   ** indicates advanced reading

Unit 6

THE UNITED STATES EXPANDED
TO THE PACIFIC (1783-1853)

"OLD AMERICA seems to be breaking up and moving westward," reported a British traveler in 1817. From every one of the original states families set out to find new homes in the wilderness. On every road to the frontier thousands of wagons rolled westward.

"Wa-a-a-gons, *ho!*" With this call in their ears Americans were packing up and setting out for unknown places. What hopes drove them onward? How did people feel as they turned their backs on their old homes and followed the wagon tracks that led to Kentucky or Ohio or Oregon?

In this Unit you will read the story of the Westward Movement and the great waves of settlement that carried the frontier to the Pacific Coast. As you read it keep in mind why Americans felt the urge to move and the main routes they traveled. You will see the United States acquiring land and expanding to the shores of the Pacific; and you will discover the leaders of the Westward Movement.

255

Chapter 14

RESTLESS PIONEERS PUSHED THE FRONTIER WESTWARD

"THIS is the country for a man to enjoy himself," a young Englishman wrote his brother in 1818. He went on to say that in America, "you may see prairie sixty miles long and ten broad at two dollars an acre that will produce seventy to one hundred bushels of Indian corn per acre. . . ."

The young Englishman did not write anything about the severe hardships and suffering connected with the settlement of the West. Instead, he wrote with enthusiasm: "If you knew the difference between this country and England you would need no persuading to come hither. The poorest families [enjoy] beef, fowls, pies, eggs, pickles, tea, coffee, and good bread. . . . Is it so in England?"

With letters like this going back to England, more and more settlers were coming to America. In America, families were on the move, too, heading West. What kind of roads did they have to follow? Who blazed the trails?

As you read this chapter try to get a clear picture of the pioneers who went West. Where did they come from? Why did they leave their old homes? What kind of vehicles did they use? What routes did they choose? Who were their leaders?

Americans kept moving west. Strange as it seems, many Americans paid little attention to the War of 1812. They were the Americans who were heading west. They had turned their backs on Europe and plunged into the wilderness. Year by year pioneers pushed the *frontier*, or edge of civilization, farther west.

The *westward movement* is one of the key facts of American history. Jamestown and Plymouth Colony were founded by people who moved west from Europe. Later, most of their sons and daughters moved inland. From colonial times on, each generation had a desire to travel west. They wanted to see "the other side of the mountain" or find out what the world looked like across the river.

The edge of settlement did not move west in a straight line, of course. Sometimes people simply hurried through the wilderness and started a settlement hundreds of miles away from the old frontier. For instance, California and Oregon were settled long before the Rocky Mountain region.

But most of the time the population moved in a westerly direction. There were three definite stages or "waves" of settlement:

(1) The first and slowest wave carried the frontier westward to the place where the Appalachian (AP eh LAYTCH yun) Mountains began. In early colonial days settlers started to move away from the coast. For a long time the mountains blocked further westward expansion. Early settlers lacked machines and tools to build roads and carry their belongings over mountains. And they were afraid of Indians and Frenchmen lurking along mountain trails.

(2) The second, more rapid wave of settlement began when the French were driven from the Ohio and Mississippi Valleys in 1763. During and after the Revolution, Americans traveled northwest into Ohio and southwest into Kentucky and Tennessee. Year after year settlers kept moving to the land between the Great Lakes and Gulf of Mexico.

(3) The third wave was the greatest and fastest of all. It carried the frontier across the Great Plains and the Rocky Mountains to the Pacific Ocean. The gold rush to California in 1849 and the covered wagons bound for Oregon were part of the last wave of settlement.

As the frontier moved west hunters, trappers, and fur traders came first. They were adventurous men who knew how to keep alive in the wilderness. Friendly Indians often showed them the best trails and hunting grounds. And the hunters and traders carried back word of good land they had found.

Later came farmers who cut down trees to "make a clearing" where they could plant crops. Then it was time for hunters and trappers to move on. As the farms increased, towns and villages developed. Busy cities appeared on land that had been wilderness a few years earlier.

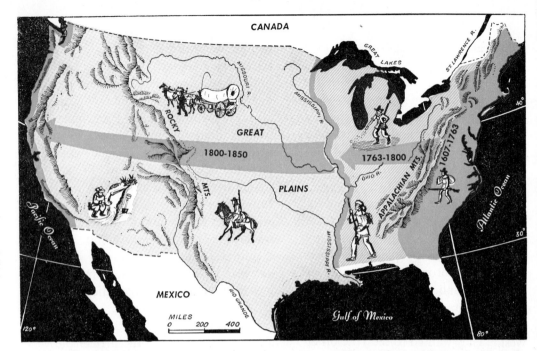

This map shows the three "waves" of westward expansion. First, settlement reached the Appalachians, then spread to the Mississippi, and finally reached the Pacific.

The process of settlement went on, all over the country, from colonial days until 1890 or about the time your grandparents were born. Then the westward movement practically came to an end, for nearly all the land had been claimed and settled. But to understand America today you must understand the westward movement: why people moved west, how they lived, and what they tried to accomplish.

The westward movement began in colonial times. To understand how the westward movement began, imagine that it is the year 1720. You have just arrived in America. What do you see and hear?

In back of you roars the Atlantic Ocean which you have just sailed across. Around you are a few houses and shops. Most people you meet are farmers. Proudly they point to a small area of plowed fields around their homes. It has taken years of hard work to cut down trees and clear the land.

Ahead you see the wilderness, a huge mass of trees. If you walk a mile or so into the forest you find yourself in a dark, frightening place. Tall trees shut out the sky. You hurry back to the cleared land.

But as days and years go by, you cannot forget the forest. It draws your thoughts as it does those of other settlers. You long to find out more about this unknown region. Perhaps it contains gold or silver!

THE WESTWARD MOVEMENT

The land must be rich. If trees were cut down you could easily raise big crops. You'd be rich.

Thus the frontier beckoned to Americans from the beginning. The land beyond the settlements seemed to say, "Come and claim me!" The pioneers had hardly learned how to keep alive in the New World before the more daring among them began a westward march. Wherever they could they followed river valleys.

In Massachusetts, men and women who wanted more land or more liberty moved west to the Connecticut Valley. In Pennsylvania, farmers in search of fertile soil followed winding trails west to the valley of the Susquehanna (SUS kweh HAN ah) River. In New Amsterdam, many traders disliked the tax demands and interfering ways of the Dutch governors. They escaped by moving westward across the Hudson to New Jersey. Others went north to the Mohawk Valley, where they founded the villages of Schenectady (skeh NEK tah dih) and Utica.

In the southern colonies there was also a movement to the West. Many Virginians found their way to the beautiful Shenandoah (SHEN an DOH ah) Valley. And Maryland pioneers took the "river road" along the Potomac as far west as where the city of Cumberland now stands.

Adventure and desire for new lands drew Americans to the West. People from every colony took part in the westward movement. As soon as a settlement was a few years old, some families started to move away. Others followed them. Soon they had new villages miles to the West.

Why were Americans so ready to

A pioneer family is shown below traveling up the Connecticut River to a home in the wilderness, braving unknown danger and hardship. Water transportation was usually safer and easier than travel over land, but Indians sometimes attacked settlers in boats.

Hunters and trappers were usually the first men to bring back word of new lands. They sometimes exaggerated, but their reports stimulated settlement of the West.

keep moving? Two reasons were a desire for adventure and the wish to obtain new land.

In every settlement there were a few restless men who liked to get away from their neighbors. Farming had no attraction for such men. They wanted adventure. They found it by hunting or trapping or trading. When they came back to the settlement they told of land that waited for an owner beyond the frontier.

And every eastern settlement held men who wanted better land for farming. Some were late-comers who found the best land already taken. Others had worn out the soil of their farms by planting the same crop year after year. New land will stand such planting for a time; but after a few years the soil "wears out" and refuses to grow another good crop. As Washington wrote in 1791:

The aim of farmers in this country is not to make the most of the land, which is everywhere cheap, but to make the most from labor, which is dear. A farmer in England, where land is dear and labor cheap, improves his land highly that he may reap large crops from a small piece of ground. In this country much land is scratched over but never cultivated or improved.

Danger and hardship slowed up the first attempts to reach the West. Need for new land caused a steady stream of Americans to move westward. For a while the presence of French to the north and in the Ohio Valley slowed up the march of pioneers. Not until the French were driven out could settlements be made far inland.

After 1763, English settlers no longer had to worry about French enemies. But there were still many obstacles. Today, it is hard to realize how hard it was to travel and to build new homes less than 200 years ago. Here are three problems that faced early pioneers:

THE WESTWARD MOVEMENT

(1) Men and women who made new homes in the wilderness had to clear away the forest and make the land support them. Then the old folks stayed at home, while the young went farther west.

(2) The pioneers had to drive back Indians who claimed the whole country as a hunting ground. Almost every mile of the westward march was marked by the graves of Indians and white people killed in the struggle for the land.

(3) There were no roads beyond the frontier. Every new settlement was like an army that dares not advance without first making sure of a "lifeline" of supplies. The forests supplied material to build houses, and there was usually plenty of wild game for food. But for tools, guns, and other necessities, settlers required a town nearby where they could trade products of their farms for what they needed. / As there were few steamboats until after 1815 and few railroads until the 1840's, growth of inland towns was slow.

The Appalachian Mountains were a barrier to settlement. The most serious obstacle that blocked early westward advance was the Appalachian Mountains. Today you can cross the mountains in a few hours by train or automobile, or in a few minutes by airplane. But 200 years ago, people had to travel on foot or on horseback or ride in a wagon. The mountains seemed to mark the end of their westward march.

The Appalachians are a mass of wooded hills and rock-capped mountains. They extend southwest from New England to Georgia and Alabama. Several ranges make up the Appalachian chain. The White Mountains of New Hampshire, the Green Mountains of Vermont, and the Adirondack (AD ih RON dak) Mountains of New York are part of the Appalachians. So are the Alleghenies in Pennsylvania, the Blue

The map below shows the frontier in colonial days when settlers were moving west to the edge of the Appalachian barrier.

This map shows paths across the Appalachians to the West. Note New York State route, Cumberland Gap, and southern route.

The Appalachians are rugged and forbidding in places. Here settlers are shown making their way over a mountain trail.

Ridge Mountains of Virginia, and the Great Smokies in the Carolinas and Tennessee.

Pioneers found ways to cross the mountains. To early settlers the mountains seemed to say "So far you may come, but no farther." But before long a few people tried to cross the rugged peaks. First to accept the challenge were the hunters and fur traders.

Sometimes they followed an Indian trail for a while. Most of the time they had to chop and push their way through the forest. At last they reached the top of the Appalachians. Below they saw a beautiful country that seemed to spread out endlessly to the west. Hunters called it the

"country beyond the mountains," and later "the New West."

After a time hunters and traders learned there were easier ways to cross the mountains. Instead of cutting paths and climbing tall peaks, they looked for "gaps" and valleys between the mountains. Gradually there developed several main routes that people took to the West. You can trace these routes on the map on this page.

One route led through New York. There the Mohawk Valley provided a fairly level way west to the flat land around Lake Erie. From there it was not difficult to travel south and west to the Ohio River. This river was called the "Gateway to the West" because boats could travel

262   THE WESTWARD MOVEMENT

down its waters for a thousand miles.

For the pioneers from Virginia and North Carolina, the Cumberland Gap provided a way to Kentucky and Tennessee. The great hunter, Daniel Boone, made this route popular.

Far to the south lay the shortest and easiest route. There the mountains tapered off into a coastal plain. Settlers from South Carolina and Georgia followed this route to the rich land that is now Alabama and Mississippi.

Whatever route they chose, pioneers were almost certain to have trouble with Indians along the way. They often tried to avoid trouble by agreeing to buy land from the chief of one of the tribes. But one chief could not represent all the tribes that shared the land. Other tribes did not understand or recognize the purchase. They would attack any settlers who entered their region.

Everywhere on the frontier, from North to South, a bloody struggle went on year after year. The pioneers fought for land they felt belonged to them. Hadn't they bought it in good faith? From their point of view they were in the right.

The Indians also felt they were in the right. Men and women who followed blood-soaked trails into Indian country knew they were risking death every minute along the way. Nevertheless, the lure was so strong that every year more wagons headed west.

Daniel Boone blazed a trail to Kentucky. The most famous of the woodsmen and pathfinders was Daniel Boone. His grandfather had followed William Penn to Pennsylvania. From there Daniel Boone's father moved the family to Virginia and then to the North Carolina frontier.

A friendly hunter told young

The picture below shows a pioneer family attacked by Indians on the frontier. The early settlers needed strong walls and plenty of courage to fight off such attacks.

DANIEL BOONE (1734–1820)

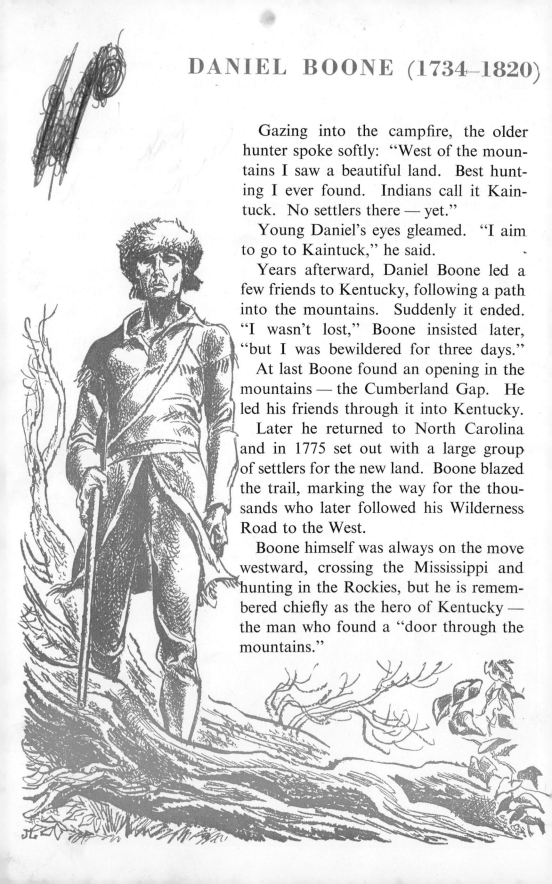

Gazing into the campfire, the older hunter spoke softly: "West of the mountains I saw a beautiful land. Best hunting I ever found. Indians call it Kaintuck. No settlers there — yet."

Young Daniel's eyes gleamed. "I aim to go to Kaintuck," he said.

Years afterward, Daniel Boone led a few friends to Kentucky, following a path into the mountains. Suddenly it ended. "I wasn't lost," Boone insisted later, "but I was bewildered for three days."

At last Boone found an opening in the mountains — the Cumberland Gap. He led his friends through it into Kentucky.

Later he returned to North Carolina and in 1775 set out with a large group of settlers for the new land. Boone blazed the trail, marking the way for the thousands who later followed his Wilderness Road to the West.

Boone himself was always on the move westward, crossing the Mississippi and hunting in the Rockies, but he is remembered chiefly as the hero of Kentucky — the man who found a "door through the mountains."

Daniel Boone about a land beyond the mountains that the Indians called "Kentucky." He described its forests, sunny clearings, and rich game. Years afterward, Boone made his way to Tennessee. From there he traveled with difficulty to Kentucky.

Later, Boone found an easier path or "a door through the mountain wall." It led through the Cumberland Gap. Boone marked the route for a road from Tennessee to Kentucky. It was called the *Wilderness Road*. Boone led a group of settlers over the road in 1775. On the Kentucky River they built a fort called Boonesboro.

Many settlers followed Boone through the Cumberland Gap and down the Wilderness Road. In 1792 Kentucky was admitted to the Union — the first state organized in the land west of the Appalachians.

Settlers reached Tennessee from North Carolina. A few years before Boone blazed his trail to Kentucky settlers from Virginia and North Carolina began to move into Tennessee. During the Revolution, the number increased. Many moved west to avoid capture by British troops who had conquered much of Georgia and the Carolinas.

Leader of the Tennessee settlers was James Robertson. On his first trip west he explored the region along the Cumberland River. It was Indian country then, but Robertson felt it would be a fine spot for a settlement. He persuaded more than 100 families to move to this region.

In February, 1779, the group gathered near the Holston River in northwestern North Carolina. There were 250 men, and 130 women and children. All they knew was that they were going far away into Indian country to start a settlement on the banks of a wide river. Robertson told them the land was rich and that there were wild animals to hunt.

To reach the place, the men would have to push their way over winding trails for hundreds of miles. It was decided that the women and children should go by boat. The way by boat was much longer, but safer. So, on the banks of the Holston, the fathers and older boys said goodbye to the women and children. Imagine how they must have felt as they turned for one last look at their families before they plunged into the woods!

The journey over land took months; every mile was dangerous. Many men were killed by Indians as they scouted their way forward. Those who lived had to go on, leaving comrades buried beside the trail. How could they turn back? They were determined to have cabins built, and a little corn planted, when their families arrived.

Nashville was founded during the Revolution. Meanwhile, in 20 roughly-made flatboats, the women and children began the long journey. They were guarded by a few men with rifles. Down the Holston they floated into the Tennessee River. And that river (as you can see by the map on page 262) flows south to Alabama before it changes its course to the west, and then to the north. On its broad current they entered the Ohio River. Now the boats had to be rowed upstream, against the current, to the inflowing Cumberland River. Here at last was the "home river"; but where was the home?

Such a journey — about 2000 miles as the rivers ran — had never before been made by women and children! Here or there, as the boats rounded a bend, Indian arrows from the nearest side of the river turned the voyage into a flight. Twenty-six of the company were killed; five more died of hardship. At last, from the first boat — the *Adventure* — there rose a joyous shout. On the riverbank ahead the travelers saw a column of smoke. There the men were waiting.

Hardly were families re-united before they set to work. Some cleared land for cornfields; others turned the village into a fort by building a stockade. There was no time to mourn the dead while the living were in constant danger.

The men worked in the fields, rifles at hand. Girls and boys watched the encircling forest. From sunset to sunrise sentinels kept guard in the fort. But in spite of this, nearly 100 people were killed or captured by Indians in the first year. Only a third of the original pioneers were left; yet not one, so far as is known, left the settlement.

The village they started became the city of Nashville. It grew from a frontier fort to the capital city of Tennessee. There were hundreds of early villages of which as brave a story might be told. With blood and sweat, pioneers turned the wilderness into a land of plowed fields and thriving towns.

Democracy moved west with the pioneers. Settlers who moved west

Pioneers moved westward on many rivers. Below is shown a group traveling on the Tennessee. Note the horses and cow which the settlers knew would be very valuable in the new land.

carried few possessions. There was little room in their wagons or boats for bulky furniture and tools. But something invisible and precious traveled with every pioneer: the English and American tradition of freedom.

The Northwest Ordinance provided for democratic government in the Northwest Territory. The same rights were extended to other territories. Almost everywhere on the frontier people elected officials and ran their local governments. As soon as the population was large enough the territory could become a state. And inhabitants of the new state had the same rights and privileges as people in the original thirteen states.

Take for example the town Nashville, that you have just read about. Soon after the first settlers arrived they called a meeting to decide how to run their government. They were following a custom that was old when the colonies began. Remember how the Pilgrims held a meeting on board the *Mayflower?* The Pilgrims chose a democratic government, where everyone could state his opinion and vote. The people of Nashville chose the same basic plan. In most cases it was the type of government they were accustomed to "back east."

Westerners believed in equality. In many ways the West was more democratic than the East. In some eastern settlements many people were prevented from voting by *property qualifications*, which meant that only men who owned a certain amount of property could vote. But people on the frontier had no patience with property qualifications. They said, "If democracy is a good thing, we can't have too much of it."

Westerners believed in *manhood suffrage*, or the right of every man to vote. When Kentucky became a state, manhood suffrage was written into its constitution. Later Ohio, and then other western states entered the Union with manhood suffrage. Slowly, the eastern states adopted manhood suffrage, too.

But what about the women? In Europe and in older parts of the United States women could not vote. The old idea was that women were inferior in intelligence to men and should not concern themselves with matters outside their home. On the frontier, however, women had to work just as hard as the men. They proved themselves intelligent and willing to do their share in building new communities. Why, then, should they not have the vote?

For a long time even in the West, there was resistance to *woman suffrage*, or giving women the right to vote. But in 1869 the territory of Wyoming included woman suffrage in its constitution. For this reason Wyoming is called the "Equality State." Colorado, Idaho, and Utah soon adopted the idea. But it was not until 1920 that an amendment to the United States Constitution [113] gave women the right to vote — fifty one years after Wyoming did so! The West took the lead in giving the vote to men and women.

Westerners became prominent in national affairs. Many people in the East regarded the frontier with fear and jealousy. They knew the West was growing rapidly, but they did not want westerners to have a part in the federal government. However, when western states were admitted to the Union they gained the right to send representatives to Congress.

Many western Congressmen were fine, outstanding leaders. They were good speakers and not afraid to say what they thought. Some of the greatest Americans grew up on the frontier.

The first westerner to gain great power in national affairs was Andrew Jackson. He was the first President who was born in real poverty. His parents had moved from northern Ireland to the frontier. Andrew was born in a log cabin on the border between North and South Carolina. His father was killed a few days before Andrew was born in 1767.

Jackson was a restless, hot-tempered lad, and often in trouble. Yet most people liked him. Self-confident and straightforward, he showed himself a leader even as a boy. His mother had taught him to read and write; his relatives persuaded him to go to school for a few terms. But he soon found he needed more education.

In those days, especially on the frontier, the quickest way to success was to become a lawyer. Jackson bought law books and read them in a hurry. Before he was 20 he was practicing law.

The next year Jackson moved to Tennessee. He soon became a leading lawyer and helped write a constitution for Tennessee. He was elected to the United States Senate at 31, and later became a judge.

Jackson was the first westerner to become President. You have already read about Jackson's part in the War of 1812. After the Battle of New Orleans he was a hero to all Americans. His friends set to work to make him President.

Eastern politicians laughed at the idea. But they soon had to take it seriously. The wiping out of property qualifications meant the "common man" could vote. And the common man liked Andy Jackson! In 1828 Jackson won the election.

Never before had Washington seen such excitement! Crowds came to see their hero become President. Here is the way a spectator described the occasion:

. . . we saw the General and his company advancing up the avenue . . . crowds thronging around him. At the moment the General entered the Capitol the shout that rent the air still rings in my ears. When the speech was over, and the President made his parting bow, the barrier that separated the people from him was broken down; they

268

rushed up the steps all eager to shake hands with him. With difficulty he made his way through the Capitol and down the hill to the avenue. Such a parade followed him! Country men, farmers, gentlemen mounted and dismounted, boys, women and children, black and white, carriages, wagons and carts pursuing him to the White House.

Jackson gave some government jobs to his friends. Jackson had eight stormy years as President. He made mistakes and he liked his own way. His enemies called him "King Andrew." But, under Jackson, the people gained new power.

Many men who followed Jackson to Washington came for a selfish reason. Because they had helped him get elected, they expected him to appoint them to government jobs.

Jackson was inclined to do as they wished. When he became President he found that many federal officials had been in office 20 or 30 years — since the time of Jefferson and even Washington! Some old office-holders did not like Jackson and did not try to carry out his policies. You can imagine how "Old Hickory" felt about that! So he dismissed some of them and appointed his friends to their jobs.

Other Presidents had dismissed officials, but they did not do it so noisily as Jackson did. And, unfortunately, Jackson did not always make sure the man he appointed to a job was capable of doing the work.

There is an old saying that "to the victors belong the spoils." This means that whoever wins a war is entitled to seize the property of those who lose. Some people claimed Jackson was applying the *Spoils System* to politics. They meant that, because he had won the election, he

Andrew Jackson, President-elect, is shown below on his way to Washington to his inauguration. He had to travel by coach, for railroads were just beginning to be built. All along the way people turned out to honor the first chief executive born in the West.

was giving many of his friends jobs.

Jackson defended his action on the ground that it was fair to give as many people as possible a chance to hold office. He thought almost anybody who was honest was capable of doing a good job for the government. Many later Presidents agreed with Jackson. The Spoils System became firmly established and led to many problems.

Jackson fought for the common man. Jackson's aim was to help the common people. He fought against anything he felt was against the interests of ordinary Americans. That is the reason he fought and destroyed the Bank of the United States.

The Bank was part of Alexander Hamilton's financial program. It was a great success at first. But in later years it became unpopular. Jackson thought the Bank was helping a few rich people in the East at the expense of people in the West.

The Bank's charter was due to *expire*, or run out, in a few years. To continue in business, the Bank needed a new charter. Congress passed a bill granting the charter.

Would Jackson *veto*, or vote against, the bill? "He won't dare!" friends of the Bank predicted. But he did. He sent the bill back to the Senate with a warning that such laws were setting "section against section, interest against interest, and man against man in a fearful commotion which threatens to shake the foundations of our Union."

The people agreed with Jackson. He was triumphantly re-elected in 1832. Soon after the election he ordered the Secretary of Treasury to stop depositing government money in the Bank.

But where could the government keep its money? Jackson decided to deposit it in certain state banks. People who did not like Jackson called these banks "Pet Banks."

The loss of government deposits was such a blow that the Bank of the United States soon came to an end. Jackson had won his "War."

Like most westerners, Jackson was deeply devoted to the Union. In the older parts of the United States, especially in the South, people tended to love their states more than the nation. But in the West, loyalty to the nation came first.

As you will learn in Unit 8, Jackson acted swiftly when South Carolina threatened to leave the Union. "Our federal Union!" he said on one occasion, "It must be preserved!" The West approved Jackson's stand. Long after "Old Hickory's" death another westerner, Abraham Lincoln, led the fight to keep America united.

CHAPTER SUMMARY

Americans kept moving west. From colonial days until about 1890, hunters, traders, and then farmers with their families, moved west. Some were lured by adventure; others longed to obtain new land. But danger and hardship made the Westward Movement slow in colonial time.

There were three definite waves of settlement. The first and slowest wave carried the frontier westward to the place where the Appalachian Mountains begin. The second moved the frontier to the Mississippi. The third and fastest carried the frontier to the Pacific Ocean.

Three main routes led to the land beyond the Appalachians. The northern route followed the Hudson and Mohawk Valleys across New York state to Lake Erie and Ohio River. The middle route led from Virginia and North Carolina into Kentucky by way of the Cumberland Gap. This was the route of Daniel Boone's Wilderness Road. The most southerly route led from South Carolina and Georgia to Alabama and Mississippi.

The West was more democratic than the East. Property qualifications for voting were abolished on the frontier. Western territories and states were the first to let women vote.

Jackson was the first great leader to come out of the West. Jackson won the Presidency in 1828. He believed in the common man. He destroyed the Bank of the United States.

The Language of History

Make sure you understand the meaning of each of the following as it is used in this chapter.

1. frontier
2. Pet Banks
3. woman suffrage
4. Spoils System
5. property qualifications
6. manhood suffrage

What Happened When

Connect each of the following dates with important events in history.

1. 1775
2. 1792
3. 1828
4. 1869

Who's Who in History

Be sure you know the part each of the following played in the Westward Movement.

1. Daniel Boone   **2.** James Robertson   **3.** Andrew Jackson

Study Questions

1. What were the three "waves" or stages of the Westward Movement?

2. Give two reasons why in colonial days settlers hesitated to move west.

3. About what year did the Westward Movement practically come to an end?

4. What criticism did Washington make in regard to the way early farmers used American soil?

5. Describe three routes by which settlers reached the land beyond the Appalachian Mountains.

6. Explain two ways in which the western part of the United States was more democratic than the East.

7. Why is Wyoming called "the Equality State"?

8. Write a brief biography of Andrew Jackson discussing **(a)** his parents, **(b)** his early life and education, **(c)** his political experience in Tennessee, **(d)** his military experience, and **(e)** what he accomplished as President.

9. **a.** What is the Spoils System?
   b. How did Jackson justify the Spoils System?
   c. Give an argument against the Spoils System.

10. **a.** Why did Jackson dislike the Bank of the United States?
    b. How did he destroy the Bank?
    c. Where did he order government money to be deposited?

Chapter 15

THE UNITED STATES WON VAST TERRITORIES BY PURCHASE, SETTLEMENT, AND WAR

"ONE morning in January, 1848 as I was taking my usual walk my eye was caught by a glimpse of something shining in the bottom of the ditch. There was about a foot of water running there. I reached my hand down and picked it up; it made my heart thump, for I felt certain it was gold. The piece was about half the size and of the shape of a pea. Then I saw another piece in the water. . . . In a very short time we discovered that the whole country was one bed of gold."

The California Gold Rush of '49 was on! Following James Marshall's report of his discovery at Sutter's Mill came the most frantic and exciting part of the Westward Movement.

This chapter follows the great pathfinders as they rode, hiked, and fought their way from the Louisiana Territory to the Pacific Coast, ever increasing the territory of the United States. Who were these pioneers?

As you read you will see the United States growing by settlement and growing by conquest. What war resulted in another sweeping increase in the size of the United States? Why was it fought? What was won?

The following pages describe the last major acquisitions by which the United States reached its present continental limits.

Lewis and Clark explored the West.
After 1800 the westward movement gathered speed and force. Thanks to Boone and other pathfinders, the land between the Appalachians and the Mississippi River soon became settled. The frontier had reached the Mississippi. There it stopped, for beyond was foreign territory.

Hunters and farmers looked longingly at land across the river. Then, in 1803, came news of the Louisiana Purchase. Imagine how Americans felt when this vast land was opened to them.

Who knew what riches — and what dangers — Louisiana might contain! President Jefferson himself was as excited as a boy unwrapping a Christmas gift. He had to find out right away what there was in it!

Even before the purchase of Louisiana, Jefferson had asked Congress for money to explore the West. Some men in Congress grumbled. Eastern Federalists were not eager to spend money on western exploration. But Congress granted $2500 for an expedition.

Jefferson appointed a young army officer who was his private secretary to lead the expedition: Captain Meriwether Lewis. Lewis was a tall, blue-eyed man who appeared awkward and shy. But the President knew he was brave and dependable. Like Jefferson, Lewis had a keen interest in science. He knew a good deal about plants and minerals.

Jefferson let Lewis choose his

The picture below shows Meriwether Lewis and William Clark with their followers on the Columbia River, the great "River of the West," which they followed to the Pacific Coast.

companion for the trip. Captain Lewis knew the man he wanted: red-headed William Clark, a brother of George Rogers Clark who had won the Northwest Territory.

The two captains picked 43 husky young men for the expedition. They were a wild, rough bunch at first. Lewis and Clark gave them several months training under military discipline, for they knew the trip meant two or three years of hardship.

Jefferson instructed Lewis and Clark to find out all they could about the new territory: its soil, climate, minerals, plants, animals, rivers, and Indian tribes that inhabited it.

On May 14, 1804, the Lewis and Clark Expedition started from St. Louis, which was then a little fur-trading town. They went by boat up the Missouri River through the territory of the Sioux (SOO) Indians. Winter they spent in the land of the Mandan Indians, in what is now North Dakota. Like most Indians, the Mandans were friendly when they first met white men.

When spring came they started out again, following the Missouri River. One day in May, 1805, they saw — far to the west — the snowy peaks of the Rocky Mountains. Here the Louisiana Territory ended, but Lewis and Clark wanted to see what lay beyond.

They crossed the Rockies and traveled through what is now Idaho and Montana. A young Indian woman named Sacajawea (sah KAH jah WAY ah) proved a most valuable member of the expedition. She was the wife of a French guide Lewis and Clark had hired.

Lewis and Clark reached the Pacific. Sacajawea marched along cheerfully, carrying her baby on her back. One day on the trail she suddenly began a dance of joy. She pointed at Indians riding toward her. "This is my tribe," she cried.

The captains learned that in childhood Sacajawea had been captured by an enemy tribe. Now she was traveling through the land of her own people, the Shoshone (shoh SHO nee) Indians. She remembered enough of the language to make friends with the Indians. One of the women had been her playmate as a child. When Sacajawea asked who was the chief of the tribe, she was told, "Camawait, your brother, who has long mourned you as dead."

The Indians could not do enough for Sacajawea and her friends! They supplied pack horses and guides to lead the expedition through the mountains. Thanks to Sacajawea's influence, Lewis and Clark traveled over thousands of miles of wild country without great difficulty. They followed west-flowing streams to the Snake River which led them to the Columbia River. Then they floated down the Columbia which grew wider and wider. The Great Plains and the Rocky Mountains were far behind them.

Lewis and Clark's exploration of the Columbia River Valley later strength-

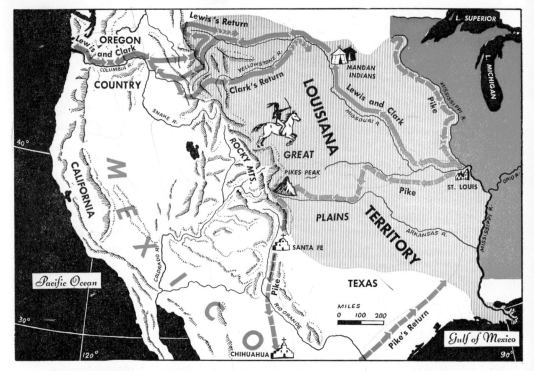

This map shows the routes of the Lewis and Clark Expedition from St. Louis to the Pacific Coast (1804–1806). Also shown are explorations of Zebulon Pike (1805–1807).

ened the American claims to the region known as the Oregon Country and helped make it part of the United States. The men traveled 4100 miles of prairie, river, Indian trail, and mountain pass. At last, in November of 1805, they saw directly to the west the waters of the Pacific Ocean! They spent the winter on the coast and then went back to St. Louis by a different way. You can follow their route on the map on this page.

Lewis and Clark did an astonishing job. In all, they traveled over 8000 miles through wild country. Part of the time game was abundant and they lived well on animals and fish they caught. At other times, especially on the Columbia, they very nearly had to starve to death.

Only one man died on the trip. The rest returned in fine condition from a journey that lasted two years, four months, and eight days!

The captains never for a moment forgot the main purpose of the expedition. They brought back a wealth of reliable information, specimens, charts, and maps. And they proved it was possible to cross the mountains to the Far West.

They blazed the trail for thousands of Americans who settled the West. Covered wagons followed the route of Lewis and Clark along the Missouri. In many ways, the history of the West really begins with the Lewis and Clark Expedition.

276

Zebulon Pike explored the Great Plains and the Rockies. While Lewis and Clark were crossing the Rockies, another man was exploring the northern part of the Louisiana Purchase. He was a 26-year-old army officer, Lieutenant Zebulon (ZEB yoo lon) Pike. He had joined the army when he was 15.

In 1805 his commander ordered him to take a few men and find the source of the Mississippi River. Pike traveled north from St. Louis into Minnesota, trying to find where the great river began. He never found the exact source of the Mississippi but he explored the northern region of the Louisiana Purchase.

The next year the army made Pike a captain. His orders were to explore the southwestern part of the Louisiana Territory. Pike's party traveled up the Arkansas River as far as where Pueblo (PWEB loh), Colorado now stands. They explored much of the Great Plains and reached the Rockies, far south of where Lewis and Clark had crossed.

One day Pike and his men caught sight of a majestic mountain. It rose 14,000 feet and seemed almost to touch the sky! The mountain is now called Pike's Peak in honor of the explorer who found it in 1806.

Later Pike pushed south to the Rio Grande (REE o GRAHN day) River, which is now the border between Texas and Mexico. Spain claimed this region, so Pike was promptly arrested as a spy! But the Spaniards soon set him free on the Louisiana border with a warning to stay out.

Pike brought back valuable information about the Southwest. He reported that the Indians west of the Mississippi were quite different from Eastern Woodland tribes. Eastern Indians traveled on foot or by canoe, but the Plains Indians were fine horsemen.

Most of their horses were descended from a few fine animals that had escaped from early Spanish explorers. (There were no horses in the Americas until the white men brought them from Europe.) Around almost every Indian village Pike saw herds of horses grazing. The boys of the tribe had to watch them and tend them. If a horse ran away, or was stolen, the boys were in disgrace.

The "Indian ponies" were tough little horses that could race over rough country like rabbits. They could live on dry grass and go all day without water.

Pike's information was valuable. Pioneers read what he had written

Zebulon M. Pike (below) helped explore the territory of the Louisiana Purchase.

about the importance of horses in the region. They brought tobacco, cloth, knives, and other goods to exchange for Indian ponies.

To cross the Plains they had to have Indian horses. Practically all travel was on horseback. Distances were so great and water holes were so far apart that it was not safe to travel on foot. A man who lost his horse was likely to die of thirst.

All this and more Pike told Americans in a long report he wrote. As a reward for his bravery, and leadership, Pike was made a general. He died leading an attack on Canada in the War of 1812.

Pike lived only 34 years but he gave his nation almost 20 years of unselfish service. Like Lewis and Clark, he was one of the great pathfinders.

The Florida border was a trouble spot. While explorers traveled to distant corners of the Louisiana Territory, the Spaniards looked on suspiciously. Spain owned Texas and Florida, and once she owned Louisiana, too. Would Americans be satisfied with Louisiana? Or would they try to take Florida and Texas, which Spain still owned? The Spaniards had reason to be fearful.

The War of 1812 increased bad feeling between the United States and Spain. During the war, Americans seized West Florida. After the war, it remained part of the United States — the only territory gained in the War of 1812.

Trouble arose on the border be-

tween East Florida and Georgia. Runaway slaves fled to Florida. And the Seminole Indians of Florida sometimes raided or burned towns in southern Georgia.

Spanish officials made little effort to stop such acts. Spain was having trouble with revolutions in her South American colonies. She could not spare troops to keep order on the Florida border.

James Monroe, who succeeded Madison as President in 1817, was eager to get control of Florida. That seemed the only way to stop Indian attacks on Georgia.

Spain gave up Florida. A crisis came in 1818, when Seminole Indians took the warpath into southern Georgia and Alabama. One war party was led by an English adventurer named Ambrister. A Scottish trader named Arbuthnot supplied the Indians with guns. Both were British citizens.

President Monroe sent General Jackson with several hundred frontiersmen to deal with the Indians. Andrew Jackson's orders were to "pacify" the border; that is, to bring peace, but not to cross the border into Spanish territory. To cross the border would be an act of war.

Jackson claimed he had a secret order from the President to take forcible possession of Florida; but the President denied any such order had been given. The truth of the matter is not known and probably never will be. At any rate, Jackson did what he thought should be done, and did it in frontier fashion.

After chasing the Indians back to Florida, he crossed the border to capture Pensacola and another Spanish fort on the Gulf coast. In one fort were the British traders who had roused the Indians, and who now thought themselves quite safe. Jackson tried them by a military court; he sentenced one to be hanged, and the other to be shot.

England was angered by such treatment of British subjects. But John Quincy Adams, Monroe's Secretary of State, persuaded the British the two traders got what they deserved. So England took no action.

Spain also was angry. To her protest, Adams responded the time had come to settle the whole matter. Spain should either control Florida, Adams said, or give it up to the United States.

Spain was not able to manage the colony, so she agreed to give it up. In return, the United States took over some five million dollars in claims against Spain. The claims were for damages Americans said they had suffered from Spaniards and Indians during the years of trouble on the border. So Spain did not receive any money for giving up Florida. The treaty was signed at Washington on February 22, 1819.

The winning of Florida added land and resources to the United States. It also ended most of the conflict with Spain. American territory now extended to the Caribbean (KARE ih

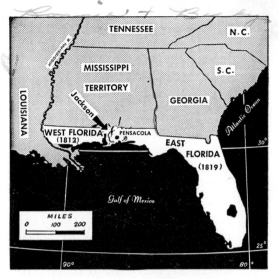

This map shows Florida, which was gained from Spain in 1819 under the leadership of Secretary of State John Q. Adams.

BEE an) Sea. The whole Atlantic coast south of Canada belonged to the United States.

Texas was ruled by Spain and then by Mexico. Spain gave up Florida partly because she was trying to crush rebellions in her colonies south of the Rio Grande River. The new nations south of the border were able to hold on to independence. But most of them had to struggle hard to establish a strong government. In Mexico the period of disorder was especially severe.

In those days the vast region of Texas was part of Mexico. When Mexico became independent in 1822, Texas became a province, or state, of Mexico. Most of the inhabitants were Indians. A Mexican governor ruled the area.

In southern Texas, Roman Catholic priests had built a few *missions* or religious settlements. There they worked hard to teach Indians the Christian faith. They built small, attractive churches; sometimes they set up schools where Indians were taught to weave cloth and raise crops. You can still see the ruins of many Spanish missions in Texas and California.

After the War of 1812 a few Americans settled in Texas. Land was cheap and well suited to cotton-growing. At first Mexican leaders welcomed Americans to Texas. They wanted to get the land settled, and they thought Americans would develop the region.

A young man named Stephen Austin received a large grant of land from the Mexican government. In return, Austin promised to bring at least 100 families to Texas. Austin did better; he brought 300 families! They settled on a fertile stretch of land between the Colorado and Brazos Rivers. You can find Austin's settlement on the map below.

Soon they were building homes, planting cotton, raising horses and cattle. They organized local governments and ran their own affairs. They did all this quietly and peacefully — just as their fathers and grandfathers had done when they started settlements on the frontier.

Austin's colony is often called the "cradle of Texas." In seven years its population grew to 3000. In 1828, Stephen Austin wrote: "Commerce begins to enliven the shores of the river, and peace and plenty everywhere prevail. Those who are here are content."

Americans moved to Texas. Several other Americans received similar grants of land. They brought hundreds of families to Texas. By 1835 five new towns had been founded. Many people moved up from old Mexico to Texas.

Leaders in Mexico City began to feel a little frightened. The new settlers were coming so fast! They worked so hard and traveled so quickly! Were they going to take over Texas? Would Mexico be able to hold on to this rich province?

The Mexican government was in a shaky condition. There were plots and revolutions. First one man, and then another, tried to run the nation. Under such conditions, a far-away province like Texas was bound to be neglected.

In many ways, Mexico did not treat Texans justly. She did not give

The map below shows Texas, which gained its independence from Mexico in 1836 and joined the United States in 1845.

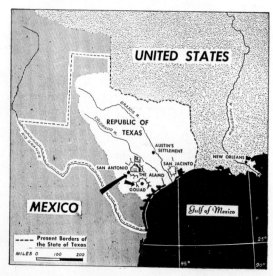

Here is how Austin, Texas looked in January 1840 when it was the capital of the young Republic of Texas. It was named for Stephen Austin, one of the founders of Texas.

them a fair share in running the government. And Texans claimed they could not get an honest trial in Mexican courts.

Little by little, misunderstandings developed. Mexico City was a long way from the Texas settlements. And communication was slow. Texas settlers did not bother to consult Mexico about many problems.

The new settlers did not even trade much with Mexico. It was difficult and expensive to ship goods 800 miles to Mexico City. It was easy and more profitable to ship them a few miles across the border to the United States. Moreover, Texas settlers usually went to New Orleans, rather than Mexico City, to buy supplies they needed.

There were other reasons why Texas and Mexico did not get along. Most — though by no means all — of the settlers had come from the United States. Few spoke Spanish. Their friends and relatives were in the United States, and they often sent their children there to school.

Another cause of misunderstand-

ing was religion. Many settlers were Protestants. They were used to freedom of worship in the United States. But under Mexican law, the Roman Catholic Church was the only church allowed in Texas.

Texas declared its independence. Texas slowly drifted toward a complete break with Mexico. In 1830 the Mexican government passed a law that made Texans angry. The law said:

1. No more settlers from the United States could come to Texas.

2. No more slaves could be brought to Texas. This was a blow at Texas cotton growers who depended on slave labor.

3. A tax must be paid on all goods coming into Texas seaports. Texans felt this was intended to discourage them from buying in the United States.

4. Soldiers would be sent to Texas and forts would be built at important points. The settlers thought the troops were being sent to spy on them. They feared they would soon

TROUBLE IN TEXAS

Samuel Houston was a hero of Texas. He won the battle of San Jacinto in 1836.

With an army of 6000 men he started out to "teach Texas a lesson."

The settlers in Texas made up their minds they would not be ruled by Santa Anna. On March 2, 1836, they held a convention and declared their independence. Then they drew up a plan of government much like that of the United States.

Sam Houston was chosen to command the armed forces, though there was no army as yet. Texas was now an independent republic. Texans had their own flag, a blue flag with one white star, so Texas was called the "Lone Star Republic."

Texans remembered the Alamo and Goliad. In the meantime Santa Anna's army reached the mission town of San Antonio. There were only 187 Texans in the town. Under command of Colonel William Travis, they tried to defend the settlement. But they were driven back to the Alamo (AH lah mo), the mission chapel which had been turned into a fort.

Inside the Alamo's thick walls the handful of Texans held off 3000 Mexican soldiers for 11 days! They killed more than 500 of the enemy. When the hopeless fight was over, the defenders were dead or dying to the last man. Among the dead were two famous scouts, Davy Crockett and James Bowie.

Next, Santa Anna marched southeast to the mission town of Goliad. There he surrounded a group of 300 Texans. They were soon forced

lose all the rights that they had.

When Mexico tried to enforce the law of 1830, fighting broke out and several people were killed. Stephen Austin was arrested and kept in prison for months. Texans held meetings to protest, and to decide on a plan of action. They began to look to Samuel Houston (HYOOS tun) for leadership.

Houston had recently come to Texas. He was a friend of Andrew Jackson and had served as governor of Tennessee. He had lived, for a time, among the Cherokee Indians. They had adopted him into their tribe and called him "The Raven," because of his dark, shining hair.

The President of Mexico at this time was Antonio López de Santa Anna (SAHN tah AN nah). Santa Anna was a dictator, that is, he had complete control of the government. He planned to smash opposition and take away all the rights of Texans to run their local affairs.

to surrender. Then they were lined up and shot.

Santa Anna thought the slaughter at the Alamo and at Goliad would frighten Texans. He expected them to give up the fight. No man ever made a worse mistake.

Thousands who had paid little attention to the trouble in Texas now became fighting mad. "Remember the Alamo! Remember Goliad!" they shouted. All over Texas, men seized their guns and rode away to join Houston's army. When news of the Alamo reached the United States many Americans hurried to join in the fight.

Within a week Sam Houston and his army were on the march. He had only about 900 men, but every one had used a rifle since boyhood. On April 21, 1836, the Texans caught up with the Mexican army. A battle took place on the bank of the San Jacinto (sahn ja SEEN toh) River.

Santa Anna was taken by surprise. The general was asleep; his men were eating and drinking. The battle lasted 20 minutes. Santa Anna's army was cut to pieces. Only two Texans were killed and 23 wounded.

Texas was a republic for nine years. Santa Anna was captured, but was soon set free and returned to Mexico. The victory at San Jacinto ended the war. The independence of Texas was won. Sam Houston became its first President. The United States and other nations recognized Texas as an independent republic.

It is interesting to note that many Spanish-speaking people helped win independence for Texas. They loved liberty and they hated Santa Anna. In the war for Texas' freedom, Spanish-speaking and English-speaking settlers fought side by side.

Like all new nations, Texas faced serious problems. The war had left a big debt. And Mexican officials would not recognize the independence of Texas. They claimed it was just a rebellious province. They warned they would declare war on any nation which took any part in Texan affairs. As you can probably guess, this warning was directed at the United States.

Many Americans had long wanted to acquire Texas. And most Texans wanted to join the United States. Nevertheless, Texas remained independent for nine years.

What caused the delay? There were two reasons: one was that the government at Washington did not want to go to war with Mexico. And

Mexican leader, Santa Anna (below) tried to crush rebellion in Texas, but failed.

Mexican leaders kept saying that if the United States took over Texas it would mean war.

The second reason for delay was the question of slavery. People in northern United States did not like slavery. They did not want to add slave states or slave territory to the Union. But Texans owned slaves. They believed they could not raise cotton without slave labor. So it was clear that Texas would want to enter the Union as a slave state.

The southern states, which favored slavery, were eager to have Texas. And the people on the frontier were always in favor of adding territory. They were coming to believe the United States must push its borders to the Pacific Ocean.

So the question of the *annexation* of Texas — that is, of adding Texas to the territory of the United States — got involved in politics. Many northerners were determined to keep Texas out. Southerners were just as determined to bring Texas in.

Texans did not like being kept waiting. In addition, they continued to have serious money troubles and they needed help. If the United States did not want Texas — other nations did!

A rumor spread that Great Britain planned to get control of Texas. This would mean the United States would have a strong foreign power on the southwestern border. That was a danger Americans had been trying to avoid since Jefferson's time.

Texas joined the United States in 1845. Annexation of Texas became a big issue in the election of 1844. One candidate for President was Henry Clay of Kentucky, who had been one of the War Hawks in 1812. The other candidate was James K. Polk of Tennessee.

Clay tried to win votes by keeping quiet about Texas. Polk came out strongly for admitting the region. This pleased the South. Polk also favored taking the Oregon Territory. This pleased the North.

Polk won. This seemed to indicate the people wanted to annex Texas. In 1845 Congress passed a "joint resolution" which declared that Texas was now a state of the Union. Thus the "Lone Star Republic" ended, and a new star was added to the American flag.

The United States had won another vast rich area and pushed its borders south and west. In a little over 40 years the nation had gained the Louisiana Territory (1803), Florida (1819), and Texas (1845). And there was more to come: Arizona, New Mexico, California and the Oregon Country.

Trouble over Texas led to war with Mexico. Mexico was angry when the United States annexed Texas. To Mexicans it looked as if Americans had been plotting all along to get control of the region. Bad feeling between the two nations grew.

Soon after Congress voted to annex Texas, Mexico "broke off

diplomatic relations." This meant that the Mexican representative left Washington, and the American representative in Mexico City was forced to return home. War was coming, slowly but surely.

To make matters worse, a bitter dispute arose about the boundary between Texas and Mexico. Texans claimed the Rio Grande was the border, and the American government backed up the claim. But Mexico declared the boundary was the Nueces (NWAY sace) River, about 50 miles north of the Rio Grande.

The land between the two rivers became a "no man's land" or disputed area. American soldiers under General Zachary Taylor were stationed near the Nueces. And Mexican troops camped south of the Rio Grande.

In an effort to avoid war, President Polk sent a representative named John Slidell to Mexico City. The President told Slidell to try to get a settlement that would reduce bad feeling. He also told Slidell to try to buy California, which Mexico controlled.

Before Slidell arrived in Mexico, news of his instructions "leaked out." Mexicans were insulted. It was bad enough to lose Texas; now Americans wanted California too! So the Mexican government refused to "receive" Slidell; no official would talk to him.

When President Polk heard how Slidell had been treated, he was angry. He ordered General Taylor to advance to the Rio Grande. Mexican soldiers crossed the river on April 25, 1846. They attacked one of Taylor's scouting parties and killed several Americans. When news of the attack reached Washington, Congress declared war.

General Taylor and General Scott won great victories. The Mexican War lasted for two years but there was never much doubt about the outcome. The United States army was stronger and more successful than it had been in the War of 1812. American military leaders planned and skillfully carried out campaigns that crushed Mexican resistance.

General Taylor was probably the most popular hero of the war. He had been in the army almost 40 years when the war began. His men called him "Old Rough and Ready."

Taylor did not wait for news of the declaration of war. When his scouts were attacked, he prepared for battle. He defeated the Mexicans and drove them back across the Rio Grande. Later he captured the military strong-

General Zachary Taylor (below) was one of the great heroes of the Mexican War.

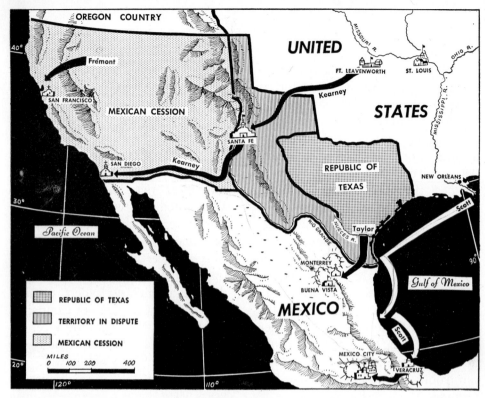

This map shows the most important battles of the Mexican War, 1846–1848. Trace the campaigns of Generals Zachary Taylor, Winfield Scott, and Stephen Kearny.

hold at Monterrey (MAHN teh RAY) in northern Mexico. And the next year he won a victory against great odds at Buena Vista (BWAY nah VEES tah). You can follow Taylor's campaign and the other campaigns of the Mexican War on the map on this page.

Another famous leader was General Winfield Scott. While Taylor was fighting in northern Mexico, Scott was heading a campaign in the South. He landed a few miles south of Veracruz (VARE ah KROOZ) and quickly captured the strongly fortified city.

Then Scott and his men fought their way hundreds of miles through mountains to the capital of Mexico. Many of his men died of disease and wounds, but Scott captured Mexico City in September of 1847. United States' Marines stood guard over "the halls of Montezuma."

The commander of the Mexican army was Santa Anna — the same general who ordered the slaughter at the Alamo and at Goliad. Before the Americans arrived, Santa Anna fled. But other Mexicans fought bravely. At the Battle of Chapultepec (chah POOL tay PECK), just outside Mexico city, 100 boys from a military school tried to hold back the American advance. None was over 18 years of age, but they all

286

died in the fight to save their city.

Americans won the Southwest and California. All the fighting did not take place in old Mexico. There were campaigns in California and the Southwest, too. In those days, Mexico controlled the region between Texas and the Pacific Ocean.

Americans had long had their eyes on this vast, undeveloped region. The government at Washington had offered to buy California. The nation was eager to expand to the Pacific Ocean. But Mexico would not sell.

When the war began, American military leaders realized that here at last was a chance to get control of the Southwest. An army officer named Stephen Kearny (KAR nee) was ordered to lead an expedition into New Mexico. Kearny followed the Santa Fe (FAY) trail from Missouri and Kansas to New Mexico.

For years American traders had been traveling over this trail. They took wagon loads of goods and sold them at a big profit in Santa Fe. Some of the traders settled in New Mexico.

Kearny crossed desert and mountain country with about 1600 men. They captured New Mexico without much trouble. American settlers welcomed them. They took the city of Santa Fe without a fight. Then Kearny left part of his army in New Mexico and pushed on to California.

American settlers in California were already rebelling against Mexican rule. An American explorer, John C. Frémont (free MAHNT) happened to be in California in 1846. He helped the rebels set up what they called the "Bear Flag Republic."

Soon afterward American warships appeared near the California coast. They landed troops and proclaimed the territory part of the United States. A few months later Stephen Kearny reached southern California and completed the con-

The picture below shows the capture of Mexico City, September 13–14, 1847. American troops are forcing their way into the enemy capital and the "halls of Montezuma."

quest of the region. Thus a few hundred men won the Southwest and California, and pushed the borders of the United States to the Pacific.

What kind of a land was California? Why were Americans interested in it and why did they find it easy to capture the region? The answers are to be found in the early history of California.

Spanish influence was strong in the Southwest. Like Arizona and New Mexico, California was a romantic land. Today, when you visit the Southwest or California, you can still find evidence of Spain's influence. Many houses are built in the style of old Spanish ranch houses. (This style of architecture has recently become popular in other parts of America also.) Most of the names of rivers, mountains, and towns are Spanish. They begin with *San* or *Santa*, the Spanish word for Saint. And some of the villages and churches are among the oldest in the United States.

Long before the English colonies were founded, Spaniards brought their language, customs, and religion to the Southwest. They called the region the Territory of New Mexico. Spanish governors ruled it from their palace in Santa Fe.

When Mexico won independence from Spain, a Mexican governor appeared in the old palace, which is still standing today. But the land remained almost empty. On the western and southern borders there were a few settlements, but the rest of the territory had never been explored.

In many parts of California and the Southwest you can see the ruins of small churches called missions. These were established by the *padres* (PAHD rayz), or priests, who made the long journey from Mexico City to help the Indians. (Padre is a Spanish word that means "father.") They taught the Indians the Christian

Below is a drawing of one of the early Spanish missions in California. Note the simple, pleasant style of architecture, the Spaniards on horseback, the priest blessing Indians.

faith. They also taught them how to make gardens and establish orchards on the dry soil by bringing water in ditches from the hills. Some of the padres were killed; some died of hunger or thirst; but others continued their work.

California was a land of missions and great estates. Outstanding among such men was Father Junípero Serra (hoo NEE peh ro SARE ah). He was called the hero of California because he planted civilization there after Spanish officials had failed. He was growing old when he was sent to establish the mission of San Diego (1769). Before his work ended, other padres had helped him to gather thousands of Indians into 18 missions, scattered along the coast from San Diego north to San Francisco. Each of the larger missions had its church, school, and hospital, its tile-roofed houses clustered around the plaza (square or park), its neighboring Indian village, its outlying grain fields, and on a hill overlooking the harbor, its *presidio* or military camp.

When Mexico became independent, the missions were neglected. The buildings crumbled into ruins. But some settlements around the missions grew into thriving towns. Many leading cities of California, Arizona, and New Mexico were founded by Spanish priests.

The pioneers of the Southwest were people of the upper class, or nobility, who came from Spain in quest of free land. Slowly they made their way up from Mexico. They established ranches along the southern border of what is now New Mexico, and around every mission in southern California. Usually they settled in a valley which offered the two essentials of ranching: grass and water. Soon their cattle were numbered by tens of thousands.

Most of the early ranches (granted by favor of the government, and still called Spanish Grants) were so large an owner could ride all day on a fast horse without going beyond his own land. Here in a fine house the *don*, or owner, lived comfortably with his family. At a distance were the *adobe* (ah DOH bih), or sun-dried, houses of his servants. The *vaqueros* (vah KAY rohs), or cowboys, lived in adobe houses too.

The dons were famous for hospitality. Travelers were welcomed; they were encouraged to stay a week or a month, but they must never offer to pay for food or lodging. Stories of the Spanish dons — of their pride, their hospitality, and their good manners — still influence the way of life in the Southwest.

California attracted Americans. For a long time California and the Southwest made little progress. Only a few Spaniards and Mexicans lived there. As long as Spaniards controlled the region, they forbade Americans to enter. However, a number of trappers and scouts found their way into the territory.

After 1822, when Mexican rule began, the number of American immigrants increased. Small groups crossed the Rockies and came down mountain passes to California. Mexican officials in California let them stay, mostly because they lacked the troops to drive them out.

By 1846 about 500 Americans were living on the California coast. American interest in the land grew steadily.

Mexico's hold on the region was weak. California, like Texas and New Mexico, was too far from Mexico City to receive much attention from the Mexican government. Communication was slow; it took weeks, sometimes months, for a message from Mexico to reach California. The population of California was small; there were only about 8000 Mexicans and 24,000 Indians in the whole territory. Most of them seem to have felt little loyalty to their faraway rulers.

On the other hand, Americans who had recently come to California were intensely loyal to the United States. When the Mexican War broke out they seized the opportunity to start a revolt. The timely appearance of General Kearny and the cooperation of American warships helped bring California under American control.

A few days before Mexico officially gave up claim to California, one of the most exciting events in American history took place. Gold was discovered in California! The news spread everywhere and started the Gold Rush of 1849. The sleepy, out-of-the-way land suddenly became the center of world attention. California was on her way to becoming one of the leading states in the Union.

The United States gained much territory from Mexico. The conquest of California, Taylor's victorious campaign in the north, and Scott's capture of Mexico City finally convinced the Mexicans they had no chance to win. Indeed, it began to look as if the United States might take over all Mexico. Santa Anna had to leave the country in disgrace. New leaders took charge and asked for peace.

At a village near Mexico City a treaty was signed in 1848. Thus the Mexican War came to an end. In the treaty, Mexico gave up all claims to Texas and the provinces of New Mexico and California. The *Mexican Cession*, or land given up by Mexico, included what is now New Mexico and California as well as parts of Utah, Nevada, Arizona, and Colorado.

In return for the territory, the United States paid Mexico fifteen million dollars. The United States also agreed to pay American citizens over three millions dollars that Mexico owed them. The border between Mexico and the United States was fixed along the Rio Grande River and thence to the Pacific.

Mexicans accepted the treaty; they

The '49ers kept on the move! Here is an artist's idea of the way the miners of 1849 looked as they searched the hills for gold in California during the famous gold rush.

had no choice. But they hated the United States for the loss of some of their richest territory. Today, Mexico and the United States are friends, but some Mexicans still remember with bitterness the unhappy events of 1846–1848.

The treaty of 1848 did not settle all disputes between Mexico and the United States. There continued to be quarrels and troubles along the border. And no one was quite sure where the boundary line ran in the Southwest.

The Gold Rush of '49 and California's rapidly growing population created a demand for a railroad through the Southwest to the Pacific coast. The best route for such a railroad lay south of New Mexico and Arizona, in Mexican territory. The United States offered to buy the land for ten million dollars. A railroad man named James Gadsden was sent to Mexico City to arrange the purchase.

Mexico needed money, so she agreed. In 1853 the *Gadsden Purchase* was completed. It added a strip of land to southern Arizona and New Mexico. It was the last piece of territory the United States got from Mexico.

The Mormons settled in Utah. During the Mexican War some Americans started a settlement in the Rocky Mountain region. The settlers belonged to a religious group called the Mormons or, more correctly, the Church of Jesus Christ of Latter Day Saints. The Mormon religion was founded by Joseph Smith.

Smith was born in Vermont in

1805. When he was 14 he moved with his family to Palmyra (pal MY rah), New York. Smith was intensely interested in religion, and he had many visions.

Smith told later how an angel appeared to him one day, led him to a hill near his father's farm, and told him to dig in the ground. Smith reported that he found golden plates containing sacred writings. These writings he translated; they were the source of a book Smith later published called *The Book of Mormon*.

Many people laughed at Joseph Smith. But some believed him and helped him found a new religion. The Mormons moved westward, hoping to find a friendly locality.

In Illinois, Smith and his followers founded a settlement. But they had trouble with neighbors who did not like the new religion. Smith was murdered by a mob. A new leader, Brigham Young, took charge. The Mormons decided to move to the Far West and find a new home, far from any other settlements.

Brigham Young (below) led the Mormons to Utah. Under his strong leadership, they established prosperous settlements.

From Illinois, Brigham Young led a pioneer group of 140 men and three women. They followed the Oregon Trail to South Pass in the Rocky Mountains. There they turned southwest on what later became the trail to California.

They reached a valley, encircled by mountains, on the shore of Great Salt Lake. Brigham Young declared, "This is the place." The Mormons cleared the sage-brush and made their first permanent camp. The loneliness of the hidden valley was one reason the Mormons chose it. Here, in Utah, they thought, they could live in peace.

The first work of the advance party was to dig canals. In this way, water could be brought from the mountains to *irrigate*, or to make fertile by watering, a few acres of desert soil. Food crops were planted, and riders carried back word that everything was ready for the great journey. Then from distant Illinois 1000 wagons set forth to cross 1500 miles of prairie and mountain.

At the end of the dangerous journey, the whole Mormon company went promptly to work. They dug more canals, planted more acres, and built mills and workshops. They intended to make the land support them, and to make whatever clothing, furniture, and tools they needed. They soon established a thriving settlement and "made the desert bloom."

At the end of the Mexican War, the United States took possession of

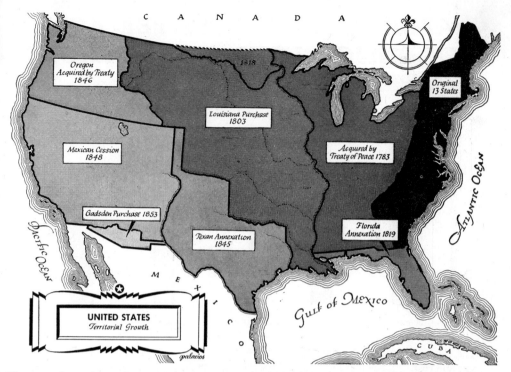

The map above shows the stages in the expansion of the United States. Beginning as 13 little states on the edge of the Atlantic, the republic spread to the Pacific in less than a century.

the whole Southwest. The land where the Mormons had settled became Utah Territory. In 1896 Utah entered the Union as a state.

Many nations claimed Oregon. North of California and west of the Louisiana Territory lay the *Oregon Country.* It included the land that is now Oregon, Washington, Idaho, and part of western Canada. Many nations claimed it. Spain claimed it because her explorers had tramped over part of the area. But Spain gave up her claim in 1819. Russia also claimed Oregon, saying it was part of Alaska. But the Russians soon withdrew from the region.

Great Britain claimed the Oregon country for two reasons: (1) Cap-

tain Cook had landed there in 1778. And (2) a British fur trading organization, the Hudson's Bay Company, had established several forts and trading posts in the region. Unlike the Russians and Spaniards, the British refused to give up their hold on Oregon.

Americans insisted that Oregon belonged to the United States. They based their claim on three facts: (1) An American sea captain, Robert Gray, discovered the Columbia River in 1792. He named the river in honor of his ship, the *Columbia.* (2) Lewis and Clark were the first who thoroughly explored the region and drew maps of it. (3) An American fur trading company started the first trading post in Oregon in 1811.

AREA*, COST & COST PER ACRE†
OF MAJOR LAND ACQUISITIONS

(*Millions of acres.   †When acquired by purchase.)

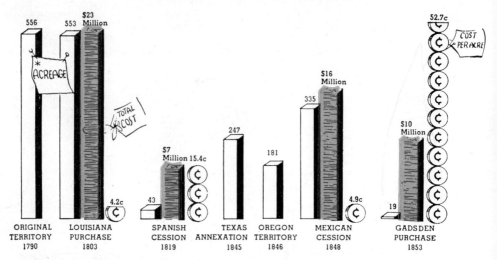

The chart above shows how the various territories acquired by the United States compare in size and cost. Notice that the Gadsden Purchase of 1853 was the most expensive per acre.

The post was named Astoria in honor of the company's founder, John Jacob Astor.

But it takes more than explorers and fur traders to conquer the wilderness. Britain and the United States realized Oregon would probably go to the nation that was able to settle it and develop it. So they both did their best to encourage people to go to Oregon.

Marcus Whitman and Jason Lee led the settlement of Oregon. American plans to settle Oregon received an unexpected boost from the Indians. Lewis and Clark had made friends with the tribes they met on their voyage down the Columbia. The wisdom of the two captains greatly impressed the Indians.

A short time later, four young Indians climbed on their horses and headed east. They rode over mountains and plains for many days. Two riders died before the journey ended. But the other two reached St. Louis. There they delivered their message: the Indians of Oregon asked that white teachers be sent to help them.

The churches were glad to answer the appeal. They sent several missionaries to Oregon. The most famous were Jason Lee, a minister, and Marcus Whitman, a physician. Their wives went with them.

Whitman and Lee established settlements and sent back word of great opportunities in Oregon. Whitman and his wife, Narcissa, were later killed by the Indians they tried to help. Jason Lee was more fortunate.

AMERICAN EXPANSION

Who's Who in History

Be sure you know the part that each of the following played in the westward movement.

1. Meriwether Lewis
2. William Clark
3. Sacajawea
4. Zebulon Pike
5. Stephen Austin
6. Samuel Houston
7. James K. Polk
8. Zachary Taylor
9. Winfield Scott
10. Joseph Smith
11. Stephen Kearny
12. John C. Frémont
13. Brigham Young
14. Robert Gray
15. John Jacob Astor
16. Marcus Whitman
17. Jason Lee

Study Questions

1. a. Trace the route of the Lewis and Clark Expedition.
   b. How did the work of Lewis and Clark help settle the West?

2. a. What region did Zebulon Pike explore?
   b. What useful information did his report give pioneers?

3. a. Give two reasons for the trouble on the border between Spanish Florida and the United States.
   b. How did Andrew Jackson put down the trouble in Florida?

4. a. Why did so many Americans go to Texas in the 1820's?
   b. Mention three reasons why misunderstandings arose between the Mexican government and Texas settlers.
   c. Explain what the Texans mean by: "Remember the Alamo!"
   d. At what battle did Texans win their independence?

5. Why did the United States delay the annexation of Texas?

6. a. State two causes of the Mexican War.
   b. What territory did the United States get as a result of the war?

7. It is said of the Mormon pioneers that "they made the desert bloom." Explain what this means.

8. a. What nations claimed the Oregon Country?
   b. Give three reasons why the United States claimed Oregon.
   c. What was meant by the slogan "54°40' or fight"?
   d. How and when did the United States acquire Oregon?

LET'S LOOK AT WHAT WE'VE LEARNED

What was the Westward Movement and what were its three main stages?

The Westward Movement is the name given the flow of population from the eastern seaboard to the Pacific Ocean. The first wave carried the frontier westward in colonial times to the foothills of the Appalachian Mountains. The second wave, which began after the defeat of the French in 1763, carried the frontier to the Mississippi River. The third wave came in the 1840's and lasted until about 1880. It carried the edge of settlement over the Great Plains and the Rocky Mountains to the Pacific Coast.

Why did Americans keep moving west?

Some wanted adventure. Most of them were seeking good land and new opportunities. Some sought freedom to try out new ideas.

How did the Westward Movement encourage the growth of democracy?

On the frontier, wealth and family influence did not mean so much as in the East. Men and women were valued for the work they did. So property qualifications disappeared on the frontier. Because women had a great part in developing the West they gained a share in the government. Women were first permitted to vote in the West.

How did the United States gain Florida?

For many years there was fighting on the border between Spanish Florida and Georgia. Finally, Spain was told to keep order or turn Florida over to the United States. In an agreement signed in 1819 Florida became part of the United States.

How did Texas become part of the United States?

Texas was under Spanish and then Mexican rule until 1836, when Texans declared their independence. They fought a short, bloody war and won their freedom. For nine years Texas was an independent nation, but Texans wanted to join the United States. Congress finally voted to annex Texas in 1845.

What were the causes and results of the Mexican War?

Mexico was angry at the United States for annexing Texas. A dispute arose over the boundary between Texas and Mexico. Fighting broke out there in April, 1846, and led to a declaration of war.

Mexico was badly beaten. In 1848 a treaty ended the war. The United States won a vast territory known as the Mexican Cession, which included California, New Mexico, and Arizona.

AMERICAN EXPANSION

How did the United States obtain Oregon?

Both the United States and Great Britain claimed the Oregon Territory. But thousands of American settlers followed the Oregon Trail to the Northwest thus strengthening the United States' claim. In 1846 Great Britain and the United States agreed to divide the territory. The United States gained the southern part, which included what are now the states of Oregon, Idaho, Washington, and part of Montana and Wyoming.

Who were some of the leaders of the Westward Movement?

Daniel Boone, who blazed the Wilderness Road to Kentucky; Sacajawea, the Indian woman who helped Lewis and Clark; Stephen Austin, who first settled in Texas; Sam Houston, the hero of Texas independence; Brigham Young, who led the Mormons to Utah; Marcus and Narcissa Whitman, who went to Oregon as missionaries.

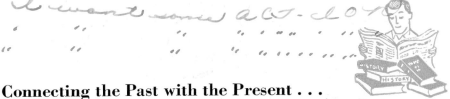

Connecting the Past with the Present . . .

How would you like to be a citizen of a small, crowded nation? It's a hard thing for Americans to imagine. In this vast land, there is a feeling of spaciousness, of "elbow room." There's a chance to expand, to move around, to find new opportunities. Because America spreads from the Atlantic to the Pacific, "from sea to shining sea," people have a feeling of freedom.

The possession of three million square miles of the world's best land has helped make the United States a leader among nations. Other governments have to respect such strength.

It was only a century or so ago that the nation reached its present boundaries. In Washington's time the United States was a small country, hemmed in by unfriendly neighbors. The expansion of the country through settlement, purchase, and war took place in the first half of the 19th century. America won the room and resources essential to a great power. Thousands of pioneers pushed the frontier to the Pacific and made the land productive.

Today the wealth and industrial capacity of the United States would astonish the pioneers of the West. However, it is largely through their efforts that the nation is big and powerful today.

Questions for Discussion and Review

1. Explain the order in which men of different occupations came to frontier regions.

2. What were the three great "waves" of settlement?

3. What were some reasons why people wished to leave their homes to move to new frontiers?

4. Tell how the new western states taught the old eastern states something about democracy.

5. **a.** What was right about Andrew Jackson's Spoils System?
   b. What was wrong about it?

6. **a.** What part did Andrew Jackson play in the acquisition of Florida from Spain?
   b. Explain the financial part of this acquisition.

7. How did Texas become part of the United States?

8. List the terms of the treaty which ended the Mexican War.

9. Why did the United States make the Gadsden Purchase?

10. Using the following headings make a chart of the territorial acquisitions described in this Unit:

Territory	Date	How Acquired

THE HISTORY LABORATORY

Here are suggestions for activities that you will find interesting and profitable.

Put the Pieces Together . . .

Make a jig-saw puzzle large enough for classroom display showing the territorial acquisitions of the United States. You can make it out of cardboard or wood and color and label it to show the different acquisitions.

WHAT AND WHEN

Boone begins Wilderness Road 1775

Louisiana Purchase 1803

Lewis and Clark 1804-06

Florida Ac[e] 1819

Yours Truly . . .

Pretend you are one of the following and write letters or advertisements urging people to settle in the West:

1. The owner of a fast sailing vessel bound for San Francisco.

2. The owner of sturdy wagons ready for the Oregon Trail.

3. An American (perhaps Stephen Austin) who has received a large grant of land in Texas.

Make a Model . . .

Make models of the famous buildings and vehicles mentioned in this Unit. Here are some suggestions: the Alamo, a mission, an army fort, a covered wagon, Sutter's Mill, an Indian village. These models can be made of clay, wood, paper, or metal.

Write a Guide Book . . .

Pretend you are to guide tourists through an old California mission. Prepare a notebook of facts about Father Junípero Serra and his Franciscan missions. Include the following Spanish words and their meanings:

vaqueros	adobe	Spanish dons
presidio	pueblo	padre

Wild Horses . . .

Uncover the story behind some of America's most famous horses by finding out what happened to a few fine animals that escaped from the early Spanish explorers. Write a report on your research including drawings or pictures. Consult the encyclopedia for information.

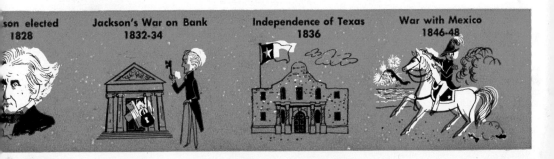

son elected 1828   Jackson's War on Bank 1832-34   Independence of Texas 1836   War with Mexico 1846-48

Keep a Diary . . .

Imagine you are a pioneer boy or girl in a typical large pioneer family on the frontier or moving in a covered wagon train on the Oregon Trail. Write a diary of your experiences. You will find these books helpful:

Children of the Covered Wagon, Mary J. Carr (Crowell, 1943).
Marcus and Narcissa Whitman, James Daugherty (Viking, 1953).
Keep the Wagons Moving, West Lathrop (Random, 1949).
Seek the Dark Gold, Jo Evalin Lundy (Winston, 1951).
On to Oregon! Honoré Morrow, (Morrow, 1946).

On the Record . . .

Secure the recording *Lewis & Clark Expedition*, distributed by Enrichment Materials, Inc., 246 5th Avenue, New York, 1, N.Y. Have it played in class. Although it is a good recording, you will find that many details have been omitted. After research prepare additions to the scripts which can be read as inserts at the proper places during a replaying of the record a week later.

Let's Read about the Westward Movement

ADAMS, SAMUEL H., *Santa Fe Trail*, Random, 1951.
BALCH, GLENN, *Indian Saddle Up*, Crowell, 1953.
COLLIER, EDMUND, *The Story of Kit Carson*, Grosset, 1953.
DAVIS, JULIA, *No Other White Men*, Dutton, 1937.
**DE VOTO, BERNARD, *The Journals of Lewis and Clark*, Houghton, 1953.
DOUGLAS, MARJORY S., *Freedom River*, Scribners, 1953.
EIFERT, VIRGINIA S., *Three Rivers South*, Dodd, 1953.
EMMONS, DELLA F. G., *Sacajawea of the Shoshones*, Binfords, 1943.
GARST, D. S., *Jim Bridger, Greatest of the Mountain Men*, Houghton, 1952.
JOHNSON, WILLIAM, *Sam Houston, the Tallest Texan*, Random, 1953.
KJELGAARD, JIM, *The Coming of the Mormons*, Random, 1953.
*McNEER, MAY Y., *Story of California*, Harper, 1944.
POLITI, LEO, *The Mission Bell*, Scribners, 1953.
STAFFELBACH, E. H., *For Texas and Freedom*, Wagner, 1952.
STEVENSON, AUGUSTA, *Zeb Pike, Boy Traveler*, Bobbs, 1953.

* indicates easy reading
** indicates advanced reading

AMERICAN EXPANSION

C A N A D A
(BRITISH)

LAKE SUPERIOR

THE NORTHWEST TERRITORY
(Organized 1787)

Mississippi River

LAKE MICHIGAN

LAKE HURON

St. Lawrence River

Fort Niagara

LAKE ONTARIO

Detroit

LAKE ERIE

NEW YORK

Mohawk Valley

VERMONT
State 1791

NEW HAMPSHIRE

MASSACHUSETTS

CONN.

R.I.

PENNSYLVANIA

NEW JERSEY

DELAWARE

MARYLAND

Ohio River

VIRGINIA

WILDERNESS ROAD

Cumberland Gap

NORTH CAROLINA

SOUTH CAROLINA

GEORGIA

U N I T E D

S T A T E S

L O U I S I A N A
(SPANISH)

Missouri River

Mississippi River

River

Area claimed by Spain

WEST FLORIDA
(SPANISH)

New Orleans

EAST FLORIDA
(SPANISH)

North

A T L A N T I C   O C E A N

40°

30°

75°

60°

50°

G U L F   O F   M E X I C O

THE UNITED STATES
IN 1783

This map shows the new American republic
as recognized by Great Britain in the Treaty
of Peace, 1783.

Note that settlers were already leaving
the original states for the West.

C U B A
(SPANISH)

90°

MAP E

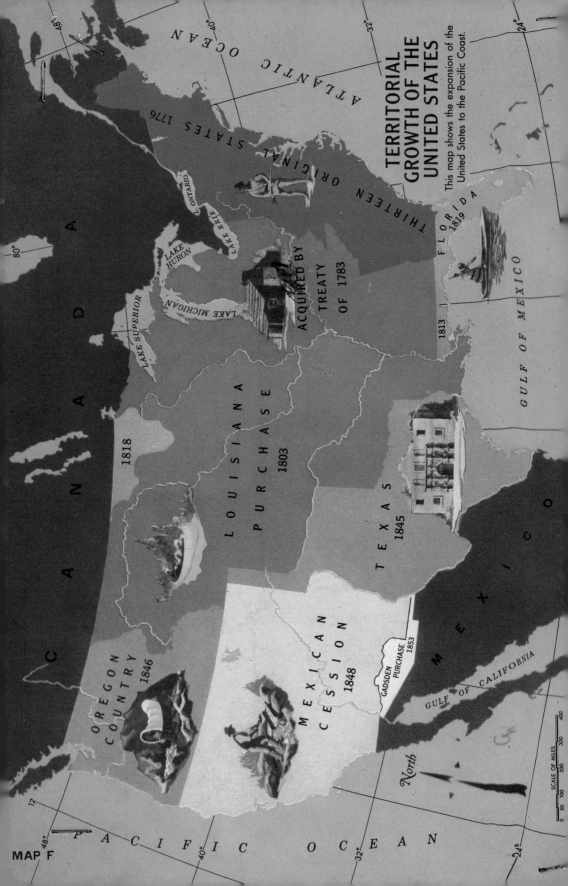

TERRITORIAL
GROWTH OF THE
UNITED STATES

This map shows the expansion of the
United States to the Pacific Coast.

ATLANTIC OCEAN

THIRTEEN ORIGINAL STATES 1776

C   A   N   A   D   A

LAKE SUPERIOR

LAKE HURON

LAKE MICHIGAN

LAKE ERIE

L. ONTARIO

ACQUIRED BY TREATY OF 1783

FLORIDA
1819

1813

GULF OF MEXICO

1818

LOUISIANA PURCHASE 1803

TEXAS
1845

M   E   X   I   C   O

OREGON
COUNTRY
1846

MEXICAN CESSION 1848

GADSDEN PURCHASE
1853

GULF   OF   CALIFORNIA

North

80°

48°

12

PACIFIC   OCEAN

48°

40°

32°

24°

SCALE OF MILES

0   50 100   200   300   400

MAP F

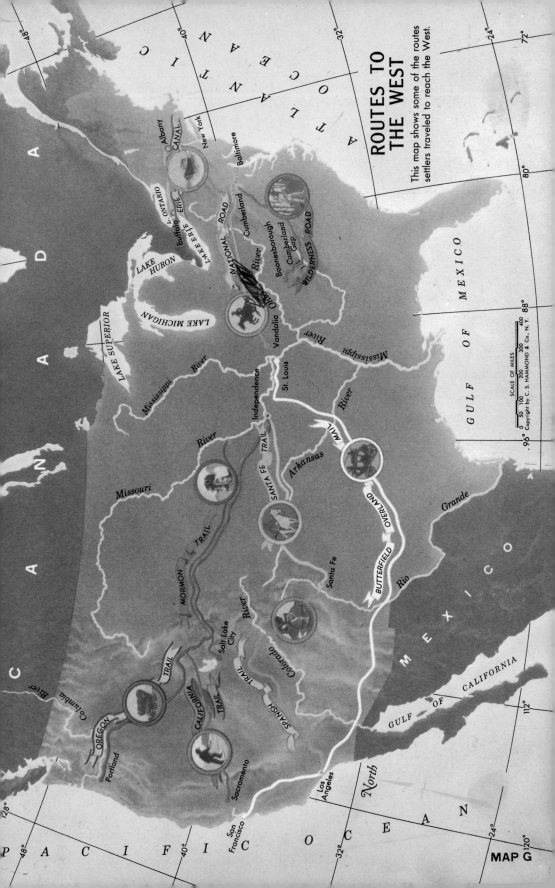

ROUTES TO THE WEST

This map shows some of the routes settlers traveled to reach the West.

SCALE OF MILES

0 50 100 200 300 400

Copyright by C. S. HAMMOND & Co., N.Y.

MAP G

BRITISH POSSESSIONS

HUDSON BAY

Mackenzie River

PACIFIC OCEAN

MEXICO

GULF OF MEXICO

CARIBBEAN SEA

ATLANTIC

North

UNITED STATES

CONFEDERATE STATES

WASHINGTON TERRITORY

OREGON

CALIFORNIA

NEVADA TERRITORY

UTAH TERRITORY

COLORADO TERRITORY

NEW MEXICO TERRITORY

DAKOTA TERRITORY

NEBRASKA TERRITORY

KANSAS

INDIAN TERRITORY

MINNESOTA

IOWA

MISSOURI

WISCONSIN

ILLINOIS

INDIANA

OHIO

MICHIGAN

KENTUCKY

TENNESSEE

ARKANSAS

TEXAS

LOUISIANA

MISSISSIPPI

ALABAMA

GEORGIA

FLORIDA

SOUTH CAROLINA

NORTH CAROLINA

VIRGINIA

WEST VIRGINIA

MARYLAND

DELAWARE

PENNSYLVANIA

NEW YORK

NEW JERSEY

MAINE

VERMONT

NEW HAMP.

MASS.

CONN.

RHODE ISLAND

Washington
Richmond

Missouri River

Mississippi River

Colorado River

Rio Grande

St. Lawrence River

Lake Superior

LAKE HURON

LAKE MICHIGAN

LAKE ERIE

L. ONTARIO

135°   105°   90°   75°   60°   60°

50°

30°

120°   105°   90°

THE CONFEDERATE STATES OF AMERICA

This map shows the states that
seceded and formed the Confederacy.
The map shows North America as
seen from the southwest, at a point
over Mexico.

MAP H

Unit 7

IMPROVED TRANSPORTATION AND COMMUNICATION STRENGTHENED AMERICA (1806-1869)

"THE TWO TRAINS pulled up facing each other, each crowded with workmen. . . . The telegraph lines had been brought to that point so that in the final spiking, as each blow was struck, the telegraph recorded it at each connected office from the Atlantic to the Pacific. Prayer was offered. When the last spike was driven . . . the engineers ran up their locomotives until they touched. . . . Thus the two roads were wedded into one great line from the Atlantic to the Pacific."

In these words General Dodge, chief engineer of the Union Pacific, reported completion of America's first transcontinental railroad.

In May, 1869, America stood united, thanks to the railroad and the telegraph. What other means of communication and transportation had been used earlier? What part did the government play in developing them? What about the telegraph which gave the world "a blow by blow" description of the event?

The answers are part of the story of the development of rapid transportation and communication — the story told in Unit 7.

303

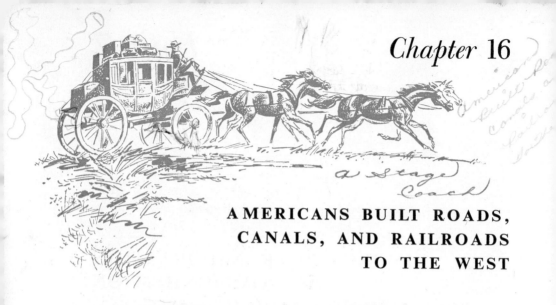

Chapter 16

AMERICANS BUILT ROADS, CANALS, AND RAILROADS TO THE WEST

We were forty miles from Albany,
Forget it I never shall,
What a terrible storm we had one night
On the E-ri-e Canal.

So sang the canal workers as they worked the barges on the Erie Canal. The time was early in the 19th century and the future was bright. The canal "craze" grew; many states rushed to dig their own canals, to bring the West closer to the Atlantic. Then, suddenly, it ended.

Strange new sounds began to be heard in the land: the hiss of escaping steam and the long, mournful whistle of a train. The railroad had become part of the Westward Movement. Who was responsible for this new means of transportation? What effect did it have?

Jefferson had predicted it would take several centuries for Americans to settle the Mississippi Valley. How long did it actually take to sweep across the Mississippi and join the Atlantic and Pacific Oceans with a railroad?

The following pages record the days when Americans were experimenting with the means of transportation to bind together their country into "one nation indivisible."

Roadbuilding began in early colonial times. Seventy years after the Revolution, the United States stretched from the Atlantic to the Pacific Ocean. By purchase, conquest, and exploration, Americans had won vast territories in the South and West. From Canada to the Gulf of Mexico, from Maine to California, the American flag waved.

But it took time for population to catch up with the flag. Many parts of the country remained empty of people long after the Mexican War and the Gadsden Purchase. There were always plenty of Americans eager to push forward and claim new lands. What held them back or at least slowed up their advance?

The answer is surprisingly simple: they had to wait for the building of a road or a waterway to the new territory. So, during the first half of the 19th century, the nation was busy building roads and canals to open up the West.

When the first settlers came to America they found only a few little paths leading into the forest. Some were made by deer and other animals. Others were made by Indians hunting through the woods.

Such trails, however, did not usually lead where the white men wanted to go. Pioneers could follow them for only a short distance. Then the trails would end, suddenly, on the side of a mountain or in the middle of a thicket.

Thus roadbuilding early became an important activity. Settlers were always cutting foot paths through the woods. Later they widened the paths so horses and two-wheeled carts could pass over them.

Sooner or later someone would try to drive a big four-wheeled wagon over one of the paths. Of course he "got stuck!" So the pioneers had to cut down more trees to straighten and widen the road.

For a while the wider road was adequate. But soon other wagons followed. Before long the road became worn down; deep ruts appeared and made travel dangerous. The settlers filled up the holes and tried to provide a firm surface with any material they could find: wooden planks, broken stones,

---

The drawing below shows a section of the Pennsylvania Road in 1751. As you can see, it was little more than a trail over the hills.

Below is a scene on the Boston Post Road in 1763. Compare it with the picture at the left noting how fast roadbuilding improved.

Here is Zane's Trace in 1797. This road led West over the mountains to Wheeling.

This wagon, the "Flying Machine," went from New York to Philadelphia in 1766.

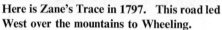

gravel, and even crushed oyster shells.

When the road came to a river, the pioneers had another problem to solve. If the stream was narrow they could build a log bridge over it. But wide rivers were too much for early road builders.

Near some rivers there were ferry men with boats to carry people and even horses to the other side. To cross other rivers, a traveler had to find a ford or shallow place where he or his horse could wade to the other side. When Thomas Jefferson rode from his home to Washington in 1801 he had to ford three rivers and swim his horse across five more.

It took time and money to build even the rough narrow roads of colonial days, and money was scarce in early America. In some colonies the government made everyone who used the roads pay a special tax. In some northern towns, able-bodied men had to give a few days work each spring to build or repair roads.

Stage coaches were popular. Ten miles a day was considered good

speed over early roads. A journey of two or three hundred miles usually took weeks. It is not surprising that some people never traveled far from the place where they were born. But most Americans were eager to see the world. In spite of trouble and expense, they kept moving.

A few years before the Revolution, stage coaches became popular. The stage coach was a large, plain, heavy carriage drawn by four horses. It could carry from eight to fourteen passengers.

The coach had to be strongly built or bumpy roads would soon shake it to pieces. One English traveler said that riding in an American stage coach was "most disagreeable . . . the motion is similar to being tossed in a blanket, often throwing you to the top of the coach, so as to flatten your hat — if not your head."

Nevertheless, stage coaches were almost always crowded. Soon there were regular stage coach routes in ten of thirteen states. It was something to boast about when one could

ROADS AND CANALS

This picture shows a stagecoach traveling near Trenton, New Jersey in 1810.

Here is shown the building of the first macadam road in America in 1823.

travel from New York to Boston in six days. One traveler described his trip like this:

I set out from Boston on the new line of stages. We reached a resting place at ten o'clock at night. After supper we went to bed, with notice that we would be called at three in the morning. Then we arose and made ready, by help of a horn lantern or a candle, to proceed over bad roads. Sometimes we had to get out to help the coachmen lift the coach out of a deep rut. We reached New York after a week's travel, wondering at the ease and speed of our journey.

At first, stage coaches traveled at the rate of two miles an hour. Later, when the roads were improved, the rate increased to six. In 1836 a trip of 300 miles took 50 hours of day-and-night travel.

Toll roads were profitable. On the frontier early roads were even worse than those in the East. Western states had no money to build the roads that were needed. So private companies were formed to build *toll roads* in the various regions.

The companies made money by requiring everyone who used the roads to pay a fee or *toll*. The toll roads were carefully built; first the top soil was scraped away; then a foundation of rocks was laid; on top of that was spread a covering of crushed stone or gravel.

A Scotchman named John McAdam invented this type of road, and in his honor such roads are still called *macadam roads*. The top of finely crushed stone was rounded so that water would run off.

Every few miles along the toll road there were gates, each with a toll-collector called a "keeper." The gate was at first a heavy post, to which was attached a bar long enough to stretch across the road. The bar was called a *pike*, and the keeper *turned* it to close the road until a traveler paid his toll. So the toll road was often called a "turnpike," or "pike."

The first toll road was the Lancaster Pike, which opened in 1793. It ran west from Philadelphia to the

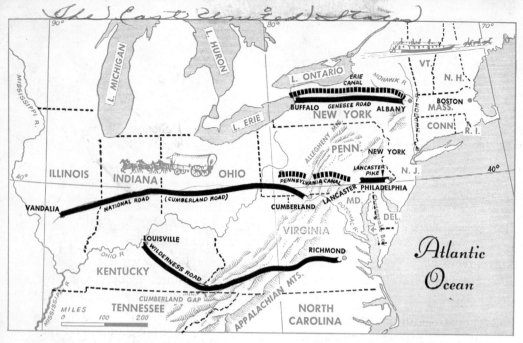

This map shows some of the routes pioneers took to the West in the first part of the 19th century. Note the Genesee Road, Wilderness Road, National Road, and Erie Canal.

frontier, a distance of 66 miles. Farther north, another road to the frontier was soon built. It was called the Genesee (JEN eh see) Road and it ran from Albany to Buffalo, New York. In the South there was the Wilderness Road from Richmond, Virginia to Louisville, Kentucky. It followed the trail Daniel Boone blazed through the Cumberland Gap.

The National Road was built at federal expense. The turnpikes helped open the West to settlers, but farmers and merchants complained about paying tolls. They thought the national government should build roads and let people use them without charge.

In those days it was feared the settlements in the Mississippi Valley might separate from the East. Western leaders pointed out that good roads would help hold the country together. So Congress agreed to pay for a road from the Potomac River to the Ohio Valley. It was called the National Road because the national government paid for it. Later it became known as the Cumberland Road because it began at Cumberland, Maryland.

Cumberland was a good starting point, for it lay midway between northern and southern states. And several short roads connected Cumberland with Baltimore and Philadelphia. The National Road was begun in 1811. From Cumberland it led over the Appalachian Mountains to the valley of the Ohio River.

It took 14 years to build 15... of road through the wilderness. ... first the government planned to build the road only as far as Wheeling. But the project was such a success that Congress voted to continue it farther west. Thousands of settlers traveled the National Road to the Ohio Valley. And back over the National Road came wagons loaded with food for the East and Europe.

Across the new state of Indiana the road led to Vandalia, Illinois. It reached Vandalia in 1833. There construction stopped, for the nation had lost interest in the project.

Because Americans had become excited about steamboats and railways, the National Road was soon forgotten. Today the old highway is a part of "U.S. 40," an automobile route that crosses America.

Canals provided cheap transportation. Thanks largely to toll companies and the national government, American roads improved greatly in the first part of the 19th century. Nevertheless, highway travel remained difficult and uncomfortable

... pos- ... travel by wat... ... was more comfortable than land travel.

It was also cheaper. It cost far less to transport goods over water than over land. This was particularly important to western farmers who had to send their products hundreds of miles to market.

Men who lived near a big river could load their goods on cheap flat boats and send them down the river to market. But people who lived miles from a waterway were out of luck. They had to pay such high transportation costs they could seldom make money on their crops.

Moreover, western farmers had to pay high prices for goods brought from the East. For example, a bushel of salt cost fifty cents on the Atlantic coast. But in the West it was so expensive that most pioneer families had to do without salt. The reason was the cost of transportation: salt had to be carried over the mountains by wagons and pack horses, and this expense added several cents a pound to the original price.

Below is a scene on the National Road which the federal government built to the West. It led from Maryland to Illinois.

Below is shown the Lancaster Pike in 1795. This was a toll road that led from Philadelphia to western Pennsylvania.

Far[...]
portation. As [...] the
problem the same solution occurred
to many: canals or artificial waterways! They said to one another,
"Why not dig waterways to connect our farms with far-away lakes
and rivers?"

It was easier said than done. A
canal is a waterway dug across land.
It must connect with a body of
water at each end.

Boats can travel along a canal,
and goods can be transported. But
a canal is not like a river. It has no
current, no rapids, no floods in the
spring or low water in summer. Instead, it is a series of level sections
of water.

The bodies of water at each end
of the canal are usually of different
levels. So too is the land between.
Therefore, *locks* must be built to
raise or lower the boats along the
way. Locks are small sections of the
canal just long enough for a canalboat to enter. At each end is a gate
to keep water from flowing in or out.

When a canalboat enters a lock,
the gates are closed behind it. Next,
a valve is opened and water is permitted to flow into the lock. The
boat rises with the water until it is
level with the water in the next lock.
The front gate is then opened, and
the boat can pass into the next lock.

It was expensive, of course, to
build canals. And it was hard, too,
in a land of forests and mountains.
But far-sighted pioneers greeted the
idea with enthusiasm.

The Erie Canal was a great success.
Washington was one of the first to
urge the building of canals. He and
his friends talked of building a canal
from Chesapeake Bay to the Ohio
River. But they were never able to
raise enough money.

Enthusiasm for canals spread
rapidly. Massachusetts built three
short canals. Then New Jersey and
Pennsylvania got busy. Each state
tried to get ahead of the other in
providing cheap transportation. But
early canals were only a few miles
long, so they were not much help to
people who wanted to reach the
West.

A New York governor named De
Witt Clinton saw that a great opportunity existed for a canal connecting East and West. And the
geography of New York State was
favorable to such a canal. At the
eastern end of the state were the
Hudson and Mohawk Rivers. At
the western end was Lake Erie. Why
not build a canal connecting the
Hudson and the Mohawk with Lake
Erie?

People laughed at the idea.
"You're crazy!" they told Clinton.
"The distance is over 350 miles. It
would take a hundred years and cost
a hundred million dollars in taxes to
build such a canal."

De Witt Clinton was not discouraged. He kept on working and
pleading. At last, in 1817, he got the
state legislature to grant money for
a canal.

It took eight years to dig the canal

and build the 72 locks needed. In 1825 the Erie Canal was completed. Clinton and other leaders sailed in triumph from Buffalo to New York City. There Clinton emptied a barrel of Lake Erie water into the Atlantic Ocean to represent the "wedding of the waters." The original canal was 363 miles long. It was 28 feet wide and four feet deep, but it soon had to be enlarged. You can trace the Erie Canal's route on the map, p. 308.

The Erie Canal cost over seven million dollars. Taxpayers grumbled at paying so much for "Clinton's Big Ditch." But the canal was a fine investment. It helped make New York the richest and most populated state. Along the canal, towns sprang up and became busy cities.

The most important result of the Erie Canal was a big increase of settlers in the Northwest Territory near the Great Lakes. Pioneers now traveled comfortably in a canalboat fitted with sleeping quarters, instead of bumping over rough roads and sleeping wherever they could. Cattle and household goods followed in another boat. The time it took to travel from New York City to Buffalo was greatly reduced.

Western settlers could now get better prices for grain, meat, and other farm products. Before the canal was built, westerners had to pay $120 a ton to get their goods to market. After the canal was finished it only cost $20 a ton. (Later the rate dropped to less than $8 a ton.) At the same time, people in the East could buy these products at lower prices because transportation cost less.

Eastern businessmen also benefited. They could ship manufactured goods to the West and sell them cheaper than ever before. Settlers in Ohio were soon buying clothing and other goods manufactured in New York State.

New York City became the nation's greatest seaport. Before the canal was built New York was far behind Boston, Philadelphia, and Charleston. But after 1825 New York forged ahead. It has remained the chief trading and financial center of the United States.

The picture below is an early drawing showing workers building a section of the Erie Canal near Lockport, New York.

Below (right) is a picture of traffic on the Erie Canal soon after it was opened in 1825. It was a success from the beginning.

At left above is shown one of John Fitch's steamboats, which never won public favor. At right is Robert Fulton, who built the first commercially successful steamboat.

Other states built canals. The success of the Erie encouraged other states to build canals. In the ten years from 1825 to 1835 more than a dozen canals were built. The nation seemed "canal crazy." Several states went deeply in debt to finance waterways that were used only a few years.

Pennsylvania had the most unusual canal. It ran across the Allegheny Mountains from Philadelphia to Pittsburgh. The mountains were so high that locks could not be used. The builders solved the problem by building a "cradle." This was a truck with wheels, operated with ropes, pulley, and a small engine. It hauled boats over the mountains.

After crossing more than thirty miles of mountains in the "cradle" the boat would be lowered to the western part of the canal. From there it floated down to Pittsburgh and the Ohio River.

John Fitch failed to interest the public in his steamboat. Water travel steadily became more important partly because many lakes and rivers were now connected by canals. But in the days of sailing ships, water transportation was slow. Something was needed to speed up travel by boat. The answer, of course, was steam power.

A Scotchman named James Watt had invented the steam engine in 1770. When news of the invention reached America many people asked, "Why not put an engine on a boat and make it turn paddlewheels that will push the boat faster than oars or sails?"

It was a good idea, but it took time to make it work. Several steamboats were invented, but they would run only a short distance and then break down. So many inventors worked on the problem and built model steamboats, that it is hard to say who deserves credit for the invention.

A Connecticut Yankee named John Fitch was one of the first to make a steamboat that really worked. But Fitch found it hard to get anyone to invest their money in his steamship.

He did not give up easily. He built a small engine and installed it in an old boat he bought on credit. In 1787 he launched his queer craft on the Delaware River. It moved along steadily at a speed of three miles an hour. People who saw it were like those who later saw the first airplane rise into the sky. They could not believe their eyes!

Fitch built three more steamboats. Each was faster and more powerful; one made trips regularly from Philadelphia, traveling 20 miles in three hours.

But travelers preferred to walk, or ride on a stage coach, for they feared the steamboat would blow up. When his fourth boat was wrecked in a storm, Fitch gave up. He died broken-hearted and forgotten.

Fulton built several steamboats. In the West settlers were raising meat, grain, and other foods in large quantities. They sent their products on flatboats that floated down the Ohio and Mississippi to New Orleans. There the flatboats had to be abandoned, for they could not be rowed or sailed back up the river against the strong current.

Westerners often remarked, "If only we had a boat that would move upstream, we would get better prices for our products, and pay less for manufactured goods." Among eastern businessmen who were thinking the same thing was Robert Livingston who had helped arrange the Louisiana Purchase. While in Paris, Livingston met a young American named Robert Fulton.

Fulton had gone to Europe to study painting but he soon learned that people were more interested in new machines than in pictures. In England Fulton saw a steam engine. He became so excited about it that he gave up painting and began studying machinery. He worked in several English factories and learned a good deal about steam engines. Next he tried his hand at inventing.

When Livingston learned what a gifted young man Fulton was, he urged him to develop a steamboat that would be profitable to operate. Livingston agreed to furnish all the money needed. Thus Fulton never had to struggle with the financial troubles that had discouraged poor John Fitch.

The two partners wasted no time. Livingston bought a boat in which Fulton installed a French engine. When they tried it on the Seine (SAYN) River that flows through Paris, the engine broke through the boat and sank to the bottom.

Fulton fished the engine up and put it in a stronger boat. The second boat was so heavy and clumsy it crawled downstream as slowly as a turtle. It would not travel upstream at all.

Fulton and Livingston resolved to keep on trying until they had a steamboat that would go. They came back to the United States and made another attempt. That also failed.

Then Fulton remembered the engine he had admired in England.

English laws forbade the export of engines. But somehow Fulton and Livingston got possession of a Watt engine. In New York they had a boat built which they called the *Clermont*. It was the largest boat ever seen on a river up to that time. When the builders heard the boat was going to run on steam power, they nicknamed it "Fulton's Folly."

The Clermont proved steamboats would work. When Fulton installed the precious Watt engine, the *Clermont* was ready. On August 17, 1807 a crowd of New Yorkers gathered to watch the launching. Some laughed and some cheered as the *Clermont* puffed slowly up the Hudson. It kept moving all the way upstream to Albany, a distance of 150 miles! The time from dock to dock was 32 hours.

The *Clermont's* first trip began the age of steam navigation. Within a month Fulton began regular passenger service on the Hudson. He gave thought to the passengers' com-

fort, too. One of his advertisements announced "A shelf has been added to each berth, on which gentlemen will please put their boots, shoes, and clothes that the cabin will not be encumbered."

Within five years steamboats were running on the Ohio and Mississippi Rivers. (Indians called them "big fire canoes.") The steamboats helped unite the new West to the East. They provided dependable transportation upstream or down, and they carried freight at low cost.

In 1819, another American ship surprised the world. The *Savannah,* a southern-owned steamship, crossed the Atlantic Ocean! It was the first time any boat had crossed the Atlantic by steam power. When the *Savannah* steamed into the harbor at Liverpool against wind and tide, the British blinked and rubbed their eyes. Until that time almost everyone thought no steamship could carry enough coal to cross the sea.

The United States had a great merchant marine. The voyage of the *Savannah* foretold the end of sailing

Below is a drawing of the *Clermont*, Robert Fulton's steamboat which proved that steam transportation was safe and practical.

Below is shown the *President*, one of the steamships that came into use after the *Clermont* made its famous trip up the Hudson.

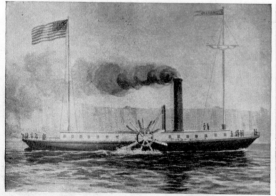

ships. But American shipbuilders were not willing to admit the fact. They kept building sailing ships and trying to improve them so they could compete with steamships.

Even in colonial days, shipbuilding was a great American industry. By 1800 the nation owned thousands of ocean-going ships. In the great seaports of the world, ships flying the American flag were constantly loading and unloading valuable cargoes. They carried lumber and fish to the West Indies, cotton to Europe, and furs to China. And they brought back sugar, tea, silks and spices.

The War of 1812 damaged American commerce, for the British navy drove most American ships off the seas. But the decline was only temporary. By 1850 the United States had more ships and sailors engaged in world trade than any Old World nation.

Discovery of gold in California in 1849 created new business for shipping companies. Thousands of gold seekers traveled by boat around Cape Horn to California. There was no Panama Canal in those days. People who wanted to go to California by boat either had to sail around South America or take a boat to the Isthmus of Panama, travel over land to the Pacific, and then take another boat north to California. Either way the trip took months, but it was safer and easier than traveling across the Great Plains and the Rockies.

Clipper Ships ruled the seas for a brief time. Fine new ships were built to carry passengers to California. Many were *clipper ships*. The clippers were fast, graceful sailing vessels. With favorable winds, they could outrun early steamships. Some clippers covered 300 miles a day — but only when the wind was "right."

The most famous builder of clipper ships was Donald McKay, a native of Nova Scotia. Like many other young Canadians, he came to New York City to seek his fortune. He got a job in a shipyard and worked ten years to become a master shipbuilder. Then McKay set up a shipyard in Massachusetts. The ships he built were long and slender, with high masts and big sails.

McKay's most famous ship was the *Flying Cloud*. In 1851 it made the trip from New York around Cape Horn to San Francisco in 89 days. No steamship of the time could equal such speed.

Nevertheless, clipper ships were doomed. British shipbuilders put stronger engines into their ships. They built their ships out of iron, which was plentiful in Britain. The British government made cash payments, or *bounties*, to help the industry. British steamships gained new speed. And they did not have to depend on the wind for power.

The American clippers could no longer compete. They soon disappeared from the seas. The era of wooden sailing ships gave way to the era of iron and steam. Because

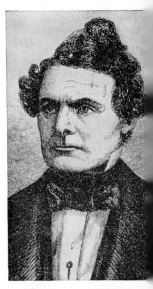

Above is shown the *Great Republic*, one of the famous, fast clipper ships built by Donald McKay (right). The swift, graceful clippers ruled the oceans for a brief period in mid-nineteenth century, but were soon replaced by more dependable steamboats.

American shipping companies refused to change with the times, they lost their leadership in world trade.

During the Civil War many merchant ships were sunk. This was the final blow. The American merchant marine became small and unimportant. Trade was lost to other nations.

Railroads originated in Great Britain. Why did Americans lose interest in ships and shipbuilding? The reason was that a great improvement occurred in land transportation. This was the railroad. The railroad transported goods and passengers quickly, comfortably, and at reasonable cost. It was the answer to the transportation problem that had hindered the nation from the beginning.

The railroad was first developed in England. In 1802 a British engineer produced what he called "a steam wagon." His neighbors called him crazy until they saw his wagon puffing over the road at ten miles an hour. Then they said he was a nuisance because, at the sight of his machine, horses ran away and people's lives were in danger.

The next step was to put the steam wagon on rails. Long before, some unknown coal miner had watched horses drawing a load of coal from the mine to a nearby highway. They had to strain to pull the cart over the soft road. So the miner laid a pair of wooden rails on top of the coal road. Over such rails one horse could easily pull the load. From that time on, carts in English mines ran on wooden rails or tracks.

The next improvement was to make rails of iron. Then someone thought of putting a kind of rim, or *flange*, on the wheels of the wagon.

ROADS AND CANALS

This helped the wagon to stay on the track.

From slow hauling of coal to fast hauling of passengers was an easy step. The first steam wagon was not very successful, but inventors kept working on the problem. They built several engines with some unexpected results: one rattled itself to pieces; another set the woods on fire; a third blew up, killing the engineer and a passenger!

But twelve years after the appearance of the first steam wagon, George Stephenson invented a practical locomotive. He called it the *Rocket*. Now the way was clear to plan a railroad. By 1830 England had several short railroads.

Americans caught railroad fever. In the United States, railroad building developed more slowly. For a while the nation was too excited over canal building to think about railroads. But several inventors became interested; they tried to build a locomotive like the English engines they had seen or heard about.

A New Yorker named Peter Cooper designed and built the first practical locomotive in America. Nicknamed the "Tom Thumb," it began running on the Baltimore and Ohio tracks in 1830. It pulled a passenger car over 12 miles of track at the breath-taking speed of 14 miles an hour! The Baltimore and Ohio was the first American railroad to carry passengers and freight. It was opened in 1830; for a short time, before Cooper finished his locomotive, the "B & O" used horses to pull its cars.

Other short lines were built in Massachusetts, Pennsylvania, and New York at about the same time. South Carolina businessmen started a railway from Hamburg, South Carolina to Augusta, Georgia. When this 136-mile railroad was completed in 1833 it was the world's longest.

Many businessmen caught what was called "railroad fever." They organized companies and started to build railroads in all directions. Of course some people opposed the railroads. Any new idea or method always meets opposition.

Men who owned stage coaches

Below is Peter Cooper's locomotive, "Tom Thumb." It had one horsepower and its boiler tubes were made from musket barrels!

Below is a scene common in early railroad days when almost everybody went "downtown to watch the train come in."

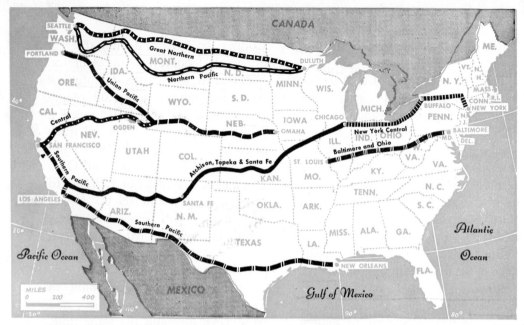

This map shows some of the famous historic American railroads. The Baltimore and Ohio which began operating in 1830 was the first to carry passengers and freight.

and canalboats feared that the railroads would ruin their business. Workers who built wagons or boats feared the railroad would throw them out of work. Farmers were afraid their cattle would be killed by the trains. Timid folks thought it was wrong for railroads to rush passengers over the country at 15 miles an hour. The human body, they insisted, could not stand such speed.

The United States became the world's greatest railroad builder. In spite of objections, the race to build railroads continued. By 1840 trains were running on at least one railroad in every eastern state. And two railroads reached out to the western territories. Most of the canals were neglected and soon became useless

ditches. People who had invested in canals were ruined. Congress helped spread the "fever" by giving large amounts of public land to railway companies.

Whenever a railroad was built, people turned out to celebrate the arrival of the first train. It was a proud day for Chicago when, in 1854, the first passengers from New York reached the city after four days of travel. Three years later crowds in St. Louis cheered as a little engine, almost covered with flags, pulled the first passengers into the city. At last the Mississippi was joined to the Atlantic by iron rails.

Once convinced of the value of railroads, the United States built more "iron roads" than all other countries combined. At the end of

318

1830, when railroad building began, there were only 23 miles of track in America. Thirty years later, trains were running on 30,000 miles of track. So the nation built an average of 1000 miles of railway every year.

That was only the beginning. The speed of building increased every year for many years. By 1916 the United States had over 250,000 miles of railway tracks. Then railroad building practically stopped, for a great network of tracks had reached all parts of the country.

In recent years a few railroads have been abandoned and total railroad mileage has decreased somewhat. But the United States still leads all other countries in railroad mileage.

Railroads were joined to form systems. In the early years, hundreds of very short railways were built to serve a few cities. There was no connection between many railroads.

If you wanted to go from Baltimore to Chicago or from Boston to St. Louis you would have to buy a dozen tickets in as many stations. And you would have to take a stage coach or a ferry to go from one railroad to another. Also, freight had to be loaded and unloaded many times. The railroads had tracks of different widths so engines and cars of one railroad could not travel on the tracks of other railroads. It was necessary to combine many of the lines into a "system" to get rid of confusion and delay.

The next step, therefore, was to unite many roads so travelers could go from one part of the country to another without having to change trains. This was soon accomplished through efforts of a few far-sighted business leaders. Of these probably the most famous was Cornelius Vanderbilt.

Vanderbilt was the son of a Dutch farmer on Staten Island, New York. By the time he was 16 he had saved enough to buy a sailboat. He used it, not for fun, but to carry passengers to New York City.

Within a few years, young Vanderbilt had six boats. He kept them busy carrying freight to New Jersey or up the Hudson River to Albany. Suddenly he sold his boats and bought a little steamer.

His friends thought he had lost his senses. But Vanderbilt saw there was now more money in steam than in sails. Soon he headed a company

The chart below shows how improved transportation has made it possible to travel across the United States in less time.

THE U. S. SHRINKS

Each symbol represents 1 day

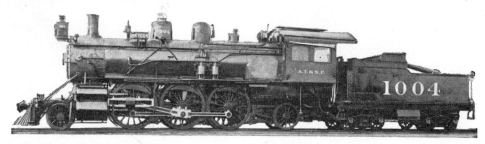

This picture shows one of the later, more powerful engines that came into use about 1901 on the Santa Fe railroad. Now out-of-date, it is used on a branch line.

that sent its steamships along the coast from Portland, Maine to New Orleans, Louisiana, and then to the Isthmus of Panama. From the Pacific side of the Isthmus, other Vanderbilt steamers carried passengers and freight to San Francisco. As chief owner of all these steamers, Vanderbilt became known as the "Commodore."

After half a lifetime in the steamboat business, the Commodore surprised his friends a second time by selling his boats. Once again he guessed what the future would bring. He realized railroads were going to be more profitable than boats.

Vanderbilt first bought enough stock in the Harlem River Railroad to control the company. Next he bought the Hudson River Railroad which ran from New York to Albany. Then he got control of the New York Central which ran from Albany to Buffalo. He soon combined the Harlem with the New York Central, and then with the Hudson River Railroad. Later Vanderbilt and his friends bought the Lake Shore, the Michigan Central, and various other railroads. The combined lines provided an all-rail route between New York City and Chicago. Thus he began the organization of the New York Central System, which is still serving America.

Railroads reached the Pacific Coast. You have seen how quickly railroads were built west to the Mississippi River. There the building stopped for several years. At the same time, thousands of pioneers and gold seekers were moving west. They needed the rapid transportation railroads could provide. But no individual or private company could raise enough money to build a railroad across the Great Plains and the Rockies.

The dangers and obstacles scared off even the most daring leaders. On the prairies, water was scarce and Indians were plentiful. Farther west, mountains, canyons, and roaring rivers seemed to say, "No road will ever be built here."

However, engineers claimed a railroad could be built, if somebody would put up the money. Only the federal government had resources to finance such an undertaking. But the government did not want to get

320   ROADS AND CANALS

into the railroad business right then.

The problem was solved in this way: Congress offered to give large stretches of western land to any company that would construct a railroad there. After the railroad was built, the company could sell the land at a good price to settlers who moved into the region. In addition, the government offered to buy shares in the company. Under certain conditions, Congress would also lend money for construction.

Two companies were formed to take advantage of the government's offer. One company began to lay track westward from Omaha, Nebraska, following the old Oregon Trail. As its name, "The Union Pacific," indicated, one object of the road was to bind the western states to the Union.

At the same time, another company began to lay rails east from San Francisco. This road, the Central Pacific, followed the Pony Express route. (You will read about the Pony Express in the next chapter.)

After six years of labor, the two building crews met near Ogden, Utah. The last stretches of the line were laid. Then, on May 10, 1869, the lines were joined by a spike of gold on one side and a spike of silver on the other. The first *transcontinental railroad*, that is, a railroad reaching from the Atlantic to the Pacific, was complete. Crowds of workers cheered as an engine steamed over the tracks. Their hard work had joined the East and West, and united the nation!

However, one railroad was not enough for the growing West. Another transcontinental road, the Santa Fe, was built over the old trail through New Mexico and Arizona to California. Then in quick succession appeared the Southern Pacific, the Northern Pacific, and the Great Northern.

The transcontinental roads played a leading part in the development of the Far West. It had taken 200 years to push the frontier from the Atlantic coast to the Mississippi River. But with railroads stretching all the way to the Pacific coast, pioneers of a later date were able to cross the wider western half of the continent — and build 17 new states — in the space of a single lifetime.

(Below) A great day dawned for the West and the whole country when the first transcontinental railroad was completed on May 10, 1869.

CHAPTER SUMMARY

Roads helped open up the West. Stagecoach travel was popular in colonial days. Many toll roads or turnpikes were built soon after the Revolution. The National Road from Maryland to Illinois was built at federal expense and completed in 1833.

The nation went "canal crazy." In the first half of the 19th century a great many canals were built. The most successful was the Erie Canal completed in 1825 which made New York State a favorite route to the West.

The United States became a world leader in shipping. The beautiful clipper ships broke all records for sailing vessels. The development of the steamboat increased the popularity of water transportation. After the Civil War the American merchant marine declined sadly.

Railroads did much to meet America's need for fast transportation at reasonable cost. The Baltimore and Ohio Railroad began operating in 1829. Great railroad systems such as the New York Central were developed. The first transcontinental railroad was the Union Pacific, completed in 1869.

The Language of History

The following words and phrases appear in Chapter 16. Be sure you understand the meaning of each.

1. turnpike
2. canal
3. bounty
4. steamer
5. macadam road
6. toll road
7. transcontinental railroad
8. railroad system
9. clipper ship

What Happened When

Connect each of the following dates with an important event in American history.

1. 1807   2. 1825   3. 1830   4. 1869

322   ROADS AND CANALS

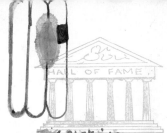

Who's Who in History

Be sure you know the part the following played in developing transportation in America.

1. John McAdam 4. De Witt Clinton 7. Cornelius Vanderbilt
2. Daniel Boone 5. Robert Fulton 8. Robert Livingston
3. John Fitch 6. Donald McKay 9. Peter Cooper

Study Questions

1. Explain how good roads helped unify the United States.

2. Trace the route of each of the following roads:
   a. Genesee Road *ALBANY-BUFF* c. National Road *Cumberland — Vand. ell.*
   b. Wilderness Road *PICH to louis* d. Lancaster Pike *Phil. to frontier*

3. Show how the completion of the Erie Canal influenced (a) the growth of cities in New York State, (b) the development of the West, and (c) the importance of New York City as a seaport.

4. Tell why each of the following ships became famous:
   a. the *Clermont* *steam* b. the *Savannah* *ATLANTIC* c. the *Flying Cloud* *NEW-YORK FRAN 89 DAYS*

5. a. In what period were the clipper ships popular? *Civil WAR*
   b. What caused the clipper ships to disappear from the oceans? *Railroads*

6. What factors caused the United States to lose her position of leadership in shipping and shipbuilding? *BRITISH* *steam* *better*

7. a. What was the first American railroad to carry passengers and freight? *B & O*
   b. When did it begin operating? *1830*

8. List the steps by which Cornelius Vanderbilt put together the New York Central Railroad System.

9. a. How was money raised to build the first transcontinental railroad? *Congress*
   b. What obstacles had to be overcome to complete it? *WATER, Ind.(etc.)*
   c. Name four transcontinental railroads. *union, Central, N, S Pacific*

10. How does the United States compare with other countries in total railroad mileage? *has more*

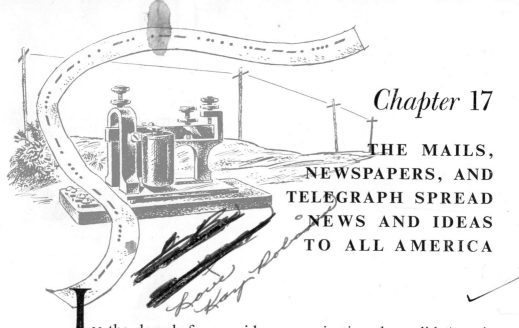

Chapter 17

THE MAILS, NEWSPAPERS, AND TELEGRAPH SPREAD NEWS AND IDEAS TO ALL AMERICA

In the days before rapid communication, how did Americans keep in touch with one another? How did mail get delivered? Who carried the news of elections and battles?

The establishment and improvement of means of communication in the United States is the story told in the following pages. It is the story of the Overland Mail and the Pony Express, of the invention of the telegraph and the laying of the Atlantic Cable, and of other great achievements in communication.

What kind of men were chosen to ride the Pony Express? Was there really such a character as Buffalo Bill?

Inventors were constantly finding ways to improve communication. Where did they find money for wires and cables? How many times did they fail and how did they find courage to keep on trying? What about newspapers — how did they make use of the new inventions? Who were the great editors who founded America's leading newspapers? What influence did they have on public opinion in America?

The answers to these questions are the subject of this chapter which deals with the growth of rapid communication in the United States and the people — pioneers, inventors, businessmen, editors — who made it possible.

News traveled slowly in early America. Steamships and railroads solved America's transportation problem in the 19th century. Now people and goods could travel rapidly and cheaply from one part of the country to another. But the nation also needed rapid *communication* — that is, speedy ways to send news and messages to distant places.

Good communication is essential in a republic. All citizens should know what their leaders are doing and saying. In addition, businessmen and farmers need to know the latest developments that may affect production and sale of goods.

Until long after the Revolution, communication was slow and undependable. There were only a few weekly newspapers, and they were full of old news from Europe. For a letter to be delivered, it took weeks and sometimes months.

When a man had to travel 300 miles, he spent weeks in preparation. He usually made his will. His family and friends gathered to bid him a tearful goodbye, for it was all too likely they would never see him again. If he were killed or died of a sudden illness, they would not hear of it until long afterward. They might not learn the details, unless a traveler happened to pass by and tell them what had occurred.

On the frontier or in remote mountainous sections, people sometimes did not find out who had been elected President until a year after votes were counted. And farmers had to plant and harvest crops without reliable weather forecasts. Merchants who shipped goods to far-away customers could only wait and pray. They had no way of knowing how or when the goods were delivered.

You will recall that the Battle of New Orleans was fought two weeks after the treaty of peace was signed. This was because it took so long for news to cross the Atlantic Ocean. Almost every activity in the United States was hindered by lack of rapid communication.

Imagine how hard it must have been for people to understand what was going on in Europe or Washington! How could they make up their minds how to vote or how to run their affairs? Life proceeded much more slowly under such conditions.

The postal service was slow and uncertain. In the early days there was little communication between colonies. Each colony was like a separate nation. The inhabitants knew little and cared less about people in other colonies from whom they were separated by miles of forest. But most colonists had relatives or friends in Europe to whom they wrote letters.

For example, when John Winthrop sailed to Massachusetts Bay Colony, he left his wife, Margaret, in England. He soon became governor of the colony, but it was several years before he was able to build a house and plant a garden for his wife. Every ship that left Boston during those years carried a letter to Margaret, and every returning ship brought two or three for John. The letters have been preserved; they tell a beautiful story of true love in Puritan days. They also give a picture of life in the new world.

It was not easy to write letters then. Paper was scarce and expensive. There were no fountain pens; everyone had to make his own pen by sharpening a goose "quill" or stiff feather.

At first, there was no such thing as a post office or mail service. If you wanted to send a letter to a friend you had to wait until a ship sailed for a port near your friend's home. Many ships were lost in storms at sea, and letters were lost with them. Today the United States Post Office has a "dead letter office" where letters are sent when no owner can be found. In colonial days the "dead letter office" was the bottom of the Atlantic Ocean!

When a ship from America arrived at a European port, the captain delivered business letters to a government official. He received a shilling for each sheet of a letter he delivered. There were no envelopes; the sheets were simply folded over and the address was written on the other side.

Other mail the captain left at the nearest store or tavern. There it remained until someone called for it. It was largely by chance, therefore, that a letter ever reached the person to whom it was sent.

The colonies gradually established a postal service. You can see why Americans became dissatisfied with such mail service. Settlers in Massachusetts did something about it: they established the first post office in America. In 1677 they passed a law which said:

It is ordered that Richard Fairbanks, his house in Boston, is the place appointed for all letters which are brought from beyond the seas or are to be sent thither, to be left with him. He is to take care that they be delivered. He shall be allowed for every letter a penny.

A double danger forced Massachusetts to take this step. For one thing, threat of Indian attack always hung over them. They wanted to have some means of warning all parts of the colony if the Indians went on the warpath.

And there was always danger of attack from the French in Canada. The governor of New France kept his soldiers ready to attack at any time. Massachusetts leaders wanted to be informed as soon as French troops crossed the border.

With such dangers facing them, it did not take long for the people of Massachusetts to establish two mail routes with regular monthly service. Other northern colonies saw the wisdom of the Massachusetts plan and developed their own mail routes. In the South it became the custom for any plantation owner who received a packet of letters to forward them to other plantations.

Here a colonial post rider is shown arriving at a lonely settlement in the 17th century.

The postmaster was an important figure in colonial life. Wherever regular mail service was established, the government hired men to carry letters. In the North, postmen rode horseback during most of the year, changing to snow shoes in winter. They received six cents a mile for carrying "official letters" from one colonial government to another. For carrying private letters they charged as much as they could get.

The first New York postmen received a small salary for carrying official letters. "He must be stout and active," said the law, and "wherever the road is not plain he must blaze a path for the guidance of travelers."

Many postmasters were store-keepers who served without pay. In colonial times and long afterward, the village store was the social center for people who lived nearby. Before the postman arrived, a crowd gathered at the store to welcome him. First he had to tell the news.

Never did a speaker have a more attentive audience! The colonists were hungry for news. They wanted to know what was happening in the big towns and in their old homes across the sea.

Anyone who received a letter was expected to read parts of it to the crowd. The news might be six months old, but to the reader and his neighbors it was fresh and exciting. Mail for distant farms was left at the store until the owner called for it or a neighbor carried it off.

Later the New England colonies passed laws which ordered that if a letter was not called for "within a reasonable time" the postmaster himself must deliver it. For this special service he might collect two pennies. This was the beginning of "rural delivery" and also of "special delivery service."

The American postal service was well-organized. Early in the 18th century the British government took charge of the postal service in the colonies and made it a branch of the London post office. Benjamin Franklin played an important part in improving the colonial postal service. He sent his newspaper to subscribers all over America. He wanted to be sure they received it within a reasonable time. Franklin managed to win appointment as deputy Postmaster General of the British colonies. He made the service more efficient and reliable.

After the Revolution it became more expensive to operate the postal system. This was mainly because Americans kept moving west and letters had to be carried longer distances.

After the Constitution was adopted in 1789 Congress set up a new and more efficient postal system. Leaders of the government realized that the postal system would probably never bring in enough money to pay expenses. Instead, Congress would have to help pay the cost of carrying the mail.

Most people were willing to pay taxes to get good mail service. They agreed with Washington when he pointed out that:

Such service would safeguard free government and the unity of our states by bringing people of all sections under the influence of letters and newspapers.

Five mail routes were established to keep the East in touch with the western frontier. Along these routes, stage coaches carried the mail wherever the roads were passable. Elsewhere the mail was carried on foot or on horseback, or even in a boat. Thus through flood or tempest or Indian danger postmen made their way. Then, as now, the motto of the postal service was "The mail must go through!"

The postal service grew with the nation. When pioneers entered the Northwest Territory there was not a post road or postal route between the Great Lakes and the Ohio. Until the first post office in the territory opened, in 1800, letters from the East were carried by any hunter or fur trader who happened to be headed in the right direction. So rapidly did the service improve, however, that in 1825 the Northwest had about 1600 post offices. Weekly mail was then delivered on 70,000 miles of post roads.

That same year, 1825, marked the beginning of an amazing mail route. It was completed 17 years later, soon after the first line of covered wagons crawled over the Oregon Trail in 1842. This route ran from Washington, D.C. across the mountains to the Ohio River. Then it traveled by steamboat down the Ohio to St. Louis. From there it went up the Missouri and the Yellowstone as far as a boat could go. Next, it wound its way over the Rockies to the Columbia River, and down the Columbia to the Pacific Coast. From Washington to the Pacific, as coach or rider or boatman went, this one mail route covered 4,500 miles.

Another famous mail route was developed in the Southwest. It was called "The Overland Mail." It led from New Orleans — across Texas, Arizona, and New Mexico — to California. When Americans began moving into the Southwest, the

The mail must go through! Here a driver of the Overland Mail is shown whipping his horses in an effort to escape Indian attackers. The date was 1858. The Overland Mail traveled from New Orleans to California, crossing desert and wilderness.

government arranged to pay a stage coach company to carry letters. The company advertised in a New Orleans paper as follows:

The San Antonio and San Diego Mail Line is now ticketing passengers through to San Francisco and intermediate stations. Passengers are forwarded in new coaches, each drawn by six mules over the entire length of our line except the Colorado Desert of 100 miles, which we cross on mule back. Fare to Fort El Paso $100, to Los Angeles $190, to San Francisco $200. Coaches leave on the 9th and 24th of each month. An armed escort travels through the Indian country with each coach train for protection.

Discovery of gold in California in 1848 put an unexpected burden on the Overland Mail. Thousands of people joined the gold rush. One route could not carry all the passengers, letters, and packages, so another route was added to the Overland Mail. This started at St. Joseph, Missouri and ran north and west, following the Oregon and California Trail. (See the map, page 331.)

Miners in California sent large amounts of gold back East on the Overland Mail. This increased the danger, for there were many attempts to rob the stage. First a mounted guard rode beside the stage. Then, for extra protection, an "express messenger" was added; he rode beside the driver with a shotgun across his knee. Even so, the stage was often "held up" by bandits or attacked by Indians. Those were the days of the "Wild West."

The Pony Express was organized. Business was good on the Overland Mail but many felt the service was too slow. After California was admitted to the Union in 1850, trade between East and West increased enormously. People needed information about business conditions.

Westerners were hungry also for news of the dispute over slavery. As you will learn in the next chapter, bitterness between North and South increased steadily; the War Between the States was about to break out. So there was a great demand for faster communication.

There was no railroad west of the Mississippi, and completion of the first transcontinental railroad was still several years in the future. Nevertheless, many people felt that faster mail service could be provided. In response to the demand, a group of businessmen started the Pony Express company in 1860. They arranged to have the mail carried by horseback riders.

The route began at St. Joseph, Missouri. It followed the Oregon-California Trail for almost 2000 miles, over plains and mountains to Sacramento, California. From there the mail traveled to San Francisco by river boat.

The cost of running the Pony Express was enormous. The government paid the company $80,000 a month to carry the mail. In addition, the company charged $5 postage for each half-ounce that a letter weighed. (Later the rate was reduced to $1.)

The company bought 500 horses and hired 180 riders. Both horses and riders were chosen for speed and endurance. Most of the riders were from sixteen to twenty years old. They earned from $100 to $150 a month; this was a high wage in those days, when a cowboy earned $20 a month.

Each rider carried a revolver and a knife to defend himself against Indians and bandits. His orders were never to fight if he could escape by running. His job was to deliver the mail!

The Pony Express carried the mail a total of 650,000 miles — and the mail was only lost once. At least two horses became heroes when they "carried the mail through" — leaving riders dead on the trail.

The Pony Express had a short, exciting life. The company built stations along the trail, 10 to 15 miles apart. As the rider approached, the station keeper brought out a fresh horse, saddled and ready to go. The rider jumped from his tired horse, grabbed the mail bags, and was on his way again in two minutes.

Usually a man rode 75 miles and then passed the mail bags to another rider. But if something happened and the next rider was unable to carry the mail, the first rider kept going. More than one rider came to a station at midnight or dawn to find the station burned, the keeper murdered, and the horses stolen. Then he had to ride on without food or rest.

The longest continuous ride was

IMPROVED COMMUNICATIONS

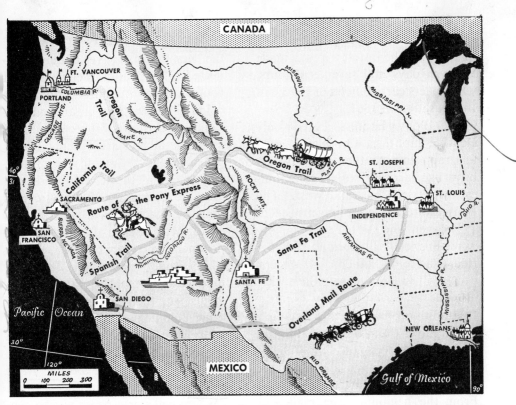

This map shows some of the famous trails to the Far West. Hunters, explorers, miners, and settlers followed these routes to reach the Southwest, California, and the Oregon Country in the nineteenth century. Notice the route of the Pony Express.

made by "Buffalo Bill," when he was eighteen. Another youngster, Jim Moore, made the fastest ride; he rode 280 miles in 22 hours.

In *Roughing It*, Mark Twain tells how he and his fellow travelers on a stage coach longed to see the Pony Express in action. At first they had no luck, because riders went streaking past "before we could get our heads out of the windows." At last came the chance they were hoping for:

Presently the driver exclaimed, "Here he comes!" Every neck is stretched further, and every eye is opened wider. Away across the endless dead level of the prairie a black speck appears against the sky, and it is plain that it moves. In a second or two it becomes a horse and rider, rising and falling, sweeping toward us nearer and nearer, growing more and more distinct; and now a flutter of hoofs comes faintly to the ear. Another instant, a whoop and hurrah from our upperdeck, a wave of the rider's hand, and the man and horse burst past our excited eyes and go winging away like a belated fragment of a storm.

The first riders took ten days to cover the entire 2000 mile distance. Later the time was cut to eight or nine days. The fastest trip was made in seven days and seventeen hours, when riders carried news of Lincoln's Inauguration in 1861.

The Pony Express lasted only eighteen months. Completion of a telegraph line to the Pacific Coast brought almost immediate communication between East and West. The Pony Express was no longer needed.

The men who started the company were financially ruined. And the riders had to find other jobs. Americans will never forget the brief, glorious time of the Pony Express. Its tradition of courageous devotion to duty lives on in the United States postal service today.

Some postmasters started newspapers.
From the beginning, the mail and the newspapers were closely connected. Soon after the first postal routes were organized, the first colonial newspaper began publication. A Boston storekeeper named John Campbell started it in 1704.

Campbell was Boston's postmaster, so he heard all the news. For several years he made a weekly list of events that he knew would interest his customers. He gave copies to the postmen who carried the mail to Maine and Connecticut. The postmen read Campbell's list in every village on their routes. People in other colonies asked for Campbell's list. He had no time to make extra copies so he had the list printed. The result was the *Boston News Letter*, which came out once a week.

Campbell's newspaper was so suc-

He rode like the wind! The Pony Express rider (below) carried the mail across the plains. Today he is a brave memory, and lives again on movie and television screens.

cessful that weekly papers were started in several colonies. Most early American newspapers were simply letters written by postmasters in the larger towns. They consisted mostly of neighborhood news and friendly jokes about people in other towns and colonies. Here is the way a Philadelphia newspaper reported an event in Massachusetts:

We hear from Amesbury, in the Bay Colony, that the generous Captain lately ordered his military company to appear at the Place of Parade, well armed with axes instead of muskets. After which he marched them into the woods, where with invincible courage they slew enough trees to make 30 cords of firewood and carted it to the waterside, in order that it could be sent to Boston for the relief of the poor.

Early newspapers carried no advertising. And they were printed at the postmaster's expense. After a while, printers took over the newspapers and made a business of it. Merchants were eager to pay the printer to advertise their products in the paper. Advertising made it profitable to run a newspaper.

Newspapers helped the cause of liberty. Even in the early days newspapers were closely connected with the rights and problems of ordinary folks. Through the newspapers, printers and their friends made known their opinion and the wishes of people they talked to. Many newspapers dared to criticize the government.

You have already learned how John Peter Zenger went to jail because he attacked a royal governor in his newspaper (page 98). When Great Britain tried to tax the colonies, protests appeared in the newspapers. When the Stamp Act was passed in 1765, colonial newspapers helped arouse people against it.

Newspapers helped hold the colonies together during the Revolution. Benjamin Franklin, owner and publisher of *The Pennsylvania Gazette,* is an example of the patriotic newspapermen who never allowed their readers to lose faith in freedom.

Newspapers influenced and molded public opinion. It was the newspapers that urged calling the Continental Congress. It was the newspapers and Tom Paine, a newspaperman, who helped the colonists make up their minds to declare independence. Indeed, newspapers were so influential during the Revolution British General Gage threatened to hang every rebel printer he found.

Newspapers increased in number and power. After the Revolution, American newspapers grew in number and importance. When the Constitution was written, it was thoroughly debated in the newpapers. Alexander Hamilton, John Jay, and James Madison wrote the *Federalist* articles in the form of letters to newspapers.

During most of Washington's administration, American newspapers were friendly to the Federalists. But after Jay's treaty was signed in 1795, many newspapers violently criticized Washington and his advisers. They increased their criticism when John Adams became President.

The Federalists could not endure newspaper attacks. To silence unfriendly newspapermen they passed the Alien and Sedition Acts (page 229). These unwise laws made the Federalists so unpopular they lost control of the federal government and never regained it.

As the United States grew, newspapers increased. On the frontier, as soon as a town was well-established, someone started a newspaper. Only six years after the Revolution ended, the Northwest Territory got its first newspaper: the *Sentinel of the Northwest*, published in what was then the little frontier town of Cincinnati, Ohio.

As more Americans learned to read, the number of newspaper readers increased. Newspapers found they had to change their style. They

Newspapers were the chief source of information about current events in the 19th century when there was no radio or television broadcasting. In the picture below a crowd has gathered to hear news of the Mexican War (1846–48) read from an "extra" edition of the local paper.

added new features — such as pictures, cartoons, and exciting stories — to appeal to the people.

America has had many great editors. Men who control newspapers have had great influence on American history. Everywhere, citizens looked to newspapers for help in making up their minds on big problems. There have been many outstanding newspaper editors whose influence extended throughout the nation.

One great editor was James Gordon Bennett, a Scotch immigrant. He started the *New York Herald* with $500 he had saved. In the beginning the *Herald* was a four-page newspaper, printed in a cellar. Bennett wrote the entire paper and sold it as well. Within a year New Yorkers were buying 15,000 copies. The *Herald* became famous for its accurate and complete reports of world events.

Another famous newspaperman was Charles Dana, editor of the *New York Sun*. He was one of the first to try to make news reports exciting and easy to read.

Horace Greeley founded the "New York Tribune." Probably the most famous of all American newspapermen was Horace Greeley, founder of the *New York Tribune*. Greeley spent his early years on a New Hampshire farm. His family was so poor he was able to attend school for only a few years.

When Horace was 14 he got a job

Horace Greeley was founder and editor of the *New York Tribune*, a widely read paper.

on a country newspaper and learned the printer's trade. When he was 20, Greeley came to New York with ten dollars — his life's savings — in his pocket. All his other possessions he carried wrapped in a large, colored handkerchief.

First, Greeley wrote articles for several newspapers. Then he started the *Tribune*. It became the most powerful newspaper in the North. Greeley had definite ideas about almost everything. He was against the spread of slavery; he liked high tariff laws; he thought the manufacture and sale of liquor should be forbidden. Greeley believed America's future lay in the new territories. "Go west, young man!"

SAMUEL F. B. MORSE (1791–1872)

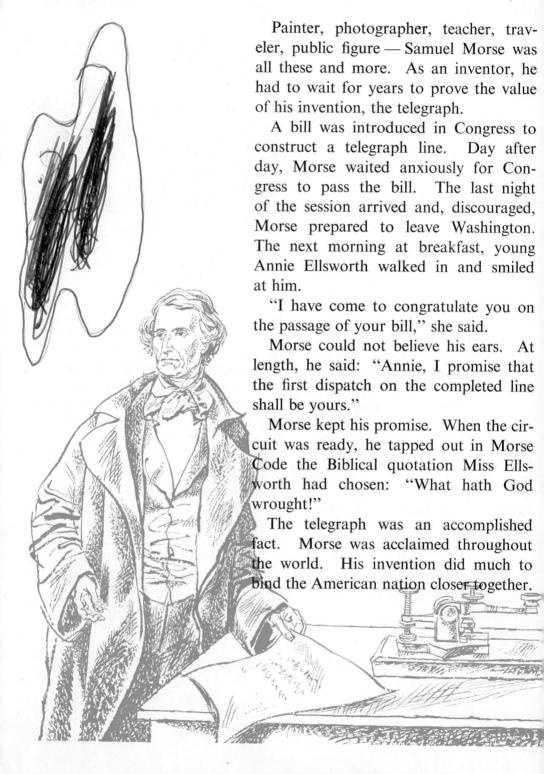

Painter, photographer, teacher, traveler, public figure — Samuel Morse was all these and more. As an inventor, he had to wait for years to prove the value of his invention, the telegraph.

A bill was introduced in Congress to construct a telegraph line. Day after day, Morse waited anxiously for Congress to pass the bill. The last night of the session arrived and, discouraged, Morse prepared to leave Washington. The next morning at breakfast, young Annie Ellsworth walked in and smiled at him.

"I have come to congratulate you on the passage of your bill," she said.

Morse could not believe his ears. At length, he said: "Annie, I promise that the first dispatch on the completed line shall be yours."

Morse kept his promise. When the circuit was ready, he tapped out in Morse Code the Biblical quotation Miss Ellsworth had chosen: "What hath God wrought!"

The telegraph was an accomplished fact. Morse was acclaimed throughout the world. His invention did much to bind the American nation closer together.

was his advice to young Americans.

Many people disagreed with Greeley, but they kept buying his newspaper. His name and that of the *Tribune* were known everywhere. Three Presidents — Lincoln, Johnson, and Grant — wrote to him about his ideas.

In 1872 Greeley was nominated for President. He did not win, but almost three million people voted for him. Brokenhearted by his defeat, he died a few weeks later. The great newspaper he founded lived on. Combined with James Gordon Bennett's *Herald*, it is now published as the *New York Herald Tribune*.

Some historians have called Greeley "a second Franklin." Both were poor boys who received little formal education. Yet they rose to wealth and high position through their ability to influence public opinion. Their careers illustrate clearly the power of the press in American life.

Morse invented the telegraph. Only a few thousand Americans read Franklin's newspaper. But every year the number of newspaper readers increased. One hundred years later, Horace Greeley's words were read by millions.

What caused the increase in newspaper reading? For one thing, Greeley was able to print news soon after it happened. A new invention brought almost immediate reports of happenings all over the country.

The new invention was the *telegraph*, an instrument that sends words thousands of miles in a few minutes by the power of electricity. The word "telegraph" comes from Greek words that mean "to write at a distance." You will understand why if you have visited a telegraph office and watched the operator; he makes clicking sounds that someone far away is listening to and translating into a written message.

Like most inventions, the telegraph was the work of many men. In 1831 a way was discovered to send an electric current over a wire. At first, nobody saw any use for this discovery. But it aroused curiosity. Other inventors tried to put the current to work.

A New Englander named Samuel Morse got excited when he heard about the experiments. Morse was in Europe at the time, studying to become a portrait painter. As a boy he had become interested in electrical experiments. Now he saw the possibilities of the latest discovery: "Why not use this lively little spark to carry a message over a wire?" he asked.

Thus began a new career for Samuel Morse. For years he spent his time and money on an instrument that would use electric sparks to make signs or letters. He lived in a bare room, always poor, often hungry. When he had to have money for food or rent he would paint a picture, sell it for anything he could get, and then go back to his lonely work.

After many years of struggle and poverty, Samuel F. B. Morse finally won recognition and honor. Here he is shown sending a message at a New York City celebration in his honor.

His wife died; relatives had to take care of his children.

The telegraph speeded up communication. Just when Morse seemed doomed to failure, a younger man named Alfred Vail came to his aid. Vail supplied money to build a new instrument. Together, Vail and Morse worked out a set of signals that could be used to send messages. The signals were "dots and dashes."

By touching a telegraph key lightly, the operator could make a "dot" signal. By holding the key down for a longer time he could make a "dash" signal. By changing the combination of dots and dashes it became possible to send a message over an electric wire. The system of dots and dashes is now known as the *Morse Code* or Morse alphabet.

Morse gave exhibitions to prove the telegraph was practical. But most people thought it was a crazy idea. He tried to get Congress to grant money for building a telegraph line; he pointed out how important it was to have rapid communication. For five years Morse argued and

begged. At last in 1843 Congress granted $30,000 for an experimental line from Washington to Baltimore.

At breakneck speed Morse and Vail had wires strung over the 40 miles between the two cities. Then Morse sat down in Washington and tapped the message, "What hath God wrought?" One of his assistants received the message over the wire in Baltimore and immediately tapped them back to Morse in Washington. It was the world's first telegram. The date was May 24, 1844.

At last America saw the value of Morse's invention. Telegraph lines were built in all directions. A huge network of wires spread over the country, bringing every city and village in touch with all the others.

Cyrus Field laid the Atlantic cable. European nations also built telegraph lines. But communication between Europe and America remained slow. Ships had to carry news and messages between the continents, and this often took weeks.

A few people asked, "Why not string a strong wire or cable across

338

the bottom of the ocean? Then we could send messages from the United States to Europe as quickly as we now send them from Maine to California!"

A Massachusetts merchant named Cyrus Field went to work on the problem. He had made a fortune as head of a paper business. He was to need this money, for it was a long, expensive undertaking to lay a cable under ocean waves.

The first attempt was a failure. Field tried again; another Atlantic cable was laid at huge cost. The first message came over it in August, 1858. Three weeks later, it suddenly snapped; somewhere, miles below the surface, the cable had broken.

In all, Field made five attempts before he got the Atlantic cable to work successfully. Thanks to his persistence, rapid communication between Europe and America was at last established.

That was only the beginning. New and better cables were laid. Cyrus Field looked west across the Pacific. Here was another and bigger ocean to be conquered! Before many years had passed, a cable linked America with Hawaii, Asia, and Australia.

There were greater things to come: the telephone, radio, and television — about which you will read in a later chapter — have improved communication beyond anything Samuel Morse or Cyrus Field dreamed about. But modern developments are all based upon the discoveries of earlier scientists and inventors.

In the picture below, Cyrus Field is seen directing laying of the Atlantic Cable. This was a gigantic task. Five attempts failed before lasting success was won in 1866.

CHAPTER SUMMARY

The postal service was started in colonial days. After the Revolution new mail routes to the West were established. The "Overland Mail" was one of the most famous routes. It led from New Orleans all the way to California. Another route, the Pony Express, had a short, colorful history. Young riders carried the mail on horseback from Missouri to California at breakneck speed.

Early newspapers had great influence. They helped arouse enthusiasm for American independence. After the Revolution they helped win friends for the Constitution. America had many famous editors: Benjamin Franklin, Charles Dana, Horace Greeley, and James Gordon Bennett. They founded great and influential newspapers.

Invention of the telegraph speeded up communication. Samuel F. B. Morse, with the financial assistance of Alfred Vail, invented the telegraph and the Morse Code. The first telegraphic message was sent in 1844. The completion of the Atlantic cable, under the direction of Cyrus Field, made possible rapid telegraph communication between Europe and America.

The Language of History

Be sure you know the meaning of the following words and phrases as they are used in this chapter.

1. communication
2. Atlantic Cable
3. the "Overland Mail"
4. Pony Express
5. telegraph
6. Morse Code

What Happened When

Connect each of the following dates with an important event in American history.

1. 1677
2. 1844
3. 1858
4. 1860

Who's Who in History

Be sure you know the part that each of the following played in the improvement of communications.

1. Buffalo Bill
2. James Gordon Bennett
3. Charles Dana
4. Horace Greeley
5. Samuel Morse
6. Cyrus Field

Study Questions

1. What did Benjamin Franklin contribute to the development of the American postal system?

2. Explain the meaning of the postal service's motto, "The mail must go through."

3. Give two examples of the way lack of rapid communication made life difficult in colonial days and in the early years of the American Republic.

4. Trace one route followed by the "Overland Mail."

5. a. What was the Pony Express?
   b. Why did it last only 18 months?

6. Why are postal employees particularly deserving of respect?

7. Connect each of the following newspapers with a famous editor or publisher:
   a. the *Pennsylvania Gazette*
   b. the New York *Sun*
   c. the New York *Herald*
   d. the New York *Tribune*

8. Give two examples of the way newspapers have influenced public opinion on important events in American history.

9. a. How did Samuel Morse come to invent the telegraph?
   b. What part did Alfred Vail play in Morse's project?
   c. How did the federal government contribute to the success of Morse's idea?

10. For what is Cyrus Field famous?

LET'S LOOK AT WHAT WE'VE LEARNED

How did good means of transportation influence the development of the United States?

The growth and improvement of transportation made it possible to settle the West. Before the population could spread out over the country, roads, canals, and then railroads had to be built.

Good means of transportation helped unify the nation. Many Americans came to feel they were "one big family," because they could travel easily and quickly from one part of the country to another.

What were some of the famous early roads to the West?

Probably the three most famous roads were: 1. the Wilderness Road from Richmond, Virginia through the Cumberland Gap in the Appalachian Mountains to eastern Tennessee and on to Kentucky; 2. the Genesee Road across central New York State from Albany to Buffalo and Lake Erie; 3. the National Road or Cumberland Road from Cumberland, Maryland to Vandalia, Illinois.

What was the canal-building era?

In the first part of the nineteenth century Americans spent huge sums to build artificial waterways. Success of the Erie Canal from Albany to Buffalo, completed in 1825, encouraged many states to go deeply in debt to build canals. The "canal craze" lasted until about 1837 when the nation turned to railroad building.

When was the United States a leader in shipping and shipbuilding and how did it lose this leadership?

In the first half of the nineteenth century American ships carried cargoes all over the world. In the 1840's and 1850's the beautiful clipper ships were the fastest sailing ships.

This leadership in shipping was lost partly because Americans were reluctant to change over to steamships as the British were doing. Another reason was the damage Confederate "raiders" did to northern merchant ships during the War Between the States. A third reason was that in the second half of the nineteenth century most Americans lost interest in shipbuilding and foreign trade. Instead they concentrated on railroad building and developing their own country.

What part has the postal service played in the growth of America?

Regular mail delivery began early in colonial times. After the Constitution was adopted, one of the first things Congress did was to provide

for building new post offices and post roads. As fast as western territories were settled, an arrangement was made for mail delivery. Among the famous postal routes across the wilderness were the Overland Mail and the Pony Express. Today the United States Post Office provides fast, dependable service to all parts of the nation.

How have American newspapers served the cause of liberty?

Since colonial days newspapers have kept Americans informed about government policies. Famous editors have not hesitated to criticize the President and other officials. Some of these great American newspapermen were: Benjamin Franklin of the *Pennsylvania Gazette;* James Gordon Bennett of the New York *Herald;* Charles Dana of the New York *Sun;* and Horace Greeley of the New York *Tribune.*

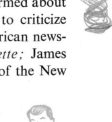

Connecting the Past with the Present . . .

"What's the news today?"
"What's the weather forecast?"
"Who won the game last night?"
"Any big sales on at the stores today?"
"What's playing at the movies this evening?"
"What's the latest from Europe? from Asia? from South America?"

Americans are always asking one another questions like this — and getting the answers. The people of the United States are among the best informed in the world thanks largely to the newspapers and the world-wide network of telegraph and cables which transmit the news.

Has a strike or mechanical trouble ever prevented the publication of newspapers in your town? If it has, then you know how uncomfortable and inconvenient it is to do without your favorite daily newspapers.

A hundred years ago most Americans were lucky if they saw a newspaper even once a week — and then it was usually a four-page affair with news from Europe and the West Coast which might be a month old. Thanks to Samuel Morse, Cyrus Field, and many great journalists, the modern newspaper in America receives the latest news as soon as it happens and reports it in words that are crisp, interesting, and easy-to-read.

Questions for Discussion and Review

1. **a.** Name four means of communication which were either invented or greatly improved between 1825 and 1870. *PO —NEW-tel-cab*
   b. List four means of transportation which came into wide use in the United States between 1800 and 1860. *turnpike- railroads steam - canals*

2. What were the reasons for the development of the toll roads? *get people to the west*

3. What was the reason for not completing the Cumberland Road (National Road) to the Mississippi River? *steam - rail*

4. Why was it that in earlier days most people preferred travel by river and canalboats to travel by highway? *cheaper, easier*

5. What were the important results of the building of the Erie Canal? Which city benefited most? Why? *became famous seaport NEW YORK*

6. What new means of transportation ended the canal era? Why? *Railroad*

7. Tell the story of the rise and fall of the "clipper ships." *British*

8. Why did the national government have to help in the building of the transcontinental railroad? *Financed*

9. List some of the difficulties faced by mailmen 150 years ago. *RIVER STATIONS*

10. What result did the invention of the telegraph have on the circulation of newspapers? *MADE PEOPLE BUY THEM More*

THE HISTORY LABORATORY

Here are some suggestions for activities to do in connection with this Unit.

Draw a Mural . . .

With others in the class, draw a mural for the wall of your classroom showing the development of transportation from the first Indian trails and canoes to modern super highways, railroads, ocean liners, and airlines.

WHAT AND WHEN

Fulton's steamboat 1807   National Road built 1815-33   Erie Canal complete 1825

Use Visual Aids . . .

Prepare a report or scrapbook illustrating the growth of means of communication. Graphs may be used to show changes in speed and number of messages; quotations will give your report "human interest"; and pictures taken from magazines will add "eye" appeal. You will find information in the books listed at the end of this Unit.

Be a Researcher . . .

Make a list of "firsts" in your community. You might include the first telegraph message, the first railroad train, the first canal boat, the first newspaper. You can add interest to your list by finding stories about these early days and including them in your report, or by taking your own photographs. You can probably get information and suggestions from your librarian and your local newspaper. Many communities have an official historian for the city or county. Find out who he or she is and arrange an interview.

Study the Local Scene . . .

Take a field trip to any place nearby where there are remains of early canals, railroads, boats, highways, telegraph lines, trains, stagecoaches, etc. Using your experiences as a background, write a story about the period of history you are studying.

Trace the Trails . . .

Select one or more of the famous routes mentioned in this Unit and write a report explaining which mountain passes, river valleys, or factors of climate made pioneers choose these routes instead of the other hundreds of possibilities.

American railroad 1830 — Invention of the telegraph 1844 — Gold Rush to California 1849 — Transcontinental railroad 1869

For Those Who Like to Write . . .

Check the list of books at the end of this Unit, pick one that interests you, read it, and then write a report on one of the following topics:

"Round the Horn to California." You sail before the mast in search of gold.

"I Rode the Pony Express." You dodge Indians to carry the mail.

"The Iron Horse Goes Through." You fight Indians, time, and the climate to join the East and West by railroad.

Calling All Space Cadets . . .

Pretend that while traveling in your space ship, you have landed on a planet which is exactly like earth except that conditions are just as they were on earth in 1825. Write a newspaper article predicting future developments.

Let's Read about the Development of Transportation and Communication

ADAMS, SAMUEL H., *Erie Canal*, Random, 1953.

ADAMS, SAMUEL H., *Pony Express*, Random, 1950.

**BURLINGAME, ROGER, *March of the Iron Men*, Scribner, 1938.

**CARLISLE, N. V., and NELSON, E. W., *Modern Wonder Book of Ships*, Winston, 1947.

FLOHERTY, JOHN J., *Make Way for the Mail*, Lippincott, 1939.

**HENRY, MARGUERITE, *Robert Fulton, Boy Craftsman*, Bobbs, 1945.

HENRY, ROBERT S., *Trains*, Bobbs, 1949.

HEWES, AGNES D., *Glory of the Seas*, Knopf, 1935.

HUNGERFORD, EDWARD, *Wells Fargo*, Random, 1949.

*HYLANDER, C. J., *American Inventors*, Macmillan, 1934.

*McNEER, MAY, *California Gold Rush*, Random, 1950.

MEADER, STEPHEN W., *Whaler 'Round the Horn*, Harcourt, 1950.

NATHAN, ADELE, *Building of the First Transcontinental Railroad*, Random, 1950.

PINKERTON, ROBERT E., *The First Overland Mail*, Random, 1953.

ROGERS, FRANCES, and BEARD, ALICE, *Heels, Wheels, and Wire*, Lippincott, 1935.

**STEVENSON, AUGUSTA, *Buffalo Bill, Boy of the Plains*, Bobbs, 1948.

WILDER, LAURA I., *Long Winter*, Harper, 1953.

* indicates easy reading   ** indicates advanced reading

Unit 8

A QUARREL ABOUT STATES' RIGHTS ALMOST DESTROYED THE NATION (1820-1877)

SEVENTY YEARS after the Revolution the United States extended from the Atlantic to the Pacific. Population was growing, production of goods was increasing, the government was strong and stable. Everything seemed to be going splendidly.

Then, just as it often does in a family, great trouble struck. An alarming crack appeared in the nation's unity. A quarrel between two sections developed into a war and threatened to tear the nation apart.

What were the early signs of trouble? Why did North and South draw farther apart? How was the Union finally restored?

Unit 8 is about the War Between the States or the Civil War. It tells the story of the quarrel that almost destroyed the American Union. As you read, try to answer these key questions:

1. What part did the dispute over slavery extension play in bringing on the war?

2. How and where was the war fought?

3. How were the states reunited and the Union restored?

Chapter 18

DISPUTES OVER
SLAVERY IN THE
TERRITORIES SPLIT
NORTH AND SOUTH

Was the United States going to collapse? For years Europeans had been saying that the republic could not endure, that the great American experiment was doomed to failure. Even Lincoln seemed to agree, for in 1858 he warned: "A house divided against itself cannot stand."

Each day added to the bitterness between North and South. By what compromise was war postponed? And why at last did compromise become impossible? What part did that angry man, John Brown, take in the events which set the North and South against each other?

As you read this chapter keep these questions in mind:

1. Why did Missouri's request for admission to the Union start a bitter controversy? Thomas Jefferson said it aroused him "like a fire bell in the night," sounding "the death knell of the Union." What did he mean?

2. Why did the North and South develop different attitudes toward the tariff?

3. How did the Mexican War lead to new controversies between North and South?

4. Why did several southern states secede as soon as Lincoln was elected?

348

The North and South differed in many ways. In early colonial days the way of life in the North was not very different from that in the South. Most people in both sections made their living by farming. Except for the "Pennsylvania Dutch," most early settlers in both North and South came from the British Isles.

As time passed, northerners and southerners drew apart. They did not raise the same crops, because the climate was different. They had to use different methods and they lived in different ways. During the Revolution and during the War of 1812, the excitement of fighting the British made northerners and southerners stand together like brothers. But that did not last. After the War of 1812 the North became interested in manufacturing. Southerners stuck to farming and concentrated on one crop — cotton.

After 1824 the people of the two sections found it increasingly hard to understand one another's point of view. They argued and quarreled. Time after time, a wise statesman named Henry Clay managed to patch things up by a settlement called a *compromise*. But each time the quarrel was worse. At last no compromise was possible. The North and South sprang at each other's throat. A terrible war raged for four years. Thousands of the finest young men of both sections died on battlefields whose names you may have heard: Bull Run, Shiloh (SHI loh), Antietam (an TE tam), Gettys-burg. The war ended at last, but bitterness lingered for a long time.

What caused the American nation to split so completely for a while? Slavery is part of the answer, but only part of it. Tariff laws had something to do with it. And people had a great deal to do with it — men like William Lloyd Garrison and John Brown.

Slavery was one answer to the South's labor shortage. One basic cause of the quarrel was probably slavery, although historians do not agree about the causes even now. *Slavery*, the dictionary says, is the state of being under control of a master who owns you and who can treat you as property. Slavery existed in ancient Greece and Rome. Sometimes men were sold into slavery after they had been captured in war; sometimes slaves were unlucky folk who got into trouble or debt. If there were not enough war prisoners to do work for which slaves were wanted, raiding expeditions would go to Africa and capture people there.

Slavery was well-known when Columbus discovered America. It was always hard to get enough workers in the colonies. The Spaniards tried to force Indians to work for them, but the Indians died or ran away. Negroes proved more enduring, so the number of Negro slaves increased. In the English colonies too, slavery soon appeared.

The first Negroes were brought to Virginia from Africa by a Dutch ship in 1619 — twelve years after the founding of Jamestown, and one year before the Pilgrims arrived. The number of Negroes increased rapidly in the South, for farmers always needed workers in the rice and tobacco fields.

The slave trade proved profitable. New England sea captains made fortunes in the slave trade. Soon the West Indies had the world's largest slave market. Each year slave ships brought thousands of Negroes from Africa. This is how many of the "slavers" worked:

An armed expedition would make a surprise attack on a village in Africa, killing all who resisted, and seizing as many young Negroes as possible. (Some slave hunters were Negro chiefs.) Around the neck of each captive was locked an iron collar. His ankles were tied together by a short chain. A heavy pole was laid on the shoulders of ten or more captives as they stood in line, and fastened to each collar. Then began the long march to the west coast of Africa. There, captives were sold to the captain of a slave ship, and a horrible trip began.

The slave ships were the worst feature of an evil business. Most were small boats in bad condition. Negroes were crowded between low decks, with little light or air. What they suffered on the long, hot voyage to the West Indies must be left to the imagination. Some died in chains. Some jumped overboard when brought on deck for a few minutes to stretch cramped muscles. Probably half the slaves shipped from Africa died on the way. But profits were enormous.

Northerners freed their slaves soon after the Revolution. In the North there were never many slaves. The farms there usually were small. The average farmer was able to handle the work with the help of his children. Only a few wealthy families wanted Negro servants or could afford them.

Because slaves were not needed in the North, it was easy to convince people that slavery was wrong and ought to be *abolished*, that is, wiped out. The Declaration of Independence declared that "all men are created equal, that they are endowed by their Creator with certain unalienable rights, that among these are life, liberty, and the pursuit of

Northern slaves won freedom early. Below is a certificate showing that a slave named William was set free in New York in 1816.

happiness." It was clear that slaves were not considered equal and did not enjoy liberty. This was contrary to the spirit of the Declaration of Independence, and, therefore, it was wrong in the eyes of many northerners. (They conveniently forgot that many of the slave traders and captains of slave ships were northerners; southerners had little to do with the slave trade.)

The next step was to pass laws to set the Negroes free, and that is what northern states did. Early in the 19th century slavery disappeared in the North.

Slavery continued to exist in the South. The problem was more difficult in the South. There were more slaves in the South — at least three times as many as in the North. In the South, farms tended to be larger than in the North. There were some big estates or plantations where many laborers were needed. Some southern planters spent a great deal of money to buy slaves. Negroes increased until whole districts became as one plantation owner said, "an island of Whites in a Sea of Blacks."

Southern white people felt uneasy about what Negroes might do. In 1831 a Negro preacher named Nat Turner led sixty slaves in an attack on Virginia plantations. Fifty-five white people were killed before Turner was captured and hanged. What would happen if thousands of slaves were suddenly set free? After two centuries of slavery, most Negroes were dependent on their owners for food and shelter. If they were let loose, they would be homeless and hungry and might do terrible things, southerners thought.

Jefferson spoke for other slave-owners when he said, "The South is holding a wolf by the ears." He meant it was dangerous to hold on to slavery and dangerous to let go. Washington was also against slavery. Not long after the Revolution he pointed out the importance of getting rid of slavery in these words:

Slaves were brought here by Europeans, and time is needed to change them into freemen — an event which no man desires more heartily than I do. Not only do I pray for it, on the score of human dignity, but I foresee that nothing but the rooting out of slavery can make the Union secure . . . joining all our states in the bond of a common principle.

Two inventions made slavery more profitable. While southern leaders like Washington and Jefferson were wondering how to get rid of slavery, two new machines made slaves more valuable in cotton growing. Southerners had started growing cotton almost as soon as Jamestown was settled, but for years they raised only small amounts. In colonial times there was not much profit in growing cotton for two reasons: (1) it was slow, hard work to separate cotton fibers from the seeds; (2) it was slow and expensive work to

Eli Whitney invented the cotton gin which made the growing of cotton more profitable.

manufacture the cloth from the cotton.

A Connecticut Yankee, Eli Whitney, solved the first problem with his cotton engine, or "gin," which he invented in 1793. Whitney's machine got rid of cotton seeds quickly and easily. An English preacher, Edmund Cartwright, solved the second problem in 1785 with his power loom. This was a simple machine which made it fairly easy to weave cotton cloth in large quantities.

Now the world could have plenty of cheap cloth for clothing. Textile mills worked night and day. British manufacturers bought all the cotton southerners raised, and called for more. In a few years the United States was shipping out more cotton than any other product. "Cotton is king!" shouted the South.

It was possible to grow cotton without slaves, and many farmers did. However, it seemed most profitable to grow it on big plantations with many slaves. But there were many small planters who owned ten slaves or less. Millions of southerners owned no slaves but hoped to become prosperous and move up into the planter class.

The planters wanted more slave territory. The planters, especially the handful of really wealthy planters, had great power in politics and society. They owned fine homes and lived pleasantly. Their way of life depended on slaves. They did not share the view of Washington and Jefferson and the North, that slavery ought to end.

Slaves became more valuable; between 1800 and 1860 the price of a farm Negro went from $500 to $1500. The planters wanted to hang on to their slaves and get more. They wanted to buy land farther west where the soil was rich. There they wanted to take their slaves and plant more cotton, for that was the way to make money. This brought up an important question: could southerners take slaves into the western territories that would some day become states?

Northerners found ways to help the slaves. The question of slavery in the territories aroused the North. Feeling against slavery had been growing slowly but steadily. Many people felt that slavery was contrary to God's wish. They formed anti-slavery societies ("anti" means "against"). They hoped to do away with slavery quietly and gradually, with justice to slave and slave owner.

Some anti-slavery workers decided Negroes would have a better chance in Africa, so they raised money to found a colony of former slaves on the west coast of Africa. Judge Bushrod Washington, a nephew of the first President, helped found the American Colonization Society; among its members were Henry Clay of Kentucky and Senator John Randolph of Virginia. In 1822 the Society began to send free Negroes to a colony they named Liberia (li BEER ih ah). (Twenty-five years later, Liberia proclaimed its independence. The capital city, Monrovia, was named in honor of President Monroe. Today, Liberia is one of the few independent nations in Africa.) But only a few thousand American Negroes went to Liberia. The anti-slavery societies could not raise enough money to send millions of Negroes to a land so far away. Liberia was not the solution to the problem of slavery.

Some people who were against slavery helped slaves escape to the North and even to Canada. (Slavery was forbidden in the British Empire.) Runaway slaves reached the North so rapidly that someone jokingly said they must be traveling by an "underground railroad."

There was no such railroad, but the name stuck; it referred to a secret method of helping slaves escape to free territory. There were "stations" along the Ohio River and in Pennsylvania, New York, Michigan, and other northern states. During the day, a runaway slave hid in a cave or hayloft. At night a white man or woman, the "conductor," would take him by boat or wagon to a "station" farther north. There the process was repeated until the Negro found freedom.

The slaves pictured below are running away from the South to an underground railroad "depot" in a free state. Each "runaway" meant the loss of hundreds of dollars to his or her owner.

Slave owners hated the underground railroad; every slave who got away meant the loss of many dollars to his owner, who also lost the slave's help in the cotton fields. Northerners who helped a slave escape felt proud of themselves for taking risks to help another human being. Southerners looked at it differently. They declared angrily that helping a slave escape was stealing.

There were "hotheads" among anti-slavery people too. They felt slavery ought to be wiped out, or abolished, immediately. They were called *abolitionists*. They had no patience with the idea of getting rid of slavery gradually. They claimed slave owners had no right to be paid for their slaves; for in the eyes of the abolitionists, slavery was a crime and slave owners were criminals.

There were not many abolitionists, and for a long time they were unpopular even in the North. Northerners who made money buying and selling cotton and making it into cloth did not want to interfere with slavery. In 1837 an abolitionist editor, Elijah Lovejoy, was killed by a mob in Alton, Illinois, because the people there did not like what he said about slavery in his newspaper.

In Boston another abolitionist, William Lloyd Garrison, edited *The Liberator*, a newspaper that demanded freedom immediately for all slaves. Garrison went so far as to burn a copy of the Constitution because it recognized the existence of slavery. Garrison was not popular in Boston. On at least one occasion he narrowly escaped injury when a mob captured him.

Slavery in the territories was the main issue. The activities of the underground railroad and the wild talk of the abolitionists made southerners angry. They thought the North was trying to steal their slaves and make it impossible to grow cotton. The truth was most people in the North — except the abolitionists — did not care if slavery existed in the southern states. But they did care about the question of slavery in the new

Below is shown the wrecking of Lovejoy's press. Elijah Lovejoy was a Quaker who edited an abolitionist newspaper in Alton, Illinois. He was killed by a mob, November 7, 1837.

William Lloyd Garrison was the most famous and most hated of abolitionist leaders.

western territories. If southerners could take slaves into the territories, northerners would have no chance there. Free workers and small farmers could not compete with slave labor. And if new slave states were formed out of the western territories, the South would gain increased power in the federal government.

The question of slavery in the territories was the heart of the matter. Southern planters wanted to take their slaves into the new lands, for the soil was good there and they would be able to raise big cotton crops and make money. The soil of the older southern states was wearing out because farmers had planted cotton over and over again.

The South was lagging behind the rest of the Union. Population grew slowly, for immigrants from Europe avoided the South. They knew they would have trouble finding jobs or getting a farm there. The North

was pushing ahead. Its population increased rapidly. There were many new factories, especially in New England. Northern prosperity worried southerners. They felt the "Yankees," or northerners, would soon run everything.

The Senate was evenly divided on slavery. Each time a new state asked to come into the Union, the question arose whether it would be slave or free. When the United States gained territory, as it did after the Mexican War, the same question came up: would the territory be slave or free?

Twice the burning question of slavery in the territories was settled by a compromise that Henry Clay thought up. The first time was in 1820 when Missouri, a part of the Louisiana Purchase, asked to come into the Union as a slave state. At that time there were only twenty-two states. Eleven were slave and eleven were free. Each state had two senators, so the United States Senate was evenly divided. (Northern states had a majority in the House of Representatives where representation was based on population.) If Missouri came in as a slave state, there would be two more senators who favored slavery. This would give the South control of the Senate. The North opposed that.

The Missouri Compromise brought peace for a time. When Missouri asked to enter the Union in 1820,

Henry Clay addresses the Senate. This picture shows the famous Kentuckian urging his fellow Senators to vote for a compromise plan to settle a dispute over slavery.

The map below shows the effect of the Missouri Compromise of 1820. Missouri came in as a slave state but the rest of Louisiana Territory north of 36° 30′ was to be free.

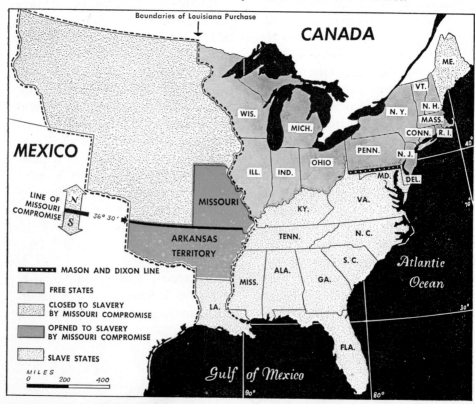

Maine was not a separate state. It was part of Massachusetts and was known as the "District of Maine." Ever since the Revolution Maine had been trying to separate from Massachusetts, but southern leaders who did not want another free state had blocked the plan. When Henry Clay, the "Great Compromiser," remembered Maine, it gave him the idea for settling the dispute over Missouri. His plan is known as the *Missouri Compromise*, or the Compromise of 1820. It provided that: (1) Maine would be admitted as a free state; (2) Missouri would be admitted as a slave state; (3) slavery would be forbidden in the rest of the Louisiana Purchase territory north of 36° 30', the southern boundary of Missouri (see map on page 356).

Congress passed the Missouri Compromise and thus asserted once more its right to forbid slavery in the territories. Earlier, in the Ordinance of 1787, Congress had said there should be no slavery in the Northwest Territory (see page 180). Missouri was not ruled by the Ordinance for it was not part of the Northwest Territory.

The Missouri Compromise settled the question of slavery in the territories for many years. It was truly a compromise, for each side won something and each side had to give up something. The South won admission of another slave state. The North won an agreement that the rest of the Louisiana Purchase north of 36° 30' would be closed to slavery.

However, the Missouri Compromise only postponed the showdown on extension of slavery.

A tariff law almost split the Union in 1832. The growing split between North and South affected other political questions. The tariff was another sore point. A *tariff* is a tax on products brought into the country from foreign lands. One purpose of the tariff is to protect American goods from foreign competition.

For example, suppose that a factory in Massachusetts makes knives to sell for $9 a dozen. But salesmen report they cannot sell the knives because English manufacturers are offering knives for $5 a dozen.

The owners of the Massachusetts knife factory may persuade Congress to put a tariff, or "duty," of 100 per cent on foreign knives. English manufacturers will have to pay a $5 tax on each dozen knives they send to the United States. This means the price of English knives will go up to $10 a dozen. Most people will then buy knives made in the United States, because they are now cheaper than English knives. This is fine for American manufacturers who make knives; it is not so pleasant for farmers who need knives and want to buy them at the lowest possible price.

As you can see, high tariffs usually helped the manufacturer but not the farmer. After the War of 1812 many factories were built in the North, but the South remained a farming section. Southerners had no use for high tariff laws.

In 1828 Congress passed a tariff law that raised taxes on imported goods to a new high. Southerners called it the "Tariff of Abominations (ah BOM ih NAY shuns)," and threatened to leave the Union. (Abomination means something that is evil or hateful.) Congress gave in and lowered the rates, but not enough to satisfy the South. South Carolina took the lead in defying the tariff law. In 1832 a state convention passed an "Ordinance of Nullification" (NUL ih fih KAY shun), declaring the tariff law would not be obeyed inside South Carolina's borders. (*Nullification* means the act of declaring a law void and of no effect.)

Andrew Jackson was then President. He was born in the South, and thought the tariff was too high;

but he was loyal to the Union and had taken an oath to defend the Constitution. He issued a proclamation warning South Carolina not to resist national authority. After ordering warships to Charleston he sent this message to a South Carolina leader:

Please give my compliments to my friends in your state. Say to them that, if a single drop of blood is shed there in opposition to the laws of the United States, I will hang the first man I catch engaged in such conduct upon the first tree that I can reach.

Jackson was bluffing, of course. He had no right to hang anyone. But his prompt action made everybody stop and think. Again Henry Clay came forward with a compromise. He suggested lowering tariff rates each year for ten years. Congress did as Clay suggested and passed the "Compromise Tariff of 1833." South Carolina repealed her Nullification Act, and everyone drew a breath of relief. But the dispute left a scar. There would be other threats of trouble when Jackson and Clay would not be on hand to settle things.

Webster and Calhoun represented opposing points of view. At about the same time as the trouble about the tariff, a big argument developed over the rights of the federal government and the rights of the states. The argument or debate took place in the Senate. Daniel Webster, the

Andrew Jackson (below) took a firm stand against a threat of secession in 1833.

Massachusetts senator, spoke for New England. He was short and dark, with flashing eyes and a deep faith in the Union. People called him "Black Dan;" he could talk for hours and hold people spellbound.

John C. Calhoun of South Carolina usually spoke for southern planters. He had taken the lead in the tariff fight. He believed in *states' rights.* This was the idea that the states were more powerful than the federal government. Calhoun and his friends reasoned that:

(1) The states existed before the federal government.

(2) The states agreed to the Constitution and set up the federal government. The federal government was just a partnership the states had created.

(3) Therefore, the federal government could not force the states to do anything they did not want to do. The federal government could do only things clearly mentioned in the Constitution.

(4) If Congress passed a law that one or more states did not approve, they could refuse to obey it, declaring it null and void and of no effect. This was the *Doctrine of Nullification.*

(5) If a state felt that belonging to the Union was no longer to its advantage, it could leave, or *secede.* This was the *Doctrine of Secession* (seh SESH un).

There was nothing new about the states' rights theory. Jefferson and Madison had talked about it in the Virginia and Kentucky Resolutions. New England leaders had talked about secession when things were not going to suit them in the War of 1812.

But Calhoun and other southern leaders were unusually serious about their belief in states' rights. They were terribly worried the North was going to have complete control of the federal government. They felt this would mean ruin for the South.

Most northerners had half-forgotten the idea of states' rights. So many new states had come into the Union it seemed silly to say the states existed before the federal government did. To men who loved the Union, secession seemed dangerous. If a state could leave whenever it felt abused, the United States would soon break up into small nations struggling and quarreling

Daniel Webster (below) represented New England in the debates over states' rights.

with one another. Powerful nations like Great Britain and France could conquer them one by one. It would be the end of the American dream of a strong free land.

Webster and Hayne debated the states' rights questions. The question of states' rights was thoroughly discussed in the *Webster-Hayne debate*. It began in the Senate on January 19, 1830; it continued for weeks. John C. Calhoun was Vice-President at the time, so he could not take part in the debate. Instead, Senator Robert Hayne of South Carolina spoke for the South. He attacked Massachusetts and other manufacturing states. He ended by declaring any state could set aside a law of Congress and leave the Union if it chose.

Webster rose to answer the attack on his state and on the idea of federal supremacy. He talked for hours. Webster's "Reply to Hayne" is one of the most famous speeches in history. Webster ended with words that rang through the North like a trumpet call: "Liberty and Union, now and forever, one and inseparable."

The Webster-Hayne debate gave both sides a chance to "blow off steam," but settled nothing. Northerners and southerners continued to suspect one another. Meantime, large numbers of Americans were moving west every year. New territories had to be organized, and each time the question of slavery came up. No matter what Congress tried to

discuss, somebody would drag slavery into it. And that, John Quincy Adams wrote in his *Diary*, was "the signal for another outburst of violent passion." Newspapers would report the angry words and there would be meetings of aroused citizens in both North and South.

The Compromise of 1850 settled another slavery crisis. The Missouri Compromise seemed to settle the question of slavery in the territories, but the matter soon came up again. In 1848 when the United States won the Southwest in the Mexican War, southerners expected the area to be open to slavery. David Wilmot, a Pennsylvania Congressman, took them by surprise when he proposed that slavery should be forbidden in all land taken from Mexico.

The *Wilmot Proviso* (pro VI zoh), as the proposal was called, raised a storm all over the country. Most northerners favored it. Southerners declared they would leave the Union if it was accepted.

In the middle of the excitement, the people of California sprang a surprise. California was part of the land won from Mexico. Nobody dreamed it would have enough population to become a state for many years. But discovery of gold sent thousands rushing to California. In a few months California demanded admission as a free state, without becoming a territory first.

Southerners called California's request "impudent." If California be-

DISPUTES OVER SLAVERY

Ready for trouble in Kansas. This picture shows pro-slavery men on their way to vote for slavery in Kansas. Anti-slavery men also went to Kansas, and violence soon broke out in the territory.

souri Compromise. It said that people who settled in Kansas and Nebraska could decide by vote whether or not to allow slavery.

The result of the law surprised everybody, but it was not a pleasant surprise. Northerners rushed to Kansas hoping to pile up votes to close the territory to slavery. Southerners came in a hurry, for they meant to open Kansas to slavery. The two groups clashed. For five years, there was burning, shooting, and murder. A fair election was impossible. Instead, the Kansas-Nebraska Act brought bloodshed. Men spoke in hushed tones of "bleeding Kansas."

The Republican Party was born 1854. The Kansas-Nebraska Act and the fighting in Kansas had another unexpected result: angry northerners

got together to form a new party. In 1854 meetings were held first at Ripon, Wisconsin and Jackson, Michigan and then in other northern states. The name "Republican Party" was adopted.

By the end of 1854 the Republican Party was organized all over the North. The old parties had tried to avoid taking a stand on slavery in the territories. This proved a mistake. Men who were against slavery walked out of the old parties.

The Republicans were not against slavery in the South, but they wanted to keep it out of territories. In 1856 the new party nominated John C. Frémont for President. He came close to winning. Republicans looked forward hopefully to the 1860 election. It looked as if they might win. Southerners felt differently. They declared they did not want to stay in the Union if "black Republicans" won.

The Supreme Court tried to settle the slavery issue. The Kansas fighting proved popular sovereignty would not work. Earlier, Congress had tried to decide the question of slavery in the territories, and that too had failed. Next, in 1857, the Supreme Court tried to settle the question in the *Dred Scott case*. This proved the worst mistake of all.

It happened this way: A slave named Dred Scott was taken by his master from Missouri to the free state of Illinois, and then to Wisconsin Territory. Later, he was brought back to Missouri and sold with his children to another master. Some white men decided to make a "test case" to find out if such actions were lawful. They went to court and demanded freedom for Dred Scott. They said that because he had lived for a time in a free state and a free territory he should be free. They lost the case in the state court but they kept fighting until they reached the United States Supreme Court.

The Supreme Court decided against Dred Scott and in favor of the southern argument. The justices headed by Chief Justice Roger B. Taney (TAW nee) said:

(1) Dred Scott was a slave and therefore not a citizen. He had no right to be heard in court.

(2) Any citizen could take his property (that is, his slaves) with him anywhere in the United States.

This meant that Congress could not forbid slavery in the territories.

The South hailed the decision with delight. Northerners thought the decision was unjust. They felt the judges had gone out of their way to interfere in the dispute. The fearsome question was: What will northern men do about a decision they regard as unjust?

The Lincoln-Douglas debates widened the gap. Northerners would not accept the Dred Scott decision. That became clear, partly through a series of debates in Illinois. In 1858 stout little Stephen Douglas ran for re-election as Senator from Illinois. Running against him was lean, lanky Abraham Lincoln. Douglas was a Democrat. He believed in popular sovereignty, and he had pushed the Kansas-Nebraska Act through Congress.

Lincoln belonged to the new Republican Party. He was not an abolitionist but he wanted to keep slavery out of the territories. He had no faith in popular sovereignty as a solution to the problem. If southern planters brought slaves into the West, poor men and their children would have little opportunity, Lincoln felt.

The nation watched the struggle between Lincoln and Douglas in Illinois. Southerners were especially interested. They wanted to know: (1) if Douglas would accept the Dred Scott decision; and (2) if he would give up his idea that the people of the territories should decide the slavery question. Douglas wanted to be President in 1860. If he stood by the Dred Scott decision — and backed down on popular sovereignty — southerners would vote for him. But he would lose the votes of many northerners and westerners. If he stuck by popular sovereignty, southerners might turn against him and put up their own candidate.

Thus there was a great deal at stake in the 1858 election in Illinois: not only the senatorship, but the Presidency of the United States later on. Douglas was nervous. He tried not to say anything about the Dred Scott decision, but Lincoln challenged Douglas to a series of debates. At Freeport, Illinois, he asked Douglas the fatal question: Do the people of a territory have the right to permit or to forbid any slavery?

Douglas answered: "No matter what the decision of the Supreme Court may be on that abstract question, still the right of the people to make a slave territory or a free territory is complete. I hope Mr. Lincoln deems my answer satisfactory."

Mr. Lincoln found it quite satisfactory — but the South did not! Southerners were through with Stephen Douglas. He might win the Illinois senatorship — and he did — but he could never be President. The Lincoln-Douglas debates split the North and South farther apart.

"Uncle Tom's Cabin" aroused the North. Men and women who watched the newspapers to find out what Douglas said to Lincoln were mostly educated, serious-minded

Lincoln debates Douglas. The picture below shows the scene at one of the famous Lincoln-Douglas debates in 1858. It was at the debate in Freeport, Illinois that Douglas announced his "Freeport Doctrine" on slavery in the territories which cost him the Presidency in 1860.

"I AM GOING THERE".
Death of little Eva.

Everybody wept when little Eva died in the play, *Uncle Tom's Cabin*.

folks. But people everywhere were getting excited about slavery. The strict Fugitive Slave Act that formed part of the Compromise of 1850 was largely a failure. Public opinion in the North would not stand for returning runaway slaves to the owners. Abolitionists kept things stirred up; more and more northerners came to feel slavery must go.

A story about slavery helped turn thousands of northerners against slavery. The story was *Uncle Tom's Cabin* by Harriet Beecher Stowe. Mrs. Stowe was the sister of Henry Ward Beecher, a minister and anti-slavery leader. She had never lived in the South but she lived in Cincinnati, Ohio where she met many runaway slaves. *Uncle Tom's Cabin* appeared in 1852, soon after passage of the Fugitive Slave Act. It became the most widely read novel in the United States. Many northern news-

papers printed it as a serial, thus bringing it into almost every home.

Soon *Uncle Tom's Cabin* was made into a play and acted out in every northern town. Millions who had never given a thought to slavery wept at the suffering of Uncle Tom and hissed the cruel deeds of Simon Legree the slave driver.

The high point of the play was the scene in which a Negro mother, Eliza, fled with her child over the ice cakes of a swollen river, chased by bloodhounds. *Uncle Tom's Cabin* gave a highly exaggerated picture of slavery. But it never failed to arouse anger in northerners who read the book or saw the play.

John Brown's raid set armies marching. Among those who burned with hatred of slavery was a man named John Brown. He brooded about slavery until he became somewhat crazy. For a while he kept a "station" on the underground railroad in Ohio. He went to Kansas where, in cold blood, he killed five pro-slavery men. Two of Brown's sons were killed in Kansas.

Brown came back east with one idea in his mind: he thought God had chosen him to raise an army of slaves and lead them against their masters. He gathered about 20 men on a farm near Harper's Ferry, Virginia. He chose Harper's Ferry because a government *arsenal* or storehouse for guns was located there. Brown planned to seize guns for slaves he thought would join him.

DISPUTES OVER SLAVERY

It seemed impossible that Brown could capture a government stronghold. Yet his first success was startling. He waited and watched until his chance came to seize the arsenal when its defenders were off guard. But no slaves gathered to use the guns. With a shock Brown learned they would not follow him or fight for their freedom. Then a company of U.S. Marines led by Colonel Robert E. Lee marched in. They quickly retook the arsenal. Brown was wounded, and most of his followers were killed. Tried in Virginia for treason and murder, he was found guilty and hanged in 1859, less than two years before the war between South and North began.

John Brown had more influence dead than he had alive. One of his admirers wrote a marching song and set it to a catchy tune that everyone could easily sing. The song begins:

John Brown's body lies a-moldering in the grave,
His soul goes marching on.

Northern boys sang the words as they marched to war. Later Julia Ward Howe borrowed the tune for her "Battle Hymn of the Republic." Mothers and fathers sang it when their sons left to fight for the Union.

To many abolitionists, John Brown was a saint who had given his life in a fight against evil. Southerners felt Brown was a wicked trouble-maker who would arm slaves to attack white people. They thought all northerners were plotting to do what Brown had tried to do.

Brown's raid helped set off the explosion called the War Between the States, or the Civil War. For years, anger had been growing.

John Brown goes to the gallows. The picture below shows the scene at his execution, December 2, 1859 as a result of his raid at Harper's Ferry. To the North he was a martyr, but to the South he was a traitor. His raid and death helped bring on the War Between the States.

Jefferson Davis of Mississippi was elected President of the Confederate States.

Southerners, or at least the leaders, were determined to keep their slaves and spread slavery to the territories. Many northerners had come to hate slavery; they were determined to keep it out of the territories. A clash was certain.

The Republican victory in 1860 caused the South to secede. The national government did nothing to stop the rush toward war. President James Buchanan was a weak, hesitating man. He wrung his hands and wept —and did nothing. Years before, Jackson's prompt action had stopped a drift toward breaking up the Union. But Buchanan merely waited, hoping the storm would not break during his term.

In 1860 came a presidential election. Douglas was the Democratic candidate and Lincoln was the Republican. Southerners would not vote for Douglas. They thought he had betrayed them in his reply to Lincoln at Freeport, Illinois. They put up their own candidate, a pro-slavery man named John Breckinridge. There was a fourth candidate in the race, John Bell of Tennessee, candidate of the new and short-lived Constitutional Union Party.

Lincoln was elected. Excitement spread like a forest fire. Southerners had warned they would leave the Union if the Republicans won. Would they keep their word?

Eleven southern states seceded in 1861. The South answered swiftly. No sooner was Lincoln's election known than South Carolina called a convention. Delegates gathered quickly; on December 20, 1860, they passed a resolution which declared that ". . . the union now subsisting between South Carolina and other states under the name of the United States of America is hereby dissolved."

Almost at once six other states followed South Carolina out of the Union: Alabama, Florida, Georgia, Louisiana, Mississippi, and Texas. In February, 1861, their delegates met at Montgomery, Alabama. There they organized a new nation, the Confederate States of America, or the *Confederacy*. Jefferson Davis of Mississippi became President of the Confederacy.

Two months later, in April, 1861, four more states left the Union: Arkansas, Tennessee, North Caro-

368

lina, and Virginia. They left because federal soldiers had invaded the seceded states. The people of these states were sad to leave, but they believed the national government had no right to use force against a state. The capital of the Confederacy was moved to Richmond, Virginia.

Thus, the Union formed in the days of the Revolution, which had grown into a strong nation, now fell apart. The split had been a long time coming. It began with the dispute over admission of Missouri in 1820. The fight over the tariff in the 1830's left bad feeling. The abolitionists and the work of the "underground railroad" made southerners angry. After the Mexican War one event

after another increased the bitterness: the strict Fugitive Slave Act in 1850, publication of *Uncle Tom's Cabin* in 1852, the Kansas-Nebraska Act in 1854 and the bloodshed in Kansas that followed, the Dred Scott decision in 1857, the Lincoln-Douglas debates in 1858, John Brown's raid in 1859, and finally the election of Lincoln in 1860. These events led the nation down the road to war.

Could the War Between the States have been avoided? Historians are still arguing about it. Andrew Jackson and Henry Clay, with the help of other leaders, stopped the drift toward war in the 1830's and 1850's. Could they have stopped it in 1860 if they had been alive? No one knows the answer.

end.

The chart below shows how the North and South compared in resources at the beginning of the War Between the States. The North enjoyed many advantages the South did not have.

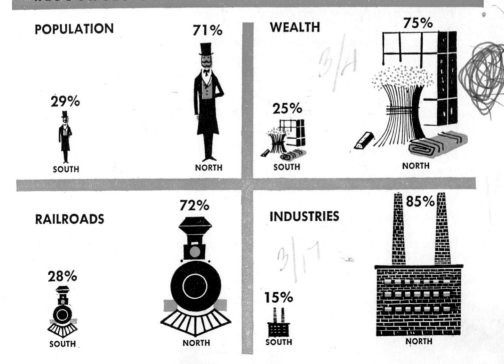

RESOURCES OF THE NORTH AND SOUTH IN 1860

POPULATION 71% 29% SOUTH NORTH

WEALTH 75% 25% SOUTH NORTH

RAILROADS 72% 28% SOUTH NORTH

INDUSTRIES 85% 15% SOUTH NORTH

CHAPTER SUMMARY

Sectionalism, slavery, and states' rights differences drove a mighty wedge between North and South. The Senate was evenly divided on the issue of slavery, but compromises by Congress postponed secession and war. They failed, however, to bring understanding, tolerance, and cooperation. The Supreme Court's decision in the Dred Scott case added to the trouble.

Violent words and actions by extremists of both sides made matters worse. Bloodshed in Kansas and John Brown's raid brought war nearer. *Uncle Tom's Cabin* dramatized the evils of slavery for northerners.

A new political party, the Republican Party, appeared in 1854. It stood firmly against the further spread of slavery. Its candidate for President, Abraham Lincoln, won the election in 1860, mostly because the Democrats split over the question of the extension of slavery.

Eleven southern states seceded from the Union. The South feared that the control of the United States Government was now in the hands of an unfriendly party. They formed the Confederate States of America.

The Language of History

Be sure you understand the meaning of each of the following words and phrases as they are used in Chapter 18.

1. compromise
2. slavery
3. abolitionist
4. tariff
5. secession
6. nullification
7. underground railroad
8. states' rights
9. popular sovereignty

What Happened When

Make sure you know the important events connected with these dates:

1. 1619
2. 1793
3. 1820
4. 1832
5. 1850
6. 1854
7. 1857
8. 1858
9. 1859
10. 1860

Who's Who in History

Tell the part each of the following played in the trouble over slavery:

1. Henry Clay
2. John Brown
3. Dred Scott
4. Daniel Webster
5. John C. Calhoun
6. Stephen Douglas
7. Abraham Lincoln
8. William Lloyd Garrison
9. Harriet Beecher Stowe

Study Questions

1. Why did the invention of the cotton gin make it harder to get rid of slavery?

2. Explain why the abolitionists were unpopular even in the North.

3. **a.** Why did southern planters want to take slaves into the western territories?

   b. Why were northerners determined to keep slavery out of the territories?

4. Why were both the North and the South willing to accept the Missouri Compromise?

5. **a.** Why did most southerners feel that tariff laws were unfair?

   b. Why did most northerners like high tariff rates?

6. Explain why the South was angered by **(a)** the Wilmot Proviso and **(b)** California's demand for admission to the Union.

7. Why did the North and South accept the Compromise of 1850?

8. **a.** What did the Supreme Court say in the Dred Scott decision?

   b. How did the Dred Scott decision cause Stephen Douglas to lose his chance to be President?

9. President James Buchanan has been described as "the weakest chief executive in the history of the United States."

   a. Why is Buchanan considered a weak President?

   b. What was the situation when he left office?

   c. Who succeeded Buchanan as President?

10. **a.** What event was the immediate reason for the secession of the South?

    b. What were the underlying causes for the break between North and South?

Chapter 19

" . . . THAT from these honored dead we take increased devotion to that cause for which they gave the last full measure of devotion — that we here highly resolve that these dead shall not have died in vain — that this nation, under God, shall have a new birth of freedom — and that government of the people, by the people, for the people, shall not perish from the earth."

Thus Lincoln ended his Gettysburg Address. His voice carried over the field where a few months before a terrible battle had been fought. Where is Gettysburg? Why was the battle of Gettysburg so important? Why is it called the turning point of the war?

The war raged on more than a year after Gettysburg. What were the big campaigns of the Civil War? How was the South able to hold out so long when food was scarce and supplies lacking? Who were the great generals on both sides?

After the war came Reconstruction — the Tragic Era. How did the victorious North treat the South? How does Reconstruction still influence southern politics today?

You will find the answers in this chapter which tells the story of the Civil War and Reconstruction.

372

The North would not agree to let the Union break up. The War Between the States, or the Civil War as it is more commonly known, began at Fort Sumter, South Carolina, on April 12, 1861. It ended at Appomattox (AP oh MAT uks), Virginia, on April 9, 1865. The South surrendered unconditionally. But the most remarkable fact was not the victory of the North; it was the fact the South held out for four years.

The North had almost every advantage: wealth, population, factories, food. The South was weak in everything except courage and leadership. But southern armies won time after time. They invaded the North twice, carrying the war into Maryland and Pennsylvania. More than once northerners were ready to give up and let the southern states go.

One man held the North steady against disappointment and defeat. His name was Abraham Lincoln. He saved the Union, though a murderer's bullet cut him down in the moment of triumph.

In his first speech as President, Lincoln made it clear he would not allow the Union to be broken. He said to the southerners, "In your hands, my dissatisfied countrymen, and not in mine is the momentous issue of civil war. The government will not assail you. . . . You have no oath registered in heaven to destroy the Union, while I have the most solemn one to 'preserve, protect, and defend' it."

Lincoln learned to love the Union. What manner of man was Abraham Lincoln and what had created in him such a devotion to the Union? Strange as it seems, he was born in what was considered a southern state. He spent his early years in the backwoods of Kentucky. His father, Tom Lincoln, was good-natured but careless and somewhat lazy.

Twice while Lincoln was a child the family moved westward. They followed the frontier to Indiana and then to Illinois. Partly because he moved around so much, Lincoln did not become primarily attached to any one state. He learned to be loyal to the whole country.

Young Abe had to work hard ploughing, hoeing, chopping. By catching a term or two at a country school when he could be spared from work, Lincoln spent about six months in school. "And that," he said, was the only schooling I ever had." At 18 he was famous because of his skill in splitting rails for fences that protected corn fields from hungry cattle. Four hundred rails, in trade, was the price of a shirt. If Abe wanted a suit he had to split 4000 rails to pay for the cloth.

Once when an Indian tribe went on the warpath, young Lincoln marched off to fight the Black Hawk War. When he came back, he reported in his humorous way that he had fought battles with mosquitoes and had saved one old Indian from being shot.

Lincoln became a lawyer and went into politics. Until Lincoln was 21, all he earned belonged to his family. Then, by the custom of the frontier, he was free to shift for himself. He found a job keeping the village store at New Salem, Illinois. People liked him. Slowly Lincoln's ambition grew. He decided to become a lawyer. He walked fifty miles to borrow a law book which he studied by the firelight at night because he was too poor to buy candles.

Soon Lincoln was trying cases before a court. He became the best

Lincoln was a champion railsplitter. The statue below shows him as a young man when he earned his way splitting rails for fences.

known lawyer in his part of Illinois. He showed a remarkable ability to make other people see the right or wrong of each side as plainly as he saw it himself.

Lincoln was elected to the Illinois legislature four times and became a leader in state politics. Later he served as a member of the House of Representatives in Washington. He was a stranger there, "lost in the crowd," as he said.

Outside of his own state, people paid no attention to Lincoln until he ran against Stephen Douglas for the position of Senator from Illinois. The Lincoln-Douglas debates (page 364) made Lincoln famous. People asked, "Who is this tall, ugly man? He thinks straight and talks sense. He makes the mighty Douglas look like a fool!"

Lincoln's chief aim was to save the Union. Largely because of his success against Douglas the Republicans nominated Lincoln for President in 1860. Southerners did not trust Lincoln. They thought he wanted to destroy slavery at any cost. It was true Lincoln did not like slavery but he was not an abolitionist. He feared slavery might spread into free states and territories, but he hoped that southern states would gradually free the slaves.

Lincoln saw America as a great free nation where every boy and girl would have a chance to learn and become happy and useful. If the Union broke up, everything would be lost. So while he hated slavery Lincoln would not lift a finger to destroy it if such action threatened the Union. In 1862, after a year of war, Lincoln declared:

My paramount object in this struggle is to save the Union and is not either to save or destroy slavery. If I could save the Union without freeing any slaves, I would do it; and if I could save it by freeing all the slaves I would do it; and if I could save it by freeing some slaves and leaving others alone, I would also do that.

The South seceded in a hurry. Lincoln could not make southerners believe he did not want to hurt them. Without waiting to see what the new president might do, southern states began to leave the Union as soon as he was elected. They felt that all was lost. The North, with its population of twenty-two million (compared with nine million in the South) could carry any national election. From now on the North would control both the Presidency and Congress. More new states were entering the Union from northern territories than from southern territories. The "balance of power" in the Senate had been destroyed. Southerners could see no future for their section in the Union, so they seceded.

Many northerners were willing to let the southern states go. Horace Greeley, editor of the *New York Tribune*, said, "If a majority of southern white people decide by an honest vote to leave the Union, they

should be allowed to do just that."

When secession became a fact men and women everywhere asked, "Will it be peace or war?" The guns at Fort Sumter gave the answer.

The war began at Fort Sumter. Fort Sumter was one of the fortifications the federal government had built to guard the harbor of Charleston, South Carolina. In the spring of 1861, the fort was running short of food. The governor of South Carolina told the commander, Major Robert Anderson, that he must turn

Lincoln was a man of strength and sadness. The picture below shows him when he was President in the War Between the States.

The war begins! At 4:30 in the morning, April 12, 1861, southern guns started firing at Fort Sumter in the harbor of Charleston, South Carolina. This gun was the first to reply.

the fort over to southern officials. Anderson tried to delay; he offered to compromise, but it was no use. Jefferson Davis, head of the Confederacy, warned that he would regard any attempt to send help to the fort as an act of war. Lincoln paid no attention. He announced he was sending an unarmed ship with supplies.

The southern commander in Charleston, General Beauregard (BO reh gahrd) then gave orders to attack. At 4:30 in the morning on April 12, 1861, southern guns began to fire on the little fort. For two days they kept it up. Anderson had to surrender.

The next day Lincoln called for 75,000 volunteers to uphold the Union. Davis called for 100,000 to defend the Confederacy. North and South, men rushed to join the armies. The Civil War had begun. The question of states' rights versus national authority would have to be settled on the battlefield.

The South had fine generals. In spite of its wealth and population, the North was at a disadvantage when war began. The federal army consisted of only a few thousand trained soldiers. Many officers resigned to fight for the South. Among them was Robert E. Lee of Virginia.

Lee proved to be one of the most valuable assets of the South. He was a military genius. During most of the war, Lincoln searched for a

376   WAR BETWEEN NORTH AND SOUTH

Virginia's Robert E. Lee was head of the Military Academy at West Point in 1852-3.

general who could beat this able man.

Lee was born on a Virginia plantation in 1807, two years before Lincoln was born in a Kentucky log cabin. When he decided to become a soldier, President Jackson himself appointed Lee to West Point.

Lee was graduated with high honors, fought brilliantly in the Mexican War, and then became Superintendent of West Point. Later he spent six years fighting Indians in Texas. He was home on leave at the time of John Brown's raid and took charge of the troops that arrested Brown.

He returned to his regiment, but when Texas left the Union Lee came home again. For thirty years he had served the Union. What was he to do now? Did he owe his loyalty to the nation or to his home state of Virginia?

Many others were asking the same question. It was perhaps the hardest question that ever faced Americans. In the so-called "border states" between North and South — Maryland, Kentucky, Missouri — one man might answer by enlisting in the Union army, while his brother joined the Confederates.

Lee did not like secession, but when Virginia left the Union he felt he had to stand by his state. He soon became Commander-in-Chief of Confederate troops.

The war was fought in the East and West and on the sea. More Americans died in the Civil War than in any other war, including even World War II. There were 150 great battles and hundreds more that would have been considered great in earlier wars. In the following pages you will read about only a few battles. You will learn about the three main *campaigns*, or war plans, that the North developed and carried out.

The three campaigns were: (1) the *blockade*, or the effort to close southern ports so the South could not get supplies from Europe or send cotton to foreign markets; (2) the *war in the East*, or the attempt to capture Richmond, the southern capital; (3) the *war in the West*, or the drive to get control of the Mississippi River.

As you read about the three campaigns, consult the map on page 380 to get a clear picture of the battle area. It is important to remember that the North fought an *offensive* war and the South fought a *defensive* war. In other words, the North attacked and invaded the South, trying to force the southern states back into the Union; southerners fought to drive the invaders out of their territory. That is why most of the big battles, except Gettysburg, were fought in the South. Southerners had the advantage of fighting on land they knew well, but this meant many southern towns and farms were destroyed while the North suffered little from the war.

Northern ships blockaded the South. The South was almost entirely a farming region at the time of the Civil War. There were few factories. Southerners concentrated on raising cotton. They had to buy manufactured goods and even some food from other parts of the world.

The North raised plenty of food and could get large amounts of wheat from the new western states which sided with the North in the war. Northern factories supplied guns, clothing, and other supplies that the Union armies greatly needed.

Where could the South get war supplies? Southerners did not worry at first. They felt sure France and Great Britain would send them military goods in exchange for cotton. Cotton mills in Europe needed millions of bales every year to keep running.

Northern leaders realized the importance of foreign trade to the South. To stop the shipping of cotton they planned to capture as many southern ports as they could and to blockade the rest. To *blockade* means to close the harbors of an enemy. This is done by stationing warships where they can stop ships from going out or coming in.

The Union navy blockaded over 200 ports from Virginia to Texas. It was a big job to guard such a long coastline, but the blockade was effective. A few fast ships called "blockade runners" managed to dodge the Union warships, but they could supply only a small part of the need. Slowly but surely the blockade starved the South into defeat.

The South tried to break the blockade. Southerners tried desperately to break the blockade. They took an

The Ironclads battle it out! Below the U.S.S. *Monitor* and the *Virginia* (formerly the *Merrimac*) are shown fighting near Hampton Roads, Virginia, March 9, 1862.

The U.S.S. *Kearsarge* sinks the *Alabama*, July 17, 1864! This picture shows the end of the Confederate raider (left) which had destroyed dozens of Northern merchant ships.

old ship, the *Merrimac*, covered the sides with iron rails, and mounted five guns on each side. On March 8, 1862, the *Merrimac* (which southerners renamed the *Virginia*) steamed into the harbor at Hampton Roads, Virginia. It attacked Union ships blockading the harbor. Their guns made no impression on the *Merrimac*. It rammed and sank one northern ship, drove another aground, and scattered the rest. At sunset it withdrew; the captain planned to come back and finish the battle in the morning. It looked as if the *Merrimac* might break the blockade.

That night another ironclad, the Union *Monitor*, appeared at Hampton Roads. It was a queer looking boat that John Ericsson, a Swedish immigrant, had designed. In the center it had a small iron gun tower that could turn in any direction. The *Monitor* looked, as someone said, like "a cheesebox on a raft," but it was a real warship.

At dawn, when the *Merrimac* re-

turned, the *Monitor* blocked her path. For hours the two monsters hammered away at each other. Neither could do much harm to the other. They used up all their ammunition. The battle of Hampton Roads ended in a draw. But the *Merrimac* withdrew and later was sunk to avoid capture. The attempt to break the blockade had failed. The North could produce many ships like the *Monitor*. The South did not have machines or resources to build more ironclads.

The battle between the *Monitor* and the *Merrimac* was the first battle between two ironclads. It proved wooden warships were a thing of the past. All over the world, nations began to build ironclad ships.

After the battle between the *Monitor* and the *Merrimac*, northern warships continued to blockade the South. That of itself was enough to decide the war. Southern armies kept fighting for three more years. They won victories, but without help and supplies from foreign lands, they could not meet Union armies on equal terms.

The North wanted to capture Richmond. The land battles of the Civil War were fought in the East near the seacoast, and in the West along the Mississippi River. Most of the time the war in the East was quite separate from the war in the West. The reason was geography. The Appalachian Mountains separate the seacoast from the Mississippi Valley. Only a few roads crossed the moun-

tains in those days. Military leaders in the West kept in contact with the East only by telegraph, and telegraph lines often broke down or were cut by the enemy.

Thus, to understand the Civil War you must study the war in the East and then the war in the West. The South was defeated section by section.

The war in the East began soon after the firing on Fort Sumter. It dragged on for years, costing thousands of lives. The South fought hard and well. For the North, it

The map below shows the Civil War campaigns in the East. Northerners strove to conquer Richmond and to defend Washington. The South's aim was to drive out northern troops. Twice Lee invaded the North but had to retreat after Antietam (1862) and Gettysburg (1863).

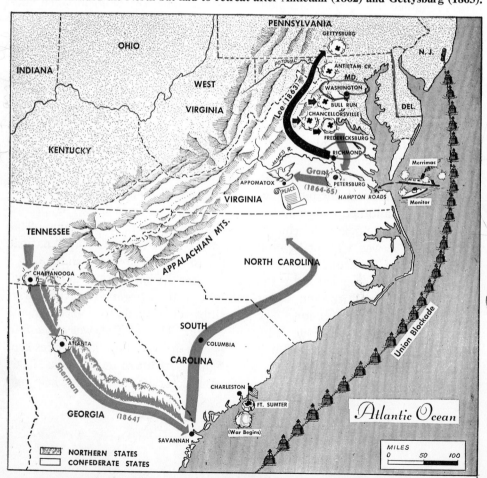

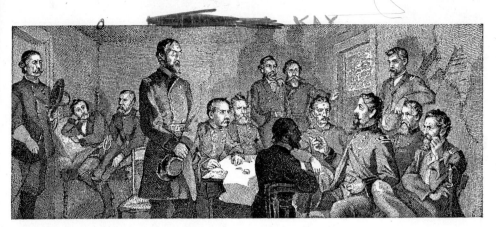

General Meade holds a council of war. This picture shows Northern officers planning the strategy that won the battle of Gettysburg (1863), the turning point of the Civil War.

was the most discouraging part of the war. There were few victories and many disappointments.

The aim of the war in the East was the same on both sides. Union leaders thought they could win the war by capturing the southern capital, Richmond. Southerners thought they could end the war by capturing Washington. The two cities are about 100 miles apart. Washington is on the Potomac River. Richmond is almost directly south, on the James River. Most of the land between was covered with woods. Several rivers cut through the land, and there were almost no bridges. It was a difficult region for warfare. The two armies moved back and forth, fighting and retreating and fighting again.

The first big battle was fought at Bull Run on July 21, 1861. Thousands of northerners had answered Lincoln's call for volunteers. They lacked training and good leaders, but nobody realized the fact. People in the North boasted the war would be over in ninety days. So the raw northern army marched into northeastern Virginia. Not far from Washington they met southern troops at a little creek called Bull Run. The southerners had better leaders and they were fighting on their own ground. They drove the Union troops back and won a surprise victory.

Gettysburg was the turning point of the war. Southern hopes rose high after Bull Run. Most northerners realized they were in for a long, hard war. Lincoln put General George B. McClellan in charge of Union armies. McClellan drilled his men thoroughly. The next year (1862) he moved south toward Richmond. The southern army under General Lee promptly started north. That scared McClellan. Within sight of Richmond, he turned back to protect Washington. Lee pushed ahead and invaded the North. At the battle of Antietam (an TE tam) in Maryland, southern armies were defeated.

LEE'S INVASION OF THE NORTH

Northern reinforcements rush to the battlefield. Here a New York regiment is shown hurrying to replace a battery destroyed by Pickett's charge at Gettysburg.

Lee then had to retreat to Virginia.

The next year (1863) the Union army tried again to capture Richmond. It was driven back at the battle of Chancellorsville, Virginia. Chancellorsville was a costly victory for the South, however. One of the most brilliant southern generals, "Stonewall" Jackson, was accidentally shot by his own troops. Jackson had been responsible for many earlier victories. Next to Robert E. Lee, he was the South's best general. That summer Lee led southern armies north a second time. He got as far as southern Pennsylvania before he was defeated at Gettysburg in July, 1863.

In many ways, Gettysburg was the most important battle of the war. Lee threw everything he had at the North. The fighting lasted three days. On the third day, Lee found ammunition was running low. He ordered General George Pickett to make a bayonet charge. Fifteen thousand southern fighters followed Pickett up a hill called Cemetery Ridge.

Pickett's Charge was one of the most daring in history. Marching directly into the fire of northern guns, southerners forced their way to the center of the Union troops in a hand-to-hand fight. For twenty minutes they held their ground. But Union guns kept firing. The southerners had to fall back. Almost the

382

whole division was wiped out. Lee had gambled and lost. He led his shattered army south once more. From that day on, the southern cause declined. Gettysburg was the beginning of the end.

However, the war in the East lasted almost two years more. Union armies kept trying to conquer Richmond, but southerners held them back. Lee knew how to use every advantage of geography. He saved Richmond from capture until the last days of the war.

The North won control of the Mississippi River. Fighting in the West began later than in the East and ended more quickly. The South was beaten in the West first. Then Ulysses S. Grant, the man most responsible for the victory on the Mississippi, moved east and finished the campaign to capture Richmond. Remember that all the while the Union navy blockaded southern ports, making it harder for the South to fight.

To understand the war in the West study the maps on page 302H and page 384. Most of the southern states are east of the Mississippi River. But three southern states, Texas, Arkansas, and most of Louisiana, lie west of the river. Union forces held the northern part of the Mississippi Valley. If they could push south they would split the Confederacy in two parts. They could cut Texas, Arkansas, and Louisiana off from the rest of the South. People in the Southwest would not be able to help the Confederate armies. It would be one more step in the process of defeating the South piece by piece.

One of the first to see the possibilities of the western campaign was Ulysses S. Grant. Grant was a graduate of West Point. He had fought bravely in the Mexican War, but had to resign from the army because of personal troubles. When the Civil War started, Grant became the leader of a group of volunteers in Illinois. After some delay he won permission to move south. In February, 1862, he captured Fort Donelson in western Tennessee. Then he pushed farther south. Two months later, at Shiloh, in southwestern

Brother fought against brother in the Civil War. Below are shown (from left to right) a Kentucky rifleman, a Louisiana Zouave, a Massachusetts foot soldier, and a Washington artilleryman. Northern troops usually wore blue and southerners wore gray.

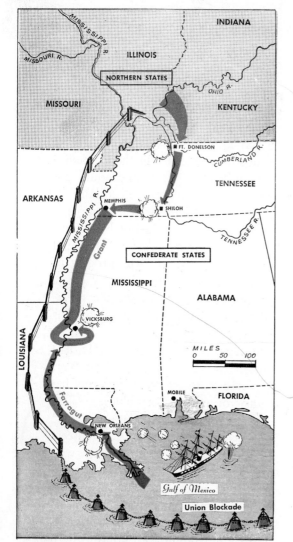

Tennessee, a southern army surprised and nearly defeated him. Fresh troops arrived in time to win the battle for the North.

While Grant and his men were coming down the Mississippi Valley, northern warships were fighting their way up the river from the South. In April, 1862, a fleet under command of David Farragut captured New Orleans and destroyed southern forts at the mouth of the river. Both ends of the Mississippi were now under northern control. But in between, a long stretch of river belonged to the Confederacy. The strongest southern forts guarding the river were at Vicksburg, Mississippi. Grant made up his mind to take Vicksburg. The town held out for months. Grant tried every method he could think of. He surrounded Vicksburg and attacked it from the rear. No food or help of any kind could get into the city. At last, on July 4, 1863, Vicksburg surrendered. (One day earlier, the battle of Gettysburg had ended in defeat for Lee.)

After the fall of Vicksburg, southern resistance on the Mississippi collapsed. The North won control of the river. The Southwest was split off from the South. Lincoln proudly announced: "The father of waters flows unvexed to the sea."

Grant and Lee fought it out. The war in the West was practically over. But in the East fighting went on. Lincoln could not find a general to beat Lee.

Grant (above) was largely responsible for the success of the western campaign that split the Confederacy (map, top).

He decided to give Grant a chance. In March, 1864, the stocky little man took command of Union armies.

Grant was a stubborn fighter. His only plan was to attack and keep on attacking regardless of the cost. He hammered his way south, losing men by the thousands. "I propose to fight it out on this line if it takes all summer," he told Lincoln in 1864. It took him all summer and all winter too.

Lee's armies were getting food and supplies from Georgia. One of the officers Grant had left in Tennessee, General William Tecumseh Sherman, begged for a chance to knock Georgia out of the war. When he received permission he and his armies marched southeast through Georgia, destroying everything. They set fire to the city of Atlanta and marched on to the seacoast. Sherman did not stop there. He marched up the coast, invading South Carolina and then North Carolina. You can follow Sherman's march on the map, page 380.

Lee and his armies were pushed into an ever smaller space. The West was gone; Georgia was gone, Grant's armies had almost surrounded Richmond. Lee led his army west, hoping to join troops in North Carolina. But Grant caught up with him at Appomattox (AP oh MAT uks), not far from Richmond.

Lee realized it was hopeless to go on fighting. The war had been lost at Gettysburg and Vicksburg almost two years before. He agreed to

Here are three Civil War scenes. The top picture shows a typical fortification erected by Union forces. In the center picture, "Stonewall" Jackson leads his men at Bull Run. The bottom picture shows Sherman's march through Georgia.

FINAL BATTLE IN THE SOUTH

385

ABRAHAM LINCOLN (1809–1865)

From log cabin to White House, from birth in the Kentucky woods to death in a Washington theater — so ran the story of Abraham Lincoln. In between he was a farmworker, a country lawyer, a representative in Congress, and finally the President of the United States.

Failure was often Lincoln's lot. He failed as a storekeeper; he did not win reelection to Congress. Stephen Douglas beat him in the race for Illinois Senator. Lincoln said of his defeat that he felt "like the boy who stubbed his toe. It hurt too bad to laugh, and he was too big to cry."

Lincoln loved the Union. He would not permit the nation to break up. He hated war but when the Civil War came he kept the North fighting battle after battle to crush the doctrine of secession.

There was no meanness in Lincoln. He wanted the South to come back into the Union easily and quietly. When a crowd gathered at the White House to rejoice that the war was over Lincoln asked the band to play "Dixie" saying, "I've always thought it one of the best tunes I ever heard."

meet Grant in a nearby farmhouse. Lee rode in on a white horse, Grant on a dark horse. For a few minutes the two men talked of the "good old days" when they had been comrades in the Mexican War. Then Grant pulled up a table and wrote a few sentences giving surrender terms.

He asked southerners to lay down their arms and promise to be loyal to the Union. Lee asked that his men be allowed to keep their horses. Grant agreed, saying they would be needed "for the spring plowing."

Lee immediately signed the surrender; in his stately way, he told Grant he appreciated the generous terms. Then the two men rode away in different directions. The date was April 9, 1865.

The end of the war brought the problems of reconstruction. The Civil War was over. There remained the task of rebuilding, or *reconstruction*. The South had to come back into the Union. War damage had to be repaired. Negroes had to learn to live as free men.

During the war Lincoln had acted against slavery. On January 1, 1863, soon after the battle of Antietam, he published an order called the *Emancipation Proclamation*. This declared that all slaves in any state fighting the Union were free. As northern armies advanced into southern territory they set free the slaves there. When the war was over, all slaves were free. However, a new amendment was added to the Constitution to make it binding. This was the Thirteenth Amendment. It said that "neither slavery nor involuntary servitude . . . shall exist within the United States." [97]

During the war, Lincoln, made plans for peace. He knew there would be confusion and suffering in the South. He hoped to restore order quickly and quietly. He wanted to bring the South back into the Union without delay. He hoped everybody would forget the war and concentrate on building a strong, free America. Lincoln declared:

Fondly do we hope — fervently do we pray — that this mighty scourge of war may speedily pass away. . . .

With malice toward none; with charity for all; with firmness in the right, as God gives us to see the right, let us strive on to finish the work we are in; to bind up the nation's wounds; to care for him who shall have borne the battle and for his widow, and his orphan — to do all which may achieve and cherish a just and lasting peace among ourselves, and with all nations.

Lincoln's plan for the South was dropped. Lincoln's plan was never put into effect. A crazy actor, John Wilkes Booth, killed the President five days after Lee surrendered. The murder of Lincoln was perhaps the greatest tragedy of the Civil War. If Lincoln had lived the Reconstruction might have been quite different.

Vice-President Andrew Johnson became President when Lincoln died. He was an honest, hard working man, but he had a bad temper. He

387

Death finds a President! This picture shows how the crazed actor, John Wilkes Booth, murdered Abraham Lincoln in Ford's Theatre, Washington, D.C. on the evening of April 14, 1865. In those days the chief executive was not carefully guarded.

did not get along with Republican leaders who controlled Congress. He tried to carry out Lincoln's plans, but he could not get any cooperation. Northern leaders in Congress wanted to punish the South. They also wanted to protect the Negroes and help them become self-supporting. They were afraid that if Lincoln's plan was followed the South might not treat Negroes fairly.

Johnson and Congress quarreled bitterly. Congress went ahead with its plan of treating the South severely. Another amendment, the Fourteenth, was proposed and accepted by Congress. It declared that Negroes were citizens. It also took the vote and the right to hold office from any southerner who had held office under the federal government and then had fought against the Union. This part of the Fourteenth Amendment barred most southern leaders from taking part in the new state governments. [99–102]

Congress said that all southern states must approve the Fourteenth Amendment before they could come back into the Union. Tennessee was the only southern state that ratified the amendment promptly. The others defied Congress.

Congress punished the South. Congress then passed the Reconstruction

WAR BETWEEN NORTH AND SOUTH

Act of 1867. It put the South under military rule. The South was divided into five military districts with an army officer in charge of each. Congress also arranged for new elections under military supervision. Southern states had to agree to give Negroes the right to vote. They must draw up new state constitutions that met the approval of Congress.

Slowly the southern states obeyed. (They had to obey to get rid of military rule.) Negroes gained the right to vote. Congress passed the Fifteenth Amendment which declared that:

The right of citizens of the United States to vote shall not be denied or abridged by the United States or by any state on account of race, color, or previous condition of servitude. [104]

Since many southern white leaders had lost the right to vote, a new group of men ran southern state governments. Some were "poor whites" and Negroes. Southerners called white men who rose to power during Reconstruction scalawags and carpetbaggers. *Scalawags* were southerners who had taken no part in the war or who tried to win northern favor. *Carpetbaggers* were northerners who went south after the war. The name came from the fact that they packed their belongings in cheap luggage called "carpetbags." Some were teachers or ministers who came to help the Negroes, but many were adventurers looking for money and power.

Most southerners hated the carpetbaggers and scalawags. They blamed them for raising taxes and running the states into debt. There were plenty of scandals. A story was told about one scalawag who had never had more than a few dollars before

Below is shown Andrew Johnson's little tailor shop at East Greenville, Tennessee. Here the future Vice-President worked at his trade for many years before going into politics. Born in North Carolina, he moved to the Tennessee frontier at 18 and "grew up with the country."

the war. During Reconstruction he got a state job that paid $8000 a year. In three years he deposited $100,000 in savings banks. When asked how he could save so much, he replied, "I did it, sir, by the practice of the most rigid economy."

The Reconstruction Period had a dark and a bright side. Southern white men who could not vote grew angry at the way the new state governments were run. They had no lawful way to interfere so they took an unlawful way. They formed the *Ku Klux Klan*. This was a secret society of young men. Under cover of night they rode about the country in white sheets that made them look like ghosts. They tried to frighten Negroes and keep them from voting. Later, they began whipping and even killing Negroes and scalawags.

Decent southerners got out of the Klan when they saw it was going too far. Congress passed a law in 1871 to break up the Klan. But the idea lingered on. The Ku Klux Klan still exists in some sections of the United States, but has no connection with the Klan of earlier days.

There was a brighter side to Reconstruction. In the North people raised money to build schools and train teachers for Negroes. Many southerners also helped to educate former slaves. Slowly and painfully Negroes adjusted to new conditions. Some were lucky enough to get a little land of their own; certain southerners gave small tracts of land to former slaves. However, most Negroes had to work as farm laborers. An increasing number moved to towns where they worked at jobs no one else wanted.

Every year the number of Negro college graduates increased. Others learned a trade. A few were able to save enough money to start small businesses. Progress was slow; even today the average Negro does not have as much money or education as the average white person. But remember that less than a hundred years ago most Negroes were completely ignorant and without money. They were turned loose to earn a living without much help from anyone. Negroes have made great progress during and since Reconstruction.

Reconstruction ended, but the South did not forget. Congress could not rule the South by force forever. Seven years after the war, southern white leaders regained the right to vote and hold office. A new generation of southern boys reached voting age. Once more the South could control its elections. In 1877 President Rutherford B. Hayes withdrew federal troops from the South. Hayes also appointed a southern man to be a member of his Cabinet. The Reconstruction Period was over.

But southerners did not forget the bitter days after the war. They blamed Republicans for their suffering. Most southerners joined the Democratic Party as soon as they could vote. In election after election, southerners sent Democrats to represent them in Washington. People spoke of the *Solid South*, meaning that the South voted solidly for the Democratic Party. For more than fifty years the South remembered Reconstruction and turned its back on the Republican Party.

A New South arose. After Reconstruction the South changed rapidly. Most plantations were broken up into small farms. Cotton remained the big crop, but it was not the only one. Peanuts, sweet potatoes, fruits and vegetables became important. In Virginia, Kentucky, and the Carolinas tobacco became increasingly profitable employing large numbers of workers.

After the Civil War the South developed manufacturing. Factories for making cloth appeared near the cotton fields. Southerners discovered they could make money out of the thick woods that covered much of their land. The South now supplies a great part of the wood products America needs. Discovery of oil in the Southwest brought prosperity to the region. New roads and railroads opened up remote sections. Cities grew rapidly. Today southern cities are moving ahead so fast many observers believe that America's greatest promise may be in the South.

Best of all, the changes in business and farming have made southerners feel they are partners in America. They no longer fear their section will be cheated of its fair share of wealth.

CHAPTER SUMMARY

The Civil War or War Between the States lasted from 1861 to 1865.
The North had greater wealth, resources, and manpower. The South
had better generals and the advantage of fighting on its own ground.
The blockade of southern ports greatly weakened the fighting strength
of the South. Grant and Farragut won control of the Mississippi
River and split the Confederacy. Sherman's march through Georgia
cut off another section.

Northern generals tried repeatedly to capture Richmond. The South
aimed only to drive out northern troops. Twice Lee invaded the
North, hoping to force the North to let the South alone. The battle
of Gettysburg in July, 1863, was the turning point of the war. Grant
finally wore out southern strength and forced Lee to surrender at
Appomattox in April, 1865.

Southerners suffered much during Reconstruction. They blamed the
Republicans in Congress for their sufferings. They voted solidly for
Democrats for many years. A new South arose from the ashes of the
Civil War and is today steadily growing more prosperous.

The Language of History

Be sure you understand the following words and phrases as they are
used in this chapter.

1. border states 〜 W.   **4.** defensive war D.C   **7.** carpetbaggers B. J
2. blockade D.U.   **5.** emancipation B.C.   **8.** scalawags C.C.
3. offensive war C.M.   **6.** reconstruction R.W.   **9.** Solid South M.F.

What Happened When

Make sure you know the important events connected with the following
dates.

    1. 1860   **2.** 1861   **3.** 1863   **4.** 1865   **5.** 1867   **6.** 1877

Who's Who in History

Tell the part each of the following played in the events of the Civil War.

1. Horace Greeley
2. Jefferson Davis
3. Robert E. Lee
4. John Ericsson
5. David Farragut
6. George McClellan
7. Ulysses S. Grant
8. William T. Sherman
9. Andrew Johnson

Study Questions

1. List the states that formed the Confederacy. (See map, page 302H.)
2. a. What advantages did the South have in the Civil War?
   b. Why was it almost certain that the North would win?
3. a. What were the three main campaigns of the Civil War?
   b. Which one do you think was the most important? Give reasons for your answer.
4. Select your favorite military leader of the Civil War and tell what he accomplished. (You can give a better answer if you look him up in an encyclopedia.)
5. Why is the battle of the *Monitor* and the *Merrimac* important in (a) American history and (b) world history?
6. Why is the battle of Gettysburg called the turning point of the Civil War?
7. a. What did the Thirteenth Amendment forbid?
   b. Give two provisions of the Fourteenth Amendment.
   c. What right did the Fifteenth Amendment give Negroes?
8. Why did the South turn against the Republican Party during the Reconstruction Period?
9. a. What was the purpose of the Ku Klux Klan?
   b. What methods did the Klan use?
   c. Why do law-abiding people in the North and South dislike the Klan and similar organizations today?
10. What new industries developed in the South after Reconstruction?

LET'S LOOK AT WHAT WE'VE LEARNED

Why did the North and South develop very different ways of life?

Geography was probably the basic reason for the difference in development. Because of the mild climate and good soil, the South became a cotton-growing region. Because of the need for cheap, plentiful labor, Negro slaves were imported in large numbers.

The North also developed agriculture but did not specialize in any one crop. The use of slave labor was not profitable, so there were few Negroes in the northern states. Manufacturing became important. Population increased rapidly because of immigration.

What were the causes of disagreement between the North and the South?

The most serious dispute arose over the question of slavery. Southern planters wanted to take their slaves into the new western territories and develop a new and rich cotton-growing region. Northerners wanted to keep slavery out of the territories because free workers and farmers could not compete with slave labor.

North and South also disagreed over the tariff. Northern leaders wanted high tariff rates to protect American manufactured goods against foreign competition. Southerners wanted low tariffs so they could buy manufactured goods as cheaply as possible.

What is the states' rights theory and why did the South favor it?

The states' rights theory says that the federal government in Washington should have the limited power to do only those things which the Constitution clearly permits it to do. The states existed before the federal government and joined the Union of their own free will. Therefore, argued believers in states' rights, a state can refuse to obey a federal law it does not like. If the federal government uses force the state has the right to leave the Union or secede.

Why did the southern states secede in 1860–1861?

Southerners had warned they could not stay in the Union if Abraham Lincoln were elected. They did not like Lincoln because he was a Republican and against slavery in the territories. Lincoln won the election in 1860, and eleven southern states seceded soon afterward.

What were the main events of the Civil War?

The fighting began at Fort Sumter, South Carolina, April 12, 1861. It ended at Appomattox, Virginia, April 9, 1865. The northern navy kept the South blockaded. U. S. Grant led a successful campaign to win control of the Mississippi River for the North. The North and the South fought many bloody battles in the region between Washington and Richmond. Lee tried to invade the North, but was turned back at Gettysburg, Pennsylvania in 1863. This was the turning point of the war. General Sherman marched through Georgia, burning crops and destroying cities. Early in 1865 Grant surrounded Lee's army and forced him to surrender.

What was the Reconstruction Period?

Reconstruction is the name given the time after the Civil War when the southern states came back into the Union. It was a time of suffering for the South. War damage had to be repaired. The slaves were freed. Many southern leaders could not vote. For a time the South was ruled by carpetbaggers and scalawags. A secret society, the Ku Klux Klan, tried to keep Negroes from voting. The South blamed its troubles on Republicans and for years after would vote only for Democrats.

Connecting the Past with the Present . . .

The America of today — your America — grew out of the Civil War. The war was basically a fight between those who wanted to keep America a quiet farming land and those who wanted to build a busy, industrial nation. To a large extent, it was a struggle for power between plantation owners in the South and factory owners in the North.

As soon as the question was decided, America moved forward with a great burst of energy. Railroad lines spread to the Pacific Coast. The West filled up with farmers from the East and from Europe. Great cities grew. Factory chimneys appeared even in the South. The United States surged forward to become an industrial power in the world.

Out of the blood and sorrow of the Civil War came great expansion east and west, tall skyscrapers, and the America that is here today.

The terrible conflict left scars and problems, however. Some of the questions that trouble thinking Americans today have grown out of or are connected with the Civil War. The issue of states' rights, the Solid South, the problem of segregation in public places — all these and many more are part of the legacy of the "Brothers' War" which began nearly a hundred years ago.

Questions for Discussion and Review

1. Why did slavery disappear in the North but increase in the South after 1800?
2. **a.** Why did southern leaders want slavery in the new territories?
   b. Why were northerners determined to keep slavery out of the new territories?
3. Why did most immigrants from Europe avoid the South?
4. Why did the South oppose high tariffs?
5. On what occasion did New Englanders threaten secession?
6. Under what circumstances was the Republican Party formed?
7. Abraham Lincoln once called Harriet Beecher Stowe "the little woman who made the big war." What did he mean?
8. How did John Brown's raid help bring on the Civil War?
9. Do you think the War Between the States could have been avoided? Why or why not?
10. Write a brief biography of Abraham Lincoln including **(a)** his early life, **(b)** his career as a lawyer, **(c)** the Lincoln-Douglas debates, **(d)** how he led the Union in the Civil War, and **(e)** his death.

THE HISTORY LABORATORY

Here are suggestions for activities that you will find interesting and profitable.

Boost Your Town . . .

Have a committee write a letter to a junior high school class in either the South or North. Tell them the part your town played in the Civil War and ask them to tell you what their town did. You may find information about your town in Civil War days in the local library. Perhaps your local newspaper or Chamber of Commerce can help also.

WHAT AND WHEN

"Bleeding Kansas" 1855-57

Dred Scott case 1857

Lincoln-Douglas debate 1858

Tell It in Pictures . . .

Make a scrapbook of pictures of Civil War battlefields and monuments. For pictures, write to schools or the Chamber of Commerce in Richmond, Gettysburg, Antietam, and other places connected with the events of the Civil War.

Travel Back in Time . . .

Imagine you were a fifteen-year-old living in Gettysburg in July, 1863. Tell or write the story of what you saw and felt. Consult *Mr. Brady's Camera Boy* by Rogers or *Johnny Reb* by Allen.

You Are There! . . .

Have a committee prepare an on-the-spot broadcast or telecast of the dedication of the National Cemetery at Gettysburg, November 19, 1863. If possible, use a recording device. Consult *The Perfect Tribute* by Andrews for information about the ceremonies.

You're Up in the Air . . .

Write an account of your experiences as an observer in a balloon over the Civil War battlefield. (Northern armies often used balloons for observation in the Civil War.) Consult *The Blue and the Gray* by Henry Steele Commager (Bobbs-Merrill Co., 1950) and the article entitled "Gettysburg — the Turning Point of the Civil War" in *Compton's Pictured Encyclopedia*, Volume 6.

Divide the Work . . .

1. The Bulletin Board Committee should prepare a display of pictures relating to slavery and the Civil War.

2. Have a committee arrange a program of readings about the Civil War. You might play records of famous Civil War songs such as "Battle Hymn of the Republic," "Dixie," and "John Brown's Body."

Brown's raid 1859   Ft. Sumter fired on 1861   Battle of Gettysburg 1863   Peace at Appomattox 1865

Ideas for Maps and Charts . . .

1. On an outline map of the United States show the location of each of the following:

Missouri	Bull Run	Harpers Ferry
the 36° 30′ line	Richmond	Gettysburg
Washington	Kansas	Mississippi River
Fort Sumter	Illinois	Vicksburg
Hampton Roads	Freeport, Illinois	Atlanta

2. Draw a picture map of the Civil War. Show (1) how northern ships blockaded the southern coast, (2) how Grant and Farragut won control of the Mississippi, (3) how Lee was turned back at Gettysburg, (4) Sherman's march through Georgia and the burning of Atlanta, (5) the fighting back and forth between Washington and Richmond, (6) the surrender of Lee at Appomattox. Consult the article on the Civil War in *Compton's Pictured Encyclopedia*, Volume 3, and the article on the War Between the States in the *World Book Encyclopedia*, Volume 18.

Let's Read about Slavery, the Civil War, and Reconstruction

*BONTEMPS, ARNA W., *Story of the Negro*, Knopf, 1948.

COMMAGER, H. S., and WARD, L., *America's Robert E. Lee*, Houghton, 1951.

COY, H., *The Real Book about George Washington Carver*, Garden, 1951.

FOSTER, GENEVIEVE, *Abraham Lincoln*, Scribner, 1950.

HARTMAN, GERTRUDE, *Machines and the Men Who Made the World of Industry*, pages 14–23, Macmillan, 1939.

**HOWARD, JOHN T., *Our American Music*, Crowell, 1946.

JACKSON, PHYLLIS, *Victorian Cinderella; the Story of Harriet Beecher Stowe*, Holiday, 1947.

KANTOR, MACKINLAY, *Lee and Grant at Appomattox*, Random, 1950.

LONG, L., *David Farragut, Boy Midshipman*, Bobbs, 1950.

LORANT, STEFAN, *Lincoln: A Picture Story of His Life*, Harper, 1952.

NICOLAY, HELEN, *Boy's Life of Abraham Lincoln*, Crofts, 1906.

NORTON, S., and COURNOS, J., *Candidate for Truth: The Story of Daniel Webster*, Holt, 1953.

PACE, MILDRED, *Clara Barton*, Scribner, 1941.

SEIFERT, SHIRLEY, *Captain Grant*, Lippincott, 1946.

WASHINGTON, BOOKER T., *Up from Slavery*, Doubleday, 1901.

* indicates easy reading
** indicates advanced reading

WAR BETWEEN NORTH AND SOUTH

Unit 9

THE UNITED STATES WON GREAT INDUSTRIAL POWER (1834-1950)

"FOR A LAD of twelve to rise and find his way to the factory and begin to work while it was still dark and not be released until after darkness came in the evening was a terrible task. But I was young and had my dreams."

Thus Andrew Carnegie recalled his first job. Out of his dreams grew the great American steel industry. In Pittsburgh, Chicago, Birmingham, Buffalo, Youngstown, and dozens of other cities, the glare of steel furnaces reddens the sky. Because Carnegie found a way to make steel cheap and plentiful, other industries — the manufacture of automobiles and airplanes and countless other important products — became practical.

This Unit traces the development of American industry from its earliest days. As you read keep in mind these key questions:

1. What part did geography and the location of resources play in the growth of manufacturing?

2. Who were the "founding fathers of industry"?

3. How did new machines and products change American life?

399

Chapter 20

NEW INVENTIONS AND
BUSINESS METHODS
INCREASED THE
SUPPLY OF GOODS

"How do you turn on the light?" Probably you've heard someone ask that question when he or she entered a darkened room. It was Thomas Edison who made it possible for people to turn on the light. His invention of the electric light is one of the greatest inventions in history. When did he make the discovery? What else did he invent?

Edison's life story is part of this chapter which deals with early developments and certain key inventions in American manufacturing. The Industrial Revolution began in England but it spread to the United States. Who was "the Father of American Industry"? How did he manage to build English-style machines in America in spite of British laws against it?

The textile industry was the first to be revolutionized by new methods and machinery. What American invention made it possible to supply enough cotton fiber for the new machines? And who was the first American to demonstrate the usefulness of standardized, interchangeable parts?

The impact of the Industrial Revolution was felt on the farms as well as in the town. What new machines made the farmer's work easier? What new problems appeared when farm production increased?

Machines changed American life.
After the Civil War the United States
changed rapidly. Everything began
to move faster. Factories multiplied;
inventions increased; and America
became a leading industrial nation.

All America seemed to be moving
to the cities. And from foreign
lands came thousands of immigrants,
seeking new opportunities in factories. Thus the United States
changed from a land of small farms
and small businesses to a nation of
great cities and busy factories.

What brought about such rapid
change? The answer lies in one
word: machines. Until after the
Civil War most Americans did their
work and earned their living by hand
labor. Electricity was just a word in
the dictionary, and oil was something
old folks used to ease the pains of
rheumatism. Here is the way one
citizen described life in Ridgefield,
Connecticut about 100 years ago —
before the machine age began:

Nearly all of us were farmers. Even
those not making a living by the land
had each a farm, or at least a garden,
with pigs, chickens, and cattle. Wages
were about 50¢ a day, and generally
were paid in meat or vegetables or other
articles; seldom in money, which was
scarce. There was not a factory of any
kind in the whole township.

As a matter of course, we had a
fattened ox ready for winter. This
means that the ox, poor thing, would
be eaten during the winter. One full
barrel of meat was salted down; the
rest was slightly salted and hung up in
the chimney to become dried or hung
beef. All vegetables came from our
own garden; our fuel came from our
own woodland. Sugar was supplied
partly from our maple trees, but more
sugar came from the West Indies.
There was no baker in the town. Each
family made not only its own bread,
cakes, and pies, but its own soap,
candles, butter, and cheese.

The making of linen and woolen
cloth was also a domestic work. We
raised our own flax and wool, dressed
it, and spun it. A little spinning wheel,
turned by a foot pedal, had its place in
every home. Weaving was done by a
traveling workman who came to the
house, put up his loom, and stayed until
the season's work was done. Twice a
year, in spring and autumn, a tailor
came and made clothing for the men
and boys. A dressmaker and a milliner
came in their turn to fit out the female
members of the family.

That was the way Americans lived
in the time of your great-grand-
parents. Today, in the same Connecticut township, most people work
in New York or one of the other
cities nearby. Those who still farm
the soil own tractors and harvesters.
Almost everyone has an automobile;
many families own two.

Homes are lighted by electricity,
and often heated by oil. Food is
stored in freezers and electric refrig-
erators. Canned goods line the
kitchen shelves. For goods farmers
do not raise on their own land, they
can telephone or drive to stores in
the village a few miles away. Beef
from Kansas, fruit from Florida and

Life was hard but peaceful and secure in the "good old days." This picture shows how many American farm families lived in the 19th century. Everyone had chores to do.

California, and other products from all over the world are available there.

All these changes resulted from new inventions that made it possible to produce more food with less work. A little over a century ago, the average American farm produced only enough food to feed three families. Today, thanks to labor-saving inventions, an average farm produces enough food for fourteen families. Some large farms produce enough wheat or potatoes for hundreds of families.

Freedom encouraged the growth of inventions. New and useful inventions appeared soon after the War of Independence ended in 1783. Each year the number of new develop-

ments increased. Winning independence had an encouraging effect on Americans. Now they were on their own!

Farmers and workers looked at their tasks with keen, questioning eyes. How could that job be done faster and better? How could this piece of land be made to produce a bigger crop? Americans were free to question and experiment. No one interfered or forbade them to try new methods. And men whose inventions succeeded often won great riches.

The combination of freedom to experiment and the promise of great wealth resulted in a flood of new inventions. In the factories and on the farms, machinery brought increased comfort and pleasure. People did

NEW INVENTIONS

not have to work so hard or so long; they had more leisure time.

Best of all, inventions created jobs: factories had to be built in which to make the new machines; and workers had to be hired at good wages to make the machines. Thus the whole nation moved upward to new levels of comfort and prosperity.

The Industrial Revolution began in England. The United States was not the first country to build factories and use machinery on a large scale. The change from hand labor to machine labor, and from small shop to factory production, began in Great Britain. These changes make up the *Industrial Revolution*.

Since the days of Queen Elizabeth and even earlier, British scientists had been working and experimenting. They discovered several new scientific principles. Toward the end of the 18th century a few mechanics and businessmen began putting these principles to practical use. They invented machines that would do the work of many men, and do it more quickly and easily.

Workers in the *textile* or cloth-making business were the first to change from hand labor to machine labor. For centuries, clothmaking had been an important industry in Britain. Almost every home had a spinning wheel. Mothers taught their daughters how to twist or spin the fibers of raw wool, flax, or cotton into yarn — then to weave the yarn into cloth by means of a hand loom.

Most women learned how to weave coarse cloth or "homespun," but they did not weave often enough to become very skilful. A few men specialized and became expert weavers. They traveled from house to house, weaving into cloth the yarn the women had spun. In the colonies, such weavers were in great demand. Many a colonial town sent word to England offering any weaver 30 acres of land if he would come over and weave cloth.

Spinning and weaving took so long that there was never enough cloth to meet the demand. Merchants were always urging the weavers to turn out more cloth. The trouble was that the weavers had to wait for the spinners. No matter how hard the spinners tried, they could not spin yarn so fast as a skilled weaver could use it up. So weavers often had to sit idle for hours, waiting for yarn.

Three inventions changed the manufacture of cloth. An Englishman named James Hargreaves found the answer to the problem of the shortage of yarn. Hargreaves was a weaver. As he sat waiting for his wife to spin yarn, he tried to figure out a way to speed up the spinning process.

About 1765, Hargreaves invented a machine run by a hand-turned wheel. It spun eight to eleven threads at once and wound them on as many spindles. The machine worked well. In honor of his little daughter, Hargreaves named his invention the

"Spinning Jenny," a fitting name.

Other weavers, whose wives or daughters could not furnish them with enough yarn, were jealous. They warned Hargreaves that he must work as others worked. When he refused, they broke into his house and smashed his spinning jenny. But Hargreaves' idea lived on. Other machines were soon in operation. In a few years spinning by hand became a thing of the past in England.

One trouble with the spinning jenny was that the threads it spun broke easily. A few years later, Richard Arkwright, an English barber, solved this problem. Arkwright invented a jenny which spun 20 or more strong threads at once. Next he built a mill, in which he constructed a jenny that took its power from a waterfall. A crowd of angry hand workers destroyed the mill, fearing that they might lose their spinning jobs.

Arkwright promptly built a larger mill. He hired watchmen to guard it. The mill soon made him rich and King George III made Arkwright a knight.

The new spinning machine produced yarn so fast that hand weavers could not use all of it. As a result, spinning mills had to cut down their output. And their workers had to go on "part time." This caused considerable hardship among the workers.

This problem was solved by Edmund Cartwright, an English clergyman. "The world must have weaving johnnies to keep up with its spinning jennies," Cartwright declared. After years of study and experiment, he made a weaving machine that would do the work of a dozen weavers.

Cheap cotton cloth for all the world! Below is a scene in an early 19th century English factory. Printed calico cloth is being produced to sell for a few cents a yard. British ships carried such cloth to customers everywhere and so helped build Britain's power in the world.

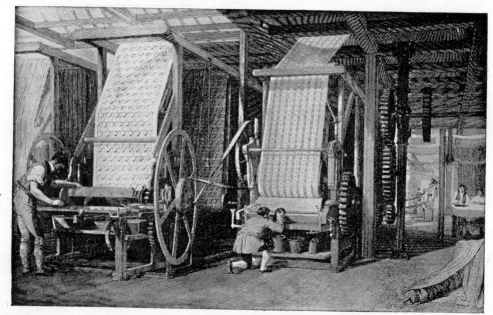

Spinning and weaving machines made Britain the first great manufacturing country. English cloth was sold all over the world. Money poured into the British Isles. To hold this advantage, Parliament forbade the export of any machine.

Businessmen in other lands wanted to know how the weaving machines worked. They offered a big reward to any British weaver who would tell them the secret. To prevent this, Parliament passed another law, forbidding any spinner or weaver to work for foreigners. Such laws helped Britain hold her place as the leading manufacturing nation. Her mills could make and sell cloth at half the price demanded in countries where weaving and spinning were done by hand.

Slater built the first American factory. In spite of all obstacles, Americans managed to find out how to build the new machines. Here is how it happened: a young English weaver named Samuel Slater heard that Americans were offering a reward to any man who could make cloth by the English method. Slater was a skilful weaver; he had learned the trade from Richard Arkwright's partner in the cotton business. But he could earn only two shillings a day. So young Slater kept his eyes and ears open. He soon learned all the secrets of the new machinery.

Slater watched for a chance to leave England. He grew a beard to

America owes much to Samuel Slater (top) and his mill (center). In the bottom picture young Slater proudly shows Moses Brown his nearly finished carding machine.

change his appearance. Then one night he slipped on board a ship sailing for America. He did not dare to bring drawings or models, but inside his head he carried all the information needed.

When he landed in America, Slater heard that a Quaker, Moses Brown of Rhode Island, had been trying for years to spin cotton yarn by machinery. He wrote to Brown, offering to show him how to make yarn as good as any made in England. The next mail brought a reply. "If thou canst do this thing," wrote the earnest manufacturer, "I invite thee to come to Rhode Island and have the credit and profit of introducing cotton manufacturing into America."

Slater accepted the invitation. Moses Brown and his family supplied the money and the first mill was built at Pawtucket, Rhode Island in 1790. In a few months the mill was producing fine cotton yarn.

Other mills were built and Slater became a partner in the firm. He married an American girl. She became so interested in her husband's affairs that she invented a machine to spin sewing thread.

When Slater died many years later, President Andrew Jackson called him "the father of American industry." Today if you visit Rhode Island, you can still see Slater's first little mill. Not much bigger than a modern garage, it is known as "the cradle of American industry."

Eli Whitney invented the cotton gin in 1793. One of the chief problems of early textile manufacturers was to find enough raw cotton to keep their mills busy. Cotton buyers searched the markets of Europe, India, and Africa, but always came back with less than was needed. At that time, little cotton was grown in America. It could easily be grown in the southern states; but the slow work of separating cotton fiber from its

Eli Whitney and the cotton gin helped fasten slavery on the South. At left, below, the Connecticut school teacher is shown working on a machine to remove seeds from cotton bolls. At right, below, is one of his early cotton gins.

clinging seeds made cotton cloth too expensive.

An American inventor solved this problem. His name was Eli Whitney. You have already read how his cotton gin brought prosperity to the South. Here is how he happened to invent it:

Whitney was a New England boy who was always "tinkering," that is, mending an old thing or inventing something new. He was skilful with tools and seemed to understand a machine after one look at its parts. When his father's watch stopped, Eli waited for a chance to take it apart and see what ailed it. His chance came on a Sunday when the family went to church, leaving him at home. When they came back the watch was running as well as ever. His father was so pleased that he turned the family workshop over to Eli!

When the War for Independence began, Eli Whitney was only 11 years

Picking cotton is hard, dull work as the picture below shows. Demand for cotton increased greatly because of the cotton gin.

old. But he did a man's work by making nails. These were greatly needed because the foreign supply was cut off by British warships. Later Eli paid his way through college by making men's canes, and large pins which women wanted as hat fasteners.

After college days Whitney headed south, intending to teach school. He happened to visit a plantation in Georgia owned by Mrs. Greene, widow of Nathanael Greene, the great Revolutionary War general. There he heard a planter say that southerners would supply the world with cotton if only they had a machine to separate fiber from seeds.

Have you ever seen cotton growing? Eli Whitney never had. He was interested to learn that it comes from the field in the form of fluffy bolls or pods in which fine fibers are closely wrapped around the seeds. It was dull work for a slave to take a boll in his fingers and pick out the fiber bit by bit. At the end of a long day's work, his basket might hold only a pound of cotton. It was no wonder that the price of cotton was so high.

Mrs. Greene urged young Whitney to work on the problem. Within a few days he built a model of a machine to remove seeds from cotton. Whitney called his invention an engine, but it was soon shortened to "gin."

In its original form the "gin" was a frame, about four feet long, through which ran a wooden roller turned by a handle. Around the roller were rings of fine metal spikes, each with a hook at the end. Just above the roller was a row of bars, set close together. When cotton bolls were placed on the bars and the roller was turned, every spike would reach up, catch a bit of fiber, and pull it down through the bars. The seeds, being too big to get through, were left dancing on the bars like jumping beans.

Of this labor-saving machine, Whitney wrote to his father:

I made one with which a man will clean 10 times as much cotton as he can in any way before known. A large machine of the same kind may be turned by water power or by a horse with the greatest ease, and one man will then do more than 50 men by the old method.

Before the "gin" appeared, America produced about 190,000 pounds of cotton a year. Today, with Whitney's invention in use, a fair cotton crop is about 15 million bales each weighing about 500 pounds, a total of over seven billion pounds.

Factories in the South and elsewhere change this huge mass of raw material into a great variety of goods. They spin, weave, and dye it to make dresses, thread, machine belts, cord fabrics for automobile tires, and even the inner layer in paved roads. It has rightly been said of the cotton gin that "no other invention ever so quickly transformed an industry or created such enormous wealth."

A new idea revolutionized American industry. Eli Whitney invented the cotton gin in 1793, when George Washington was President. The invention made cotton one of America's most important crops. Whitney himself never made much money out of his invention. The machine was so easy to build that people copied it and paid Whitney nothing.

Whitney went to court and tried to win legal protection, but he had no luck. At last he gave up the fight and went back to New England. He had lost almost all his money. But Whitney was not discouraged. He borrowed money to build a little machine shop in New Haven, where he began to make guns.

In those days almost every man owned a gun or rifle. But no two guns were alike, for they were made by different gunsmiths. Even guns made by the same gunsmith were different, because each gun was made separately. The same was true of the muskets soldiers used.

If any part of a gun was broken, the whole weapon had to be sent to the gunsmith for repair. This meant delay and expense, and meanwhile the gun was of no use. Guns had been made that way for four hundred years. But to Whitney's inventive mind it seemed foolish and unnecessary.

In 1795 Whitney won a government contract to make 10,000 muskets for the army. This was a huge order for his little shop, but Whitney did not rush into the job. First he sat down and did some hard thinking. He "borrowed" some ideas that had been tried in British factories. When he had thought the problem through, he went to work.

First he made a military musket in ten parts. Next, he made nine exact copies of every part. Then he asked for a meeting with the Secretary of War and his advisors to explain his plan. What a meeting it must have been!

Whitney appeared with ten heavy bags. He took a gun stock or handle from one bag, a gun barrel or metal tube from a second, and other parts from each of the other bags. In a few minutes he put the parts together. The gun was almost ready for use. Then he took a handful of triggers out of the last bag. "Pick one," he said, "and I'll finish the gun!"

The officials looked at one another. Had Whitney's troubles caused him to lose his mind? "Surely," said the Secretary of War, "only one of those triggers is the one made for that gun?"

Whitney smiled. "Go ahead, pick out any one," he urged. So one was chosen. Swiftly and expertly Whitney put it into the gun. Then he took it out and put in another trigger. One after another he fitted each trigger into the gun. Thus he demonstrated his idea that gunsmiths should make parts of the same size and shape. Then the parts could be put together quickly wherever and whenever needed.

This was the beginning of the idea of standardized, interchangeable parts. It soon became the rule in most American industries. Today you take it for granted that the parts of your bicycle, automobile, or radio should be made to standard, exact measurements. If one part breaks or wears out, you take your machine to a repair shop or send it back to the factory. There a new part is slipped into place and the machine is ready to use again. Eli Whitney's idea has become the basis of modern American industry.

New England became a manufacturing center. The War of 1812 helped the growth of American manufacturing. Because the nation was at war with Britain, it was impossible to buy English cloth. So Americans had to make their own.

Hundreds of mills were built, most of them in New England. They produced so much cotton cloth that the price went down to seven cents a yard — compared with forty-two cents for handwoven cloth. Mill owners grew rich. New England became, and long remained, the textile center of the United States.

Samuel Slater's success encouraged people to invest their savings in cotton mills. At the beginning of the War of 1812, a Boston merchant named Francis Lowell decided that cotton mills were a better investment than sailing ships. He built a big factory at Waltham, Massachusetts. Lowell's cotton mill was the first —

in the world where cotton was spun into yarn and then woven into cloth under one roof. This saved time, labor, and expense. It was another step toward modern mass production.

Elias Howe invented the sewing machine in 1845. Boys and girls from nearby farms found jobs in the Lowell mill. One day the factory manager hired a sixteen-year-old lad named Elias Howe. Elias was small and lame, but he proved to be a good worker. He progressed from job to job until he was repairing the mill machinery. But two years later, when business was poor, Elias was "laid off." He went to Boston and found a job repairing watches.

One day Howe heard a customer remark that a man who could invent a machine to sew cloth would make a fortune. The problem interested Howe. He began to work on it in his spare time.

By now Howe had a wife and three children to support. He had such faith in his idea that he quit his job and spent all his time working on the sewing machine. He borrowed money to buy needed materials.

At last, in 1845 the machine was finished. In a demonstration, Howe proved that his little machine could sew faster and straighter than five women who were famous for their sewing.

Next, Howe got a patent for his invention and tried to sell his sewing machines. People admired them but would not buy; the price was too high. Because the parts were made by hand, Howe had to charge $300 for each sewing machine. In those days, few families could afford to pay such a sum. And tailors and dressmakers tried to stop Howe from selling the machines because they feared his invention would put them out of work.

Then a man named Singer got the idea of selling sewing machines on the installment plan. Thousands of machines were sold. And as production increased it was possible to lower the price. Eli Whitney's idea of "standardized parts" was adopted with great success.

Elias Howe (below) won wealth and fame as inventor of the sewing machine.

Below is Elias Howe's first sewing machine, which he patented in 1846.

The sewing machine created new industries. Imagine how the average woman felt when at last she was able to own a sewing machine! She could sew shirts, coats, and dresses for her family in half the time. The sewing machine gave her almost as much help as a maid. In homes all over the world, Elias Howe's invention lightened the heavy burden of women's work.

It did even more than that: it created new industries. For example, ready-made shoes scarcely existed before 1845. Almost everyone went to a shoemaker and had shoes made by hand. After the invention of the sewing machine, hundreds of shoe factories were built. They used large, powerful sewing machines and turned out dozens of pairs of shoes every day.

The ready-made clothing industry also resulted from Howe's invention. Tailors and other garment workers bent over rows and rows of sewing machines, turning out suits and dresses that sold for a moderate price. Thus the invention of the sewing machine did three things: (1) it lightened work; (2) it increased the supply of cheap comfortable clothing; and (3) it created thousands of factory jobs.

Americans experimented with electricity. Another factor that increased factory production of goods was the use of electric power. The first sewing machines, like most other machines of 100 years ago, were operated by hand or foot power. A handle was turned or a pedal was pumped to provide energy to operate the machine. The use of electric power to run machines was a great step forward. It speeded up production and reduced the physical labor needed.

The existence of electricity was known for centuries before mankind learned how to put it to work. Probably the man who was most successful in putting electricity to work was Thomas Alva Edison. He was born in Ohio and grew up on the Michigan frontier. He was always asking questions about every-

Less work for mother! The lady below rejoices in owning her first sewing machine.

Today's sewing machine (below) is light and compact. Compare with early models.

THOMAS ALVA EDISON (1847–1931)

"I find what the world needs; then I go ahead and try to invent it," was the motto of the world's most successful inventor, Thomas Edison. For sixty years he worked — often twenty hours a day — taking out over 1000 patents.

Edison hardly remembered a time when he wasn't experimenting. From childhood on, everything connected with electricity stirred his curiosity.

At the age of 23, Edison invented the stock market ticker — and sold it for $40,000! Immediately he opened a laboratory. He grew famous as invention after invention poured from his shops: the phonograph, the electric motor, waxed paper, a motion picture projector, a perfected typewriter — and countless more.

On October 21, 1879 Edison's career reached a climax: the first incandescent light bulb burned for forty hours. Within three years electric lighting began to appear in American cities.

Edison became one of the world's most honored men. It is said that one out of every nine workers in the United States owes his job to an Edison idea.

thing. He read many books and seldom forgot useful information.

At the age of twelve, Edison went to work. He sold newspapers, candy, and sandwiches to passengers on the Grand Trunk Railway. One day young Edison saw a baby playing on the railroad track. He pulled the child to safety just before a fast train roared by. As a reward, the baby's father offered to teach Edison the trade of telegraph operator.

Edison soon learned to send and receive messages rapidly; but he was not satisfied. He had to know how the instrument worked — and why. That was the beginning of his experiments with electricity.

Edison invented the electric light in 1879. Edison spent all he earned on books and equipment. He was always shabby; he seemed an impractical dreamer. For five years he wandered around America as a telegraph operator, working in many places. He was always thinking hard about his ideas for inventions.

When he was twenty-two, Edison managed to get money to fit up a small workshop in New Jersey. There he worked and thought for 60 years. Out of that workshop, which slowly grew into a chain of laboratories and factories, came more than 1000 important inventions. Most were not original inventions; they were improvements on ideas others had suggested. But they added greatly to the comfort and pleasure of millions of people.

Perhaps the most familiar and useful of his inventions was the *incandescent* electric light bulb. "Incandescent" means intensely bright, or glowing with heat, without being burned up. It is the filament, or thread of a light, that is incandescent; the filament glows when an electrical current passes through it.

Other men had attempted to make such a light. But they used a filament that burned to ashes in a few moments. Edison experimented many years; he tested a thousand materials before finding one that stood the test of long use. This was a shred of bamboo fiber, which first had to be charred by heat until it became like charcoal. It served until recent years when its place was taken by the metal filaments now in use.

People today are so used to pressing a switch and getting a light that it is hard to imagine the excitement when the electric light was invented. Newspapers announced an exhibition of the new lighting system at Menlo Park, New Jersey, near Edison's home. The railroad ran special trains, and people crowded to see the wonderful sight of street lights that went on or off at the turn of a switch!

Among Edison's other inventions were the phonograph, dictaphone, and stock market ticker. He also played an important part in the development of motion pictures. For centuries artists and inventors had been trying to find some way of arranging pictures to give the impression of movement. Several devices were developed that were really the ancestors of modern motion pictures.

One of these devices was the *kinetoscope.* Here is how it worked: one hundred or more pictures were taken of a running horse, or of soldiers on the march, or of a steamboat coming into the harbor. The

Thomas Edison invented the phonograph (below) and made several pioneer films such as *The Record of a Sneeze* (bottom).

pictures were bound together on one side, like the pages in a tiny book. By snapping the pages under your thumb, the pictures would run together.

The next stage was called a "peep show." To make it, a large number of tiny pictures were pasted together in a roll. The roll was then placed in a slot machine. When you wanted amusement you dropped a penny in the slot. Then you looked into the eye-piece, turned a crank, and the horse or the soldiers or the steamboat seemed to pass before you.

Seeing one of these toys, Edison thought, "Why not throw such pictures on a screen, so that a roomful of people could enjoy the sight?" With the help of other inventors he soon changed the kinetoscope into the moving picture.

At the first public showing, the pictures amazed the audience. People in the front seats jumped up screaming when a locomotive or a running horse seemed to rush at them. Such was the beginning of the "movies," which became one of America's leading industries.

Machinery helped the farmers. While new products, industries, and amusements were developing in the cities, progress was also taking place on the farms. New and better ways of planting, cultivating, and harvesting crops came into use in the 19th century.

One of the first improvements was made in making plows. The plow

1833 FIRST STEEL PLOW ON RECORD
Was made of strips of steel from a crosscut saw.

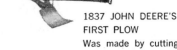

1837 JOHN DEERE'S FIRST PLOW
Was made by cutting a diamond-shaped piece from a broken steel mill saw to form the moldboard and share. It scoured well in sticky soils.

THE STEEL PLOW

1830 WOOD AND IRON PLOWS CLOGGED
In the rich prairie soils of the midwest. Some blacksmiths began to use smooth steel for plow surfaces.

1838 ORIGINAL STEEL PLOW
One of three made by John Deere in 1838 and believed to be substantially identical with his first one.

The chart above shows some of the stages in the development of the modern steel plow. The early American farmer used a wooden plow that had an iron "share." President Thomas Jefferson was one of the first to encourage efforts to improve the plow.

has always been the farmer's most important tool. It opens the soil to receive new seeds.

Before history began, some forgotten inventor made the first plow. He probably took a small tree stump and chopped off all the roots except one. He sharpened the root to a point, or "share," and attached a handle. Then he dragged the crude plow over a field. The share, pointed into the ground, loosened the soil and prepared it for planting.

Up to the time America was colonized, only one improvement had been made on the ancient plow. A handmade share of oak replaced the natural root; and the point of the share had a metal cover to keep it from wearing out.

The plow of colonial times must have been cruelly hard to work with. It consisted of a twelve foot log, with an iron-pointed share about four feet long.

One American, Charles Newbold, worked half his life to improve the plow. Finally he succeeded; he built a plow with a share of cast iron bolted to an oaken bar. One of the first patents granted by the national government was given to Newbold.

Newbold's invention worked better and lasted longer than the old plow; but farmers would not use it. They said the iron share would poison the ground and encourage the growth of weeds.

Thomas Jefferson was always ready to try out new ideas on his planta-

IMPROVING THE PLOW

tion. He was not afraid to try using the cast-iron plowshare. Jefferson did not find it easy to work with, but he felt the idea was practical. He wrote to his friend, Jethro Wood, to suggest a few changes.

Wood set to work and, in 1819, produced a plow that was lighter and more lasting than any other. All parts were made of metal. By this time most farmers had forgotten their fear that an iron share would poison the soil, so Wood's invention was widely used in eastern states.

When pioneers moved into the Ohio Valley they found the soil was deep and rich — but it was covered by a very tough sod. The new plow did not work well there because its cast-iron share often failed to cut through the grass roots. Instead, it left a ragged furrow, turning up a foot or two of earth and only scratching over the next foot or two. John Deere found the answer to this problem.

Deere was a blacksmith who had followed the frontier from Vermont to Illinois. There he made several unsatisfactory plowshares; finally in 1837 he made one that cut the sod cleanly, leaving a straight furrow. His invention worked well from the start. Thousands of farmers used it to turn a vast prairie region into fields of corn and wheat.

Thus the work of many inventors helped develop a modern, efficient plow. Thanks to the labors of Newbold, Wood, Deere, and others, the farmer at last had a plow that could cut clean, straight, furrows.

And the companies that manufactured plows did not forget Eli

The chart below shows some of the effects of improved farm machinery from 1775 to the present. One man using the latest modern equipment can plow eight acres in less time than two men with several oxen could plow one acre in 1775.

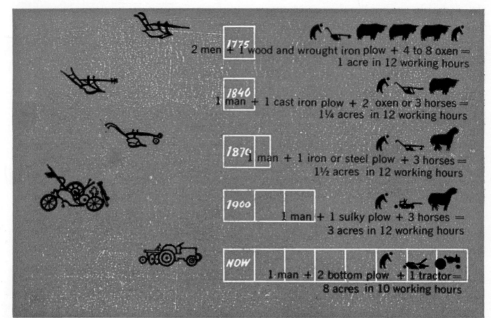

2 men + 1 wood and wrought iron plow + 4 to 8 oxen = 1775
1 acre in 12 working hours

1 man + 1 cast iron plow + 2 oxen or 3 horses = 1840
1¼ acres in 12 working hours

1 man + 1 iron or steel plow + 3 horses = 1870
1½ acres in 12 working hours

1 man + 1 sulky plow + 3 horses = 1900
3 acres in 12 working hours

1 man + 2 bottom plow + 1 tractor = NOW
8 acres in 10 working hours

Whitney's principle of interchangeable parts. They made plows of parts that could be replaced if broken.

McCormick invented the reaper.

Farmers also needed efficient tools to cut grain when it became ripe. For thousands of years, farmers had cut wheat, barley, or rye with a short curved blade called a sickle or a longer blade called a scythe (SYTH). It was slow work to harvest a crop with such tools.

When American pioneers pushed across the Appalachians to the Ohio and Mississippi Valleys they found a vast region well suited to the growing of wheat. In those days, wheat was scarce and expensive. Few could afford to eat white bread made from wheat flour. Most folks had to be content with yellow bread, made from cornmeal.

The pioneers longed to plant huge fields of wheat. But wheat was hard to harvest. It took time to cut down the grain in even a small field of wheat. "If somebody would just invent a machine to harvest a big field in a hurry," westerners often remarked, "our great prairies could produce enough wheat to feed all America — and maybe the world!"

Some people did more than talk. A Virginian named Robert McCormick worked on the problem in his blacksmith shop in his spare time. He never succeeded in getting a machine that would work, but he inspired his son, Cyrus, to work on the problem.

At first the boy had no better luck than his father. In fact, the first machine he tried out ruined a field of ripe wheat! But Cyrus didn't get discouraged. He tried again.

At last, in 1831, Cyrus McCormick invented a successful *reaper*. It consisted of a narrow iron bar with forward pointing teeth and a cutting blade of steel. As the bar moved into the wheat field, a wheel kept the blade sliding back and forth. Wheat stems were caught between the teeth; the blade cut them instantly and quickly. (A barber's clippers work on the same plan but on a smaller scale.)

At its first trial McCormick's reaper was pulled by a horse. Behind the cutting bar the grain dropped in large piles. A man followed the reaper; he raked and tied the wheat into bundles or sheaves. McCormick's reaper cut far more grain than several men could harvest with sickles or scythes.

Making farm machines became a big business.

McCormick had trouble selling his machine at first. Because the reaper had to be made by hand the price was high. McCormick quit farming and invested all his time and money in the business. But after a few years the machine became popular. By 1860 McCormick was selling 35,000 reapers a season and making a yearly profit of one million dollars.

Best of all, McCormick's invention brought wheat bread to every Ameri-

The reaper proves successful! This picture shows Cyrus McCormick demonstrating how his invention works. The reaper helped make America a leading grain growing area.

can table. And it led to the development of new industries such as flour milling and bread baking. It encouraged settlers to go west and start new farms in the great prairie country beyond the Mississippi. The reaper's influence on the westward movement was great.

Improvements came rapidly. A *binder* was added that raked up the grain and made it unnecessary for a man to follow the machine. Later came the development of the *thresher*. This was a device that separated the grain from the straw or chaff.

Finally the reaper, binder, and thresher were put together in one machine. Today it is called a *combine*. It cuts and rakes the wheat, threshes it, and puts it into bags.

Methods of pulling the machine also improved. The early reapers and threshers were pulled by horses. But the modern "combine" is pulled by a tractor or has its own engine built into the particular machine.

Manufacturing farm machines grew into a big business. As production increased, the prices came down. Soon, most farmers could afford to own at least some modern tools.

Farmers in other lands were amazed at the efficiency of American agricultural machines. Orders poured in from all over the world. A famous German leader, Otto von Bismarck, ordered one of the early combines. He followed it around his farm, smoking a pipe and saying not a word. At the end of the second day, he burst out:

Wonderful, that is wonderful! Now I understand everything, all but one point. Tell me, how can a machine without fingers tie up a bag?

Farm machines brought new problems. American farmers too must have wondered how a machine could perform tasks with almost human skill and at super-human speed.

418

But they did not ask many questions, for they were too busy buying and using the new devices. A farmer with two or three helpers could harvest more than 400 acres of grain with a combine and a tractor. The Middle West became America's "bread basket." "Bumper" or extra large crops of wheat and other grains flooded the world markets.

Sometimes, in some places, the new machines brought ruin and heartache. Farmers went in debt to buy machinery. Then they harvested such big crops the price of grain went down, and they had little to show for their work except a pile of debts. This was the beginning of the "farm problem" that still troubles America.

However, few people wanted to give up the new machines and go back to the old, hard days of hand labor and small crops. Farmers in New England and in the South even expressed envy of the Middle West where the type of agriculture (grain farming) made it possible to do most farm jobs by machine. But in time, ways were found to use tractors and certain other agricultural machinery to plant and harvest other crops besides grain.

In old England, workers rioted and destroyed new machines. But in America most people have welcomed new machinery. In the long run machines almost always create far more jobs than they eliminate. That is not much comfort to workers who today and tomorrow must search for new ways to earn a living. But as your study of American history has shown, increased use of machinery usually means increased prosperity for all concerned.

The map below shows where the chief farm products of the United States are grown. The land produces enough to feed all Americans, plus a big surplus to sell abroad.

CHAPTER SUMMARY

The Industrial Revolution began in England but soon reached America. It began in the textile industry; machinery replaced hand labor. New inventions brought rapid, sweeping changes. At Pawtucket, Rhode Island in 1790 Samuel Slater built the first factory in the United States. Eli Whitney invented the cotton gin in 1793. He also popularized the idea of using standardized, interchangeable parts in manufacturing.

The War of 1812 encouraged the growth of American industry. Most of the factories were built in New England. Howe's invention of the sewing machine led to the development of shoe manufacturing and the ready-made clothing industry.

Edison experimented with electricity. In 1879 he invented the electric light. He also invented the phonograph and helped develop the motion picture.

New machines appeared on the farm. Newbold, Deere, and others improved the plow. In 1831 Cyrus McCormick invented the reaper out of which developed the modern "harvester." Farm machinery helped increase the supply of wheat and other foods. This sometimes caused overproduction and lower prices.

The Language of History

Be sure you know the meaning of each of the following words and phrases as they are used in Chapter 20.

1. Industrial Revolution
2. incandescent bulb
3. spinning jenny
4. cotton gin
5. reaper
6. combine
7. plow
8. motion picture
9. farm machinery

What Happened When

Connect each of the following dates with an important event in American history.

1. 1790   2. 1793   3. 1831   4. 1845   5. 1879

420

HALL OF FAME.

Who's Who in History

Make sure you know the part each of the following played in the development of America.

1. Eli Whitney
2. Samuel Slater
3. Elias Howe
4. Thomas Edison
5. John Deere
6. Cyrus McCormick

Study Questions

1. **a.** Where did the Industrial Revolution begin?
   b. What industry was the first to change from hand to machine labor?
   c. Name two inventions that encouraged the growth of manufacturing.

2. State two contributions Eli Whitney made to the advance of manufacturing.

3. Why is Samuel Slater called the "Father of American Industry"?

4. What new industries developed partly as a result of the invention of the sewing machine?

5. In what ways would your life be poorer and more difficult if Edison had never lived?

6. How did the invention of the reaper speed up the settlement of the West?

7. Why did the use of machinery sometimes increase the farmers' problems?

THE AUTOMOBILE, AIRPLANE, AND NEW METHODS OF COMMUNICATION HELPED BUILD MODERN AMERICA

W HEELS and wire, rubber and oil, yards of strong linen cloth — nothing pretty or romantic about such things. Yet they helped make an age-old dream come true — the dream that man could fly. The scoffers and doubters said to Wilbur and Orville Wright, "It'll never work." But the two young mechanics went ahead and made their airplane fly.

That was in 1903. Within a comparatively few years airplanes were big business. But the airplane, like the automobile, could never have developed so fast and so successfully had it not been for the earlier development of the steel, rubber, and petroleum industries. This chapter tells the story of the growth of America's big enterprises. As you read it try to answer the following key questions:

1. How and when did Americans learn to make huge quantities of steel at reasonable cost?

2. What part did geography and resources play? Why did Pittsburgh become a steel center and Detroit "the motor city"?

3. What improvements in communications were made in the same period that America's great industries were developing?

4. Who were the leaders in each industry and how did they use the resources and opportunities the United States offered?

Many factors aided American development. You live in the Machine Age. And you live in the land where machines have reached their highest development. Every day, probably every hour, you use a machine or the products of machines.

Yet, many boys and girls in some Old World lands seldom see modern machines. They live much as their ancestors did centuries ago. Machines are scarce and expensive, and most work is done by hand.

How did it happen that the United States became the world's leader in manufacturing? The Industrial Revolution began in Britain. However, after 1865 the United States caught up with and soon passed Great Britain in production of manufactured goods. What conditions helped America to forge ahead?

Freedom to experiment and the chance of winning great wealth encouraged American inventors. Other factors were important too. To develop great industries, natural resources must be available. The United States had huge deposits of coal and iron and almost every mineral needed by industry.

A manufacturing nation also needs many workers, both skilled and unskilled. The United States had little trouble finding workers. Every year thousands of immigrants came from Europe to work in American factories, stores, and mines. And as harvesters and tractors reduced the number of workers needed on the farm, men and women from the country came to the city seeking factory jobs. Thus a plentiful labor supply, and a wealth of natural resources, aided American industrial development.

Still, something more was needed to develop great industries: clever, capable leaders. Here again the United States was fortunate. In the history of almost every great American industry you will find one or more far-sighted leaders who made the most of opportunities America offered.

You have already met some of these men: Cornelius Vanderbilt, Cyrus McCormick, Thomas Edison. There were many others. Almost all were poor boys; many were immigrants. In the growth of America's big industries, particularly those connected with new ways of travel and communication, "self-made men" played a great part.

Carnegie made steel cheap and plentiful. You have seen how a great network of railroads spread across America in the 19th century. Later came the automobile which provided comfortable, convenient transportation everywhere in the country. The development of the railroads and the automobile industry required huge amounts of high quality steel at a reasonable price.

Steel making is one of America's basic industries. Without it, the modern world could scarcely exist. Yet steel manufacturing on a large scale began less than 100 years ago.

Here is a picture story of the steel-making process that Bessemer (top left) discovered and Carnegie (top right) put to use. In the center is a Bessemer converter; and the bottom picture shows an early steel mill.

Early machines and railroads were built of iron, which was heavy and broke easily. Steel was too expensive to use until a new method of making it was discovered. This was the *Bessemer process.* In this process, a blast of air was blown through melted iron to remove impurities. The oxygen in the air absorbs the impurities. An Englishman, Henry Bessemer (BES eh mer), discovered the method in 1855. At about the same time an American named William Kelly also discovered it. A young railroad official named Andrew Carnegie (kar NAY gih) saw its possibilities.

As a child, Carnegie had come to America from a Scotch village. His family was so poor he had to go to work when he was thirteen. Step by step, he rose to become a high official of the Pennsylvania Railroad when he was only twenty-five. Then he suddenly gave up his job and went into another business.

The Civil War had just ended. Carnegie saw that new industrial developments were starting. He realized the nation would need much iron and steel. He had already saved his money and invested it so carefully that he had several thousand dollars. This was his *capital* — money saved out of income to use in producing new goods.

With his capital, Carnegie built a steel mill near Pittsburgh, Pennsylvania. He was the first to try the Bessemer process in America. Thanks to Carnegie's leadership, the

NEW INDUSTRIES

United States forged ahead in steel production. Steel became and has remained a great source of America's strength. And Carnegie gave away most of the money he made. His great fortune was used to found libraries and colleges.

Horseless carriages appeared. For many years the railroads were Carnegie's best customer. No one dreamed that another form of transportation would soon become the greatest steel user of all. This was the automobile.

It is hard to say who invented the automobile. In the 18th and 19th centuries, inventors of many countries were trying to build a "horseless carriage." At first they used steam engines to provide the power needed. But steam engines were heavy and noisy. Laws were passed to discourage their use. Not until the gasoline engine was invented could the modern automobile be developed.

The gasoline engine is smaller and weighs less than the steam engine.

Instead of burning coal to boil water and make steam, it burns gasoline mixed with air, causing a series of rapid explosions. Have you ever watched an outboard motor boat speed over the water? If you have, you know how much power a tiny gasoline engine can create.

As soon as the principle of the gasoline engine became well-known, inventors set to work to make it turn the wheels of a wagon. In England and in France, cars were developed that traveled by gas or electric power. In the 1890's several American inventors built "horseless carriages."

In Springfield, Massachusetts, Charles Duryea (door YA) and his brother, J. Frank, completed a car in 1893. It was a small one-seater; the engine was under the seat. Barnum and Bailey bought the Duryea's "motor wagon" to exhibit it in their circus.

At about the same time, Elwood Haynes designed a motor vehicle. It appeared on the streets of Kokomo,

In the 1890's "horseless carriages" seemed almost as fantastic as space ships seem today. Below are shown two early automobiles, the Duryea (left) and an 1897 model Oldsmobile (right). Collecting and studying old autos is an increasingly popular hobby.

"Where's the fire?" the policeman seems to be asking the early traffic violator (above, left). At right is shown a 1901 Oldsmobile. Compare with the 1897 model on p. 425.

Indiana in 1894, chugging along at the great speed of eight miles an hour! One trial was enough for the townspeople. The smoke and smell of the queer thing and, worst of all, the explosions, frightened horses and set the dogs to barking. Haynes was orded to tow his "carriage" out of town. Today you can see Haynes' automobile at the Smithsonian Institution in Washington, D.C.

Henry Ford built a low-cost auto. Meantime a Detroit mechanic named Henry Ford was working in a workshop he built in his backyard. "I'm going to build a horseless carriage and I'll make it cheap enough so every man in the country can have one!" he told his wife.

Success came slowly. Ford gave up his job to devote all his time to building cars. He borrowed Eli Whitney's idea of standard, interchangeable parts and developed it beyond anything Whitney had ever dreamed of. Ford watched every penny, trying to cut the cost of

building cars so he could sell them cheaply.

In 1909, Ford produced his *Model T.* The price was low and it soon captured the market. More than fifteen million Model T's were sold within 20 years. Henry Ford became the greatest automobile producer in the world. More than any other man he "put America on wheels."

The automobile influenced other industries. Ford made his men work hard and fast, but he paid high wages. He believed that high wages created buying power. This is the way he reasoned: if he wanted his workers to buy Ford cars, he had to pay them enough so they could afford to drive automobiles.

Ford's idea worked! He became not just a millionaire but a billionaire. And the Ford Motor Company became one of the biggest and richest in the world.

Thousands of workers found jobs in Ford factories. In a few years Detroit grew from a small town to a

426

Here is a 1905 Buick "touring car." Only a few people could enjoy such elegance for the early autos were very expensive.

city of more than a million people. Today a big share of the profits of the Ford Company is paid to the Ford Foundation, which conducts many worth-while projects for the benefit of humanity.

In the days of the horseless carriages no one dreamed that within a short time they would create an industry of enormous size. By 1951 more than 40 million autos were in use in the United States. And eight million trucks and buses were doing work formerly done by horses and oxen.

What this new industry means in the way of more jobs, with more money earned and spent, is hard to estimate accurately. One large company, General Motors, employs 175,000 people in its factories.

The automobile also caused a boom in other industries. Steel mills are kept busy rolling out metal for automobile engines and bodies. Textile mills sell millions of yards of material to cover automobile seats. And the making of rubber for auto-mobile tires has become a giant industry.

Goodyear learned how to vulcanize rubber. People have known about rubber for a long time. Columbus reported that he had seen Indians playing with a ball that bounced. Much later an English scientist discovered that the stuff would rub out pencil marks. (That is how it came to be called "rubber.") But no one really saw much use for the elastic material made from the gum of certain tropical trees.

"Raw rubber" has three serious faults: (1) it becomes sticky in hot weather; (2) it becomes hard and breaks in very cold weather; (3) it loses its bounce when exposed to the air for a long time. An inventor named Charles Goodyear spent nearly twenty years trying to find a way to correct these faults. He had to borrow money to buy raw rubber for his experiments. At one time he was thrown into prison because he

Ford's first factory is shown below.

could not pay bills which he owed!

One day in 1842, Goodyear had an accident — a lucky accident, as it turned out. He dropped a cup of rubber mixed with sulfur on a red-hot stove. A horrible smell arose.

When Goodyear started to scrape up the mess something caught his attention. He examined the mixture carefully. It proved stronger and more elastic than raw rubber; moderate heat or cold did not affect it. By chance he had stumbled on the answer! The way to preserve the best qualities of rubber was to heat it with sulfur.

Goodyear called the process *vulcanizing* after Vulcan, the Greek god of fire. The inventor died in debt, long before the automobile created a big demand for rubber. But people all over the world are still benefiting from his work. Imagine what it would be like to ride in a car without rubber tires!

(Below) Charles Goodyear accidentally discovered the process of vulcanizing rubber. The year of the discovery was 1842.

Oil became an essential industry. Another enterprise that became big business, thanks to the automobile, was the petroleum or oil industry. For centuries, observers had noticed an oily scum floating on the surface of some streams or oozing out of rocky ground. Some people used such oil as medicine for colds, aching joints or baldness. A few burned it in lamps to light their homes.

The supply of petroleum was small until someone got the idea of drilling oil wells. In 1859 a man named Edwin Drake drilled the first oil well in Titusville, Pennsylvania. That was the beginning of the great petroleum industry.

It was cheap and easy to make kerosene from the oil. Kerosene lamps soon replaced candles and whale-oil lamps. And the heavier oil proved to be an excellent grease or lubricant for machines to prevent friction. Thus the demand for oil products kept increasing.

A young Cleveland businessman, John D. Rockefeller, formed the Standard Oil Company to refine and transport oil. It soon became a big corporation; but that was only the beginning! The growth of the automobile industry created an enormous new demand for petroleum products. Oil fields were opened up in California, Texas, Oklahoma, Louisiana, and other parts of the country. Today, oil is almost as vital as steel to the nation's business.

Without oil, machines would soon break down, because their moving parts would grind to bits or melt from the heat. During the Second World War, gasoline and oil were *rationed* — that is, civilians were allowed only a small amount so there would be plenty of gasoline and oil to run military machines.

Thanks to the demand for petroleum products, John D. Rockefeller became one of the world's richest men. Like Andrew Carnegie, he gave much of his wealth to make America a better place to live. Schools, colleges, medicine and other scientific research all received millions from the Rockefeller family.

Rapid changes brought new problems. The making of steel, rubber, and petroleum became great basic industries, largely because of the popularity of the automobile. Thus the automobile changed American life and business. It is important to remember that these developments have all come within the last 50 or 100 years. Because changes came so fast, people found it hard to keep up with the world. New problems developed — problems of traffic, housing, and labor.

The Wright brothers invented the airplane. While Henry Ford was building his first cars in Detroit, two other mechanics were dreaming about an even more daring kind of transportation. They were the Wright brothers, Wilbur and Orville. They wanted to build a "flying machine."

This is a reproduction of Drake's first oil well at Titusville, Pennsylvania.

The Wright brothers ran a bicycle repair shop in Dayton, Ohio. Their neighbors laughed at the two boys who talked always about flying and spent all their spare cash on books about the subject.

There had always been a dream that men might fly like birds. The ancient Greeks had a story about a boy named Icarus (ICK ah rus) who wanted to fly. His father made him wings out of beeswax and feathers, but Icarus flew so high the sun melted the wax. That was the end of Icarus! But not the end of stories about flying.

Some scientists said that it was not possible for man to fly. The human body, they said, could not stand the strain. But the Wright brothers did not care what the great men said; they were too busy thinking about a machine that would carry them through the air.

They studied the air currents. Then they built a *glider*, or cloth covered frame, that supported them when they jumped from a hilltop

The brothers took their machine to Kitty Hawk Hill in North Carolina, because there the wind blew strong and steadily. On December 17, 1903, all was ready. They cranked the engine; Orville climbed aboard. The whirling propeller pushed the craft through the air for 12 seconds; the airplane traveled 120 feet. It was the first successful flight by an airplane carrying a human being.

Only five persons watched the experiment. Yet the little flight revealed a secret for which the world had waited ages. Men could fly! The Wright brothers knew how. Soon they had a machine which carried them through the air at 50 miles an hour.

Other inventors rapidly improved the airplane. Less than 20 years after the first flight at Kitty Hawk, an American naval officer crossed the Atlantic in a "flying boat." That same year, two British fliers made the first non-stop flight across the Atlantic. And four years later, American naval officers took two "flying boats" on a seven-month journey around the world.

The most surprising of all solo flights came in 1927. A young pilot, Charles Lindbergh, flew from New York to Paris in one "hop." His daring flight made "Lucky Lindy" a world hero. Today you can see Lindbergh's little one-engine plane "The Spirit of St. Louis" in the Smithsonian Institution in Washington, D.C.

Here are shown the Wrights' first glider (top), their Dayton, Ohio shop (center), and the flight at Kitty Hawk, North Carolina.

into a strong breeze. "How can we keep it going?" they asked each other. They decided to use a whirling propeller driven by a gas engine. For support they made two pairs of glider-like wings, one pair above the other, and put the engine between them.

Meanwhile, inventors of many countries were busy with the idea of turning the airplane into a military weapon. They succeeded so well that, during the First World War (1914–1918), planes fought and destroyed one another high above the fighting armies. During the Second World War (1940–1945) the airplane became a terrible instrument of destruction. Bombing planes carried death and destruction to cities far from the battlefield.

At sea a new type of ship appeared: the airplane carrier. From its top deck planes took off to fight an enemy fleet. Thus, airplanes have changed the nature of naval battles. No longer do ships have to wait for enemy fleets to appear. Instead, bombers carry the battle to ships hundreds of miles away.

Airplanes were important in other ways in the war. They carried supplies across the ocean in several hours. They dropped soldiers by parachute behind enemy lines. And they saved thousands of wounded soldiers and sailors by rushing them to hospitals in a few minutes.

The airplane industry developed. At first businessmen paid little attention to airplanes. But after Lindbergh's flight across the Atlantic, they realized that the new invention offered new and faster transportation. They began to invest money in airlines and airplanes. The airplane industry grew rapidly. By 1930, forty new companies had been formed, some to build airplanes, others to carry mail, passengers, or freight.

Soon the airlines became crowded and dangerous. There were so many accidents that Congress passed the *Civil Aeronautics Act*. This law gives the federal government wide control of airplane manufacturing and operation. Pilots and planes must be licensed by the Civil Aeronautics Administration. Pilots who break any of the regulations may be forbidden to fly. The number you now see on the wings of a plane is the license number issued by the federal government.

Today air travel has become commonplace. It is no longer news that a person can eat breakfast in New

Airplanes and pilots improved rapidly, as the pictures below illustrate. At left is Charles Lindbergh with his plane, *The Spirit of St. Louis,* in which he flew to Paris in 1927. At the right is an army airforce bomber, the "Stratofortress," in flight.

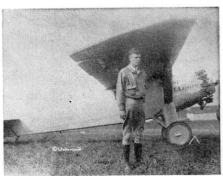

This map shows the major commercial airlines in the United States. The network of airlines makes it possible to reach almost any part of the country in a few hours.

York and enjoy dinner that evening in Los Angeles. Businessmen make overnight trips to London or Paris and thousands of Americans fly to Europe for two-week vacations. Almost every day another air record is broken.

Recently the speed of passenger planes has been doubled by the jet plane. This machine uses no revolving propeller to pull itself forward. Instead, it "kicks" itself along, like a skyrocket, by rapid explosions of mixed gas and air in a tube at the back of the plane.

Some jet planes are called supersonic (SOO per SAHN ik), which means "faster than sound." You can hear an ordinary plane coming before you see it because the sound of its motor runs ahead of it. But you can't hear a supersonic plane until after it has passed.

Jet planes are used in war to protect bombers, which are slower, from enemy fighters. British airlines are already using jet planes to carry passengers long distances. The future seems to promise faster and faster travel. The Air Age has only begun!

Bell invented the telephone in 1876.

Along with faster travel have come improvements in communication. In the 1840's, Samuel Morse and his electric telegraph conquered space and made it possible to send messages over the miles almost instantly. This soon led to the Atlantic cable and sending messages across the ocean by electricity.

But the inventors were not satisfied. If you could send clicking sounds over a telegraph wire, they said, why couldn't you send the hu-

432

man voice over a wire just as well?

Alexander Graham Bell was one of those who puzzled over the problem. Bell had been born in Scotland the same year that Thomas Edison was born in Ohio. His father ran a school for deaf-mutes, or people who could not hear or talk. Alexander became his assistant.

When he was 23 Bell came to America and started his own school for deaf-mutes. He wanted terribly to teach his pupils to talk. He thought that if he could show them the vibrations or movements made by the human voice, they would learn to speak by producing similar vibrations.

Bell tried to find some electrical apparatus that would record sound vibrations. A young mechanic named Thomas Watson became interested in the problem. Together, Bell and Watson spent all their spare time and money on experiments. They worked almost four years. Then they stumbled on a clue.

Here is how it happened: Bell was experimenting with an electrified wire. He was trying to catch signals from Watson in the next room. Watson happened to touch Bell's wire with another wire. Bell heard a faint buzzing sound. "Zing! Zing!" came over the wire. Bell rushed into Watson's room shouting, "What did you do? Do it again!" Another touch produced another "Zing!" They had discovered the principle of the telephone.

They still had to improve their materials and methods. They worked for weeks building a little machine. Then one March night, in 1876, Alexander Graham Bell stood in an upstairs room and called softly into the machine: "Watson, come here, I want you." Downstairs, Watson heard the message perfectly. It was the first time the human voice had spoken a clear complete message over the telephone!

Telephones became big business. Strange as it seems, people paid little attention to Bell's discovery. They

Alexander Graham Bell (below, left) invented the telephone. At the right, below, is the model of an instrument he and Thomas A. Watson built in 1875.

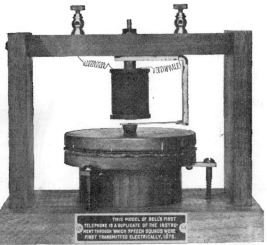

THIS MODEL OF BELL'S FIRST TELEPHONE IS A DUPLICATE OF THE INSTRUMENT THROUGH WHICH SPEECH SOUNDS WERE FIRST TRANSMITTED ELECTRICALLY, 1875.

called it a toy. In an effort to win public interest, Bell showed his invention at the Philadelphia Centennial Exposition. This was sort of a fair, held in 1876, to celebrate the hundredth birthday of the Declaration of Independence.

The Emperor of Brazil, Dom Pedro, visited the Exposition and stopped to look at Bell's machine. Bell asked the Emperor to listen. Then he went some distance away and spoke into the machine. Dom Pedro cried out, "Heavens, it talks!"

When the newspapers told the story of how an American inventor had scared the Emperor, nearly everyone wanted to see and use the telephone. Bell and his friends formed a company. They built telephone lines across the country. The invention changed American life. It put people in constant touch with one another.

The telephone has become America's favorite means of communication. In 1950 over 56 billion telephone conversations took place in the United States — 372 per person. Many — perhaps ten percent — were long distance calls from city to city, even from country to country. And almost every call meant a saving of time or travel.

To manufacture so many telephone instruments; to install them in homes and offices; to set up the poles along country roads or to bury the wires in city streets — all this, and much more, meant a new industry of enormous size. It gave employment to millions.

The invention of the telephone led to other inventions. The wireless telephone came into use. This helped make radio and television possible. Thus the Scotch immigrant, Alexander Graham Bell, brought gifts beyond price to his adopted country.

Marconi invented the wireless. In the 19th century, communication took three giant steps forward. In the 1840's, the invention of the telegraph by Morse made it possible to send dot and dash messages long distances at the speed of electricity. In the 1860's, Cyrus Field's work of laying the Atlantic cable made it possible to send messages across the ocean. And, in the 1870's, the invention of the telephone enabled people to send their voices over the

The chart below illustrates the rapid growth of industry in the United States during the 19th century. Note how the percentage of national income produced by farming decreased as manufacturing grew and thousands of people moved to the cities.

GROWTH OF INDUSTRY IN THE 19TH CENTURY
(Share of national income provided by each division)

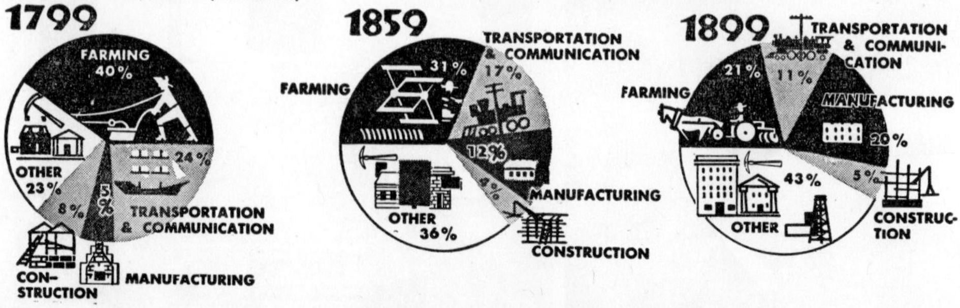

1799
FARMING 40%
OTHER 23%
8%
5%
24%
TRANSPORTATION & COMMUNICATION
CON-STRUCTION
MANUFACTURING

1859
FARMING 31%
TRANSPORTATION & COMMUNICATION 17%
12%
4%
OTHER 36%
MANUFACTURING
CONSTRUCTION

1899
FARMING 21%
TRANSPORTATION & COMMUNICATION 11%
MANUFACTURING 20%
OTHER 43%
5%
CONSTRUCTION

The wireless led to the radio. Marconi (left) invented wireless telegraphy; de Forest (right) perfected the radio tube.

wires to places many miles distant.

No longer did a person have to wait weeks or months for information to come by mail. Now he could get an answer in minutes or even seconds! But still inventors were not satisfied. The telegraph and telephone required miles of wires. Without such wires it was impossible to send messages quickly. And there was no way to communicate with large numbers of people at the same time.

An Italian inventor named Guglielmo (gool YEL moh) Marconi (mahr KOH nee) found the answer. In the 1890's he found a way to send electric messages through the air. This "wireless" message could go anywhere over land or sea. Only three things were necessary: electric power, a sending station, and a receiving station.

Practically all ships now carry instruments for sending and receiving wireless messages. Thus a ship keeps in touch with other ships and with land. When a ship is threatened by fire or storm, the wireless operator sends out the danger signal: *SOS*.

On receiving it, all other wireless stations within hearing are silenced. The operator then taps out a message telling the location of his ship.

Radio "direction-finders" are now also used to determine the direction from which the wireless message comes. The nearest ship then goes to its rescue, or a patrol ship is sent out from the nearest land station. In the number of lives saved alone, wireless telegraphy is counted among the world's great inventions.

Radio broadcasting began. From Marconi's wireless telegraph to radio was only a short step. Other inventors sought a way to send the human voice directly through space. So many men worked on radio at the same time, it is hard to say who invented it.

Among the inventors was Lee De Forest, who perfected the vacuum tube, or "tube without air." The sounds that come by electric wave to your radio are very faint. In the vacuum tube these faint sounds are magnified, or made loud enough, for you to hear.

Stations KDKA in Pittsburgh and WWJ in Detroit were the first to broadcast to the nation. In the presidential election of 1920, KDKA sent out news of the vote counting every hour. Americans liked the idea so much they began to buy and build radios in large numbers.

Soon there were dozens of stations, each broadcasting when and however it pleased. Their broadcasts

EARLY RADIO BROADCASTING

Television has brought a great variety of entertainment into millions of American living rooms.

often "jammed" one another, so listeners heard only yelps and howls. After seven years of this confusion, Congress created the Federal Communications Commission, or FCC.

The FCC regulates radio broadcasting. Stations must get permission from the FCC to broadcast. Each station is given a definite *wave length* that it must use. It must not interfere with the wave length of other stations.

More quickly than any other invention, radio became part of American daily life. During the Second World War it gave almost hourly news of what the army, navy, and air force were doing far away. News of the first bombing raid on Tokyo, for example, was broadcast in the United States before the bombing planes had returned from their mission.

On many a battlefront in Europe, generals kept in touch by radio with every regiment under their command. In the jungles of the Pacific islands every scouting party carried a "walkie-talkie." This sending and receiving radio set allowed scouts to report the enemy's position and to receive orders from headquarters.

In time of peace radio is also useful. Together with the newspapers, it keeps the American people informed of all important news — from weather reports to international affairs. Also, radio is widely used in schools and lecture halls as a new means of education. And police cars, equipped with radio, patrol city streets; such cars are ready at a moment's notice to go where danger threatens.

Radio has created a new industry. More than 3000 stations are now broadcasting programs in the United States. And over 110 million home

436

and auto radios have been sold here.

Today, radio is everywhere. A turn of a switch brings you fine music, or news, or the latest jokes. You take it for granted; if you have a television set, radio may even seem a little old-fashioned. But nationwide broadcasting is younger than your parents! It is one of the modern developments that have transformed American life in recent years.

Television is the latest advance in communication. Most of the inventions you have been reading about came into use long before you were born. But you yourself have witnessed the growth of the newest and, in some ways, the most exciting development: television. Before 1945, most Americans had never seen a television broadcast.

Long ago, scientists realized that television was possible. Soon after Morse invented the telegraph, inventors began to talk about the possiblity of "seeing by telegraph." Over seventy years ago, a German received a patent for a system that included many features now used in television broadcasting.

In the 1920's, research workers in several countries developed ways of sending and receiving pictures. An American, Philo Farnsworth, invented the first Orthicon tube, which is the heart of the TV camera. He conceived the idea when he was studying physics in high school!

Television broadcasting existed on a small scale in the 1930's, but World War II interrupted progress. At the end of the war there were only six television stations in the United States. Now there are hundreds, some of them broadcasting in color. Television has become a giant enterprise. Through television, millions of Americans now "sit in" at meetings of Congress and watch the nomination and inauguration of the President. Schools and colleges use television as an aid in teaching. Political campaigning has felt TV's influence; politicians who make a good impression on television win many votes.

Television has created thousands of jobs; in the future it will require the services of perhaps a million highly trained workers in many fields. Like other modern inventions, television seems likely to bring continued and rapid changes in American life.

Radar helps the airforce keep watch. The picture below shows a radar site in Japan. The planes are "Thunderjets" guarding the islands against attacks.

CHAPTER SUMMARY

The United States became a leader in manufacturing after 1865. Factors which encouraged industrialization were (1) freedom to experiment, (2) a wealth of natural resources, (3) a plentiful supply of labor, and (4) capable leaders.

New methods became the foundation of big industries. Andrew Carnegie used the Bessemer Process and made Pittsburgh a steel center. Henry Ford built a low-cost car and helped make Detroit the center of the automotive industry. Charles Goodyear discovered how to vulcanize rubber. The petroleum industry became one of America's key enterprises. New products and developments came so rapidly that serious problems developed.

The Wright brothers made a successful airplane flight. At Kitty Hawk, North Carolina in 1903 the Air Age began. Alexander Graham Bell invented the telephone in 1876; it became a big business. Marconi, an Italian inventor, found a way to send messages without wires. Radio broadcasting soon began, to be followed in recent times by the latest advance in communication, Television.

The Language of History

Make sure you understand the meaning of each of the following words and phrases as they are used in this chapter.

1. Bessemer Process *B.S.*
2. vulcanizing *C.M.*
3. Civil Aeronautics Act *X.C.*
4. capital *V.G.*
5. Model T *D.M.*
6. vacuum tube *C.C.*
7. rationed *R.W.*
8. supersonic *E.K.*
9. glider *S.C.*

What Happened When

Connect each of the following dates with an important event in American history.

1. 1842   2. 1859   3. 1876   4. 1903   5. 1909   6. 1920

HALL OF FAME.

Who's Who in History

Be sure you know the part that each of the following played in the development of communication, transportation, and industry.

1. Andrew Carnegie
2. Charles Goodyear
3. Guglielmo Marconi
4. Henry Ford
5. Lee De Forest

6. Philo Farnsworth
7. Wilbur and Orville Wright
8. Alexander Graham Bell
9. Charles Lindbergh

Study Questions

1. Write a brief biography of Andrew Carnegie including **(a)** his early life, **(b)** how he obtained capital to build his first mill, **(c)** the process he used, **(d)** his contribution to the growth of manufacturing, and **(e)** how he disposed of his fortune.

2. What was Henry Ford's influence on **(a)** everyday life, **(b)** the wage level, and **(c)** the number of jobs available for workers?

3. Why is the production of oil and related products one of the most important industries in the United States?

4. When, where, and by whom was the first successful airplane flight made?

5. Mention three ways in which Alexander Graham Bell's invention changed life in America.

6. **a.** Who developed wireless telegraphy?
   b. Who perfected the vacuum tube?
   c. When did regular radio broadcasting begin?

7. It has been said, "There is nothing very new about television. Scientists knew about the possibility many years before the first television program was broadcast." Explain why this is so.

LET'S LOOK AT WHAT WE'VE LEARNED

What is meant by the Industrial Revolution? *a change in industry*

The Industrial Revolution was a revolution in the ways of producing goods. It began in Great Britain near the end of the 18th century and consisted of a change from hand labor to machine labor.

Where and when did manufacturing get started in the United States?

Samuel Slater built the first American factory in Pawtucket, Rhode Island in 1790. The War of 1812 greatly encouraged the growth of manufacturing. Americans could not get manufactured goods from Britain and had to make their own.

How did Thomas A. Edison help develop modern America?

Edison found ways to put electricity to work. He invented the electric light, the phonograph, the dictaphone, the stock market ticker, and hundreds of other useful machines. He also played an important part in the development of motion pictures.

What new ideas and inventions helped the farmers?

Lightweight, efficient metal plows were developed through the efforts of many inventors.

In 1831, Cyrus McCormick invented a reaper that cut grain faster and more efficiently than could be done by hand. Later other features were added until the combine was developed. The combine cuts and rakes wheat, threshes it, and puts it into bags.

What new problems did farm machinery help create?

With the new machines it became possible to harvest huge crops. Often farmers could not sell all they raised. This was especially discouraging because farmers often had gone into debt to buy harvesters and tractors.

What was Henry Ford's contribution to the development of America?

He produced huge numbers of cheap, efficient automobiles. This made it possible for the average American to buy a car. Ford also created thousands of jobs for automobile workers. The automobile stimulated the growth of steel and rubber factories. Automobiles used great quantities of oil and gasoline, which stimulated the petroleum industry. Textile factories, glass factories, paint factories, and dozens of other manufacturing enterprises received big orders from automobile makers.

When and where was the first airplane flight with a human being?

At Kitty Hawk Hill, North Carolina on December 17, 1903 the Wright brothers flew an airplane for 120 feet. This was the beginning of the Age of Flight.

Who were some of the famous men who contributed to the growth of new industries?

Eli Whitney invented the cotton gin and developed the idea of interchangeable parts in manufacturing. Elias Howe invented the sewing machine in 1845. Andrew Carnegie made steel cheap and plentiful. Charles Goodyear discovered the process of vulcanizing rubber. John D. Rockefeller organized the petroleum industry. Alexander Graham Bell invented the telephone. Guglielmo Marconi found a way to send messages by wireless. Lee De Forest perfected the vacuum tube, thus furthering the development of radio. Philo Farnsworth invented the Orthicon tube used in television cameras.

Connecting the Past with the Present . . .

Have you ever spent a vacation in a remote spot where there was no electricity? Perhaps it seemed fun to light kerosene lamps or candles in the evening. However, when the novelty wore off the dim light probably began to seem very inconvenient.

Can you imagine what America would be like today without the electric light? Factories would have to close at the end of the day. Streets would be dark and dangerous at night. Few automobiles would be on the road after sundown. The fire department would be busy putting out fires started by lamps and candles. At home, you and your family would probably stay close together near the lamps or fireplace. If you wanted to go up or down stairs you would have to light a candle or lamp and move slowly lest you fall or start a fire.

Thomas Edison made life much easier and more pleasant for everyone when he invented the electric light. Thanks to him you can press a button and make a room as bright as day. You can enjoy the excitement of a brightly lit city after dark. You can read for hours after sundown. You can walk briskly and confidently down a city avenue lined with street lights. All this and much more are the result of the long hours Thomas Edison spent in his laboratory.

UNIT REVIEW

Questions for Discussion and Review

1. What were three good results of the change from hand to machine labor during the 19th century?
2. What industry was the first to feel the changes of the Industrial Revolution?
3. How did most workmen in Britain regard the new labor-saving inventions?
4. Explain how the idea of interchangeable parts revolutionized industry.
5. Make a list of the inventions of Thomas Edison adding any about which you know even though they are not mentioned in this book.
6. What were two important results of the invention of the "harvester"?
7. What conditions in the United States after the Civil War helped bring about rapid development of industry?
8. How has the growth of the auto industry affected other industries?
9. What is the purpose of the Civil Aeronautics Act?
10. Why was the Federal Communications Commission established?

THE HISTORY LABORATORY

Here are some suggestions for activities that you will find interesting and profitable.

Picture Gallery — A Class Project . . .

On the walls of your room or the hall arrange pictures and drawings which show the invention or improvements in the manufacturing of the following:

textiles	oil	airplanes
sewing machines	movies	radio
phonograph	plow	wireless

WHAT AND WHEN

Slater's mill
1790

Whitney's cotton gin
1793

McCormick's r
1831

Surprise Box . . .

Have everyone in the class put into a box a card on which is written a fact in this Unit that he or she found of great interest. Pass the box around the room so that all students may take turns reading the unusual facts.

After this, have the class choose the most interesting statements of fact and put them in a scrapbook.

See for Yourself . . .

Organize a field trip to see any of the activities carried on by industries whose growth has been discussed in this Unit. Many industries are anxious to show their facilities to interested students.

I Remember When . . .

Invite some of the older people in your community to come to your classroom and tell about their first experiences with automobiles, radios, electric lights, movies, and other modern inventions.

Calling All Authors! . . .

Write a story on one of the following topics:

"Our First Sewing Machine." Imagine you are the mother of a large family. Tell how Elias Howe's new invention affected your life.

"Across the Deep." Imagine that you were one of the first fliers to solo across an ocean.

"I'm a Ham." Tell about the experiences of a "ham" operator.

"Rich Strike." Tell the story of an oil well you discovered and brought into production.

Sewing machine 1845   Edison's electric light 1879   Early automobiles 1893   First airplane flight 1903

Honor Roll of American Industry . . .

Several students can work together to produce a booklet containing biographical sketches of the founders of American industry.

Things to Come . . .

The changes of the past century have gone far beyond the expectations of the dreamers of 1860. Gaze into your crystal ball and tell the class how people will live in 2000.

Models Museum — A Group Project . . .

Bring to the classroom for exhibition models showing the development of automobiles, airplanes, and inventions, mentioned in this Unit. Short, clear labels will make the models more interesting.

Let's Read about Modern Inventions

BATE, NORMAN, *Who Built the Highway?*, Scribner, 1953.
BURLINGAME, ROGER, *Inventors Behind the Inventor*, Harcourt, 1947.
BURLINGAME, ROGER, *Machines That Built America*, Harcourt, 1953.
FLOHERTY, JOHN J., *Aviation from the Ground Up*, Lippincott, 1950.
FLOHERTY, JOHN J., *Flowing Gold*, Lippincott, 1945.
**GRACE, DICK, *Visibility Unlimited*, Longmans, 1950.
HARLOW, ALVIN F., *Andrew Carnegie*, Messner, 1953.
LATHAM, JEAN LEE, *The Story of Eli Whitney*, Aladdin, 1953.
**LONGSTREET, STEPHEN, *A Century on Wheels*, Holt, 1953.
*MEADOWCROFT, ENID L., *The Story of Thomas Alva Edison*, Grosset, 1953.
MEYER, JEROME S., *Picture Book of Radio and Television and How They Work*, Lothrop, 1951.
OTTO, MARGARET, and OTTO, STUART, *The Tractor Book*, Morrow, 1953.
PERRY, JOSEPHINE, *Rubber Industry*, Longmans, 1946.
PERRY, JOSEPHINE, *Steel Industry*, Longmans, 1943.
SHIPPEN, KATHERINE B., *Mr. Bell Invents the Telephone*, Random, 1952.
WILLIS, C. H., and SAUNDERS, L. S., *Those Who Dared*, University of North Carolina Press, 1935.

* indicates easy reading
** indicates advanced reading

Unit 10

THE GROWTH OF INDUSTRIES CREATED NEW PROBLEMS IN AMERICA (1875-1952)

"WHAT *are* these people talking about?" Alexander Hamilton would say if he attended a meeting of businessmen or workers or even government officials today. Hamilton was a fine businessman and a brilliant Secretary of the Treasury, but he never heard of most of the problems which confront the business world today.

"What do they mean by anti-trust laws? And what's collective bargaining the working men keep asking for? The farmers too — what do they mean by the AAA and why do they want government aid? What are slums and housing projects and immigration quotas? I don't understand any of this!"

This Unit is about the developments in business, labor, and farming since 1865 and the problems which they have created. As you study it keep in mind these key questions:

1. Why did the government begin to regulate business?
2. Why did the farmers need help?
3. What new problems appeared with the rapid growth of cities?
4. Why did the United States decide to restrict immigration?

Chapter 22

THE GOVERNMENT BEGAN
TO REGULATE BUSINESS
AND TO HELP THE FARMER

"I N the interest of the whole people, the nation should assume power of regulation over all corporations doing an interstate business," Theodore Roosevelt told Congress in 1901.

Western farmers were demanding that the government make rules for the railroads. Citizens everywhere were calling on Congress to restrict business practices. What did Congress do? What was the Interstate Commerce Commission? What did the Sherman Act say? How does the Pure Food and Drug Act affect your life?

As years passed, more restrictions were placed on business. What new laws were passed in Franklin Roosevelt's administration? What was the NRA? Why was it declared unconstitutional?

The farmers had been among the first to demand regulation of business. But they were not satisfied with railroad regulation alone. What other laws did Congress pass to aid the farmer?

The farmer's land was one of the nation's natural resources along with oil and timber and coal. These resources were being used up at an alarming rate. What did Theodore Roosevelt do about this waste? What is meant by conservation?

This chapter takes a look at fifty years of American development. In it you will read of the effect the government has had on business, agriculture, and conservation.

Businessmen had to deal with new problems. New inventions and industries caused sweeping changes in American life after 1865. Men like Thomas Edison and Andrew Carnegie created opportunities and luxuries for the American people. But there were new problems too. Noisy overcrowded cities grew up around the factories. Accidents increased. And disputes arose that sometimes led to violence between workers and employers.

Businessmen themselves found life more difficult as business grew bigger. *Competition*, or trying to get business away from someone else, became severe: business firms tried to win customers from one another by cutting prices. The government made rules and regulations for business; taxes rose, and the need for keeping records increased. It is not surprising that some businessmen looked back longingly to "the good old days" when running a business was not so complicated!

Corporations and combinations were formed. Other business leaders, however, regarded new problems as a challenge. They looked for ways to increase production and reduce expenses. They found that it was more efficient to organize a large business as a *corporation*.

A corporation is a form of business organization. Instead of one or two owners, a corporation has a great many owners called *stockholders*. Anyone can become a stockholder by buying a share of the corporation's stock. The stockholders choose a board of directors to run the corporation for them. The directors, in turn, hire a manager. If the business is successful, the stockholders receive a share of the profits called a *dividend*. If it fails they lose only their investment. They enjoy *limited liability* which means they are not held personally responsible for the corporation's debts. In a single enterprise or a partnership the owners can lose everything they own if the business fails. This can not happen to stockholders of a corporation.

The corporation has many advantages. It can obtain huge amounts of capital by selling stock. And a corporation can continue in business for a very long time. The original stockholders may sell their stock or pass it on to their children. A manager or a director may die, but this does not upset the business as it would if there were only one or two owners.

The advantages of the corporation were so attractive that most of the big business firms were organized in this way. Later, some leaders began to ask: Why not join several corporations in the same industry and make one giant combination? The combination would be even more efficient and profitable. It would do away with wasteful competition and price cutting. Over the years many such combinations were formed. They became known as *trusts*.

The trusts were unpopular. The trusts soon ran into trouble. Small businessmen, who could not sell their products so cheaply as the giant combinations, complained bitterly. And other people feared the power of the trusts. They pointed out that the trusts enjoyed a *monopoly* — that is, the trusts had such control of the production of certain commodities they could raise or lower prices at will. For example, anyone who wanted to buy kerosene or gasoline had to pay the price set by Standard Oil. This caused a demand for government regulation: "There ought to be a law!" cried many farmers and owners of small business firms. As a result, several states and finally the federal government passed laws against trusts.

A small business was begun. To understand more clearly what this meant to individuals, consider the case of David Gibbons and his son, Peter.* David was born on a farm in western New York a few years before the Civil War. His father and mother had left Ireland during the terrible potato famine of 1849.

By working hard and saving every penny, the family had managed to buy a little farm. David had two older brothers and four younger sisters. When he was ten years old his father got him a job in a blacksmith's shop. He earned only a few pennies a day, and every cent he earned was needed at home.

David soon decided he would rather be a blacksmith than a farmer. He worked hard and learned his trade thoroughly. By the time he was nineteen he was strong, capable, and self-confident.

For almost a year David had been "keeping company" with Mary Lee,

"The smith, a mighty man is he," wrote the poet, Longfellow. The picture below shows a popular blacksmith shop in the 19th century when horses were numerous and an important factor in the life of America.

* Gibbons was not their real name.

whose father ran the village store. To support a wife David felt he ought to have his own shop. When he heard that a town nearby had no blacksmith, he borrowed a horse and rode over to investigate. What he saw pleased him.

"It's a new place and growing fast," he told Mary Lee. "It's right near the main road to the West. Lots of people going west need a blacksmith to repair their wagons or shoe their horses. If I only had more money saved . . ."

"Maybe Pa would help us," suggested Mary Lee. And "Pa" did. Within a year travelers noticed a bright new sign on the road: "D. Gibbons, Blacksmith." David was busy all day at his forge, and next door to the shop Mary Lee proudly kept house.

The business came to a sudden end. Business was good. The Gibbons paid off their debts in a few years. They did not have to buy much food, for David's parents had given them a cow and some chickens and they had a big garden. The Gibbons' bank account grew slowly but steadily. Soon David had so much business he hired a boy to help.

"David works too hard, and he doesn't take care of himself," Mary Lee often complained. After Peter was born, David worked harder than ever. He said, "I want my son to have the things I missed!" So he got up at dawn and often worked until long after dark. His shop was too small for all the business. David wanted to enlarge it and hire a man to help him, but he could not yet afford this. Instead, he tried to do two men's work himself.

One dreary March day he caught a cold that turned into pneumonia. There were no "wonder drugs" in those days, and the doctor could do little. David died and Mary Lee tried to sell the business. A blacksmith in a nearby town bought some of David's tools for a few dollars, but no one wanted the shop. It stood empty and dark. What had been a profitable business suddenly was worth almost nothing because the owner was no longer there.

In the story of Gibbons' blacksmith shop you can see some advantages and disadvantages of the single owner type of business. David was his own boss. He collected all the profits. But when he needed money to enlarge his shop he did not have it. And when he died the business ended.

A corporation had its troubles. David's son, Peter, never tried to start his own business. When he was sixteen he went to the city and took a course in bookkeeping. Then he found a job in the office of a small factory. One day he asked his fellow workers: "Who owns this business, anyway?" "Why, the stockholders," he was told. Peter learned that anyone could buy stock in the company, which was organized as a corporation. He made up his mind to save his money and buy company stock.

In time Peter became manager of the company and a large stockholder. When money was needed to build a new mill Peter persuaded the directors to sell more stock and thus obtain the necessary money. When Peter himself needed money to send his children to college he sold some of his stock at a fair profit.

The company grew fast. It employed several hundred men and women. Sometimes serious disputes arose between the management and the workers. Several times the workers threatened to *strike*, that is, refuse to work if their demands were not met. Sometimes they demanded a pay increase. Sometimes they wanted shorter hours or better working conditions. In most cases a way was found to settle the dispute without a strike. Once, when their wages were cut, the workers did go on a strike. Peter said that the company had to reduce wages because competition was so severe; other corporations were cutting prices and trying to get all the business.

Peter's firm met increasingly stiff competition. Gradually a company several hundred miles away became the biggest and most powerful in the industry. It cut prices and drove several competitors out of business.

A new "Dime Store" opens! The picture below shows a scene in one of the early Woolworth Stores. This company introduced modern methods of selling in many American towns. "Penny profits on huge sales" was the motto of the new type of business.

It was soon called the "trust." A day came when Peter had to tell the directors and stockholders that their company could no longer compete with the trust.

"Well, 'if you can't lick 'em, join 'em,' is my motto," one director said. The others agreed. As a result, they joined the trust. They exchanged their stock for *trust certificates* and kept on getting dividends.

By this time Peter was growing old and tired, so he retired. He was not happy about the way his business career had ended. He felt the trust had used unfair methods. "The small businessman is the backbone of America," he declared, "There ought to be a law to protect him!"

The corporation met the needs of modern business. The story of Peter Gibbons illustrates some advantages and disadvantages of the corporation. The company for which he worked found it easy to obtain money to expand and hire additional workers. And the company kept on going in spite of many changes in management. People who invested in the company were able to sell their stock when they wished. They got back all they had invested plus a profit. Of course this would not be true of all stocks. Many times stocks go down in value and people have to sell them for less than they paid. Peter's company was successful so the stockholders made money. But there is always risk involved in buying stocks. Because Peter's company had plenty of capital it could buy new machines, hire an efficient manager, and keep up-to-date in methods. Then, too, the company was not a "one man show." The manager consulted with the directors; together they decided on a policy.

On the other hand there were disadvantages. Peter was never his own master in the way his father had been. He had to report to directors and stockholders and carry out their orders. When the company was prosperous Peter received only a small part of the profits.

Nevertheless, the corporation was clearly better suited to modern needs and conditions than other forms of business organizations. Its advantages were greater than its disadvantages, especially from the investor's point of view. So in most of the new industries, such as automobile making, the corporation has been the favorite way of organizing a business.

However, the single owner type of organization did not disappear. The small family-owned business is still the most common type in the United States. Think over the business firms in your town. Probably many of the grocery stores, restaurants and repair shops are owned and operated by individuals. But you will probably find that big factories, super markets, and "chain stores" are organized as corporations.

Some railroads used unfair methods. Managers of corporations, such as

Peter Gibbons, had to think about public opinion and government regulation. There was no doubt about it; the number of laws passed to regulate business was increasing.

Railroads were the first to experience strict regulation. In those days there were no trucks and airplanes, so people had to ship their products by railroad. And they had to pay whatever rates the railroads asked.

The farmers, especially those in the West, were at the mercy of the railroads. Some railroad managers took advantage of the situation and charged higher rates to carry farm products than they charged to carry manufactured goods. They also charged a higher rate per mile to carry goods a short distance than to carry them a long distance.

To stop this, one state passed a law that required railroads within its borders to charge the same rates to all shippers. Railroad owners got around the state law in this way: first they offered the same freight rates to both farmers and manufacturers. Then they returned to the manufacturer a sum of money, small or large according to the size of the freight bill. The money that was returned was called a *rebate*. Thus, big businessmen still paid less than farmers for the same service.

Another practice that helped make railroad leaders unpopular was the policy of giving passes to influential people. This began innocently enough, as a way of honoring or showing respect for high government officials. But when railroads spread over the country and states began to regulate them, railroad officials began sending passes to almost everyone with influence. It seemed to the public as if railroads were trying to bribe important people. The granting of passes finally was forbidden by law, but not before the practice had done much harm to the railroads' reputations.

Another unfair practice, called *pooling*, was often used in cases where two or more railroad lines crossed a state. At first each road tried to get as much business as possible by offering low rates for passenger or freight service. After a while the railroads saw the advantage of *pooling* or combining their interests and charging all shippers the same rate. This did away with competition. The railroads made bigger profits, but the public had to pay very high rates for freight and passenger service. This caused hardship, especially in the new western states. Western farmers made up their minds to do something about the situation.

Farmers formed the Grange. The farmers already had an organization to work for their interests. It was called the "Patrons of Husbandry." (Patron sometimes means a protector or guardian; husbandry is another name for farming.) The organization was made up of many small groups called "Granges." (Grange is an old name for land on which

GOVERNMENT REGULATION

grain is grown.) And the farmers who belonged were called "grangers." A man named Oliver Kelley started the organization in 1867.

Kelley was a Massachusetts man who went west and cleared land for a farm on the Minnesota frontier. Later the federal government hired him to travel through the West and South and report on farming conditions. Kelley noticed that many farmer families were lonely and unhappy because they lived far from other people. He started the first granger society to provide a chance for farmers to get together and hear a lecture or a concert or have a picnic. But like people everywhere the farmers preferred to talk about their own problems. Sooner or later they always began talking about railroads and how to get lower rates.

The Grange became powerful. Women joined the new organization on equal terms with men. Soon there was a "Grange" in almost every part of America. Total membership was over two million. Political leaders paid attention to the grangers' demands, because they wanted the members to vote for them.

The grangers asked the states to pass laws requiring the railroads to charge fair rates and to treat all customers alike. They pointed out that a farmer had almost nothing left after he paid for sending his

"Mr. Chairman, Mr. Chairman!" several members seem eager to speak at the local Grange meeting (below). This session was held in the schoolhouse near Edwardsville, Illinois in the days when Grangers were demanding railroad regulation.

This was one of the many cartoons the Grangers used in their attacks on the railroads in the 1870's. The Grange is pictured as a farmer trying to awaken people to the danger of letting railroads operate without state or federal regulation.

goods to market. For example, an Illinois farmer might ship corn to Boston or Philadelphia. There it sold for 70 cents a bushel but the farmer received only 15 cents a bushel. The railroad received 52 cents; the wholesale dealer who bought western corn and sold it to eastern customers got 3 cents a bushel.

Grangers demanded regulation of railroads. In 1870 the Grangers persuaded the Illinois legislature to pass a law to *regulate* or make rules for railroads. It set up a Commission with power to force railroads to charge the same rate for carrying farm products they charged for carrying manufactured goods. Five other states passed similar laws which were known as the "Granger" laws.

However, the railroads found ways to avoid obeying the Granger laws. They were big and powerful. Their tracks ran across the whole country. The problem was too big for any one state or even several states. The farmers soon realized that successful regulation would have to be done by the national government. The Grangers appealed to Congress. They pointed out that the Constitution [27] says "Congress shall have power to regulate commerce with foreign nations, and among the several states." The railroads, said the farmers, were carrying on commerce among the several states. Therefore Congress should regulate them.

At first the leaders of Congress were unwilling to do as the Grangers asked. Railroad leaders fought hard to keep Congress from doing anything to regulate rates. They said it was an old American custom for the government to let business alone. They argued that they had the right to charge what they liked for carrying the farmer or his goods. If the farmer didn't want to pay, he could walk or hire a wagon.

Congress passed the Interstate Commerce Act in 1887. The Grangers replied that railroad service had become a necessity. Whole towns and sections depended on the railroads for transportation. People had to be protected from unfair rates, so it was the government's duty to step into the dispute to try to settle it.

Because the Grangers worked steadily for what they wanted and because they controlled many votes, they finally got the law they wanted. In 1887, Congress passed the Interstate Commerce Act. This law was not enforced for many years but today it regulates the railroads quite strictly. It provides that:

1. Passenger and freight rates must be fair, or reasonable.

2. Rebates, pooling, and other such attempts to avoid equal treatment of shippers and passengers must stop.

3. Railroads must publish a list of rates to be offered to all alike.

4. Railroads must get the government's approval before they can change their rates.

5. If any railroad disobeys any part of the Act, its officials may be brought into court and, if found guilty, may be imprisoned or fined.

The ICC has great power. To carry out the provisions of this Act five men were appointed by the President. Later the number was increased to eleven. They are members of the *Interstate Commerce Commission*, commonly known as the ICC. Their duty is to supervise the business of all railroads operating in more than one state.

The Commission keeps on file (where anybody may see them) all passenger and freight rates. Every railroad must make an annual report to the Commission. In case of a

dispute between a railroad and a shipper or a passenger, the Commission may decide which side is right.

The ICC has been supervising the railroads for more than sixty years. It is perhaps the most active of the many federal commissions that now regulate business. It tries to look out for the passengers' comfort. It requires every railroad to inspect its cars frequently, and to provide them with heat, light, drinking water and fresh air. Because of its good work, the ICC has been given new powers and duties. It regulates not only railroads but all trucks and buses that carry freight or passengers from one state to another.

Rockefeller organized the oil industry. Railroad leaders learned they had to accept government regulation. Later, other industries had to accept it also. Certain industries became unpopular because of methods the public felt were unfair. Such unpopularity led almost always to government regulation.

One of the first of the big business corporations was the Standard Oil Company. This was the company which John D. Rockefeller founded.

To get oil out of the ground and prepare it for use three things had to be done: first, the oil had to be produced or removed from the ground; second, it had to be refined and purified; and third, it had to be sold. Rockefeller was wise enough to see that time, money, and labor might be saved by putting the whole process under one management. So he formed the Standard Oil Company of Ohio by combining his own refinery, which turned out 1500 barrels a day, with twenty others that turned out 12,000 barrels daily. Refining companies of other states joined the Rockefeller company because it was making big profits.

The next step was to get control of the oil business by persuading, or forcing, several oil-producing companies to join Standard Oil. The usual method was to offer a fair price for a well or refinery. If the owner accepted this offer, his business became part of Rockefeller's organization. If he refused, the Standard Oil Company would offer oil to his customers at a very low price. The independent owner could not afford to sell oil for such a low price so he would lose his customers. Thus Rockefeller would "freeze" him out of his business.

Another method Rockefeller used to force other companies out of business was to make secret bargains with the railroads. Standard Oil Company would agree to ship so many thousand carloads of oil every day. To get this profitable business a railroad would agree to charge Standard Oil lower freight rates than it charged any rival company. (In those days there were no pipelines; oil was shipped by railroad.) In some cases the railroad even paid Standard Oil a part of the profit it made by carrying oil for other companies. By such methods, Standard Oil was able to absorb other companies or put them out of business by underselling them. It could then set its own price on oil products because it controlled most of the wells and refineries in the country.

Company after company was brought under the Standard Oil management, until about three-fourths of the oil industry — its wells, refineries, pipelines, tank cars — had come under the control of Standard Oil. That was only the beginning. The popularity of the automobile created a new market for petroleum products. In the early days of the oil industry, gasoline was thrown away as a waste product of kerosene. But when automobiles came into general use, the sale of gasoline became increasingly profitable. The business of Standard Oil kept growing.

Monopolies increased. The success of Standard Oil encouraged owners of other industries to combine under a single management. The chief purpose of every monopoly was to control the production and selling price of some article people needed.

Here are a few examples: many small sugar companies united to form the American Sugar Refining Company; factories for making farm machinery were joined to make the International Harvester Company; factories for making matches combined into the Diamond Match Company.

So rapid was the growth of big business that within thirty years many products needed every day — salt and sugar, matches and tobacco, shoes and sewing machines, chewing gum and tombstones — were each more or less under the control of a trust.

There are many arguments in favor of trusts and monopolies. They have improved the quality of many foods, tools, and clothing. They often lowered the price of goods to the public; at the same time they made money for their stockholders. By employing trained men for research, or experiment, they estab-

John D. Rockefeller (below) was the founder of the Standard Oil Company which became the largest in the petroleum industry.

"The bad trusts must go!" Here are some of the cartoons used in the fight against monopoly in the days of President Theodore Roosevelt. The trusts were pictured as completely heartless and greedy. Cartoons like these helped bring about increased regulation of business.

lished industries and created jobs.

However, some trusts behaved in a way that made the public angry. They charged as much for their products as they thought people would pay or, as the railroad men used to say, "as much as the traffic will bear." As a result, most people came to feel that all trusts, good and bad alike, should be regulated for at least two reasons. First, they put too much power into the hands of a few men, which is dangerous in a democracy. Second, they often gave a small businessman the hard choice of joining them or going out of business. It was neither fair nor wise to permit big businesses to swallow up small enterprises.

Since early colonial days, small businesses have played a very important part in American life. Even today, small business firms outnumber big companies fifty to one. The nation could not get along without small business firms. It was the government's duty to keep the trusts from crushing "the little fellow."

Congress passed the Anti-Trust Act of 1890. By 1890 many citizens had turned against the trusts. Popular demand for action was overwhelming. So, in that year, Congress passed the Anti-Trust Act, usually known as the Sherman Act in honor of Senator Sherman of Ohio who proposed the law. The Anti-Trust Act forbade combinations that restrained competition. Persons who set up a combination that controlled prices and production could be fined or sent to prison.

For several years the Sherman Act was not enforced. Congress seemed to feel that by passing the law it had done all that was necessary. Big business firms and monopolies kept on growing. From 1897 to 1901 the number of trusts increased from

458   GOVERNMENT REGULATION

63 to 246. Public demand for action against trusts seemed to die down. The country was prosperous, and in good times people are inclined to let business alone.

During the administrations of President Cleveland and President McKinley the trusts were allowed to operate as they pleased. But the government's attitude changed when another man became President.

Theodore Roosevelt fought the trusts. One summer day in 1901 news of a terrible crime shook the nation: in Buffalo, New York, as President McKinley stood shaking hands with a long line of citizens attending the Pan-American Exposition there, an insane man stepped up to him and shot him. The President lived for several days but medical science was not far enough advanced at the time to save him.

When McKinley died, Vice-President Theodore Roosevelt became President. "Teddy" Roosevelt was a man of great energy and determination. He announced that he was going to enforce the Anti-Trust law. He wisely pointed out that there were good trusts and bad trusts. The good trusts he intended to leave alone. But he warned the bad trusts to expect no mercy.

Roosevelt tried hard, but he did

"We demand that big business give people a square deal," said President Theodore Roosevelt (below). During the period he was in the White House (1901–1909) "Teddy" worked hard to enforce the Sherman Anti-Trust Act of 1890 and to break up the "bad" trusts.

Food and Drug officials try to protect American health. (Top) A chemist examines medicine. (Above) Flour is inspected.

not have much success against the trusts. He had the Attorney General start suits against several "bad" trusts, but the government lost most of the law suits. The language of the Sherman Anti-Trust Act was not very clear, so it was hard to prove a big corporation really had broken the law.

President William Howard Taft, who followed Theodore Roosevelt, continued the attack on the trusts. During his administration the government won a case against the Standard Oil Company. As a result, the "granddaddy of the trusts" was broken up into several companies. The trusts suffered a defeat but the problem of monopolies did not disappear. However, big business had to accept regulation for the public good.

The Pure Food and Drug Act protects the nation's health. Since the first anti-trust law of 1890, many laws about business have been passed. All were intended to benefit the public, but some had little effect.

One of the most famous laws to regulate business was the Pure Food and Drug Act. It was passed when Theodore Roosevelt was President. At that time, certain meat-packing companies were selling food products which were not fit to eat, and certain drug manufacturers were selling "patent medicines" as a sure cure for almost every disease. Some of the patent medicines contained dangerous drugs.

The Pure Food and Drug Act provided for inspection of all food products sold in *interstate commerce* — that is, products produced in one state and shipped to dealers and customers in other states. The officials who inspect the products try to make sure that no impure or harmful food is offered for sale. The law also provided that patent medicines and cosmetics or beauty preparations must have a printed label telling what they contain.

The Pure Food and Drug Act, which has since been enlarged and strengthened, helps protect the health of the nation. Most people agree that laws such as the Pure Food and Drug Act are necessary, but they do not agree about other government regulations.

Americans disagree about regulation of business. In almost every meeting of Congress there are debates about government regulation of business. In general, members of the Republican Party tend to be against increased government regulation, while Democrats tend to be more friendly to the idea. But the division is not clear cut. Many Democratic leaders, particularly those in the South, do not want to increase the government's power over business.

Outside of Congress — in factories, schools, clubs, and other meeting places — the argument goes on. Many Americans fear the power of big business. Others are just as afraid of the growing power of the government to regulate business. When times are bad and thousands of men and women lose their jobs, government regulation is likely to increase. People ask: "Why doesn't the government do something?"

In the 1930's the United States and the rest of the world experienced a severe depression. The Republican Party was in power when the trouble began. In the election of 1932 the Democrats won, mostly because people blamed the Republicans for the depression.

Franklin Roosevelt, who became President in 1933, urged Congress and the people to join him in a nation-wide attack on the depression. He called his program the *New Deal.* At his request, Congress passed many laws providing for severe regulation of business. Banks and stock markets had to submit to strict supervision. Under the National Recovery Administration or NRA almost every industry had to draw up and obey "codes of fair competition." The codes forbade price cutting and other practices considered unfair. After two years, however, the Supreme Court declared the NRA unconstitutional.

As the nation recovered from the depression, resistance to government regulation increased. This was probably one of the reasons for the success of the Republican candidate, Dwight D. Eisenhower, in the election of 1952. Under President Eisenhower, some government regulations have been abolished or moderated. But business leaders

contend that it is still hard to run an enterprise and obey all the laws Congress has passed to restrain business activity.

How far should the government go in regulating business? How can Congress and the President protect the welfare of the public without discouraging business enterprise? Certain laws, such as the Pure Food and Drug Act, have been fairly successful. Others, such as the NRA, have failed to help business or the public. One thing appears certain: the question of regulation of business will continue to be a big issue in America for years to come.

Federal laws helped the farmers. While business was growing bigger, American farmers were running into difficulties. As more land in the West was brought under cultivation and more farm machinery was used, production of wheat, corn, and other grains increased enormously. When the supply of a product increases, the price is likely to go down. Thus, while farmers produced bigger crops, they had to sell them for lower prices.

Imagine how a farmer felt when he had only a few dollars to show for a year's hard work! He was sure someone was to blame; he thought something should be done. Farm organizations kept up a steady demand for government action to help agriculture.

The federal government had already taken its first step to aid the farmers by helping them get land. During the Civil War the Homestead Act of 1862 was passed. It offered any citizen over 21 (or anyone over 21 who intended to become a citizen) 160 acres of western land free if he would live on the land and farm it for five years.

In the same year, 1862, Congress

They built "a little old sod shanty on a claim." The four sisters shown below claimed land in Custer County, Nebraska under the Homestead Act of 1862. There were few trees on the Great Plains so the pioneers had to build shelters of earth or "sod."

also passed the Morrill Act. This law granted huge stretches of western land to each state (except the southern states which had left the Union). The states could sell the land but the money they received had to be used to set up agricultural schools and colleges.

Thanks to the Morrill Act there are a great many agricultural or "land grant" schools. In these schools young men and women learn the most efficient methods of farming. Students are taught the latest and best ways to raise vegetables and fruits, grain, cattle, hogs, and chickens, ducks and other birds. They find out the crops that grow best on different kinds of soil. They study insect pests and how to fight them. They learn how to run farms of all kinds, large and small.

The land grant colleges also give training in veterinary medicine or the treatment of disease in animals. Many of these schools also maintain "experimental stations" where scientists study farm problems and try to develop new plants and improve crops and breeds of cattle. Schools and colleges established under the Morrill Act have greatly increased the quality and quantity of American farm production.

The Department of Agriculture carries on many activities. However, the farmers wanted quicker, more direct aid than the Morrill Act could supply. So Congress created the Department of Agriculture some

These students at a land grant college are learning how to judge poultry correctly.

years after the Civil War. The head of the Department is called Secretary of Agriculture. He is an important member of the President's Cabinet.

The Department of Agriculture carries out a big program of activities, all aimed at helping the farmer. It has grown until it is now one of the largest and busiest parts of the government. It collects information about farming all over the world. It even sends explorers to search for new food plants that American farmers might grow profitably. Alfalfa, millet, and several new varieties of wheat and fruit were brought to America because of such searching.

The Department also publishes

The world is their garden! Department of Agriculture experts (above) search the West Indies for plants that may be grown on American farms. At right, below, a scientist examines varities of wheat grown experimentally at an agricultural station.

thousands of booklets of information about specific farm problems. And farmers can get help in a hurry when an emergency arises. If a fruit farmer sends word that insects are destroying his trees, or a rancher reports that mountain lions are killing his stock, the Department of Agriculture sends trained men to help. To guard the public health it stations other trained men at every port of entry to make sure that no disease is brought in with foreign plants or animals.

Farmers depend on the Weather Bureau. Until recently the Department of Agriculture provided the nation with weather reports. In 1940 the Weather Bureau was transferred to the Department of Commerce. The Bureau performs a number of services that help Americans in all walks of life, and it is particularly important to farmers.

In country areas the weather report is vitally important. The accuracy of a forecast may mean the difference between profit and loss on the farm. A wise farmer will not plant early vegetables or shear the wool from his sheep when the Bureau predicts a cold wave. He will not cut his hay or wheat if he hears that a storm is on the way. He demands, of course, that weather forecasts be accurate. The Weather Bureau does its best.

The Bureau has observers in all parts of the country. They send to Washington daily reports on temperature, moisture in the air, clouds, winds, and barometer pressure. Thus the Bureau can warn of the approach of heat waves, blizzards, hurricanes and other storms and floods. From Alaska to the Virgin Islands, Weather Bureau experts are constantly collecting information that may affect tomorrow's weather and next season's harvest.

The AAA tried to decrease farm production. The depression of the 1930's brought many new laws to help the farmers. The government acted to help agriculture because the depression had hit the farmers earlier and harder than it hit the rest of the nation.

In the 1920's, soon after the end of the First World War, foreign markets for American wheat, corn, and cotton began to shrink. American farmers found it increasingly hard to sell their crops. Prices went down; farm income decreased swiftly and sharply. Nearly everywhere farm families felt the pinch. "Eat it up, wear it out, do without," became the rule.

In 1933, at the urging of President Franklin D. Roosevelt, Congress passed the Agricultural Adjustment Act, usually called the AAA. This law provided that the government would pay farmers to grow *less* cotton, wheat, corn, tobacco, pea-

A Weather Bureau worker (below) learns the night wind's direction and velocity by sending up a candle attached to a balloon.

nuts, and potatoes. The idea was to raise the prices of farm products by decreasing the supply.

The Supreme Court declared the first Agricultural Adjustment Act unconstitutional. Congress then passed a second Agricultural Adjustment Act that overcame the Supreme Court's objections. Under the provisions of the second AAA, the government also paid farmers for improving land and working to save soil from *erosion* or being worn away by wind and water.

World War II brought farm prosperity. Many Americans disliked the AAA intensely. They felt it was wrong to destroy food or to plant smaller crops. But the program did succeed in raising farm incomes.

During the Second World War the farm situation changed completely. At home and in foreign countries demand for food increased tremendously. American farmers were called upon to meet this demand. They bought more land, raised bigger crops, and earned large profits.

During this boom, the government continued most of its farm aid program. Then, in 1953 and 1954, demand for American farm products decreased. Farm income began to drop once more. Again farmers demanded emergency help.

Why is it that farmers always seem to be raising too much or too little? Basically, the trouble seems to be this: American farmers can raise more than people inside the United States can use. Therefore, a large part of American crops must be sold in foreign lands. However, most of the time foreigners cannot afford American farm products.

As long as the American government gives or lends huge amounts of corn, wheat, cotton, and other goods to foreign nations, American farmers are prosperous. This is what happened during World War II and for a few years afterward. However, when foreign nations stop buying or borrowing American products, prices drop. Surplus crops pile up. So far no one has found a satisfactory solution. Like the problem of regulating business, the farm problem will probably continue to challenge Americans in the years ahead.

Natural resources were used carelessly. Making farming successful and profitable is closely tied up with the problem of *conservation*, or wise use of soil and other natural resources such as water, wild life, forests, oil and minerals. Stop and think about the things you use — your food, your clothes, your house, your bicycle, your books and magazines, even the school bus you ride. Where do all these things come from? Each one was made out of materials that originally came from the soil.

All civilization rests upon the soil. And the United States more than any country in the world depends on natural resources. The steel for trucks, passenger cars, and other modern machinery comes from iron ore. Oil and gasoline, so essential to keep the machines moving, come from petroleum deposits deep in the earth. From coal mines comes fuel for heat and power. Swift flowing rivers produce electricity for many industries.

Imagine what would happen if any one of these resources became unavailable! Has the electricity ever been shut off for a few minutes or hours in your town? If it has, you know how it interfered with almost every activity.

When the supply of other resources such as wood or oil is reduced, you do not feel the effects so quickly or so severely. But the damage is great, nevertheless. That is why it is terribly important that natural resources be used wisely. Unfortunately, it is only in the last fifty years that most Americans have become aware of the need for conservation.

When the first settlers arrived, it seemed to them that America's resources were unlimited. The soil was deep and rich. Tall trees covered the land for miles and miles. It was said that a squirrel — if he were strong and determined enough — could travel through the tree tops from the Atlantic Ocean to the Mississippi River without ever touching the ground!

In the forests lived countless wild animals. Rivers and lakes were full of fish. The sky was often darkened by the flight of huge flocks of birds. Beyond the Mississippi, great herds of buffalo roamed the grassy plains.

Surrounded by so much natural wealth, you can understand how Americans grew careless. They

The map below shows the location of certain major natural resources of the United States. The national wealth includes adequate supplies of many important minerals and materials.

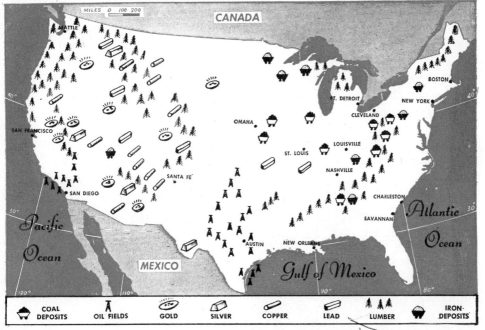

Enemies at work! These pictures show the damage that can be done to natural resources by erosion and fire. At left, once valuable farm land has been ruined by gullies and the washing away of top soil. At right, flames eat up a California forest.

needed wood to build homes and keep warm; they had to clear the land of trees in order to plant crops. So they chopped and burned down the trees as fast as they could.

As Americans moved west they plowed up the grasslands to plant wheat and corn. Wherever they lived they planted the same crop over and over: cotton or wheat or corn. After years of this, the soil wore out. It produced smaller and poorer crops. And disasters occurred: terrible floods washed away homes and good farm land; dust storms sprang up suddenly and blew away dry, loose topsoil. Thus the nation began to pay the price of unwise use of natural resources.

Waste of resources leads to disaster. To understand how careless use of a natural resource can cause loss to thousands of people, imagine that a forest fire has started in a distant corner of your state. Perhaps a careless camper neglected to stamp out a fire; or someone in a passing car tossed a lighted cigarette into dry underbrush. The fire burns slowly and quietly at first. Suddenly it shoots up into a roaring blaze. It eats away acres of grass and timber. In a few days nothing is left in the area but stumps and gray skeletons of trees. The squirrels, deer, and other animals die for lack of food and refuge.

When the rains come, there are no trees and tree roots to help soak up the water and hold it in the soil. So the water races down hills and slopes, pouring into the rivers. And rivers rise over their banks, flooding the land and causing loss of life and property. Fertile soil is washed away down the rivers. It clogs harbors and kills the fish.

After the flood, little water remains in the soil to nourish crops on nearby farms. So the stalks of corn and wheat are small and of poor quality.

468

Farmers cannot earn a living; they begin to abandon their farms and move away.

Factories also feel harmful effects from the water shortage. Lumber mills move away when the supply of timber decreases. You and your neighbors may have trouble finding clean drinking water when the rivers become filled with dirt washed down from the bare hills that once were covered with trees. Thus everybody is likely to suffer because one natural resource was wasted.

The conservation movement began. America was so big and full of riches that almost three hundred years passed before people realized the need for conservation. Toward the end of the 19th century a few observers began to warn the nation. In 1891 Congress passed laws giving the President power to create *forest reserves* or national forests where trees would be protected so the nation would not run out of wood. A little later the Department of Agriculture established the Forest Service to guard national forests against fire and disease. But most people paid little attention.

It was Theodore Roosevelt who really made the nation do something to stop waste of national resources. "Teddy" Roosevelt was a New Yorker, who had lived for several years on the frontier. He saw with his own eyes the destruction of forests and wild life through carelessness and greed. It made him angry. Afterward, when he became President, he made up his mind to do something about it.

Theodore Roosevelt was an expert in what is called "public relations." That is, he knew how to win friends for his ideas. He set the stage carefully to gain the public's attention: In May, 1907 he summoned dozens of the country's leaders to the White House. State governors, Supreme Court justices, Congressmen, writers, and scientists — all met in the White House. They talked about one topic: How to save America's dwindling store of natural wealth. Arguments sometimes got hot; the newspapers reported excitedly day by day what scientist X had called Congressman Y and what the President told the Governors. It all served to center attention on conservation.

He guards America's heritage. The forest ranger (below) watches constantly for signs of fire that might destroy timber.

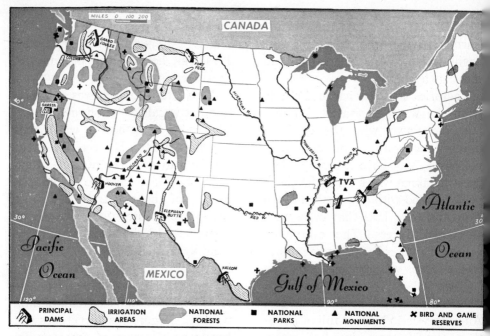

| PRINCIPAL DAMS | IRRIGATION AREAS | NATIONAL FORESTS | ■ NATIONAL PARKS | ▲ NATIONAL MONUMENTS | ✕ BIRD AND GAME RESERVES |

This map shows the location of national parks and some of the important dams the federal government has built. The national parks serve a dual purpose: they preserve natural resources and also provide a vacationland for thousands of Americans.

Conservation programs expanded widely. Theodore Roosevelt did more than talk about conservation. He added millions of acres to the national forests and also set aside lands containing mineral resources.

The presidents who followed Theodore Roosevelt continued to support conservation. Gradually the policy broadened to include protection of wild life, and wise use of land, minerals, and water power. National parks were established to preserve areas of unusual beauty for the use of the public. The map on this page shows the location of the national parks.

During the depression of the 1930's conservation efforts were greatly expanded. The Tennessee Valley Authority, generally known as the TVA, was set up to stop floods and soil erosion in the region through which the Tennessee River flows. This is a hilly area that includes parts of six states. The map on this page shows the region served by the TVA.

Thousands of unemployed young men joined the Civilian Conserva-

Below is a profile of the Tennessee River showing location of dams built by the TVA to prevent floods. Before the dams were built, floods did great damage to the area. Can you name the states where the dams are located?

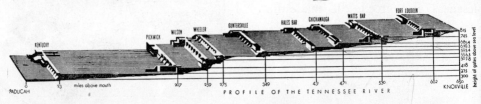

tion Corps or CCC which planted trees, dug ditches, and fought forest fires. Farmers too were encouraged to join the movement. Under the Soil Conservation Act, Congress offered to pay farmers for planting soil-building crops (such as alfalfa) and using fertilizer to restore the richness to their land.

Efforts were made to prevent *erosion* (ee RO zhun) or the wearing away of land by wind and water. Erosion has already ruined more than fifty million acres of American farm land, an area as big as Idaho. Every year erosion costs the United States almost half a billion dollars.

By careful planning and by using special methods of cultivation such as contour plowing, strip cropping, and terracing, farmers can save their land from erosion. These methods of planting are difficult and require much labor, but they bring good results.

Good citizenship includes conservation. State governments as well as the national government have adopted conservation policies. Many have created state parks where people can picnic and camp. And many citizens have formed private organizations that work to save America's natural resources. The Izaak Walton League and the Audubon Society work to protect wild life. There are also garden clubs, science clubs, nature associations and soil conservation societies.

Young people too are working actively to save natural resources.

The Boy Scouts give a merit badge in conservation. Girl Scouts and Campfire Girls include conservation in their activities. The 4-H Clubs and Future Farmers devote much attention to protection of natural resources.

Thus the conservation movement has grown into a great nationwide effort. But the job has only begun. America's natural wealth is still disappearing. Forest fires eat up millions of feet of timber each year. And priceless topsoil is still being washed and blown away. Americans agree that conservation is a good idea, but more than mere agreement is needed. Every one must work for conservation and support the program. Conservation and good citizenship go hand in hand.

These Boy Scouts (below) are learning how the annual rings on a pine stump tell the story of the tree's development.

CHAPTER SUMMARY

Western farmers demanded lower railroad rates. They formed the Grange and exerted much political influence. To regulate railroads, Congress passed the Interstate Commerce Act in 1887.

Many corporations were organized after 1865. Some big business firms gained great power and became trusts. Rockefeller organized the Standard Oil Company which controlled the petroleum industry. Congress passed the Sherman Anti-Trust Act of 1890. Theodore Roosevelt tried to break up the bad trusts.

Franklin Roosevelt's New Deal program brought increased regulation. Banks, stock markets, and other businesses were affected. The National Recovery Act, which set up codes of fair competition, was declared unconstitutional by the Supreme Court.

The federal government tried to help the farmers. The Homestead Act of 1862 made it possible for farmers to obtain free land in the West. The Department of Agriculture helps farmers develop new crops. Conservation became important. Theodore Roosevelt aroused the nation to the need to take care of natural resources.

The Language of History

Make sure you know the meaning of the following words and phrases as they are used in Chapter 22.

1. competition
2. corporation
3. dividend
4. limited liability

5. trusts
6. monopoly
7. rebate
8. pooling

9. Grange
10. interstate commerce
11. erosion
12. conservation

1492 ...?
1497 ...?
1519 ...?

What Happened When

Connect each of the following dates with an important event in American history.

1. 1862   2. 1887   3. 1890   4. 1907   5. 1933

Who's Who in History

Make sure you know the part each of the following played in the events discussed in this chapter.

1. Oliver Kelley
2. John D. Rockefeller
3. William McKinley
4. Theodore Roosevelt
5. William H. Taft
6. Franklin Roosevelt

Study Questions

1. State two advantages of the corporation.
2. a. Why were the trusts unpopular?
   b. What law forbade trusts?
3. Explain why western farmers felt that the federal government should make rules for the railroads.
4. Mention two powers of the Interstate Commerce Commission.
5. Why was Theodore Roosevelt a popular President?
6. How does the Pure Food and Drug Act help protect the health of Americans?
7. a. Name *three* laws Congress passed to help the farmers.
   b. Give the provisions of *one* of these laws.
8. How did Theodore Roosevelt awaken Americans to the need for conservation?
9. Explain how each of the following aimed at conserving natural resources: (a) the policy of creating forest reserves, (b) the TVA, (c) the Soil Conservation Act.
10. What can the average citizen do to help the cause of conservation?

Chapter 23

AMERICAN WORKERS JOINED LABOR UNIONS

Would you rather work for a small company or a big company? There are arguments for and against each choice. A big company offers greater opportunity, but there is more chance of labor trouble. Why is it that as a business gets bigger disagreements between workers and employers seem to increase?

Today's "labor problem" is a fairly recent development, but labor unions are not new in America. However, since the Civil War unions have grown larger and more powerful and are organized all over the country. Why do many workers feel they need big unions? Who were the men who organized them?

Right now you probably do not belong to a union, nor are you an employer. Perhaps you never will join a union. What has the labor problem to do with you and all the millions of Americans who are neither union members nor employers? How do strikes affect the public?

Congress has passed laws regarding hours, wages, and working conditions. Why should the government interfere in such matters?

You will find the answers to these questions in the following chapter which deals with the growth of the big labor organizations and the laws passed to regulate them.

Labor troubles grew with business activity. Almost every day you probably hear or read about disputes between workers and employers. Trouble between capital and labor — that is, between those who manage a business and those who carry out their orders and receive wages — has increased greatly in the last hundred years. It is a problem that involves a great many Americans.

When a business grows large and hundreds or even thousands of workers are hired, chances of misunderstandings seem to increase. The officials who manage a big business cannot possibly know all the men who work for them. And the workers see "the big bosses" only once in a while and then from a distance. So both management and workers may feel strange and suspicious. They do not understand one another's problems.

For example, take the case of Harry Wright who works in the paint department at Plant Number Four of a large automobile factory. He wants a raise in pay. He'd also like to have a longer lunch hour. He thinks the company should install showers so he could really clean up after work. If you point out that this would cost money, he replies, "The company's got lots of money. Why don't they let the workers get the benefit of it?"

John Watson, the general manager of Plant Number Four, is eager to "beat the production record" and turn out more automobiles. He also wants to keep expenses down. If you tell him the workers need more money, he shakes his head and says, "The company can't afford it! Taxes are terribly high. We've got to buy a lot of new machines. And our men are getting five cents an hour more than other companies in this industry pay!"

The stockholders who own the company are scattered all over the world. They pay little attention to Plant Number Four. What they want is dividends. They have invested their savings in the stock of the automobile company. Their money built Plant Number Four and created Harry Wright's job. They (or their representatives on the Board of Directors) hired John Watson to run Plant Four. If he doesn't earn profits for them some one will probably get up at the next meeting of the stockholders or the Board of Directors and demand, "Let's get a new manager — a fellow who can show results!"

Strikes are costly. In a big business, workers, management, and stockholders are likely to want different things. It is easy to see why conflicts develop. Harry Wright and his fellow workers may form a *union* and make a united demand for higher pay. That is, they get together and agree to demand a raise. They choose a spokesman to present their demands to the employers. And they try to get John Watson and other officials to sit down with their leader and talk things over. This is known as *collective bargaining*. It is really bargaining for a group because a representative of the union bargains for all the workers.

If John Watson and other officials refuse to increase wages, the union may call a *strike*, which is a united refusal to work. The union members may *picket* the plant. This means that several workers will walk back and forth in front of each entrance, carrying signs urging other workers to join the strike.

While the strike goes on, Plant Number Four does not make any automobiles. Harry Wright loses his pay. The company and the stockholders lose profits. And customers who want new cars find they have to wait several weeks and then perhaps pay a higher price. During a strike, everybody loses: workers, owners, and the public generally. Therefore it is to everyone's interest to prevent strikes.

Labor unions have a long history. When your great-grandfather was young, there was little labor trouble. Most business firms were small. The average businessman had only a few employees — five or ten at most. They usually worked together closely and understood one another's problems. Of course, relations were not always peaceful. Even in colonial days there were employers and workers who tried to take advantage of one another. And more than three hundred years ago workers in certain trades such as shoemaking began to organize unions.

The early unions were small and weak. They included only workers in one city or locality. Most workers did not feel the need for a union.

The old time blacksmith shop (below) was an example of a small business firm. The owner and his employees understood one another's problems. There was seldom any serious "labor trouble." There were no laws against hiring children, and everyone worked long hours.

At "Bell Time" these workers had to hurry to their places in a 19th century factory. Note that men and women, old and young, even children were employed. They all carried lunch pails, for factory lunchrooms were unknown. They worked from dawn to dusk.

Wages and working conditions were generally better in America than in Europe, because the country was growing fast. There were seldom enough workers to fill all the jobs.

After the American Revolution unions became more numerous. Some of them even called strikes to get higher wages or shorter hours. For a long time strikes were regarded as unlawful. But in 1842 a Massachusetts judge ruled that unions were lawful and that they could call a strike.

Some unions grew larger and took in members in many cities. Shortly before the Civil War several national trade unions were started. Printers, stone cutters, cigar makers and other skilled workers formed unions that spread over most of the country. In 1860 the shoemakers' union called a strike for higher wages. It spread all through the New England states. Twenty-thousand workers — including many women — refused to work until their demands were fully met.

Railroad workers formed strong organizations. During and after the Civil War, union membership increased rapidly. At this time railroad workers began forming unions or "brotherhoods," according to the kind of work they did. In 1863 the men who drove railroad engines formed the Brotherhood of Locomotive Engineers. It is now one of the strongest unions in America and has about 60,000 members. Like other railroad unions, the Brotherhood of Locomotive Engineers is an independent union — that is, it has no connection with other industries.

Only men who are qualified to drive a locomotive can join the Brotherhood of Locomotive Engineers. They pay dues and elect delegates to represent them at a national meeting held every three years. The delegates elect a few officers to lead the organization.

Railroaders work hard, earn good pay, and belong to unions or "brotherhoods."

These officers have power to make decisions for the Brotherhood. All members must obey the leaders their delegates have elected. The Brotherhood publishes a weekly newspaper to keep members informed about their work. There is also a pension or retirement system to provide incomes for members when they are too old to work.

From the beginning, the Brotherhood has insisted on collective bargaining. Representatives chosen by the engineers sit down with officials of the railroad companies. They discuss wages and working conditions; if they reach an understanding, a written agreement or *contract* is signed by the railroad officials and union leaders.

The Knights of Labor had a short, exciting life. The Brotherhood of Locomotive Engineers, like most of the older unions, is a *trade union* or *craft union*. In such unions only workers in a particular trade or craft can become members. But when men like Rockefeller put several small businesses together to make one big business, some labor leaders asked, "Why shouldn't the unions combine and form one big union that all workers could join? Then we'd be strong enough to fight the big companies!"

Uriah Stephens, a tailor of Philadelphia, was one of the men who asked the question. In 1869 he called a meeting at which a new labor organization was started. It was called the Knights of Labor, and it soon became big and powerful.

The Knights of Labor welcomed all workers, men and women of all races, skilled and unskilled. By 1886 the Knights of Labor had over 700,000 members. Their motto was "an injury to one is the concern of all," and they tried to defend all workers.

A younger leader named Terence Powderly took Stephen's place. Powderly was a man of high ideals and courage. He led the Knights of Labor into many fights for shorter hours and better working conditions. For a time he was quite successful. But then the tide turned; the Knights called many strikes that failed.

People began to say that the Knights had gone too far; that they were a dangerous group. Members stopped paying dues. By 1890 the organization was falling to pieces, and a little later it had disappeared.

Gompers organized the A.F. of L. in 1886. Many leaders of craft unions had been against the Knights of Labor from the beginning. They did not like the idea of one big union for skilled and unskilled workers. Some of these union leaders formed a national organization made up of many separate trade unions. Later this developed into the American Federation of Labor, generally called the A.F. of L.

The A.F. of L. was founded in 1886; its first president was Samuel Gompers. It was quite different from the Knights of Labor, which it gradually replaced as the leading labor organization in the United States. First of all, it was composed not of individual workers but of craft unions — carpenters in one, plumbers in another. Second, the A.F. of L. was more conservative than the Knights of Labor. It did not try to take a direct part in politics as the Knights tried to do.

The A.F. of L. leaders tried not to become involved in controversies. They worked quietly and steadily to get higher wages and better working conditions for the skilled workers in their unions.

The A.F. of L. has had a long, successful life. It is still a powerful, growing organization. In some of its member unions, unskilled laborers have been admitted; but the A.F. of L. is chiefly made up of workers in trades that demand the thorough

learning of some particular skill.

The organization of the A.F. of L. is very complex. Take, for example, the case of Edward Martin, a carpenter in Boston, Massachusetts. He wants to join the A.F. of L. but he cannot do so directly. First he must become a member of the Boston Carpenters' union. This

The first Labor Day parade (below) took place September 16, 1882. Samuel Gompers, founder of the A.F. of L. (bottom), helped establish the holiday.

SAMUEL GOMPERS (1850–1924)

A great part of the history of the labor movement in America is the story of one man: Samuel Gompers. From his arrival in the United States at the age of 13 until he died, he labored to improve the lot of workingmen and women.

At 14 he became a member of the Cigar-Makers Union. In time he made it one of the most successful unions in America.

Working tirelessly, Gompers, in 1881, organized 25 craft unions into the American Federation of Labor. From 1886 until his death he missed only one year as its president. The A.F. of L. grew in that time to a powerful body of over 100 unions with 8,500,000 workers.

Gompers originated and supported a number of labor laws: the eight hour day for government employees, state laws regulating work hours, the creation of Labor Day as a workingman's holiday. He was also largely responsible for the idea of a Labor Department in the government.

Gompers always thought of himself as a workingman. As he said, "The labor movement is made up of men and women of all sorts of natures and experiences. Their welfare depends on solidarity."

These shoemakers (members of the A.F. of L. Boot and Shoe Workers Union) attended a convention in 1919. Gompers (fourth from left, front row) welcomed them.

union is a member of the Boston Central Labor Union and of the Massachusetts Federation of Labor. It is also part of a national union called the United Brotherhood of Carpenters and Joiners. Does this seem too involved for you to understand? You may be sure that many union members themselves are puzzled by the complicated way the A.F. of L. is organized.

Once a year the A.F. of L. holds a convention. Edward Martin and other union carpenters are represented by delegates their national union sends to the convention. Other national unions also send delegates. The delegates elect the president and other officers of the A.F. of L. These officers in turn run the national business of the A.F. of L.

Officers are elected for only one year, but they can be reelected every year as long as the delegates want them in office. Samuel Gompers, the first president of the A.F. of L.,

was reelected every year but one from 1886 until he died in 1924.

The C.I.O. organized workers according to industries. In his long years of service to labor, Gompers won the respect of most Americans. He was called "the father of organized labor in the United States." But many people felt his policies were too limited. "What about unskilled workers in the factories?" they asked. "What does the A.F. of L. do for them?"

That was a hard question. As manufacturing increased, the number of unskilled factory workers

George Meany (below, right) succeeded William Green (left) as A.F. of L. head.

The shift changes! Workers leave as others arrive at a General Motors plant.

grew rapidly. Thousands came to America from Europe every year. Many were poor and ignorant. Clearly they needed help, but Gompers and other leaders did not feel their unions could admit them.

When Gompers died in 1924, William Green became president of the A.F. of L. He followed Gompers' policy of keeping most unskilled workers out of A.F. of L. unions. But discontent was growing. A few labor leaders decided it was time for a change. They wanted to form *industrial unions* or unions that all the workers in an industry could join regardless of the kind of work they did.

John L. Lewis, the head of the Mine Workers, was one of those who wanted to organize industrial unions. Lewis was a vice-president of the A.F. of L., but he did not agree with William Green on this issue.

Their dispute turned into a serious quarrel.

Lewis and others who favored industrial unions left the A.F. of L. in 1935. They had already formed an organization called the Committee for Industrial Organization. In 1938 it was reorganized as the Congress of Industrial Organizations. It is almost always called the C.I.O.

The C.I.O. is composed of national industrial unions. It tries to organize workers according to the industry where they are employed. For example, the United Automobile Workers, one of the unions in the C.I.O., welcomes all workers in the automobile industry regardless of the work they do.

The C.I.O. grew rapidly. Within a few years it had several million members. As you might guess, the leaders of the A.F. of L. and the leaders of the C.I.O. did not get along too well together. There were many disputes. Each organization claimed the other was trying to "steal" its members. The American labor movement has been weakened by such quarrels. There have been attempts to heal the split, but so far none has succeeded. However, there are signs that the two organizations are learning to work together more smoothly.

The Wagner Act guaranteed collective bargaining. The dispute between the A.F. of L. and the C.I.O. created new troubles for the federal government. When some workers in a factory or store wanted to join an A.F. of L. union and others wanted to join the C.I.O., the government tried to settle the question. More and more frequently the President and other officials had to try to settle disputes between unions and employers.

Why should the government get involved in labor troubles? The answer seemed to be that somebody had to try to prevent strikes. The world today is so closely tied together that a big strike hurts almost everybody. And when violence breaks out during a strike, as it often does, innocent people may get hurt. The government must interfere to keep order and protect the public. Therefore, in recent years, Congress has passed many laws that relate to workers and their problems.

The depression of the 1930's caused suffering and unemployment among wage earners. President Franklin D. Roosevelt approved in general of the aims of labor unions. In 1935 he persuaded Congress to pass the National Labor Relations Act which protected the right of workers to organize or join unions. The law is often called the Wagner Act in honor of Senator Wagner of New York who introduced it.

The Wagner Act guaranteed workers the right of collective bargaining. You will notice that the emphasis was on the rights of *workers*. For this reason it seemed to many people a one-sided law. Employers complained that, under the Wagner Act, labor had all the rights and the boss had all the duties.

The Taft-Hartley Act amended the Wagner Act. Many people felt that labor leaders took advantage of the

Workers and bosses talk it over. Below is shown a labor-management conference at Standard Oil Company's Bayonne, New Jersey refinery. Such meetings may prevent strikes.

law and recklessly called strikes the nation could not afford. After a long period of argument, Congress in 1947 passed the Labor-Management Relations Act. It is generally known as the Taft-Hartley Act in honor of Senator Robert Taft of Ohio and Representative William Hartley of New Jersey who introduced it.

The Taft-Hartley Act made several changes in the Wagner Act. In general, it was less favorable to labor unions. It required union leaders to publish financial reports showing how much money the unions collected and how the money was spent. It forbade certain types of strikes. In cases where a strike might endanger the nation's health or safety the President could order labor unions to postpone the strike for 80 days. It was hoped that during the "cooling off" period the employer and the union would find a way to settle their dispute.

Labor leaders disliked the Taft-Hartley Act. They worked hard to get it repealed or withdrawn, but Congress refused. There are many different opinions about the Taft-Hartley Act. It has not stopped strikes, but the number of strikes has declined. It has not ended labor trouble, but labor leaders and employers seem more willing than before to discuss their problems and try to reach a compromise.

The Social Security Act was passed in 1935. The Wagner Act and the Taft-Hartley Act aroused furious arguments for and against government interference in labor affairs. But there was not much criticism of another law Congress passed for the benefit of working men and women. This was the Social Security Act of 1935. It tried to protect workers against the danger of poverty in old age or periods of unemployment.

Years ago, when most people lived on farms or in small towns, they did not worry much about old age or unemployment. They could raise enough food for their families. They usually owned their homes or paid low rent, so they felt reasonably sure of a place to live.

The situation changed completely when a worker moved to the city and took a job in a factory. Now he had no land for a garden. He and his family probably lived in an apartment for which he paid high rent. If he lost his job, he might soon be without a penny for food or rent. And when he became too old to work his children had to support him or he had to go to the poorhouse.

To protect workers against such dangers the Social Security Act contained three provisions: (1) it set up old age pensions or retirement allowances; (2) it established a system of unemployment insurance; (3) it set up a program of aid for such groups as the blind.

Many groups receive benefits. The old age pension plan works as follows: a small percentage of a worker's pay is *deducted* or subtracted before he receives it. His employer also has to pay the government a small percentage or "payroll tax." Contributions of the worker and the employer go to build up a pension fund which the federal government supervises. When a worker reaches 65 he can stop work and begin receiving a retirement allowance from the pension fund.

The system of *unemployment insurance* works a little differently. The worker does not have to contribute, but his employer has to pay a tax to support an unemployment insurance fund. If the worker loses his job he receives a weekly allowance from the fund for several months while he looks for work. Unemployment insurance is a fed-eral-state project. The states play an important part in this part of the program. The federal government collects money from employers and then turns part of it over to each state which has set up a system of unemployment insurance. The states use the money to make payments to people who are out of work. Each state's system is different, so the amount an unemployed worker receives and the length of time he may receive it varies from state to state.

The Social Security Act also arranges for payment to crippled children, needy blind persons, and widowed mothers of small children. Thus the law provides help for many people in time of need. It is a law that affects almost everyone.

How the Social Security System Functions

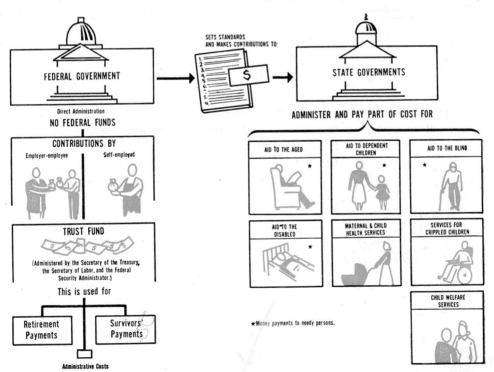

This chart shows some of the activities of the Social Security System. Not shown is the unemployment insurance part of the program that is run by the states.

CHAPTER SUMMARY

Labor troubles increased as business grew bigger. Many labor unions existed before the Civil War. Railroad workers formed organizations called Brotherhoods. The Knights of Labor was organized in 1869. It welcomed all workers into one big union. The organization only lasted a few years.

Samuel Gompers organized the American Federation of Labor. It is made up of skilled workers organized in local trade unions. A group of unions from the A.F. of L. formed the Congress of Industrial Organizations. It is made up of skilled and unskilled workers organized according to industries.

The National Labor Relations Act gave workers many rights. Often called the Wagner Act, it guaranteed collective bargaining for workers. It was amended by the Taft-Hartley Act which was less favorable to labor unions. Labor leaders disliked it very much.

The Social Security Act was passed. It provided for old age pensions and retirement allowances; a system of unemployment insurance; and a program of special benefits for handicapped groups such as the blind and crippled.

The Language of History

Be sure you know the meaning of each of the following words and phrases as they are used in this chapter.

1. union
2. strike
3. picket
4. collective bargaining
5. railroad brotherhoods
6. trade or craft union
7. industrial union
8. Taft-Hartley Act
9. contract

What Happened When

Connect each of the following dates with an important event in American history.

1. 1886   2. 1935   3. 1938   4. 1947

Who's Who in History

Identify each of the following and explain the part he played in the American labor movement.

1. Uriah Stephens
2. Samuel Gompers
3. John L. Lewis
4. Robert F. Wagner
5. William Green
6. Robert Taft

Study Questions

1. Explain what is meant by "disputes between capital and labor."

2. Why is labor trouble more likely to develop in a large corporation than in a small business?

3. "During a strike everybody loses." Do you agree or disagree with this statement? Give reasons for your answer.

4. Why did the Knights of Labor fail?

5. Write a paragraph about the A.F. of L. telling (a) when it was founded, (b) how it is organized, and (c) the names of two presidents of the A.F. of L.

6. State two differences between the A.F. of L. and the C.I.O.

7. a. What did the Wagner Act provide?
   b. Why did many people criticize the Wagner Act?

8. a. Give two provisions of the Taft-Hartley Act.
   b. How do labor leaders feel about the Taft-Hartley Act?

9. How does the Social Security Act help the unemployed?

10. Explain how the Social Security Act helps protect workers against extreme poverty when they grow too old to work.

Chapter 24

THE GROWTH OF CITIES
CHANGED AMERICAN
WAYS OF LIFE

"RED tongues of flame began to shoot upward. . . . The fire was moving north like ocean surf on a sand beach. Billows of fire were rolling over the business places of the city and swallowing their contents. Men and women were hurrying from the burning quarter, some with bundles of clothes, others dragging trunks along the sidewalks, children trudging by their sides or borne in their arms."

Thus an eye-witness described the great fire which destroyed Chicago in 1871. How was it possible for a fire to do so much damage? Other cities, too, suffered from terrible fires. What conditions created fire hazards?

Other threats hung over American cities in the 19th century. Disease killed thousands almost every year. Crimes of all kinds increased. What efforts were made to correct such conditions?

In spite of all dangers people kept moving to the cities. What attracted them? Many of the newcomers were immigrants. Why did native born Americans demand that immigration be restricted? What action did Congress take? What contributions have immigrants made to American life? You will find the answers in this chapter which discusses the rapid growth of American cities and the problems that resulted.

Americans moved to cities. If Benjamin Franklin had come back to life sixty years after his death he would have felt at home in the America of 1850. He would have noticed changes, of course, but he would have been pleased at the way the nation had grown and spread westward. He would probably nod his head and say, "Yes, things are going very well. These people know how to work and they are making a success of life!"

Franklin would have understood the way people lived in 1850, for it was not greatly different from the way they lived in 1790. Except in the Northeast where factories were becoming numerous, most Americans lived and worked on farms. There were some factories but they were mostly small scale enterprises. Life in America was comparatively quiet and slow-moving.

But imagine how Franklin would feel if he came back to America today. He would probably be confused and frightened if he found himself in one of the cities where most Americans now live and work. "Why, what's going on?" he would demand shakily. "Where did all these people come from? And what are all these dreadful swift monsters flying by? Automobiles you say? I never heard of them! It's so terribly noisy I can't think. This is America you say? I don't believe it! My America was a green and pleasant place, peaceful and quiet."

In earlier times nearly every American earned his living by farming. Today, scarcely 16 out of 100 are farmers; the others work in factories, stores, or offices. This change came about in a rather brief period — from about 1870 to 1930.

One reason for the change from country life to city life was the fact that most towns were located in

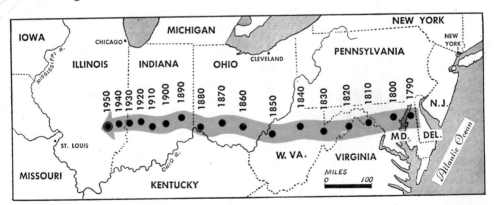

This map shows the westward movement of the *center of population.* This is the point through which a straight line drawn in any direction from boundary to boundary would leave approximately equal numbers of people on each side. Each census since 1790 has shown the center of population moving westward. Where do you think it will be located in 1960?

places which offered good transportation by land or water. When a man planned a new factory he usually arranged to build it where he could get raw material (cotton or wool, for example) and send his product (cloth) to market as quickly and cheaply as possible. So he came to the town. Soon afterward, men and women came from the farms and from foreign lands to get jobs in the new factory.

Another reason why people moved to town was because the farm offered only one way of earning a living, while the town offered many different ways. As towns grew, they needed more storekeepers, builders, clerks, mechanics, bankers, doctors, teachers, and lawyers. In town a person could choose his way of earning a living.

Also, towns and cities offered greater opportunity for fun and for education. Theaters, museums, fashionable stores, schools and universities — all these attracted people to the city.

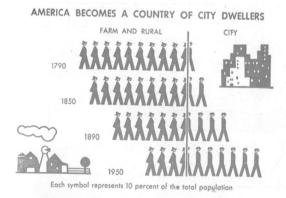

AMERICA BECOMES A COUNTRY OF CITY DWELLERS

FARM AND RURAL   CITY

1790

1850

1890

1950

Each symbol represents 10 percent of the total population

This chart illustrates the movement of people from farms to cities. The rapid change created many difficult problems.

Detroit became the motor city. Detroit provides a good example of how little towns grew into industrial cities. A French explorer, Antoine de la Mothe Cadillac (KAD ih lak), built a fort at Detroit in 1701. (Detroit is a French word meaning narrow strait or passageway connecting two large bodies of water. As you can see on the map on page 493, the name is appropriate; Detroit stands on the shore of the little river that connects Lake Erie and Lake St. Clair.)

Cadillac hoped his fort would become a center of the fur trade with the Indians. He also hoped it would strengthen France's hold on the Great Lakes region, but this was not to be.

Detroit saw plenty of fighting in the early days. The British took it from France during the French and Indian War. A little later, Chief Pontiac besieged the fort throughout the summer of 1763. Long after the Revolution the British gave up Detroit to the Americans; then they took it back early in the War of 1812. General William Henry Harrison recaptured it for the Americans in 1813. After that the war drums were silent and Detroiters turned their attention to peaceful pursuits.

The little settlement grew into a busy trading center. Notice on the map on page 493 how conveniently Detroit is located for trade with the East and the West, as well as with Canada. From Detroit it is easy

British - France
France - Pontiac
British - American
America - British
America

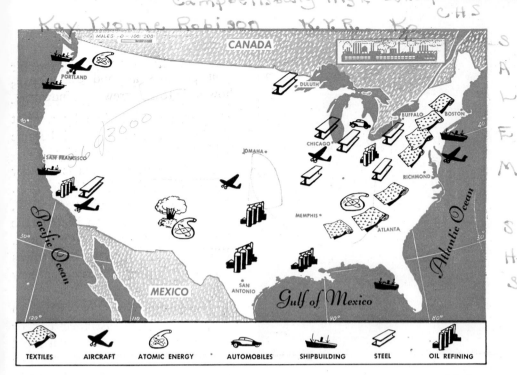

This map shows location of some of the leading industries. What factors encouraged industrialization in the Northeast? What discouraged it in the Rocky Mountain area?

and cheap to ship goods up and down the Great Lakes. So Detroit increased in size and importance.

But not until the coming of the automobile did Detroit really shoot ahead. In 1880 it had 116,340 people — about as many as Canton, Ohio or South Bend, Indiana has today. Then came Henry Ford! He was the man who made Detroit world famous.

When Ford started to build autos in Detroit, he found the place well suited to his purposes. He could get raw materials from nearby mines and factories. He could ship cars to distant customers by way of the Detroit River and the Great Lakes.

Many other auto makers followed Ford's lead. One company after

another — Packard, Cadillac, Chrysler, Hudson — built factories near his. From all over America, especially from farms in the South and Middle West, men and women hurried to Detroit.

"Have you heard? Henry Ford's paying men eight dollars a day!" someone would report excitedly to the crowd in a country store. "Yes, and it's not hard work," another man would add. "You just do one job and you learn how in a couple of days. My sister's boy is working there. He's bought his own car already!"

The story of Detroit's opportunities spread even to foreign lands and brought thousands of immigrants to the "Motor City." Detroit became

STORY OF DETROIT

491

These cars are nearing the end of the assembly line at Ford's Dearborn factory.

the automobile capital of the world. Today more than half of America's cars and trucks are built in Detroit.

For a long time the auto makers bought all their steel from Pittsburgh. But Detroit now has some steel mills of its own. Detroit makes many other products for America and the world: chemicals, stoves, medicines, paint, aluminum and brass products, to mention only a few.

Thus the little fort on the Detroit River grew into a great city. By 1930 more than one and one-half million people lived in Detroit. Today the number is approaching two million and Detroit is the fifth largest city in the United States.

Cities sprang up all over America. A similar story of rapid growth could

be told of other cities. Chicago, for example, was wiped out by Indians in 1813, and almost completely destroyed a second time by a great fire in 1871. Nevertheless it became America's second largest city.

Birmingham, Alabama is another example. It was founded in 1871. Only an overgrown village in 1900, it has surged ahead to become the iron and steel center of the South. In almost every state there are towns that grew to big cities when new industries moved in.

Everywhere Americans liked to boast about how fast their city or state was growing. But such rapid growth had its disadvantages. For one thing, it created a housing problem. Where were all the people who moved into a city going to live?

Many people crowded into existing buildings. Homes built for one family were made into apartments or rooming houses. Factory owners and private builders hurriedly put up cheap structures called *tenements* where dozens of families found shelter.

The danger of fire and disease increased under such conditions. In

A terrible fire swept Chicago in 1871. The young city consisted mainly of flimsy wooden buildings that burned quickly.

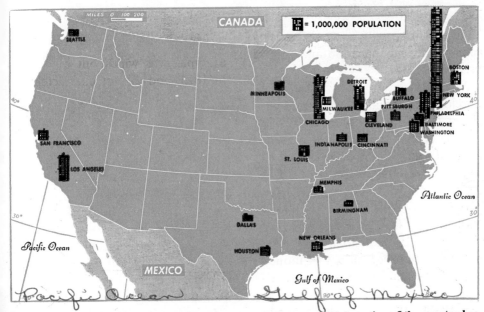

This map shows some of the large cities of the United States. Which section of the country has the largest number of big cities? Which section has the fewest cities? What are the reasons for this? How many cities have over one million people?

many cities the water supply was not sufficient. People in the tenements did not get much sun or air; many became ill. Children did not want to stay in dark, crowded rooms so they roamed the streets and often got involved in crimes.

A housing problem developed. Sections of the city where poor people lived in crowded tenements came to be called "the slums." Almost every city has slums where families of five or six people live in only one or two rooms. The death rate is high. Many babies die before they reach school age. Until recently there were no playgrounds near the slums. The only place children could play was the narrow, dirty street.

Why would people live in such places? The reason usually was that they could not help themselves. Many newcomers to America could not speak English and did not know their way around. Confused and frightened, they huddled together in tenements near the factory where they worked. They did not have enough money to pay high rents for a decent place to live.

Slums are a danger to everyone, even those who live several miles away. Disease germs breed rapidly in the dark, dirty rooms. And people who get little sun or good air have less resistance to disease. They become ill. Often their diseases spread to people in other parts of the city. And sometimes from the dark slums come gangs of criminals who rob and kill honest citizens.

Thus slums really cost everyone money and endanger life and property.

Why do cities allow slums to develop and remain? Why not get rid of them once and for all? The answer is that the problem is complicated and cannot be solved over night. Before slums are torn down other homes must be found for the people who live there. And the owners must be paid a fair price for their property. All this takes time and huge sums of money — money that must come from tax-payers.

In the face of such obstacles it is remarkable that cities have made progress in getting rid of slums. But thanks to the efforts of many sincere men and women, the drive to provide decent housing for poor families has succeeded in getting rid of some of the worst slums.

Riis told "how the other half lives." A young newspaperman was one of the first to make Americans aware of conditions in the slums. He was Jacob Riis (REES) who came to New York from Denmark when he was 21. Riis had hardly any money so he had to exist in a dirty tenement.

For several years Riis worked as a laborer. He saved his money and studied in his spare time. Seven years after he landed in America, Riis became a reporter on a leading New York newspaper. Though he moved to a better part of the city, he never forgot the slums. He wrote articles and books that aroused many readers and made them want to improve their city. Theodore Roosevelt read Riis's first book, *How the Other Half Lives.* Roosevelt became his friend and fellow worker in the fight for better housing.

In one report Riis told of "five or six little people huddled in one bed" as if they were wild animals in a den. In another, he reported "a whole family, parents and children, lying lengthwise or crosswise in the same bed — all but one boy for whom there was no room. He slept on a pile of rags, wearing all his clothes to keep warm."

Work for better housing brought results. Another pioneer in efforts to improve slum conditions was Jane Addams. The daughter of a pros-

Below are two views of the slums in the late 19th century. At left is a picture Jacob Riis took of a necktie factory in New York City in 1889. At right is a street scene in a crowded area. Modern laws and housing projects have done much to correct such conditions.

perous doctor, she chose to spend her life helping the poor. In the heart of Chicago's slums, she found an old run-down mansion known as Hull House. She turned it into a social center for the neighborhood.

Jane Addams organized classes in music and art for youngsters. She taught their mothers how to cook and budget the family income. She started classes where their fathers learned to speak English. A day nursery was set up to care for children whose mothers had to work.

Hull House became a meeting place for dozens of clubs for young workers. Men and women who lost their jobs came there and Jane Addams helped them find new opportunities. Always her aim was "to help the people help themselves." She showed them ways to improve their homes, develop their abilities, and thus live richer, happier lives. Hull House became a model for similar centers or "social settlement houses" in other cities.

Individuals like Jacob Riis and Jane Addams gradually convinced the nation that "the slums must go!" "Housing projects" were built where low income families could enjoy clean, attractive apartments for moderate rents. Sometimes the city government built the project. Sometimes the state supplied the money. Certain wealthy individuals made large contributions.

During the depression of the 1930's, the federal government became active in the movement to provide low cost housing. Congress gave millions to help cities build housing projects. Then private business firms, such as the big insurance companies, found it was a good investment to build apartments for families with moderate incomes.

As a result of these efforts, slums are everywhere on the decline. Today, thousands of city families enjoy clean, roomy apartments in modern housing projects. Still, the fight against slums is not over. In 1954 it was estimated that in New York City one person in five still lived in a slum.

Every big city still has tenements and tumble-down houses. Whenever a new industry or a war-time "boom" brings many newcomers, houses and apartments may be overcrowded and

Plenty of fresh air and play space! Compare this modern housing project with the slum conditions pictured on the opposite page. Improving housing conditions is difficult and expensive, but progress is being made in getting rid of slums.

From the Old World to the New. Emigrants are shown boarding a New York bound ship in Hamburg, Germany many years ago.

the housing problem becomes acute once more. But Americans have learned slums do not pay and they have made up their minds to get rid of them.

Immigrants settled in cities. Many, though by no means all, of the people who settled in the slums were newcomers to America. After 1865, factories and mines needed an ever-increasing number of workers. From faraway lands came masses of eager *immigrants* or people who moved to America from foreign lands. They were attracted by stories of good jobs and high wages.

Many of the "greenhorns," as the new immigrants were called, had a hard time learning American ways.

But most of them soon became hard-working citizens. They wanted more than anything else to belong, to become part of America, the land of their dreams. But it was not easy. They did not understand American methods and traditions. Some had a hard time learning English. And they often were cheated and exploited when they first arrived.

Immigrants who came to America before 1890 had an easier time than those who have come in more recent years. Earlier immigrants usually went to work on farms. Most of them saved enough to buy a farm, or they obtained some free land under the Homestead Act.

Before 1890 most immigrants came from the British Isles and western

CHANGES IN AMERICA

Europe. The potato famine of the 1840's caused thousands of Irish to come to the United States. And the failure of the Revolution of 1848 made many freedom-loving Germans flee their "Fatherland" for America. A little later, bad times and business failures in Scandinavia encouraged many Swedes and Norwegians to seek a new start in America. All these groups adjusted to American life without great difficulty.

"New" immigrants met new problems. The story was different for workers from southern and eastern Europe who came after 1890. These groups — the Italians, Poles, and various Slavic nationalities — made up what was called the "New Immigration." (Those who came from northern and western Europe before 1890 made up the "Old Immigration.")

When the "new" immigrants arrived, after 1890, almost all the good land had been claimed. Because of the new machines, farm workers were not needed. So Italians, Poles, and Slavic groups had to find jobs in factories or mines. Because most of the new immigrants had had little chance to attend school in their old homes, they found it hard to learn to read and write English.

Many citizens feared that the new "wave" of immigrants was a danger to American democracy. They said the newcomers lacked knowledge and experience to vote intelligently. American workers complained that foreigners took their jobs and pulled down the scale of wages because they would work for low pay. Labor leaders asked the government to reduce the number of immigrants coming into the country.

Congress began to restrict immigration. Ever since colonial days there had existed a certain amount of distrust of immigrants. Why, you may ask, should any American feel prejudice against immigrants? After all, the United States is a nation of immigrants. All Americans, even the Indians, are either immigrants or descendants of immigrants.

Nevertheless, many people born in America tended to be critical of newcomers. One reason was the fact that a number of criminals and half-witted people had been coming to America. This situation caused Congress in 1882 to pass a law that forbade idiots, beggars, and criminals to enter the United States. However, the total number of immigrants who came to America con-

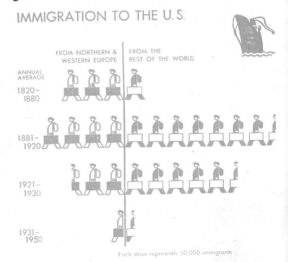

IMMIGRATION TO THE U.S.

FROM NORTHERN & WESTERN EUROPE | FROM THE REST OF THE WORLD

ANNUAL AVERAGE
1820–1880

1881–1920

1921–1930

1931–1950

Each man represents 50,000 immigrants

Until 1890, most immigrants to America came from northern and western Europe.

Changes In America

tinued to increase each year until World War I.

In the early 1880's, the public became excited about the immigration of Chinese workers or "coolies." Contractors had brought in thousands of Chinese to work on western railroads. The Chinese accepted low wages and lived in a way that cost very little. For this reason, other workers feared and hated them. There were riots and killings. Public opinion forced Congress to pass a law in 1882 that forbade immigration of Chinese laborers.

Thus began a long series of laws to regulate immigration. In 1917 a new law required foreigners to pass a *literacy* (LIT er ah see) *test* to prove they could read and write.

The flood of immigrants was reduced to a trickle. After the First World War conditions in Europe were very bad and the number of foreigners who wished to come to America was enormous. But the United States could not provide jobs and homes for so many newcomers.

Therefore, Congress passed stricter laws to keep out immigrants. A *quota* (KWOH tah) system was adopted in 1924. This limited the number of immigrants admitted each year from any country to two percent of the number of immigrants from that country who were living in the United States in 1890. The percentage was called a *quota*.

Here is an example: About 2,500,000 German immigrants were living in the United States in 1890. Two percent of 2,500,000 is 50,000. Therefore the number of Germans who would be admitted under the quota law was 50,000 a year.

During the 1930's, immigration laws were made even more severe. Millions of Americans were out of work, and the government was determined not to add to the unemployment problem by admitting new job seekers. During this period the number of foreigners in the United States actually declined. This was because many immigrants who lost their jobs decided to return to their homelands.

After World War II, a new problem arose. Thousands of Europeans had lost their homes during the war. Many had to flee from their own countries because of German or Russian persecution. They were called "displaced persons" or DP's. Most of them wanted to come to the United States. Congress passed a special act to admit several thousand displaced persons in addition to the yearly quota.

In 1952, Congress passed a new immigration law, known as the *McCarran-Walter Act*. It kept many of the provisions of the 1924 law, including the quota system. Under the new law, no more than 154,657 immigrants could be admitted to the United States in one year.

Immigrants enriched American life. It is important to remember that to a great extent it was immigrants who built modern America. An amazing number of the bewildered "greenhorns" who landed in the United States without money or friends later became outstanding citizens. If you examine a list of leading Americans in any field — science, painting, music, business — you will find several immigrants among them.

Earlier you have read about several immigrants who made important contributions to American life: Andrew Carnegie, Alexander Graham Bell, John Ericsson, Samuel Gompers. Other, more recent immigrants who have enriched America include: Enrico Fermi (en REE koh FARE mih), a scientist born in Italy, whose research aided greatly in the development of atomic power; Michael Pupin (poo PEEN), a one-time shepherd boy in Hungary, whose inventions improved communication by telephone and radio; Irving Berlin, who came from Russia at the age of four and wrote songs that all America sings; Leopold Stokowski (stoh KOW skih), who was born in London of Polish and Irish parentage and who became conductor of the Philadelphia Orchestra; William Knudsen (NOOD sun) of Denmark, who became President of General Motors, and who served as a high government official during World War II, directing production of war materials.

What names can you add to the list of foreign-born citizens who have become famous? If you read the newspapers carefully, almost every

Here are two immigrants who made important contributions to America: (top) Leopold Stokowski, and Samuel Gompers (below).

day you will learn of men and women who came to America a few years ago and who are now helping build a stronger, richer nation.

Education for all became an American ideal. Closely connected with the problem of immigration was the growth of education in the United States. Immigrants and their children needed instruction in American traditions and methods of government. In recent years training for citizenship has become one of the chief aims of American education.

Even in colonial times people were concerned about education. Massachusetts Bay Colony required every settlement of fifty families to provide

Horace Mann, "the father of the public schools," worked for better education for everybody.

an elementary school. The schools of New England early became famous for their high standards.

Outside New England, communities established free schools more slowly. For a long time it was felt that parents should pay for their children's schooling. Many people believed it was not right to tax one man for the education of another man's children.

However, most Americans gradually came to believe that free public education benefited all people whether they had children or not. Today, the public school system is based on the idea that in a democracy children must be educated, not only for their own good, but to safeguard freedom. The democratic form of government depends on intelligent, well-informed citizens.

How and why did Americans become so convinced of the value of education? It did not happen by accident. Many men and women worked hard to win public approval for more and better schools.

Horace Mann was the "father of the public schools." One of the first and greatest leaders in the fight for free schools was Horace Mann who was born in Massachusetts in 1796. From harsh experience he knew how difficult it was for a poor person to get an education, no matter how bright and ambitious he or she might be.

As a boy, Horace Mann longed to attend one of the private schools, then called academies, where students prepared for college. This seemed an impossible dream, for his parents were terribly poor. Horace was needed at home to work on the farm.

Until he was 15, Horace Mann attended school for only eight or ten weeks a year. Eager for knowledge, he begged the minister of the village church to lend him books. The minister showed him how to study and make the most of what he read.

Sometimes, by working extra hard and going without enough food, Horace saved enough to attend a private school for a few weeks. But he was over twenty years old when he was able to enter college.

Later Mann became a successful lawyer and was elected to the Massachusetts legislature. At last he had a chance to do something for education! He persuaded the legislature to establish a State Board of Education — the first of its kind. The Board had power to make rules and set up standards for public schools in the state. It could compel every town to improve its schools.

Horace Mann knew the law would not enforce itself. Someone must see to it that the new Board really did what was expected. So in 1837 he gave up his profitable law practice to serve as secretary of the new State Board of Education at a very small salary. He realized that the success of any school depends on the teachers, so one of the first things he did was to set up a school for training teachers at Lexington, Massachusetts. It was the first "normal school" or teacher training institution in America.

Under Mann's direction, Massachusetts schools became the model for all the states. Every state — and most towns and cities within each state — set up a Board of Education.

Other leaders advanced the cause of education. In Connecticut, a man named Henry Barnard accomplished many of the improvements in education Mann had suggested. Barnard believed the national government, too, should take an interest in education. Largely through his efforts, Congress set up an agency to collect information about education

"Readin', writin', and 'rithmetic" were taught in this Pennsylvania school in 1835.

throughout the country. This became the United States Office of Education.

In New York State, Governor DeWitt Clinton worked to improve and extend the state's system of public schools. (He was the same DeWitt Clinton who persuaded New York State to build the Erie Canal, as you read on page 310.) There were also many women who worked tirelessly to win public support for education. One of the most famous was Mary Lyon, founder of Mt. Holyoke College.

Like Horace Mann, Mary Lyon was born on a Massachusetts farm toward the end of the 18th century. In those days most parents did not feel it was necessary to educate their daughters. Mary Lyon was taught to spin and weave; she became such an expert she was able to support herself by working at her loom. But she longed more than anything else

to go to school and become educated.

For years Mary Lyon saved every penny she could, but she was twenty years old before she had enough money to attend an academy. She learned so much faster than the other pupils that she was asked to become an assistant teacher. Mary Lyon loved teaching; she was able to inspire her students with her enthusiasm for learning. She became famous and successful, but she was not satisfied. She wanted to start her own school — a school for girls.

Mary Lyon was a good businesswoman as well as a fine teacher. She persuaded several individuals to give money and land. In 1837 the new school opened in South Hadley, Massachusetts. It was called Mt. Holyoke Female Seminary. As its principal, Mary Lyon received a salary of $200 a year or about $4 a week. She never got rich, but she helped greatly to advance education in the United States.

Educational opportunities have increased greatly. Thanks to the efforts of Horace Mann, Henry Barnard, Mary Lyon and others, schools and colleges were built in all parts of the country. Today, American education is "big business." In 1951 almost 23 million students attended public schools; nearly one million teachers taught in these schools.

Horace Mann and Mary Lyon would be amazed at the new developments in education. They never

Mary Lyon believed in education for women. She founded Mount Holyoke Seminary.

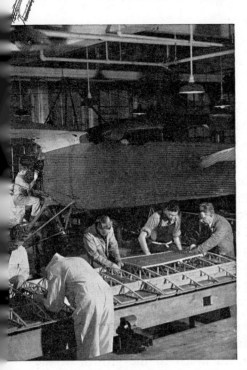

These boys in a Brooklyn technical school are learning to become highly paid aviation workers. Vocational training is part of modern American education. Most cities now have several schools where boys and girls can learn various trades.

heard of junior high schools, centralized schools, or vocational schools, which now occupy a very important place in American education.

Modern life is so full of problems and changes that individuals need advanced training to succeed. A hundred years ago, when most Americans were farmers, a man or woman who could not read or write could earn a good living and be considered fairly successful. Today, a person who has not graduated from high school is considered practically uneducated. He is at a worse disadvantage than was his great-grandfather who could not read or write.

Since World War II, the number of students in schools and colleges has increased enormously. This is partly because the population has grown, but it also reflects the average American's interest in education. Under the "G.I. Bill," veterans of World War II were able to attend college free. Thousands took advantage of this opportunity.

Not only young people enrolled in schools and colleges. The "adult education movement" is growing as fast or faster than other branches of American education. Thousands of workers attend evening or Saturday classes to gain new skills or become better informed. Eagerness to keep on learning, and willingness to make sacrifices to gain an education have become part of American tradition.

CHAPTER SUMMARY

Cities grew rapidly after the Civil War. Factories were built in or near cities. People came from farms and from foreign lands to work in the cities. Housing shortages appeared. Slums developed in all the larger cities. Reformers made great efforts to abolish slums.

Immigrants created a problem. After 1890 most of the free land was gone, so immigrants stayed in the cities. Before 1890 most immigrants came from northern and western Europe. The "new immigration" after 1890 was mostly from southern and eastern Europe.

Congress restricted immigration. By a series of laws the number of immigrants admitted to the United States was greatly reduced. The quota system was established. The McCarran-Walter Act of 1952 regulates immigration very strictly.

The number of public schools increased. Horace Mann was called the "Father of the public schools" because of his work to improve education. Henry Barnard also contributed much to the growth of the public schools. Mary Lyon founded Mt. Holyoke Seminary to give girls also a chance to obtain higher education. Many new types of schools have appeared in recent years. School enrollments have increased greatly. The Adult Education movement has made great progress.

The Language of History

Be sure you know the meaning of each of the following words and phrases as they are used in Chapter 24.

1. tenement 3. new immigration 5. displaced persons
2. slums 4. literacy test 6. quota

What Happened When

Connect each of the following dates with an important event in American history.

1. 1701   **2.** 1890   **3.** 1924   **4.** 1952

Who's Who in History

Identify each of the following and explain the part he or she played in American history.

1. Jane Addams
2. Jacob Riis
3. Irving Berlin
4. Horace Mann
5. Mary Lyon
6. Henry Barnard

Study Questions

1. Give two reasons why cities increased rapidly in population after 1870.

2. Why did the rapid growth of cities create a housing problem?

3. Why has Congress passed many laws to limit immigration?

4. Make a list of five famous immigrants and tell what each contributed to the development of America.

5. Horace Mann has been called "the Father of the American public school system." Do you think he deserves the title? Give reasons for your answer.

6. Explain why conditions in modern America encourage a great many people to keep on studying.

7. Outline the history of Detroit telling (a) when and by whom it was founded, (b) the geographic advantages which encouraged the early development of trade, and (c) why it became "the Motor City."

8. Explain how bad housing encouraged the increase of crime.

9. Why did the immigrants who came after 1890 find it harder to succeed in America than those who came earlier?

10. After World War II many schools and colleges became overcrowded. What caused this condition?

LET'S LOOK AT WHAT WE'VE LEARNED

Why did the corporation form of business organization become popular?

It has many advantages. It can obtain huge sums of capital by selling stock. It does not end when one of its leaders dies. Liability is limited.

Why did the national government begin to regulate railroads?

Western farmers demanded regulation of railroads. Congress passed the Interstate Commerce Act of 1890, setting up the Interstate Commerce Commission to regulate railroad rates and business methods.

Why was the Sherman Anti-Trust Act passed?

The public disliked the trusts and demanded that they be regulated. In 1890 Congress passed the Sherman Act, prohibiting restraint of trade. The law proved hard to enforce.

Other laws were passed to regulate business. The Pure Food and Drug Act protects the public health and welfare. During the depression of the 1930's many other laws were passed to regulate banks and the Stock Market. Today, thousands of local, state, and federal laws regulate business.

How has the government tried to help the farmer?

Congress passed the Homestead Act of 1862 and the Morrill Act. It set up the Department of Agriculture. During the depression of the 1930's Congress passed two Agricultural Adjustment Acts which aimed to decrease production of surplus crops and raise farm income.

Why is conservation so important?

In colonial times and until the end of the 19th century Americans wasted natural resources. President Theodore Roosevelt drew attention to the need for conservation. Today there are many programs to save resources.

What are the most important national labor organizations?

The first big national labor organization was the Knights of Labor which did not last. It was succeeded by the American Federation of Labor which is made up of local trade unions. The Congress of Industrial Organizations organized skilled and unskilled workers into industrial unions.

How has the government regulated labor?

The Wagner Act of 1935 guaranteed collective bargaining. The Taft-Hartley Act of 1947 made important changes. The Social Security Act of 1935 provided many benefits for workingmen and women.

What problems arose from the rapid growth of cities?

Overcrowded houses turned into slums. Fire, disease, and crime became serious problems. To remedy this, many cities built low-cost housing projects.

How did Congress reduce the amount of immigration?

Beginning in 1882 Congress passed laws to regulate immigration. In 1924 the Quota System was adopted. Today immigration is severely restricted.

How were educational opportunities increased?

The public school system was greatly expanded thanks to men like Horace Mann. The Adult Education movement made rapid progress. Enrollment in schools and colleges increased steadily.

Connecting the Past with the Present . . .

"It's over the hill to the poorhouse for him." Have you ever heard someone make a remark like that about a person who's been unfortunate in his financial affairs? In the past many people did have to go to the poorhouse or poorfarm in their old age. They could not save enough to take care of themselves when they were too old to work. Unless their children were able to support them, these old folks had to go to the poorhouse. For such people this meant not only heartbreak, but disgrace and failure.

Thanks partly to the Social Security Act, poorhouses have become less in number, and you do not have to worry about being dependent in your old age. You will receive a small pension when you reach sixty-five. It will be paid from money deducted from your pay each week or month as long as you work. You can't spend it ahead of time. Out of the sad experience of earlier generations Americans have learned to value security in old age and to see that everyone has a chance to enjoy it.

Be sure you register with the Social Security Administration when you are ready to take a job.

UNIT REVIEW

507

Questions for Discussion and Review

1. a. What are the advantages of organizing a business as a corporation?
   b. What are the disadvantages?
2. Why were western farmers more dependent on railroads than eastern farmers?
3. List the main provisions of the Interstate Commerce Act.
4. What was the purpose of the Sherman Act?
5. What was the NRA?
6. List some ways the federal government has helped farmers.
7. Explain some of the causes of the growth of cities after 1900.
8. Tell some of the problems which slums created.
9. Explain the way the quota system of immigration works.
10. Who are the DP's?

THE HISTORY LABORATORY

Here are suggestions for activities that you will find interesting and profitable.

Prepare for Your Old Age ...

Write to the nearest Social Security Administration field office for information about social security. Then tell the class what pensions they may be eligible to receive when they reach sixty-five.

Hall of Fame ...

Make a *Directory of Famous Americans* born in foreign lands who immigrated to the United States and won fame and fortune. Your project may cover people living or dead in all fields of endeavor.

WHAT
AND
WHEN

Homestead Act
1862

A.F. of L. founded
1886

Interstate Commerc
1887

Study Your Community — A Class Project . . .

Make a survey to find how many of the companies in your community are organized as corporations, partnerships, and single proprietorships. Find out why each company prefers its form of organization and report your conclusions to the class.

Labor's Story . . .

Invite members of the A. F. of L. and the C. I. O. to answer your prepared questions about their organizations and activities. If possible, have them visit your classroom to participate in a panel discussion.

Look at Your Town . . .

If there is a run-down or slum area in your community, ask older people in the community how it came to be; find out if there are any plans to improve it and make a list of the problems which it is causing.

Minute Biographies . . .

Write short biographies of some of the famous men mentioned in this Unit. Find the dates of birth and death of the person about whom you are writing. This will help you locate him in time and connect him with other famous people of the period. For example, to get a clear picture of Andrew Carnegie it is helpful to know that he was a successful young businessman at the end of the War Between the States, and that at about the same time John D. Rockefeller was in the grocery business in Cleveland.

Use several reference books and compare the information you find in each.

n Anti-Trust Act
1890

Theodore Roosevelt's Presidency
1901-1909

Conservation conference
1907

Immigration Quota Law
1924

Be a Reporter . . .

If there is a Grange in your community, visit it and report to the class on its history and present activities. Compare its influence today with its political influence in about 1880.

Let's Read about Capital, Labor, and the Farmer

*ANGELO, VALENTI, *Bells of Bleecker Street*, Viking, 1949.

BAILEY, RALPH EDGAR, *Tony Sees It Through*, Dutton, 1953.

EMERY, ANNE, *County Fair*, Macrae Smith, 1953.

ERDMAN, LOULA G., *The Edge of Time*, Dodd, 1950.

*EVANS, EVA, *All About Us*, Capitol, 1947.

FENTON, CARROLL, and FENTON, MILDRED, *The Land We Live On*, Double-day, 1944.

HAGEDORN, HERMANN, *Boy's Life of Theodore Roosevelt*, Harper, 1922.

HUBBARD, MARGARET ANN, *Halloran's Hill*, Macmillan, 1953.

JUDSON, CLARA, *They Came From Scotland*, Houghton.

JUDSON, CLARA, *They Came From Sweden*, Houghton.

JUDSON, CLARA, *Theodore Roosevelt*, Wilcox and Follett, 1953.

LAMPMAN, EVELYN, *Elder Brother*, Doubleday, 1951.

*LAWSON, ROBERT, *They Were Strong and Good*, Viking, 1940.

*LENSKI, LOIS, *Prairie School*, Lippincott, 1951.

McLELLAND, ISABEL, *Ten Beaver Road*, Holt, 1948.

MELBO, IRVING, *Our Country's National Parks*, Bobbs, 1950.

**OSBORN, FAIRFIELD, *Our Plundered Planet*, Little, Brown, 1948.

SCHNEIDER, HERMAN, *Everyday Weather and How It Works*, McGraw, 1951.

**SEARS, PAUL B., *Deserts on the March*, University of Oklahoma, 1947.

SHIPPEN, KATHERINE, *Great Heritage*, Viking, 1947.

STEVENS, WILLIAM O., *Famous Humanitarians*, Dodd, 1953.

VAN DERSAL, WILLIAM, and GRAHAM, EDWARD, *The Land Renewed*, Oxford, 1946.

VAN DERSAL, WILLIAM, and GRAHAM, EDWARD, *Wild Life for America*, Oxford, 1949.

WISE, WINIFRED E., *Jane Addams of Hull House*, Harcourt, 1935.

* indicates easy reading
** indicates advanced reading

Unit 11

AMERICA BECAME A WORLD POWER (1898-1945)

"WESTWARD the course of empire takes its way." For more than two centuries Americans kept moving west and acquiring new territory until they reached the Pacific Coast. Where would they go next? What new lands would they acquire?

Westward across the Pacific lay beautiful, rich islands. Southward, in and around the Caribbean Sea which one President called "our front yard," other undeveloped regions seemed to offer great opportunities. This Unit tells how and where the United States acquired new possessions.

As you study the Unit keep in mind the following questions around which the material is organized:

1. What new territory did the United States acquire after the War Between the States?

2. How did victory over Spain affect the United States?

3. Why were Americans interested in the Far East?

4. How did the United States get along with the other nations in the Western Hemisphere?

511

Chapter 25

AMERICA GAINED
DISTANT TERRITORIES AND
FACED NEW PROBLEMS

Do you know anyone from Puerto Rico? Have you ever dreamed of driving up the Alcan Highway to Alaska? Or spending a vacation in Hawaii?

You can travel to and from these places without a passport for they are all American territory and the American flag flies over them just as it does over your home town.

How did the United States get lands so far away? That is the story of this chapter — the story of American overseas possessions and how they were acquired. It is not entirely a happy, peaceful story.

Why did the United States go to war with Spain in 1898? Could war have been avoided? Where was the war fought? What were the famous victories?

The war with Spain marks a great dividing line in American history. What change occurred in the world position of the United States after the war? Why did the nation become deeply involved in Far Eastern affairs after 1898? What new foreign policies were developed to meet the challenge of changing times?

The answers to these questions are all part of the subject matter of this chapter which tells how Americans gained distant territories and faced new problems.

512

Alaska was purchased from Russia in 1867. While the United States was growing into a strong industrial nation it was also acquiring overseas territory. In the first half of the 19th century the United States expanded rapidly and reached the Pacific Ocean. The Gadsden Purchase of 1853 (page 291) completed the rounding out of the country's borders.

However, many Americans were still hungry for land. They looked around for "new worlds to conquer." For a few years, the argument about slavery and states' rights occupied almost everyone's attention. However, when the Civil War was over, some people began to dream about gaining new territory. They were called *expansionists* because they wanted the United States to get bigger or expand.

William Seward, Lincoln's Secretary of State, was an expansionist. In 1867 Seward heard that Russia wanted to sell Alaska, the northwest corner of North America. How did it happen that Russia owned Alaska? The map on this page will give you a clue to the answer.

Notice that Bering Strait separates Alaska from Asia. This part of Asia, called Siberia, belongs to Russia. It has been called the back door to America. Along this way ancestors of the American Indians are believed to have come to America in the days before history (page 4).

About 35 years before the American Revolution, the Russian *czar* (ZAR) or ruler sent a group of men to explore eastern Siberia. The head of the expedition was Vitus Bering (BARE eeng), a native of Denmark. He sailed along the coast of northeastern Siberia and discovered the channel now called Bering Strait in his honor. Later he sailed across to Alaska.

Bering was the first white man to visit the region. As a result, Russia claimed Alaska. Later, a few fur traders and adventurers from Siberia founded settlements there.

However, the Russian government neglected Alaska. The colony was so far away from the Russian capital that it was expensive to send men and supplies. And the Russians were afraid that the British fleet might attack Alaska. They knew that if this happened they were not strong enough to defend their colony.

In those days (long before Com-

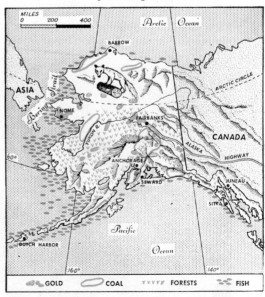

This map shows Alaska, which was purchased from Russia in 1867 for $7,200,000.

munists got control) Russia was on good terms with the United States. This was chiefly because both countries feared Great Britain. During the Civil War, when the British government was friendly to the South, the Russians sent their fleet to New York harbor. This seemed to hint that Russia would help the North fight Great Britain if the British interfered in American affairs. Actually, Russia was bluffing; nevertheless, Americans felt friendly to Russia at the time.

So when the Czar offered to sell Alaska, Secretary Seward welcomed the idea. At his urging, Congress agreed to pay the price — $7,200,000 — that the Russians asked. A treaty was signed and in 1867 Alaska became part of the United States.

Alaska proved a treasure house. Some people grumbled that the price (less than two cents an acre) was too high. Newspapers called Alaska Seward's "million dollar ice box" and "Seward's Folly."

Seward let them have their fun. He felt sure his "ice box" was packed with good things. Time proved him right. The immense land — about three times as big as France or Germany — was rich in resources. In a recent year, Alaska shipped out furs worth 12 million dollars, minerals worth 35 million, and fish worth 100 million. Next to the Louisiana Purchase, Alaska was probably the biggest real estate bargain in history.

Today, Alaska is called "the land of the future." Its population is still small — less than that of Buffalo, N.Y. — but it is growing steadily. Alaska is organized as a territory. This means that the people have their own governor and make

Vitus Bering was shipwrecked (below) and died on an island in Bering Sea soon after his discovery of Alaska. Russia claimed Alaska because of his visit there.

Juneau, Alaska's capital, has a good harbor.

their own laws. They also send a delegate to Congress. Thus, Alaska is governed the way the western lands were governed before they entered the Union as states.

It is expected that Alaska will some day become a state. The people of Alaska are waiting impatiently for that day. They believe that more than anything else, "Alaska needs statehood!"

A beginning was made in Samoa. Alaska was the last piece of land the United States acquired in North America. But it was only the beginning of expansion outside the borders of the United States. Americans looked westward to the islands in the Pacific Ocean. Missionaries longed to convert natives of such islands to Christianity; businessmen wanted to sell them American products. And a few far-sighted observers realized that the Navy needed *bases* or fortified locations on friendly islands where American ships could get coal, fresh water, and other supplies, and make repairs.

A beginning was made in the Samoan (sah MO ahn) Islands in the South Pacific. These islands lie on the route followed by ships traveling from United States to Australia. You can locate them on the map, page 516.

American ships began stopping at Samoa more than a hundred years ago. In 1878 the United States persuaded Samoans to let Americans establish a naval base at Pago Pago (PAHN goh PAHN goh) on the island of Tuituila (TOO too E lah). American influence in Samoa gradually increased; in 1899 the United States took over Tuituila and several smaller islands. Thus the nation gained a good naval base in the Pacific.

Hawaii attracted Americans. Most Americans were hardly aware of the existence of Samoa. They were more interested in a group of islands nearer home. These were the beautiful, rich islands of Hawaii (hah WY ee), which lay some 2000 miles southwest of California.

The Hawaiian Islands seemed ideal for missionary work as well as trade; they would also make a fine naval base. The English explorer, Captain Cook, had discovered the islands in 1788, but the natives remained independent under the rule of their own royal family.

Soon after the American Revolution, merchant ships and whaling vessels from New England began stopping at Hawaii for food and

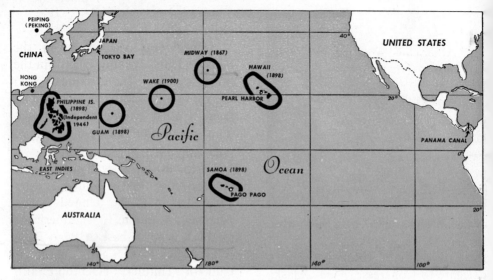

This map shows American possessions in the Pacific Ocean. Beginning with Pago Pago, Samoa in 1878, the United States gained many Pacific bases in the late 19th century. Find Hawaii, Guam and Wake. How and when was each acquired?

water. They found a broad, deep harbor. It was called *Pearl Harbor*, a name fated to ring loud in later American history.

Hawaii is called the "Paradise of the Pacific" because of its lovely scenery and pleasant weather. Many American sailors and traders liked the islands so well they settled there permanently. They opened stores, bought land, and developed sugar plantations. Religious leaders also were interested in Hawaii. In 1820 a group of New England missionaries went there and converted many natives to the Christian religion.

Other nations, especially Great Britain, did not like the growing power of the United States in the islands. There were rumors that the British were going to seize Hawaii. Some people thought the

United States should seize the island first. Americans who had settled there were eager to raise the stars and stripes over their new home. The native ruler of Hawaii, Queen Liliuokalani (LEE lee oo oh kah LAH nee) did not like Americans; she tried to govern in an old-fashioned, undemocratic way that soon led to trouble.

Hawaii became an American territory. In 1893 Americans in Hawaii started a revolt that drove the Queen from her throne. Then they asked the United States to *annex* or take over the islands. They expected a welcome, but were disappointed.

Grover Cleveland, who was then President, did not believe in acquiring overseas territory. And he felt the Hawaiian people and their

516   OVERSEAS TERRITORIES

Queen had not been treated fairly. The Americans who led the revolt had not consulted many natives. But they had sought and received help from American troops on a warship that happened to be in Honolulu harbor. All this displeased Cleveland; he blocked the annexation of Hawaii.

However, the next President, William McKinley, approved the idea of adding new territory. Soon after he took office, a treaty was signed, and in July 1898, Hawaii was annexed. Two years later, Hawaii became a territory; the people gained the right to make their own laws and send a delegate to Congress.

Hawaii has grown steadily in wealth and population. Tourists flock there, for Hawaii is a wonderful vacation land. Thousands of Chinese and Japanese as well as Americans and Europeans have settled in Hawaii. Thus, the population is a mixture of many racial groups. Today the people of Hawaii are waiting impatiently for the day when the territory will become a state of the United States.

Spain was unfriendly to the United States. One reason why President McKinley and Congress were eager to annex Hawaii in 1898 was the fact that a war was going on. During a war, islands with good harbors are especially useful as naval bases. The war was the Spanish-American War of 1898, which added several other islands to the list of American overseas possessions.

Why did the United States and Spain go to war with each other? The reasons reach far back in American history. In early days, there was trouble with Spain over navigation of the Mississippi River. A little later came the dispute over the Florida border that ended with Florida becoming a part of the United States in 1819. And the Spanish government always resented the Monroe Doctrine of 1823 which helped prevent Spain from winning

Most Hawaiians welcomed annexation by United States in 1898. Below, Hawaiian children enjoy kindergarten.

back her Latin American colonies. Thus, over a long period, bad feeling between Spaniards and Americans kept increasing.

Cuba was another source of trouble between the United States and Spain. Cuba is a long, narrow, curving island in the West Indies. Notice on the map (page 527) that Cuba is not far from southwestern Florida and lies at the entrance to the Gulf of Mexico. This location makes Cuba very important to the United States. If powerful enemies should ever get bases on Cuba it would be easy for them to invade Florida or other places along the Gulf of Mexico. For safety's sake, therefore, many Americans felt that the United States should control Cuba.

But Spain wanted to keep Cuba. Cuba and the nearby island of Puerto Rico (PWAIR toh REE koh) were all that remained of the great American empire Spain had once possessed. And Cuba was a rich island; her fertile soil could produce huge crops of sugar. Many Americans invested large sums of money to develop Cuban sugar plantations. The United States tried several times to buy Cuba, but Spain would not listen. A Spanish leader declared that "sooner than see the island transferred to any power, Spain would prefer seeing it sunk in the ocean."

Cuban rebels won American sympathy. Many Cubans wanted to be independent like the United States and the nations of South America. Under Spanish control, the island was badly governed. Most of the

Cuban rebels burn a sugar mill. This picture shows an incident in a rebellion against Spanish rule that began in 1868. Years of fighting and devastation preceded the winning of Cuban independence. The United States became involved in the struggle.

LET GO OF HIM, M'KINLEY!

This cartoon appeared in the *New York Journal* two days after the battleship *Maine* was blown up in Havana harbor. President McKinley is pictured as trying to hold back Uncle Sam who wants to fight Spain, shown as a vulture. Newspaper articles and cartoons like this one did much to arouse "war fever" in the people of the United States.

people were poor farm workers who could neither read nor write. There were many revolts which Spain crushed with great cruelty. One revolt dragged on ten years and brought terrible suffering to Cuba.

In 1895, another revolt broke out. Once again, fire and hunger, disease and death swept over the island. The American people felt angry and disgusted. President Grover Cleveland told the Spaniards to settle the dispute promptly, or the United States would have to interfere. Cuba, he pointed out, was so near United States that the warfare was "like a fight in our front yard."

American newspapers published daily reports of Cuban misery and Spanish cruelty. Some stories were true, but many were false or greatly exaggerated. The newspapers got most of the reports from Cuban leaders who wanted the United States to interfere. They described the cruel things Spanish soldiers did to Cubans, but told little of what Cubans did to Spanish soldiers when they got the chance.

The fighting and destruction caused great loss of life and property. Americans in Havana, Cuba's largest city, found themselves in great danger. To protect them, President McKinley (who had now succeeded President Cleveland) sent the battleship *Maine* to Havana.

Meanwhile, a new group of men

TROUBLE IN CUBA

This headline appeared in a New York paper when the *Maine* was blown up. Note claim of "proof" that Spaniards destroyed the ship. Actually the cause was never learned.

had taken over the Spanish government. They realized something had to be done to improve conditions in Cuba. They started several reforms and promised Cubans a chance to govern themselves. But it was too late. A strange tragedy ended any chance of peaceful settlement.

America went to war with Spain (1898). At midnight on February 15, 1898, while the battleship *Maine* was at anchor in Havana harbor, an explosion sent her to the bottom. More than 250 officers and sailors died. Next morning, American newspapers told in big headlines how the battleship had been "blown up" and American sailors "murdered" in time of peace. From the commander of the *Maine* came a quiet word asking Americans to "withhold judgment" — that is, to accuse no one until the cause of the disaster was known.

To this day, no one knows how the ship was destroyed. Spanish officials claimed the *Maine's* sides were blown out by an explosion of her powder magazine. Other investigators stated her sides were blown in by a torpedo or a bomb. There was a possibility that Cuban rebels might have set off the explosion hoping the United States would blame Spain and so give the Cubans support in their fight for freedom.

Many people jumped to the conclusion that Spanish officials had planted a mine beneath the *Maine*. This was almost certainly not true. Spanish leaders were trying desperately to avoid war with the United States. They had nothing to gain by destroying the *Maine*.

Unfortunately, people did not stop to think and reason. From the

This is the battleship *Maine*, whose destruction led to war with Spain in 1898.

streets, from the newspapers, even from the halls of Congress, rose a clamor for war. "Remember the Maine!" became the battle cry.

Spanish leaders offered new concessions. They were willing to do almost anything to avoid war with the United States, which they knew they would lose. But Americans had no faith in Spain's promises.

Suddenly, as if impatient of delay, President McKinley sent a message to Congress saying, "In the name of humanity, and in behalf of American interests, the warfare in Cuba must stop." Congress passed a resolution declaring that Cuba must be independent, and that Spain must withdraw her troops from the island. This meant war, which Congress formally declared a few days later, on April 25, 1898.

Dewey won a great victory at Manila. The United States went to war to free Cuba, but the first big battle took place in the Philippine Islands thousands of miles away, across the Pacific Ocean. Spain owned the Philippines, and it is an old rule of warfare to hit the enemy where he least expects it.

For several years before the Spanish-American War, the United States had kept a few warships near the coast of Asia to protect American trade with China and Japan. These ships were called the "Asiatic Squadron." The commander was George Dewey, a Vermont man who had served under David Farragut in the

Admiral Dewey's fleet enters Manila Bay, the Philippines, at dawn May 1, 1898.

War Between the States (1861–1865).

When war began, the "Asiatic Squadron" was near Hong Kong on the Chinese coast. On the day Congress declared war, Dewey got a cable from Theodore Roosevelt, who was then Assistant Secretary of the Navy. Roosevelt ordered him to go to the Philippine Islands, about six hundred miles away. He was to seize the harbor of Manila and destroy the Spanish ships there.

At daybreak, on May 1, 1898, Dewey's six ships steamed past the Spanish forts guarding the entrance of Manila Bay. "You may fire when ready, Gridley," Dewey told the captain of the ship in the lead. Thus began the famous Battle of Manila Bay. One observer reported that "American guns were fearfully accurate and destructive, but the Spanish gunners couldn't hit anything but the ocean."

By noon the Spanish fleet was destroyed. Eight Spanish ships were

THEODORE ROOSEVELT (1858–1919)

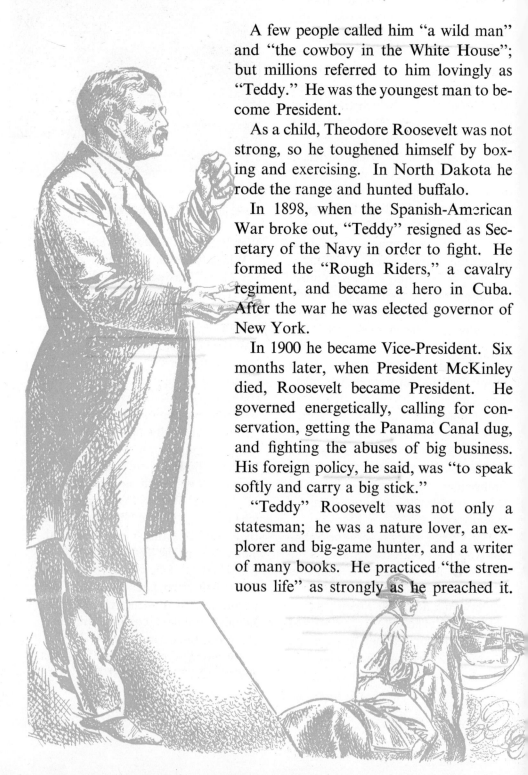

A few people called him "a wild man" and "the cowboy in the White House"; but millions referred to him lovingly as "Teddy." He was the youngest man to become President.

As a child, Theodore Roosevelt was not strong, so he toughened himself by boxing and exercising. In North Dakota he rode the range and hunted buffalo.

In 1898, when the Spanish-American War broke out, "Teddy" resigned as Secretary of the Navy in order to fight. He formed the "Rough Riders," a cavalry regiment, and became a hero in Cuba. After the war he was elected governor of New York.

In 1900 he became Vice-President. Six months later, when President McKinley died, Roosevelt became President. He governed energetically, calling for conservation, getting the Panama Canal dug, and fighting the abuses of big business. His foreign policy, he said, was "to speak softly and carry a big stick."

"Teddy" Roosevelt was not only a statesman; he was a nature lover, an explorer and big-game hunter, and a writer of many books. He practiced "the strenuous life" as strongly as he preached it.

sunk, and half the sailors were killed or wounded. Not one American ship was seriously damaged. Not one American was killed; only eight were wounded. It was a smashing victory. Europe was amazed. Every American felt a thrill of pride in Dewey's achievement.

Spain was badly beaten. In the meantime, about 15,000 American soldiers had landed in Cuba. They lacked training and equipment, and they lacked medical supplies and the right foods. Many became ill with malaria and yellow fever. But in spite of handicaps, they won battles.

The hardest fights were at El Caney (el kah NAY) and San Juan (san HWAHN) Hill near the city of Santiago (SAHN tee AH go). At San Juan Hill, a volunteer group called the "Rough Riders" won fame; this was partly because one of their officers was "Teddy" Roosevelt. He had resigned from the Navy Department to organize the Rough Riders and take part in the actual fighting. The Rough Riders included many of Roosevelt's western friends — cowboys and ranchers — plus a few college men.

While battles were raging, the Spanish ships in Santiago harbor tried to escape. But the American Navy was waiting for them. Every Spanish ship was destroyed. American troops then surrounded the city. Santiago had to surrender.

Next, an American army was sent to the island of Puerto Rico, east of

This photograph taken in 1898 shows Colonel "Teddy" Roosevelt and his Rough Riders at the battle of San Juan Hill.

Cuba. The Spanish governor there surrendered without a fight. By this time Spain had had more than enough. Her ships were sunk, her army had surrendered, and her colonies were lost. She asked for terms of peace. Her defeat on land and sea was accomplished in 90 days.

At the peace table, Spanish representatives agreed, without protest, to give up all claim to Cuba and Puerto Rico. They tried hard to hold on to the Philippines, but had to give them up in return for 20 million dollars.

The United States won new possessions. Many leaders in Congress and a large section of the American public did not want to annex the Philippines. They pointed out that the United States had fought the war to free Cuba, not to win control of foreign people on the other side of the earth. However, President McKinley and his advisers were expansionists. They believed annexation of the Philippines would mean new markets and opportunities for American business. They also believed it was America's duty to teach Filipinos the ways of democracy.

The argument in the Senate went on for some time. This delayed the treaty of peace, since, according to the Constitution [63], two-thirds of the Senate must approve all treaties. But the treaty finally won the required number of votes, and the United States took over the Philippines.

Thus the United States gained several new possessions. Puerto Rico and the Philippines were the most important. The nation also won Guam, a small island in the western Pacific. In the same year, the Hawaiian Islands were annexed. And a little later, the Navy took possession of Wake Island in the central Pacific.

It is important to remember that Cuba became an independent republic. It did not become part of the United States, although American influence in Cuban affairs remained strong.

The war left many problems. War always brings far-reaching changes. While it may settle a few questions, it almost always raises new and more difficult ones. The Spanish-American War of 1898 was no exception. It involved the United States in problems no one had foreseen.

For one thing, Americans found they had to fight a long bloody war in the Philippines. Like most other people, the Filipinos wanted to govern themselves. They expected to become independent when Spain was defeated. But President McKinley and his advisers felt the Filipinos lacked education and experience; so the United States decided to keep control for a while.

The Filipinos had a capable, determined leader named Aguinaldo (ah ge NAHL doh). He had been fighting Spaniards for years. Now he organized resistance against the United States.

The Filipinos knew they had no chance of winning a regular battle so they split up into small groups of guerillas (guh RILL luz). They hid in the mountains or the jungle and struck suddenly when least expected. The guerillas were savage fighters.

The warfare dragged on for two years; it was an ugly struggle, much like the Indian wars of colonial days. Aguinaldo was finally captured and his followers surrendered. But it took years to win the friendship and respect of the Filipinos.

Americans built schools and roads, fought disease and developed industries, but still the Filipinos were

UNCLE SAM—By gum, I rather like your looks.

This cartoon in a Denver newspaper shows Uncle Sam in an imperialistic mood.

dissatisfied. They admitted a government of their own probably would not be so efficient as American rule; but they preferred an inefficient government of their own to foreign control.

American leaders promised the Filipinos they would become independent as soon as they proved able to govern themselves. Step by step, the Filipinos were allowed to take more power in running the islands.

At last in 1934, Congress passed a law providing for the Philippines to become independent in 12 years. That seemed a long delay to Filipino leaders. Then came World War II. The islands put up a strong resistance to the Japanese but they were quickly conquered. Most Filipinos remained loyal to the United States; they did their best to help defeat Japan. Thus they earned the right to be a partner in the struggle for a better world.

Soon after the War ended the American government officially withdrew. The Philippine Islands became independent on July 4, 1946 — one hundred seventy years after the 13 American colonies declared their independence. Thus each year the United States and the Republic of the Philippines celebrate their birthday or Independence Day on July 4.

The Filipinos have not forgotten how easily Japan conquered their islands in World War II. They realize they would need help to fight off a future attack. On the other hand, the United States wanted to

Emilio Aguinaldo led a bloody revolt against American rule in the Philippines. Years later the islands won independence.

keep bases in the Philippines. So in 1947 the American and Filipino governments made a 99-year treaty. It provides that United States may have certain military and naval bases in the Islands and it assures the Philippines of American protection.

Americans helped Cuba recover. Like the Philippines, Cuba involved the United States in new problems after the Spanish-American War. The beautiful island had suffered terrible damage. In 1898, practically all the sugar plantations, where most Cubans earned their living, lay in ruins. Thousands of people were hungry and homeless. Yellow fever, malaria, and other diseases plagued the unhappy natives.

Like the Filipinos, Cubans hoped to become independent immediately. But American leaders insisted that Cubans were not ready to run their own affairs. President McKinley appointed an army doctor, General

Leonard Wood, to govern Cuba.

Under Wood's direction, schools were opened, roads were built, and plantations were brought back into production. American soldiers removed wreckage left by war and cleaned up the dirt where disease germs bred. In three years, under General Wood's leadership, Cuba made greater progress than in 300 years of Spanish rule.

At this point American leaders decided to let the Cubans run their own affairs. American soldiers withdrew and Cuba became a free republic. However, the United States insisted on keeping two pieces of Cuban territory for use as naval bases. It was also made clear to the Cubans that if they started fighting among themselves American soldiers would return.

American doctors conquered yellow fever. One of the most exciting things that occurred in Cuba during the period of American occupation had nothing to do with war. Nevertheless it was a great victory. Here is what happened:

Yellow fever had been killing hundreds of people in Cuba and other Caribbean lands for almost 300 years. No one knew what caused the disease, so no one knew how to keep it from spreading. A Cuban doctor named Carlos Finlay thought the disease was spread by mosquitoes. He pointed out that if a mosquito happened to bite a person suffering from yellow fever it might carry off some of the germs. The next person bitten by the mosquito would then become ill with yellow fever.

"What a crazy idea!" Dr. Finlay's neighbors cried. "How could a little mosquito cause such a terrible disease?" No one would listen to the doctor. When American doctors came to Cuba in 1898 Finlay tried to convince them, but for a long time they too laughed at him. They tried everything they could think of to stamp out yellow fever — but nothing worked.

At last a young doctor named Jesse Lazear (lah ZEER) said, "Maybe old Dr. Finlay's got the right idea! Why don't we try it out?" There was only one way to test the theory and Dr. Lazear offered himself for the experiment. He exposed his arm to a mosquito which he knew had just bitten a yellow fever victim. In a few days he was dead of the disease. He was a true hero, for he gave his life to save his fellow men.

But further proof of Finlay's theory was needed. Dr. Walter Reed, who had worked with Dr. Lazear, conducted other experiments. He proved beyond a doubt that a certain type of mosquito spread the disease. This knowledge made it easier to control yellow fever.

Under Dr. Reed's direction, Cubans and Americans cleaned up places where germ-carrying mosquitoes bred. And they worked at top speed putting screens in windows of homes and hospitals to keep out the mosquitoes. Thanks to this work, which has continued ever since, yellow fever ceased to be a serious danger in Cuba and in many other parts of the West Indies.

A canal across Panama was needed. More and more the attention of the American people was turning to the Caribbean area. They liked General Wood's work in Cuba. They were proud of the victory over yellow fever. And they were eager for new achievements.

There was one project that everyone agreed would bring great benefits to the Caribbean region as well as to the United States. This was a canal across the Isthmus of Panama. Notice the map, on this page; only a narrow strip of land separates the Atlantic and Pacific Oceans at this point.

A canal linking the two oceans would aid commerce because it would make it possible for goods and people to travel from the Atlantic to the Pacific Ocean easily and quickly. Because there was no canal, ships still had to travel around South America to get from one ocean to the other. In time of war this created a dangerous situation.

In the Spanish-American War it took 71 days for the battleship *Oregon* to travel from San Francisco to Cuba. Navy men asked: "What would happen if a much stronger power than Spain should send its battle fleet across the Atlantic?" No one liked to think about such a possibility. But it was clear a canal

would add greatly to the nation's safety by enabling warships in the Pacific and the Atlantic to join forces at short notice.

There were many difficulties to be overcome. The idea of a canal across the Isthmus of Panama was not new. Balboa, discoverer of the Pacific

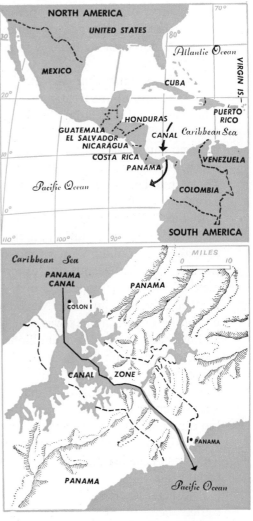

This map shows the route of the Panama Canal which connects the Atlantic and Pacific Oceans. It was opened in 1914.

Ocean, had suggested it. And during the California Gold Rush of 1849 there was talk about it. But in those days the nation lacked money and power to attempt such a big undertaking.

In 1850, the United States made a treaty with Great Britain providing for a canal to be built and controlled by the two countries. The ink was hardly dry on the treaty before Americans decided it was a mistake. They did not want to build a canal with Britain.

But for a long time the British refused to give up the treaty. Meanwhile, no canal was built. To build a canal of its own, the American government must somehow get rid of the 1850 treaty. This was obstacle number one in the canal project.

In the 1880's a group of Frenchmen tried to dig a canal in Panama. Just about everything went wrong in the attempt. Thousands of workers died of disease or collapsed in the heat of Panama's jungles. Machinery broke down; money was stolen and wasted. After losing millions, the French gave up the attempt.

However, the French company still held some rights in Panama. Any group or nation that wanted to build a canal in Panama would first have to buy out the French company. This was obstacle number two in the canal project.

Another question that had to be settled before anyone could start digging a canal was this: in what part of the Isthmus should the canal be built? The narrowest part of the Isthmus was just north of the South American continent; this region was part of the province of Panama. And Panama belonged to Colombia, the northernmost nation of South America. It was in Panama that the French had tried and failed to build a canal. Could the United States succeed where great French engineers had failed?

Some Americans felt doubtful. They argued, "It would be easier to build a canal farther north on land that belongs to Nicaragua (NICK ah RAH gwah). The Isthmus is wider there, but part of it is covered by a big lake. We could link up the canal with the lake. It wouldn't be necessary to dig all the way across the Isthmus." To this day, some observers believe the canal should have been built in Nicaragua, but in the end the shorter route was chosen. But to build a canal in Panama it was necessary to get Colombia's permission. Colombia was in no hurry to grant permission. This was obstacle number three.

Columbia refused a treaty. Theodore Roosevelt was President when Congress voted to build a canal joining the Atlantic and Pacific Oceans. Thus it became his job to (1) get rid of the 1850 treaty with Great Britain; (2) persuade the French company to sell its rights; and (3) get Colombia's permission to build a canal across Panama.

OVERSEAS TERRITORIES

The first obstacle was easily overcome. Relations with Great Britain had been growing more friendly since the Spanish-American War. The British realized that a canal would help world trade. They agreed to tear up the old treaty and make a new one permitting the United States to build a canal alone.

Roosevelt got around the second obstacle by persuading Congress to pay the French company 40 million dollars for their rights in Panama "Too much money," many people grumbled. Roosevelt agreed, but he was in a hurry to get the canal started.

The third obstacle — Colombia — proved unexpectedly difficult. Roosevelt and his Secretary of State, John Hay, offered to pay Colombia 10 million dollars for a narrow strip of land or *Canal Zone* across Panama. A treaty was drawn up and signed by Colombia's representative in Washington. But the Colombian government refused to approve.

Apparently leaders in Colombia hoped to get more money out of the United States. They thought that by delaying they could force the United States to pay any price they wanted. After all, they reasoned, Colombia owned the canal strip; it was one of their nation's most valuable resources. They were going to get all they could.

Theodore Roosevelt was not a patient man. He called the Colombians "bandits" and blackmailers. He swore he would build the canal

in Nicaragua. He decided to give up trying to make a treaty with Colombia.

Panama becomes independent. The thought of losing the canal frightened people in the province of Panama. They were eager to have the canal built across their land. They had long been discontented under Colombia's rule. This was the last straw. They revolted and declared Panama independent.

Troops from a United States warship kept Colombian soldiers from landing in Panama to fight the rebels. Then Theodore Roosevelt hurriedly recognized the independence of Panama. Fifteen days after the revolution, on November 18, 1903, the new republic of Panama made a treaty leasing the Canal Zone to the United States for ten million dollars plus a yearly rental of $250,000.

As you might guess, this made Colombia angry. And other republics in Central and South America felt shocked. The affair did much damage to the reputation of the United States in foreign lands. Inside the country, too, there were many who felt Theodore Roosevelt had treated Colombia unjustly.

The Colombians did not let the world forget their grievance; they complained bitterly. Several times it was proposed that Congress or the President should end the quarrel. Nothing was done until 1921 when Warren Harding was President and Theodore Roosevelt was dead. Then a new treaty was made giving Colombia $25,000,000 as a sort of payment for her lost province.

Building the canal was very difficult. When the diplomatic barriers were out of the way, the building of the canal could begin. It was one of the biggest engineering jobs in history. Difficulties were enormous. Only the development of steam shovels and other power driven tools made

Colonel William Gorgas (above) directed mosquito control work (top) that made the Canal Zone a healthier place to work.

it possible to conquer the natural obstacles.

One part of the canal was nearly 100 feet above the sea; this made it necessary to build huge locks to raise or lower ships from one level to another. In places land was rocky and hilly. It was necessary to cut through mountain peaks, blasting away tons of rocks with dynamite. At times, heavy rains brought landslides that killed workers and ruined months of toil.

Although the United States took possession of the canal property in May, 1904, actual digging did not begin for more than two years. However, the time was not wasted. The men in charge made careful preparations that resulted in health, efficiency, and speed later on.

In the very beginning it was realized that disease was the biggest menace. The canal strip was a hot, wet jungle where yellow fever and other tropical diseases flourished.

In Cuba, a few years before, Dr. Walter Reed and his assistants had shown how to clean up disease-breeding areas. A doctor who had served as chief sanitary officer in Cuba was put in charge of the fight against disease in Panama. He was Colonel William Gorgas (GAWR gas) of the Army Medical Corps.

Colonel Gorgas and his men drained lakes, swamps, ponds, and ditches. Over those they could not drain they spread a film of oil that destroyed larvae (LAHR vee) or baby mosquitoes and mosquito eggs.

Here Colonel George Washington Goethals is pictured directing the building of the Panama Canal. What do you think the first president would think of his namesake?

Rats and fleas were killed. Rubbish was burned. Sewers were built and drinking water was purified. Gorgas insisted that all buildings and even trains must have screens.

Thanks to this energetic campaign, there was not one case of yellow fever in Panama after 1906; malaria and other tropical diseases ceased to be serious threats. The Canal Zone, once a place of sickness and death, became as disease-free as any place under the American flag. Thus Gorgas and his staff won a victory against disease.

The Canal is a key point of American defense. The actual digging of the canal took seven years. Another army officer, General George Washington Goethals (GO thulz), was the engineer-in-chief. Patient and untiring, he kept at his gigantic task in the face of difficulties that seemed endless. Finally, on October 10, 1913, President Woodrow Wilson pressed an electric button in the White House, more than 4000 miles away. This sent a flash over the wires and set off a charge of dynamite which blew up a temporary dike or

Here is the "Panama Story" in pictures. At top is Col. Goethals and a partly finished section of the canal. Next are shown two views of the digging of Culebra Cut; and (bottom) an aircraft carrier is shown going through the completed canal.

barrier. Water rushed into "the Big Ditch." The Panama Canal was completed. The map on page 534 shows the route of the Canal.

After four centuries, Balboa's dream had come true. The "westward passage" to the Pacific, which explorers had sought in vain, now existed, thanks to the skill of American engineers.

On August 15, 1914, the Canal was opened to commerce. Within a year more than 2000 ships passed through. That was only the beginning. In 1952 more than 7000 ships traveled through the Canal — an average of almost 20 a day.

The Panama Canal is of immense military value. Through it, the United States can shift its naval strength quickly from ocean to ocean. Without the Canal it might not have been possible to defeat Japan and win back the Philippines in World War II.

However, the Canal also adds to America's defense problems. The Army, Navy, and Air Force must be on the watch at all times to protect the Canal. One enemy bomb could wreck a lock or dam and block the Canal for weeks. An atomic or hydrogen bomb might destroy the whole Canal in a few minutes.

Therefore, defense of the Canal has become a key point of American military planning. Thousands of men are at work all the time, building air bases and setting up antiaircraft guns and listening posts. Every hour of the day and night, air-

OVERSEAS TERRITORIES

planes and boats patrol approaches to the Canal. And American leaders are still giving thought to the idea of building a canal in Nicaragua. Perhaps in the not-too-distant future the United States will have a second or "spare" canal in Nicaragua.

The United States established bases in the Caribbean. Because of the Panama Canal and problems connected with its defense, the United States became interested in all the lands around the Caribbean Sea. Look carefully at the map on page 534. Notice that the Caribbean Sea is near the Panama Canal; notice also that ships from Europe and the United States must travel through the Caribbean to reach the Canal.

There are many islands in the Caribbean; any one of them could become a base for attack on the Canal if it fell into enemy hands. If an enemy nation could get control of Cuba or Puerto Rico or the Virgin Islands, it could build airfields there and send out airplanes to bomb the Canal. Thus it is important to all Americans that the United States should control the Caribbean area and entrances to it. It is necessary to have naval bases there so warships guarding the region can get supplies and make emergency repairs.

After the Spanish-American War the United States obtained naval bases in Cuba. Another base was established on Puerto Rico after the island came under the rule of America.

In 1917, Congress passed a law that enabled Puerto Ricans to take a great step forward. They became American citizens and gained power to run their own affairs. Thus Puerto Rico became a territory, with a government somewhat like that of Hawaii and Alaska.

Today, Puerto Rico is self-governing. A few Puerto Ricans would like to become independent, but most of the people are content with American rule. Some would like their island to become a state of the United States, but this does not seem likely. The future of Puerto Rico is still undecided.

The United States bought the Virgin Islands. East of Puerto Rico lies a group of small islands called the Virgin Islands. One of the islands, St. Thomas, has a fine harbor. The map on page 534 shows the location of the Virgin Islands. Until World War I the islands belonged to Denmark. This worried some Americans, for in the hands of a strong enemy the Virgin Islands might become a base for attack on the Panama Canal. When war broke out in Europe, fear grew that Germany might seize the islands from little Denmark. Therefore the United States hurriedly offered to buy them for 25 million dollars. Denmark agreed, and the islands became an American possession in 1917.

The Virgin Islands are valuable

chiefly because of their location. Natural resources are lacking and the people are very poor. But purchase of the Virgin Islands gave the United States another naval base.

Thus the nation developed a line of defense across the Caribbean Sea. Airplanes and warships based in Cuba, Puerto Rico, and the Virgin Islands constantly patrol the Atlantic and the Caribbean Sea to make sure no enemy approaches American shores or the Panama Canal from the East.

"But," you may object, "enemies might attack from the other side, across the Pacific! What about protection there?"

The armed services have spared no effort to protect the Pacific approaches to the Canal. North and south of the Canal, from California to islands off the coast of Ecuador (ECK wah dawr) in South America, there are bases fortified with modern weapons.

And westward across the Pacific the United States has island bases with airplanes and warships always on patrol, watching the sky and the water for any suspicious movement. Notice on the map on page 516 how American bases dot the Pacific: Hawaii, Midway, Wake, Guam, the Philippines, and many more. The line of American defenses marches almost to the shores of China and Japan.

Americans wanted to trade with the East. In the 20th century the United States became a power in the Pacific.

This map shows the possessions of the United States in the Caribbean Sea. Puerto Rico was acquired after the Spanish-American War, and Cuba became a republic under American protection. The Virgin Islands were purchased from Denmark in 1917.

agreed — or pretended to agree — to the Open Door Policy.

The Communists took over China. Thus there was a long tradition of friendship between the United States and China. When Japan attacked China in the 1930's the United States sent money and weapons to help the Chinese. In the Second World War the two nations were allies, fighting against the dictators.

A tragic break in the friendship came after the Second World War when Communists or "Chinese Reds" seized control of China. Under Russia's direction they did all they could to stir up hatred against the United States. American missionaries and merchants had to flee. Many did not escape and are still in Chinese prisons or have been killed.

Do the Chinese people believe the Communist lies? Or do they remember American kindness and long for the day when they can be friends with the United States and the free world? That is a question no one can answer today. Americans can only hope that in the long run China will break away from communism and the Chinese people will remember and cherish their century-old friendship with the United States.

Japan was a hermit nation. American relations with Japan began somewhat later than relations with China. In the early days Japan was less attractive to American traders than was China. No one knew much about the "Island Kingdom" except that it consisted of four large and many small islands off the coast of northeastern Asia. Japan was called a "Hermit Nation" because she tried to have little to do with the rest of the world.

Shipwrecked sailors who landed in Japan were driven back into the sea or tortured to death. Foreign ships were not permitted to enter any Japanese port, not even for food and water.

In 1852 when Millard Fillmore was President, the United States decided to do something about the situation. It was decided to send an expedition to Japan to try to make an agreement providing for two things: (1) decent treatment for shipwrecked sailors; and (2) establishment of trade. To command the expedition President Fillmore chose Matthew Perry, a naval officer. (He was a younger brother of Oliver Perry who won the Battle of Lake Erie in the War of 1812).

Perry opened up Japan. Fillmore wisely gave Perry command of four sturdy warships. The Japanese dared not attack such a fleet. On July 8, 1853 Commodore Perry sailed into Tokyo (TOH kyoh) Bay and delivered a letter from President Fillmore addressed to the Japanese Emperor. Then he sailed away to China, saying he would be back in the spring with more ships.

The Japanese were frightened and

impressed. They had never seen such powerful ships. When Perry came back in February, 1854 with seven ships, they were ready to talk business. The Americans brought exciting presents: a miniature telegraph and a model of a steam engine. The Japanese gave the Americans silk garments to take home to their wives and dolls for their children.

After a dinner on Perry's ship, the treaty was signed. Japan promised to be kind to shipwrecked sailors and to open two ports to trade.

Thus the Hermit Nation joined the modern world. And so began a swift rise to power that is one of the most amazing in history. Within fifty years Japan became a modern industrial nation, selling its cheap manufactured goods all over the earth. It also built up a strong, well-trained army and a big navy. The Japanese accomplished so much so fast because they were hard workers and clever at copying other people's ideas.

Japan took the road to war. Unfortunately, the Japanese did not care for peaceful ideas. They chose to copy aggressive, greedy nations such as Germany. Military officers got

control of the Japanese government; they proceeded to fight a series of wars aimed at making Japan master of Asia.

First they fought China in 1894 and seized the big island of Formosa (fawr MO sah). Next they fought Russia and easily defeated the Czar's badly-led troops. Then they invaded the peaceful peninsula of Korea, northeast of Japan. Korea became a Japanese province and the Korean people were treated almost like slaves.

In 1931 Japan seized Manchuria (man CHOOR ih ah), an outlying province of China on the border of Siberia. Manchuria is rich in coal, iron, and other materials Japan needed to strengthen her military power. Six years later Japan started out to conquer the rest of China, seizing practically all Chinese seaports and industrial cities. Then, grown mad with power and greed, Japan attacked the United States at Pearl Harbor in December, 1941.

Thus to a considerable extent Japan was responsible for World War II. How she joined forces with other power-mad nations and how she was defeated will be told in the next unit.

Commodore Perry opened up Japan. Here he is shown negotiating with Japanese representatives at Yokohama in 1854. He won a treaty promising trade and friendship.

CHAPTER SUMMARY

After the Civil War the United States gained land in many parts of the world. Alaska was purchased from Russia in 1867. Part of the Samoan Islands came under American rule. Hawaii was annexed in 1898.

The United States went to war with Spain in 1898. "Remember the *Maine*" was the battle cry. Spain was thoroughly beaten. At the end of the war the United States acquired the Philippines, Guam, Wake, and Puerto Rico. Cuba became a republic under American protection. The Philippines became independent in 1946.

American doctors in Cuba conquered yellow fever. A canal was built in Panama and opened in 1914. The United States acquired many bases for defense of the Canal. The Virgin Islands were purchased from Denmark in 1917.

Americans became interested in trading with the Far East. The United States developed the Open Door Policy. Relations between China and America were very friendly until the Communists took over China after World War II. Commodore Perry opened up Japan in 1853-4.

The Language of History

Be sure you know the meaning of each of the following words and phrases as they are used in this chapter.

1. expansionist
2. naval base
3. Rough Riders
4. Canal Zone
5. guerrillas
6. indemnity

What Happened When

Connect each of the following dates with an important event in American history.

1. 1853-4
2. 1867
3. 1898
4. 1903
5. 1914
6. 1917

Who's Who in History

Be sure you know the part the following played in history.

1. Liliuokalani	**5.** Theodore Roosevelt	**9.** William Gorgas
2. Grover Cleveland	**6.** Aguinaldo	**10.** George Goethals
3. William McKinley	**7.** Leonard Wood	**11.** Caleb Cushing
4. George Dewey	**8.** Walter Reed	**12.** Matthew Perry

Study Questions

1. Discuss the purchase of Alaska explaining **(a)** how the territory happened to belong to Russia, **(b)** the date of the purchase from Russia, and **(c)** the price paid.

2. **a.** Where are the Samoan Islands?
   b. How and when did the United States obtain part of Samoa?
   c. Of what value is Samoa to the United States?

3. Write a paragraph about the Hawaiian Islands telling **(a)** location, **(b)** how and when they became American territory, **(c)** the value of the islands to the United States.

4. **a.** Why did the United States go to war with Spain in 1898?
   b. Mention two important battles of the war.
   c. What territory did the United States gain by the peace treaty?

5. How and when did the Philippines become an independent nation?

6. Discuss the building of the Panama Canal telling **(a)** how the United States obtained land on which to build it, **(b)** the natural obstacles that had to be overcome, **(c)** the work done by Dr. Gorgas, and **(d)** the contribution of Colonel Goethals.

7. **a.** Why is the Panama Canal so important to the defense of America?
   b. What measures have been taken to defend the Canal?

8. How and when did the United States acquire the Virgin Islands?

9. Why have American businessmen been greatly interested in the Far East?

10. Why did President Fillmore send Commodore Perry to Japan? What did Perry accomplish?

11. Why was the Communist victory in China a serious blow to the United States?

OVERSEAS TERRITORIES

Chapter 26

THE UNITED STATES TRIED TO BE A GOOD NEIGHBOR

"I<small>N</small> the field of world policy I would dedicate this nation to the policy of the good neighbor — the neighbor who resolutely respects himself and because he does so respects the rights of others — the neighbor who respects his obligations and respects the sanctity of his agreements in and with a world of neighbors."

In these words Franklin D. Roosevelt summarized an important and remarkably successful development in American foreign affairs, the Good Neighbor Policy.

Why and when did Americans become aware of the need to be on good terms with the neighbors? What obstacles had to be overcome? What unhappy memories made it difficult to establish good relations with the nearest neighbors, Canada and Mexico?

The Good Neighbor Policy has not been 100% successful. There is always an exception. In this case, it is Argentina. Why is Argentina "the problem child of the Americas"? How are other Latin-American countries governed?

You will find the answers to these questions in this chapter which tells the story of America's neighbor nations — their patriots and ways of life — and describes how the United States has tried to be a good neighbor to them.

America became a world power.
When William Seward arranged the purchase of Alaska in 1867 he was a happy man. If he could have looked ahead he might have felt even happier, for in the following years the United States acquired many overseas possessions: Puerto Rico, the Philippines, Hawaii, Guam, and the Virgin Islands.

You may ask, "What did it all add up to? What difference does it make to me and to the people I know?" The answer is that it changed everybody's life and the life of generations to come. Partly because of the new possessions and partly because of its constantly growing industrial strength, the United States became a *world power*.

What does that mean? Just this: a world power is a nation that has possessions and interests in many parts of the earth. It rules over people in distant lands; it has influence on events thousands of miles from its shores. And almost anything that happens around the globe affects a world power nation. Spain, for example, was the greatest power when America was discovered.

She took possession of large parts of the New World, ruling over the natives, and still exercising great authority in Europe. Now, centuries later, the United States occupies a position somewhat similar to that of Spain four hundred years ago.

It is a serious thing for a nation to become a world power. A world power is likely to be involved in troubles and wars all over the globe. Most Americans were slow to understand this. They did not realize that an important change had occurred in the position of their country. They thought the United States could still go its own way, paying little attention to what happened in Europe or Asia. But those days were gone. The United States had to take on new responsibilities to protect her possessions and to try to keep peace in the world.

American foreign policy changed after 1898. The Spanish-American War of 1898 marks the great dividing line in American foreign policy. From the time of Washington until the 1890's the United States tried to follow the first President's advice to "steer clear of permanent alliances with any portion of the foreign world."

The same advice was echoed by the Monroe Doctrine of 1823, which warned Old World nations not to interfere in the Americas. Plainly stated, American foreign policy was "Let us alone and we will let you alone."

UNCLE SAM—THAT'S A LIVE WIRE, GENTLEMEN!

In this cartoon Uncle Sam warns England and Germany not to interfere in America.

However, in 1898 when the United States went to war to help Cuba, and later took Puerto Rico and the Philippines, a great change occurred. No longer was the nation following a policy of neutrality and isolation — or keeping "hands off" other nations' affairs. Instead, the American government seemed to be saying, "We're strong enough to play a leading part in world affairs and we're going to do so!"

Americans found they had to pay attention to neighbor nations north and south. After all, a country with world-wide interests and obligations must make sure its borders are safe. Gradually the United States worked out a policy toward its neighbors.

In the days when the frontier was being settled and most Americans lived on farms, the best thing you could say about any man was: "He's a good neighbor." This meant he was friendly; he respected your rights as well as his own; he stood ready to help you in time of trouble or danger.

Today the United States is trying to be a good neighbor to nations on the American continents. This is known as the "Good Neighbor Policy." You can help make this policy a success. How? By learning all you can about other American nations. As a good citizen you need to understand the people who live north and south of your country's borders.

Canada is rich in resources. First, consider Canada. This great neighbor to the north is even larger than the United States. It has 3,845,144 square miles compared to 3,082,809 square miles for the United States. But it has only about 15 million people, compared to the more than 160 million inhabitants of the United States. Thus for every Canadian there are more than 10 Americans.

Canada, like the United States, extends from east to west across the North American continent. Most Canadians live in the southern part of the country near the border between the United States and Canada. This border is remarkable in two ways: (1) it is more than 4000 miles long; and (2) nowhere are there soldiers or fortifications.

Canada has a great treasure of natural resources, which are mostly still untouched. It has long been known that Canada is rich in forests, farmland, coal, gold, copper, iron, and other minerals. But in recent years the world has been startled to learn that western Canada also contains huge oil deposits. And there is exciting news of uranium (you RA nih um) discoveries in remote parts of Canada. Uranium, as you probably know, is needed to produce atomic power.

Canada has a democratic government. Canada consists of ten *provinces* or states, plus the Northwest Territories and the Territory of the Yukon. Canada is a self-governing part of the British Commonwealth of Nations; the Canadian provinces, except Quebec, were originally settled by people from the British Isles. Later, immigrants from Germany, Russia, and other parts of Europe came to Canada, but British influence remained the strongest.

In all the Canadian provinces, except Quebec, the people speak English and live in a way like that of the United States. They read many of the same books; their children can go to free public schools. They believe in democratic government, freedom of speech, freedom of press and freedom of religion. They wear the same kind of clothes, use the same inventions, and listen to many of the same radio and television programs.

Like people in the United States, Canadians are fond of sports — baseball in summer, hockey in winter. Canadians and Americans are probably more alike than any other two peoples. If you have traveled in Canada you know that — except in Quebec — it is hard to realize you are really in some foreign country.

The French founded Quebec. Quebec is quite different from the rest of Canada. It is the oldest province, for it was founded by French settlers in 1608, twelve years before the Pilgrims settled Plymouth. Today, the people of Quebec still speak French. Most are descendants of Frenchmen who came to Canada in the 17th and 18th centuries. They proudly called themselves French Canadians, remembering that Canada was once known as New France.

When France had to withdraw from North America in 1763, her colonists became British subjects. But they remained faithful to the language and religion of their homeland. Today, French as well as English is the language of Canada. On government buildings in Ottawa, Canada's capital, all signs are written in both French and English.

Tories fled to Canada after the Revolution. The first British settlers came to Canada long after the

These pictures show western Canada's growing industrial power. At left is the Corra Linn dam, British Columbia. At right are towers for purifying oil at the new LeDuc oilfield near Edmonton, Alberta.

French. The American War of Independence caused the first big immigration of English-speaking settlers to Canada. Tories or colonists who were loyal to the king had to leave the United States in a hurry. Many fled over the border to Canada, leaving behind their homes and most of their possessions.

The Tories had to start all over, clearing the land, building new homes, and establishing towns in Canada. In time they became prosperous once more; they built thriving little towns in Nova Scotia, New Brunswick and Ontario. But they did not forget what happened to them during the Revolution. They wanted no friendship with the United States.

Canada and the United States became friends. For years there was bad feeling between Americans and Canadians. They quarrelled often about the boundary line. The land between the two countries was mostly covered with forest so no one knew exactly where the line should run.

All is peaceful along the U. S.-Canadian border. Detroit is seen from the Windsor, Ontario side of the Detroit River.

However, the Canadians and Americans were sensible people. They found a peaceful way to settle their disputes, a method called *arbitration*. It works like this: both countries choose several arbitrators or judges who listen to all the arguments and then decide how the question should be settled. The judges are usually high officials of neutral nations. Their job is something like that of an umpire in a baseball game.

Thanks to arbitration, many disputes between Canada and the United States were settled peacefully. After the War of 1812 both sides agreed it was a waste of money to keep warships on the Great Lakes. This was known as the *Rush-Bagot Agreement* of 1818. Since that time the border has been unfortified.

The United States and Canada have really learned to live in peace. In the last fifty years people on both sides of the border have drawn together. Their men fought side by side in two World Wars. Now they are working together for peace.

Perhaps you have traveled across the "Peace Bridge" at Buffalo or the Ambassador Bridge at Detroit — into the province of Ontario. Or if you live near the West Coast you may have seen the International Peace Arch which links the state of Washington and the Province of British Columbia; it bears a famous inscription: "Children of the Same Mother." Along the border are other monuments recalling the long period of peaceful relations between

545

Here is one of the bridges on the Alcan Highway. Built in World War II, the road connects British Columbia and Alaska.

the two countries which had existed.

Everywhere in northern United States you will find broad highways leading to Canada. The traveller who follows them finds welcome and fair treatment on the other side of the border. Every year new roads are built into distant parts of the north land.

One of the most interesting of these new roads is the Alaska Highway, often called the Alcan Highway. It stretches 1520 miles from British Columbia west and north to Fairbanks, Alaska. (You can trace it on the map on page 547.) U.S. Army engineers built the Alaska Highway as a military supply route during World War II, when it was necessary to rush supplies to Alaska for defense against a possible attack by Japan. Today the Alaska Highway connects with several roads leading across Canada and into the United States.

More and more Americans visit Canada on their vacations. And thousands of Canadians visit the United States. Perhaps you are thinking, "That's fine, but do we really get anything out of all this visiting?" The answer is, "Yes!" Canada has long been one of the United States' best customers. Canadians buy huge quantities of American farm machines, typewriters, oranges, and other American products. And citizens of the United States buy wood and paper, oil, nickel, apples, cheese and other products of Canada.

Thus many factors strengthen friendly relations between Canada and the United States: a common language, similar ideas and habits, a long tradition of friendship, good transportation, and a thriving trade.

Spain ruled Latin America. Relations with nations to the south present more problems than relations with Canada. Canadians and Americans speak the same language and both nations were once British colonies. Most nations to the south started out as colonies of Spain, and their people still speak Spanish. Two exceptions are Brazil and Haiti. Brazil was long a colony of Portugal, so its people speak Portuguese. And because Haiti was ruled by France for many years, its people speak French.

The nations south of the United States make up what is known as *Latin America* because the inhabitants speak languages based on Latin. Mexico, the Caribbean region, Central America, and South America are all part of Latin America. Latin Americans gained their independence later than the United States did. In fact, it was the success of the American Revolution that inspired early Latin American patriots to dream of freedom from Spain. But Spain kept a tight grip on her colonies for a long time. Any young man who dared speak about independence soon found himself in prison; if he managed to escape, he had to flee to Europe or the United States.

At last a day came when Spain had to turn her attention away from Latin America. During the Napoleonic Wars (1803–1815), Spain was conquered by Napoleon. The Spanish king was driven from his throne; the country was in a state of confusion.

Spain's colonies won their freedom. Among Latin American exiles in

Paris, London, and New York the message traveled fast: "Now is the time to strike a blow for freedom!" And so began the *Wars of Liberation*, as the Latin American struggle for independence is called.

In Mexico, in Central America, and in parts of South America fighting broke out. It lasted for years. Slowly the courage and stubborn determination of the rebels brought victory. By 1823 the Wars of Liberation were over and most of Latin America was free.

The greatest hero of Latin America's struggle for independence was Simón Bolívar (boh LEE vahr). From Mexico to Argentina he is called *El Libertador* or "the Liberator," and almost every town has a statue of Bolívar on horseback.

Bolívar was born on July 24, 1783 in Venezuela (VEN ee SWE lah). He

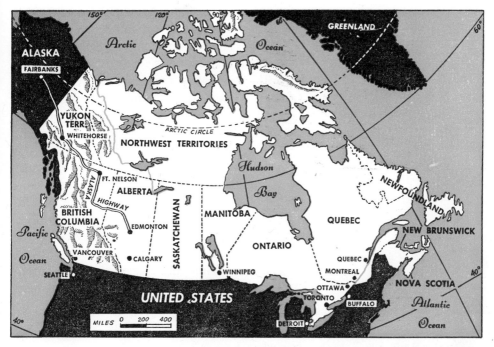

This map shows the vast extent of the Dominion of Canada. This northern neighbor is somewhat larger than the United States, but has a much smaller population.

belonged to a rich and noble family who sent him to study in Spain. When Simón was 18 his uncle arranged a marriage for him, as was the custom. His bride was the lovely young daughter of a great Spanish family. Proudly, Bolívar took her home to Venezuela. But their happiness was short-lived. In a few months she died of yellow fever.

Heartbroken, young Bolívar decided to devote his life to freeing his native land from Spain. For years Bolívar fought battle after battle in northern South America. When he had driven the Spaniards out of the region that is now Colombia, Venezuela, and Ecuador (ECK wah dawr), Bolívar turned his attention southward. There, another great soldier, José San Martín (ho ZAY sahn mahr TEEN), had already won independence for Argen-

tina and Chile. Bolívar united San Martín's troops with his own and led a vigorous campaign in Peru that ended Spain's rule in South America.

Bolívar gave his entire fortune to the war. He also gave his health. Years of fighting and hardship wore out his slender body; he died of tuberculosis in 1830 at the age of 47. Today, Latin Americans regard Bolívar with the same respect and gratitude that people in the United States feel for Washington.

There are 20 republics in Latin America. Independence brought new problems to Latin America. The people lacked experience in political affairs. Most of them were very poor and had never had a chance to go to school. As you might expect, they found it hard to run a government. And they did not remain united, as Bolívar had hoped. Instead, Latin America became divided into weak republics, separated in some cases by high mountains or dense jungles.

Today there are 20 republics in Central and South America. Each has an interesting history; each has made contributions to the world's culture and wealth. A few, like Brazil and Chile, have marched forward steadily and now have considerable influence in the world. Others, like Paraguay and Ecuador, have lagged behind; they count for little in world politics.

Time and space are lacking for a detailed study of all the Latin Ameri-

Simón Bolívar (1783–1830) is "South America's George Washington." His armies freed the continent of Spanish rule.

can nations. But in the following pages you will find a discussion of the more important republics.

Mexico is a next-door neighbor. To citizens of the United States, the most important country in Latin America is Mexico — because Mexico is nearest. Mexico is a big country, one-fourth as large as the United States. It has almost twice as many people as there are in New York State.

Mexico is rich in natural resources; drilling oil and mining silver, copper, lead and zinc are big industries. But the typical Mexican is still a farmer, scratching a bare living from a small patch of dry soil.

Most Mexicans have both Spanish and Indian ancestors. And almost everywhere in Mexico you can see reminders of ancient Indian civilizations, and also of the influence of Spanish conquerors. Indian temples, lovely Spanish churches, snow-capped mountains and masses of tropical flowers make Mexico a fascinating place to visit.

Perhaps you know someone who has driven down the Pan-American Highway from Texas to Mexico City. It is a wonderful trip, one that is increasingly popular. Americans who visit Mexico usually come home with a new respect and understanding of the problems south of the border. This is all to the good, for relations between Mexico and United States have often suffered because neither nation understood

The Palace of Fine Arts in Mexico City took 27 years to build. It houses the works of Mexico's most famous artists.

the point of view of the other one.

Mexicans found it hard to forget or forgive the loss of Texas and the Mexican War of 1846 (pp. 279–88). Americans were impatient with Mexico's frequent revolutions and the way Mexican leaders borrowed money they could not or would not repay.

Morrow won Mexico's friendship. Bad feeling between the two nations was so well known that in World War I a German diplomat offered to help Mexico get back Texas and California if she would fight against the United States. Mexico ignored the offer, but Americans did not. They suddenly realized the danger of being on bad terms with the folks next door.

However, the situation in Mexico was so confused and Mexicans were so unfriendly it seemed hopeless to try to improve relations. But one man was able to change the whole picture in a few months. He was Dwight Morrow, a banker who had gone to college with Calvin Coolidge. In 1927 President Coolidge appointed him Ambassador to Mexico.

Someone asked scornfully what Morrow could do in such a job. "I know what I can do for the Mexicans," Morrow answered firmly, "I can like them."

He did — and the Mexicans liked him. He traveled about Mexico, observing, listening, and learning. Crowds gathered to cheer the American whose kindness had won their hearts. A new spirit of cooperation began to develop.

About this time Charles Lindbergh made his famous flight to Paris and became a hero to all the world. Morrow arranged to have the young man fly to Mexico City. Mexicans gave an overwhelming welcome to "the conqueror of the Atlantic." In Mexico, Lindbergh met and fell in love with Anne Morrow, the ambassador's daughter. Soon they were married. Like everybody else, the Mexicans love a romance; the whole incident helped greatly to improve relations with the United States.

American friendship with Mexico has continued to grow. Cordell Hull, who was Secretary of State in the 1930's, encouraged trade between the two nations by getting tariff rates reduced. In World War II, Mexico proved a true and valuable friend. When the Japanese attacked American ships at Pearl Harbor, Mexico declared war on Japan. Mexican officials worked steadily with American leaders drawing up plans to ward off enemy attack.

Mexican harbors and airports were put at the use of American ships and airplanes. Thousands of Mexicans crossed the border to work in American fields and war factories. Mexican airmen helped drive the Japanese out of the Philippines. Thus, in a time of danger, the United States found a good neighbor on the southern border.

Central America contains the Panama Canal. South of Mexico lie the six republics of Central America. Reading downward on the map on page 554, they are: Guatemala (GWAT tuh MAH lah), Honduras (hahn DOO ras), El Salvador, Nicaragua (NICK ah RAH gwah), Costa Rica (KOHS tah REE kah), and Panama. They occupy land between North and South America.

The people of the region are mainly Indians (except in Costa Rica). They raise tropical products, most of which they sell to the United States. The bananas you eat, and the chicle which makes your chewing gum easy to chew, probably came from Central America.

The United States' chief interest in Central America is the Panama Canal. That waterway is almost as precious to Central America as to the United States. It has brought increased trade and profits to the area.

Most people in Central America

Central America has lots of bananas! Here the fruit is being washed before shipment to markets in the United States.

Good news! At their old home this El Salvador family learns they are to have a new house in a government project.

are friendly to the United States. They hope their rich northern neighbor will soon build a second canal across the Isthmus. Nicaragua has signed a treaty giving the United States the right to build such a canal.

However, the Central American republics have many troubles. Only Costa Rica has been able to establish a sound, democratic government. In the other countries, discontent and poverty have often led to revolutions and dictatorship.

Communists work constantly to stir up hatred of the United States. On the whole, however, the Good Neighbor Policy has succeeded in Central America.

Cuba, Haiti, and Santo Domingo are Caribbean nations. East of Central America are three island republics: Cuba, Haiti, and the Dominican (doh MIHN ih kun) Republic. Cuba owes her independence to the United States, as you read in the story of the Spanish-American War. After

the war the United States continued to supervise the island's affairs. Many Cubans resented what they felt was American interference. Since 1934, however, the United States has let Cuba alone, giving help and advice only when asked.

The Good Neighbor Policy has paid dividends in Cuba. During World War II the Cuban government declared war on the enemies of the United States and cooperated fully in defense plans.

East of Cuba in the Caribbean Sea is a large, beautiful island on which are two nations: Haiti and the Dominican Republic. Haiti was once a French colony. When Napoleon was busy trying to conquer Europe a Negro slave named Toussaint L'Ouverture (too SAN loo VEHR TYOOR) saw a chance to strike for freedom. He led a bloody uprising in which thousands of French soldiers died. Toussaint was captured and died in a French prison, but his people won freedom.

Unfortunately, Haiti never found

Toussaint L'Ouverture (1744–1803) is the national hero of the Republic of Haiti. He led a rebellion against French rule that finally won independence, although Toussaint himself was captured and died in a French prison.

another leader like Toussaint. Soldiers, politicians, would-be dictators have fought for control, and the people have sunk deeper into debt. In recent years, however, the situation in Haiti seems to have improved.

The Republic of Haiti occupies the western part of the island. On the eastern side is the Dominican Republic, sometimes called Santo Domingo (SAN toh doh MIHNG oh). It is larger than Haiti and was formerly a Spanish colony.

Columbus visited Santo Domingo on his first voyage to America. It is said the first white settlement in America, the first church, and the first college were all founded in Santo Domingo.

Like Haiti, the Dominican Republic has had troubles and changes in government. Today the country is ruled by a dictator named Trujillo (troo HE yoh).

At various times the United States has sent troops to both Haiti and the Dominican Republic to keep order and protect American citizens during uprisings. But after the Good Neighbor Policy was adopted such action ceased. At present both countries are peaceful and friendly to the United States.

There are ten South American Republics. South of Central America lies the continent of South America. There are ten South American republics. Study carefully the map on page 554 and you will find Colombia, Venezuela, Brazil, Ecuador, Peru, Bolivia, Paraguay (PAIR ah gway), Uruguay (YOO roo gway), Chile (CHIHL ih), Argentina (AR jen TEE nah).

South America has all varieties of climate. The lands in the northern part are mostly hot and wet; farther south the climate becomes temperate; at the extreme southern end, it is

A GOOD NEIGHBOR

very cold. Seasons in South America are the opposite of those in the United States. When winter is on its way in North America, summer is coming in the republics far to the south.

South America has many natural resources but they are mostly undeveloped. Because the mountains are high and there are many jungles and deserts, the continent has few good roads. And without good roads people find it hard to carry on business and industry. They tend to stay at home and live as their ancestors did. That is what has happened in many parts of South America.

South America is moving forward. Today there are signs of progress in South America. The airplane provides transportation to many places where it would be almost impossible to build roads. And the radio is bringing news and ideas to people in remote settlements.

In recent years South American musicians, movie stars, teachers, and athletes have won fame in the United States. But too many Americans still think South America is a land of bandits and revolutions. Actually the people of South America are friendly, cultured, and polite. They have many beautiful cities and universities that were already old when Jamestown was founded.

Their way of life is different from that in the United States, partly because of differences in climate and location and partly because their lands were under the influence of Spain or Portugal for centuries. Because of these differences misunderstandings have sometimes developed. However, in the past quarter of a century the United States has tried hard to be friends with South American nations and has succeeded fairly well. Their enthusiastic cooperation during and since World War II proved the value of the Good Neighbor Policy.

It would require a book much larger than this one to tell the story of all the republics of South America. For that reason, only the "big three" will be discussed: Argentina, Brazil, and Chile, often called the *ABC powers.*

Argentina is proud and sensitive. Argentina, the "A" of the ABC countries, is the neighbor most distant from the United States. It occupies the southeastern part of South America. Notice on the map, page 554, what a long country Argentina is; it stretches southward more than 2000 miles, from the edge of the warm tropics almost to the cold, dreary Antarctic.

Argentina is a prosperous country. It raises wheat and cattle that help to feed people in distant parts of the world. The Argentinians are a proud people. Unlike most other Latin American nations there is little Indian blood in the population. Most Argentinians are descended from the early Spanish settlers or

This map shows the nations of Central and South America. There are 20 republics and several European possessions. Note that South America lies *east* as well as south of most of the United States, and so is much closer to Africa and Europe. What problems does this create in making plans for the defense of the American continents against attack?

A GOOD NEIGHBOR

from the large number of Italians and Germans who moved to Argentina in the last century.

Argentinians are proud of their schools, their growing commerce, their art and literature. They are especially proud of their capital city, Buenos Aires (BWAY nohs I rays), a name that means in Spanish "the city of beautiful airs."

You have probably noticed that proud people get their feelings hurt rather easily. That seems to be the case with Argentina. Its relations with its neighbors, including the United States, have been stormy. The main trouble seems to be that Argentina wants to be the leading American nation, though other nations are larger and more powerful.

The people of Argentina do not have a democratic government. They are ruled by a dictator named Juan Perón (HWAHN pay ROHN), who uses the army to enforce his will. In Argentina people do not have freedom of speech or of the press.

As you might expect, Juan Perón and his friends do not like the United States. There are two main reasons for their hostility. First, Perón and his advisers resent the growing influence of the United States in South America. They also resent the friendship between the United States and Brazil, Argentina's powerful neighbor. The second reason for Argentina's hostility is that the United States does not buy much from Argentina. This is because Argentina produces many products

Radio helps fight illiteracy. These women in Colombia are listening to lessons on the only radio in their village.

that American farmers also produce: beef, hides, wheat, and corn. American tariff laws limit the amount of Argentine beef that can come into the United States.

During World War II Argentina was frequently accused of helping enemies of the United States. Since the end of the war the United States has tried to make friends with Argentina, but without much success. Argentina remains the only South American country that does not seem to be friendly to the United States.

The root of the trouble is the fact

Almost everyone works hard in Ecuador. This mother keeps her child bundled close to her as she does the milking.

Buenos Aires, capital of Argentina, is one of the most beautiful cities in the world. It was founded 47 years before the Pilgrims settled Plymouth. Above is a view of "Ninth of July Avenue," named in honor of Argentina's independence day.

that Argentina is ruled by a dictator and the United States is a democracy. Sometime in the future when democratic government is restored in Argentina the two countries should be able to establish a genuinely friendly relationship.

Brazil is big and friendly. Argentina's neighbor, Brazil, is the largest country in South America. It is slightly larger than the United States; in fact, Brazil is the fourth largest nation in the world — only Russia, China, and Canada are larger.

Everywhere you go in Brazil you get the impression of bigness. The capital of Brazil, Rio de Janeiro (RE oh day zhah NA roh) has a harbor big enough to shelter all the world's navies at once. Brazil's big coffee plantations supply three-fourths of the world's coffee. Brazil's

jungles, inhabited only by a few Indian tribes, cover an area as large as Europe.

Brazil's great river, the Amazon, is more than 3000 miles long and carries more water than any other river in the world. The Amazon is so wide and deep that big ships can sail up its waters for 2000 miles.

The Portuguese discovered and claimed Brazil in the 17th century. They found numerous Indian tribes in the region. Many Portuguese colonists came to Brazil. They established sugar plantations and imported Negro slaves to do the work.

In more recent years, thousands of Germans and Italians have come to Brazil. And you may be surprised to learn that a number of people have left the United States for Brazil. After the War Between the States a

556

number of southern planters moved there.

Today, the population of Brazil is a mixture of all these groups. But almost all of them speak Portuguese and they get along with one another in a cheerful, friendly way.

Brazil became independent of Portugal in 1825. Then, and for more than a century afterward, Brazilians lived mainly by farming and mining. From the vast rich land came huge quantities of rubber, fruit, cotton, gold, and diamonds, as well as coffee. Almost all Brazil produced was sold to the United States and Europe.

In the past 20 years Brazilians have taken to manufacturing. With money borrowed from the United States they built a steel mill, the largest in South America. They decided to make their own cotton into cloth instead of shipping it to foreign lands. Today Brazil has more than 300 cotton mills.

World War II encouraged this industrial development. Because many merchant ships were sunk by submarines and others were busy carrying war materials to Europe and the South Pacific, Brazil could not get manufactured goods from Europe or the United States. It became impossible to buy tools, clothing, and machines. So Brazilians had to get busy and manufacture such things for themselves, just as people in the United States learned to do during the War of 1812.

Brazilians are friendly people. They get along with one another and with most other nations. Relations between the United States and Brazil are especially cordial. In 1917 when the United States became involved in World War I, Brazil promptly declared war on the enemies of the United States.

In World War II Brazil again proved to be a good neighbor. She opened her harbors and airfields for American use. She did her best to

This is Brazil's capital, Rio de Janeiro, as seen from Sugar Loaf Mountain. Note the beautiful, large harbor. Natives of Rio are called "cariocas" in honor of the Carioca Mountain range that surrounds the city. Rio was founded 400 years ago.

supply products needed in war; Brazilian young men enlisted in the army, navy and air force. Brazilian pilots became famous for their skill and daring; a division of the Brazilian army fought gallantly in the long campaign to drive the Germans out of Italy.

Chile is ambitious and progressive. Compared to Brazil, Chile seems small and remote. But it is an important, progressive nation. As you can see on the map on page 554, Chile is a narrow ribbon of land. It occupies the southwestern part of South America between the high Andes mountains and the Pacific.

The "ribbon" is over 2600 miles long; it stretches south from Peru all the way to Cape Horn. But most of the way Chile is only about 100 miles wide from east to west. At its widest point the country is only about 250 miles wide. It is sometimes said of Chile that "its head is burning while its feet are freezing." There are about six million people in Chile. They are descended from the original Indian inhabitants and Spanish conquerors who came south from Peru in the 16th century.

The Indians of Chile were fierce and warlike. It took Spain more than a hundred years to subdue them. The Chilean people have inherited this fighting ability. Chile has won several wars against her neighbors; her army and navy are strong and efficient.

Chile's national hero was Bernardo O'Higgins, son of an Irish merchant and a Chilean woman. He led the Chilean rebels in their fight against Spain. Later, with Bolívar and San Martín, he won independence for Chile in 1818.

For five years O'Higgins ruled Chile fairly and efficiently. But the Chileans did not want to be ruled by one man. They adopted a constitution in 1823 and O'Higgins retired, asking nothing for himself.

Since the days of O'Higgins, Chile has had a stormy history. For years a few big landowners ran the government. But in recent years the common people have gained some representation.

Chile had many boundary dis-

"The Christ of the Andes," statue on the border, reminds Argentina and Chile of their promise to live in peace.

Latin America badly needs trained mechanics. These Ecuadorian students are receiving instruction in auto repairing.

putes with her neighbors. In 1904 Chile and Argentina finally settled their quarrel and promised they would fight no more. As a sign of their intentions, a beautiful statue, known as the Christ of the Andes, was erected on the border, high in the Andes mountains. Since that day, Chile and Argentina have been good neighbors.

In other ways Chile has made great progress. Mining is a big industry, for the long narrow land is a treasure house of minerals the world needs: copper, coal, and iron. Chile also has vast deposits of nitrates (NI trayts). Nitrates are made into fertilizers which farmers use to enrich the soil. Chile ships large amounts of nitrates and minerals to customers in many parts of the world.

The people of Chile are famous for their energy and ambition. Some of them began to say "Why should we ship our resources out of the country? Why don't we start manufacturing and use them ourselves?"

The answer was, of course, that it takes money to build factories and most Chileans were very poor. But gradually manufacturing was started. The United States helped by lending money. Today Chile, like Brazil, has steel mills and cotton mills, and is on her way to becoming an industrial nation.

Most Chileans are still very poor, at least by North American standards. They work on farms or in factories for low wages. But the situation is improving. Many laws have been passed to improve working conditions.

Education has improved, too. More and more Chilean children are going to school and they are staying in school longer. Chile's leaders have proved they believe in democracy. They want to provide new opportunities for the nation.

Chile did not take an active part in World War II. But when the war was over she became a member of the United Nations and has worked hard for world peace.

Chile supports the Good Neighbor Policy with vigor. She has sent her most capable leaders to Pan-American conferences. Chile is one of the strongest supporters of the old Pan-American Union and of the new Organization of American States, which works to encourage cooperation among the American nations.

The Good Neighbor Policy is a success. In this chapter you have made a rapid survey of the neighbors of the United States. From Canada on the north to Chile in the far south is a long way. The neighbor nations present a great variety of problems, opportunities, and interests.

However, with one or two exceptions they are ready, willing, and able to cooperate with United States in developing trade and defending the American continents. Every American has a right to be proud of the good relations between the United States and the other American nations.

CHAPTER SUMMARY

The United States became a world power after 1898. The Good Neighbor Policy has been developed to maintain friendly relations with other American nations. It has been quite successful. This was shown in World War II when most of the neighbor nations gave active support to the United States.

Canada is rich in resources and has a great future. In the past many Canadians were unfriendly to the United States. Today Canada and the United States are very friendly and carry on a thriving trade with each other.

Latin America is the region south of the United States. Spanish is spoken by most of the people there. The region won independence in the Wars of Liberation which ended in 1823. Bolívar is the great hero of Latin America.

Relations with Mexico have improved greatly in recent times. The United States is vitally interested in Central America because of the Panama Canal.

The ABC powers are Argentina, Brazil, and Chile. Argentina has proved hard to get along with, but Brazil and Chile are friendly nations.

The Language of History

Be sure you know the meaning of each of the following words and phrases as they are used in this chapter.

1. world power
2. French Canadian
3. arbitration
4. Latin America
5. Good Neighbor Policy
6. Wars of Liberation
7. The Liberator
8. ABC Powers

What Happened When

Connect each of the following dates with an important event in American history.

1. 1608
2. 1823
3. 1867
4. 1898
5. 1927

Who's Who in History

Be sure you know the part each of the following played in the history of Latin America.

1. Simon Bolívar
2. José San Martín
3. Toussaint L'Ouverture
4. Rafael Trujillo
5. Juan Perón
6. Bernardo O'Higgins

Study Questions

1. a. What territory did the United States acquire after the Spanish-American War?

   b. Explain why it was more difficult after 1898 for the United States to remain neutral when wars broke out in other parts of the world.

2. Write a paragraph about Canada touching on (a) her natural resources, (b) the size of the population, (c) differences between Quebec and the rest of Canada, (d) the type of government Canada has, and (e) relations between Canada and the United States.

3. a. Why do most of the people of Latin America speak Spanish?

   b. When and how did the nations of Latin America win independence?

   c. Who is the great hero of Latin America?

   d. How many republics are there in Latin America?

4. a. Why are good relations with Mexico vitally important to the United States?

   b. What did Dwight Morrow accomplish in Mexico?

5. State two reasons why Central America is important to the United States.

6. Why did the United States send troops to Haiti and the Dominican Republic on certain occasions?

7. How is Argentina governed?

8. How does Brazil compare in size and development with other nations?

9. What handicaps has Chile had to overcome to become a modern, progressive nation?

10. Explain what the Good Neighbor Policy is. Is it a success?

LET'S LOOK AT WHAT WE'VE LEARNED

What important possessions did the United States acquire in the period between the Civil War and World War I?

1. Alaska, purchased from Russia in 1867; 2. Part of the Samoan Islands, annexed in 1899; 3. Hawaii, annexed in 1898; 4. Guam, Wake, and Puerto Rico, taken from Spain after the Spanish-American War; 5. The Panama Canal Zone, leased from Panama in 1903; 6. The Virgin Islands, purchased from Denmark in 1917.

(The Philippine Islands which were acquired from Spain in 1898 were given their independence in 1946.)

What were the causes and results of the Spanish-American War?

Americans sympathized with the Cubans who were trying to win independence from Spain. The United States battleship *Maine* was blown up in Havana harbor and Americans blamed Spain. Newspapers published stories of Spanish atrocities in Cuba that inflamed American public opinion.

As a result of the war the United States became a world power with possessions in the Pacific and the Caribbean.

Why was the building of the Panama Canal a tremendous achievement?

Many diplomatic obstacles had to be overcome before it was possible to lease land for the Canal. Tropical diseases had to be conquered. Landslides and mountain barriers proved great obstacles.

What part does the Panama Canal play in American defense?

It is a key point in American military planning. It strengthens the defense of the United States because the Navy can quickly send warships from the Atlantic to the Pacific.

However, it is necessary to defend the Canal itself. Many bases and fortifications have been set up in the Caribbean and in the Pacific to protect all approaches to the Canal.

Why and when did the United States become interested in the Far East?

Soon after the Revolution American ships began trading with China. Americans wanted to sell their products to the millions who live in the Far East and also buy the products of the region.

In 1853–54 Commodore Perry led an expedition to Japan and persuaded the Hermit Nation to open her doors to world trade.

A GOOD NEIGHBOR

What troubles have developed in American relations with the Far East?

The United States developed the Open Door Policy which said that all nations should have equal rights to trade in China. This proved hard to enforce. The Japanese wished to take over China. This was one reason why Japan attacked Pearl Harbor in 1941.

China and the United States fought on the same side in World War II but after the war the Communists gained control and made China unfriendly to the United States.

How did American foreign policy change after 1898?

The United States became a world power with possessions in distant parts of the world. It became very difficult to remain neutral when other countries went to war. The United States found it was very important to be friends with neighbor nations. The Good Neighbor Policy was adopted and has been quite successful.

Connecting the Past with the Present . . .

You live on the world's main street. Events that happen in the most distant parts of the world influence your life. A Communist victory in Southeast Asia, a revolution in Central America, a flood in Western Europe — each of these may affect your life and will almost surely affect the taxes you or your family must pay.

Why does the United States have to get involved in troubles all over the globe? Why must young Americans stand guard in Korea and France and dozens of other remote spots?

It all goes back to 1898 and the Spanish-American War. The United States became a world power at that time. Since then, the United States has grown rich and powerful and has had to take on great responsibilities. Therefore you and other Americans, especially young Americans, must bear a share of the burden of keeping the world peaceful and orderly.

Living on the world's main street is not just a succession of troubles, however. It has its privileges, too. You have the opportunity to travel and to work and serve in many lands. You have the respect of many nations who look to you to guard their freedom and safety. Most of all, you have the chance to make this a better world for everyone living in it.

Questions for Discussion and Review

1. What were the causes of the Spanish-American War?
2. How would you rate the Spanish army and navy of 1898?
3. What were the results of the Spanish-American War?
4. How did the Philippines become an independent nation?
5. Using the following headings make a chart of the possessions of the United States:

   Possession   Date Acquired   How Acquired   Principal Products

6. How was yellow fever brought under control?
7. How was China changed from America's ally in World War II to an enemy in the Korean War?
8. Using the following headings make a chart of the nations of the Western Hemisphere including the United States:

   Country   Language   Principal Products   Large Cities

9. Because the United States is a world power all Americans have extra responsibilities. What are some responsibilities which you have that a teen-ager in Peru does not have?

THE HISTORY LABORATORY

Here are some suggestions for activities that you will find interesting and profitable.

Plan a Fiesta

Arrange a party featuring the customs of any of the nations studied in this Unit. For instance, have a fiesta complete with songs, dances, foods, costumes, and games.

WHAT AND WHEN

Opening of Japan
1853-54

Alaska purchased
1867

Spanish-Americ[an]
1898

For Those Who Like to Draw . . .

Draw a pictorial map of Latin America or part of Latin America. Illustrate the resources, products, and ways of life.

Draw a map or chart to illustrate how the Panama Canal saves weeks of ocean travel on the trade routes of the world.

Prepare a Scrapbook . . .

Make a scrapbook of news reports and stories about the Western Hemisphere. Arrange it topically under such headings as politics, economics, natural resources, society, and sports.

A Latin-American Directory . . .

Make a "Who's Who" of important people of the Western Hemisphere. This should include the present leaders of each government with their titles.

Dig Out the Facts . . .

Discover the details of the experiments of Dr. Lazear and Dr. Reed that proved yellow fever was carried by mosquitoes. Report your findings to the class.

Arrange a Display . . .

Prepare a bulletin board tour of cities of the Western Hemisphere for your class. Pictures can be obtained from travel folders, magazines, and newspapers.

Front Page Report . . .

Write an eye-witness account of events in the Spanish-American War as you saw them when you were a war correspondent.

Open Door Policy
1899

Panama Canal
1914

Virgin Islands purchased
1917

PUERTO RICO VIRGIN ISLANDS

CARIBBEAN SEA

Sports Fans Special . . .

Write a sports column which includes the following information:

1. The extent to which baseball is played in the nations of the Western Hemisphere.

2. Some of the all-time great athletes who have come from the Western Hemisphere nations outside of the United States.

3. The extent to which bull fighting, association football (soccer), and ice hockey are played in neighbor nations.

Traveler's Tales . . .

Invite people who have visited nations you are studying to come to the classroom and tell about their travels. You will find that many former servicemen can tell you about these countries and illustrate their talk with souvenirs and photographs.

For Those Who Like to Write . . .

Write a biography of any of the famous people studied in this Unit.

Let's Read about the United States as a World Power

BONNER, MARY, *Canada and Her Story*, Knopf, 1950.
BROWN, ROSE, *Land and People of Brazil*, Lippincott, 1946.
**BURLINGAME, ROGER, *Mosquitoes in the Big Ditch*, Winston, 1952.
CONSIDINE, BOB, *Panama Canal*, Random, 1951.
CROCKETT, LUCY H., *Teru; a Tale of Yokohama*, Holt, 1950.
EDELMAN, LILY, *Japan in Story and Pictures*, Harcourt, 1953.
GALT, THOMAS, *Volcano*, Scribner, 1946.
GILBERT, KENNETH, *Arctic Venture*, Holt, 1950.
GILL, R., and HOKE, H., *The Story of the Other America*, Houghton, 1951.
*GILL, R., and HOKE, H., *Paco Goes to the Fair*, Holt, 1940.
GOETZ, DELIA, *Other Young Americans*, Morrow, 1948.
HAHN, EMILY, *The Picture Story of China*, McKay, 1946.
*HOFFMAN, FLORIA, *Primitivo and His Dog*, Dutton, 1950.
LONGSTRETH, T. M., *The Scarlet Force*, Macmillan, 1953.
*O'NEILL, HESTER, *Picture Story of Alaska*, McKay, 1951.
PARISH, HELEN, *At the Palace Gates*, Viking, 1949.
ROSS, PATRICIA, *Made in Mexico*, Knopf, 1952.
SPENCER, CORNELIA, *Japan*, Holiday, 1948.

     * indicates easy reading   ** indicates advanced reading

Unit 12

THE UNITED STATES BECAME THE LEADER OF THE FREE WORLD (1917-1954)

"AMERICANS have the advantage over the French because of their long legs," said a French officer after American troops won a big battle in World War I.

It was the first time American troops had appeared in Europe and foreigners were surprised by how well the "Yanks" fought.

Americans, too, might well have been startled by their own strength. From a nation devoted to neutrality America developed into the leader in the fight for freedom. But it didn't happen overnight. What was the first break in American neutrality? How did the United States get into World War I? What was American feeling about the peace treaty and the League of Nations?

The world "blew up" again in 1939. How did World War II affect America? After Germany and Japan surrendered, there was no real peace. Who was the new enemy of freedom in the world? How did war start in Korea? Why was the United States involved?

The answers are in this Unit: The story of America's fight in two wars and her rise to world leadership.

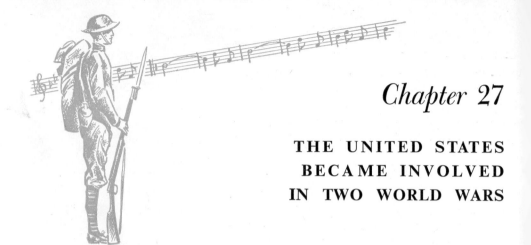

Chapter 27

THE UNITED STATES
BECAME INVOLVED
IN TWO WORLD WARS

"The sky over the battlefield, both before and after dawn, aflame with exploding shells, star signals, burning supply dumps and villages presented a scene at once picturesque and terrible. Here, at last, an American army was fighting under its own flag. Confidence in our troops dispelled every doubt of ultimate victory."

So General John J. Pershing described the beginning of the first victorious American attack in World War I. How did America get into the war? Why was a century old tradition of neutrality forsaken?

With victory came the terrible problem of establishing peace in the world. President Wilson sailed to Europe with high hopes of arranging a just peace treaty and setting up a League of Nations. What became of Wilson's hopes? How was the idea of a League of Nations received in the United States?

Revolutions in Russia brought a dictatorship; later in Italy and Germany, dictators took over the government. Once again the world pressed closer to war. What did Americans do when Britain and France declared war on Germany? What brought America into World War II? The answers are part of the story of America's part in two world wars — the story told in this chapter.

murder led to war in 1914. While the United States was gaining new possessions and becoming a world power, certain European nations were also trying to expand. They wanted colonies and markets. Chief among these was Germany.

The Germans were hard, skilful workers. They produced large quantities of steel, chemicals, and other manufactured goods. They wanted to sell their goods in foreign lands. They also wanted more land and resources. These aims brought them into conflict with France, Britain, and Russia who also wanted foreign markets and additional territory.

There was bitterness between France and Germany for another reason. In 1870 the Germans had defeated France and seized Alsace-Lorraine (AL sas-lah RAYN), a region rich in coal and iron. The French never forgot their loss. They were determined to get Alsace-Lorraine back.

There were conflicts between other nations also. Russia and Austria-Hungary were each trying to gain land and influence in eastern Europe. Italy desired to annex territory that belonged to Austria-Hungary.

As a result of these and other conflicting interests, Europe became divided into two systems of *alliances*. An alliance is an agreement — often a secret agreement — between two or more nations. They promise to help one another in war and peace. An alliance is usually directed against some other nation or group of nations. Germany and Austria-Hungary formed one alliance. They agreed to work together to get what they wanted. Later Turkey and Bulgaria joined their side. Opposing them were France, Great Britain, and Russia. They formed an alliance.

Both groups worked feverishly to build up armies and navies. Each was determined to keep the other side from gaining land or influence. Thus Europe became a "powder keg." Almost any dispute could cause an explosion.

That was the situation in the summer of 1914 when Archduke Francis Ferdinand, the heir to the Austrian throne, set out with his wife to visit Bosnia. Bosnia was a province on the border between Austria and Serbia (now part of Yugoslavia). Serbia was very friendly with Russia. The Serbians felt Bosnia should belong to them and not to Austria-Hungary.

The people of Bosnia were unhappy under Austrian rule. A young man named Princip (PREEN tsip) thought he might win freedom for the province by killing the Archduke. He obtained guns in Serbia, and then went to Sarajevo (SAH rah yeh voh), the capital of Bosnia. There on June 28, 1914, he shot and killed Francis Ferdinand and his wife.

The leaders of Austria-Hungary blamed Serbia for the murder. They said the Serbians had encouraged and aided Princip. They made humiliating demands; when Serbia

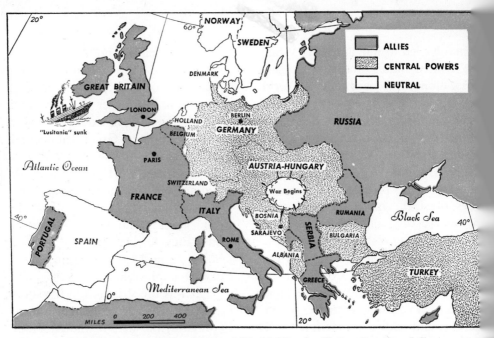

This map shows Europe at the beginning of World War I. Notice the size of Germany and the Austro-Hungarian Empire. Why were they called the *Central Powers?*

(encouraged by Russia) refused to do all the things demanded, Austria-Hungary declared war on Serbia.

True to her alliance, Germany sided with Austria-Hungary. Russia backed up Serbia; then France, true to *her* alliance, backed up Russia and declared war on Germany. Great Britain sided with France and Russia, partly because of her alliance and partly because the Germans invaded little Belgium on their way to attack France. (Britain had promised long before to protect Belgium against any attackers.)

Thus, in a few weeks, most of Europe was at war. France, Great Britain, and Russia were known as the *Allies*. After a year's delay, Italy joined their side. Germany, Austria-Hungary, and Turkey were known as

the *Central Powers* because they were located in Central Europe. Most of the fighting took place in France and Belgium and on the sea. The conflict, now called World War I, lasted from 1914 to 1918. The suffering, destruction, and death were beyond anything the world had seen up to that time.

America tried to remain neutral. When the Archduke was killed, Americans paid little attention. Many newspapers did not even put the news on the front page. When the war spread over Europe, Americans considered it none of their business. They were going to remain neutral just as George Washington had advised long before. The United States did remain neutral for almost

TWO WORLD WARS

three years. But at last the nation became involved, and the United States sent an army to fight in Europe for the first time in her history.

Why did the United States get drawn into the war after three years of neutrality? There were many reasons. Most — but by no means all — Americans sympathized with the Allies. They did not like the aggressive way German leaders talked and acted. They were horrified by the invasion of little Belgium. However, the chief reason was *submarine warfare.*

The German Navy was too small and weak to defeat the British Navy, so Germany built many submarines or "undersea boats" which attacked and sank Allied merchant ships, often without warning. In 1915, near the coast of southern Ireland, they sank the big British passenger ship, the *Lusitania.* More than 100 Americans traveling on the *Lusitania* were drowned. This aroused great anger in the United States. "Wholesale murder on the high seas," a New York newspaper called it.

Then German submarines began attacking American merchant ships carrying food and supplies to Britain and France. President Wilson protested vigorously, and for a time the Germans stopped their attacks. But the fighting in Europe grew desperate. Germany could not get supplies from the United States because British warships stopped American ships from carrying cargoes to the Central Powers. Ameri-

Boastful Emperor or *Kaiser* Wilhelm II (below) led Germany to war in 1914. He fled to Holland when defeat came in 1918.

cans were angry at the British for interfering in this way, and President Wilson protested strongly. However, the British did not sink ships without warning, killing passengers and seamen, as the Germans did.

The United States entered the war in 1917. Early in 1917 Germany announced she would wage "unrestricted submarine warfare." This meant that submarines would sink without warning any American ship they saw on the high seas. President Wilson's patience was at an end. He ended relations with Germany.

In March the nation heard that five unarmed American ships had been sunk. The President reluctantly asked Congress to declare war. Sadly he told his secretary, "My message today was a message of death for our young men." Congress did not take long to decide. On April 6, 1917 the United States declared war on Germany.

The Germans thought they could defeat the Allies and end the war before the United States could get an army to France. They made the fatal mistake of underestimating American ability to get things done in a hurry. There were only 200,000 men in the American Army when war was declared, but in little more than a year the number grew to four million. Hundreds of factories were built in a few months. American men and women worked overtime to turn out guns, airplanes, ships, and war materials.

Men were drafted in World War I. Here Sec. of War Baker draws a number. The plan was similar to Selective Service today.

Three months after Congress declared war, the first American troops marched through Paris on their way to battle. By December, 1917 more than 100,000 had arrived. That was only the beginning. By the middle of 1918, 10,000 American soldiers were arriving in France every day. Meantime, the American Navy was chasing submarines and protecting troop ships. Soon the submarines became the hunted instead of the hunters; they had to hide to avoid being sunk.

Early in 1918 German military leaders decided to try to end the war in a hurry. They staged a "big push" on British and French lines, hoping to drive clear across France to the seacoast. American troops fought with British and French regiments in several battles of this campaign: at Belleau (beh LO) Wood and Château Thierry (shah TOH tyeh RE), Americans helped slow up the Germans.

The turning point came at what is known as the Second Battle of the Marne. As you can see on the map, below, the Marne is a river in north-eastern France. It flows west to join the Seine (SAYN) River at Paris. More than 85,000 American soldiers took part in the fight that kept the Germans from sweeping down the Marne Valley and conquering Paris.

Strengthened by the arrival of thousands of Americans in France, British and French military leaders were able to take the offensive — that is, to attack the Germans instead of just fighting to delay or hold back the enemy's advance. In August, 1918 American troops were organized into a separate army and given one section of the battlefront to defend. The American army and air forces in France made up what was called the *American Expedi-*tionary Force or the AEF. The commander-in-chief of the AEF was General John J. Pershing.

Born in Missouri just before the Civil War, Pershing was graduated from West Point and fought the Sioux Indians on the frontier. He took part in the Spanish-American War and then went to the Philippines where he spent several years fighting to put down rebellion there. Later he was sent to the Mexican border to try to capture the bandit chief, Pancho Villa (PAWN choh VEE yah). Pershing's training and experience helped transform the hastily-assembled American troops into an efficient fighting force.

In September, 1918 Pershing led the first distinctly American offen-

This map shows the chief battlefields of World War I. Most of the fighting took place in Belgium and France. Germany was not invaded until after the Armistice. American troops played a decisive part in the battles of the Argonne and the Marne.

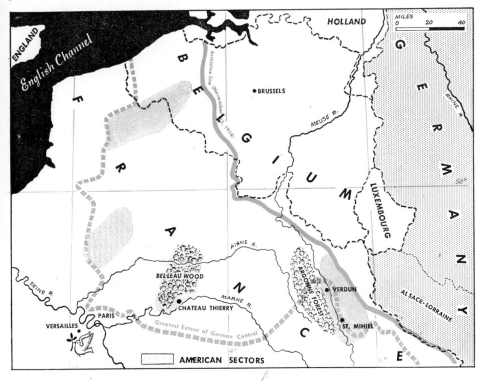

World War I was big and grim as these pictures show. (Top) Soldiers "go over the top," charging from trenches. (Center) Tanks roll forward. (Bottom) Men and supplies advance in the Argonne.

sive. The assignment was to capture an area known as the *Saint Mihiel Salient* (san mee YEL SALE ih ent) which the Germans had held for a long time. Within twenty-four hours the Americans surrounded the area and cut off the German's retreat. They captured 16,000 prisoners and 443 guns, but the cost was high. Seven thousand Americans were killed or wounded.

After this brilliant success American troops moved west to the section of the battlefield between the Meuse (MEWZ) River and the Argonne (AHR gawn) Forest. They were ordered to capture a railroad that was the main line of supply for many German regiments. More than a million Americans took part in the Meuse-Argonne offensive. They helped force the Germans to withdraw all along the battlefront. By the first week of November, 1918 the enemy was "on the run." German military leaders realized the situation was hopeless and asked for an *armistice* (AHR mis tis) or "cease fire" agreement.

The United States did not join the League of Nations. How was peace to be made with the Germans? Months before, the President had offered a plan in a message to Congress. It consisted of *Fourteen Points* which set forth the fundamental changes Wilson believed must be made to insure permanent peace. Here are three of the most important points: (1) The President asked for an end to the secret treaties and alliances which had divided Europe into enemy camps. (2) He demanded a reduction of armies and navies. (3) He asked that an international organization or *League of Nations* be set up to settle disputes between nations. Wilson's plan was accepted as the basis of the peace treaty, but unfortunately, many points were disregarded later.

The Germans surrendered on November 11, 1918. In memory of this, Americans celebrate a holiday known as Armistice Day — or more recently as Veterans Day — on November 11. Three weeks later, President Wilson and a group of advisers sailed for Paris and the Peace Conference.

Wilson had a hard time at Paris. The other leaders, especially Clemenceau (KLAY man SO) of France, cared little for Wilson's Fourteen Points. They wanted to get everything they could from the enemy, forgetting that this was likely to lead to another great war in time to come.

After many months of bitter argument, representatives of the victorious nations presented Germany with a treaty of peace. It was called the *Treaty of Versailles* (ver SAH y'). It provided for severe punishment of Germany. The Germans had to sign, but they made up their minds to get revenge.

Germany lost much valuable territory including Alsace-Lorraine. She also had to agree to pay a huge amount of *reparations* (rep uh RAY shuns) or compensation for damage done in the war. The Austro-Hungarian Empire was broken up, and most of its land was given to other countries. The Polish people regained their independence; a new nation called Czechoslovakia (CHECK oh sloh VAH kih ah) was created. Serbia gained vast territories and became known as Yugoslavia.

President Wilson did not like

Here are the "Big Four" at the Paris Peace Conference, 1919. Left to right, Orlando of Italy, Lloyd George of Britain, Clemenceau of France, President Wilson of the United States.

some parts of the Treaty of Versailles, but he was proud of one provision. This was the creation of the League of Nations, an organization to work for world peace. However, when Wilson brought the treaty back to America, he found that many people, especially the Republican leaders in the Senate, did not want to belong to the League. (Wilson was a Democrat and a majority of the Senate was Republican.) They said that taking part in an international organization was contrary to the advice Washington had given the nation in his Farewell Address (page 227). Wilson tried hard, but he lost the fight. He really gave his life to the cause. He traveled about the country pleading for the League. In Pueblo, Colorado he was taken ill and had to give up. For the rest of his life he was a helpless invalid. The Senate refused to approve the Treaty of Versailles and the United States never entered the League of Nations.

After World War I, the United States tried to return to the old policy of isolation (i soh LAY shun) it had followed during most of the 19th century. This proved difficult because the nation was now a world power with interests and possessions in many parts of the world. European nations resented American efforts to keep out of international affairs. They said, "Your President Wilson insisted we set up the League of Nations. Now you refuse to join it or help us work for world peace!"

So the Allies who had fought against Germany and won a great victory now began to quarrel. Relations between Japan and the United States became especially troublesome. The Japanese were eager to

This map shows Europe in 1918. What new nations appear? Which nations have shrunk?

gain power in Asia. Japan had joined the Allies in the war against Germany and felt entitled to a reward. They wanted to control China but the United States opposed this.

Efforts to build a permanent peace failed. The First World War was scarcely over before threats of another conflict appeared. Although the United States refused to join the League of Nations, American leaders tried in other ways to remove some of the causes of trouble. In 1921, the Washington Arms Conference was held to reduce the size of navies and try to bring about peace in the Far East. Two treaties were signed; for a time the world felt a thrill of hope, but the treaties were soon disregarded by Japan.

In 1927 the United States and France signed an agreement promising to "outlaw war" and settle disputes peaceably. Many other nations signed this *Peace Pact of Paris* as it was known. However, there was no way to make nations keep their promise so it had little influence on events.

During the 1920's people felt somewhat hopeful about the possibility of avoiding future wars. The United States was prosperous. Most Americans were making money. In Europe there was great activity rebuilding homes and factories ruined in the war. Americans loaned millions to European nations for the purpose. This was in addition to huge amounts of money, food, and weapons the United States had loaned Europe during the war. How were these *war debts* to be repaid? That became one of the most vexing problems among nations. No solution was found. The European nations, except Finland, never finished paying their debts — much to the disgust of American taxpayers.

The League of Nations was weak. The League of Nations was organized soon after World War I. The United States never joined it, but most nations did. The League had its headquarters in Geneva, Switzerland. There, representatives of member nations met and discussed world problems much as the United Nations does today.

In Holland the League set up a *World Court* to hear cases arising out of disputes between nations. At Geneva, the nations gained valuable experience in working together and learning to talk over problems. The League was successful in settling a few disputes, but it failed to correct the big causes of war.

Why did the League fail? Chiefly because it always worked under three great handicaps. The first was the fact that membership did not include all important nations. The United States never joined; Russia belonged for several years and then was expelled for aggressive acts against Finland. Germany was allowed to join a few years after the war but later left in anger. Japan quit when

CROSS-CURRENTS IN OUR FOREIGN RELATIONS AFTER WORLD WAR I

① We refused to sign Versailles Treaty ...

① ... though President Wilson had taken a leading part in writing it.

② We refused to join the League of Nations ...

② ... but did participate in many League activities.

③ We raised our tariff rates ...

③ ... but spent record totals on travel and investment abroad.

④ We refused to join the World Court ...

④ ... but were co-sponsor of the Kellog-Briand pact "outlawing war" in settlement of disputes.

⑤ We refused to completely cancel War Debts owed us by our Allies ...

⑤ ... but sponsored and supported Disarmament Conferences.

The League discusses the Italian invasion of Ethiopia. Baron Aloisi, the Italian delegate, is shown stating Italy's case. The League condemned the invasion, and Italy angrily resigned.

a League committee criticized her for taking over Manchuria (see page 538).

A second great handicap was the League's own organization. To take any action, all member nations had to agree. A unanimous vote was necessary. This was the same defect that had weakened the Articles of Confederation (page 180) and it proved just as damaging to the effectiveness of the League.

The third and most serious handicap was the lack of power to enforce the League's decisions. The League had no army, navy or air force. It could not make nations stop fighting. For example, when Italy attacked Ethiopia (EE thih O pih ah), an African country, the League of Nations condemned Italy's act. But the Italian government paid no attention. Ethiopia was quickly conquered and made into an Italian colony while the League stood by helplessly.

In spite of all the bloodshed of World War I, the seeds of war re-mained: bad feeling among nations, greed for land, competition for markets, and the desire for revenge. To make matters worse, the world suffered from a severe business depression in the 1930's. In every country there were large numbers of jobless people. It became harder and harder to sell goods. Banks failed, factories closed, while government leaders searched desperately for some way to feed and clothe the needy.

Dictators gained power in Italy and Germany. In the emergency some people lost faith in themselves and their government. They cried out for a strong leader who would take care of them. In Italy and Germany, where the depression was especially severe, this led to the creation of dictatorships or "one man rule."

In Italy a man named Mussolini (MOOS soh LEE nee) organized a sort of private army he called the "Blackshirts." The Blackshirts were *Fascists* (FASH ists). They were against letting the common people have any part in the government. They believed in having a strong leader and putting through their program by force.

The Blackshirts were men who were dissatisfied for various reasons. Some were soldiers who had come back from the war and had been unable to find jobs. Some were small businessmen who were afraid Italy would collapse into communism as Russia had already done. Others were office workers or laborers who had lost their jobs. They followed Mussolini blindly. He used them to seize control of the government and make himself master of Italy. Then he began to build up Italy's army and navy. This served two purposes: (1) it provided jobs for the unemployed; and (2) it gave Mussolini more power in foreign affairs. If weaker nations refused to do as he wished he could use his military power to crush them.

However, with all his loud talk and threats, Mussolini could not bring prosperity to Italy. The people dared not complain, for anyone who did was imprisoned. Freedom vanished when Mussolini and his Blackshirts took charge. Worst of all, Mussolini steadily led the nation down the road to war. It was he who launched the attack on Ethiopia in 1935.

In Germany, much the same sort of thing happened that had happened earlier in Italy. Many Germans never really accepted their defeat in World War I. A republic was established in Germany, but it was not successful, partly because the people lacked experience in governing themselves.

A few years after the war there occurred a terrible *inflation* (in FLAY shun) or sudden, sharp rise in prices. German money became practically worthless. It took a basketful of paper bills to buy a magazine. People who had saved their money for years found they had nothing; their savings would scarcely buy one meal. Germany's *middle class*, that is the people who were neither very rich nor very poor, was made penniless.

Then, a few years after the disastrous inflation, came the depression. Millions of Germans lost their jobs. They blamed the government. They wanted a new leader. They found one, a house painter and ex-soldier named Adolf Hitler. He had failed at almost everything, but he had the ability to make speeches which seemed to cast a spell over the Germans. He told them they had not been defeated but had been betrayed. He blamed everything on the Jews. He promised to lead the Germans to victory and prosperity.

Hitler built up his private army known as the "Brown Shirts." Soon he was head of a political party, the National Socialist or *Nazi* (NAH tsee) Party.

The Nazis got control of the German government in 1933; and soon set up a dictatorship. Almost all rights were abolished; people had

580

only duties. Everyone had to do as Hitler said. The Jews were terribly persecuted. Hitler claimed they were responsible for all of Germany's troubles, and encouraged everyone to abuse them. Meantime, thousands of unemployed young men were put into uniform as "Storm troopers." Anyone who dared oppose Hitler was either killed or thrown into a concentration camp.

Like Mussolini, Hitler took an aggressive, war-like attitude in world affairs. For a time the democratic, western nations tried to get along with Hitler and Mussolini. Leaders of France and Great Britain hoped that by giving in on certain points they could keep the dictators from starting another war. They did not interfere when Italy attacked Ethiopia in 1935. They let Hitler rearm Germany and send troops into the Rhine River Valley, although this was forbidden in the Treaty of Versailles. The policy of giving in to the dictators soon came to be known as the *appeasement* (uh PEEZ ment).

The dictators made alliances. As time went by, Mussolini and Hitler drew closer together. They formed an alliance called the *Axis* to get what they wanted. Later Japan joined their alliance. As Germany, Italy, and Japan lined up together, the free nations felt they had to stand together to oppose them. Thus the old system of alliances was revived. The great powers of the world became divided into two camps. Once again, the United States tried to keep from taking sides, but it was clear to most observers that when a showdown came, America would join the free nations and oppose the dictatorships.

Where did Russia fit into the picture? After World War I, Russia was an outcast nation. In 1917 a revolution had occurred in Russia. The Czar's government was ended. For a few months a group of moderate-minded men tried to set up a

The dictators talked big. Adolf Hitler (left) is shown preaching his doctrine of hate. Benito Mussolini (right) clenches his fist to show the power he claimed Italy would have under his rule. Both men were able to lead their people blindly down the road to war.

Hitler celebrated his 50th birthday in 1939. He is shown at extreme left, reviewing a parade in his honor. Note the soldiers' characteristic "goose step" or stiff-legged parade step. Five months after this picture, Hitler's troops invaded Poland and started World War II.

republic. However, they were soon driven out by extreme radicals or *Communists*. The Communists set up a dictatorship, destroying all private rights. They took control of the land and the factories. They refused to pay the debts of the former Russian government. Worst of all, they tried in every way they could to overthrow the governments of other nations. The first head of the Russian Communists was Nikolai Lenin (NEE koh LI LEN in). When he died, a tough, gangster-like fighter named Joseph Stalin (STAH leen) managed to get control of the government and made himself dictator of Russia.

For many years Hitler claimed to hate Communism. He said he was arming Germany to protect her from Communism. Mussolini also claimed to be an enemy of Communism. But Hitler and Mussolini had much in common with Stalin, the Communist leader. They were all dictators. They all hated freedom. They all wanted to defeat Britain, France, and the United States. They all wanted to grab land and power.

So, in 1939 Hitler made a deal with Stalin. They agreed that neither Germany nor Russia would attack each other. If either nation went to war with a third power the other would remain neutral. This meant that if Germany attacked one of her neighbors — Poland or France — Russia would keep out of the dispute.

This was a great advantage to Hitler, because the Germans were always afraid of being attacked from east and west at the same time. That was what happened in World War I when France and Russia both went to war with Germany at the same time. By the German-Russian Pact of 1939, Hitler made sure the eastern approach or "back door" was secure against invasion.

It was Hitler's aim to annex the territory of his weaker neighbors. He had seized most of Czechoslovakia in 1938. Poland was next. In the Treaty of Versailles some German land, including the seaport of Danzig (DAHN tsik) had been given to the newly-revived state of Poland. This was called the *Polish Corridor*. A few days after signing the German-Russian Pact, Hitler de-

TWO WORLD WARS

manded of Poland that she give up the Polish Corridor. British and French leaders advised the Poles to resist, promising help if Germany attacked Poland.

World War II began in Poland. In the late summer of 1939 Europe was once more a "powder keg," ready to blow up, just as it had in 1914. Hitler struck the match when he sent his armies marching into Poland on September 1, 1939. Britain and France demanded that he withdraw. Hitler refused, blaming all the trouble on the British because they had encouraged Poland to resist. So on September 3, 1939, Britain and France declared war on Germany. The Second World War had begun.

The Polish people fought like heroes, but they could not stop the German war machines. Hitler had built up a highly efficient army, equipped with the latest and deadliest of weapons. He had many *panzer* (PAHN zur) divisions. These consisted of hundreds of tanks and artillery pieces mounted on fast trucks. Foot soldiers were moved to battle in trucks and armored cars. These divisions were supported by many bombing planes which flew close to the ground. The panzer divisions would attack one point and break through the Polish lines; then they would spread out, smashing communications and disorganizing the Polish troops.

In less than four weeks the Nazis conquered Poland. They called it "lightning war" and warned other nations to expect the same treatment if they dared oppose Germany. Meantime, the Russians had invaded Poland from the East. Russia and Germany divided Poland between them.

After the conquest of Poland, there was little fighting for several months. Then in the spring of 1940 German armies, without warning, invaded Holland and Belgium. Holland was conquered in four days; Belgium resisted for two weeks and then had to surrender. The Nazis raced into northern France, easily defeating the French and British armies. The British had to get their army out of France to avoid capture. By heroic efforts they withdrew some 300,000 men by way of the port of Dunkerque (DUN kirk).

Up to this point Italy had remained neutral, in spite of the alliance with Germany. Now Mussolini thought

The British rescued their army at Dunkerque. The picture below shows how hundreds of little boats helped the withdrawal after France was defeated in 1940.

Winston Churchill's leadership helped save Britain from defeat in 1940. At left, the gallant old man talks to the nation. He is wearing his famous "siren suit" or air raid outfit. At right is a view of London after a German air attack, which left many buildings burning and in ruins. Hitler hoped such raids would make it easy to invade Britain, but he was disappointed.

his chance had come. He declared war on France and Great Britain. Italian troops invaded southern France as the Germans neared Paris. And so France fell in June, 1940. The Germans and their Italian helpers were masters of western Europe.

Next Hitler tried to conquer Great Britain. He sent thousands of airplanes to bomb British cities and railroads. They did enormous damage, but the British refused to surrender. They had found a stout-hearted leader, Winston Churchill, who became Prime Minister in May, 1940. Churchill dared Hitler to do his worst, saying, "We shall defend our island whatever the cost . . . we shall fight on the beaches . . . we shall fight in the fields and in the streets, we shall fight in the hills; we shall never surrender . . ."

Americans helped the Allies. While this was going on, Americans were officially neutral. However there was little doubt where American sympathies lay. Most Americans hoped they could keep out of the quarrel, but they feared this was unlikely. The cruelty of Hitler and Mussolini, their ruthless disregard of the rights of humanity, aroused disgust and anger in the United States. Sooner or later Americans would have to take up arms against the enemies of freedom and decency.

The nation began to prepare its defenses. Congress voted millions for ships, planes, and guns. In answer to Prime Minister Churchill's appeal, the War Department sent Great Britain large amounts of surplus or out-of-date weapons.

The feeling grew that America could not let Hitler continue to

584

trample on the free nations. In March, 1941 Congress passed the *Lend-Lease Act*. This permitted the President to sell, lend, transfer, or lease war supplies to any nation whose defense he considered vital to American safety. In other words, the United States would supply weapons to any nation that was fighting the dictators. Steadily America was moving away from the idea of staying neutral.

The nation began to strengthen its defenses. In September, 1940 Congress passed the *Selective Service Act*. This required all men between 21 and 35 to register for military service. It was the first time in peace that the United States had ever "drafted" or required men to serve in the armed forces.

So far Japan was taking no active part in World War II. But Japan was a dictatorship like Germany, Italy, and Russia. No one man in Japan was so powerful as Hitler or Mussolini, but a small group of military leaders ruled the country and oppressed the people. It was to be expected that Japan would side with the Axis nations.

Then, after the fall of France, Japan signed a military alliance with Germany and Italy. It was clear that the alliance was directed against the United States. Japan felt that sooner or later she must fight America in order to be free to seize China. (As you read on page 537, the United States was helping China resist Japanese attacks.)

Hitler's terrible air attacks on Britain lasted from the summer of 1940 until the spring of 1941. Then the attacks became less violent. Had the Germans given up hope of conquering Britain? Were they running short of planes or gasoline? What was Hitler up to now? The world learned the answer on June 22, 1941. With dramatic suddenness he turned and sent his armies eastward, invading Russia. He did this in spite of the fact that only two years before he had made a treaty of friendship with Stalin.

Taken by surprise, the Russians fell back. The Germans pushed hundreds of miles into Russia, conquering some of her richest provinces and cities. Britain and the United States rushed supplies to Russia to help her resist the Germans. When winter came, German victories came to an end. The terrible cold accomplished what nothing else had so far been able to do: it stopped the Nazi advance. The German army "bogged down" in Russia.

Japan attacked without warning December 7, 1941. Meantime relations between the United States and Japan were growing steadily more unfriendly. When the Japanese invaded France's colony of Indochina (so called because it lies between India and China), President Roosevelt took action that practically stopped all trade with Japan. This was intended as a warning to the Japanese leaders, but it had no effect.

In November, 1941 Secretary of State Hull began discussions with two Japanese representatives in an attempt to find a way to improve relations. The Japanese demanded that the United States abandon China and resume trade relations. In response, Hull demanded that Japan stop interfering in China and get out of Indochina. The Japanese asked for time to study Hull's proposals.

Meantime the Japanese army and navy went ahead with plans for a secret attack on the United States. President Roosevelt made a direct appeal to the Japanese emperor, asking him to preserve the peace. Americans were still hoping that the President and Secretary Hull would succeed in their efforts when terrible news came over thousands of radios: "Japan has attacked Pearl Harbor!"

It was a sneak attack. Without warning, early Sunday morning, on December 7, 1941 Japanese forces bombed the American naval base in Hawaii. Nineteen ships, including eight battleships, were hurt or destroyed. More than 100 planes were destroyed; 3581 soldiers, sailors, and civilians were killed or wounded.

They had no chance to defend themselves. On the same day Japan launched attacks on the Philippines, Guam, and Midway Island.

The next day Congress declared war on Japan. Germany and Italy hastened to declare war on the United States. Thus at the end of 1941 the nation was once more at war. In many ways, World War II was a continuation of World War I, and the period in between — from 1919 to 1941 — was merely a "long armistice" and not a real peace.

The causes of both wars were much the same: greed for land and trade, rivalry of neighbor nations, the military spirit, and a system of alliances. In both wars the United States tried to remain neutral but was eventually drawn into the fight. World War I brought great changes. It speeded up American life, encouraging the growth of factories and cities. World War II had even more far-reaching effects.

Remember Pearl Harbor! This picture shows some of the burning and damaged ships at America's great naval base in Hawaii after Japan's sneak attack, December 7, 1941.

CHAPTER SUMMARY

World War I lasted from 1914 to 1918. Chief causes were rivalry for land and markets, desire for revenge, and alliances that divided Europe. The murder of Archduke Francis Ferdinand was the immediate cause.

German submarine attacks involved America in the war in 1917. American troops under General Pershing helped defeat the German armies in 1918. President Wilson offered a peace plan called the Fourteen Points.

The Treaty of Versailles punished Germany. A League of Nations was set up, but the United States never joined. Efforts were made to remove causes of war, but failed.

The Communists gained control of Russia in 1917. Mussolini became dictator of Italy. Hitler got control of Germany partly because of the depression. Europe again became divided by alliances.

Hitler's invasion of Poland began World War II (1939–45). Germany conquered western Europe, than attacked Russia. The United States supplied Lend-Lease Aid to combat Hitler. The United States entered World War II after Japan attacked Pearl Harbor, December 7, 1941.

The Language of History

The following words and phrases appear in this chapter. Be sure you know the meaning of each.

1. AEF
2. Axis
3. fascist
4. alliance

5. inflation
6. depression
7. appeasement
8. armistice

9. League of Nations
10. World Court
11. Fourteen Points
12. reparations

What Happened When

Be sure you know the important events connected with each of the following dates.

1. 1914
2. 1917

3. 1918
4. 1929

5. 1933
6. 1935

7. 1939
8. 1941

Who's Who in History

Be sure you know the part each of the following played in the history of the world.

1. Woodrow Wilson
2. Nikolai Lenin
3. Joseph Stalin
4. John J. Pershing

5. Benito Mussolini
6. Archduke Francis Ferdinand
7. Adolf Hitler
8. Winston Churchill

Study Questions

1. **a.** What were the underlying causes that led to World War I?
   b. What was the immediate cause or "match that exploded the powder keg"?

2. **a.** Which nations were called the Central Powers in World War I?
   b. Which nations were called the Allies?

3. Why and when was the United States drawn into World War I?

4. **a.** What was Wilson's peace plan called?
   b. Give two provisions of his plan.

5. Why did not the United States join the League of Nations?

6. Show how each of the following helped bring about World War II:
   a. The world-wide depression of the 1930's.
   b. The growth of dictatorships.
   c. The desire for revenge.
   d. The desire for territory.

7. **a.** Which nations were called the Axis powers in World War II?
   b. Which nations fought against Hitler?

8. **a.** Why were the Germans able to win many victories in the early years of the war?
   b. What was the purpose of Lend-Lease Aid?

9. **a.** What deal was made between Hitler and Stalin?
   b. How and when was the agreement broken?

10. Why did the Japanese attack Pearl Harbor?

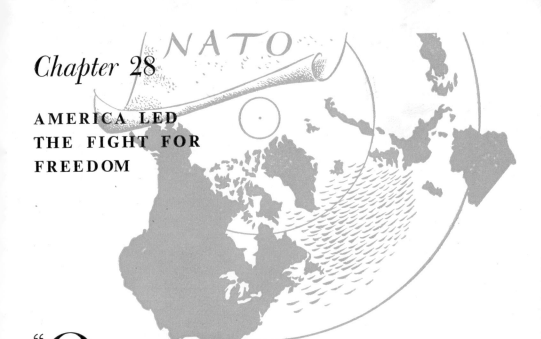

Chapter 28

AMERICA LED THE FIGHT FOR FREEDOM

"OBSERVERS in the tail of our ship saw a giant ball of fire rise as though from the bowels of the earth, belching forth enormous white smoke rings. Next they saw a giant pillar of purple fire, 10,000 feet high, shooting skyward with enormous speed. . . . There came shooting out of the top a giant mushroom that increased the height of the pillar to a total of 45,-000 feet." Thus a reporter described an atomic explosion over Japan in 1945. A week later World War II was over.

Actually, World War II was two wars: one in Europe, one in the Pacific. Why did the United Nations throw everything into the European War first?

The war over, the United States for the first time in its history prepared to enter an organization of nations. When was the United Nations planned? How does it work?

After the war, Russia became unfriendly: in the UN, she abused the veto; in satellite countries she destroyed freedom. What did the United States do about the spread of Communism? What happened when South Korea was attacked?

The answers to these and many other questions make up the story of this chapter: the recent history of the United States.

589

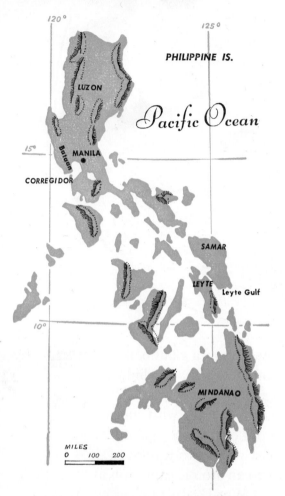

MILES
0   100   200

There was hard fighting in the Philippines. At Bataan, Corregidor, and Leyte Gulf, thousands of Americans fought bravely and died during the Second World War.

Other defeats followed Pearl Harbor. When the First World War ended in 1918 the United States went wild with joy. There were parades and celebrations in every village and town. Newspaper headlines screamed, "PEACE!" Fathers and mothers demanded, "Bring our boys home!"

Americans everywhere vowed,

"Whatever happens in Europe, we are going to keep out of it! No more foreign wars for us!"

Yet twenty-three years later the United States was involved in another world conflict. Japan's sudden attack on December 7, 1941 hurled the nation into the middle of the most terrible war in history.

The bombs that fell on Pearl Harbor did more than sink ships. They startled Americans out of dreams of remaining neutral. The nation had to fight for its very life. President Roosevelt proposed the name, *United Nations*, to describe all the countries fighting against Hitler and his friends. (The same name was later given to the international peace organization formed at the end of the war.)

Pearl Harbor was only the first of many disasters. The Japanese swept everything before them in their drive to conquer the Pacific area. The American Navy suffered such a blow at Pearl Harbor it could do little to stop the Japanese advance for many months.

Guam and Wake Island were quickly conquered in spite of the heroic resistance of American troops there. The Japanese landed in the Philippines and captured Manila, the capital, in less than a month. The American commander, General Douglas MacArthur, retreated to Bataan (buh TAN) Peninsula. There he set up headquarters in the fortress of Corregidor (kuh REG ih DORE) on Manila Bay. For more than three months American troops held out

590

against Japanese attacks. Food ran short; the number of sick and wounded grew. At last the men of Bataan had to surrender and start a "death march" to Japanese prisons.

Before the surrender, General MacArthur was ordered by President Roosevelt to leave the Philippines secretly and go to Australia. There he took command of troops in the Southwest Pacific. The troops were mostly Americans, Australians, and New Zealanders. Britain was too busy fighting Germany and Italy to spare many soldiers for the war in the Pacific. Russia remained at peace with Japan until the last days of the war. It was MacArthur's job to organize the fight to drive the Japanese back.

However, it was a long time before MacArthur's troops were able to take the offensive in the Pacific. Japan swiftly took over Southeast Asia and nearby islands. Indochina, Burma, Thailand (TAH ee land) or Siam, the Dutch East Indies — all were quickly conquered. Australia was threatened. Early in June, 1942 the Japanese bombed Dutch Harbor in Alaska. A few days later they occupied the islands of Attu and Kiska in the Aleutian (ah LOO shun) Island chain southwest of Alaska.

A victory was won in North Africa. Why didn't Americans throw their full strength into the war against Japan? Why was the flow of war supplies to the Pacific area a mere trickle? The answer was that America had to fight on two fronts. World War II was really two wars — the war in the Pacific and the war in Europe and Africa.

The military experts decided soon after Pearl Harbor that the war in Europe must be won first. Soldiers and sailors in the Pacific could only hope to delay or hold back the Japanese advance until victory in Europe was assured.

Why was it so important to win the fight against Hitler first? Partly because the Germans had conquered Western Europe (except Britain) and were threatening to conquer Africa next. And, as you can see on the map, page 592, the west coast of Africa is not far by airplane from the east coast of South America. If Hitler could get control of the port of Dakar (dah KAR) in French West Africa, he might try to bomb Brazil and capture landing fields. From there he could move north and attack the United States. You can see why American leaders were determined to stop the Germans from conquering Africa.

British leaders were equally determined, but for a different reason. The German advance in Africa was threatening the Suez (soo EZ) Canal.

Watching for submarines! These sailors on a U.S. warship are shown on guard to prevent attacks on merchant vessels carrying war supplies across the Atlantic in 1943.

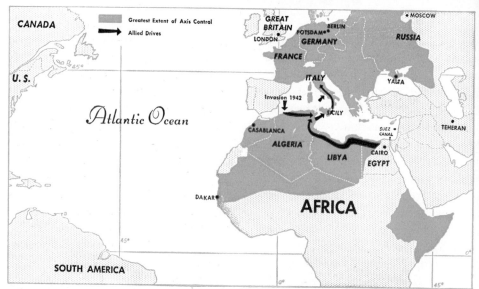

This map shows how close the Germans came to conquering all of Europe and Africa in World War II. Note how near Dakar, West Africa is to the eastern coast of South America. It was feared the Germans might use it as a base for an invasion of Brazil.

British ships going to and from India and Australia must pass through the Suez Canal or go all the way around Africa. The Suez was part of Britain's "lifeline" or communication with her Empire. It must not fall into German hands.

By the summer of 1942 the Germans had conquered much of North Africa and were heading for the Suez. They were also spreading down the west coast toward Dakar. American and British leaders made careful plans. In November they landed thousands of troops in North Africa. General Dwight D. Eisenhower was in charge of the campaign. In six months hard fighting the Germans were thoroughly beaten. Their leader, Erwin Rommel, the so-called "desert fox" fled; 250,000 Axis troops surrendered.

United Nations forces invaded Italy. The African victory gave the United Nations a base from which to invade Europe. The next step was an invasion of the island of Sicily (SIS uh lih) which, as you can see on the map on this page, lies between North Africa and Italy.

In July, 1943 United Nations troops landed in Sicily. They won control of the island in six weeks.

Sicily, in turn, served as a base for the invasion of Italy. In September, 1943 British and American forces landed in southern Italy and began to fight their way north. But the battle for Italy turned out to be unexpectedly difficult. Much of Italy is a land of rugged mountains and rushing rivers. Winter in the mountains was bitterly cold. Heavy rains washed out roads and bridges. The

American-British advance up the peninsula was slow and painful. Every mile was won at terrific cost. The Italian people, who had never been enthusiastic about the war, turned against Mussolini. He was arrested but soon escaped to join the Germans. (Later he was recaptured and shot.)

A new Italian government, which was set up, made peace in September, 1943. But the German troops who were in control of Italy continued to fight. They clung stubbornly to Italy's rocky hills and made the Americans and British pay for every mile they advanced.

The campaign in Italy dragged on and victory seemed far away and uncertain. Clearly, if Hitler was to be decisively defeated, Americans and British must invade France and carry the war into Germany.

Meanwhile, German armies in Russia were learning the taste of defeat. The Russian winter was terribly cold. The Germans lacked clothing and equipment suitable for fighting in such a climate. They had to retreat. Russian armies, aided by weapons and supplies from America, were able to recapture town after town. When summer came in 1943 the Germans tried to launch another attack, but it failed miserably. They were driven back to Poland.

France was invaded on D-Day, 1944. At last the tide was turning against the Germans. They were on the run in the East. Now was the time to attack from the West.

In the early years of the war Hitler's Nazis had conquered France, Belgium, Holland, and Luxembourg. The people of the conquered lands were restless and longing for freedom. However, the Germans had strong defenses. A military invasion of western Europe would be a tremendous and costly undertaking.

President Roosevelt and Prime Minister Churchill held several conferences to discuss such an invasion and to make plans for peace. The first of these meetings took place at Casablanca (CAHS ah BLAHNG kah), North Africa in January, 1943. There the invasion of Sicily and Italy was planned, and the possibility of an invasion of France was mentioned. The following August

President Franklin Roosevelt (left) and Prime Minister Winston Churchill (right) met at Casablanca, North Africa in 1943.

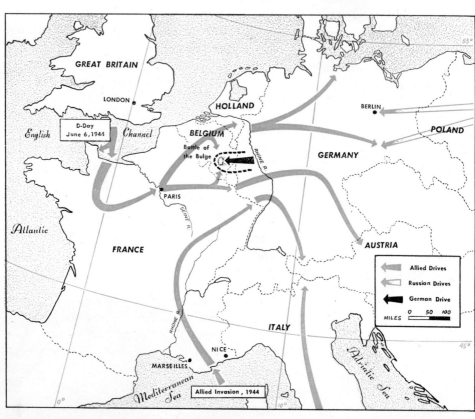

This map shows the major World War II campaigns in western Europe. Germany was forced to surrender in May, 1945 after American and British troops, landing in northwestern and also in southern France, invaded from the west, while Russian armies invaded from the east. Above the map are shown U.S. B-17 Flying Fortresses on a bombing raid over Berlin, and below is shown a ruined Berlin street in 1945.

Roosevelt and Churchill met again, this time at Quebec, Canada. There the leaders decided definitely that it would be necessary to invade France in order to defeat Hitler.

On November 22, 1943 Roosevelt and Churchill met again in Cairo (KY roh), Egypt. China's leader, Chiang Kai-Shek (TSHANG ky-SHEK), was present, for one of the topics discussed at the Cairo meeting was the war in the Far East.

A few days after the Cairo Conference, Roosevelt and Churchill went to Teheran (teh Y'RAN), the capital of Iran. Premier Stalin of Russia also came to the Teheran Conference. At this meeting Roosevelt and Churchill agreed that American and British troops would invade northern France and that there would also be an invasion of southern France. The Russians agreed to "step up" their offensive against eastern Germany at the same time. Stalin also promised to declare war against Japan. The conference also discussed plans for an international organization to keep the peace — that is, a new and stronger League of Nations.

In January, 1944 General Eisenhower became Supreme Commander of all United Nations* forces in Europe. It was his job to plan the invasion of France. Careful, detailed preparations were made. Everything was done in secrecy.

At last "D-Day" came — June 6, 1944, the day of the invasion. Almost 200,000 soldiers, sailors, and airmen took part. American, British, and Canadian troops landed on the beaches of Normandy in northwestern France. The Germans did their best to drive them back into the sea, but nothing could stop the United Nations* advance. Within a month a million troops had landed and were racing across France.

In August, 1944 another United Nations army invaded southern France between Marseilles and Nice. It pushed up the Rhone River Valley to join the troops that had landed in northern France. Paris was liberated and the Germans were driven back to their own borders.

Then began the Battle for Germany. American, British, and Canadian armies invaded Germany from the west and north. The Russians invaded from the east. The Germans were doomed, but they would not give in. In December, 1944 they suddenly attacked American troops near the border between Belgium and Germany. The Americans, many of whom lacked battle experience, were taken by surprise. The Germans "broke through" and pushed deep into Belgium. This was the famous "Battle of the Bulge." The German drive was stopped after a few weeks, but at great cost. About 77,000 Americans were killed, wounded or captured.

In the spring of 1945 the United Nations* launched new attacks and German resistance slowly crumbled. At this time American and British

---

* *United Nations* was the official name for countries fighting Hitler. They were not the same as the membership of the *United Nations organization* formed after the war.

France was invaded on D-Day, 1944. Here the first wave of troops is shown landing at "Omaha Beach" on the French coast.

commanders began to have serious trouble with the Russian military leaders who showed little friendliness or willingness to cooperate. This was a hint of difficulties to come, but few people realized it as yet.

Roosevelt died just before victory was won in Europe. With victory in Europe in sight, Americans everywhere were saddened by the sudden death of President Franklin Roosevelt. He had been President longer than any other man. First elected in 1932, early in the depression, he was reelected in 1936 and won a third term in 1940. Thus he broke the "no third term" tradition that Washington and Jefferson had started. In 1944 Roosevelt won a fourth term.

When Roosevelt died on April 12, 1945, Vice President Harry S. Truman became the chief executive. Fighting in Europe continued for a few more weeks. Early in May Hitler committed suicide; Berlin was captured. German armies began to surrender. May 8, 1945 was "V–E Day," the date of complete victory in

Europe. Germany surrendered unconditionally and was divided into four "occupation zones," each under control of one of the victorious nations.

The United Nations* took the offensive in the Pacific. The war in the Pacific was far from over. The Japanese advance had been stopped in the last part of 1942. In 1942 and 1943 the American Navy won several victories: the Battle of Coral Sea, the Battle of Midway, the Battle of Guadalcanal (GWAH dahl kah NAL), the Battle of Bismarck Sea, and many others. Large numbers of Japanese warships and planes were destroyed.

These victories made it possible for troops to land on important islands in the vast area between Australia and Japan. The plan was to seize certain "key" islands. These would serve as bases or "stepping stones" for the recapture of the Philippines and eventually the invasion of Japan. This plan of campaign was known as *island hopping*.

The Navy, Air Force, and the Army all worked together to push the Japanese back. It was a long, bloody fight, because the area to be reconquered was enormous; and for a long time only a limited amount of supplies came from America because the war in Europe had first call.

In 1944 the American advance gained new force and speed. The island of Guam was recaptured in July. The Air Force began a steady bombing of Japanese cities. In

596   * United Nations was the official name for countries fighting Hitler. They were not the same as the membership of the *United Nations organization* formed after the war.

October American troops landed in the Philippines. At their head was General MacArthur who, in the dark days of 1941, had promised, "I shall return." It took months and cost many lives to recapture the Philippines. To gain control of the surrounding waters the American Navy fought the last and greatest naval battle of the war, the Battle of Leyte (LAY tay) Gulf. Most of Japan's remaining warships were sunk. Early in 1945 United States forces recaptured Manila.

Two atom bombs forced Japan to surrender. As you can see on the map on this page, the Japanese islands lie almost directly north of the Philippines. "On to Tokyo"

became the slogan of the Americans.

Now, the Japanese fought harder than ever to save their homeland. It looked as if the conquest of Japan would be long and bloody. On July 26, 1945 President Truman and the British Prime Minister, who were meeting with Stalin in Potsdam, Germany, warned Japanese leaders to surrender or be destroyed. They refused. Eight days later an American plane flew high over the Japanese city of Hiroshima (HEE roh SHEE mah). It dropped one bomb and sped away. Few people bothered to look up; American planes had been raining bombs on the city for weeks.

But this bomb was different! There was a blinding flash, visible almost 200 miles away. The air was

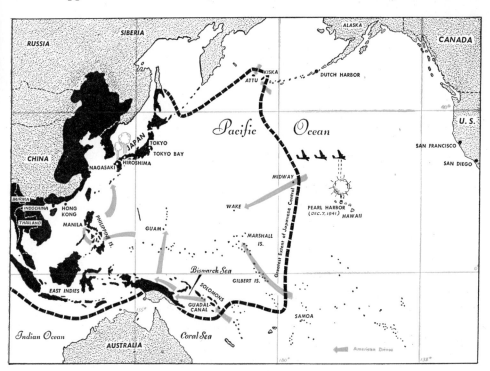

This is a map of World War II campaigns in the Pacific. The dotted line shows the huge area Japan conquered early in the war. Arrows show how and where Americans took the offensive and forced the Japanese back to their home islands.

The Atomic Age begins! This mushroom-like cloud was created by the atomic bomb dropped on Nagasaki, Japan in 1945.

full of flames. Boiling clouds of white smoke shot up 40,000 feet. The city seemed to fall apart. Buildings crumbled; houses disappeared. More than 160,000 people were killed or injured. Three days later another bomb was dropped on a second Japanese city, Nagasaki (NAH gah SAH ke). One third of the city was destroyed and 75,000 people were killed or wounded.

Too late the Japanese leaders realized they should have heeded the Potsdam warning. They surrendered to the United Nations on August 14, 1945. The formal surrender was signed on the United States battleship *Missouri*. American troops marched into Japan and took over the country.

The Atomic Age began in 1945. How was it possible that one bomb could destroy a city and two bombs could force an entire nation to surrender? The answer was: *atomic power*. Even before World War II, scientists had known that enormous power was locked inside the *atoms* or tiny invisible particles which make up all matter. If a way could be found to smash the atom, *atomic energy* would be released for use in making *atomic bombs*. Such bombs would be thousands of times more destructive than any weapon the world had ever seen.

German scientists had set to work to make an atomic bomb even before the war began. British and American scientists started later but worked more efficiently. President Roosevelt backed up the attempt with the enormous wealth and resources of the United States. More than two billion dollars were poured into the project. For years the best scientific brains worked to develop the A-bomb. The whole enterprise was carried out in complete secrecy. Most people had never even heard of the power in the atom until August, 1945. The bombs that fell on Hiroshima and Nagasaki began a new period of history — the Atomic Age.

The Communists claimed credit for victory. Russia took no part in the fight against Japan until after the first atomic bomb was dropped. Then, on August 8, 1945, the Communists hurriedly declared war on Japan and marched into Manchuria, the rich industrial region which Japan had seized from China before World War II. They seized factories and supplies and imprisoned thousands of Japanese soldiers. The Russian people were told that their armies alone had conquered Japan. A "faked" photograph was printed in Communist newspapers which made it appear as if the Japanese had surrendered to Russian commanders.

The Communists had already claimed they alone had defeated the Germans. Now they were trying to steal credit for victory in the Far East, where they had done very little to help in the long struggle against Japan. Russia's unfriendly attitude toward the Western nations was becoming steadily more apparent. However, when World War II ended, most Americans were not willing to admit the possibility of future trouble with Russia. They wanted to get along with other nations and have permanent peace on earth. They no longer dreamed of remaining neutral and isolated. They realized a world organization to maintain peace must be set up — something stronger and more efficient than the League of Nations had ever been. They hoped the Russians would cooperate in maintaining peace.

Roosevelt and Churchill met often. While the war was still in its early stages, President Roosevelt and Prime Minister Churchill began planning for peace. On January 6, 1941 President Roosevelt made his famous "Four Freedoms" speech to Congress. He said:

We look forward to a world founded upon four essential human freedoms.

The first is freedom of speech and expression — everywhere in the world.

The second is freedom of every person to worship God in his own way — everywhere in the world.

The third is freedom from want . . . which will secure to every nation a healthy peace-time life for its inhabitants. . . .

The fourth is freedom from fear . . . a world wide reduction of armament . . . so that no nation can

"Freedom from want" is one of the Four Freedoms the American people enjoy.

FREEDOM FROM WANT

commit aggression against any neighbor.

Several months later, in August, 1941, the President met with Prime Minister Churchill on a warship in the Atlantic Ocean near Newfoundland. There they drew up a list of principles they felt should be the basis for a lasting peace.

Their plan was called the *Atlantic Charter*. It consisted of eight points or declarations of what the United States and Britain aimed to do to prevent future wars. Among the most important were promises to encourage international trade, oppose aggression, and secure the Four Freedoms for individuals everywhere.

Later, as you have seen, Roosevelt and Churchill held conferences at Casablanca, Quebec, Cairo, and Teheran. In February, 1945, when the war in Europe was nearly over, there was another big meeting, this time at Yalta in southern Russia. Roosevelt and Churchill and their top advisers went to Yalta to discuss post-war plans with Stalin. It was decided to go ahead and make definite arrangements for a new international organization which President Roosevelt suggested should be called the United Nations. Perhaps he hoped the name would remind the nations which had fought together against Hitler that they should remain united to keep the peace. The name was soon shortened to "UN." This is the name which it is usually called today.

The United Nations was created. In August, 1944 (several months before the Yalta Conference) representatives of the United States, Great Britain, Russia, and China met at Dumbarton Oaks, a stately old house near Washington, D. C. They prepared a preliminary plan for the new organization to maintain peace. In April, 1945 a meeting was called at San Francisco to consider the Dumbarton Oaks plan. Representatives from fifty nations came to the San Francisco Conference.

There were many hot arguments at San Francisco. The Russian delegates caused many difficulties. Eventually agreement was reached, but the Russians' unfriendly attitude created some doubt about the new organization's chance of success.

The delegates to the San Francisco Conference worked over the Dumbarton Oaks plan and finally adopted a *charter* or basic plan for the UN.

The UN Charter went into effect October 24, 1945. It provided for an organization made up of six main divisions: (1) the General Assembly; (2) the Security Council; (3) the Economic and Social Council; (4) the International Court of Justice; (5) the Trusteeship Council; (6) the Secretariat.

The Assembly and the Security Council consider threats to peace. Each division of the United Nations has its own special duties, but all work toward the same goal, which is to prevent wars. The *General Assembly* has a great many members. It is made up of representatives of all nations that belong to the United Nations. Each member nation has one vote, so all have equal power in the General Assembly. It is the duty of the Assembly to discuss any problem or situation that might lead to war. After a thorough discussion the Assembly may recommend that the Security Council take action.

The *Security Council* is much smaller than the Assembly but it has more power. Its chief duty is to secure and maintain peace. It has eleven members. The five most powerful nations — the United States, Great Britain, Russia, France, and China — are permanent members. This means they are always represented in the Security Council. There are six "non-permanent" members elected by the Assembly for two years. Thus every nation has a chance to serve on the Security Council some time.

According to the Charter, the Security Council must always be "in session" or ready to act if war threatens. In case of a dispute between nations the Charter says that the Council "may take such action by air, sea, or land forces as may be necessary to maintain or restore international peace."

On paper the Security Council seems very powerful. But one little word has kept it weak and divided. The word is *veto*, meaning the power to forbid action. All the permanent members have the right to veto or forbid the Security Council to take action. This means that any one of the five most powerful nations can prevent the Security Council — and through it, the United Nations — from doing anything to stop aggression or correct a situation that might lead to war.

It was expected that the veto would be used very seldom, but the Russians have greatly abused it. They have used it as a weapon to oppose the United States and Great Britain in

President Franklin Roosevelt (seated second from left) is shown signing the United Nations Declaration in 1942. This was the first step taken to organize the United Nations. Standing are the representatives of 26 nations who also signed.

meetings of the United Nations.

The UN carries on many activities.
A third division of the United Nations is the *Economic and Social Council*, often called ECOSOC. It works to correct economic and social conditions which are causes of bad feeling and unhappiness in the world. For example, the World Health Organization, which is part of ECOSOC, tries to stamp out diseases such as malaria and tuberculosis. The Food and Agriculture Organization, which is also part of ECOSOC, sends agricultural experts and machinery to help people in underdeveloped areas increase and improve their crops.

The *International Court of Justice* is another division of the United Nations. It meets in Holland and tries to settle legal questions — such as boundary disputes — that might lead to war.

A fifth division of the UN is the *Trusteeship Council*. Its duty is to see that people in certain remote areas under United Nations' supervision receive fair treatment. For example, the Marshall Islands in the central Pacific are a "trust territory." In World War II, the United States captured them from the Japanese, who had taken them from Germany in World War I. The Islands are now ruled by the United States under the supervision of the United Nations. If the Marshall Islanders feel they are being treated unfairly they can appeal to the Trusteeship Council, where it will be investigated.

Last, but by no means least of the divisions of the UN, is the *Secretariat* (sek reh TARE ih aht). This is the division that administers or manages the UN, keeping records and carrying out the wishes of the General Assembly and the Security Council. It is headed by the Secretary-General who is appointed by the General Assembly. He has a large staff of experts and assistants. The first Secretary-General was Trygve Lie (TRIG vee LEE) of Norway. In 1953 he was succeeded by Dag Hammarskjöld (dahg HAHM ahr sheeld) of Sweden.

The chart on page 610 shows the organization of the UN. Note how many separate agencies and commissions carry out its work. However, the most important thing to remember about the UN is its purpose: to prevent war and to work always to eliminate conditions which may lead to war. It strives to apply advanced knowledge and the most up-to-date methods to solve the world's problems.

It is well to keep in mind also that the UN is still very young. It did not come into existence until late in 1945, so it is younger than you are. It has managed to settle several serious disputes and to bring about improvements in many areas. If nations and individuals will only give whole-hearted support to the UN it may in the future achieve the purpose stated in its Charter, which is "to save succeeding generations from the scourge of war." However, if the UN does not receive such support it may fail as the League failed.

Communism spread rapidly after the war. Hopes for world peace suffered disappointment after disappointment in the years following World War II. Russian leaders refused to cooperate with the Western nations. They were determined to spread Communism and gain control of other countries. They set up or encouraged Communist governments in neighboring nations until all of eastern Europe was under Russian influence.

In this region, freedom has vanished. Just as in Russia, the people of the new Communist states have no rights, only duties. There are no free elections. People who dare criticize the government are likely to be sent to a "slave labor camp" where they are forced to work until they die. The East European countries which have fallen under Russia's control are known as satellite (SAT uh lite) nations. They include Estonia, Latvia, Lithuania, Poland, Czechoslovakia, Hungary, Rumania, Bulgaria, and Albania. East Germany, too, is under Russian control.

The Communist leaders allow very little information about conditions in eastern Europe to reach the Western nations. Winston Churchill remarked in 1946 that Russia had separated the Communist world from the free nations of the West by "an iron curtain." The phrase has become popular as a description of Communist secrecy. There is, of course, no real curtain, but the separation between East and West is very real.

The rapid growth of Russian influence alarmed American and British leaders. They realized they must act quickly or all Europe might go Communist. In March, 1947 President Truman urged Congress to grant money to European nations in danger of being taken over by Communists. This idea became known as the *Truman Doctrine*. At the President's request Congress granted 400 million dollars to help Greece and Turkey, whose independence was threatened by Russia.

Other European nations were in danger. France, for example, suffered great damage in the war. Many of her factories and railroads lay in ruins. Thousands of Frenchmen were hungry, cold, and out of work. Communist agents were busy spreading lies and urging people to overthrow the government. In Belgium, Holland, and Italy the situation was much the same.

In Great Britain the danger of Communism was not great, but the need for money and tools to help the nation rebuild was urgent.

The Marshall Plan aided European recovery. What could be done to stop the spread of Communism? Secretary of State George Marshall offered a plan in a speech at Harvard University in June, 1947. He said

With American Marshall Plan aid, Europeans went to work to rebuild after World War II. This picture shows Italians repairing bombed-out transportation facilities.

that the United States would supply tools, food, and money to help European nations rebuild farms, industries, and homes. The nations must develop their own programs and prove they were willing to help themselves. This was the *Marshall Plan*. It was in many ways quite successful. The nations of Western Europe grasped eagerly at the chance to get on their feet again. In a few years they were producing big crops and their factories were working overtime.

The Russians seek to control Germany. Russia bitterly denounced the Marshall Plan. She refused to let any of the nations under her control take part in it. The struggle between Communism and freedom, between East and West, went on all over the world. It was called the *cold war* because the two sides were officially at peace. It was not a "shooting war" or a "hot war." Nevertheless it was a fierce, deadly conflict for control of the world.

The Russians were particularly anxious to get control of all Ger-

many. They tried everything they could think of to get the American, British, and French occupying forces to leave Germany. The city of Berlin became the key point in the struggle. The Russians controlled one section or "zone" of the city and the Western nations controlled other sections. But at the end of the war the Russians had managed to get control of all roads leading to Berlin.

In June, 1948 the Russians closed all roads to Berlin on the excuse that they had to repair bridges. They would not let anyone from western Europe or America travel or bring supplies over the roads to Berlin. They hoped in this way to starve the

Financed by American aid these cranes are repairing the port of Dunkerque, France, which suffered great war damage.

occupying troops and force them to leave.

But American ingenuity and skill easily defeated the clumsy plan. With the help of the British, they organized the "Berlin Airlift." They carried tons of food, fuel, and other supplies to western Berlin by airplanes. For almost a year planes flew into the Berlin airport every few minutes. It was a superb demonstration of the strength and determination of the Western powers. In May, 1944 the Russians ended the blockade. The Berlin Airlift cost a great deal of money but it won a great victory for the West.

Western nations joined NATO. Russia's aggressive methods caused the Western nations to draw closer together. On April 4, 1949 just before the airlift ended, representatives of twelve of the Western nations signed an agreement called the *North Atlantic Treaty.* The nations that signed were the United States, Great Britain, Canada, France, Belgium, Holland, Luxembourg, Italy, Denmark, Norway, Iceland, and Portugal. They promised to defend one another against any attack and to build up strong defenses.

General Dwight D. Eisenhower was appointed commander of the armed forces of the *North Atlantic Treaty Organization* or *NATO.* He went to France and took charge of western Europe's defenses against Communism. Later, when he came home to run for President his efforts to build up Europe's military strength continued under the leadership of officers he had helped train.

The Communists won control of China. It was clear that the Western nations meant business. Greece and Turkey joined the Atlantic Pact. Strong, united action blocked the Communists from gaining control of any more territory in Europe. But in the Far East, the situation was different. China came out of World War II weak and confused. The Communists steadily gained power. By 1950 they had control of all China — a vast region inhabited by hundreds of millions of people.

The Chinese Communists were very friendly to Russia. They took orders from the Moscow government. Thus the Communists were in control of two of the largest countries, plus many smaller countries on Russia's border.

Now the Communists tried to take over smaller countries around China. Korea (ko REE ah), which occupies a peninsula southeast of Manchuria, was next on the list. Korea had been conquered by Japan in 1910. At the end of World War II Russian armies marched into northern Korea. American troops held southern Korea, but soon withdrew. The South Koreans set up a republic friendly to the United States.

The dividing line between Communist North Korea and the Republic of South Korea was the 38th parallel of latitude. (Study the map

DWIGHT EISENHOWER (1890–   )

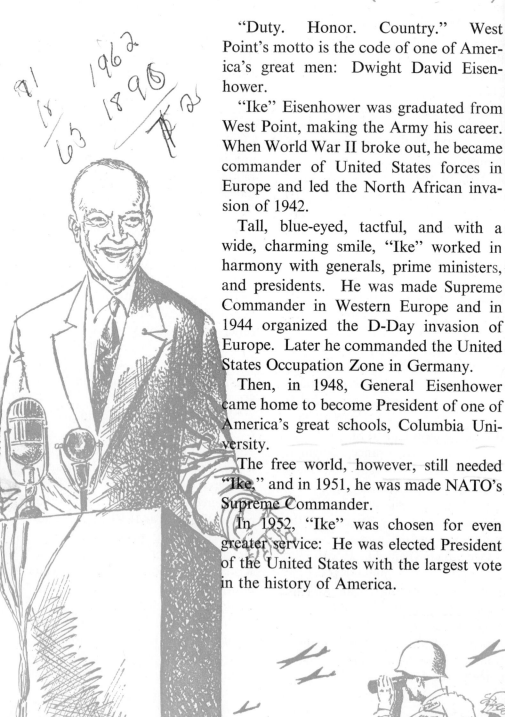

"Duty. Honor. Country." West Point's motto is the code of one of America's great men: Dwight David Eisenhower.

"Ike" Eisenhower was graduated from West Point, making the Army his career. When World War II broke out, he became commander of United States forces in Europe and led the North African invasion of 1942.

Tall, blue-eyed, tactful, and with a wide, charming smile, "Ike" worked in harmony with generals, prime ministers, and presidents. He was made Supreme Commander in Western Europe and in 1944 organized the D-Day invasion of Europe. Later he commanded the United States Occupation Zone in Germany.

Then, in 1948, General Eisenhower came home to become President of one of America's great schools, Columbia University.

The free world, however, still needed "Ike," and in 1951, he was made NATO's Supreme Commander.

In 1952, "Ike" was chosen for even greater service: He was elected President of the United States with the largest vote in the history of America.

at right.) South Korea was weak and struggling. Communist leaders thought it would be easy to overrun the region and force it behind the iron curtain. So on June 25, 1950 the North Korean army suddenly invaded South Korea.

The UN helped South Korea. South Korea lacked weapons and troops to oppose the tanks and well-organized armies of North Korea. On rolled the Communist war machine, capturing the capital, Seoul (SOLE). But the United Nations came to the aid of South Korea. The Security Council condemned North Korea and ordered the members of the UN to help South Korea. A United Nations army was organized under the command of General Douglas MacArthur.

How did it happen that the Russians failed to veto UN aid to Korea? The answer is that the Russians had been boycotting or staying away from the meetings of the Security Council because the UN refused to admit the Communist government of China as a member. In the absence of the Russians it was possible for the Security Council to act and it did so. (The Russians have since attended Security Council meetings very regularly.)

Red China aided North Korea. Thus began a long, bitter struggle to drive the Communists out of South Korea. It was a difficult region for fighting. The land was mountainous and there

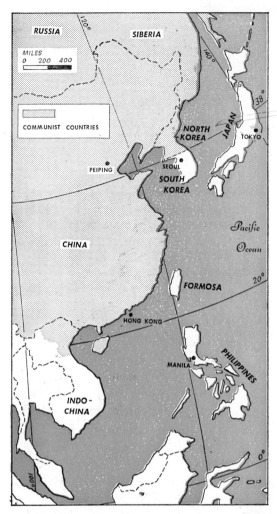

This map shows eastern Asia split between communist and non-communist powers.

were few roads. The winters were terribly cold. Nevertheless the United Nations forces won many victories. They forced the North Koreans to retreat until all of Korea was nearly free once more. But then thousands of Chinese Communists came pouring into Korea. They really started another war. MacArthur and his troops had to retreat south again in bitter cold

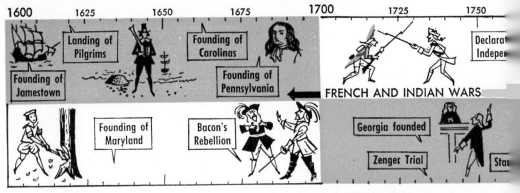

| 1600 | 1625 | 1650 | 1675 | 1700 | 1725 | 1750 |

Founding of Jamestown
Landing of Pilgrims
Founding of Maryland
Founding of Carolinas
Bacon's Rebellion
Founding of Pennsylvania
FRENCH AND INDIAN WARS
Georgia founded
Zenger Trial
Declara Indepe
Stan

Here is another time line like the one on page 50. It covers the time from 1600 to 1955 and shows only the most important events. Note how crowded the last 25 years have been. Try to

weather, giving up step by step the land won only a few weeks before.

An armistice was signed in Korea. New troops and supplies soon arrived to strengthen the United Nations forces. The retreat stopped. MacArthur and his men won back some territory. Then the war came to a standstill. Neither side could advance or win a big victory. The lines of battle were near the border between North and South Korea. It was decided to arrange a truce or "cease fire" agreement.

Negotiations went on for more than a year. As usual the Communists used unfair methods, "stalling," and name-calling. At last, in July, 1953, the fighting stopped. But there was no permanent peace in the Far East.

In other parts of Asia Communist groups constantly are working to win power. They have been stopped from advancing in Europe so they are concentrating on the Far East. The possession of China gives them a great advantage and a

base from which to attack nearby countries.

A plan for control of atomic weapons was rejected. After World War II ended scientists continued research in atomic power. Many peacetime uses were discovered. In medicine, certain by-products of atomic research called "radio-active isotopes" (EYE soh topes) were used with some success in treating diseases such as cancer. It proved possible to produce electric power by using atomic energy.

In Russia, too, research in atomic power went on. Communist spies were able to get much information about discoveries in American and British atomic research. A "race" to make bigger and more terrible bombs seemed to be developing. The United Nations created a commission to study the problem of control of atomic weapons.

The American delegate to the UN Atomic Energy Commission was Bernard Baruch (bah RUKE). He proposed a plan by which the United

WORLD LEADERSHIP

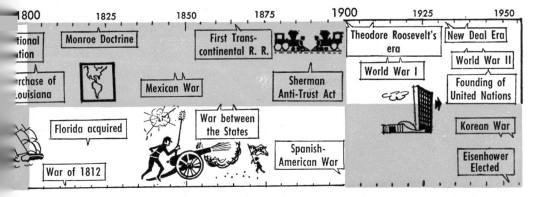

see relations between events — for example, why World War I was followed by another terrible war and how this led to the creation of the UN.

States would turn over its atomic bomb secrets *provided* a system of international control and inspection was established so other nations could not make atomic bombs secretly. The Russians refused to agree to any inspection, so the Baruch Plan was not accepted and the atomic arms race went on.

Hydrogen bombs were manufactured. Meanwhile, something even more terrible than atomic bombs was being developed. This was the *Hydrogen* or *H-bomb.* In November, 1952 American military forces set off a hydrogen explosion on a tiny Pacific island. It was probably the most violent man-made explosion in history. According to reports from men who saw it, the explosion began with a flash of light brighter than the sun, followed by a wave of unbearable heat. Thousands of tons of earth were blown up toward the sky. A huge mushroom-shaped cloud of smoke appeared. The island became a mass of flames — and then disappeared, completely and permanently. Remember, this was just a tryout — a small hydrogen explosion. What might happen if several larger hydrogen bombs were exploded?

Then in August, 1953 came news that the Russians too had exploded an experimental type of hydrogen bomb. It was believed the Russians had not advanced so far in research as American and British scientists, but they were coming close. The development of such terrible weapons has made it more than ever essential that efforts for world peace should succeed. The possibilities of hydrogen bomb warfare are frightful beyond words.

America has gained strength. How long will the struggle between the Communist nations and the free world go on? Will it turn into World War III? No one knows. Men and women of good will hope that it will be possible to avoid another world war which might destroy mankind.

However, most Americans realize it is not enough to hope. The nation

ORGANS OF THE UNITED NATIONS

PRINCIPAL ORGANS AND SUBSIDIARY BODIES

SECURITY COUNCIL

INTERNATIONAL COURT OF JUSTICE

TRUSTEESHIP COUNCIL

GENERAL ASSEMBLY

UNITED NATIONS CHILDREN'S FUND (UNICEF)

OFFICE OF THE UNITED NATIONS HIGH COMMISSIONER FOR REFUGEES

SECRETARIAT

ECONOMIC AND SOCIAL COUNCIL

SPECIALIZED AGENCIES

Here are the buildings of the United Nations headquarters in New York City.

This picture shows the inauguration of Dwight D. Eisenhower as President, January 20, 1953 at the Capitol in Washington. First row, left to right: Ex-President Truman, Chief Justice Vinson, Mr. Eisenhower, and Vice-President Nixon.

must prepare its defenses and become so strong the Communist nations would not dare to attack. Hard experience has shown that the Communists respect only strength. They will try to get control of any nation that seems weak or confused. "The chain snaps at its weakest link" is their motto. Therefore America must be strong herself and must help friendly nations to build up their strength.

During and since World War II, the United States has grown steadily in wealth and power and population. Factories have multiplied; improved methods and new inventions have increased production. World War I stimulated American industry so that the United States became one of the leading nations of the earth. World War II carried the process much farther so that today the United States is the strongest, richest, and most advanced nation. Russia, with all her boasting and threats, is far behind in ability to produce goods.

This does not mean that Americans can afford to "slow down" and take their leadership for granted. It does mean, however, that the people of the United States can and should have faith in their ability to meet the challenge of the future.

Dwight D. Eisenhower became President. In 1952 the American people went through one of the most exciting political campaigns in their history. The cold war, American participation in the UN, the fight in Korea — all these and many other issues were thoroughly discussed. The Democratic Party had been in power for almost twenty years — through the depression, World War II, and the Korean War. "It's time for a change," declared the Republicans, who had been out of office since 1933. They nominated Dwight D. Eisenhower for President.

General Eisenhower had served the country long and faithfully. A graduate of West Point, he made the army his career. His leadership helped win victory in Europe in World War II. After the war he became President of Columbia University. Later he obtained a leave of absence to go to Europe and direct the building up of defenses in western Europe to prevent the spread of Communism.

In 1952, somewhat reluctantly, he returned from Europe to campaign for the Presidency. He was inexperienced in politics, but he was the man Americans wanted to lead them. He won a decisive victory and was inaugurated as President in January, 1953. A few months later, the Korean War came to an end.

There were still many terrible problems ahead, but most Americans felt a great increase in confidence. They knew they were a strong and capable people. They had managed to hold back the spread of Communism first in Europe and in Korea. At the helm in Washington they had a beloved leader whose bright smile and steady voice created confidence. The nation faced the future with faith and determination.

CHAPTER SUMMARY

Japan conquered much of the Pacific and southeast Asia in 1942. The United Nations concentrated on defeating Germany first. They invaded North Africa, then Sicily, then Italy.

France was invaded on D-Day, 1944. German troops were driven back. Germany surrendered May 8, 1945. United Nations forces won many victories in the Pacific. The dropping of two atom bombs forced Japan to surrender in August, 1945.

Wartime conferences were held at Casablanca, Quebec, Cairo, Teheran, Yalta, and Potsdam. The United Nations organization to maintain peace was established at San Francisco in 1945. The UN's effectiveness has been hampered by Russia's abuse of the veto.

The Communists gained control of Eastern Europe and China. The United States helped European nations gain strength by Marshall Plan aid. Russia tried to drive the western powers out of Berlin but was defeated by the Berlin Airlift. The western nations set up NATO.

North Korean Communists invaded South Korea in June, 1950. The UN came to South Korea's aid. Chinese Communists joined the fight. An armistice was signed in July, 1953.

The Language of History

Be sure you know the meaning of each of the following words and phrases as they are used in this chapter.

1. liberate	5. Truman Doctrine	9. surrender
2. atom	6. Marshall Plan	10. four freedoms
3. veto	7. Baruch Plan	11. iron curtain
4. satellite	8. United Nations	12. aggression

What Happened When

Connect each of the following dates with an important event in American history.

1. 1945   **2.** 1950   **3.** 1953

Who's Who in History

Be sure you know the part each of the following played in American history.

1. Douglas MacArthur   3. Chiang Kai-shek   5. George Marshall
2. Dwight Eisenhower   4. Harry S. Truman   6. Bernard Baruch

Study Questions

1. Why was Japan able to conquer so much territory in a few months?

2. Give two reasons why Britain and America were determined to keep the Germans from winning control of Africa.

3. **a.** Why did the campaign to conquer Italy prove long and costly?
   b. Discuss the D-Day invasion including **(a)** the date, **(b)** place, **(c)** leader, and **(d)** results.

4. **a.** What was meant by "island hopping"?
   b. Mention three United Nations victories in the Pacific area.
   c. How and when was Japan forced to surrender?

5. **a.** What were the "four freedoms"?
   b. Give two provisions of the Atlantic Charter.

6. Trace the establishment of the United Nations telling **(a)** what was done at Yalta, **(b)** at Dumbarton Oaks, **(c)** at San Francisco.

7. List the six main divisions of the UN and tell one function of each.

8. **a.** What was the purpose of the Marshall Plan?
   b. When and by whom was it proposed?
   c. What were the results?

9. **a.** What is the purpose of NATO?
   b. List five members of NATO.

10. Trace the history of the Korean War telling **(a)** when it began, **(b)** causes, **(c)** how the UN aided South Korea, **(d)** geographic conditions that affected fighting, **(e)** part played by Chinese Communists, and **(f)** date of the armistice.

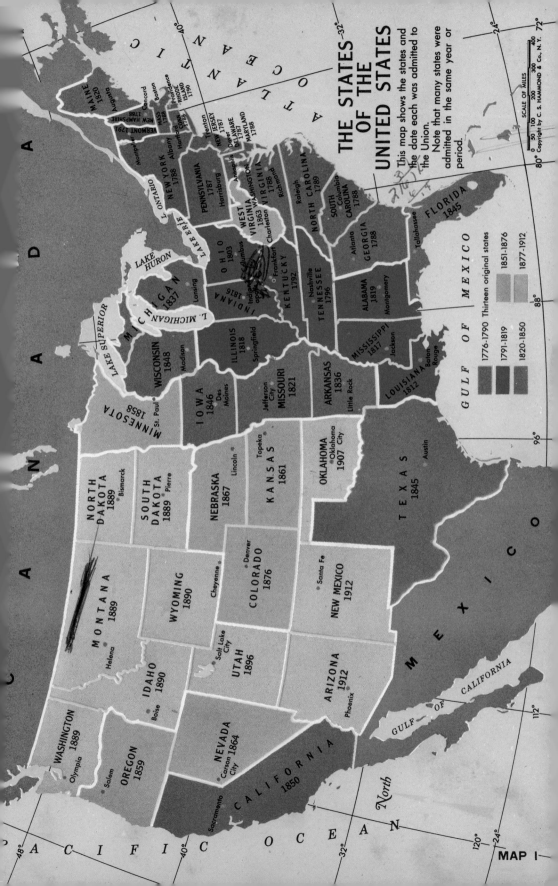

THE STATES OF THE UNITED STATES

This map shows the states and the date each was admitted to the Union.

Note that many states were admitted in the same year or period.

SCALE OF MILES

0 50 100 200 300 400

Copyright by C. S. HAMMOND & Co., N.Y.

1776-1790 Thirteen original states	1851-1876
1791-1819	1877-1912
1820-1850	

MAP I

States and dates

MAINE 1820 · Augusta

NEW HAMPSHIRE 1788 · Concord

VERMONT 1791 · Montpelier

MASS. 1788 · Boston

CONN. 1788 · Hartford

RHODE ISLAND 1790 · Providence

NEW YORK 1788 · Albany

PENNSYLVANIA 1787 · Harrisburg

NEW JERSEY 1787 · Trenton

DELAWARE 1787 · Dover

MARYLAND 1788 · Annapolis

WEST VIRGINIA 1863 · Charleston

VIRGINIA 1788 · Richmond

NORTH CAROLINA 1789 · Raleigh

SOUTH CAROLINA 1788 · Columbia

GEORGIA 1788 · Atlanta

FLORIDA 1845 · Tallahassee

OHIO 1803 · Columbus

INDIANA 1816 · Indianapolis

KENTUCKY 1792 · Frankfort

TENNESSEE 1796 · Nashville

ALABAMA 1819 · Montgomery

MISSISSIPPI 1817 · Jackson

LOUISIANA 1812 · Baton Rouge

MICHIGAN 1837 · Lansing

WISCONSIN 1848 · Madison

ILLINOIS 1818 · Springfield

IOWA 1846 · Des Moines

MISSOURI 1821 · Jefferson City

ARKANSAS 1836 · Little Rock

MINNESOTA 1858 · St. Paul

NORTH DAKOTA 1889 · Bismarck

SOUTH DAKOTA 1889 · Pierre

NEBRASKA 1867 · Lincoln

KANSAS 1861 · Topeka

OKLAHOMA 1907 · Oklahoma City

TEXAS 1845 · Austin

MONTANA 1889 · Helena

WYOMING 1890 · Cheyenne

COLORADO 1876 · Denver

NEW MEXICO 1912 · Santa Fe

IDAHO 1890 · Boise

UTAH 1896 · Salt Lake City

ARIZONA 1912 · Phoenix

WASHINGTON 1889 · Olympia

OREGON 1859 · Salem

NEVADA 1864 · Carson City

CALIFORNIA 1850 · Sacramento

CANADA

MEXICO

ATLANTIC OCEAN

PACIFIC OCEAN

GULF OF MEXICO

GULF OF CALIFORNIA

LAKE SUPERIOR

LAKE HURON

LAKE MICHIGAN

LAKE ERIE

LAKE ONTARIO

North

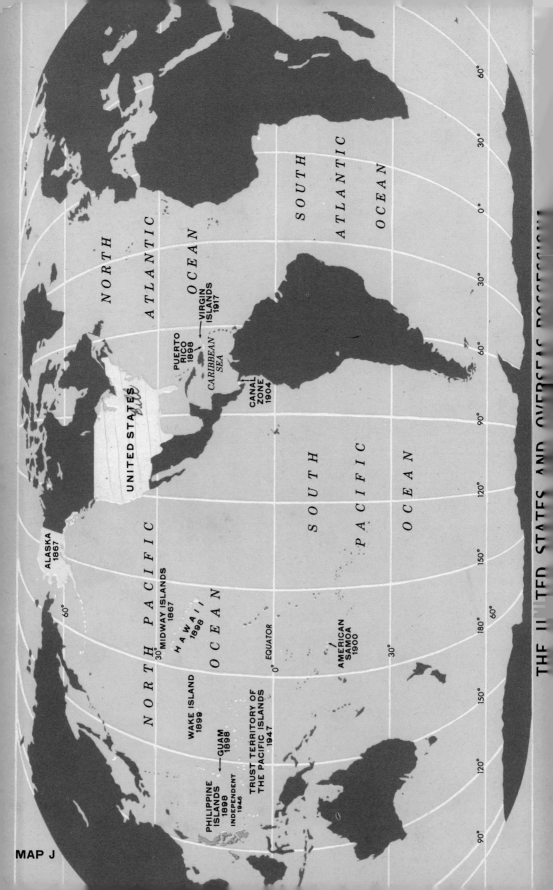

MAP J

THE UNITED STATES AND OVERSEAS POSSESSIONS

NORTH ATLANTIC OCEAN

SOUTH ATLANTIC OCEAN

NORTH PACIFIC OCEAN

SOUTH PACIFIC OCEAN

UNITED STATES

ALASKA
1867

MIDWAY ISLANDS
1867

HAWAII
1898

WAKE ISLAND
1899

GUAM
1898

TRUST TERRITORY OF
THE PACIFIC ISLANDS
1947

PHILIPPINE
ISLANDS
1898
INDEPENDENT
1946

AMERICAN
SAMOA
1900

EQUATOR

PUERTO
RICO
1898

VIRGIN
ISLANDS
1917

CARIBBEAN
SEA

CANAL
ZONE
1904

60°   30°   0°   30°   60°   90°   120°   150°   180°   150°   120°   90°

60°   30°   0°

EQUATOR

30°

THE UNITED STATES TODAY

This map shows the modern United States. A map of the United States, such as this, might be drawn on your blackboard.

The red areas are the National Parks.

SCALE OF MILES
50 100 200 300 400

Copyright by C. S. HAMMOND & Co., N.Y.

MAP K

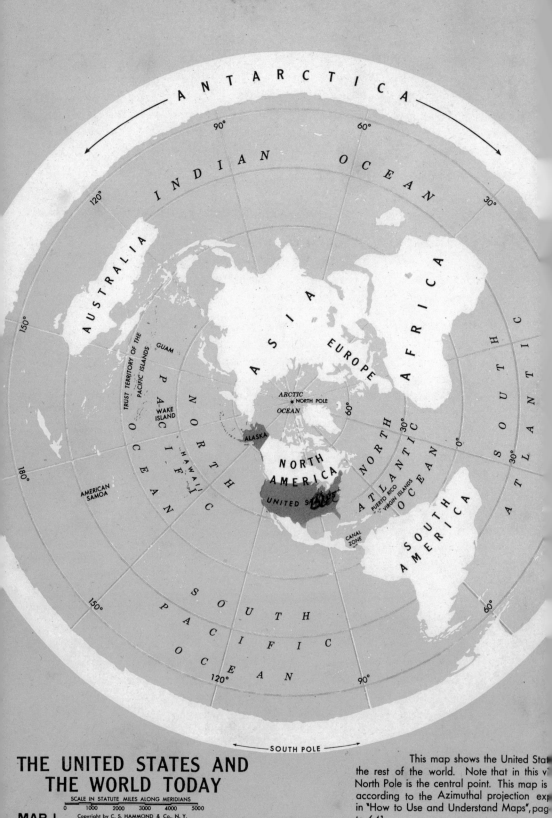

ANTARCTICA

INDIAN OCEAN

90°   60°

120°   30°

AUSTRALIA

150°

TRUST TERRITORY OF THE PACIFIC ISLANDS

GUAM

WAKE ISLAND

ARCTIC   NORTH POLE
OCEAN

ALASKA

180°

PACIFIC   OCEAN

NORTH

HAWAII

AMERICAN SAMOA

NORTH
AMERICA

UNITED STATES

AFRICA

EUROPE

ASIA

AFRICA

30°

ATLANTIC

PUERTO RICO
VIRGIN ISLANDS

0°

30°

OCEAN

CANAL ZONE

SOUTH
AMERICA

SOUTH

ATLANTIC

60°

150°

SOUTH

PACIFIC

OCEAN

120°   90°

SOUTH POLE

THE UNITED STATES AND
THE WORLD TODAY

SCALE IN STATUTE MILES ALONG MERIDIANS
0   1000   2000   3000   4000   5000

MAP L   Copyright by C. S. HAMMOND & Co., N. Y.

This map shows the United Sta[...]
the rest of the world. Note that in this v[...]
North Pole is the central point. This map is [...]
according to the Azimuthal projection ex[...]
in "How to Use and Understand Maps", pag[...]
to 641.

LET'S LOOK AT WHAT WE'VE LEARNED

What were the causes of World War I?

Secret alliances divided Europe into two jealous, armed camps. Each nation wanted more land and markets. France wanted to regain Alsace-Lorraine. The immediate cause was the murder of Archduke Ferdinand.

Why did the United States become involved in World War I?

German submarines sank American ships without warning. After many protests and warnings, the United States declared war in 1917.

Why did not the United States join the League of Nations?

The Senate refused to approve the Treaty of Versailles which set up the League. Many Americans feared that joining the League would involve the United States in foreign wars.

How did dictators gain power in Russia, Italy, and Germany?

Revolutions occurred in Russia in 1917, and Communists won control. Lenin became dictator; when he died, Stalin grabbed power.

In Italy, the Fascists overthrew the lawful government and abolished freedom. Mussolini became dictator. In Germany, defeat, inflation, and economic depression made the people despair. Hitler made himself dictator by promising the Germans revenge and prosperity.

What conditions led to World War II and how did the United States get involved?

The democratic nations tried to appease Hitler by letting him move in on smaller neighbors. Germany, Italy, and later Japan, formed the Axis alliance. Hitler made a deal with Russia. Then the Germans invaded Poland. Great Britain and France declared war on Germany.

Americans tried to remain neutral, but they sympathized with Britain and France and gave Lend-Lease aid. The United States encouraged China to resist Japan. This finally led to war when Japan attacked the naval base at Pearl Harbor on December 7, 1941.

How was World War II won?

In Europe, carefully planned invasions beginning with North Africa led to victory. After invading Sicily, American and British landed in Italy. On June 6, 1944 northwestern France was invaded. United Nations troops drove across France into Germany.

Hitler had attacked Russia in 1941. But the terrible winter and

Lend-Lease aid from America helped Russia drive the Germans back. The combined East-West attack forced Germany to surrender in May, 1945.

In the Pacific, "island hopping" United Nations forces won key islands, driving the Japanese back to their homeland. The dropping of atom bombs on two Japanese cities forced Japan to surrender in August, 1945.

Where and when was the United Nations set up and how is it organized?

Plans were made during the war and at Dumbarton Oaks. At the San Francisco Conference in April, 1945, the UN Charter was adopted. The UN consists of six divisions. Each of them has a special function, but all work to prevent war.

When and why was the Korean War fought?

In 1950 Communists from North Korea invaded South Korea. The United Nations sent aid to South Korea and a bitterly fought war began. When the UN forces had almost won, Chinese Communists entered the fight. Neither side was able to win a clear victory, and an armistice was signed in July, 1953.

Connecting the Past with the Present . . .

Now, to add up the score. What does the story of America mean to you? What can you gain from it that will help you in the future?

America has always been a land of opportunity. From the very beginning, Americans have dared to try new paths and meet unknown dangers. "The cowards never started and the weaklings died on the way" is the motto of California, but it applies to all America. Your ancestors, whether they came here in 1620 or 1920, were people of courage or they would not have dared to leave their old homes. Their courage and hard work helped build a great nation that your generation will soon lead. The problems you face are different but no more frightening than those which challenged the pioneers.

Even more than a land of opportunity, the United States is a land of freedom. Americans have always fought for the right to believe and speak as they wish. Generations of Americans have defended those rights. Today some forces in the world want to abolish freedom.

Remember, men such as Nathan Hale, Horace Mann, Abraham Lincoln, and Woodrow Wilson built a free America. This is your heritage. It is your duty and privilege to preserve and defend it for those who will come after you.

616

Questions for Discussion and Review

1. Explain how alliances caused a dispute between two nations to develop into World War I.
2. Why did the United States join the Allies instead of the Central Powers in World War I?
3. Did the Treaty of Versailles treat Germany too harshly or too generously? Give reasons for your opinion.
4. How did the traditional policy of isolation help prevent the United States from joining the League of Nations?
5. What conditions encouraged many Germans and Italians to accept dictatorship?
6. What did Japan hope to gain by attacking the United States?
7. Describe the part Russia has played in the work of the United Nations.
8. How is membership in the UN Security Council determined?
9. Why is the Berlin Airlift considered a victory for the western nations over Russia?
10. Compare the reasons for the failure of the League of Nations with the difficulties the UN has had in taking action to prevent war.

THE HISTORY LABORATORY

Here are some suggestions for activities that you will find interesting and profitable.

Set Up a Current Events File . . .

Have a library committee establish a research center for this Unit by collecting books, magazines, newspapers which contain information about recent United States history. Make it available to schoolmates for project work.

The Inquiring Reporter . . .

Discover what life was like on the home front during World War II by asking neighbors, relatives, and friends. Report to the class.

Cartoonists' Delight . . .

Draw a cartoon or cartoon strip showing the need for all people to think seriously about the problems presented by the atom bomb and the hydrogen bomb.

Good Evening, Ladies and Gentlemen! . . .

Pretend you are an experienced United Nations reporter. Prepare a large chart like the one on page 610 and use it to illustrate a report on how the United Nations is organized.

Cartographers' Delight . . .

Make maps which show the extent of the conquests of Hitler, Mussolini, and Japan, or the spread of Communism. Textbooks, encyclopedias, magazines, and newspapers will provide the facts and ideas you need.

Place the Face . . .

Find pictures of famous military and civilian leaders of recent history and create a Photo Quiz to test your classmates, schoolmates, teachers, parents, and friends.

Science and the Future . . .

Help your classmates understand their future in the atomic age by reporting the latest developments in civilian and military use of atomic energy. Illustrate your report with charts, maps, or models.

WHAT AND WHEN

World War I
1914-18

World-wide depression
1930's

CLOSED
NO HELP
WANTED

World War I
1939-45

Listen to the Record . . .

By records bring the music of the period from 1914 to the present into your classroom. Many people will be able to suggest and provide the music and records you will need. One or two selections for each ten years should make a good program.

Let's Read about the United States as the Leader of the Free World

COOKE, DAVID C., *Young America's Aviation*, McBride, 1951.

DEJONG, DOLA, *The Level Land*, Scribner, 1952.

EDMONDS, W. D., *They Fought with What They Had*, Little, 1951.

**EISENHOWER, D. D., *Crusade in Europe*, Doubleday, 1948.

*FISHER, LOIS, *You and the United Nations*, Children's Press, 1947.

HATCH, ALDEN, *Red Carpet for Mamie*, Holt, 1954.

HATCH, ALDEN, *Woodrow Wilson; a biography for young people*, Holt, 1947.

**HAYES, C. J. H., *Brief History of the Great War*, Macmillan, 1943.

HUNT, GEORGE P., *Story of the U. S. Marines*, Random, 1951.

KUGELMASS, J. A., *Ralph H. Bunche, Fighter for Peace*, Messner, 1952.

MEADER, STEPHEN W., *The Long Trains Roll*, Harcourt, 1944.

POTTER, ROBERT D., *Young People's Book of Atomic Energy*, Dodd, 1952.

PYLE, ERNIE, *Here Is Your War*, Holt, 1943.

STERLING, DOROTHY, *United Nations, N.Y.*, Doubleday, 1953.

TIME, INC., Life's *Picture History of World War II*, Simon and Schuster, 1950.

WHITE, WILLIAM L., *They Were Expendable*, Harcourt, 1942.

* indicates easy reading
** indicates advanced reading

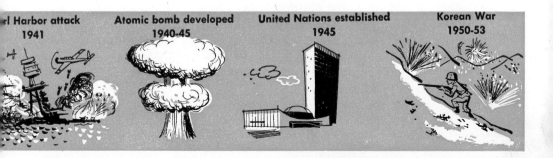

| l Harbor attack | Atomic bomb developed | United Nations established | Korean War |
| 1941 | 1940-45 | 1945 | 1950-53 |

THE DECLARATION OF INDEPENDENCE

In Congress, July 4, 1776,

THE UNANIMOUS DECLARATION OF THE
THIRTEEN UNITED STATES OF AMERICA

WHEN in the Course of human events, it becomes necessary for one people to dissolve the political bands which have connected them with another, and to assume among the Powers of the earth the separate and equal station to which the Laws of Nature and of Nature's God entitle them, a decent respect to the opinions of mankind requires that they should declare the causes which impel them to the separation.

We hold these truths to be self-evident, that all men are created equal, that they are endowed by their Creator with certain unalienable Rights, that among these are Life, Liberty and the pursuit of Happiness. That to secure these rights, Governments are instituted among Men, deriving their just powers from the consent of the governed, That whenever any Form of Government becomes destructive of these ends, it is the Right of the People to alter or to abolish it, and to institute a new Government, laying its foundation on such principles and organizing its powers in such form as to them shall seem most likely to effect their Safety and Happiness. Prudence, indeed, will dictate that Governments long established should not be changed for light and transient causes; and accordingly all experience hath shewn, that mankind are more disposed to suffer, while evils are sufferable, than to right themselves by abolishing the forms to which they are accustomed. But when a long train of abuses and usurpations, pursuing invariably the same Object, evinces a design to reduce them under absolute Despotism, it is their right, it is their duty to throw off such Government, and to provide new Guards for their future security. Such has been the patient sufferance of these Colonies; and such is now the necessity which constrains them to alter their former Systems of Government. The history of the present King of Great Britain is a history of repeated injuries and usurpations, all having in direct object the establishment of an absolute Tyranny over these States. To prove this, let Facts be submitted to a candid world.

He has refused his Assent to Laws, the most wholesome and necessary for the public good.

He has forbidden his Governors to pass Laws of immediate and pressing importance, unless suspended in their operation till his Assent should be obtained; and when so suspended, he has utterly neglected to attend to them.

He has refused to pass other Laws for the accommodation of large districts of people, unless those people would relinquish the right of Representation in the Legislature, a right inestimable to them and formidable to tyrants only.

He has called together legislative bodies at places unusual, uncomfortable, and distant from the depository of their Public Records, for the sole purpose of fatiguing them into compliance with his measures.

He has dissolved Representative Houses repeatedly, for opposing with manly firmness his invasions on the rights of the people.

He has refused for a long time, after such dissolutions, to cause others to be elected; whereby the Legislative Powers, incapable of Annihilation, have returned to the People at large for their exercise; the State remaining in the mean time exposed to all the dangers of invasion from without, and convulsions within.

He has endeavoured to prevent the population of these States; for that purpose obstructing the Laws for Naturalization of Foreigners; refusing to pass others to encourage their migrations hither, and raising the conditions of new Appropriations of Lands.

He has obstructed the Administration of Justice by refusing his Assent to Laws for establishing Judiciary Powers.

He has made Judges dependent on his Will alone, for the tenure of their offices, and the amount and payment of their salaries.

He has erected a multitude of New Offices, and sent hither swarms of Officers to harass our People, and eat out their substance.

He has kept among us, in times of peace, Standing Armies without the Consent of our legislatures.

He has affected to render the Military independent of and superior to the Civil Power.

He has combined with others to subject us to a jurisdiction foreign to our constitutions, and unacknowledged by our laws; giving his Assent to their acts of pretended legislation:

For quartering large bodies of armed troops among us:

For protecting them, by a mock Trial, from Punishment for any Murders which they should commit on the Inhabitants of these States:

For cutting off our Trade with all parts of the world:

For imposing taxes on us without our Consent:

For depriving us in many cases, of the benefits of Trial by Jury:

For transporting us beyond Seas to be tried for pretended offences:

For abolishing the free System of English Laws in a neighbouring Province, establishing therein an Arbitrary government, and enlarging its Boundaries so as to render it at once an example and fit instrument for introducing the same absolute rule into these Colonies:

For taking away our Charters, abolishing our most valuable Laws, and altering fundamentally the Forms of our Governments:

For suspending our own Legislatures, and declaring themselves invested with Power to legislate for us in all cases whatsoever.

He has abdicated Government here, by declaring us out of his Protection and waging War against us.

He has plundered our seas, ravaged our Coasts, burnt our towns, and destroyed the lives of our people.

He is at this time transporting large armies of foreign mercenaries to compleat the works of death, desolation and tyranny, already begun with circumstances of Cruelty and perfidy scarcely paralleled in the most barbarous ages, and totally unworthy the Head of a civilized nation.

He has constrained our fellow Citizens taken Captive on the high Seas to bear Arms against their Country, to become the executioners of their friends and Brethren, or to fall themselves by their Hands.

He has excited domestic insurrections amongst us, and has endeavoured to bring on the inhabitants of our frontiers the merciless Indian Savages, whose known rule of warfare is an undistinguished destruction of all ages, sexes and conditions.

In every stage of these Oppressions We have Petitioned for Redress in the most humble terms: Our repeated Petitions have been answered only by repeated injury. A Prince, whose character is thus marked by every act which may define a Tyrant, is unfit to be the ruler of a free People.

Nor have We been wanting in attentions to our British brethren. We have warned them from time to time of attempts by their legislature to extend an unwarrantable jurisdiction over us. We have reminded them of the circumstances of our emigration and settlement here. We have appealed to their native justice and magnanimity, and we have conjured them by the ties of our common kindred to disavow these usurpations, which would inevitably interrupt our connections and correspondence. They too have been deaf to the voice of justice and of consanguinity. We must, therefore, acquiesce in the necessity which denounces our Separation, and hold them, as we hold the rest of mankind, Enemies in War, in Peace Friends.

We, therefore, the Representatives of the united States of America, in General Congress Assembled, appealing to the Supreme Judge of the world for the rectitude of our intentions, do, in the Name and by Authority of the good People of these Colonies, solemnly publish and declare, That these United Colonies are, and of Right ought to be Free and Independent States; that they are Absolved from all Allegiance to the British Crown, and that all political connection between them and the State of Great Britain is and ought to be totally dissolved; and that, as Free and Independent States, they have full Power to levy War, conclude Peace, contract Alliances, establish Commerce, and to do all other Acts and Things which Independent States may of right do. And for the support of this Declaration, with a firm reliance on the Protection of Divine Providence, we mutually pledge to each other our Lives, our Fortunes and our sacred Honor.

THE CONSTITUTION OF THE UNITED STATES

Preamble. We the people of the United States, in Order to form a more perfect Union, establish Justice, insure domestic Tranquility, provide for the common defence, promote the general Welfare, and secure the Blessings of Liberty to ourselves and our Posterity, do ordain and establish this CONSTITUTION for the United States of America.

ARTICLE I

[1] *Section 1.* All legislative Powers herein granted shall be vested in a Congress of the United States, which shall consist of a Senate and House of Representatives.

[2] *Section 2.* The House of Representatives shall be composed of Members chosen every second Year by the People of the several States, and the Electors in each State shall have the Qualifications requisite for Electors of the most numerous Branch of the State Legislature.

[3] No Person shall be a Representative who shall not have attained to the Age of twenty-five Years, and been seven Years a Citizen of the United States, and who shall not, when elected, be an Inhabitant of that State in which he shall be chosen.

[4] Representatives and direct Taxes shall be apportioned among the several States which may be included within this Union, according to their respective Numbers, which shall be determined by adding to the whole Number of free Persons, including those bound to Service for a Term of Years, and excluding Indians not taxed, three fifths of all other Persons. The actual Enumeration shall be made within three Years after the first Meeting of the Congress of the United States, and within every subsequent Term of ten Years, in such Manner as they shall by Law direct.

The Number of Representatives shall not exceed one for every thirty Thousand, but each State shall have at Least one Representative; and until such enumeration shall be made, the State of New Hampshire shall be entitled to chuse three, Massachusetts eight, Rhode-Island and Providence Plantations one, Connecticut five, New-York six, New Jersey four, Pennsylvania eight, Delaware one, Maryland six, Virginia ten, North Carolina five, South Carolina five, and Georgia three.

[5] When vacancies happen in the Representation from any State, the Executive Authority thereof shall issue Writs of Election to fill such Vacancies.

[6] The House of Representatives shall chuse their Speaker and other Officers; and shall have the sole Power of Impeachment.

[7] *Section 3.* The Senate of the United States shall be composed of two Senators from each State, chosen by the Legislature thereof, for six Years; and each Senator shall have one Vote.

[8] Immediately after they shall be assembled in Consequence of the first Election, they shall be divided as equally as may be into three Classes. The Seats of the Senators of the first Class shall be vacated at the Expiration of the second Year, of the second Class at the Expiration of the fourth Year, and of the third

Class at the Expiration of the sixth Year, so that one third may be chosen every second Year; and if Vacancies happen by Resignation, or otherwise, during the Recess of the Legislature of any State, the Executive thereof may make temporary Appointments until the next Meeting of the Legislature, which shall then fill such Vacancies.

[9] No Person shall be a Senator who shall not have attained to the Age of thirty Years, and been nine Years a Citizen of the United States, and who shall not, when elected, be an Inhabitant of that State for which he shall be chosen.

[10] The Vice President of the United States shall be President of the Senate, but shall have no Vote, unless they be equally divided.

[11] The Senate shall chuse their other Officers, and also a President pro tempore, in the Absence of the Vice President, or when he shall exercise the Office of President of the United States.

[12] The Senate shall have the sole Power to try all Impeachments. When sitting for that Purpose, they shall be on Oath or Affirmation. When the President of the United States is tried, the Chief Justice shall preside: And no Person shall be convicted without the Concurrence of two thirds of the Members present.

[13] Judgment in Cases of Impeachment shall not extend further than to removal from Office, and disqualification to hold and enjoy any Office of honor, Trust or Profit under the United States: but the Party convicted shall nevertheless be liable and subject to Indictment, Trial, Judgment and Punishment, according to Law.

[14] *Section 4.* The Times, Places and Manner of holding Elections for Senators and Representatives, shall be prescribed in each State by the Legislature thereof; but the Congress may at any time by Law make or alter such Regulations, except as to the Places of chusing Senators.

[15] The Congress shall assemble at least once in every Year, and such Meeting shall be on the first Monday in December, unless they shall by Law appoint a different Day.

[16] *Section 5.* Each House shall be the Judge of the Elections, Returns and Qualifications of its own Members, and a Majority of each shall constitute a Quorum to do Business; but a smaller Number may adjourn from day to day, and may be authorized to compel the Attendance of absent Members, in such Manner, and under such Penalties as each House may provide.

[17] Each House may determine the Rules of its Proceedings, punish its Members for disorderly Behavior, and, with the Concurrence of two thirds, expel a Member.

[18] Each House shall keep a Journal of its Proceedings, and from time to time publish the same, excepting such Parts as may in their Judgment require Secrecy; and the Yeas and Nays of the Members of either House on any question shall, at the Desire of one fifth of those present, be entered on the Journal.

[19] Neither House, during the Session of Congress, shall, without the Consent of the other, adjourn for more than three days, nor to any other Place than that in which the two Houses shall be sitting.

[20] *Section 6.* The Senators and Representatives shall receive a Compensation for their Services, to be ascertained by Law, and paid out of the Treasury of the United States. They shall in all Cases, except Treason, Felony and Breach of the Peace, be privileged from Arrest during their Attendance at the Session of their respective Houses, and in going to and returning from the same; and for any Speech or Debate in either House, they shall not be questioned in any other Place.

[21] No Senator or Representative shall, during the time for which he was elected, be appointed to any civil Office under the authority of the United States, which shall have been created, or the Emoluments whereof shall have been encreased during such time; and no Person holding any Office under the United States, shall be a Member of either House during his Continuance in Office.

[22] *Section 7.* All Bills for raising Revenue shall originate in the House of Representatives; but the Senate may propose or concur with Amendments as on other Bills.

[23] Every Bill which shall have passed the House of Representatives and the Senate, shall, before it become a Law, be presented to the President of the United States; if he approve he shall sign it, but if not he shall return it, with his Objections to that House in which it shall have originated, who shall enter the Objections at large on their Journal, and proceed to reconsider it. If after such Reconsideration two thirds of that House shall agree to pass the Bill, it shall be sent, together with the Objections, to the other House, by which it shall likewise be reconsidered, and if approved by two thirds of that House, it shall become a Law. But in all such Cases the Votes of both Houses shall be determined by Yeas and Nays, and the Names of the Persons voting for and against the Bill shall be entered on the Journal of each House respectively. If any Bill shall not be returned by the President within ten Days (Sundays excepted) after it shall have been presented to him, the Same shall be a Law, in like Manner as if he had signed it, unless the Congress by their Adjournment prevent its Return, in which Case it shall not be a Law.

[24] Every Order, Resolution, or Vote to which the Concurrence of the Senate and House of Representatives may be necessary (except on a question of Adjournment) shall be presented to the President of the United States; and before the Same shall take Effect, shall be approved by him, or being disapproved by him, shall be repassed by two thirds of the Senate and House of Representatives, according to the Rules and Limitations prescribed in the Case of a bill.

Section 8. The Congress shall have Power

[25] To lay and collect Taxes, Duties, Imposts and Excises to pay the Debts and provide for the common Defence and general Welfare of the United States; but all Duties, Imposts and excises shall be uniform throughout the United States;

[26] To borrow Money on the Credit of the United States;

[27] To regulate Commerce with foreign Nations, and among the several States, and with the Indian Tribes;

[28] To establish an uniform Rule of Naturalization, and uniform Laws on

the subject of Bankruptcies throughout the United States;

[29] To coin Money, regulate the Value thereof, and of foreign Coin, and fix the Standard of Weights and Measures;

[30] To provide for the Punishment of counterfeiting the Securities and current Coin of the United States;

[31] To establish Post Offices and post Roads;

[32] To promote the Progress of Science and useful Arts, by securing for limited Times to Authors and Inventors the exclusive Right to their respective Writings and Discoveries;

[33] To constitute Tribunals inferior to the supreme Court;

[34] To define and Punish Piracies and Felonies committed on the high Seas, and Offences against the Law of Nations;

[35] To declare War, grant Letters of Marque and Reprisal, and make Rules concerning Captures on Land and Water;

[36] To raise and support Armies, but no Appropriation of Money to that Use shall be for a longer Term than two Years;

[37] To provide and maintain a Navy;

[38] To make Rules for the Government and Regulation of the land and naval Forces;

[39] To provide for calling forth the Militia to execute the Laws of the Union, suppress Insurrections and repel Invasions;

[40] To provide for organizing, arming, and disciplining, the Militia, and for governing such Part of them as may be employed in the Service of the United States, reserving to the States respectively, the Appointment of the Officers, and the Authority of training the Militia according to the discipline prescribed by Congress;

[41] To exercise exclusive Legislation in all Cases whatsoever, over such District (not exceeding ten Miles square) as may, by Cession of particular States, and the Acceptance of Congress, become the Seat of the Government of the United States, and to exercise like Authority over all Places purchased by the Consent of the Legislature of the State in which the Same shall be, for the Erection of Forts, Magazines, Arsenals, dock-Yards, and other needful Buildings; — And

[42] To make all Laws which shall be necessary and proper for carrying into Execution the foregoing Powers, and all other Powers vested by this Constitution in the Government of the United States, or in any Department or Officer thereof.

[43] *Section 9.* The Migration or Importation of such Persons as any of the States now existing shall think proper to admit, shall not be prohibited by the Congress prior to the Year one thousand eight hundred and eight, but a Tax or Duty may be imposed on such Importation, not exceeding ten dollars for each Person.

[44] The Privilege of the Writ of Habeas Corpus shall not be suspended, unless when in Cases of Rebellion or Invasion the public Safety may require it.

[45] No Bill of Attainder or ex post facto Law shall be passed.

[46] No Capitation, or other direct, Tax shall be laid, unless in Proportion to the Census or Enumeration herein before directed to be taken.

[47] No Tax or Duty shall be laid on Articles exported from any State.

[48] No Preference shall be given by any Regulation of Commerce or Reve-

ue to the Ports of one State over those of another: nor shall Vessels bound to, or from, one State, be obliged to enter, clear, or pay Duties in another.

[49]   No Money shall be drawn from the Treasury, but in Consequence of Appropriations made by Law; and a regular Statement and Account of the Receipts and Expenditures of all public Money shall be published from time to time.

[50]   No Title of Nobility shall be granted by the United States: And no Person holding any Office of Profit or Trust under them, shall, without the Consent of the Congress, accept of any present, Emolument, Office, or Title, of any kind whatever, from any King, Prince, or foreign State.

[51]   *Section 10*.   No State shall enter into any Treaty, Alliance, or Confederation; grant Letters of Marque and Reprisal; coin Money; emit Bills of Credit; make any Thing but gold and silver Coin a Tender in Payment of Debts; pass any Bill of Attainder, ex post facto Law, or Law impairing the Obligation of Contracts, or grant any Title of Nobility.

[52]   No State shall, without the Consent of the Congress, lay any Imposts or Duties on Imports or Exports, except what may be absolutely necessary for executing its inspection Laws: and the net Produce of all Duties and Imposts, laid by any State on Imports or Exports, shall be for the Use of the Treasury of the United States; and all such Laws shall be subject to the Revision and Controul of the Congress.

[53]   No State shall, without the Consent of Congress, lay any Duty of Tonnage, keep Troops, or Ships of War in time of Peace, enter into any Agreement or Compact with another State, or with a foreign Power, or engage in War, unless actually invaded, or in such imminent Danger as will not admit of Delay.

ARTICLE II

[54]   *Section 1*.   The executive Power shall be vested in a President of the United States of America.   He shall hold his Office during the Term of four Years, and, together with the Vice President, chosen for the same Term, be elected, as follows

[55]   Each State shall appoint, in such Manner as the Legislature thereof may direct, a Number of Electors, equal to the whole Number of Senators and Representatives to which the State may be entitled in the Congress: but no Senator or Representative, or Person holding an Office of Trust or Profit under the United States, shall be appointed an Elector.

[56]   The electors shall meet in their respective States, and vote by ballot for two Persons, of whom one at least shall not be an Inhabitant of the same State with themselves.   And they shall make a List of all the Persons voted for, and of the Number of Votes for each; which List they shall sign and certify, and transmit sealed to the Seat of the Government of the United States, directed to the President of the Senate.   The President of the Senate shall, in the Presence of the Senate and House of Representatives, open all the Certificates, and the Votes shall then be counted.   The Person having the greatest Number of Votes shall be the President, if such Number be a Majority of the

whole Number of Electors appointed; and if there be more than one who have such Majority and have an equal Number of Votes, then the House of Representatives shall immediately chuse by Ballot one of them for President; and if no person have a Majority, then from the five highest on the List the said House shall in like Manner chuse the President. But in chusing the President, the Votes shall be taken by States, the Representation from each State having one Vote; A quorum for this Purpose shall consist of a Member or Members from two-thirds of the States, and a Majority of all the States shall be necessary to a Choice. In every Case, after the Choice of the President, the person having the greatest Number of Votes of the Electors shall be the Vice President. But if there should remain two or more who have equal Votes, the Senate shall chuse from them by Ballot the Vice-President.

[57] The Congress may determine the Time of chusing the Electors, and the Day on which they shall give their Votes; which Day shall be the same throughout the United States.

[58] No Person except a natural born Citizen, or a Citizen of the United States, at the time of the Adoption of this Constitution, shall be eligible to the Office of President; neither shall any Person be eligible to that Office who shall not have attained to the Age of thirty-five Years, and been fourteen Years a Resident within the United States.

[59] In Case of the Removal of the President from Office, or of his Death, Resignation, or Inability to discharge the Powers and Duties of the said Office, the same shall devolve on the Vice President, and the Congress may by

Law provide for the Case of Removal, Death, Resignation, or Inability, both of the President and Vice President, declaring what Officer shall then act as President, and such Officer shall act accordingly, until the Disability be removed, or a President shall be elected.

[60] The President shall, at stated Times, receive for his Services, a Compensation, which shall neither be encreased nor diminished during the Period of which he shall have been elected, and he shall not receive within that Period any other Emolument from the United States, or any of them.

[61] Before he enter on the Execution of his Office, he shall take the following Oath or Affirmation: — "I do sol- "emnly swear (or affirm) that I will "faithfully execute the Office of Presi- "dent of the United States, and will to "the best of my Ability, preserve, pro- "tect and defend the Constitution of the "United States."

[62] *Section 2.* The President shall be Commander in Chief of the Army and Navy of the United States, and of the Militia of the several States, when called into the actual Service of the United States; he may require the Opinion, in writing, of the principal Officer in each of the executive Departments, upon any Subject relating to the Duties of their respective Offices, and he shall have Power to grant Reprieves and Pardons for Offences against the United States, except in Cases of Impeachment.

[63] He shall have Power, by and with the Advice and Consent of the Senate, to make Treaties, provided two thirds of the Senators present concur; and he shall nominate, and by and with the Advice and Consent of the Senate, shall

appoint Ambassadors, other public Ministers and Consuls, Judges of the supreme Court, and all other Officers of the United States, whose Appointments are not herein otherwise provided for, and which shall be established by Law: but the Congress may by Law vest the Appointment of such inferior Officers, as they think proper, in the President alone, in the Courts of Law, or in the Heads of Departments.

[64] The President shall have Power to fill up all Vacancies that may happen during the Recess of the Senate, by granting Commissions which shall expire at the End of their next Session.

[65] *Section 3.* He shall from time to time give to the Congress Information of the State of the Union, and recommend to their Consideration such Measures as he shall judge necessary and expedient; he may, on extraordinary Occasions, convene both Houses, or either of them, and in Case of Disagreement between them, with Respect to the Time of Adjournment, he may adjourn them to such Time as he shall think proper; he shall receive Ambassadors and other public Ministers; he shall take Care that the Laws be faithfully executed, and shall Commission all the Officers of the United States.

[66] *Section 4.* The President, Vice President and all civil Officers of the United States shall be removed from Office on Impeachment for, and Conviction of, Treason, Bribery, or other high Crimes and Misdemeanors.

ARTICLE III

[67] *Section 1.* The judicial Power of the United States, shall be vested in one supreme Court, and in such inferior Courts as the Congress may from time to time ordain and establish. The Judges, both of the supreme and inferior Courts, shall hold their Offices during Good Behavior, and shall, at stated Times, receive for their Services, a Compensation, which shall not be diminished during their Continuance in Office.

[68] *Section 2.* The judicial Power shall extend to all Cases, in Law and Equity, arising under this Constitution, the Laws of the United States, and Treaties made, or which shall be made, under their Authority; — to all Cases affecting Ambassadors, other public Ministers and Consuls; — to all Cases of admiralty and maritime Jurisdiction; — to Controversies to which the United States shall be a Party; — to Controversies between two or more States; — between a State and Citizens of another State; — between Citizens of different States, — between Citizens of the same State claiming Lands under Grants of different States, and between a State, or the Citizens thereof, and foreign States, Citizens or Subjects.

[69] In all Cases affecting Ambassadors, other public Ministers and Consuls, and those in which a State shall be Party, the supreme Court shall have original Jurisdiction. In all the other Cases before mentioned, the supreme Court shall have appellate Jurisdiction, both as to Law and Fact, with such Exceptions, and under such Regulations as Congress shall make.

[70] The Trial of all Crimes, except in Cases of Impeachment, shall be by Jury; and such Trial shall be held in the State where the said Crimes shall have been committed; but when not committed within any State, the Trial shall

be at such Place or Places as the Congress may by Law have directed.

[71] *Section 3.* Treason against the United States, shall consist only in levying War against them, or in adhering to their Enemies, giving them Aid and Comfort. No Person shall be convicted of Treason unless on the Testimony of two Witnesses to the same over Act, or on Confession in open Court.

[72] The Congress shall have Power to declare the Punishment of Treason but no Attainder of Treason shall work Corruption of Blood, or Forfeiture except during the Life of the Person attained.

ARTICLE IV

[73] *Section 1.* Full Faith and Credit shall be given in each State to the public Acts, Records, and judicial Proceedings of every other State. And the Congress may by general Laws prescribe the Manner in which such Acts, Records and Proceedings shall be proved, and the Effect thereof.

[74] *Section 2.* The Citizens of each State shall be entitled to all Privileges and Immunities of Citizens in the several States.

[75] A person charged in any State with Treason, Felony, or other Crime, who shall flee from Justice, and be found in another State, shall on Demand of the executive Authority of the State from which he fled, be delivered up to be removed to the State having Jurisdiction of the Crime.

[76] No Person held to Service or Labour in one State, under the Laws thereof, escaping into another, shall, in Consequence of any Law or Regulation therein, be discharged from such Service or Labour, but shall be delivered up on Claim of the Party to whom such Service or Labour may be due.

[77] *Section 3.* New States may be admitted by the Congress into this Union; but no new State shall be formed or erected within the Jurisdiction of any other State; nor any State be formed by the Junction of two or more States, or Parts of States, without the Consent of the Legislatures of the States concerned as well as of the Congress.

[78] The Congress shall have Power to dispose of and make all needful Rules and Regulations respecting the Territory or other Property belonging to the United States; and nothing in this Constitution shall be so construed as to Prejudice any Claims of the United States, or of any particular State.

[79] *Section 4.* The United States shall guarantee to every State in this Union a Republican Form of Government, and shall protect each of them against Invasion; and on Application of the Legislature, or of the Executive (when the Legislature cannot be convened) against domestic Violence.

ARTICLE V

[80] The Congress, whenever two thirds of both Houses shall deem it necessary, shall propose Amendments to this Constitution, or, on the Application of the Legislatures of two thirds of the several States, shall call a Convention for proposing Amendments, which, in either Case, shall be valid to all Intents and Purposes, as Part of this Constitution, when ratified by the Legislatures of three fourths of the several States, or by Conventions in three

fourths thereof, as the one or the other Mode of Ratification may be proposed by the Congress; Provided that no Amendment which may be made prior to the Year One thousand eight hundred and eight shall in any Manner affect the first and fourth Clauses in the Ninth Section of the first Article; and that no State, without its Consent, shall be deprived of its equal Suffrage in the Senate.

ARTICLE VI

[81] All Debts contracted and Engagements entered into, before the Adoption of this Constitution, shall be as valid against the United States under this Constitution, as under the Confederation.

[82] This Constitution, and the Laws of the United States which shall be made in Pursuance thereof; and all Treaties made, or which shall be made, under the Authority of the United States, shall be the supreme Law of the Land; and the Judges in every State shall be bound thereby, any Thing in the Constitution or Laws of any State to the Contrary notwithstanding.

[83] The Senators and Representatives before mentioned, and the Members of the several State Legislatures, and all executives and judicial Officers, both of the United States and of the several States, shall be bound by Oath or Affirmation, to support this Constitution; but no religious Test shall ever be required as a Qualification to any Office or public Trust under the United States.

ARTICLE VII

[84] The Ratification of the Conventions of nine States, shall be sufficient for the Establishment of this Constitution between the States so ratifying the Same.

DONE in Convention by the Unanimous Consent of the States present the Seventeenth Day of September in the Year of our Lord one thousand seven hundred and Eighty seven and of the Independence of the United States of America the Twelfth. *In Witness* whereof We have hereunto subscribed our Names,

G:º WASHINGTON —
*Presidt, and Deputy
from Virginia* [1]

ARTICLES IN ADDITION TO, AND AMENDMENT OF, THE CONSTITUTION

ARTICLE I

[85] Congress shall make no law respecting an establishment of religion, or prohibiting the free exercise thereof; or abridging the freedom of speech, or of the press; or the right of the people peaceably to assemble, and to petition the Government for a redress of grievances.

ARTICLE II

[86] A well regulated Militia, being necessary to the security of a free State, the right of the people to keep and bear Arms, shall not be infringed.

ARTICLE III

[87] No Soldier shall, in time of peace be quartered in any house, without the consent of the Owner, nor in time of war, but in a manner to be prescribed by law.

[1] The remaining signatures are omitted.

ARTICLE IV

[88]   The right of the people to be secure in their persons, houses, papers, and effects, against unreasonable searches and seizures, shall not be violated, and no Warrants shall issue, but upon probable cause, supported by Oath or affirmation, and particularly describing the place to be searched, and the persons or things to be seized.

ARTICLE V

[89]   No person shall be held to answer for a capital, or otherwise infamous crime, unless on a presentment or indictment of a Grand Jury, except in cases arising in the land or naval forces, or in the Militia, when in actual service in time of War or in public danger; nor shall any person be subject for the same offence to be twice put in jeopardy of life or limb; nor shall be compelled in any Criminal Case to be a witness against himself, nor be deprived of life, liberty, or property, without due process of law; nor shall private property be taken for public use, without just compensation.

ARTICLE VI

[90]   In all criminal prosecutions, the accused shall enjoy the right to a speedy and public trial, by an impartial jury of the State and district wherein the crime shall have been committed, which district shall have been previously ascertained by law, and to be informed of the nature and cause of the accusation; to be confronted with the witnesses against him; to have compulsory process for obtaining Witnesses in his favor, and to have the Assistance of Counsel for his defence.

ARTICLE VII

[91]   In suits at common law, where the value in controversy shall exceed twenty dollars, the right of trial by jury shall be preserved, and no fact tried by a jury shall be otherwise re-examined in any Court of the United States, than according to the rules of the common law.

ARTICLE VIII

[92]   Excessive bail shall not be required, nor excessive fines imposed, nor cruel and unusual punishments inflicted.

ARTICLE IX

[93]   The enumeration in the Constitution, of certain rights, shall not be construed to deny or disparage others retained by the people.

ARTICLE X

[94]   The powers not delegated to the United States by the Constitution, nor prohibited by it to the States, are reserved to the States respectively, or to the people.

ARTICLE XI

[95]   The Judicial power of the United States shall not be construed to extend to any suit in law or equity, commenced or prosecuted against one of the United States by Citizens of another State, or by Citizens or Subjects of any Foreign State.

ARTICLE XII

[96] The Electors shall meet in their respective states, and vote by ballot for President and Vice-President, one of whom, at least, shall not be an inhabitant of the same state with themselves; they shall name in their ballots the person voted for as President, and in distinct ballots the person voted for as Vice-President, and they shall make distinct lists of all persons voted for as President, and of all persons voted for as Vice-President, and of the number of votes for each, which lists they shall sign and certify, and transmit sealed to the seat of the government of the United States, directed to the President of the Senate; — The President of the Senate shall, in presence of the Senate and House of Representatives, open all the certificates and the votes shall then be counted; — The person having the greatest number of votes for President, shall be the President, if such number be a majority of the whole number of Electors appointed; and if no person have such majority, then from the persons having the highest numbers not exceeding three on the list of those voted for as President, the House of Representatives shall choose immediately, by ballot, the President. But in choosing the President, the votes shall be taken by states, the representation from each state having one vote; a quorum for this purpose shall consist of a member or members from two-thirds of the states, and a majority of all the states shall be necessary to a choice. And if the House of Representatives shall not choose a President whenever the right of choice shall devolve upon them, before the fourth day of March next following, then the Vice-President shall act as President, as in the case of the death or other constitutional disability of the President. The person having the greatest number of votes as Vice-President, shall be the Vice-President, if such a number be a majority of the whole number of Electors appointed, and if no person have a majority, then from the two highest numbers on the list, the Senate shall choose the Vice-President; a quorum for the purpose shall consist of two-thirds of the whole number of Senators, and a majority of the whole number shall be necessary to a choice. But no person constitutionally ineligible to the office of President shall be eligible to that of Vice-President of the United States.

ARTICLE XIII

[97] *Section 1.* Neither slavery nor involuntary servitude, except as a punishment for crime whereof the party shall have been duly convicted, shall exist within the United States, or any place subject to their jurisdiction.

[98] *Section 2.* Congress shall have power to enforce this article by appropriate legislation.

ARTICLE XIV

[99] *Section 1.* All persons born or naturalized in the United States, and subject to the jurisdiction thereof, are citizens of the United States and of the State wherein they reside. No State shall make or enforce any law which shall abridge the privileges or immunities of citizens of the United States; nor

shall any State deprive any person of life, liberty, or property, without due process of law; nor deny to any person within its jurisdiction the equal protection of the laws.

[100] *Section 2.* Representatives shall be apportioned among the several States according to their respective numbers, counting the whole number of persons in each State, excluding Indians not taxed. But when the right to vote at any election for the choice of electors for President and Vice-President of the United States, Representatives in Congress, the Executive and Judicial officers of a State, or the members of the Legislature thereof, is denied to any of the male inhabitants of such State, being twenty-one years of age, and citizens of the United States, or in any way abridged, except for participation in rebellion, or other crime, the basis of representation therein shall be reduced in the proportion which the number of such male citizens shall bear to the whole number of male citizens twenty-one years of age in such State.

[101] *Section 3.* No person shall be a Senator or Representative in Congress, or elector of President and Vice-President, or hold any office, civil or military, under the United States, or under any State, who, having previously taken an oath, as a member of Congress, or as an officer of the United States, or as a member of any State legislature, or as an executive or judicial officer of any State, to support the Constitution of the United States, shall have engaged in insurrection or rebellion against the same, or given aid or comfort to the enemies thereof. But Congress may by a vote of two-thirds of each House, remove such disability.

[102] *Section 4.* The validity of the public debt of the United States, authorized by law, including debts incurred for payment of pensions and bounties for services in suppressing insurrection or rebellion, shall not be questioned. But neither the United States nor any State shall assume or pay any debt or obligation incurred in aid of insurrection or rebellion against the United States, or any claim for the loss or emancipation of any slave; but all such debts, obligations and claims shall be held illegal and void.

[103] *Section 5.* The Congress shall have power to enforce, by appropriate legislation, the provisions of this article.

ARTICLE XV

[104] *Section 1.* The right of citizens of the United States to vote shall not be denied or abridged by the United States or by any State on account of race, color, or previous condition of servitude.

[105] *Section 2.* The Congress shall have power to enforce this article by appropriate legislation.

ARTICLE XVI

[106] *Section 1.* The Congress shall have power to lay and collect taxes on incomes, from whatever source derived, without apportionment among the several States, and without regard to any census or enumeration.

ARTICLE XVII

[107] *Section 1.* The Senate of the United States shall be composed of two Senators from each State, elected by the people thereof, for six years; and each Senator shall have one vote. The electors in each State shall have the qualifications requisite for electors of the most numerous branch of the State Legislature.

[108] *Section 2.* When vacancies happen in the representation of any State in the Senate, the executive authority of such State shall issue writs of election to fill such vacancies: Provided, That the Legislature of any State may empower the executive thereof to make temporary appointment until the people fill the vacancies by election as the Legislature may direct.

[109] *Section 3.* This amendment shall not be so construed as to affect the election or term of any Senator chosen before it becomes valid as part of the Constitution.

ARTICLE XVIII

[110] *Section 1.* After one year from the ratification of this article the manufacture, sale, or transportation of intoxicating liquors within, the importation thereof into, or the exportation thereof from the United States and all territory subject to the jurisdiction thereof for beverage purposes is hereby prohibited.

[111] *Section 2.* The Congress and the several states shall have concurrent power to enforce this article by appropriate legislation.

[112] *Section 3.* This article shall be inoperative unless it shall have been ratified as an amendment to the Constitution by the legislatures of the several states, as provided in the Constitution, within seven years from the date of the submission hereof to the states by the Congress.

ARTICLE XIX

[113] *Section 1.* The right of the citizens of the United States to vote shall not be denied or abridged by the United States or by any state on account of sex.

[114] *Section 2.* Congress shall have power, by appropriate legislation, to enforce the provision of this article.

ARTICLE XX

[115] *Section 1.* The terms of the President and Vice-President shall end at noon on the 20th day of January, and the terms of Senators and Representatives at noon on the 3rd day of January, of the years in which such terms would have ended if this article had not been ratified; and the terms of their successors shall then begin.

[116] *Section 2.* The Congress shall assemble at least once in every year, and such meeting shall begin at noon on the 3rd day of January, unless they shall by law appoint a different day.

[117] *Section 3.* If, at the time fixed for the beginning of the term of the President, the President elect shall have died, the Vice-President elect shall become President. If a President shall not have been chosen before the time fixed for the beginning of his term, or if the President elect shall have failed to qual-

ify, then the Vice-President elect shall act as President until a President shall have qualified; and the Congress may by law provide for the case wherein neither a President elect nor a Vice-President elect shall have qualified, declaring who shall then act as President, or the manner in which one who is to act shall be selected, and such person shall act accordingly until a President or Vice-President shall have qualified.

[118] *Section 4*. The Congress may by law provide for the case of the death of any of the persons from whom the House of Representatives may choose a President whenever the right of choice shall have devolved upon them, and for the case of the death of any of the persons from whom the Senate may choose a Vice-President whenever the right of choice shall have devolved upon them.

[119] *Section 5*. Sections 1 and 2 shall take effect on the 15th day of October following the ratification of this article (Oct., 1933).

[120] *Section 6*. This article shall be inoperative unless it shall have been ratified as an amendment to the Constitution by the legislatures of three-fourths of the several States within seven years from the date of its submission.

ARTICLE XXI

[121] *Section 1*. The eighteenth article of amendment to the Constitution of the United States is hereby repealed.

[122] *Section 2*. The transportation or importation into any State, Territory, or Possession of the United States for delivery or use therein of intoxicating liquors, in violation of the laws thereof, is hereby prohibited.

[123] *Section 3*. This article shall be inoperative unless it shall have been ratified as an amendment to the Constitution by conventions in the several States, as provided in the Constitution, within seven years from the date of the submission hereof to the States by the Congress.

ARTICLE XXII

[124] No person shall be elected to the office of the President more than twice, and no person who has held the office of President, or acted as President, for more than two years of a term to which some other person was elected President shall be elected to the office of the President more than once. But this Article shall not apply to any person holding the office of President when this Article was proposed by the Congress, and shall not prevent any person who may be holding the office of President, or acting as President, during the term within which this Article becomes operative from holding the office of President or acting as President during the remainder of such term.

ACKNOWLEDGMENTS

Lewis F. White designed the typography. William D. Hayes prepared the first general designs. Jacob Landau acted as art director. Edward Malsberg drew time lines. Rafael Palacios prepared the maps. Frances Orkin obtained photographs. James McRee prepared the index.

American Airlines, page: 549.
American Federationist, pages: 479 (bottom), 481, 499.
American Museum of Natural History, pages: 3, 5 (bottom left), 8 (bottom), 9, 10, 11.
American Museum of Photography, page: 365.
American Philosophical Society, page: 213.
American Telephone and Telegraph, pages: 433, 435.
Auto Manufacturing Association, pages: 425, 426.
Baltimore and Ohio R.R., page: 317 (left).
Bettmann Archive, pages: 183, 212, 404.
British Information Services, pages: 48, 113, 583, 584, 592.
Brown Brothers, page: 321.
John Carter Brown Library, pages: 137 (top), 177.
Bureau of Public Roads, pages: 262, 329, 546.
Capital Press Service of Ottawa, page: 544 (right).
Carnegie Institution of Washington, page: 5 (top right).
Chamber of Commerce, Ticonderoga, N.Y., page: 103.
Chase National Bank Museum of Moneys of the World, pages: 176 (right), 214 (top).
Chicago Historical Society, pages: 150, 492 (bottom).
Cities Service Co., page: 429.
Cleveland Museum of Art, page: 136.
Concord Antiquarian Society, page: 92 (bottom).
Cooper Union Museum, pages: 28, 34, 37, 47, 82, 86, 102, 189 (right), 229, 263, 312 (right), 359, 384, 388, 453.
Cornell University School of Agriculture, page: 463.
Culver Service, pages: 31, 32, 33, 154, 181, 285, 354, 363, 368, 375, 378, 381, 454, 458.
Deere Plow, page: 415.
Duncan William Collection, page: 70 (bottom).
Edison Museum, West Orange, N.J., page: 414.
Essex Institute, page: 92 (top).
Federal Hall Memorial Museum, pages: 97, 108, 139, 163, 176 (left), 188, 209.
Food and Drug Administration, page: 460.
Ford Motor Co., pages: 489, 492 (top).
Ford Museum, Dearborn, Mich., page: 430 (center).
General Motors Corp., pages: 425 (right), 426, 427, 482.
Goodyear Tire and Rubber Co., page: 428.
Graphics Institute, pages: 112, 196, 247, 294, 434, 578.
John Hancock Insurance Co., pages: 274, 332, 406 (left), 418, 427 (bottom), 450, 459, 469, 478, 500, 531.
Harper and Bros., page: 226.
Harper's Weekly, pages: 477, 517 (center).
Illinois Historical Society, page: 374.
Independence Hall Collection, Philadelphia, pages: 214 (bottom), 215.
International News Service, page: 604 (bottom).
Library of Congress, pages: 14, 17, 66, 69, 70, 116, 144, 197, 224, 269, 281, 288, 366, 385 (bottom), 402, 448, 476, 496, 571, 599.
Massachusetts Dept. of Commerce, pages: 93, 140.
Metropolitan Museum of Art, pages: 89, 132, 137 (bottom), 187, 189 (left), 235, 307 (left).
Moffett Studios, Chicago, page: 433 (left).
Morgan Library, page: 18.
Mt. Holyoke News Bureau, page: 502.
Museum of the City of New York, page: 494 (left).
National Archives, pages: 138, 230, 525, 538, 574, 575.
National Film Board of Canada, pages: 544 (left), 545.
National Life Insurance Co., pages: v, 43, 87, 88, 94, 244, 259, 291, 317 (right), 501.
National Park Serv., page: 391.
National Screen Serv., page: 15.
Nebraska State Historical Society, page: 462.
New Orleans News, page: 222.
New York Historical Society, pages: 78, 208, 239, 287, 311 (left), 312 (left), 376, 379, 520 (bottom).
New York Housing Authority, pages: 494 (right), 495.
New York Public Library, pages: 217, 245, 282, 292, 355, 358, 367, 548, 552.
New York State Museum, page: 6.
Nova Scotia Bureau of Information, page: 107.
Old Slater Mill, page: 405.
Panama Canal Official Photo, pages: 530, 532.
Pan American-Grace Airlines, pages: 556, 557, 558 (left).
Paramount Pictures, page: 12.
Pennsylvania Academy of Fine Arts, page: 79.
Pennsylvania State Dept. of Commerce, page: 109.
Philadelphia Dept. of Public Works, page: 277.
Pictograph Corporation, pages: 192, 319, 490, 497.
Pilgrim Society, pages: 71, 72.
Public Archives of Canada, page: 105.
Public Roads Administration, pages: 110, 216, 305, 306, 307, 309, 311 (right), 327.
Pyle, *Book of the American Spirit*, pages: 96, 173.
Radio Corporation of America, pages: 435, 436.
Ross County Historical Society, Ohio, page: 240.
Santa Fe R.R., page: 320.
Saturday Evening Post and Norman Rockwell, page: 98.
Schoenfeld Collection, Three Lions, pages: 385 (center), 514, 518.
Singer Manufacturing Co., pages: 43 (bottom), 411.
Smithsonian Institution, pages: 7, 8 (top), 16, 314, 316, 406 (right), 410, 416, 430.
Social Security Administration, page: 485.
Sons of the Revolution, Fraunces Tavern, New York City, pages: 141, 152, 207.
Standard Oil of New Jersey, pages: 407, 468, 483, 503.
TVA, page: 470.
Title Guarantee and Trust Co., New York, page: 77.
Underwood and Underwood, page: 431 (left).
United Artists Corp., page: 67.
United Fruit Co., page: 551.
United Nations, pages: 535, 551, 555, 558, 601, 610.
United Press (Acme), pages: 457, 579, 582, 584.
U.S. Air Force, pages: 431 (right), 437, 594 (top), 598.
U.S. Army, pages: 385 (top), 521, 572, 574, 575, 593, 594 (bottom), 596, 611.
U.S. Dept. of Agriculture, page: 464.
U.S. Dept. of Int., page: 517.
U.S. Dept. of Labor, page: 481.
U.S. Forest Service, pages: 468 (right), 471, 515.
U.S. Military Academy, West Point, page: 377.
U.S. Navy, pages: 586, 591.
U.S. Office of Ed. page: 503.
U.S. Steel Corp., page: 424.
USWB, page: 465.

HOW TO USE AND UNDERSTAND MAPS

One of the most important skills you need to acquire in order to understand the story of America is how to use a map. Maps are always drawn to show three things: direction, scale, and position or location. In addition, they may show such information as elevation or altitude, population, boundaries of states and distances between ports.

1. How can you tell what direction one place is from another?

On most maps, North is shown at the top of the page; South is at the bottom; East is on the right side; and West is on the left side. However, sometimes maps are drawn differently. When they are, you will find the points of the compass plainly marked on the map.

2. How can you tell how far one place is from another?

On most maps you will find a *scale* or line accompanied by a sentence telling how many miles each inch on the map represents. Using this scale and a ruler, you can translate distance on the map into miles. For example, suppose you wish to know the distance from New York to Albany. You measure the distance on the map between the two cities and find that it is about one and one-half inches. The scale on the map shows that one inch equals 100 miles. So the approximate distance from New York to Albany is one and one-half times 100 or about 150 miles.

3. How can you tell how far North or South a place is?

On most maps of the world or large sections of it you will find a line called the *Equator* (ee KWAY tur) that runs from east to west across

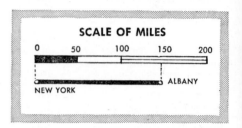

the middle of the map. This is an imaginary line or circle that map makers draw to show the middle of the earth — that is, the distance half-way between the North Pole or northernmost part of the earth and the South Pole or southernmost part. Every place on earth may be located north or south of the Equator.

To make it easier to measure the distance, map makers draw additional circles on the map. Because these lines are parallel to the Equator they are called *parallels of latitude*. There are 90 of these parallels of latitude between the North Pole and the Equator, and 90 parallels between the Equator and the South Pole. Thus, there are 180 parallels of latitude in all. You can see some of these parallels on page 614L.

The parallels are numbered in *degrees* to show their distance from the Equator. The Equator is numbered 0°. The parallels north of the

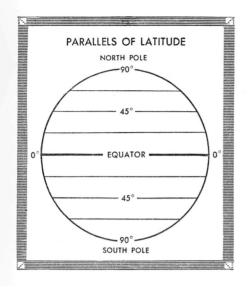

PARALLELS OF LATITUDE

NORTH POLE
90°
45°
0° — EQUATOR — 0°
45°
90°
SOUTH POLE

itch) Observatory in London. Thus a place is usually located by its distance east or west of Greenwich. There are 180 meridians of longitude extending east from Greenwich and 180 meridians of longitude west, so their are 360 meridians in all. The meridians are numbered from 1 to 180 degrees of longitude East and 1 to 180 degrees West. London, England lies on the zero meridian. Columbus, Ohio lies near the 83rd meridian *West*. This means that Columbus is 83 degrees west of London or the prime meridian. Thus, the location of Columbus, Ohio may be written as 40° N, 83° W.

On maps of smaller areas such as a state or a country it is not practical to show parallels of latitude and meridians of longitude. Instead, letters of the alphabet and numbers are used. For example, on a road map of New England such as you can obtain free from an oil company, letters from A to M are printed equal distances apart along the top and bottom of the map. Along the sides are numbers from 1 to 15.

Suppose that you want to locate

Equator are numbered from 1 to 90 degrees North; the parallels south of the Equator are numbered from 1 to 90 degrees South. Each degree of latitude is usually considered to be about 70 miles. For example, Columbus, Ohio is very near the 40th parallel so its location is 40° North latitude. This means it is about 2800 miles north of the Equator.

4. How can you tell from a map how far east or west a place is?

In addition to the parallels of latitude which run east and west, most maps of the world also have lines running north and south. These are called *meridians of longitude* (meh RID ih ans of LAHN jih tud). These lines are drawn to show distance east and west of the *prime meridian*. The prime meridian is an imaginary line running from the North Pole to the South Pole and passing through Greenwich (GREHN

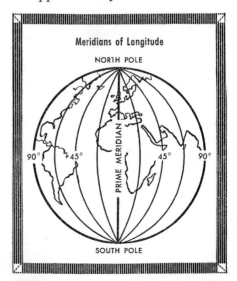

Meridians of Longitude

NORTH POLE

90° 45° PRIME MERIDIAN 45° 90°

SOUTH POLE

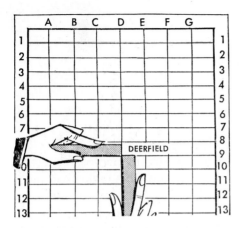

Deerfield, Massachusetts. You look at the Index or list of towns usually printed on the back of road maps. On this list you read "Deerfield, Massachusetts D–9."

If you draw a line downward on the map from "D" and another line across the map from "9" you will find Deerfield at or very near the spot where the two lines cross or intersect each other.

5. What other facts do maps show?

On many maps the population of cities is indicated by the size of type and the symbol that shows their location. For example, Chicago is usually printed in larger, blacker type than is Portland, Maine. A city that is the capital of a state is often shown with a star beside it.

Among the many special kinds of maps is the "physical map." This shows altitude or the elevation (height) of land above or below sea level. Sea level means the level the ocean would reach if it were as still as the water in a pail. On physical maps colors are often used to indicate how high a region is above sea level. Red usually indicates high mountains; a section of the map colored brown and yellow usually indicates a high land or "upland." Lowlands or plains are shown in green; light blue is used to show that a lake or ocean is not very deep, while darker blue indicates greater depth.

6. The earth is round and all maps are flat. How can you represent a round object on a flat surface?

If you want to see just what kind of problem the map maker faces when he tries to make a flat map of the world, you can take a globe, a tangerine, a small paring knife, and a fountain pen and find out yourself.

First draw the outlines of the continents on the tangerine with your fountain pen, using the globe as a guide. (You can do this easily with a tangerine because the tangerine peel is fairly dry. Orange peel is too oily. You need not try to draw the continents too carefully.) Then cut a strip down one side of the tangerine and remove the fruit through this opening, section by section. From each end of the hollow tangerine peel, at the place corresponding to a pole, cut out a small piece of peeling, about the size of a dime. Then beginning at the place where you cut out the first strip, unroll the peeling and flatten it out against the table.

You will find that in order to do this, you will have to stretch the top and bottom parts of the peel a great deal, so much so that the edges split. Something of this sort always happens in the making of a flat world map. Parts of the earth are drawn as if stretched out in comparison with other parts. Such a departure from the truth is called *distortion*.

To get around this difficulty, many different methods or map *projections* have been devised. A projection is simply a way of representing the earth or part of it on a flat surface such as a page in a book.

There are more than a dozen different projections. The ones most generally used are the *Mercator* (mer KAY tur) *projection* and the *Azimuthal* (AZ ih MUTH al).

7. What is the Mercator projection?

This is the most common method of map making. Most of the maps in this book are Mercator projection maps. In this projection all the parallels and meridians are shown as evenly-spaced lines (see below)

Notice that on this map the island of Greenland appears at the top of the map larger than the United States. Actually, however, Greenland is less than one-third as large as the United States. But on a Mercator projection map, only the equator is true to scale. The parts of the map far away from the equator are distorted or out of shape. This is because the meridians are shown as evenly-spaced straight lines instead of curved lines running together at the extreme north and south as they do on a globe.

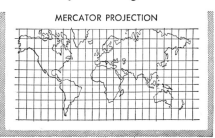

MERCATOR PROJECTION

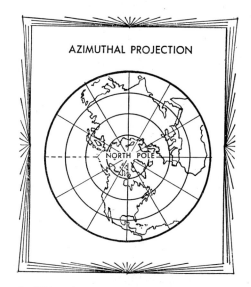

AZIMUTHAL PROJECTION

NORTH POLE

8. What is the Azimuthal projection?

This is a kind of map that has become more popular since the coming of the airplane. It is sometimes called the "Polar projection," or the "Air-age map." Such maps often show the North Pole in the center of the map! In fact, any point on the earth's surface may be taken as the center. The map shows the earth as it appears from that point. The map on page 614L is an Azimuthal projection. On it the North Pole is in the center and the rest of the world is shown as it appears from there. The most valuable feature of this projection is that it shows every point at its true direction from the center point, and all points equally distant on the map. But Azimuthal projection maps often seem very confused and confusing. Their usefulness is somewhat limited because a separate map has to be drawn for each central point selected.

641

KEY TO PRONUNCIATION

The pronunciation system used throughout *Story of Our Land and People* does away with the difficult pronunciation marks found in many dictionaries. The following KEY is based on the one developed for *The World Book Encyclopedia*, published by Field Enterprises, Inc. It is reproduced here, with minor changes, by permission of *The Encyclopedia*.

Whenever a difficult or unusual word first appears in the text, it is respelled for you and put within parentheses, like this:

Renaissance (REN ah SAHNTS)

Note that the syllable that gets the main accent is spelled in large capital letters, while the syllable that gets a secondary accent is spelled in small capital letters. Syllables without accent are not capitalized.

In this KEY, consonants remain the same if the sound they stand for is clear. If not, they are changed, as in the following example:

Nullification (NUL ih fih KAY shun)

Here the "K" takes the place of "c" and "sh" takes the place of "ti."

In the words respelled to show pronunciation, a vowel is long when it stands alone in an accented syllable. Note the "I" in this example:

Irish (I rish)

A vowel is also long when its syllable ends in silent "e." Note here the pronunciation of the "i" in the respelled word:

excise (EK size)

When a consonant follows a vowel in the same syllable, the vowel is usually short. The sound of "EK" in the word respelled below is such an example. The following KEY will help you to pronounce the vowels.

A   *or* ay as in *Abraham* (A bruh HAM); *Crusades* (kroo SAYDZ)
ai as in *tariff* (TAIR if)
a   as in *abolition* (AB o LISH un)
ah as in *saga* (SAH ga)
aw as in *Australia* (aw STRAYL ya)
E   *or* ee as in *equal* (E kwuhl); *election* (ee LEK shun)
I, y, *or* eye as in *Irish* (I rish); *Vikings* (VY kings); *isotopes* (EYE-soh topes)
i   *or* ih as in *Plymouth* (PLIM uth); *Adirondack* (AD ih RON dak)
O   *or* oh as in *Oglethorpe* (O g'l-thawp); *Ohio* (oh HI oh)
o   as in *proclamation* (PROK luh-MAY shun)
oo as in *Suez* (soo EZ)
ow as in *counterfeit* (KOWN ter fit)
oi *or* oy as in *boycott* (BOY kaht)
U   *or* yoo as in *Utah* (U tah); *fugitive* (FYOO jih tiv)
u   as in *Dunkerque* (DUN kirk)
uh represents the unaccented "a" in *alone;* "e" in *system;* "i" in *easily;* "o" in *gallop;* or "u" in *circus.* If you think of it as the "a" in *alone,* you will pronounce it rightly.

Study these examples carefully and refer to this KEY frequently.

GLOSSARY

alliance: a formal agreement between two or more governments in which they promise to help one another.

amendment: a change; an addition to, or change in a constitution.

Anti-federalists: the group of people who did not want the Constitution to be adopted.

appeasement: a foreign policy of yielding to some of the demands of an enemy to avoid war.

armistice: an agreement among warring nations to "cease fire" and stop fighting.

Articles of Confederation: a document outlining the form and powers of the national government, adopted by Congress and ratified by the states in 1781. The United States was governed according to the Articles until 1789.

Bill of Rights: a statement of certain fundamental rights and privileges guaranteed to the people.

blockade: the shutting off or blocking of a harbor by enemy warships so goods cannot get in or out.

blue laws: colonial laws against such amusements as dancing or card playing.

boycott (BOY kaht): a united refusal to buy; also, an agreement to have no dealings with a nation, company, or person.

Cabinet: in the United States, a council that advises the President.

capital: money saved out of income and used in producing new goods and services.

charter: a written plan of government; in colonial times, a document issued by the King permitting a group of people to organize a colony and run it.

checks and balances: a system by which the national government of the United States is divided into three branches: legislative, executive, and judicial. Each branch checks the power of the others.

"cold war": name given to the tension between communist nations and the democratic nations after World War II.

collective bargaining: negotiations between employer and workers to determine conditions of employment.

compromise (KAHM pro mize): settlement of a quarrel or difference of opinion by agreeing that each side will give up part of what it wants.

Confederacy or Confederate States of America: the government established by the southern states which seceded in 1861.

conservation: the preservation, protection, and planned use of natural resources.

constitution: a fundamental law or statement according to which a country or region is governed.

counterfeit (KOWN ter fit) **money:** coins or paper bills made in imitation of genuine money for the purpose of cheating.

Crusades (kroo SAYDZ): military expeditions undertaken by Christians of western Europe in the 11th, 12th, and 13th centuries. The purpose was to win control of the Holy Land (Palestine).

Declaration of Independence: a document written by a committee of which Thomas Jefferson was a member. It was adopted by the second Continental Congress on July 4, 1776. It declared the American colonies free of British control.

dictator: a person who has complete control of the government of a country.

economic (EE kho NAHM ik): connected with earning a living, that is with production, distribution, and consumption.

electoral college: a body of electors chosen by voters in the different states to choose the President and the Vice-President.

erosion (ee RO zhun): the wearing away of land by wind and water.

excise (EK size): a tax on goods manufactured or produced within the country.

executive branch: the law-enforcing part of the government.

federal form of government: a system where power is divided between the states and the national government.

frontier: the last edge of settled country, where the wilderness begins.

House of Burgesses (BUR jes es): the law-making assembly of the Virginia colony.

immigration quota (KWOH tah): a method used to limit the number of people who can enter the United States. A certain number is admitted from each country.

indentured servant or bond servant: one who agreed to work without wages for a certain number of years to pay off a debt. In colonial days many immigrants paid for their passage to America in this way.

Industrial Revolution: the change from hand labor to machine labor, and from small shop to factory production.

inflation: a sudden, sharp rise in prices, usually caused by an increase in the supply of money and a scarcity of goods.

interstate commerce: trade among the states, in which products made in one state are shipped across state boundaries and sold in other states.

isolation (ɪ soh LA shun): the name given to the foreign policy which states that the United States should keep out of European affairs.

judicial branch: the part of the government that explains or interprets the law.

labor union: an organization of workers formed to work for mutual welfare.

legislative branch: the lawmaking part of the government.

literacy (LIT er ah see) **test:** an examination a person takes to prove he can read and write.

Loyalist or Tory: an American who remained loyal to the King of England during the Revolution.

Magna Carta or Great Charter: a famous English document guaranteeing rights that King John was forced to sign in 1215.

majority rule: an accepted principle of democratic government. According to this principle the individual or policy which receives the most votes is the one elected or chosen.

manhood suffrage: the right of every adult male citizen to vote.

Middle Ages: period between ancient times and modern times; or, between the fall of Rome and the Renaissance.

minute men: volunteers ready for military service at a minute's notice during and just previous to the American Revolution.

monopoly (moh NAHP oh lih): control of the production of a commodity or service which permits the holder to fix prices.

nation: a group of people sharing the same traditions and usually speaking the same language.

nationalism: devotion to the whole country and its people.

naval base: a fortified location (usually on an island) where ships can get coal, fresh water, supplies, and make repairs.

neutral: a person, group, or nation that refuses to take sides in a dispute or war, trying instead to keep out of the quarrel.

New Deal: a phrase used to describe Franklin Roosevelt's program of reforms aimed at curing the depression.

Northwest Ordinance (also called Ordinance of 1787): A law passed by Congress under the Articles of Confederation. It provided for democratic government in the Northwest Territory.

nullification (NUL ih fih KAY shun), **theory of:** the idea that a state could declare a federal law void within its borders.

patroons: Dutch landowning families in New Netherlands (New York).

Petition of Right: a famous English document containing a declaration of the rights of the English people.

political party: a group of people who have the same ideas about the way the government should be run.

popular sovereignty (SOV rihn tee): a plan whereby the people of a territory would decide whether to admit slavery.

President: the chief executive of the United States. He is head of the executive or law enforcing branch of the government.

proprietor (proh PRI eh ter): owner or

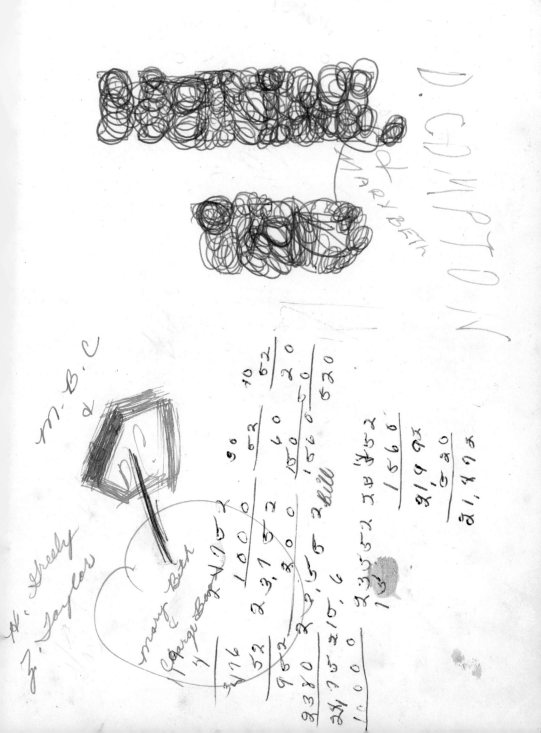

WWW

BOOM!

D. CAMPTON

& MARYBETH

M.B.C
& M.

H. Greely
Z. Taylor